西安统计年鉴

XI'AN STATISTICAL YEARBOOK

2015

中英文对照 Chinese/English

中国统计出版社
China Statistics Press

西安市统计局
XI'AN MUNICIPAL BUREAU OF STATISTICS
国家统计局西安调查队
NBS SURVEY OFFICE IN XI'AN

图书在版编目（CIP）数据

西安统计年鉴. 2015 / 西安市统计局, 国家统计局西安调查队编. -- 北京 : 中国统计出版社, 2015.8
ISBN 978-7-5037-7538-3

Ⅰ. ①西… Ⅱ. ①西… ②国… Ⅲ. ①统计资料－西安市－2015－年鉴 Ⅳ. ①C832.411-54
中国版本图书馆CIP数据核字(2015)第193028号

西安统计年鉴—2015

作　　者/ 西安市统计局　国家统计局西安调查队
责任编辑/ 陈越月
装帧设计/ 西安力天世纪品牌策划设计有限公司
出版发行/ 中国统计出版社
地　　址/ 北京市丰台区西三环南路甲6号　邮政编码/100073
电　　话/ 邮购（010）63376909　书店（010）68783171
网　　址/ http://csp.stats.gov.cn
印　　刷/ 西安一印制版有限责任公司
经　　销/ 新华书店
开　　本/ 890mm×1240mm　1/16
字　　数/ 1380千字
印　　张/ 41.25
版　　别/ 2015年8月第1版
版　　次/ 2015年8月第1次印刷
定　　价/ 260元

如有印装差错，由本社发行部调换。

《西安统计年鉴—2015》编辑部

XI'AN STATISTICAL YEARBOOK-2015
EDITORLAL STAFF

编者说明

一、《西安统计年鉴—2015》系统收录了全市、区县及开发区2014年经济、社会各方面统计数据，以及重要历史年份主要统计数据，是一部全面记载西安市国民经济和社会发展情况的大型连续性统计文献资料和重要工具书。

二、本年鉴正文内容分为二十二个篇章：（一）综合；（二）基本单位；（三）国民经济核算；（四）人口、从业人员与职工工资；（五）固定资产投资；（六）财政；（七）物价指数；（八）人民生活；（九）城市公用事业；（十）环境保护；（十一）农业；（十二）工业；（十三）能源；（十四）建筑业；（十五）运输和邮电；（十六）国内贸易；（十七）对外经济贸易和旅游；（十八）规模以上服务业；（十九）金融业；（二十）教育和科技；（二十一）文化、体育、卫生、社会福利和其他；（二十二）企业调查。同时，为方便读者使用，各篇章前设有简要说明和主要统计指标，对本篇章的主要内容、资料来源、以及历史变动情况予以简要概述，篇末附有《主要统计指标解释》。

三、本年鉴统计资料的统计标准，按当时国家统计制度执行，有关指标的涵义、口径、范围、计算方法等，在不同时期可能有所不同，使用时请注意。如国民经济行业分类按GB/T4754—2011标准执行。

四、为便于国内外读者查阅，本年鉴全部内容均采用中英文对照编辑。

五、本年鉴中国民经济核算、工业部分的2013年数据为全国第三次经济普查数据，贸易部分的2009—2013年数据为依据全国第三次经济普查调整后数据，数据与往年年鉴不同，使用时请注意。

六、本年鉴中的部分指标合计数或相对数由于单位取舍不同产生的计算误差均未作机械调整。

七、本年鉴所使用的计量单位均依据2014年相关统计报表制度。

八、本年鉴使用的符号说明："空白"表示该项统计指标无数据或数据不详；"#"表示其中项；"*"表示另有注解。

感谢社会各界长期以来对《西安统计年鉴》的广泛关注和大力支持。为进一步做好工作，更好地为广大读者服务，希望社会各界提出宝贵意见。

PREFACE

I. Xi'an Statistical Yearbook 2015 is a periodical statistic yearbook which record economic and social development of Xi'an all-around in 2014 and some selected data series in historical important years. With its features of comprehensive and intensive information, this practically provides data covering the situation of social and economic developments in Xi'an.

II. The book contains twenty-two parts, 1.General Survey; 2.Basic Unit; 3.National Economic Account; 4.Population, Employment and Wages; 5.Investment in Fixed Assets; 6.Government Finance; 7.Price Indices; 8.People's Livelihood; 9.Urban Public Utilities; 10.Environmental Protection; 11.Agriculture; 12.Industry; 13.Energy; 14.Construction; 15.Transportation, Post and Telecommunication Service; 16.Domestic Trade; 17.Foreign Trade; 18. Service Enterprises Above Designated Size; 19.Banking and Insurance; 20.Education, Science and Technology; 21.Culture, Sports, Public Health, Social Welfare Institutions and Other Social Activities; 22.Enterprises Investigation. As insert pages including statistical graphs and charts.

III. The data of various years in conformity to the statistical standards prescribed by national statistical system of the time. The meaning, scope and calculating method of indicators may have some difference in different periods, which readers must pay attention to. For example, national industries classification is carried out according to standard GB/T4754 -2011. For the sake of comparison of the old and new industry standards, we edit the division' s data in some major indicators according to standard GB/T4754 -2011.

IV. For the convenience of being consulted by foreigners, the book is Chinese-English bilingual edition.

V. In this yearbook, the data in 2013 at the part of national economic account and industry and data from 2009 to 2013 at the part of domestic trade have adjusted by Third National Economic Census, different from previous year's Yearbook, Please note that when using.

VI. Statistical discrepancies due to rounding are not adjusted automatically in this yearbook.

VII. Unit of measurement is used in this yearbook according to 2014 statistics system.

VIII. Explanations on symbols used in this yearbook:

(Blank) indicates the data not available;

# indicates the items of the total.

* indicates some other explanatory note.

Here we would like to express our sincere thanks to the people for their concerning and support to the Xi'an statistical yearbook. In order to do better and provide better service to readers, we hope that the whole society fields can propose constructive advices.

生产总值（亿元）
Gross Domestic Product (100 million yuan)

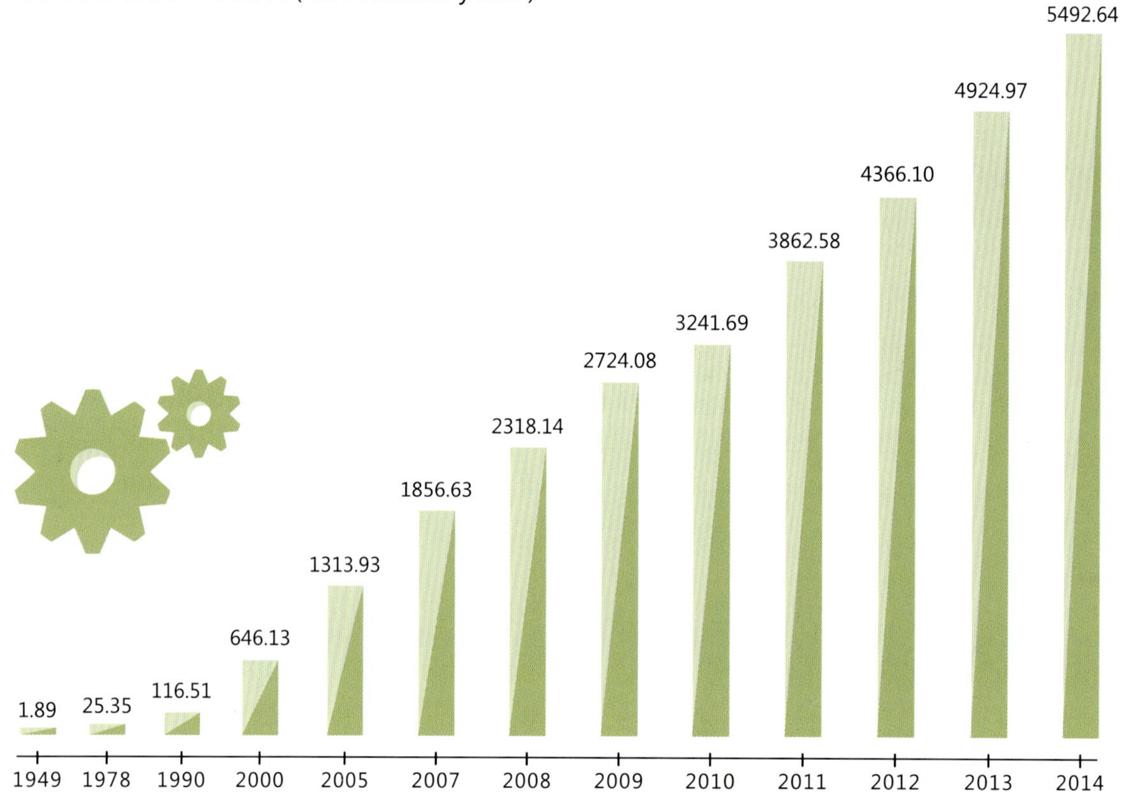

生产总值指数（以上年为100）
Indices of Gross Domestic Product (preceding year = 100)

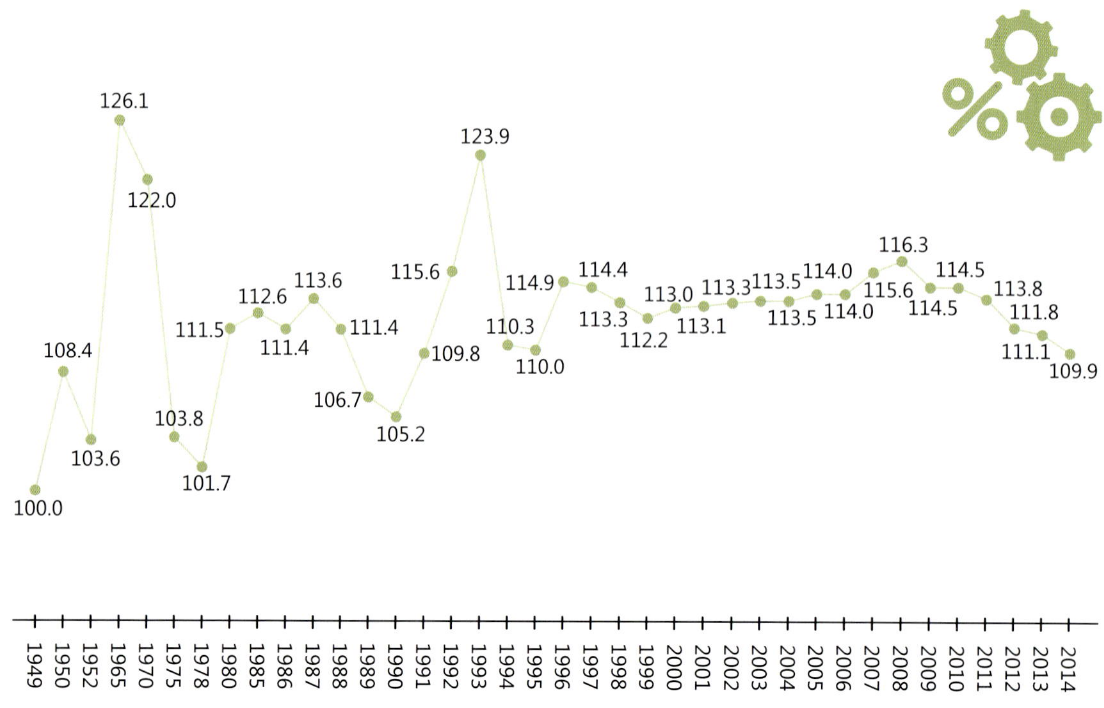

生产总值构成（%）
Composition of Gross Domestic Product （%）

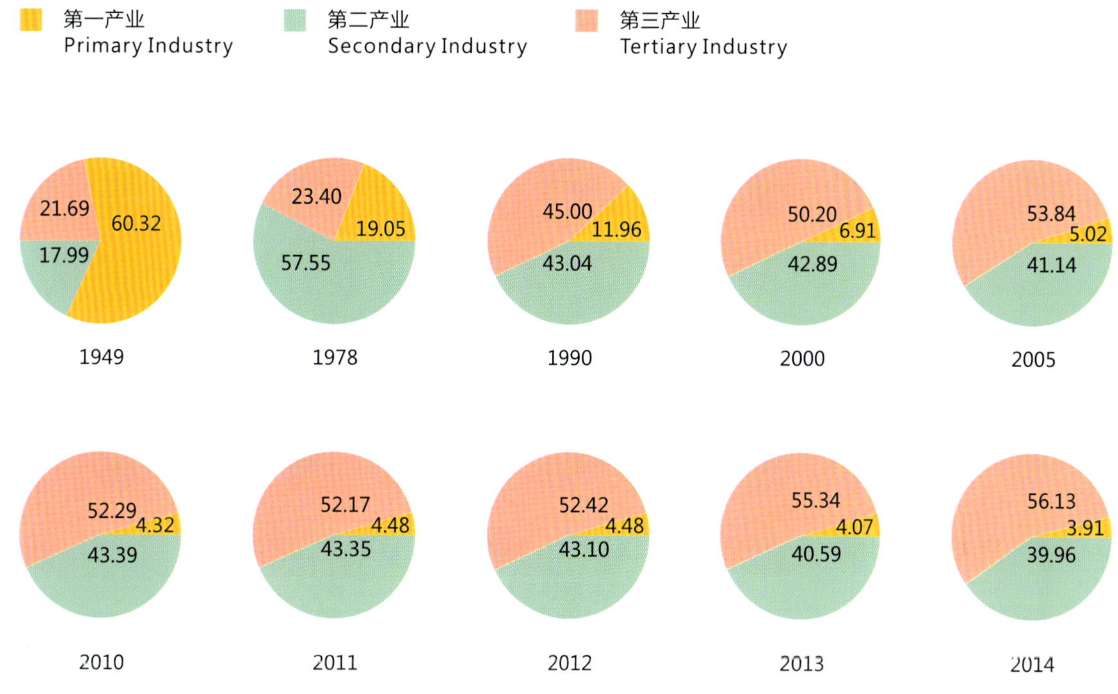

人均GDP（元/人）
Per Capita GDP（yuan/person）

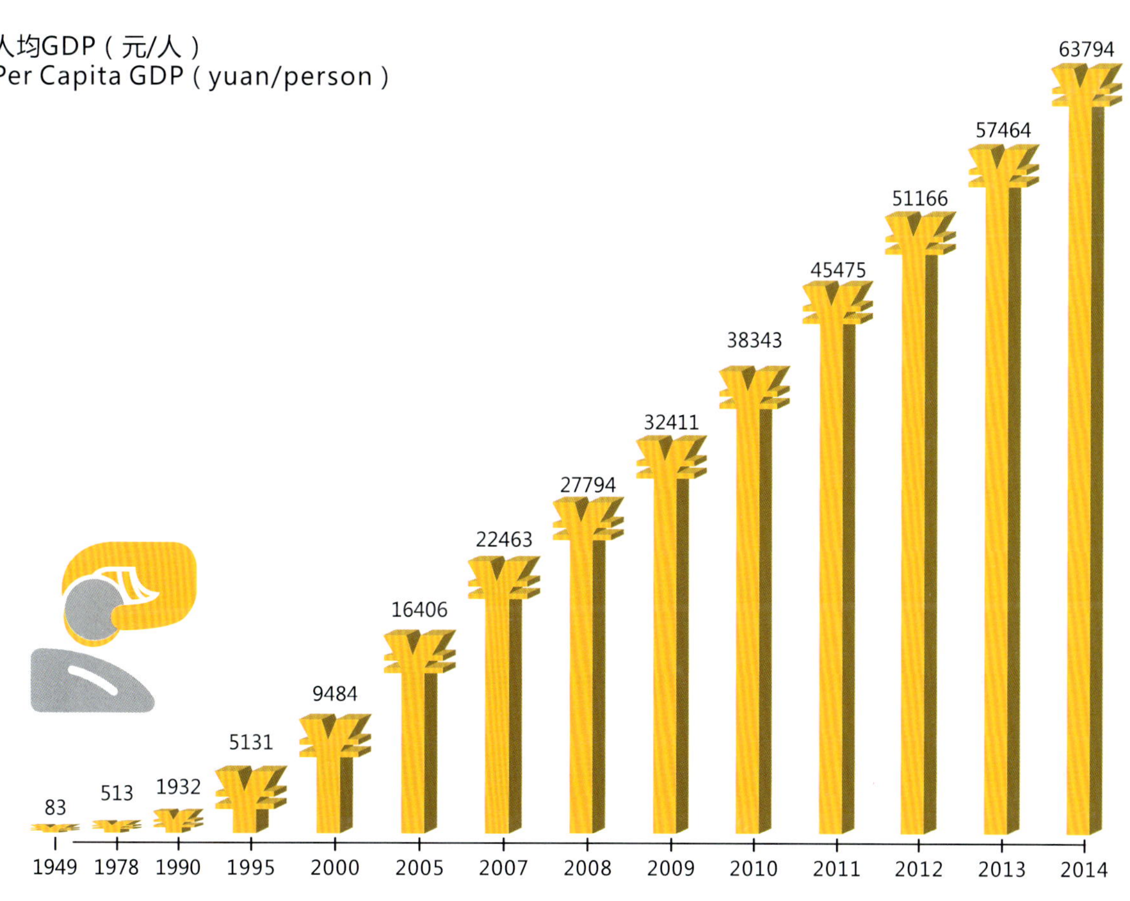

年末常住人口（万人）
Year-end Permanent Population (10 000 persons)

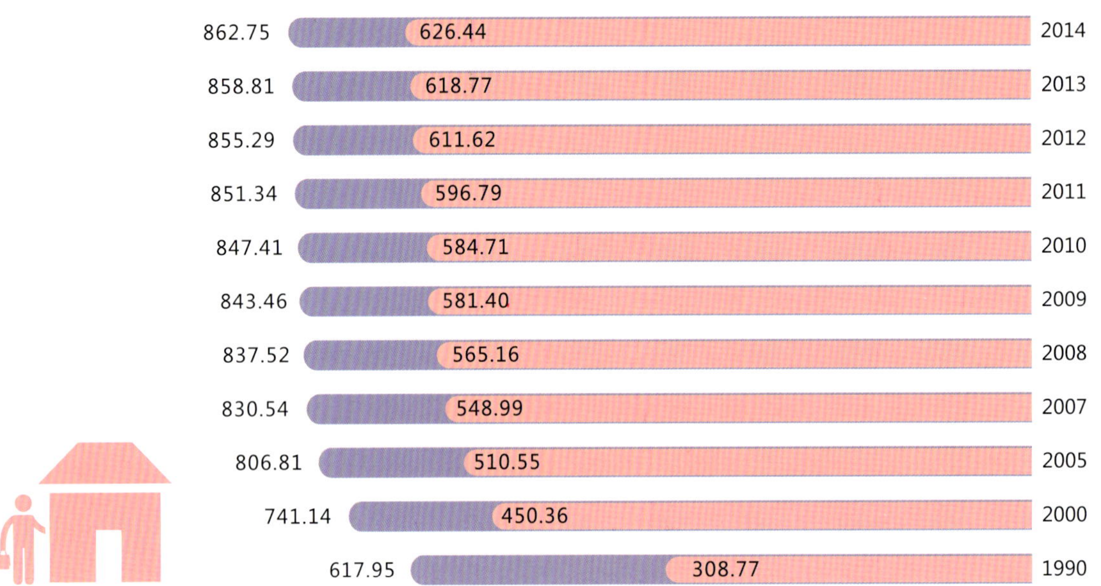

社会从业人数（万人）
Social Workers (10 000 persons)

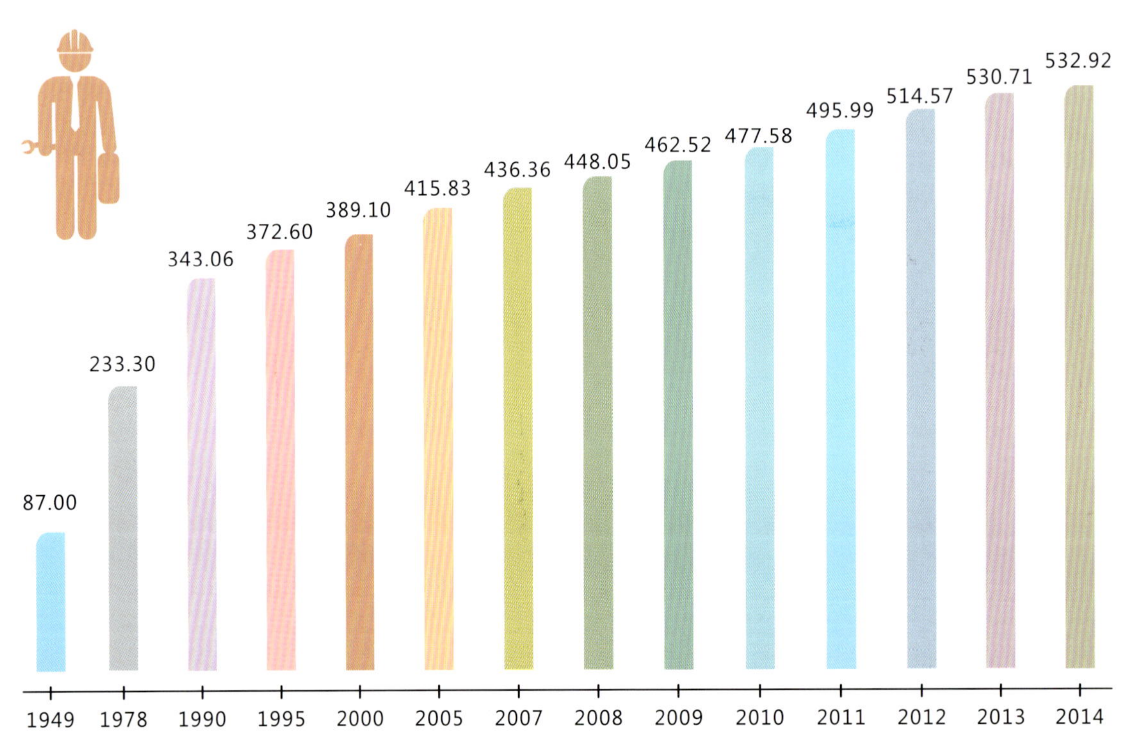

固定资产投资（亿元）
Investment in Fixed Assets (100 million yuan)

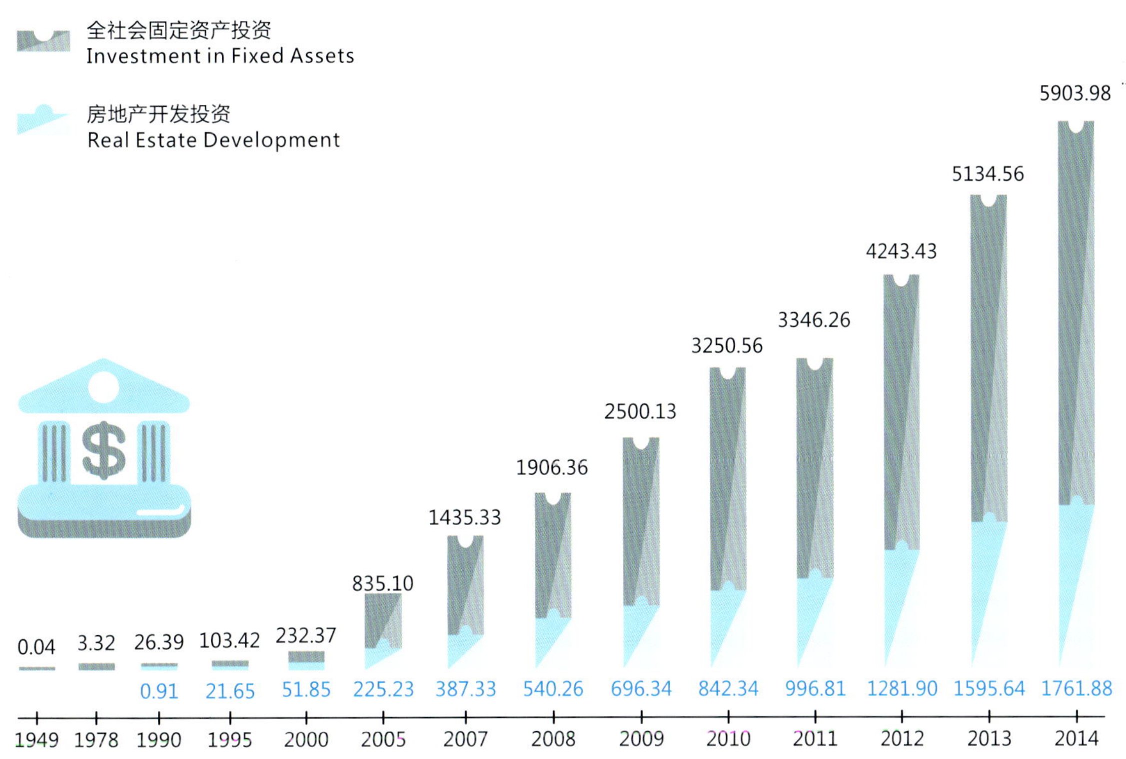

新增固定资产及住宅竣工面积
Newly Increased Fixed Assets and Residenctial Area of Completion

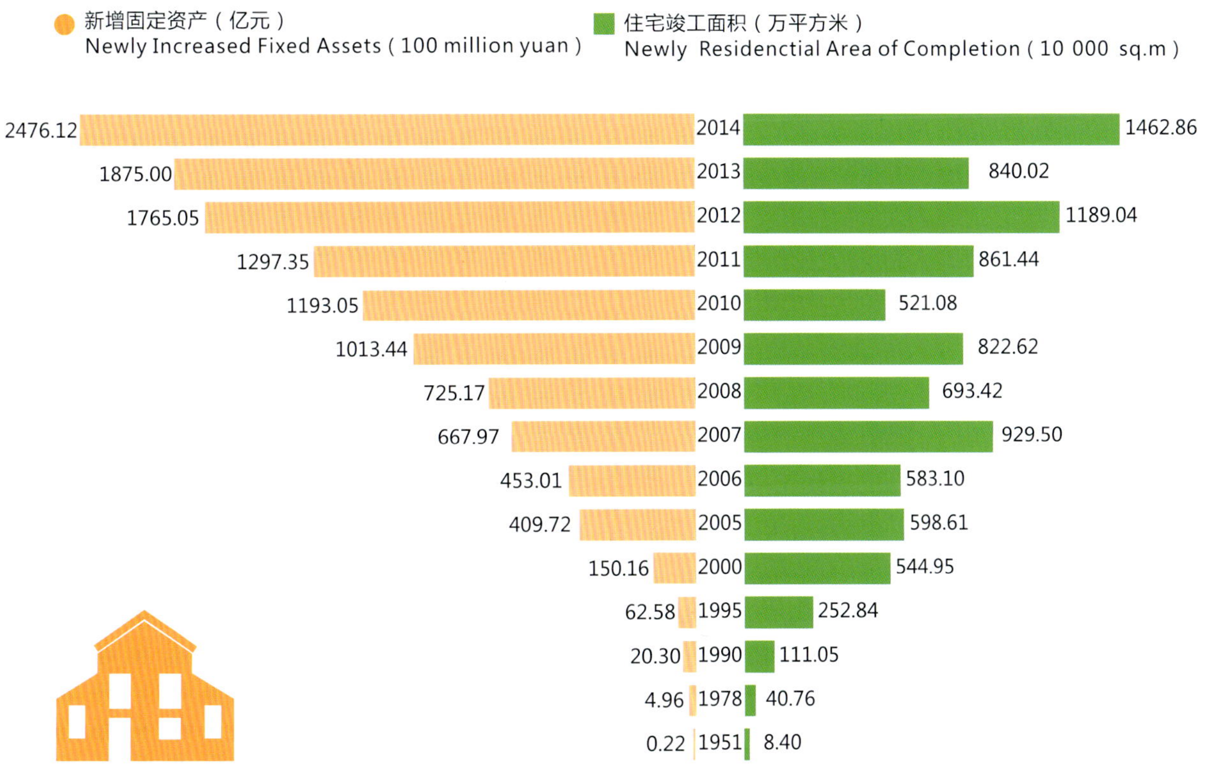

农林牧渔及服务业总产值（亿元）
Gross Output Value of Farming,Forestry,
Animal Husbandry,
Fishery and Service（100 million yuan）

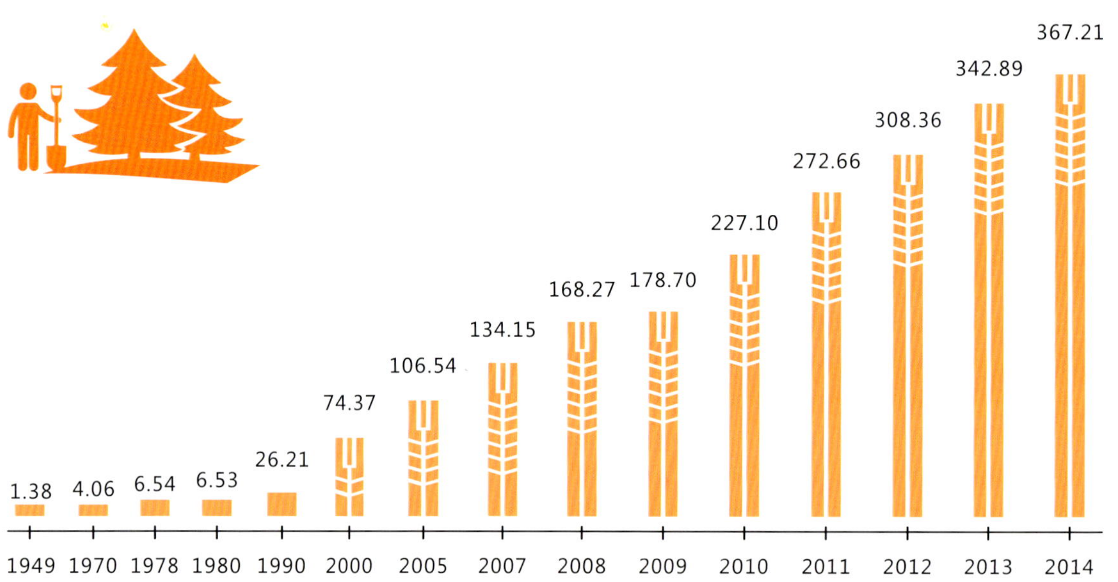

蔬菜产量（万吨）
Vegetables Product（10 000 ton）

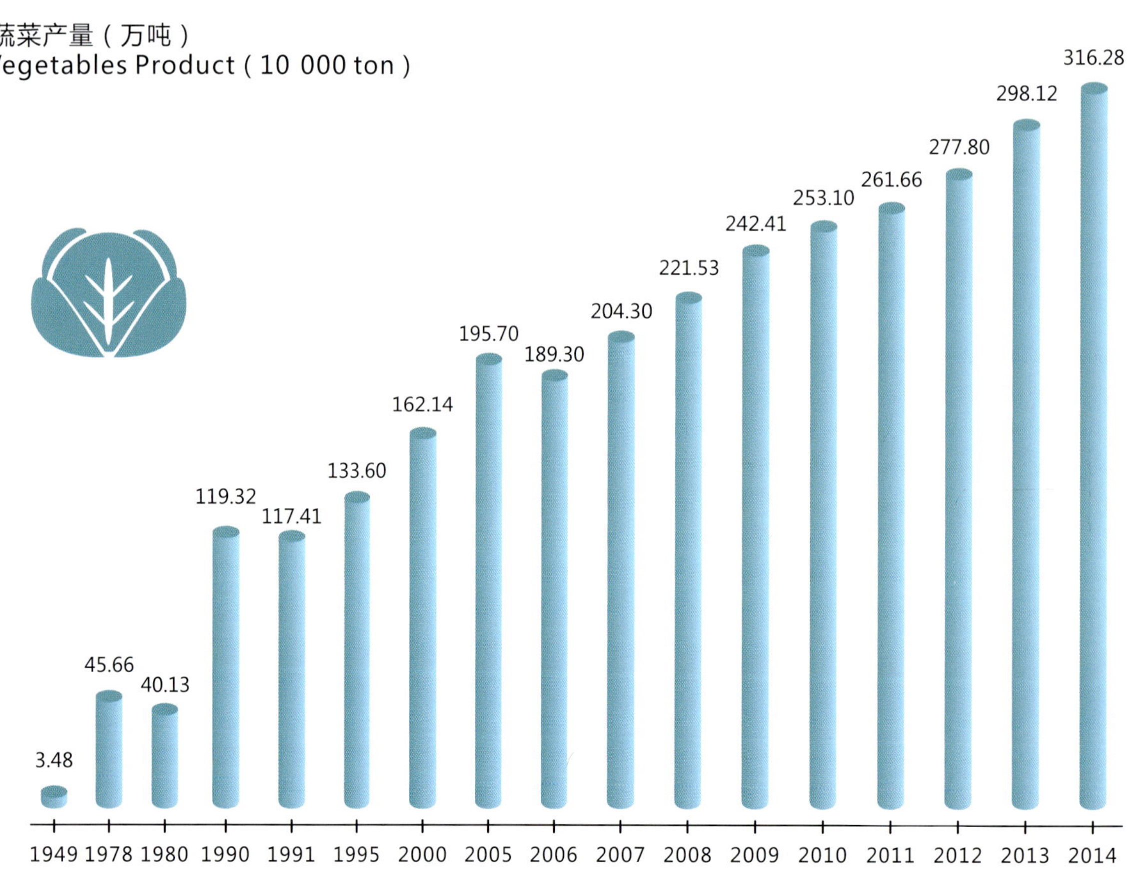

规模以上工业增加值（现价）（亿元）
Value Added of Industrial Enterprises Above Designated Size
（100 million yuan）

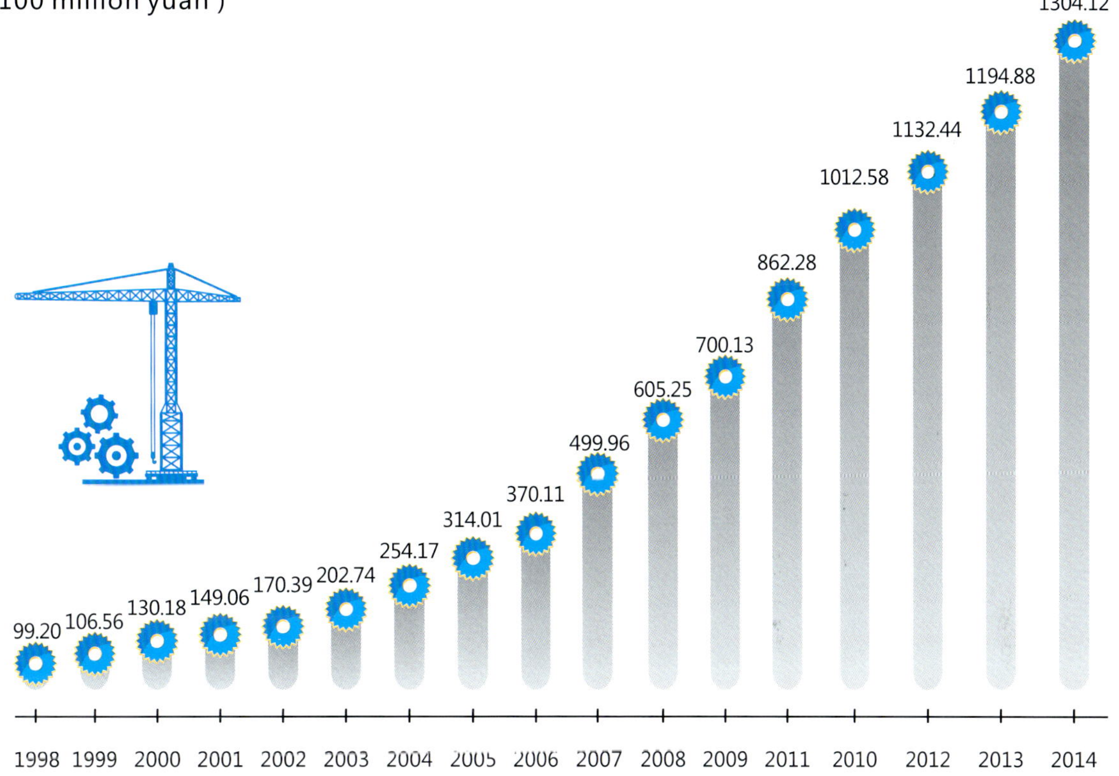

规模以上工业企业主要产品产量
Output of Major Industrial Products Of Enterprises Above Designated Size

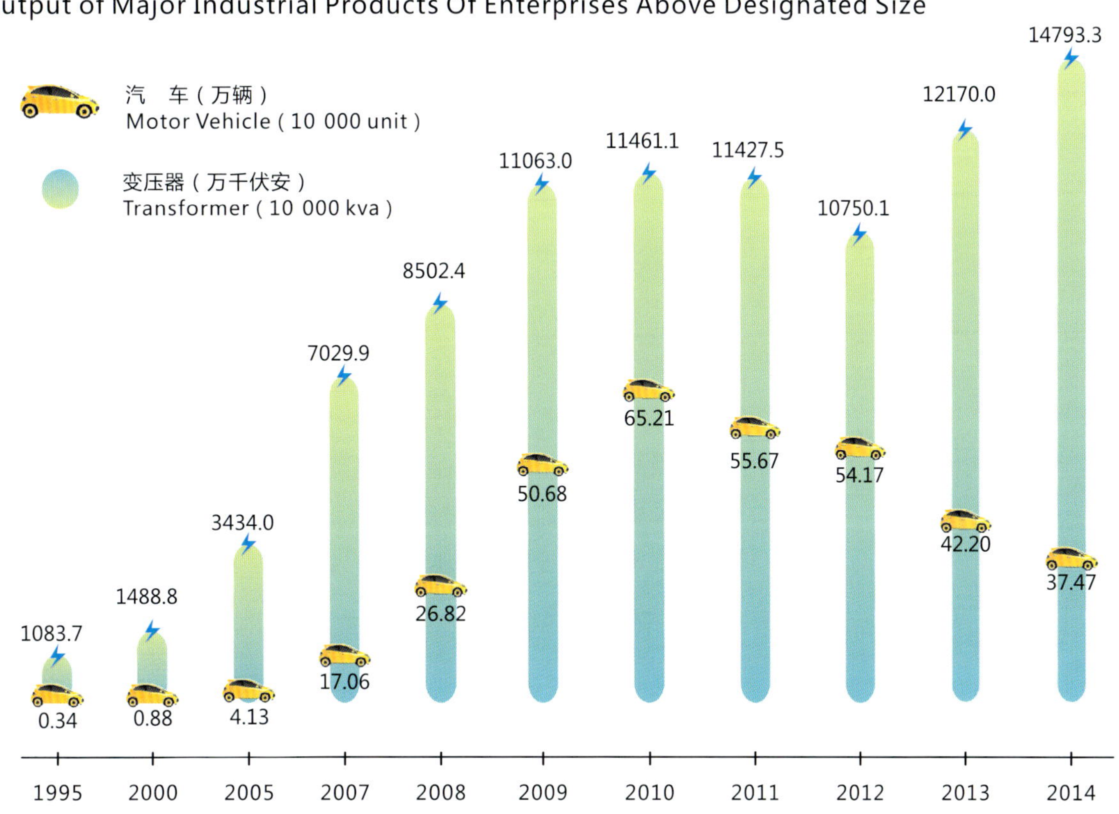

交通
Trafficed Size

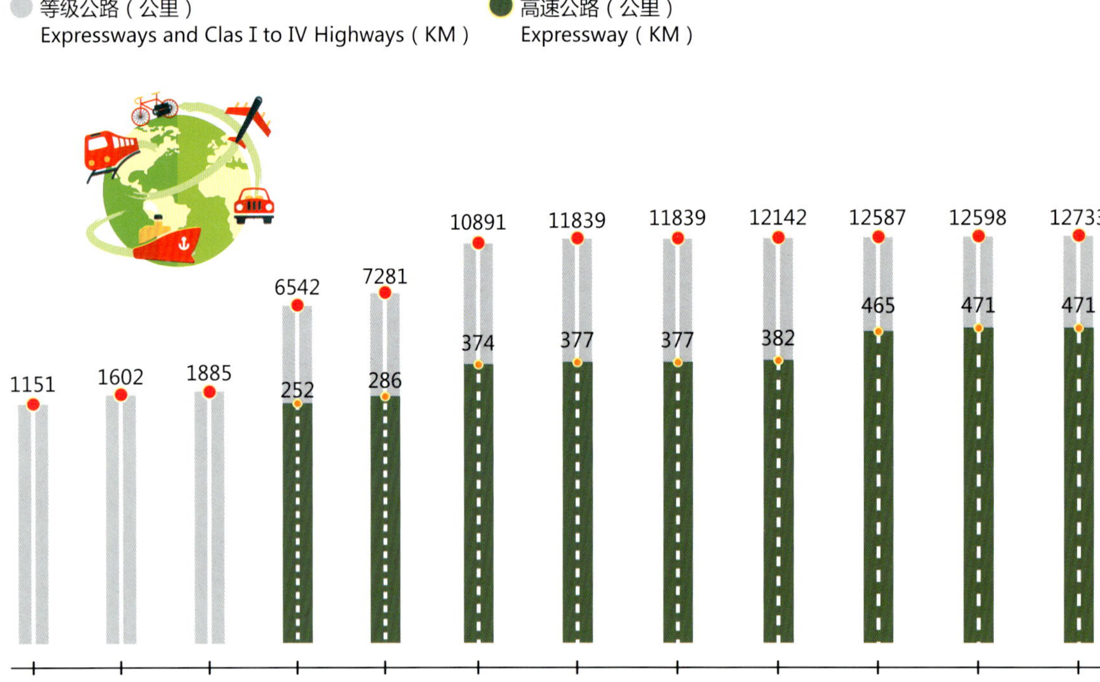

全社会车辆数（万辆）
Possession of Civil Vehicles（10 000 unit）

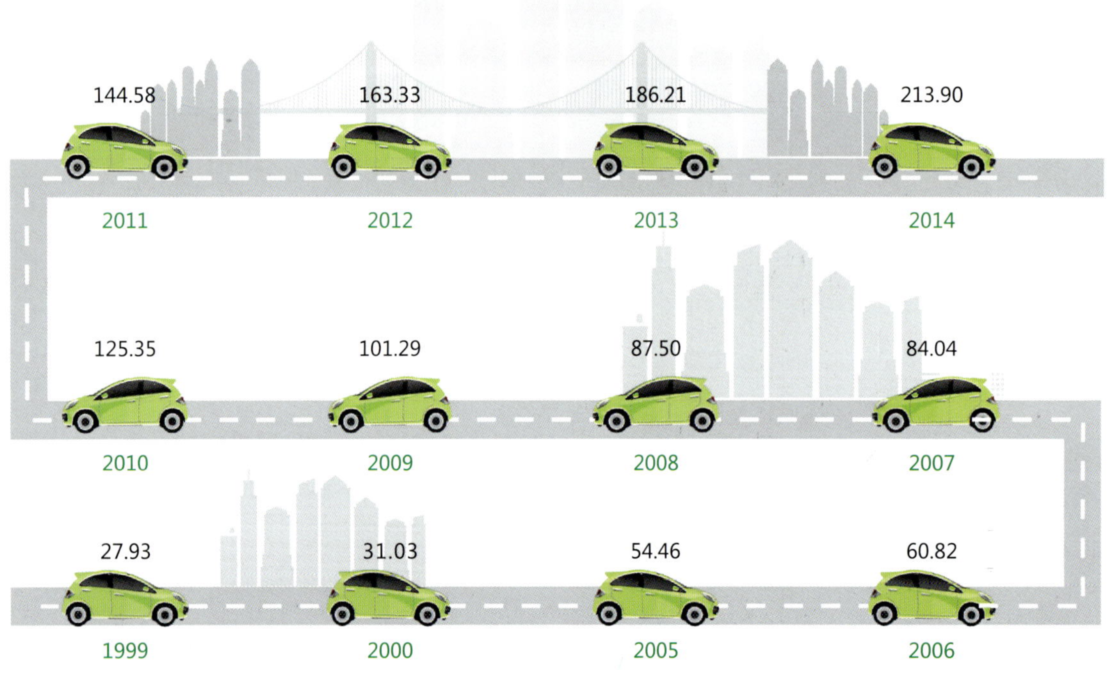

社会消费品零售总额（亿元）
Total Retail Sales of Consumer Goods (100 million yuan)

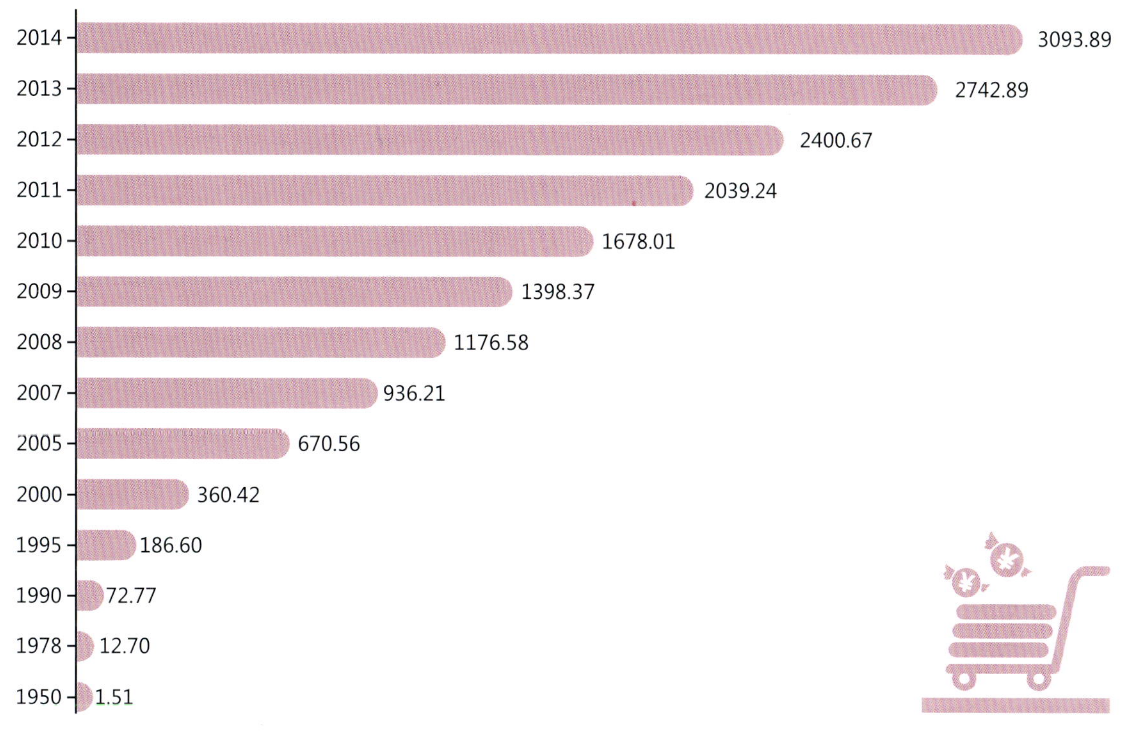

实际利用外商直接投资额（亿美元）
Foreign Direct Investment (USD 100 million)

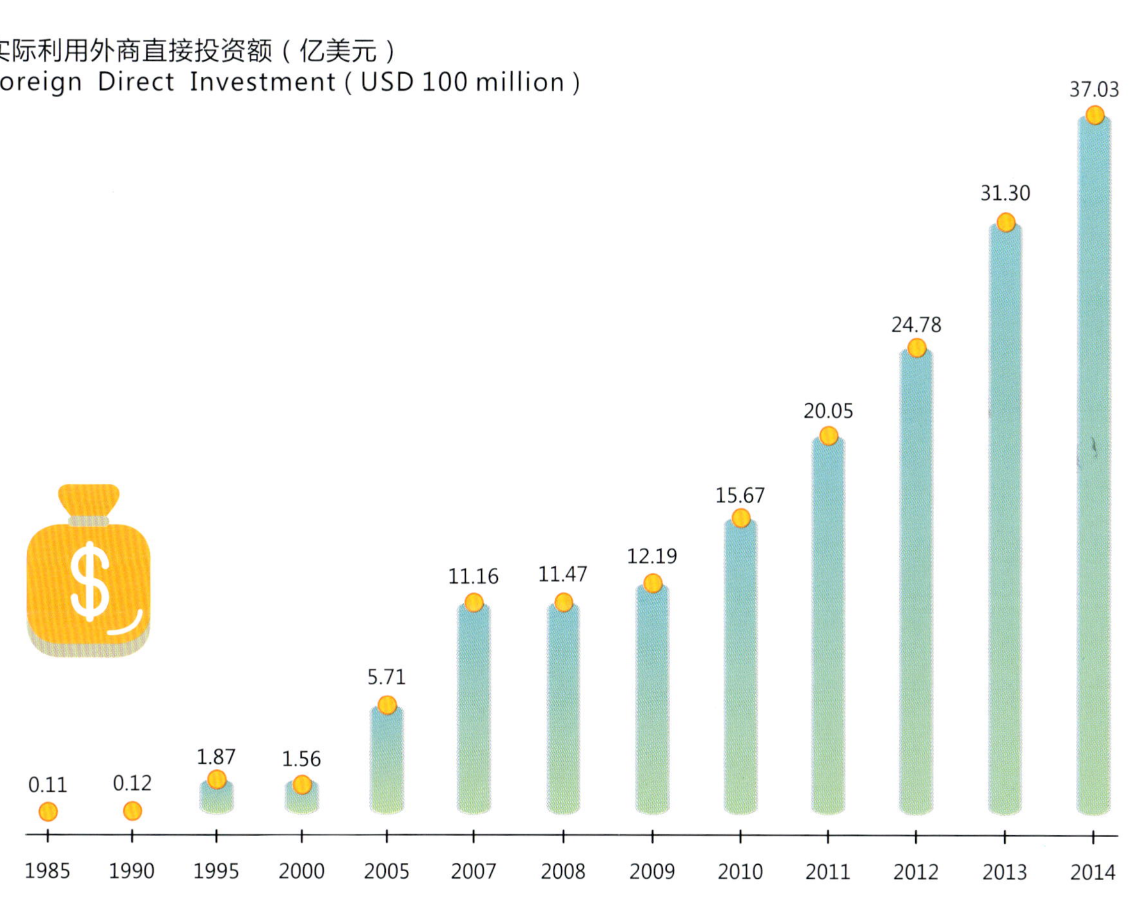

进出口总额（亿美元）
Total Value of Imports and Exports (USD 100 million)

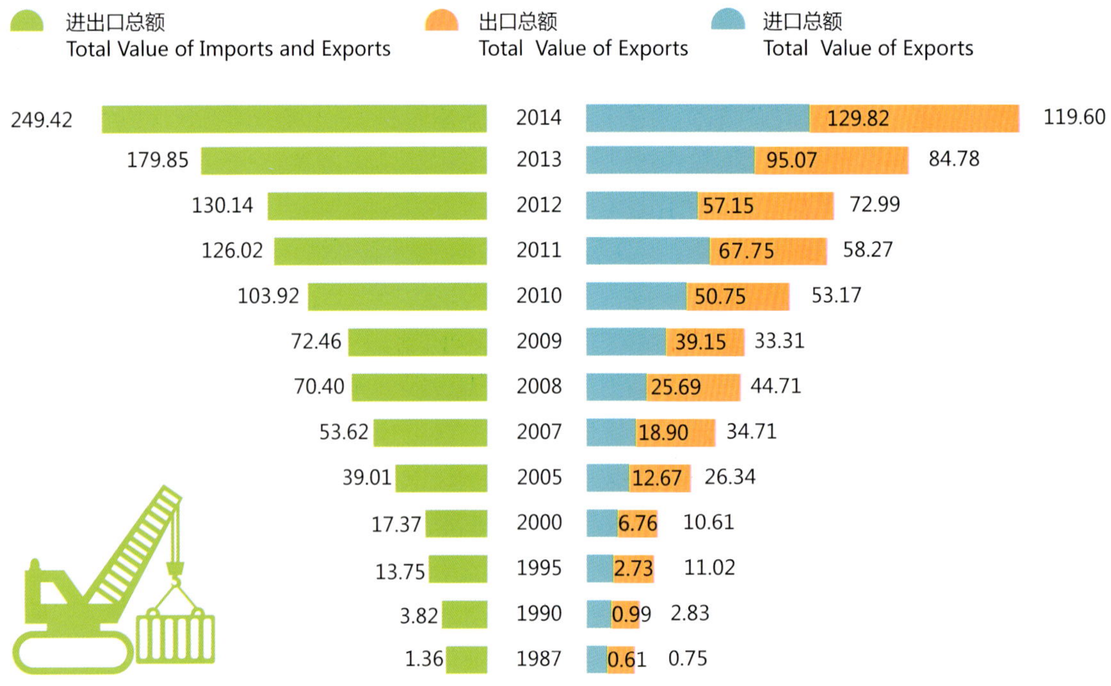

旅游人数及收入
Number of Tourists and Tourism Income

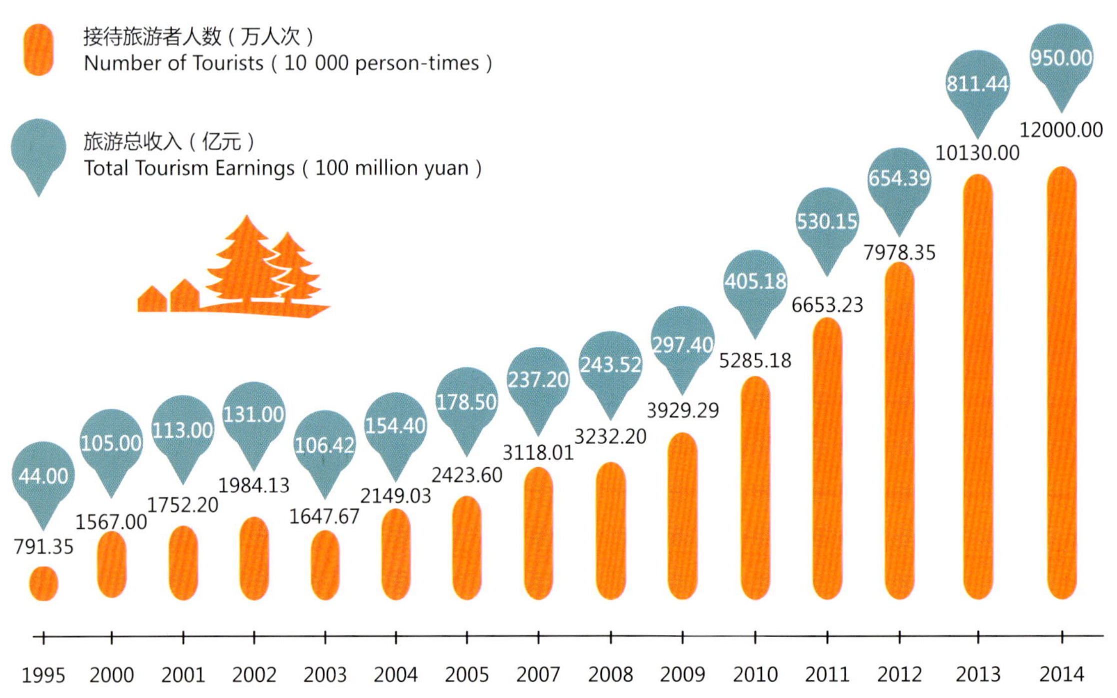

财政收支（亿元）
Government Revenue and Expenditure (100 million yuan)

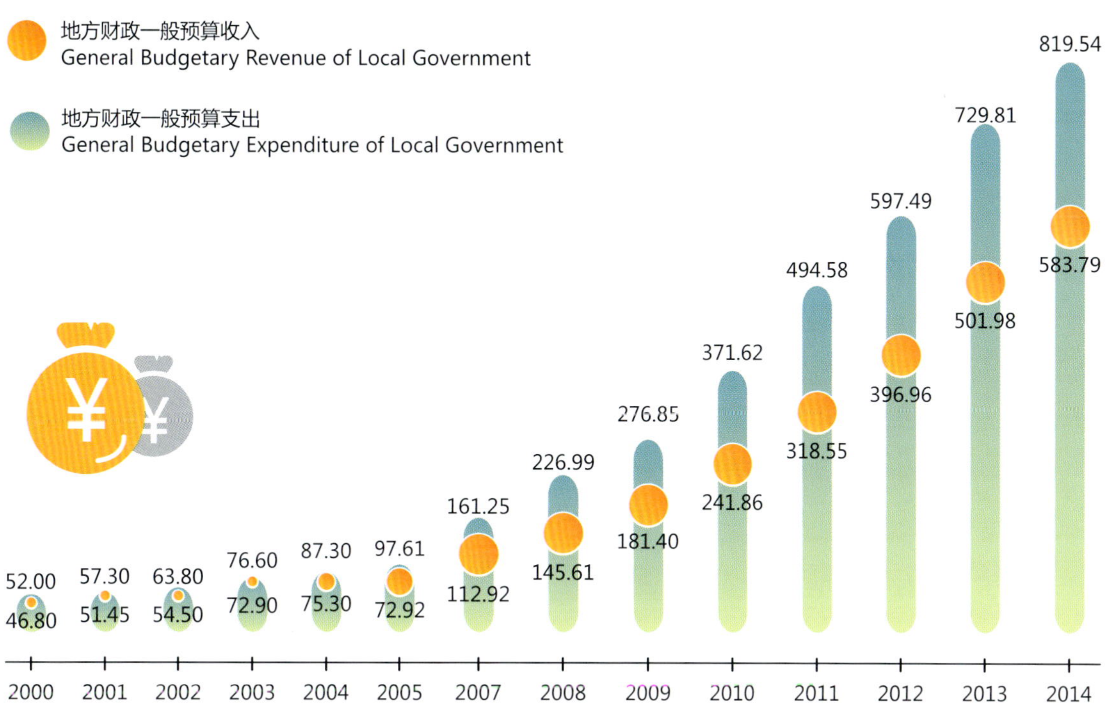

金融机构人民币存贷款年末余额（亿元）
Year-end Deposit and Loans in Financial Institutions (100 million yuan)

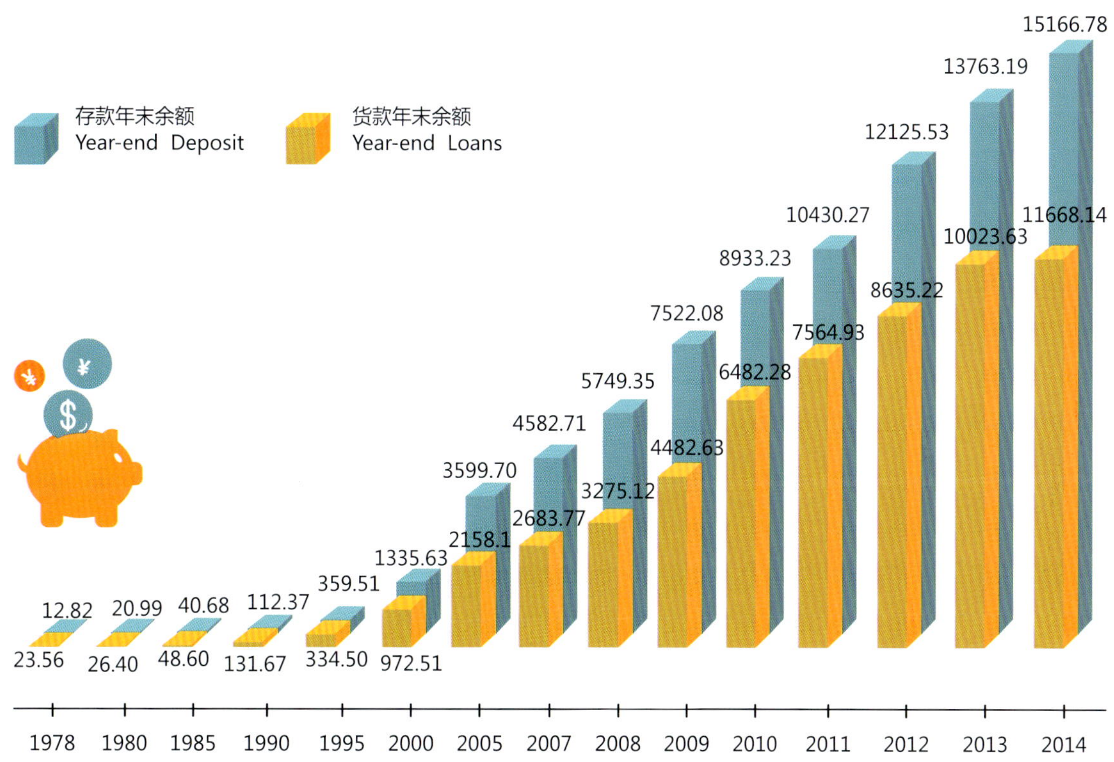

建成区面积（平方公里）
Area of Regions Built-up (sq.km)

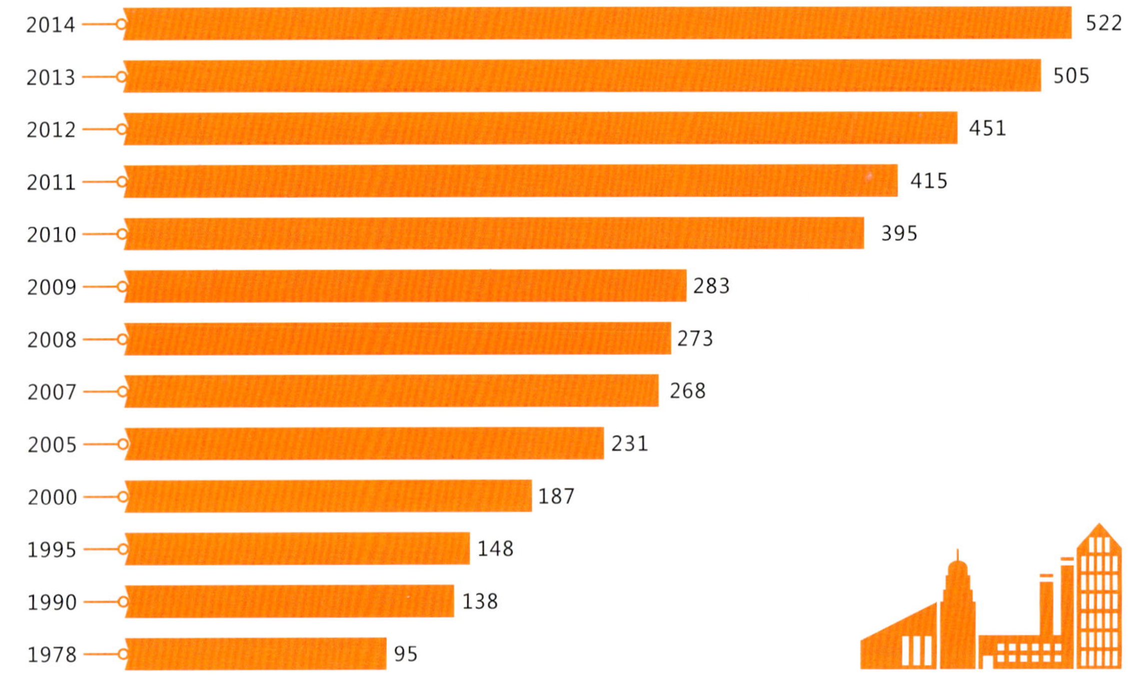

城市公共营运车辆（辆）
City Operating Vehicles (unit)

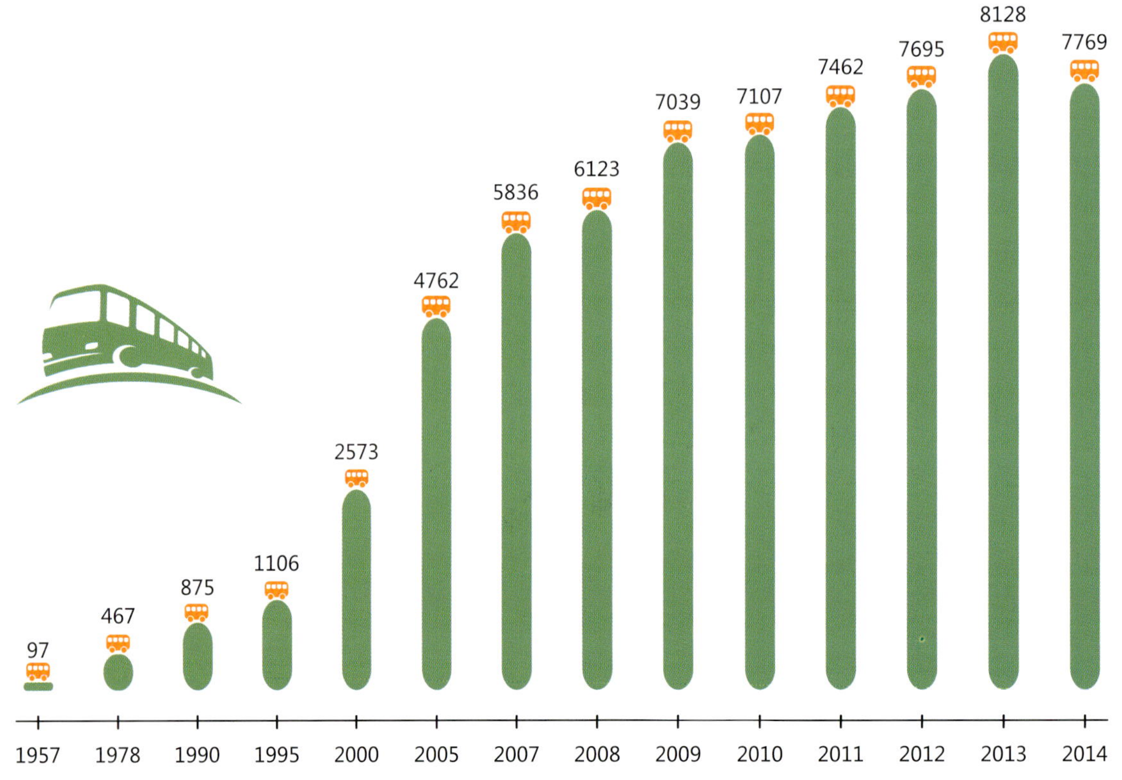

天燃气供气总量（万立方米）
Total Natural Gas Supply (10 000 cu.m)

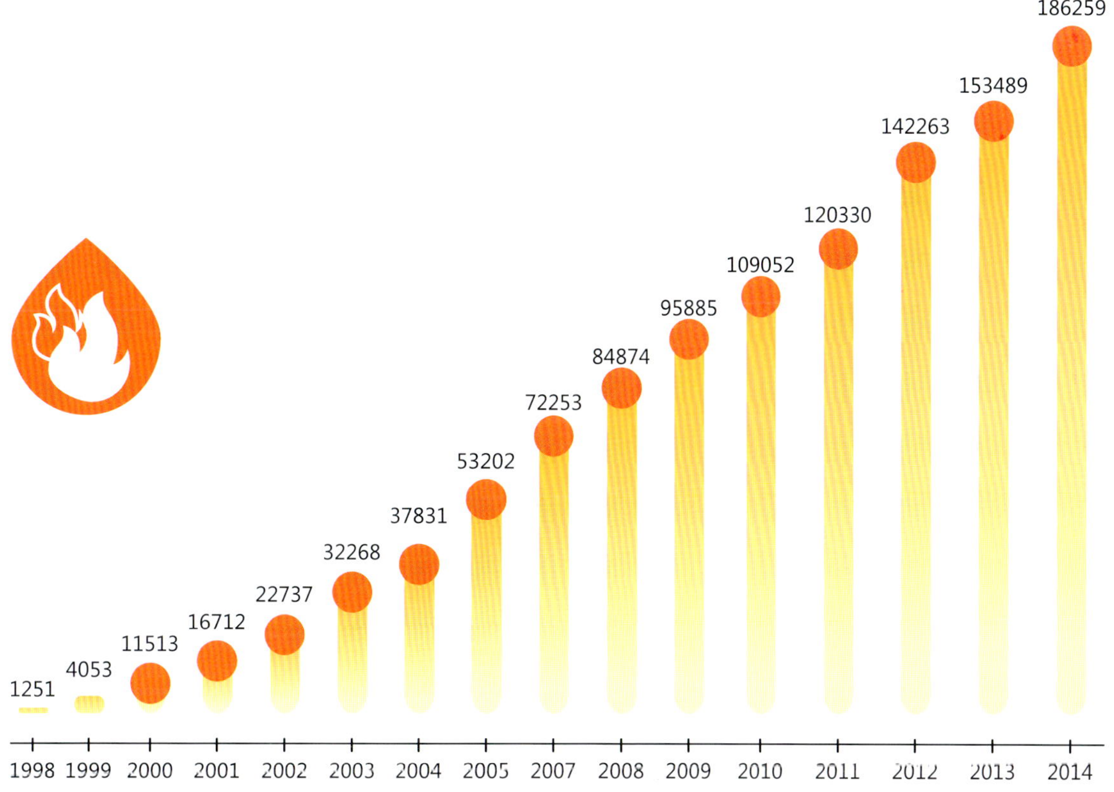

园林绿地总面积（公顷）
Total Area of Park , Gardens and Green Area (hectare)

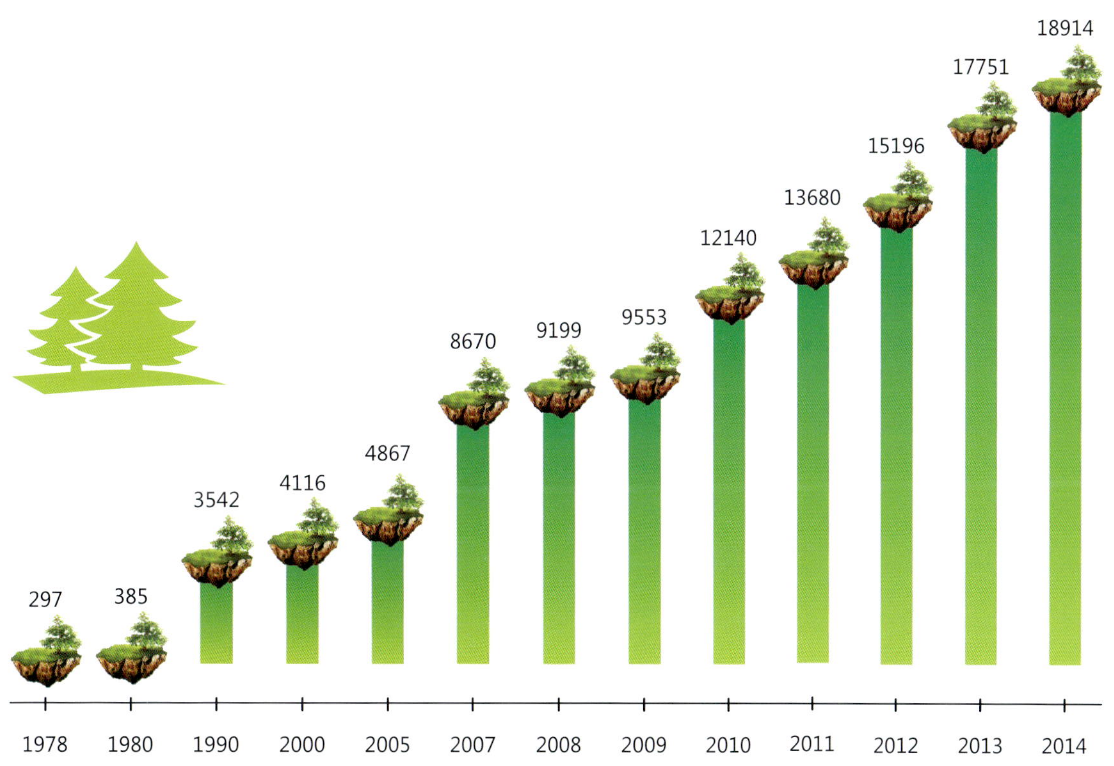

专任教师（万人）
Full-time Teachers（10 000 persons）

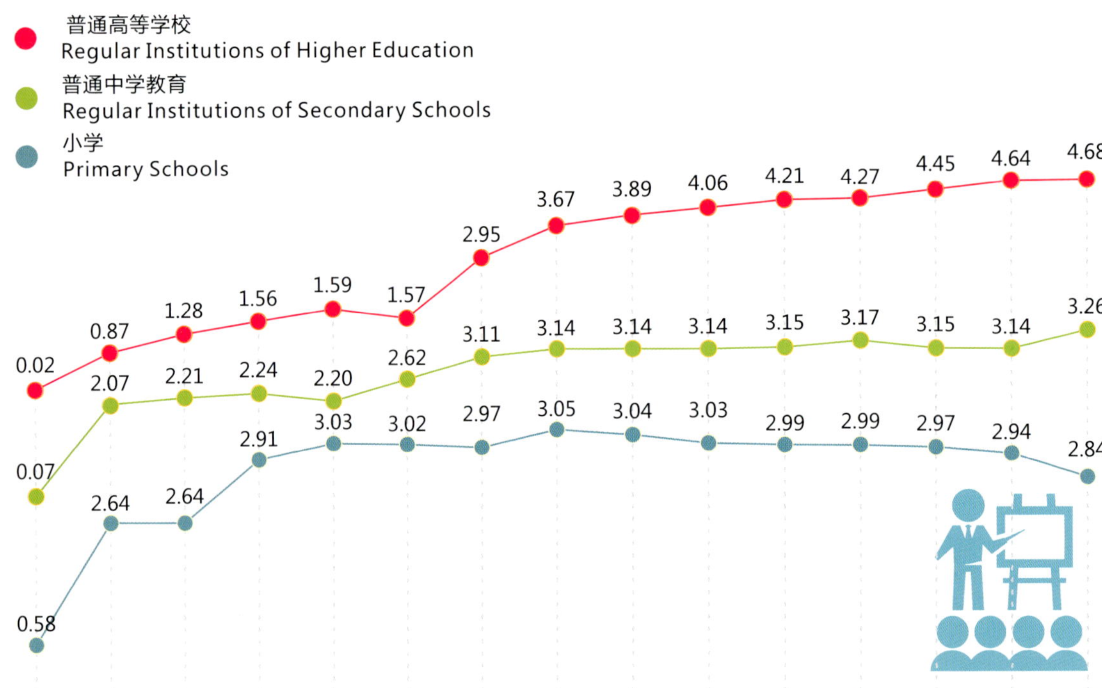

普通教育在校学生（万人）
Total Enrollment of Regular Education（10 000 persons）

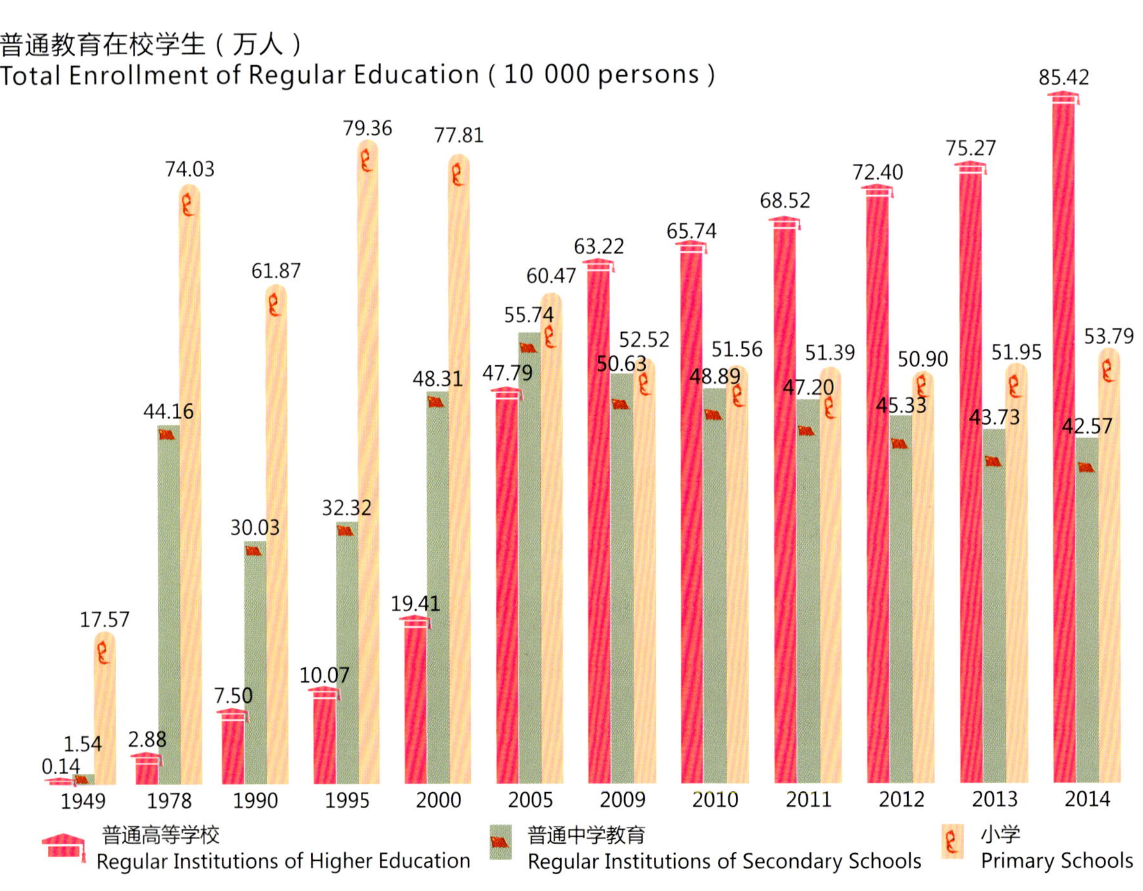

城乡居民收入（元）
The Income of Urban and Rural Residents（yuan）

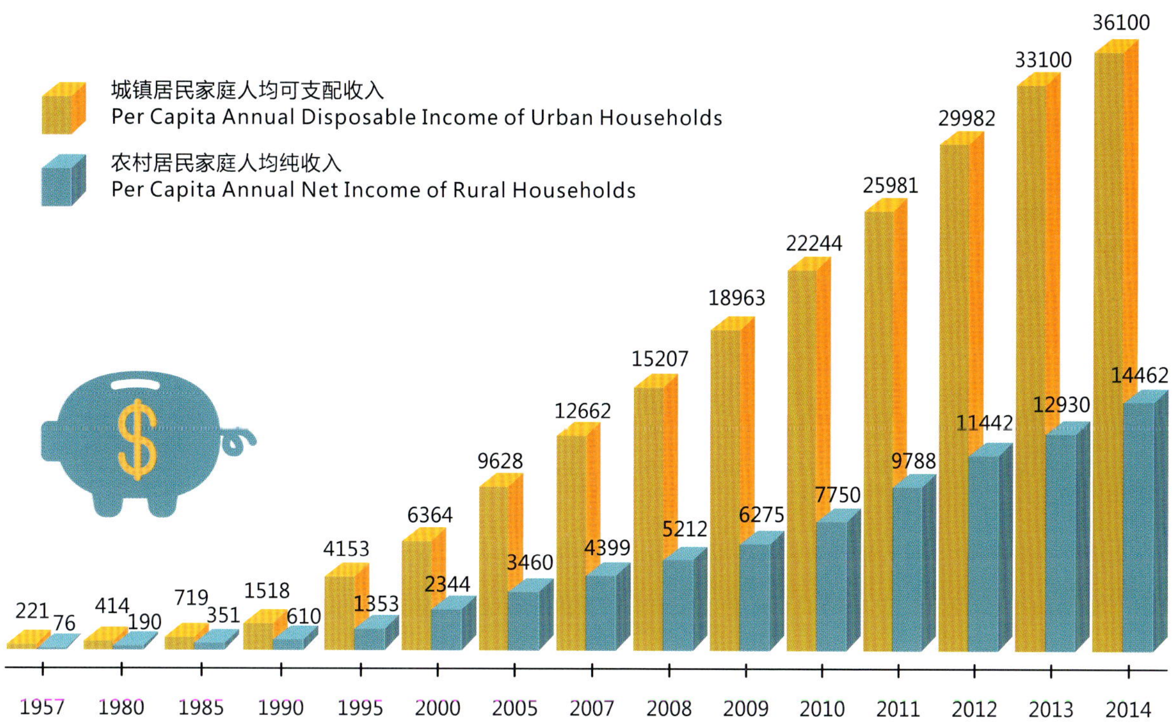

价格指数（以上年价格为100）
Price Indices（the price of preceding year=100）

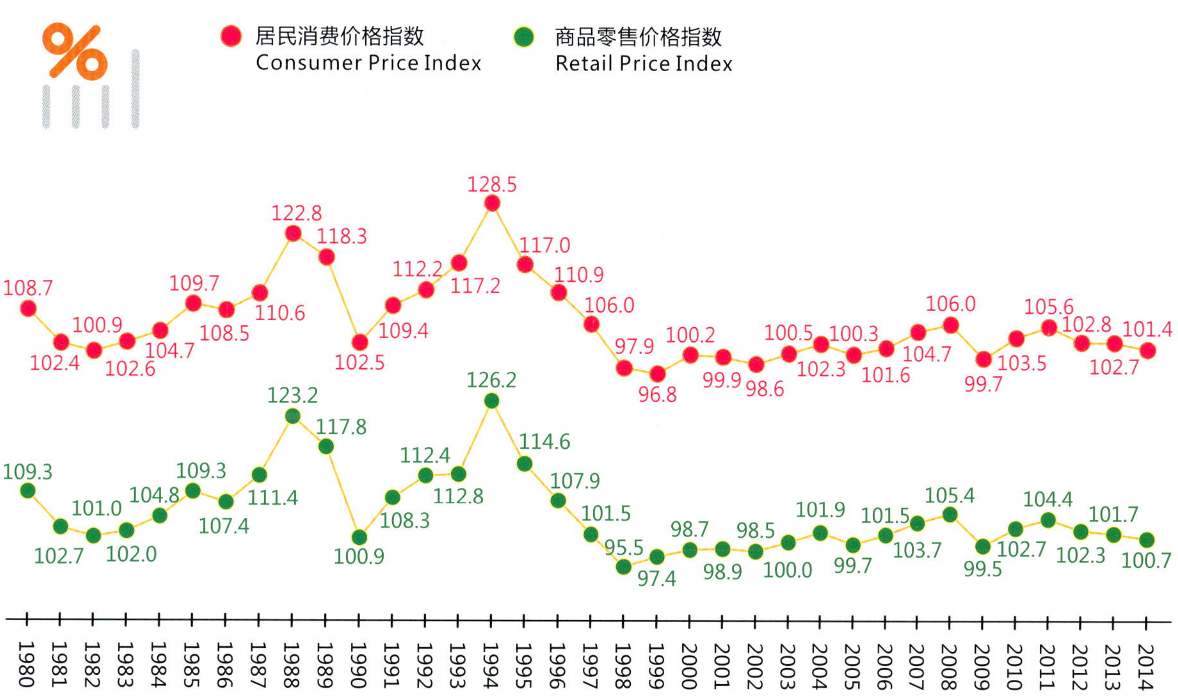

目　　录

一、综　　合

二、基本单位

三、国民经济核算

四、人口、从业人员与职工工资

五、固定资产投资

六、财　　政

七、物价指数

八、人民生活

九、城市公用事业

十、环境保护

十一、农　业

十二、工　业

十三、能　源

十四、建筑业

十五、运输和邮电

十六、国内贸易

十七、对外经济贸易和旅游

十八、规模以上服务业

十九、金融业

二十、教育和科技

二十一、文化、体育、卫生、社会福利和其他

二十二、企业调查

CONTENTS

CHAPTER 1 GENERAL SURVEY

CHAPTER 2 BASIC UNIT

CHAPTER 3 NATIONAL ECONOMIC ACCOUNTS

CHAPTER 4 POPULATION,EMPLOYMENT AND WAGES

CHAPTER 5 INVESTMENT IN FIXED ASSETS

CHAPTER 6 GOVERNMENT FINANCE

CHAPTER 7 PRICE INDICES

CHAPTER 8 PEOPLE'S LIVELIHOOD

CHAPTER 9 URBAN PUBLIC UTLITIES

CHAPTER 10 ENVIRONMENT PROTECTION

CHAPTER 11 AGRICULTURE

CHAPTER 12 INDUSTRY

CHAPTER 13　ENERGY

CHAPTER 14　CONSTRUCTION

CHAPTER 15　TRANSPORT, POSTAL AND TELECOMMUNICATION SERVICE

CHAPTER 16 DOMESTIC TRADE

CHAPTER 17 FOREIGN TRADE AND ECONOMIC COOPERATION TOURISM

CHAPTER 18 SERVICE ENTERPRISES ABOVE DESIGNATED SIZE

CHAPTER 19 FINANCIAL INTERMEDIATION

CHAPTER 20 EDUCATION,SCIENCE AND TECHNOLOGY

CHAPTER 21 CULTURE, SPORTS, PUBLIC HEALTH, SOCIAL WELFARE INSTITUTIONS AND OTHER SOCIAL ACTIVITIES

CHAPTER 22 ENTERPRISES INVESTIGATION

西安市2014年国民经济和社会发展统计公报[1]

西安市统计局　国家统计局西安调查队

2015年3月5日

2014年，面对复杂严峻的宏观环境，市委、市政府团结带领全市人民，深入贯彻落实中央、省各项决策部署，坚持稳中求进工作总基调，主动适应经济发展新常态，统筹做好稳增长、促改革、调结构、惠民生、防风险各项工作，保持了全市经济社会平稳健康发展。

一、综合

年末全市常住人口862.75万人，比上年末净增加3.94万人，其中，男性人口442.94万人，占51.3%；女性人口419.81万人，占48.7%，性别比为105.51（以女性为100，男性对女性的比例）。全年出生人口8.70万人，出生率为10.11‰；死亡人口4.71万人，死亡率为5.47‰；自然增长率为4.64‰。城镇人口626.44万人，占72.61%；乡村人口236.31万人，占27.39%。年末全市户籍总人口815.29万人，比上年增长1.0%。

初步核算，全年生产总值[2]（GDP）5474.77亿元，比上年增长9.9%。其中，第一产业增加值214.55亿元，增长5.1%；第二产业增加值2205.37亿元，增长11.3%；第三产业增加值3054.85亿元，增长9.0%。第一产业增加值占生产总值的比重为3.9%，第二产业增加值比重为40.3%，第三产业增加值比重为55.8%。

全年非公有制经济增加值2883.48亿元，占生产总值的比重为52.7%，比上年提高0.5个百分点。

图1　2010—2014年生产总值及其增长速度

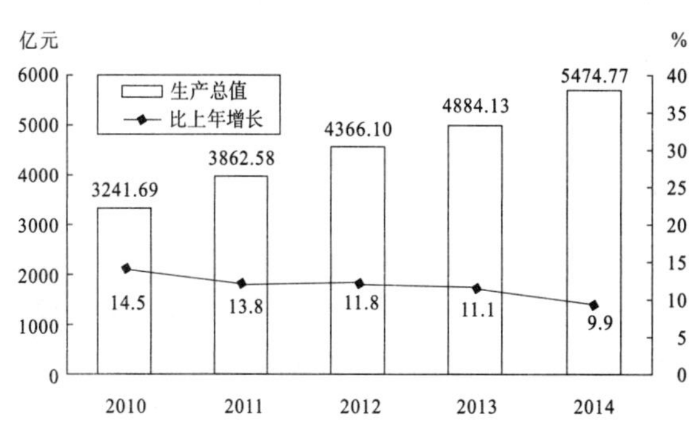

全年居民消费价格比上年上涨1.4%，其中，食品价格上涨2.9%。商品零售价格上涨0.7%。工业生产者出厂价格下降0.5%。工业生产者购进价格下降0.5%。固定资产投资价格上涨0.8%。新建住宅销售价格上涨3.7%。

图2　2014年居民消费价格月度涨跌幅度

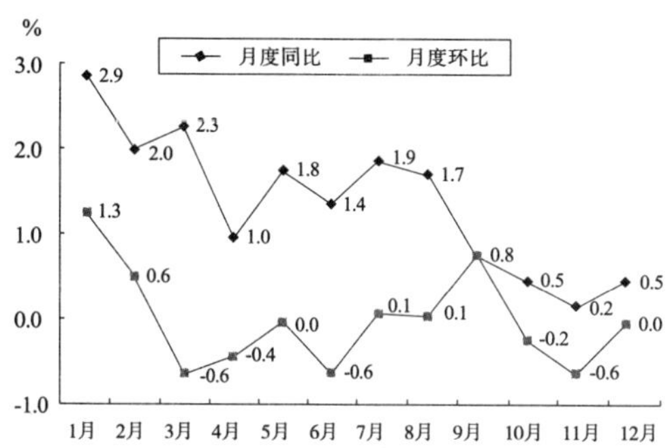

表1　2014年居民消费价格比上年涨跌幅度

指　标	涨跌幅度(%)
居民消费价格	1.4
食　品	2.9
其中：粮食	3.2
烟　酒	−1.6
衣　着	1.1
家庭设备用品及维修服务	1.9
医疗保健和个人用品	2.8
交通和通信	0.2
娱乐教育文化用品及服务	0.1
居　住	−0.2

全年城镇新增就业13.16万人，城镇失业人员再就业5.57万人。年末城镇登记失业率为3.4%。

全年财政总收入1019.56亿元，比上年增长12.9%。地方财政一般预算收入583.76亿元，增长16.3%，其中，营业税下降10.4%，增值税、企业所得税和个人所得税分别增长3.4%、15.5%和26.2%。全年地方财政一般预算支出819.50亿元，比上年增长12.3%，其中，科学技术支出增长70.8%，城乡社区事务支出增长40.0%，社会保障和就业支出增长13.6%，节能环保支出增长12.9%，一般公共服务支出下降0.9%。

二、农业

全年粮食播种面积551.46万亩，比上年下降2.9%；油料播种面积7.01万亩，下降8.6%；蔬菜播种面积101.56万亩，增长1.7%；棉花播种面积0.37万亩，下降85.7%。全年粮食产量175.61万吨，比上年下降4.1%，其中，夏粮88.05万吨，增长5.3%；秋粮87.56万吨，下降12.0%。

表2　2014年主要农产品产量及其增长速度

产品名称	单位	产量	比上年增长（%）
油 料	万吨	0.98	–2.1
蔬 菜	万吨	316.28	6.1
园林水果	万吨	99.66	4.7
肉 类	万吨	16.19	2.8
奶 类	万吨	65.80	持平
禽 蛋	万吨	13.52	–0.1
大牲畜年末存栏数	万头	21.73	2.6
猪年末存栏数	万头	95.01	–1.6
羊年末存栏数	万只	27.92	2.0
家禽年末存栏数	万只	1161.16	–1.0

三、工业和建筑业

全年全部工业增加值1523.12亿元，比上年增长10.7%。规模以上工业增加值1195.28亿元，增长11.1%。在规模以上工业中，轻工业增加值293.58亿元，增长8.9%；重工业增加值901.70亿元，增长11.8%。

图3　2014年规模以上工业增加值增速（累计同比）

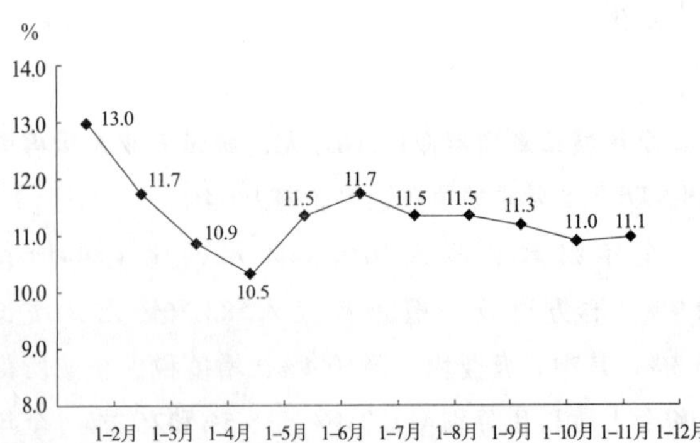

全年规模以上工业中，计算机、通信和其他电子设备制造业增加值比上年增长1.4倍，金属制品业增长11.9%，汽车制造业增长13.7%，铁路、船舶、航空航天和其他运输设备制造业增长21.9%。六大高耗能行业[3]增长9.4%，其中，非金属矿物制品业增长10.8%，化学原料和化学制品制造业增长35.1%，有色金属冶炼和压延加工业增长39.2%，黑色金属冶炼和压延加工业下降20.8%，电力、热力生产和供应业增长5.5%，石油加工、炼焦和核燃料加工业下降11.1%。

表3　2014年主要工业产品产量及其增长速度

产品名称	单位	产量	比上年增长（%）
发电量	亿千瓦小时	179.58	–2.5
原油加工量	万吨	148.05	–30.5
乳制品	万吨	111.01	–16.7
软饮料	万吨	204.93	–18.4
商品混凝土	万立方米	2789.14	10.9
机制纸	万吨	11.24	–35.7
交流电动机	万千瓦	792.42	37.8
饲料	万吨	116.86	11.7
合成洗涤剂	万吨	11.59	–1.1
水泥	万吨	412.69	5.5
风机	万台	0.59	226.0
汽车	万辆	37.47	–11.2
其中：轿车	万辆	26.71	–15.8
高压开关板	面	24635.00	42.3
变压器	万千伏安	14793.29	28.0
电力电缆	万千米	2.09	12.7
气体压缩机	万台	41.04	–5.3
电子元件	亿只	2.48	3.0
单晶硅	吨	2973.12	20.4

全年规模以上工业企业经济效益综合指数为289.8，比上年提高26.7个百分点。规模以上工业企业主营业务收入3768.18亿元，增长10.1%。实现利润总额176.24亿元，增长13.4%。

全年建筑业增加值731.06亿元，比上年增长11.3%。全年资质以内建筑业企业540家。

图4　2010—2014年建筑业增加值及其增长速度

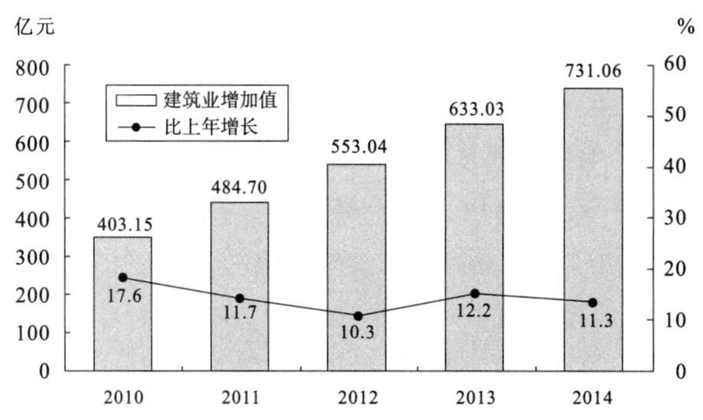

四、固定资产投资

全年全社会固定资产投资5903.98亿元，比上年增长15.0%，扣除价格因素，实际增长14.1%。其中，固定资产投资（不含农户）5824.53亿元，增长15.2%；农户投资79.45亿元，增长0.2%。

图5　2014年固定资产投资（不含农户）增速（累计同比）

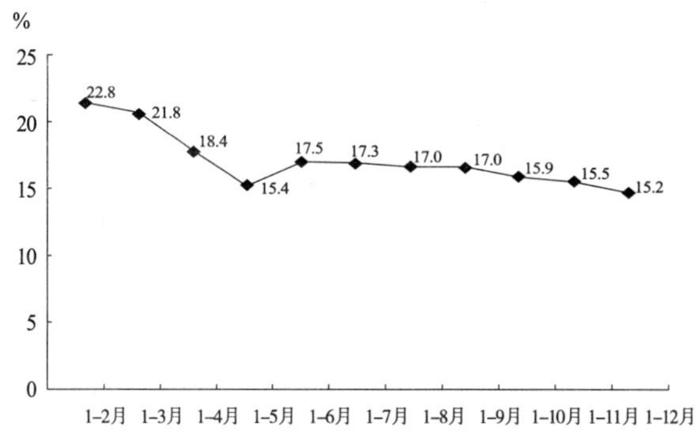

在固定资产投资（不含农户）中，第一产业投资75.15亿元，比上年增长2.7%；第二产业投资1261.70亿元，增长28.3%，其中，工业投资1205.53亿元，增长38.8%；第三产业投资4487.68亿元，增长12.2%。

表4　2014年重点行业固定资产投资及其增长速度

行　业	投资额（亿元）	比上年增长（%）
农、林、牧、渔业	86.04	3.0
制造业	1012.39	47.3
交通运输、仓储和邮政业	336.15	18.8
信息传输、软件和信息技术服务业	68.47	43.3
批发和零售业	184.83	33.4
科学研究和技术服务业	181.48	145.2
水利、环境和公共设施管理业	411.83	–11.2
教育	83.65	19.0
卫生和社会工作	96.40	31.8
公共管理、社会保障和社会组织	36.63	–45.0

全年房地产开发投资1761.88亿元，比上年增长10.4%。房屋施工面积12422.10万平方米，增长18.8%，房屋竣工面积1533.70万平方米，增长92.8%。

表5　2014年房地产开发主要指标完成情况

指　标	单位	绝对量	比上年增长（%）
房地产开发投资	亿元	1761.88	10.4
其中：住宅	亿元	1334.43	7.5
房屋施工面积	万平方米	12422.10	18.8
其中：住宅	万平方米	9727.60	15.0
房屋新开工面积	万平方米	2460.47	–4.9
其中：住宅	万平方米	1810.44	–6.7
房屋竣工面积	万平方米	1533.70	92.8
其中：住宅	万平方米	1307.64	97.2

五、国内贸易

全年社会消费品零售总额2872.90亿元，比上年增长12.8%，扣除价格因素，实际增长12.0%。按经营地统计，城镇消费品零售额2788.61亿元，增长12.7%；乡村消费品零售额84.29亿元，增长13.5%。按消费形态统计，商品零售额2635.62亿元，增长13.4%；餐饮收入额237.28亿元，增长6.0%。

图6　2014年社会消费品零售总额增速（累计同比）

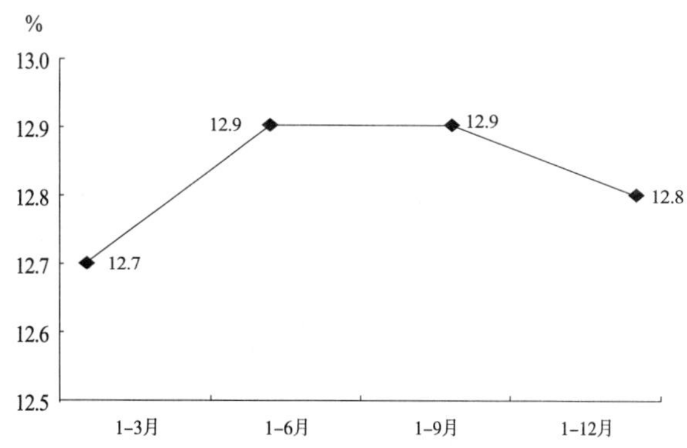

在限额以上企业商品零售额中，粮油、食品、饮料、烟酒类零售额比上年增长5.0%，服装、鞋帽、针、纺织品类增长14.7%，化妆品类增长10.7%，金银珠宝类增长8.8%，日用品类增长3.6%，体育、娱乐用品类增长3.6%，书报杂志类增长0.4%，家用电器和音像器材类下降3.0%，通讯器材类增长16.9%，家具类增长12.8%，石油及制品类增长21.9%，建筑及装潢材料类增长26.1%，汽车类增长12.6%。

六、对外经济

全年进出口总额1534.54亿元，比上年增长

37.7%。其中，出口734.62亿元，增长39.7%；进口799.92亿元，增长35.9%。

在进出口总额中，加工贸易进出口916.8亿元，增长1倍，占进出口总额的59.7%；一般贸易进出口385.9亿元，下降7%，占进出口总额的25.1%。

主要进出口商品中，机电产品出口582.6亿元，增长48.3%；进口656.6亿元，增长49.1%。农产品出口22.2亿元，下降25.6%；进口5.6亿元，下降3.4%。矿产品出口17亿元，增长11.1%；进口47.8亿元，下降6.9%。纺织服装出口14.3亿元，增长22.4%；进口0.4亿元，增长21%。

全年批准外商直接投资项目103个，批准合同外资25.53亿美元，比上年增长1.4%；实际利用外商直接投资37.03亿美元，增长18.3%。

七、交通、邮电和旅游

全年货物运输总量4.20亿吨，比上年增长12.9%。货物运输周转量623.41亿吨公里，增长9.4%。旅客运输总量2.57亿人次，增长6.8%。旅客运输周转量309.11亿人公里，增长8.1%。

表6　2014年各种运输方式完成货物运输量及其增长速度

指标	单位	绝对数	比上年增长（%）
货物运输总量	万吨	42038.55	12.9
公路	万吨	41120.03	13.1
铁路	万吨	899.87	4.9
民航（吞吐量）	万吨	18.64	4.2
货物运输周转量	亿吨公里	623.41	9.4
公路	亿吨公里	386.40	13.8
铁路	亿吨公里	235.95	2.9
民航	亿吨公里	1.07	3.6

表7　2014年各种运输方式完成旅客运输量及其增长速度

指　标	单位	绝对数	比上年增长（%）
旅客运输总量	亿人次	2.57	6.8
公路	亿人次	1.93	4.9
铁路	亿人次	0.35	13.1
民航（吞吐量）	亿人次	0.29	12.3
旅客运输周转量	亿人公里	309.11	8.1
公路	亿人公里	106.75	5.0
铁路	亿人公里	65.93	4.4
民航	亿人公里	136.44	12.7

年末全市机动车保有量213.90万辆，比上年末增长14.9%，其中，私人汽车保有量170.52万辆，增长20.7%。

全年邮政业务总收入21.39亿元,比上年增长20.8%。电信业务总收入135.67亿元，增长3.1%。年末全市固定电话用户306.66万户。移动电话用户2025.32万户，其中，3G移动电话用户[4]638.96万户。

全年接待国内外游客12001万人次，比上年增长18.5%；旅游总收入950亿元，增长17.1%。

八、金融

年末全市金融机构本外币存款余额15315.39亿元，比上年末增长10.2%。人民币存款余额15166.78亿元，增长10.2%，其中，城乡居民储蓄存款余额5698.15亿元，增长6.4%。金融机构本外币贷款余额11878.89亿元，增长16.3%。人民币贷款余额11668.14亿元，增长16.4%，其中，短期贷款余额2516.78亿元，增长8.2%；中长期贷款余额8685.74亿元，增长17.6%。

全年证券市场各类证券交易总额18874亿元，比上年增长46.9%。年末全市拥有上市股份公司31家，上市总股本356.33亿股，总市值4228.80亿元。年末股票市场累计开户数185万户，比上年末增长5.7%。

年末全市共有保险公司50家，其中，财产险23家，人寿险27家。保险专业中介机构125家。全年保费收入219.40亿元，比上年增长8.4%，其中，财产险保费收入74.18亿元，增长17.8%；人身险保费收入145.32亿元，增长4.2%。全年支付各类赔款给付104.39亿元，比上年增长57.0%，其中，财产险、人身险分别为41.71和42.68亿元，分别比上年增长20.9%和31.0%。

九、教育、科技、文化和体育

全市普通高校63所，在校学生90.53万人，毕业生23.95万人，另有研究生培养单位43个，在学研究生8.85万人，毕业生2.41万人；普通中学421所，在校学生42.57万人，毕业生14.54万人；小学1257所，在校学生53.79万人，毕业生8.29万人。小学、初中学龄人口入学率分别为99.98%和99.80%。

全年实施市级科技计划项目404项，其中，高新技术产业专项21项。重点扶持高新技术企业71家，支持建设农业科技示范园区和项目23个。全年技术市场交易额530.53亿元。申请专利量47134件，专利授权量16723件。

全市博物馆108个，公共图书馆15个，群众艺术馆2个，文化馆14个，文化站182个。地市广播电视台2座，县级广播电视台6座。

全年举办各类群众体育展示表演和竞赛活动共计

260项次，体育社团举办和承办体育赛事300项次，其中，国际性和全国性赛事40项次。新建城市社区全民健身器材配送工程91个，乡镇农民体育健身工程47个，社区全民健身路径31个。全市新增社会体育指导员6920名。已有晨晚练点1600个，健身气功站点198个，在册练功人数6118人。

2014年，我市培养输送运动员参加国际、国内各项比赛获得金牌19枚、银牌16枚、铜牌28枚。

十、卫生和社会服务

年末全市共有各类卫生机构5554个，其中，医院、卫生院381个。各类卫生技术人员7.60万人，其中，执业（含助理）医师2.48万人。卫生机构床位5.11万张。

全市提供住宿的法定社会服务机构132个，共有床位2.2万张，年末收养人数1.4万人。年末城市低保对象4.0万户、7.5万人，发放低保金4.2亿元；农村低保对象4.9万户、15.2万人，发放低保金4.1亿元。4718人纳入农村五保供养[5]，发放供养金3580.6万元。全年救助城市医疗困难群众4.4万人次；救助农村医疗困难群众17.0万人次。

十一、人民生活和社会保障

全年城镇居民人均可支配收入36100元，比上年增长9.1%，扣除价格因素，实际增长7.6%；农村居民人均纯收入14462元，比上年增长11.9%，扣除价格因素，实际增长10.4%。

年末全市城镇基本医疗保险参保人数417.70万人；城镇企业职工养老保险参保人数284.58万人；失业保险参保人数149.41万人；工伤保险参保人数142.86万人，职工生育保险参保人数98.72万人。年末参加农村新型合作医疗的农民人数407.18万人，实际参合率99.21%。

十二、城市建设、环境和安全生产

全年完成市政公用设施投资352.80亿元。新建人行天桥12座，建设公交港湾80处，新建改造绿地广场60个。

全年城市环境空气质量好于国家二级标准（良好）以上的天数211天。二氧化硫年平均浓度为32微克/标立方米，比上年下降30.4%；二氧化氮年平均浓度为47微克/标立方米，下降17.5%；可吸入颗粒物年平均浓度为147微克/标立方米，下降22.6%。全市集中式饮用水源地的水质达标率为100%。区域环境噪声等效声级均值为55.2分贝，道路交通噪声等效声级均值为68.0分贝。

全年共发生各类安全生产事故[6]1330起，死亡205人，受伤453人，经济损失3578.49万元。

注释：

［1］本公报数据为初步统计数，部分数据因四舍五入的原因，存在着分项与合计不等的情况。

［2］生产总值、各产业增加值绝对数按现价计算，增长速度按不变价格计算；根据第三次全国经济普查结果和国家统计局2012年制定的《三次产业划分规定》对相关数据进行了修订。

［3］六大高耗能行业分别为：化学原料和化学制品制造业、非金属矿物制品业、黑色金属冶炼和压延加工业、有色金属冶炼和压延加工业、石油加工炼焦和核燃料加工业、电力热力生产和供应业。

［4］3G是指第三代蜂窝移动通信系统（3rd-generation，简称3G），3G移动电话用户是指报告期末在计费系统拥有使用信息、占用3G网络资源的在网用户。

［5］农村五保供养是指老年、残疾和未满16周岁的村民，无劳动能力、无生活来源又无法定赡养、抚养、扶养义务人，或者其法定赡养、抚养、扶养义务人无赡养、抚养、扶养能力的村民，在吃、穿、住、医、葬方面得到的生活照顾和物质帮助。

［6］安全生产事故包括道路交通事故、火灾事故、农机事故和工矿商贸事故。

资料来源：本公报中物价数据来自国家统计局西安调查队；城镇新增就业、登记失业率、社会保障数据来自西安市人力资源和社会保障局；财政数据来自市财政局；进出口数据来自西安海关；利用外资数据来自市商务局；铁路运输数据来自西安铁路局；公路运输数据来自市交通运输局；民航运输数据来自西安咸阳国际机场；机动车数据来自市车管所；邮政业务数据来自市邮政局；电信数据来自中国移动西安分公司、中国电信西安分公司、中国联通西安分公司、陕西铁通西安分公司；旅游数据来自市旅游局；货币金融数据来自中国人民银行西安分行营业管理部；证券数据、保险业数据来自市金融办；教育数据来自市教育局；科技数据来自市科技局；艺术表演团体、公共图书馆、文化馆、广播、电视数据来自市文化广电新闻出版局；博物馆数据来自市文物局；体育数据来自市体育局；卫生、新农合数据来自市卫生局；社会服务、低保和五保供养数据来自市民政局；城市建设数据来自市城乡建设委员会；环境监测数据来自市环境保护局；安全生产数据来自市安全生产监督管理局；其他数据均来自市统计局。

Statistical Communique of Xi'an City on 2014 National Economic and Social Development

Xi'an Municipal Bureau of Statistics and NBS Survey Office in Xi' an

Mar. 5th, 2015

In 2014, Faced with a complicated and severe marcosituation, the municipal party committee and municipal government of Xi'an unite and lead the people of the city, conscientiously implement the deployment policy of CPC Central Committee and Shaanxi Province, insist on the tone of maintaining stability of overall the work, strive to improve the quality and efficiency of economic operation, initiatively adapt to the new normal of the economy, make overall plan on steady growth, promoting the reform ,restructuring, benefiting people' s livelihood and risk prevention. The city's economic and social development maintained stability and health.

I. General Outlook

The resident population of Xi' an city at the end of 2014 was 8.6275million,up by 39.4 thousand against the previous year, 4.4294million male and 4.1981 million female, accounted for 51.3 percent and 48.7 percent respectively. The sex ratio was 105.51(granted the female was 100).The born population in the whole year was 87.0 thousand, and the birth rate was 10.11‰ .The death population in the whole year was 47.1 thousand, and the death rate was 5.47‰, the natural growth rate was 4.64‰. The urban population was 6.2644million, accounted for 72.61 percent; the rural population was 2.3631 million, accounted for 27.39 percent. The total household population was 8.1529 million, up by 1.0 percent by previous year.

In 2014, the gross domestic product (GDP) preliminarily estimated was 547.477 billion Yuan, up by 9.9 percent against the previous year. Analyzed by different industries, the value added of the primary industry was 21.455 billion Yuan, up by 5.1 percent; the value added of the secondary industry was 220.537 billion Yuan, a rise of 11.3 percent; and the value added of the tertiary industry was 305.485 billion Yuan, up by 9.0 percent. The value added of the primary industry accounted for 3.9 percent of the GDP, that of the secondary industry accounted for 40.3 percent, and that of the tertiary industry accounted for 55.8 percent.

The value added of non-public sectors of the economy is 288.348billion, accounted for the proportion of GDP is 52.7 an increase of 0.5 percent over the previous year.

Table 1 the GDP and Growth Rate between 2010–2014

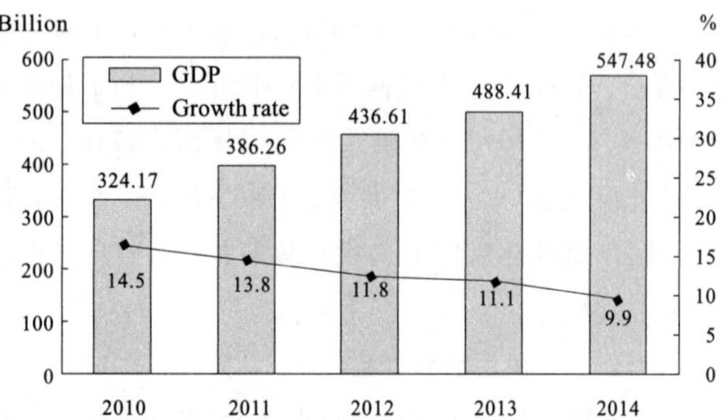

The general level of consumer prices in Xi'an was up by 1.4 percent against the previous year. Of this total, the prices for food went up by 2.9percent; the retail prices for commodities up by 0.7 percent; the producer prices for manufactured goods went down 0.5 percent; The purchasing prices for manufactured goods went down by 0.5 percent. The fixed asset investment price went up by 0.8 percent and the price of newly founded house increased by 3.7 percent.

Table 2 The rate of increase and decrease of CPI in 2014

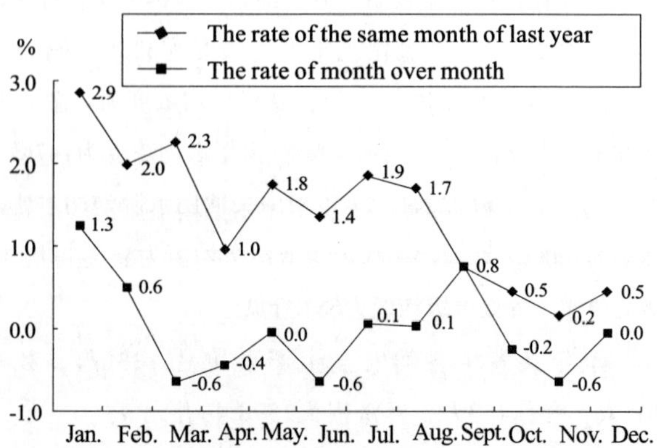

Sheet 1 Up and fall extent of Residents Consumer Price Indices with previous year(2014)

Item	2014(%)
Consumer Price Index	1.4
Food	2.9
#Grain	3.2
Tobacco and liquor	-1.6
Clothing	1.1
Household facilities and maintaining services	1.9
Medical, Health and Personal Articles	2.8
Transportation and Communication	0.2
Recreation, Education and Cultural articles and Services	0.1
Residence	-0.2

In 2014, the newly increased employed people in urban areas in Xi'an numbered 131.6thousand. The number of reemployment of laid-off workers was 55.7 thousand, the urban unemployment rate through unemployment registration was 3.4 percent at the end of 2014.

The financial revenue totaled 101.956 billion Yuan, an increase of 12.9 percent as compared with the previous year. The General Budget Revenue of Regional Finance reached 58.376 billion Yuan, up by 16.3 percent. Of this, business tax was down by 10.4 percent, the value added tax, income tax of enterprises and individual income tax were up by 3.4percent, 15.5 percent and 26.2 percent respectively. The General Budget Expenditure of Regional Finance totaled 81.950 billion Yuan, up by 12.3 percent. Of this total expenditure, the expenditure on technology and science was up by 70.8 percent; that on urban and rural community affairs was up by 40.0 percent, that on social security and employment was up by 13.6 percent, that on environmental protection was up by 12.9 percent, that on general public service went down 0.9 percent.

II. Agriculture

In 2014, the sown area of grain was 55.146 thousand hectares, a decrease of 2.9 percent as compared with the previous year; the sown area of oil-bearing crops was 70.1 thousand hectares, a decrease of 8.6 percent; the sown area of vegetables was 1015.6 thousand hectares, up by 1.7 percent; the sown area of cotton was 3.7 thousand hectares, a decrease of 85.7 percent. The total output of grain in 2013 was 1.7561 million tons, a decrease of 4.1percent. Of this, the output of summer crops was 0.8805 million tons, went down by 5.3 percent, and that of the autumn grain was 0.8756 million tons, an increase of 12.0 percent.

Sheet 2 Mail Product of Agriculture Production in 2014

Name of Product	Units	Output	Increase over the last year (%)
Oil	10,000 tons	0.98	-2.1
Vegetable	10,000 tons	316.28	6.1
Fruit	10,000 tons	99.66	4.7
Meat	10,000 tons	16.19	2.8
Milk	10,000 tons	65.80	Stay level
Poultry eggs	10,000 tons	13.52	-0.1
Year-end Cattle on hand	10,000 head	21.73	2.6
Year-end Pig on hand	10,000 head	95.01	-1.6
Year-end Sheep on hand	10,000 head	27.92	2.0
Year-end Fowl on hand	10,000 head	1161.16	-1.0

III. Industry and Construction

In 2014, the value added by the industrial sector was 152.312 billion Yuan, up by 10.7 percent over the previous year. The value added of industrial enterprises above the designated size was 119.528 billion Yuan, up by 11.1percent. Of this, the value added of the light industry was 29.358 billion Yuan, up by 8.9 percent; that of the heavy industry was 90.170 billion Yuan, up by 11.8 percent.

Table 3 Growth of Above-scale Industrial added Value in 2014

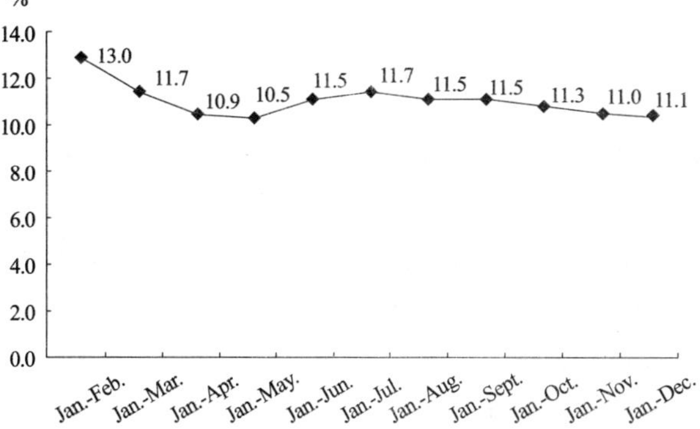

In 2014, of the industrial enterprises above designated size, the growth of value added for manufacture of computer, communication and other electrical devices was up by 40 percent over the previous year; for manufacture of material products was up by 11.9 percent; for manufacture of car up by 13.7 percent; for manufacture of transport equipment up by 21.9 percent; The growth of the value added for the major six high energy consuming industries were 9.4 percent, of which, that of the manufacture of non-metallic mineral products was 10.8 percent, manufacture of raw chemical materials and chemical products 35.1 percent, smelting and pressing of ferrous metals 39.2 percent, smelting and pressing of non-ferrous metals 20.8 percent, production and supply of electric power and heat power 5.5 percent and 11.1 percent for processing of petroleum, coking, processing of nuclear fuel.

Sheet 3 Output of Major Industrial Products above designated size in Xi' an(2014)

Name of Product	Units	Output	Increase over the last year (%)
Electricity	100 million kilo watt-hour	179.58	-2.5
Crude Oil Processing	10,000 tons	148.05	-30.5
Dairy	10,000 tons	111.01	-16.7
Soft Drink	10,000 tons	204.93	-18.4
Commercial Concrete	10,000 cubic meter	2789.14	10.9
Machine-made paper and Cardboard	10,000 tons	11.24	-35.7
AC motors	10,000 Kilowatt	792.42	37.8
Feed	10,000 tons	116.86	11.7
Synthetic detergent	10,000 tons	11.59	-1.1
Cement	10,000 tons	412.69	5.5
Draught fan	10,000 units	0.59	226.0
Motor vehicle	10,000 units	37.47	-11.2
#Car	10,000 units	26.71	-15.8
High voltage switch board	unit	24635.00	42.3
Transformer	10,000 kilovolt amperes	14793.29	28.0
Electric cable	10,000 km	2.09	12.7
Gas compressor	10,000 units	41.04	-5.3
Electronic component	100 million units	2.48	3.0
Mono-crystalline silicon	ton	2973.12	20.4

The composite index on economic benefits of the industrial enterprises above the designated size in 2014 was 289.8, an increase of 26.7 percent over the previous year. The main business income of the industrial enterprises above designated size is 37.6818 billion Yuan, up by 10.1 percent over the previous year. The profit was 17.624 billion Yuan, up by 13.4 percent.

In 2014, the added value by construction sector was 7.3106 billion Yuan, an increased of 11.3 percent over the pervious year. The total number of the qualified contractors and professional building contractor companies was 540.

Table 4 the value added of construction and growth rate between 2010–2014

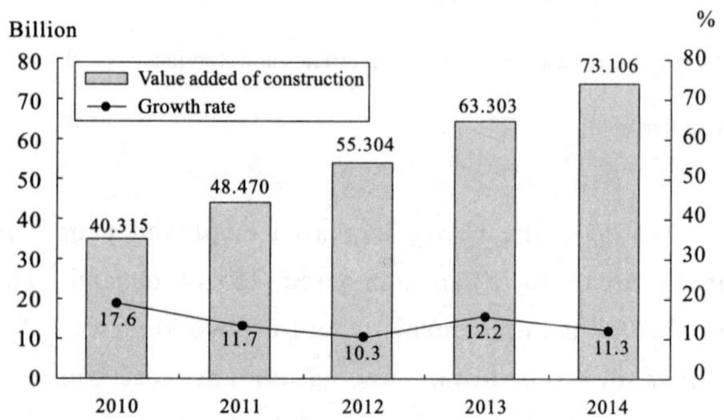

IV. Investment in Fixed Assets

The completed investment in fixed assets of the city in 2014 was 590.398 billion Yuan, up by 15.0 percent over the previous year. The real growth was 14.1 percent after deducting the price factors. Of the total investment in urban areas was 582.453 billion Yuan, up by 15.2 percent. Farmers Investment was 7.945 billion Yuan, up by 0.2 percent.

Table 5 Growth Rate of Fixed Asset Investment (excluding farmers) in 2014

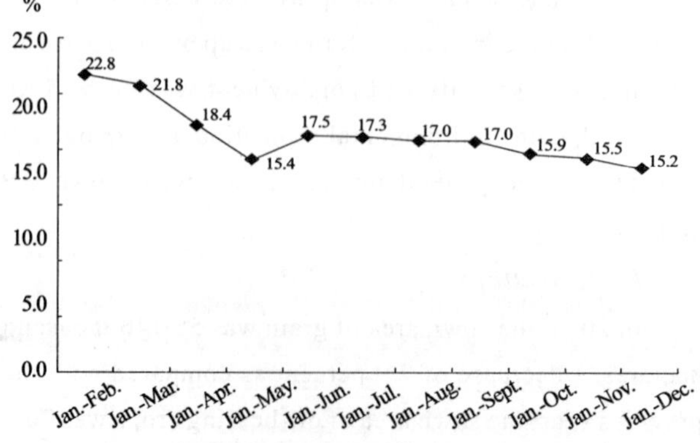

In whole investment, the investment in the primary industry was7.515 billion Yuan, up by 2.7 percent against the previous year; in the secondary industry, it was 126.170 billion Yuan, up by 28.3 mpercent, of which industrial investment was 120.553 billion Yuan, up by 38.8 percent; in the tertiary industry, it was 448.768 billion Yuan, up by 12.2 percent.

Sheet 4 the investment in fixed assets and growth rate in key industries in 2014

Industries	Investment (100 million Yuan)	Growth rate (%)
Agriculture, Forestry, Animal husbandry and fishery	86.04	3.0
Manufacturing	1012.39	47.3
Transportation, storage and postal services	336.15	18.8
Information transmission, computer services and software industry	68.47	43.3
Wholesale and retail trade	184.83	33.4
Accommodation and catering industry	181.48	145.2
Water Conservancy, environment and public facilities administration industry	411.83	-11.2
Education	83.65	19.0
Sanitations, social security and social welfare	96.40	31.8
Public administration and social organizations	36.63	-45.0

In 2014, the investment in real estate development was 176.188 billion Yuan, up by 10.4 percent; housing construction area was 1242.210 million square meters, up by 18.8 percent; the sold area of commercial housing was 153.370 million square meters, decreased by 92.8 percent.

Sheet 5 Mail Indicators of Real estate development and sales in 2014

Item	Units	Absolute Number	ncrease over the last year (%)
Investment in Real Estate Development	100 million Yuan	1761.88	10.4
#Residential Building	100 million Yuan	1334.43	7.5
Floor Space of Commercial Houses Construction	10,000 sq.m	12422.10	18.8
# Residential Building	10,000 sq.m	9727.60	15.0
Floor Space of Newly Construction	10,000 sq.m	2460.47	-4.9
# Residential Building	10,000 sq.m	1810.44	-6.7
Floor Space of Commercial Houses Completed	10,000 sq.m	1533.70	92.8
# Residential Building	10,000 sq.m	1307.64	97.2

V. Domestic Trade

In 2014, the total retail sales of consumer goods reached 287.290 billion Yuan, a growth of 12.8 percent over the previous year or a real growth of 12.0 percent after deducting price factors. An analysis on different areas showed that the retail sales of consumer goods in urban areas stood at 278.861 billion Yuan, up by 12.1 percent, and that in rural areas reached 8.429 billion Yuan, up by 13.5 percent. Grouped by consumption patterns, the income of retail sales of commodities was 263.562 billion Yuan, up by 13.4 percent; that of catering industry was 23.728 billion Yuan, up by 6.0 percent.

Table 6 The total retail sales of social consumer goods growth rate in 2014

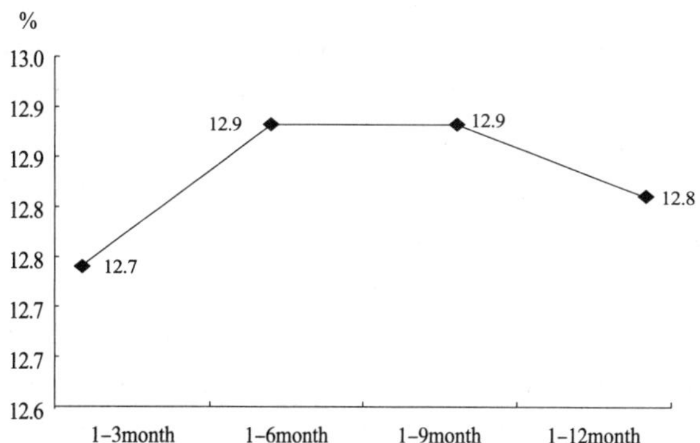

Of the total retail sales by wholesale and retail enterprises above designated size, the sales of food, beverage, wine and cigarette was up by 5.0 percent; clothing, shoes, hats, and needle textiles up by 14.7 percent; cosmetics up by 10.7 percent; gold,silver and jewelry up by 8.8 percent ; daily necessities up by 3.6 percent; sports-recreation up by 3.6 percent; books, newspapers and magazines up by 0.4 percent; electric and electronic appliances for household use and audio-video equipment down by 3.0 percent; telecommunication equipment up by 16.9 percent; furniture increased by 12.8 percent; oil and oil products up by 21.9 percent; building decoration materials up by 26.1 percent and motor vehicles up by 12.6 percent.

VI. Foreign Economic Relations

In 2014, the total value of imports and exports reached 153.454 billion US Dollars, up by 37.7 percent over the previous year. Of this, the value of exports was 73.462 billion US Dollars, up by 39.7 percent, and that of imports was 79.952 billion US Dollars, decreased by 35.9 percent.

In total imports and exports, the value of processing

trade was 91.68 billion US Dollars, up by 100 percent, accounted for 59.7 percent of import and export whole value of Xi' an region. The value of imports and exports of general trade was 38.59 billion US Dollars, decreased by 7 percent, accounted for 25.1 percent of import and export whole value of Xi' an region.

Of the main import and export commodities, the value of exports of electromechanical products was 58.26 billion US Dollars, an increase of 48.3 percent; that of imports of electromechanical products was 65.66 billion US Dollars, up by 49.1 percent. The value of exports of agricultural product was 2.22 billion US Dollars, a decrease of 25.6 percent; that of imports of agricultural products was 0.56 billion US Dollars, down by 3.4 percent. The value of exports of mineral products was 1.7 billion US Dollars, up by 11.1 percent; that of imports of mineral products was 4.78 billion US Dollars, increased by 6.9 percent. The value of exports of textile products was 1.43 billion US Dollars, an increase of 22.4 percent; that of imports of textile products was 0.4 million US Dollars, up by 21 percent.

In 2014, there were 103 Foreign Direct Investment projects approved in Xi'an; the contracted Foreign Direct Investment was 2.525 billion US dollars, an increase of 1.4 percent compared with the previous year; the realized Foreign Direct Investment was 3.703 billion US dollars, up by 18.3 percent.

VII. Transportation, Post, Telecommunications and Tourism

In 2014, the total freight traffic reached 0.420 billion ton, up by 12.9 percent over the previous year. The total goods transportation turnover reached 62.341 billion ton-kilometers, up by 9.4 percent over the previous year. The Total passenger transport reached 0.257 billion, up by 6.8 percent over the previous year. The passenger transport turnover reached 30.911 billion person-kilometers, up by 8.1 percent over the previous year.

Sheet 6 The Total Freight Traffic and growth rate created by Kinds of transport Mode in 2014

Index	Unit	Amount	Growth rate (%)
The Total Freight Traffic	10,000 tons	42038.55	12.9
Highway	10,000 tons	41120.03	13.1
Railway	10,000 tons	899.87	4.9
Airway	10,000 tons	18.64	4.2
Goods Transportation Turnover	100 million ton-kilometers	623.41	9.4
Highway	100 million ton-kilometers	386.40	13.8
Railway	100 million ton-kilometers	235.95	2.9
Airway	100 million ton-kilometers	1.07	3.6

Sheet 7 The Total Passenger Traffic and growth rate created by Kinds of transport Mode in 2014

Index	Unit	Amount	Growth rate (%)
The Total Passenger	100 million person	2.57	6.8
Highway	100 million person	1.93	4.9
Railway	100 million person	0.35	13.1
Airway	100 million person	0.29	12.3
The passenger transport turnover	100 million person-kilometers	309.11	8.1
Highway	100 million person-kilometers	106.75	5.0
Railway	100 million person-kilometers	65.93	4.4
Airway	100 million person-kilometers	136.44	12.7

The total number of motor vehicles for civilian use reached 2139.0 thousand by the end of 2014 up by 14.9 percent, of which private-owned vehicles numbered 1705.2 thousand, up 20.7 percent.

The revenue of post services totaled 2.139 billion Yuan, an increase of 20.8 percent over the previous year. That of telecommunication services was 13.567 billion Yuan, up by 3.1 percent. At the end of 2014, there were 3.0666 million fixed telephone users; there were 20.2532 million mobile phone users, of which the number of telecom and China Unicom 3G[4] mobile phone was 6389.6 thousand.

The total of domestic tourists was 120.01 million person-times, up by 18.5 percent. The revenue from tourism totaled 95.0 billion Yuan, up by 17.1 percent.

VIII. Financial Intermediation

Savings deposit in RMB and foreign currencies in all items of financial institutions totaled 1531.539 billion Yuan at the end of 2014, an increase of 10.2 percent as compared with the end of the previous year. The savings deposit in RMB stood at 1516.678 billion Yuan, an increase of 10.2 percent, of which the savings deposit of urban and rural residents was 569.815 billion Yuan, up by

6.4 percent. Loans in all items of financial institutions in RMB and foreign currencies reached 1187.889 billion Yuan, an increase of 16.3 percent as compared with the end of the previous year. The loans in RMB stood at 1166.814 billion Yuan, an increase of 16.4 percent, of which the short-term loans totaled 251.678 billion Yuan, up by 8.2 percent, and medium -and- long term loans reached 868.574 billion Yuan, up by 17.6 percent.

The trading volume of stock exchange market was 1887.4 billion Yuan in 2014, an increase of 46.9 percent as compared with the previous year. There were 31 listed companies in Xi'an at the end of 2014 of which the total capital stock was 35.633 billion shares, and the total market value was 422.880 billion Yuan. There were 1.85 million accounts in stock market at the end of 2014, an increase of 5.7 percent as compared with the end of the previous year.

By the end of 2014, there were 50 insurance institutions, of which the number of property insurance was 23, and that of life insurance was 27. There were 125 intermediary organs of insurance. The received by the insurance companies totaled 21.94 billion Yuan in 2014, up by 8.4 percent. Of this, the revenue from property insurance was 7.418 billion Yuan, up by 17.8 percent; that from life insurance was 14.532 billion Yuan, up by 4.2 percent. In total, insurance companies paid an indemnity worth of 10.439 billion Yuan, up by 57 percent over the previous year, of which the worth of property insurance and life insurance were 4.171 billion Yuan and 4.268 billion Yuan respectively, up by 20.9 percent and 31 percent respectively.

IX. Education、Science & Technology and Culture

There were 63 general universities and colleges, with 905 thousand general tertiary education enrollments, including 239.5 thousand graduates; there were 43 post-graduate training units, with 88.5 thousand students in school and 24.1 thousand graduates. There were 421 general middle schools and high schools, with 425.7 thousand junior high education enrollments and 145.4 thousand graduates; there were 1257 primary schools, with 537.9 thousand primary education enrollments and 82.9 thousand graduates. The enrollment rates for school-age population of primary school and junior high school were 99.98 percent and 99.80 percent respectively.

404 science and technology projects were carried out in 2013 (including 21 projects of high technology). Of this, 71 technology demonstration towns and 23 important direction projects of industry science and technology in districts and counties implemented. The turnover in technology market reached 53.053 billion Yuan. 47134 patents were applied in 2014, including of 16723 patents accredited.

By the end of 2014, there were 108 museums, 15 public libraries, 2 Mass Art Museum, 14 Cultural center, 182 culture stations. There were 2 municipal radio and television stations and 6 county radio.

260 mass sports performances and competition activities were organized in 2014, and 300 sports competition were organized and host by sports associations, including 40 international and national sports competition. In 2014, there were 91 newly built fitness projects, 47 fitness projects for township farmers, and 31 public national fitness paths of community built. The number of social sports instructors had increased6920. There were 1600 sites for morning and evening exercise and 198 sites for fitness Qigong, with 6118 taking part in fitness Qigong.

In 2014, the delegation of Xi'an won 19 gold medals、16 silver medals and 28 bronze medal in the National and international Games.

X. Health and Public Service

At the end of 2014, there were 5554 health institutions in Xi'an, including 381 general hospitals and health centers. There were all 76 thousand health care workers, including 24.8 thousand practicing (assistant) doctors. General health centers in Xi'an possessed 51.1 thousand beds.

There were 132 social welfare adoption class units, with a total of 22 thousand beds, and 14 thousand people were in them at the end of the year. There were 40 thousand of urban low-income households, with 75 thousand people, and 420 million Yuan were distributed to them. There were 49 thousand of village low-income households, with 152 thousand people, and 410 million Yuan were distributed to them. 4718 people were in the rural five guarantees [5] and 35.806 million Yuan were distributed. 44 thousand urban residents and 170thousand rural residents gained medical relief.

XI. Living Conditions and Social Security

In 2014, the annual per capita disposable income of urban households was 36100 Yuan, growth of 9.1 percent over the previous year, or a real increase of 7.6 percent when the factors of price increase were deducted. And that of rural households was 14462 Yuan, growth of 11.9 percent over the previous year, or a real increase of 10.4 percent.

By the end of 2014, a total of 4.1770 million people participated in urban basic health insurance program; a total of 2.8458 million people participated in basic pension program for staff and workers of enterprises; a total of 1.4941 million people participated in unemployment insurance programs; a total of 1.4286 million people participated in work accident insurance; a total of 987.2 thousand people participated in maternity insurance programs for staff and workers. The number of farmers taking part in the new cooperative medical care system in rural areas reached 4.0718 million, with a participation rate of 99.21 percent covered.

XII. Urban Construction, Environment and Work Safety

The total investment of municipal utilities was 35.28 billion Yuan.12 pedestrian bridges, underground passages and 80 bus bays were newly built. In urban areas was newly added 60 green squares were reformed and newly built.

In 2014, there were 211 days with air quality better than standard Grade II.The annual mean concentration of Sulfur dioxide, Nitrogen dioxide and respirable particulate matter was 0.032 Mg / cu.m, 0.047 Mg / cu.m and 0.147 Mg / cu.m, a decrease by 30.4 percent, 17.5 percent and 22.6 percent. All of water quality of reference water source reached the state standard. The average value of sound level equivalent of regional environmental noises was 55.2 decibel, and the average value of sound level equivalent of transportation noises was 68.0 decibel.

In 2014, various kinds of work accidents amounted to 1330, Of this, there were 205 people dead and 453 people injured, the property losses was 35.7849 million Yuan.

Notes:

1. All figures in this Communiqué are preliminary statistics.

2. Gross domestic product (GDP) and value added as quoted in this Communiqué are calculated at current prices, whereas their growth rates are at constant prices. According to the third national economic census and the 《regulation on classification of three sectors》 revised by national statistics bureau in 2012.

3. Six highly energy-consuming industries are: manufacture of raw chemical materials and chemical products, manufacture of non-metallic mineral products, smelting and pressing of ferrous metals, smelting and pressing of non-ferrous metals, oil processing, coking and nuclear fuel processing, and production and supply of electricity and heat.

4. 3G refers to the third generation cellular mobile communication system (3rd - generation, referred to as \"3G\"), the 3G mobile phone users refers to those who own using information in the billing system of the final report, and take up the 3G network resources in the network.

5. Rural five guarantees is refers to the elderly,disabled,and those under the age of 16 villages, without labor ability, the source of life, and has no fixed support, raising, the obligation of maintenance, or its legal support, raising, the obligation of maintenance support, raising, the villages of bring up ability,who gain help in the care of life and material such as eat,wear, live, medical such as eat, wear, live, medical. and buride. 6. work accidents include traffic accidents, fire accidents, agricultural machinery accidents ,mines and commercial and trade accidents.

6. Production safety accidents includs road traffic accidents, fires, agricultural accidents and mining accidents.

Data Sources:

In this communiqué, data of price are from NBS Survey Office in Xi'an ;data of newly increased employed people, unemployment rate through unemployment registration and social security are from the Xi'an Municipal Bureau of Human Resources and Social Security; financial data are from the Xi'an Municipal Bureau of Finance; data of imports and exports are from the Xi'an Customs; data of utilizing foreign capital are from the Xi'an Municipal Bureau of Business; data of railway transportation are from the Xi'an Municipal Bureau of Railways; data of highway transportation are from the Xi'an Municipal Bureau of Transport; data of air transport are from the Xi'an- Xian yang International Airport; data of motor vehicles for civilian use are from the Xi'an vehicle administration; data of post services are from the Xi'an Municipal Bureau of post; data of telecommunications are from Xi'an branch of China Mobile、 China Unicom、 China Telecom, and Shaanxi CTT; data of tourism are from the Xi'an Tourism

Administration; data of monetary and financial are from business management department for Xi'an branch of the People's Bank of China; data of listed companies and insurance are from Xi'an Municipal Finance Office; data of education are from the Xi'an Municipal Bureau of Education; data of technology are from Xi'an Municipal Bureau of Technology; data of art-performing groups, public libraries, culture centers, radio and television are from the Xi'an Municipal Bureau of Culture, Radio, Press and Publication; data of museum are from Xi'an Municipal Bureau of Heritage; data of sports are from the Xi'an Municipal Bureau of Sport; data of health and new cooperative medical care system in rural areas are from the Xi'an Municipal Bureau of Health; data of central heating area and green area are from Xi'an Municipal Urban and Rural Construction Committee; data of sewage treatment in urban and environment monitoring are from the Xi'an Municipal Bureau of Environmental Protection; data of work safety are from the State Administration of Work Safety; all the other data are from Xi'an Municipal Bureau of Statistics.

1 综　合

GENERAL SURVEY

资料整理：栗海燕
Data management：Li Haiyan
数据审核：陈　英
Data audit：Chen Ying

第一部分　综合

一、简要说明

本章资料主要包括西安市行政区划、自然地理、自然资源、气象、国民经济和社会发展等综合资料，由西安市统计局综合处根据局内各专业处及有关部门统计资料进行整理和编辑。

二、主要指标

生产总值（亿元）	5492.64	比上年增长	9.9%
农林牧渔及服务业总产值（亿元）	367.21	比上年增长	5.1%
规模以上工业增加值（亿元）	1304.12	比上年增长	11.1%
全社会固定资产投资额（亿元）	5903.98	比上年增长	15.0%
社会消费品零售总额（亿元）	3093.89	比上年增长	12.8%
财政一般预算收入（亿元）	583.79	比上年增长	16.3%
财政一般预算支出（亿元）	819.54	比上年增长	12.3%
出口总额（亿美元）	119.60	比上年增长	41.1%
城镇居民人均可支配收入（元）	36100	比上年增长	9.1%
农村居民人均纯收入（元）	14462	比上年增长	11.8%

1　GENERAL SURVEY

Ⅰ.Brief Introduction

This chapter consists of mainly unified data of administrative divisions, natural geography, natural resources, meteorology, national economy and social development of Xi'an city. It is compiled by Integration Division according to the reported data from other divisions of the Xi'an Bureau of Statistics and other departments of the municipal government.

Ⅱ. Major Indicators

		Increase over Preceding Year
Gross Domestic Product (100 mil. Yuan)	5492.64	9.9%
Gross Output Value of Farming, Forestry, Animal, Husbandry and Fishery (100 mil. Yuan)	367.21	5.1%
Gross Industrial Added Value (100 mil. Yuan)	1304.12	11.1%
Investment Fulfilled In Fixed Assets (100 mil. Yuan)	5903.98	15.0%
Total Retail Sales of Consumer Goods (100 mil. Yuan)	3093.89	12.8%
Local Government Revenue (100 mil. Yuan)	583.79	16.3%
Local Government Expenditures (100 mil. Yuan)	819.54	12.3%
Total Value of Exports (USD 100 mil.)	119.60	41.1%
Per Capita Annual Disposable Income of Urban Households (Yuan)	36100	9.1%
Per Capita Net Income of Rural Residents (Yuan)	14462	11.8%

1-1 行政区划（2014年）

Administrative Division（2014）

单位：个 (unit)

地 区	Region	乡镇及街道办 Township and Urban Subdistrict Office	镇数 Town	街道办事处 Urban Subdistrict Office	村民委员会 Villagers' Committee	社区居委会 Neighbourhood Committee
西安市	**Xi'an**	**178**	**67**	**111**	**2947**	**828**
（一）市区	**Urban**	**105**	**2**	**103**	**1337**	**764**
新城区	Xincheng	9		9		105
碑林区	Beilin	8		8		103
莲湖区	Lianhu	9		9	3	131
灞桥区	Baqiao	9		9	218	42
未央区	Weiyang	10		10	97	104
雁塔区	Yanta	8		8	82	130
阎良区	Yanliang	7	2	5	80	23
临潼区	Lintong	23		23	284	41
长安区	Chang'an	22		22	573	85
（二）四县	**Four Counties**	**68**	**65**	**3**	**1501**	**48**
蓝田县	Lantian	22	22		519	9
周至县	Zhouzhi	22	22		376	14
户 县	Huxian	16	16		518	21
高陵县	Gaoling	8	5	3	88	4
（三）沣东新城	**Fengdongxincheng**	**5**		**5**	**109**	**16**

注：本表数据来源市民政局。

1-2 土地面积和常住人口密度（2014年）

Statistics on Land Area and Density of Permanent Population（2014）

地 区	Region	土地面积 Area 绝对数（平方公里）Absolute Value (sq.km)	比重（%）Proportion (%)	常住人口（万人）Total of Permanent Population (10 000 persons)	常住人口密度（人/平方公里）Density of Permanent Population (person/sq.km)
西安市	**Xi 'an**	**10096.81**		**862.75**	**854**
（一）市区	**Urban**	**3581.22**	**35.5**	**662.06**	**1849**
新城区	Xincheng	30.13	0.3	59.86	19867
碑林区	Beilin	23.37	0.2	62.40	26701
莲湖区	Lianhu	38.32	0.4	70.68	18445
灞桥区	Baqiao	324.50	3.2	60.82	1874
未央区	Weiyang	264.41	2.6	82.28	3112
雁塔区	Yanta	151.44	1.5	119.74	7907
阎良区	Yanliang	244.55	2.4	28.53	1167
临潼区	Lintong	915.97	9.1	67.16	733
长安区	Chang'an	1588.53	15.7	110.59	696
（二）四县	**Four Counties**	**6515.59**	**64.5**	**200.69**	**308**
蓝田县	Lantian	2005.95	19.9	52.30	261
周至县	Zhouzhi	2945.20	29.2	57.57	195
户 县	Huxian	1279.42	12.7	56.60	442
高陵县	Gaoling	285.03	2.8	34.22	1201

注：本表土地面积数据来源市国土资源局。

1-3 自然状况和资源（2014年）

Nature Conditions and Resources（2014）

指　标	Item	2014
一、自然状况	**Nature Conditions**	
土地总面积（平方公里）	Total Land Area (sq.km)	10096.81
#市区面积	Urban Area	3581.22
气候（市区）	Climate (Urban)	
年平均气温（℃）	Average Annual Temperature (℃)	15.2
年降水量（毫米）	Total Annual Precipitation (mm)	660.3
日照总时数（小时）	Total Sunshine Time (hour)	1941.8
平均风速（米/秒）	Average Wind-speed (m/sec.)	2.3
二、自然资源	**Natural Resources**	
年末实有耕地面积（千公顷）	Cultivated Area Year-end (1 000 hectare)	360.73
林业用地面积（千公顷）	Area of Forestry (1 000 hectare)	508.39
全市水面面积（千公顷）	Whole Water Area (1 000 hectare)	5.18
水资源总量（亿立方米）	Total Water Resource (0.1 billion cu.m)	21.92
#天然地表水资源总量	Total Savageness Surface Water Resource	17.77
地下水资源总量（亿立方米）	Total Ground Water Resource (0.1 billion cu.m)	11.98

注：2013年市气象局位于市郊新站启用，本年鉴气象资料为新站监测数据。
全市水面面积包括湖泊、水库、鱼塘、城市段河流面积等。
本表数据来源市气象局、林业局、水务局等。

1-4 气象情况（2014年）

Climate Condition（2014）

地 区	Region	平均气温（℃）Average Temperature（℃）	日照时数（小时）Sunshine Time (hour)	降水天数（天）Raining days (day)	年降水量（毫米）Total Annual Precipitation (mm)	平均风速（米/秒）Average Wind-speed (m/second)
市 区	Urban	15.2	1941.8	88	660.3	2.3
临潼区	Lintong	16.1	2239.0	44	559.9	1.5
长安区	Chang'an	14.1	1804.6	111	792.4	1.3
蓝田县	Lantian	14.1	1927.2	108	738.1	1.2
周至县	Zhouzhi	13.5	1878.9	102	733.8	1.0
户 县	Huxian	14.3	2148.7	127	727.1	1.6
高陵县	Gaoling	15.0	1949.8	116	544.6	1.4

注：本表数据来源市气象局。

1-5 市区及县各月平均气温（2014年）

Average Temperature of Xi'an and the Districts of each Month（2014）

单位：℃ (℃)

月 份	Month	市区 Urban	临潼 Lintong	长安 Chang'an	蓝田 Lantian	周至 Zhouzhi	户县 Huxian	高陵 Gaoling
一月	January	2.9	2.4	1.3	0.6	1.2	1.8	2.1
二月	February	2.3	1.9	1.6	1.8	1.4	1.8	2.3
三月	March	12.0	11.8	10.7	11.1	10.4	10.6	11.8
四月	April	16.1	15.5	14.9	15.1	14.6	14.9	16.1
五月	May	21.1	20.9	19.6	19.4	19.3	19.9	20.8
六月	June	26.0	25.7	24.6	24.8	24.0	25.2	26.2
七月	July	29.1	28.9	28.8	28.9	27.8	28.9	29.2
八月	August	25.1	24.6	24.4	24.8	23.5	24.3	25.1
九月	September	20.3	19.9	19.6	20.0	18.9	19.6	20.4
十月	October	16.4	15.6	14.9	15.4	14.1	15.3	16.2
十一月	November	8.9	8.6	7.4	7.1	6.8	7.9	8.6
十二月	December	2.2	2.2	0.9	-0.1	0.4	1.2	1.5

注：本表数据来源市气象局。

1-6 市区及县各月日照时数（2014年）

Sunshine Duration of Xi'an and the Districts of each Month（2014）

单位：小时 (hour)

月 份	Month	市区 Urban	临潼 Lintong	长安 Chang'an	蓝田 Lantian	周至 Zhouzhi	户县 Huxian	高陵 Gaoling
一月	January	181.5	214.3	134.3	155.2	198.3	204.5	182.0
二月	February	55.4	59.7	28.6	50.8	38.6	46.0	43.1
三月	March	162.5	211.1	150.3	173.2	175.8	184.8	186.0
四月	April	126.0	150.8	100.6	136.3	124.1	129.8	124.0
五月	May	209.3	250.0	193.6	197.8	216.6	221.0	204.3
六月	June	193.9	233.6	178.3	202.5	198.2	223.6	203.4
七月	July	288.0	334.1	302.8	286.2	287.8	307.9	279.0
八月	August	191.4	207.3	199.1	200.5	199.0	227.8	191.4
九月	September	112.0	126.0	90.2	102.2	71.8	113.9	87.3
十月	October	105.0	148.1	123.6	127.1	98.6	150.2	120.1
十一月	November	141.0	113.9	121.6	122.8	110.2	137.5	135.0
十二月	December	175.8	190.1	181.6	172.6	159.9	201.7	194.2

注：本表数据来源市气象局。

1-7 市区及县各月降水天数（2014年）

Precipitation Days of Xi'an and the Districts of each Month（2014）

单位：天 (day)

月 份	Month	市区 Urban	临潼 Lintong	长安 Chang'an	蓝田 Lantian	周至 Zhouzhi	户县 Huxian	高陵 Gaoling
一月	January	1	1	1	1	1	1	1
二月	February	10	4	15	13	4	17	19
三月	March	9	4	12	10	8	9	10
四月	April	10	4	9	11	14	16	15
五月	May	5	2	9	8	10	13	7
六月	June	9	2	10	10	12	12	9
七月	July	6	3	9	9	6	6	5
八月	August	7	5	10	11	12	10	9
九月	September	15	11	17	16	16	17	18
十月	October	7	2	7	7	10	12	9
十一月	November	8	4	11	10	9	13	10
十二月	December	1	2	1	2		1	4

注：本表数据来源市气象局。

1-8 市区及县各月降水量（2014年）

Amount of Precipitation of Xi'an and the Districts of each Month（2014）

单位：毫米 (mm)

月 份	Month	市区 Urban	临潼 Lintong	长安 Chang'an	蓝田 Lantian	周至 Zhouzhi	户县 Huxian	高陵 Gaoling
一月	January	0.3	0.1		1.1			
二月	February	16.2	19.0	26.1	25.6	30.4	21.4	16.4
三月	March	13.9	16.5	22.5	38.4	32.1	24.4	14.8
四月	April	65.6	78.5	74.8	64.8	104.2	104.7	63.5
五月	May	53.4	20.1	69.5	91.9	53.6	46.8	51.2
六月	June	62.7	30.3	53.8	52.0	47.5	45.1	30.0
七月	July	80.3	15.0	103.3	56.8	22.0	23.2	53.6
八月	August	96.8	90.6	112.7	138.7	132.3	146.7	89.5
九月	September	230.3	240.5	260.6	199.1	266.0	258.2	183.2
十月	October	20.8	20.2	21.5	26.3	18.4	21.2	22.2
十一月	November	19.5	28.2	46.5	42.7	26.8	34.9	19.4
十二月	December	0.5	0.9	1.1	0.7	0.5	0.5	0.8

注：本表数据来源市气象局。

1-9 市区及县各月平均风速（2014年）

Average Wind Velocity of Xi'an and the Districts of each Month（2014）

单位：米/秒 (m/s)

月 份	Month	市区 Urban	临潼 Lintong	长安 Chang'an	蓝田 Lantian	周至 Zhouzhi	户县 Huxian	高陵 Gaoling
一月	January	2.0	1.3	1.4	1.2	1.1	1.6	1.1
二月	February	2.4	1.5	1.1	0.8	0.8	1.5	1.5
三月	March	2.3	1.5	1.5	1.4	1.2	1.6	1.2
四月	April	2.3	1.5	1.2	1.3	1.0	1.6	1.1
五月	May	2.5	1.8	1.5	1.4	1.3	1.8	1.1
六月	June	2.3	1.6	1.4	1.3	1.0	1.7	1.0
七月	July	2.8	1.8	1.5	1.5	1.4	2.0	2.1
八月	August	2.6	1.6	1.2	1.3	0.9	1.7	1.9
九月	September	2.4	1.3	1.2	1.0	0.6	1.5	1.7
十月	October	2.2	1.3	1.3	1.2	0.5	1.5	1.7
十一月	November	2.0	1.4	1.2	1.0	1.0	1.4	1.3
十二月	December	2.1	1.6	1.5	1.2	1.1	1.6	1.3

注：本表数据来源市气象局。

1-10 主要年份国有土地使用权出让、划拨情况

The Transfer and Allocation of State-Owned Land Use Right in Main Years

项　　目	Item	2007	2008	2009	2010	2011	2012	2013	2014
国有土地使用权出让	**Lease of the Use Right of State-owned Land**								
出让地块(宗)	Land leased (item)	333	278	297	386	474	581	550	506
协议	Agreement	171	119	100	173	133	80	90	109
招标	Invitation for Bid	1	3		3				
拍卖	Auction	3	5	1	11				
挂牌交易	Listed Transaction	158	149	196	199	341	500	460	397
出让面积（公顷）	Area of Totally Leased Land (hectare)	843	809	1047	1364	1386	1853	2195	1789
土地使用权出让总收入（万元）	**Total Revenue from Leasing of the Use Right(10 000 yuan)**	**267666**	**309181**	**284405**	**358098**	**334069**	**218817**	**292945**	**183901**
国有土地使用权划拨	**Administrative Allocation of the Use Right of State-owned Land**								
划拨地块（宗）	Land Allocated (item)	100	102	79	108	253	154	234	152
划拨面积（公顷）	Area of Land Allocated(hectare)	388	455	1721	1027	1426	1617	1986	1739

注：本表数据来源市国土资源局。

1-11 主要年份国民经济和社会发展总量与速度指标

指　标	Item	总量指标 Total quantity index 1995	2000	2005	2009
人口与就业	**Population and Employment**				
人口	**Population**				
年底总人口(万人)	Population at the Year-end (10 000 persons)	648.21	688.01	741.73	781.67
非农业人口	Non-agricultural Population	255.71	285.79	333.14	370.66
农业人口	Agriculturral Population	392.50	402.22	408.59	411.01
男性人口	Male Population	334.75	355.18	382.02	399.28
女性人口	Female Population	313.46	332.83	359.71	382.39
就业	**Employment**				
全社会从业人员数(万人)	Employment(10 000 persons)	372.6	389.1	415.83	462.52
#全部单位在岗职工人数	Number of Employed Staff and Workers	141.17	109.62	119.73	129.62
城镇登记失业人数	Registered Unemployed in Urban Areas	5.92	3.85	8.45	10.02
宏观经济	**Macroeconomic Indicator**				
国民经济核算(亿元)	**National Accounts(100 mil. yuan)**				
地区生产总值（亿元）	Gross Domestic Product(100 mil. yuan)	330.35	646.13	1313.93	2724.08
第一产业	Primary Industry	41.40	44.65	66.01	110.38
第二产业	Secondary Industry	135.33	277.13	540.50	1144.75
#工业	Industry	112.50	218.44	420.00	816.92
第三产业	Tertiary Industry	153.62	324.35	707.42	1468.95
在生产总值中：最终消费	Total Consumption	239.64	414.43	766.62	1403.10
资本形成总额	Total Investment	151.55	287.82	839.01	2281.91
固定资产投资	**Investment in Fixed Assets**				
全社会固定资产投资总额(亿元)	Total Investment in Fixed Assets(100 mil. yuan)	103.42	232.37	835.10	2500.13
按城乡划分：城镇	According to the Division of Urban and Rural：Urban Area	88.50	203.01	776.33	2367.58
#房地产	Real Estate	21.65	51.85	225.23	696.34
农村	Rural Area	14.92	29.36	58.77	132.55
按经济成分划分	According to the Division of Economic Component				
国有经济	State-Owned	69.08	159.60	373.70	932.91
集体经济	Collective-Owned	9.78	14.65	59.23	289.91
个体经济	Self-employed Individual	11.13	24.40	79.04	97.86
其他经济	Other	13.43	33.72	323.13	1179.45
财政	**Public Finance**				
地方财政一般预算收入（亿元）	General Budgetary Revenue of Local Government (100 mil. yuan)	18.21	46.80	72.92	181.40
地方财政一般预算支出（亿元）	General Budgetary Expenditure of Local Government (100 mil. yuan)	18.42	52.00	97.61	276.85
物价指数(上年=100)	**Price Indices(preceding year=100)**				
商品零售价格指数	Retail Price Index	114.6	98.7	99.7	99.5
居民消费价格指数	Consumer Price Index	117.0	100.2	100.3	99.7
工业生产者出厂价格指数	Producer Price Indices (PPI) for Manufactured Goods	110.8	99.4	103.9	99.9
利用外资	**Utilization of Foreign Capital**				
利用外资签定协议额(万美元)	Amount of Foreign Capital for Utilization Through Signed Contracts or Agreements(USD 10 000)	28956	54123	121499	60027
外商实际直接投资额(万美元)	Amount of Foreign Capital Actually Utilized (USD 10 000)	18653	15633	57113	121872

注：国民经济核算2004—2008年为全国第二次经济普查修订数据。2013年为全国第三次经济普查数据。2009-2012年数据暂未修订。
总人口为户籍人口数。
2009年及以前年份财政收支为一般预算收支与基金预算收支之和。
由于2010年固定资产投资起报点的变化，指数和平均增长速度为可比口径计算。

Total and Speed Index of National Economy and Social Development in Main Years

					速度指标（%） Indices and Growth Rates（%）						
2010	2011	2012	2013	2014	指数（2014比以下各年） (2014 as percentage of the following years)				平均增长速度 Average Annual Growth Rate		
					2000	2005	2010	2013	2001-2005	2006-2010	2011-2014
782.73	791.83	795.98	806.93	815.29	118.5	109.9	104.2	101.0	1.5	1.1	1.0
374.64	391.31	392.04	409.82	418.16	146.3	125.5	111.6	102.0	3.1	2.4	2.8
408.09	400.52	403.94	397.11	397.13	98.7	97.2	97.3	100.0	0.3	-0.02	-0.7
398.80	402.52	397.58	408.78	412.46	116.1	108.0	103.4	100.9	1.5	0.9	0.8
383.93	389.31	398.40	398.15	402.83	121.0	112.0	104.9	101.2	1.6	1.3	1.2
477.58	495.99	514.57	530.71	532.92	137.0	128.2	111.6	103.6	1.3	2.8	2.8
130.70	154.33	155.28	183.60	183.22	167.1	153.0	140.2	99.8	1.8	1.8	8.8
10.46	10.37	9.60	10.13	10.84	281.6	128.3	103.6	107.0	17.0	4.4	0.9
3241.69	3862.58	4366.10	4924.97	5492.64	587.4	312.1	155.3	109.9	13.5	15.0	11.6
140.06	173.14	195.59	200.46	214.55	210.4	170.5	124.6	105.1	4.3	6.5	5.6
1406.72	1674.31	1881.75	1998.82	2194.78	668.0	329.4	159.9	109.3	15.2	15.5	12.5
1003.57	1189.61	1328.71	1376.74	1488.02	634.3	317.9	161.4	108.4	14.8	14.5	12.7
1694.91	2015.13	2288.76	2725.69	3083.31	576.4	312.7	153.9	110.7	13.0	15.2	11.4
1598.51	1856.91	2092.97									
2835.42	3264.83	3783.10									
3250.56	3346.26	4243.43	5134.56	5903.98	3208.3	892.7	229.3	115.0	29.2	31.2	23.1
3104.92	3207.97	4107.54	4982.25	5682.42	3579.7	936.1	234.1	114.1	30.8	31.9	23.7
842.34	996.81	1281.90	1595.64	1761.88	3398.2	782.3	209.2	110.4	34.1	30.2	20.3
145.64	138.29	135.89	152.31	221.56	754.9	377.1	152.2	145.5	14.9	19.9	11.1
1348.76	1204.80	1661.22	1770.84	1916.31	1515.8	647.4	179.4	108.2	18.5	29.3	15.7
326.44	258.15	194.71	219.88	203.35	1752.4	433.4	78.6	92.5	32.2	40.7	-5.8
54.73	74.64	82.72	84.43	83.28	430.9	133.0	192.1	98.6	26.5	-7.1	17.7
1520.63	1808.67	2304.78	3059.41	3701.04	13810.5	1441.2	306.2	120.6	57.1	36.6	32.3
241.86	318.55	396.96	501.98	583.79	1072.6	800.6	241.4	116.3	9.3	27.1	24.6
371.62	494.58	597.49	729.81	819.54	1403.5	839.6	220.5	112.3	13.4	30.7	21.9
102.7	104.4	102.3	101.7	100.7					-0.2	2.5	2.3
103.5	105.6	102.8	102.7	101.4					0.3	3.1	3.1
102.3	102.5	100.5	99.5	99.5					1.1	2.2	0.5
119689	120083	360264	251874	255321	471.7	210.1	213.3	101.4	17.6	-0.3	20.9
156653	200522	247800	312994	370310	2368.8	648.4	236.4	118.3	29.6	22.4	24.0

1-11 续表1

指 标	Item	总量指标 Total quantity index			
		1995	2000	2005	2009
产 业	**Industry**				
农业	**Agriculture**				
耕地面积(万亩)	Cultivated Areas(10 000 hectares)	463.97	443.37	400.17	387.89
农林牧渔及服务业总产值 (亿元)	Gross Output Value of Farming Forestry, Animal Husbandry and Fishery(100 mil yuan)	75.46	74.37	106.54	178.70
主要农产品产量(万吨)	Output of Major Farm Products(10 000 tons)				
粮 食	Grain	175.30	201.90	205.50	218.20
奶 类	Milk	13.29	24.59	42.22	61.82
油 料	Oil-bearing Crops	2.17	1.34	1.16	1.12
蔬 菜	Vegetables	133.60	162.14	195.70	242.41
水 果	Fruits	24.10	34.36	51.29	78.96
肉 类	Meat	12.78	14.76	18.20	12.62
水产品	Aquatic Products	0.85	1.14	0.94	1.30
工业	**Industry**				
全部工业总产值（亿元）	Gross industrial Output Value(100 mil. yuan)	405.90	639.48	1308.56	2827.07
规模以上工业企业主要经济指标	Main Economic Indicators of All Industrial Enterprises State Ownership and Non-state-owned above Designated Size above Designated Size				
工业增加值	Value Added of Industrial		130.18	314.01	700.13
资产总计	Total Assets		958.05	1503.85	2913.56
主营业务收入	Revenue from Principal Business		420.42	980.97	2384.52
利润总额	Profits		16.11	28.72	177.20
从业人员年平均人数 （万人）	Annual Average Employers(10 000 persons)		43.25	37.92	43.42
主要工业产品产量	Output of Major Industrial Products				
布(亿米)	Cloth(100 mil.m)	3.03	2.48	2.70	2.22
机制纸及纸板(万吨)	Machine-Made Paper(10 000ton)	36.44	5.47	22.19	47.63
发电量(亿千瓦时)	Electricity(100 million kwh)	22.00	19.00	48.00	83.21
钢材(万吨)	Steel Products(10 000ton)	31.44	10.00	24.02	110.51
汽车(万辆)	Motor Vehicle (10 000 units)	0.30	0.90	4.10	50.70
建筑业	**Construction**				
建筑业企业从业人数(人)	Number of Employed Persons(person)		136718	158311	461080
建筑业总产值(亿元)	Gross Output Value(100 mil. yuan)	42.55	105.93	326.65	1296.58
房屋建筑施工面积 (万平方米)	Floor Space of Buildings under Construction (10 000 sq.m)	601.70	793.30	1801.20	3947.01
房屋建筑竣工面积 (万平方米)	Floor Space of Buildings Completed (10 000 sq.m)	177.15	336.80	569.01	1209.88

注：规模以上工业2013年为全国第三次经济普查数据，以前年份未做修订。
由于2010年规模以上工业起报点的变化，指数和平均增长速度为可比口径计算。

continued 1

					速度指标（%）				Indices and Growth Rates（%）		
2010	2011	2012	2013	2014	指数（2014比以下各年）(2014 as percentage of the following years)				平均增长速度 Average Annual Growth Rate		
					2000	2005	2010	2013	2001-2005	2006-2010	2011-2014
383.32	377.10	369.91	366.23	360.73	81.4	90.1	94.1	98.5	-2.0	-9.0	-1.5
227.10	272.66	308.36	342.89	367.21	217.6	173.4	124.6	105.1	4.6	6.8	5.6
221.70	182.04	192.55	183.12	175.61	87	85.5	79.2	95.9	0.4	1.5	-5.7
63.37	64.80	66.64	65.77	65.80	267.6	155.9	103.8	100.0	11.4	8.5	0.9
1.20	1.17	1.02	1.00	0.98	73.1	84.5	81.7	98.0	-1.6	0.0	-4.9
253.10	261.66	277.80	298.12	316.28	195.1	161.6	125	106.1	3.8	5.3	5.7
84.78	91.14	93.21	95.18	99.66	290.1	194.3	117.6	104.7	8.3	10.6	4.1
13.65	14.46	15.17	15.74	16.19	109.8	89.0	118.6	102.8	4.2	-5.6	4.4
1.19	1.18	1.40	1.42	1.42	124.6	151.1	119.3	100.0	-3.9	5.7	4.5
3562.88	4093.32	4656.08	5042.64	5660.63	811.1	415.4	159.0	112.3	14.3	21.2	12.3
862.28	1012.58	1132.44	1194.88	1304.12		379.9	169.8	111.1		17.5	14.2
3592.13	3975.38	4775.92	5127.69	6048.34	631.3	402.2	168.4	118.0	9.4	19.0	13.9
3011.19	3381.27	3758.56	4171.21	4483.69	1066.5	457.1	148.9	107.5	18.5	25.1	10.5
245.37	172.94	167.77	211.26	226.17	1403.9	787.5	92.2	107.1	12.3	53.6	-2.0
47.11	50.42	49.23	44.27	49.53	114.5	130.6	105.1	111.9	-2.6	4.4	1.3
2.38	1.63	1.43	1.40	1.12	45.1	41.5	47.0	80.0	1.7	-2.5	-17.2
49.60	49.79	27.61	16.00	11.24	205.4	50.7	22.7	70.3	32.3	17.5	-31.0
96.94	95.01	99.48	184.50	179.58	945.2	374.1	185.2	97.3	20.4	15.1	16.7
110.77	18.48	31.29	54.30	42.87	428.7	178.5	38.7	79.0	19.2	35.8	-21.1
65.21	55.67	54.17	42.20	37.47	4163.3	913.9	57.5	88.8	35.4	73.9	-12.9
539000	372088	391199	577944	394070	288.2	248.9	73.1	68.2	3.0	27.8	-7.5
1820.35	1619.09	1874.23	2228.41	2586.33	2441.5	791.8	142.1	116.1	25.3	41.0	9.2
4592.57	6218.70	7531.07	9753.45	11182.18	1409.6	620.8	243.5	114.6	17.8	20.6	24.9
1391.91	2392.39	1985.31	2229.97	2536.71	753.2	445.8	182.2	113.8	11.1	19.6	16.2

1-11 续表2

指 标	Item	总量指标 Total quantity index			
		1995	2000	2005	2009
交通运输	**Transportation**				
货运量(万吨)	Freight Traffic(10 000 tons)	9590	6999	12051	30606
铁 路	Railways	3317	3101	540	614
公 路	Highways	6268	3890	11505	29986
民用航空	Civil Aviation	5	8	6	6
客运量(万人次)	Passenger Traffic(10 000 persons-times)	9069	8068	10479	28693
铁 路	Railways	2678	2130	1796	2585
公 路	Highways	6128	5578	8294	25271
民用航空	Civil Aviation	263	360	389	837
邮电通信业	**Post and Telecommunication Services**				
邮电业务总量(亿元)	Total Business Revenue(100 mil. yuan)	7.65	46.16	132.04	298.92
函 件(万件)	Number of Letters Delivered(10 000 pieces)	14647	8230	9526	6128
本地电话局用交换机容量 (万门)	Capacity of Local Office Telephone Exchanges (10 000 line)	58.3	204.8	457.3	441.1
本地电话年末用户(万户)	Local fixed telephone end users (million)	30.79	141.28	321.48	289.10
城市电话用户	Urban Telephone Subscribers	29.95	124.26	271.40	253.28
乡村电话用户	Rural Telephone Subscribers	0.84	17.02	50.08	35.82
移动电话用户(万户)	Number of Mobile Telephone Subscribers (10 000 subscribers)		73.10	419.96	1120.06
互联网年末宽带用户(万户)	Number of Subscribers of Intemet Services (10 000 subscribers)			33.93	116.79
国内贸易	**Domestic Trade**				
社会消费品零售总额 (亿元)	Total Retail Sales of Consumer Goods (100 mil. yuan)	186.60	360.42	670.56	1398.37
对外经济贸易	**Foreign Trade**				
进出口总额(万美元)	Total Exports and Imports(USD 10 000)	137510	173696	390146	724618
出口额	Exports	110163	106062	263441	333114
进口额	Imports	27347	67634	126705	391504
国际旅游	**International Tourism**				
国际旅游者人数(万人次)	Number of International Tourists(10 000 persons)	41.35	65.03	77.56	67.29
国际旅游收入(亿元)	Foreign Exchange Earnings from Tourism (10 000yuan)	10.38	22.41	33.54	31.05
金融业	**Financial Intermediation**				
金融机构（不含外资）人民币存款余额(亿元)	Balance of Deposits in Domestic Funded Financial Institutions (100 mil. yuan)	359.51	1335.63	3599.70	7457.71
金融机构（不含外资）人民币贷款余额 (亿元)	Balance of Loans in Domestic Funded Financial Institutions (100 mil. yuan)	334.50	972.52	2158.10	4436.50
保险公司保费收入(亿元)	insurance premium income (100 million Yuan)	4.70	13.58	44.94	122.11
保险公司赔款支出及各项给付金额(亿元)	insurance and compensation paid to Amount (100 million Yuan)	1.70	1.39	9.50	25.16

注：2006年铁路数据按新口径统计；
2006年国际互联网络用户改为互联网宽带用户。
2009—2013年社会消费品零售总额为依据全国第三次经济普查修订数据。
2014年陕西省公路运输统计方法制度改变，因此与往年数据不可比。

continued 2

					速度指标（%）				Indices and Growth Rates（%）		
2010	2011	2012	2013	2014	指数（2014比以下各年）(2014 as percentage of the following years)				平均增长速度 Average Annual Growth Rate		
					2000	2005	2010	2013	2001-2005	2006-2010	2011-2014
34323	39231	44924	50119	42039					11.5	23.3	
706	823	825	858	900					-29.5	5.5	
33610	38399	44082	49243	41120					24.2	23.9	
7	9	17	18	19					-5.6	3.1	
30294	33375	36154	38289	25719					5.4	23.7	
2781	2861	2919	3071	3511					-3.4	9.1	
26536	29358	30893	32614	19282					8.3	26.2	
977	1156	2342	2604	2926					1.6	20.2	
323.11	200.50	216.20	247.94	292.20	633.0	221.3	90.4	117.8	23.4	19.6	-2.5
8176	3061	2769	2856	2112	25.7	22.2	25.8	73.9	3.0	-3.0	-28.7
449.0	441.5	420.38	378.02	230.01	112.3	50.3	51.2	60.8	17.4	-0.4	-15.4
261.77	270.36	311.02	319.11	306.66	217.1	95.4	117.1	96.1	20.9	-4.0	4.0
228.27	238.34	277.43	286.05	269.38	216.8	99.3	118.0	94.2	20.4	-3.4	4.2
33.50	32.02	33.59	33.06	37.28	219.0	74.4	111.3	112.8	24.1	-7.7	2.7
1423.08	1614.15	1803.54	2160.67	2025.32	2770.6	482.3	142.3	93.7	41.9	27.6	9.2
146.18	184.10	202.31	267.05	277.95		819.2	190.1	104.1		33.9	17.4
1678.01	2039.24	2400.67	2742.89	3093.89	858.4	461.4	184.4	112.8	13.2	19.5	16.5
1039273	1260179	1301446	1798534	2494223	1436.0	639.3	240.0	138.7	17.6	21.6	33.9
531729	582662	729878	847819	1196005	1127.6	454.0	224.9	141.1	20.0	15.1	31.0
507544	677517	571568	950715	1298218	1919.5	1024.6	255.8	136.6	13.4	32.0	36.8
84.18	100.23	115.35	121.11						3.6	1.7	
42.40	51.28	59.89	64.16						8.4	4.8	
8863.36	10350.80	12044.68	13665.89	15064.10	1127.9	418.5	170.0	110.2	21.9	19.7	14.2
6420.72	7496.25	8559.27	9930.04	11576.30	1190.3	536.4	180.3	116.6	17.3	24.4	15.9
129.38	162.57	173.21	202.41	219.49	1616.3	488.4	169.6	108.4	27.0	23.6	14.1
26.39	37.14	47.55	66.49	80.77	5810.8	850.2	306.1	121.5	46.9	24.8	32.3

1-11 续表3

指 标	Item	总量指标 Total quantity index 1995	2000	2005	2009
教育、科技、文化	**Education, Science and Technology and Culture**				
教育	**Education**				
专任教师数(人)	Full-time Teachers(person)				
#普通高等学校	Institutions of Higher Education	15914	15679	29498	40605
普通中等专业学校	Regular Specialized Secondary Schools	2533	3172	2130	1720
普通中学	Regular Schools	21984	26230	31094	31415
小 学	Primary Schools	30270	30215	29647	30334
在校学生数(万人)	Students Enrollment(10 000 person)				
#普通高等学校	Institutions of Higher Education	11.67	19.41	53.06	70.31
普通中等专业学校	Regular Specialized Secondary Schools	3.74	6.02	6.16	7.44
普通中学	Regular Schools	32.32	48.31	55.74	50.63
小 学	Primary Schools	79.36	77.81	60.47	52.52
科技	**Science and Technology**				
高新技术企业(个)	Hi-tech Enterprises (unit)				
企事业单位累计授权专利数（件）	Accumulated patents awarded(unit)	3164	6139	11670	23962
文化	**Accumulated patents awarded(unit)**				
图书馆总藏量(千册件)	Total Collections in Library (1000 Volume-time)	2830	3214	3671	4324
文化馆、站（个）	Cultural Centers or Stations (unit)	201	251	192	197
电视节目制作时间(小时)	Time for TV Programs Production(hour)	5738	11871	27377	27131
家庭、生活、环境	**Family, People's Livelihood and Environment**				
家庭	**Family**				
家庭总户数（户籍人口）(万户)	Total Number of Households(10 000 household)	171.25	187.08	203.04	221.51
城镇常住居民平均每户家庭人口(人)	Average Household Size in Urban Areas(person)	3.88	2.99	2.93	2.84
农村常住居民平均每户家庭人口(人)	Average Household Size in Rural Areas(person)	4.60	4.30	4.22	4.07
婚姻	**Marriages and Divorces**				
结婚(对)	Register Number of Marriages(couple)	47236	46415	49962	88138
离婚(对)	Number of Divorces(couple)	4296	5161	12747	15796
居住	**Housing**				
城镇居民人均现住房建筑面积(平方米)	Per Capita Building Area of Urban Residents' (sq.m)	13.05	14.82	16.38	28.40
农村居民人均现住房建筑面积(平方米)	Per Capita Building Area of Rural Residents(sq.m)	21.77	28.31	36.73	56.73

注：2008年及以前图书馆总藏量为图书馆藏书量。

2005年以前城镇居民人均现住房总建筑面积为城镇人均住房使用面积。

2014年城乡居民人均住房面积为城乡住户调查一体化改革后新口径数据，与往年不可比。

continued 3

2010	2011	2012	2013	2014	速度指标（%） Indices and Growth Rates（%） 指数（2014比以下各年） (2014 as percentage of the following years) 2000	2005	2010	2013	平均增长速度 Average Annual Growth Rate 2001-2005	2006-2010	2011-2014
42098	42734	44487	46436	46766	298.3	158.5	111.1	100.7	13.5	7.4	2.7
1845	1723	1595	1474	1346	42.4	63.2	73.0	91.3	-7.7	-2.8	-7.6
31506	31675	31526	31419	32615	124.3	104.9	103.5	103.8	3.5	0.3	0.9
29944	29900	29651	29421	28395	94.0	95.8	94.8	96.5	-0.4	0.2	-1.3
73.30	76.60	80.73	83.83	85.42	440.1	161.0	116.5	101.9	22.3	6.7	3.9
6.75	6.11	5.43	4.66	4.07	67.6	66.1	60.3	87.4	0.7	1.9	-11.9
48.89	47.20	45.33	43.73	42.57	88.1	76.4	87.1	97.3	2.9	-2.6	-3.4
51.56	51.39	50.85	51.95	53.79	69.1	89.0	104.3	103.5	-4.9	-3.1	1.1
827	978	917	1026	1253			151.5	122.1			10.9
31999	41273	53118	69368	86639	1411.3	742.4	270.8	124.9	13.7	22.4	28.3
4465	4907	6123	6647	7585	236.0	206.6	169.9	114.1	2.7	4.0	14.2
197	196	197	198	199	79.3	103.6	101.0	100.5	-5.4	0.6	0.3
29626	43925	30091	46614	35182	296.4	128.5	118.8	75.5	18.2	1.6	4.4
226.71	234.34	239.54	245.53	250.26	133.8	123.3	110.4	101.9	1.7	2.2	2.5
2.81	2.83	2.76	2.73	2.86	95.7	97.6	101.8	104.8	-0.4	-0.8	0.4
3.94	3.97	4.09	4.09	3.54	82.3	83.9	89.8	86.6	-0.4	-1.6	-2.6
83645	94398	89877	89136	91123	196.3	182.4	108.9	102.2	1.5	10.9	2.2
19060	19421	18579	20304	21887	424.1	171.7	114.8	107.8	19.8	8.4	3.5
28.70	28.90	32.98	33.43	32.06					2.0	11.9	
66.73	67	78	81	48.83					5.3	12.7	

1-11 续表4

指 标	Item	总量指标 Total quantity index			
		1995	2000	2005	2009
生活	**People's Livelihood**				
城镇居民人均可支配收入(元)	Per Capita Annual Disposable Income of Urban Households (yuan)	4153	6364	9628	18963
农村居民人均纯收入(元)	Per Capita Net Income of Rural Residents(yuan)	1353	2344	3460	6275
城乡储蓄存款余额(亿元)	Savings Deposit of Urban and Rural Households (100 mil. yuan)	230.63	675.83	1716.76	3084.20
工资	**Wages and Welfare**				
在岗职工工资总额(亿元)	The Gross Salary of Workers (100 mil. yuan)	67.23	101.68	211.14	439.74
城镇非私营单位从业人员年平均工资(元)	Aunual Average Wage of Stuff and Workers in Urban Non-privite Enterprises(yuan)	4763	9179	17728	34032
卫生	**Health Care**				
医院、卫生院(个)	Number of Hospitals(unit)	368	426	479	415
执业（助理）医师（人）	Licensed (Assistant) Doctors (person)	18846	18750	17730	19284
医院、卫生院床位数(张)	Number of Hospital Beds(unit)	28265	28697	30087	34904
市政建设	**City Construction**				
自来水供应量(万立方米)	Volume of Tap Water Supply(10 000 cu.m)	35885	30273	35776	38307
自来水供水管道长度(公里)	Length of Water Supply Pipelines(km)	1066	2237	2315	1985
城市天然气供气量 (万立方米)	Volume of Natural Gas Supply in Urban Areas (10 000 cu.m)	8419	11513	53202	95885
公交运营汽(电)车总数(辆)	Total Number of Public Buses and Trolley Buses(unit)	977	2573	4762	7039
道路长度(公里)	Length of Paved Roads(km)	835	975	1382	2296
园林绿地面积(公顷)	Areas of Green Land(hectare)	5603	4116	4867	9553
环境、灾害	**Environment and Disaster**				
工业废水排放量(万吨)	Volume of Waste Water up to the Standard for Discharge(10 000 tons)	12479	9145	16969	13168
火灾发生数(起)	Number of Fire Disasters(case)	426	1040	2664	1485
火灾事故损失额（万元）	Fire Loss(10 000 yuan)	742.1	472.4	1565.5	1850.6
交通事故发生数（起）	Number of Traffic Accidents(case)	3065	4099	4903	2702
交通事故损失额（万元）	Loss of Traffic Accidents(10 000 yuan)	1103.2	1116.1	2024.4	851.7

注：城镇非私营单位从业人员年平均工资2012年前为城镇非私营单位在岗职工年平均工资。

continued 4

2010	2011	2012	2013	2014	速度指标（%） Indices and Growth Rates（%）						
					指数（2014比以下各年）(2014 as percentage of the following years)				平均增长速度 Average Annual Growth Rate		
					2000	2005	2010	2013	2001-2005	2006-2010	2011-2014
22244	25981	29982	33100	36100	567.3	374.9	162.3	109.1	8.6	18.2	12.9
7750	9788	11442	12930	14462	617.0	418.0	186.6	111.8	8.1	17.5	16.9
3641.09	4155.65	4787.03	5357.05	5698.15	843.1	331.9	156.5	106.4	20.5	16.2	11.8
501.76	629.35	742.16	987.80	1094.02	1075.9	518.1	218.0	110.8	15.7	18.9	21.5
37870	41679	44533	49350	54573	594.5	307.8	144.1	110.6	14.1	16.4	9.6
412	368	376	381	381	89.4	79.5	92.5	100.0	2.4	-3.0	-1.9
18763	21551	23051	23885	24820	132.4	140.0	132.3	103.9	-1.1	1.1	7.2
36796	37264	40585	44190	47075	164.0	156.5	127.9	106.5	1.0	4.1	6.4
41089	38934	45792	51372	53799	177.7	150.4	130.9	104.7	3.4	2.8	7
2416	2721	3208	3385	3500	156.5	151.2	144.9	103.4	0.7	0.9	9.7
109052	120330	142263	153489	186259	1617.8	350.1	170.8	121.4	35.8	15.4	14.3
7107	7462	7695	8128	7769	301.9	163.1	109.3	95.6	13.1	8.3	2.3
2662	2755	3119	3387	3461	355.0	250.4	130.0	102.2	7.2	14.0	6.8
12140	13680	15196	17751	18914	459.5	388.6	155.8	106.6	3.4	20.1	11.7
13840	13148	10224	8973	6340	69.3	37.4	45.8	70.7	13.2	-4.0	-17.7
1825	1920	2568	4062	3199	307.6	120.1	175.3	78.8	20.7	-7.3	15.1
2224.2	1587.2	2793.7	3011.9	4381.1	927.4	279.9	197.0	145.5	27.1	7.3	18.5
2323	2264	2446	2252	1970	48.1	40.2	84.8	87.5	3.6	-13.9	-4.0
736.6	611.9	1011.1	1143.9	1264.0	113.3	62.4	171.6	110.5	12.6	-18.3	14.5

1-12 主要年份国民经济和社会发展结构指标

单位: %

指 标	Item	1995	2000	2005
人口与就业	**Population and Employment**			
人 口	**Population**			
农业与非农业结构	Structure			
农业	Agriculture	60.55	58.46	55.09
非农业	Non-Agriculture	39.45	41.54	44.91
性别结构	Sexual Structure			
男	Male	51.64	51.62	51.50
女	Female	48.36	48.38	48.50
就 业	**Employment**			
全社会从业人员产业结构	Industrial Structure of the Whole Society			
第一产业	Primary Industry	41.17	37.78	32.78
第二产业	Secondary Industry	29.43	27.57	27.46
第三产业	Tertiary Industry	29.40	34.65	39.76
宏观经济	**Macro Economy**			
国民经济核算	**National Accounting**			
生产总值产业结构	Industrial Structure			
第一产业	Primary Industry	12.53	6.91	5.02
第二产业	Secondary Industry	40.97	42.89	41.14
第三产业	Tertiary Industry	46.50	50.20	53.84
生产总值支出结构	Structure of Gross Domestic by Expenditures			
最终消费	Total Consumption	72.54	63.99	58.35
资本形成总额	Total Investment	45.88	44.55	63.85
货物和服务净出口	Net Export of Goods and Services	-18.42	-8.54	-22.20
投 资	**Investment**			
全社会固定资产投资结构	Structure of Total Investment in Fixed Assets			
城乡结构	Urban and Rural Composition			
城镇	Urban Area	85.57	87.36	92.96
#房地产	Real Estate	20.93	22.31	27.00
农村	Rural Area	14.43	12.64	7.04
经济成分结构	Registion Status Composition			
国有经济	State-owned Enterprises Investment	66.79	68.68	44.75
集体经济	Collective-owned Enterprises Investment	9.46	6.30	7.09
个体经济	Self-employed Individual	10.76	10.50	9.46
其他经济	Other	12.99	14.51	38.69

Structural Indicators of National Economic and Social Development in Major Years

(%)

2007	2008	2009	2010	2011	2012	2013	2014
53.70	52.88	52.58	52.14	50.58	50.75	49.21	48.71
46.30	47.12	47.42	47.86	49.42	49.25	50.79	51.29
51.35	51.22	51.08	50.95	50.83	49.95	50.66	50.59
48.65	48.78	48.92	49.05	49.17	50.05	49.34	49.41
30.55	28.50	26.40	25.65	24.41	22.33	20.81	19.71
28.66	29.10	28.45	29.65	30.51	31.55	28.55	28.49
40.79	42.40	45.15	44.70	45.08	46.12	50.64	51.80
4.44	4.46	4.05	4.32	4.48	4.48	4.07	3.91
42.12	42.34	42.02	43.39	43.35	43.10	40.59	39.96
53.44	53.20	53.93	52.29	52.17	52.42	55.34	56.13
53.60	51.02	51.51	49.31	48.07	47.93		
78.18	79.28	83.77	87.47	84.52	86.65		
-31.78	-30.30	-35.28	-36.78	-32.60	-34.58		
93.40	93.72	94.70	95.52	95.87	96.80	97.03	96.25
26.09	28.34	27.85	25.91	29.79	30.21	31.08	29.84
6.60	6.28	5.30	4.48	4.13	3.20	2.97	3.75
33.22	36.45	37.31	41.49	36.00	39.15	34.49	32.46
14.43	12.95	11.60	10.04	7.71	4.59	4.28	3.44
12.75	2.65	3.91	1.68	2.23	1.95	1.64	1.41
39.60	47.95	47.18	46.78	54.05	54.31	59.58	62.69

1-12 续表1

单位: %

指　　标	Item	1995	2000	2005
财 政	**Government Finance**			
财政收入结构	Structure of Government Revenue			
中　央	Central Government		31.94	58.30
地　方	Local Governments		68.06	41.70
产　业	**Industrial**			
农　业	**Agriculture**			
农林牧渔及服务业总产值结构	Structure of Gross Output Value of Farming,Forestry,Animal Husbandry, Fishery and Service			
农　业	Farming	68.03	69.23	61.69
林　业	Forestry	0.96	1.14	1.23
牧　业	Animal Husbandry	30.29	28.58	30.96
渔　业	Fishery	0.72	1.05	0.69
农林牧渔服务业	Farming,Forestry,Animal Husbandry and Fishery			5.43
工 业	**Industry**			
工业总产值经济类型结构	Structure of Gross Output Value of Industry by Registion Status			
国有经济	State-owned Enterprises	51.04	43.00	45.21
集体经济	Collective-owned Enterprises	40.98	32.76	5.16
其他经济类型	Others	7.98	24.24	49.63
工业总产值轻重结构	Structure of Gross Output Value of Industry by Ligth Industry and Heavy Industry			
轻工业	Light Industry	40.31	48.81	31.17
重工业	Heavy Industry	59.69	51.19	68.83
工业总产值规模结构	Structure of Gross Output Value of Industry by Size of Enterprises			
大型企业	Large Enterprises	38.80	36.29	35.46
中型企业	Medium-sized Enterprises	9.14	5.14	24.67
小型企业	Small Enterprises	52.06	58.57	39.87

注：本表2008年以后财政收入结构中地方指地方财政一般预算收入。

continued 1

(%)

2007	2008	2009	2010	2011	2012	2013	2014
60.40	39.49	39.68	37.28	35.78	32.37	30.80	29.61
39.60	44.87	45.32	47.36	49.02	52.71	55.60	57.25
59.50	56.85	59.42	63.36	63.42	62.69	63.38	64.37
1.18	1.13	1.27	1.18	1.27	2.02	2.34	2.37
30.58	33.52	30.56	27.72	27.68	26.60	25.19	23.95
0.68	0.66	0.66	0.56	0.55	0.65	0.66	0.65
8.06	7.84	8.09	7.18	7.09	8.04	8.42	8.66
51.41	52.26	51.07	51.52	50.46	52.20	50.29	48.32
1.85	1.85	1.38	1.22	0.92	0.81	0.64	0.59
46.74	45.89	47.55	47.26	48.62	46.99	49.07	51.09
37.03	25.17	23.47	22.01	21.97	21.95	18.44	18.32
62.97	74.83	76.53	77.99	78.03	78.05	81.56	81.68
42.18	43.85	43.54	42.11	41.15	48.46	34.49	43.95
21.07	20.96	21.88	23.96	15.17	13.41	14.42	15.47
36.75	35.19	34.58	33.93	43.68	38.13	51.09	40.58

1-12 续表2

单位: %

指　　标	Item	1995	2000	2005
建筑业	**Construction**			
建筑业总产值结构	Structure of Gross Output Value of Construction Industry			
房屋建筑业	Building Construction	12.84	9.28	34.05
土木工程建筑业	Civil Engineering Construction	86.27	88.50	56.59
建筑安装业	Installation of Construction			
建筑装饰和其他建筑业	Decoration and others	0.89	2.22	9.36
交通运输业	**Transportation**			
客运量结构	Structure of Freight Traffic			
铁　路	Railways	29.53	26.40	17.14
公　路	Highways	67.57	69.14	79.15
民　航	Civil Aviation	2.90	4.46	3.71
货运量结构	Structure of Freight Traffic			
铁　路	Railways	34.59	44.30	26.92
公　路	Highways	65.36	55.58	73.04
民　航	Civil Aviation	0.05	0.12	0.04
国内贸易	**Domestic Trade**			
社会消费品零售总额结构	Composition of Retail Sales of Consumer Goods			
城　镇	Urban Area	88.95	87.99	90.17
农　村	Rural Area	11.05	12.01	9.83
国际旅游	**International Tourism**			
国际旅游人数结构	Structure of Tourists			
外国人	Foreigners	89.76	84.03	84.91
华侨及港澳台同胞	Overseas Chinese and Compatriots form Hong Kong, Macao and Taiwan	10.24	15.97	15.09
教育文化、卫生、人民生活	**Education and Culture，Health Care，People's Livelihood**			
教　育	**Education**			
在校学生结构	Structure of Student Enrollment			
#普通高等学校	Institutions of Higher Education	8.81	12.44	28.48
普通中等专业学校	Regular Specialized Secondary Schools	2.84	3.84	3.33
普通中学	Regular Schools	24.55	30.93	29.89
小 学	Primary Schools	59.91	49.89	32.45

continued 2

(%)

2007	2008	2009	2010	2011	2012	2013	2014
32.44	29.80	25.50	24.63	36.81	43.03	43.03	41.58
57.78	59.14	67.14	68.61	53.75	47.57	47.86	49.43
			4.39	6.70	6.49	5.86	5.32
9.78	11.06	7.36	2.37	2.74	2.91	3.25	3.67
19.09	10.11	9.01	9.18	8.57	8.07	8.02	13.65
75.93	87.45	88.07	87.59	87.96	85.45	85.18	74.97
4.97	2.44	2.92	3.23	3.46	6.48	6.80	11.38
3.90	2.20	2.01	2.06	2.10	1.84	1.71	2.14
96.07	97.78	97.97	97.92	97.88	98.13	98.25	97.81
0.03	0.02	0.02	0.02	0.02	0.04	0.04	0.05
90.32	90.43	90.49	95.91	97.08	96.97	96.81	96.85
9.68	9.57	9.51	4.09	2.92	3.03	3.19	3.15
85.09	84.78	87.81	86.97	88.43	87.91	88.26	
14.91	15.22	12.19	13.03	11.58	12.08	11.74	
29.18	30.53	31.54	32.60	29.74	31.00	33.09	33.16
3.75	3.71	3.32	3.02	2.37	2.08	1.84	1.58
25.62	24.17	22.70	21.74	18.32	17.40	17.26	16.53
26.62	25.03	23.56	22.95	19.95	19.52	20.51	20.88

1-12 续表3

单位: %

指　　标	Item	1995	2000	2005
专任教师结构	Full-time Teachers by Type			
#普通高等学校	Institutions of Higher Education	21.25	19.89	29.93
普通中等专业学校	Regular Specialized Secondary Schools	3.38	4.02	2.16
普通中学	Regular Schools	29.37	33.21	31.55
小 学	Primary Schools	40.41	38.34	30.08
人民生活	**People's Livelihood**			
城镇居民消费结构	Consumption Structure of Urban Residents			
食 品	Food	44.68	36.46	37.04
衣 着	Clothing	12.67	8.13	9.03
家庭设备用品及服务	Household facilities,Articles and Services	13.75	11.33	4.73
医疗保健	Health Care	3.27	7.23	9.45
交通和通信	Transportation and Communication	5.58	6.93	9.67
教育文化娱乐服务	Recreation,Education and Culture Articles	9.05	13.74	17.18
居 住	Residence	6.49	11.23	9.10
杂项商品和服务	Articles for Daily Use and Others	4.51	4.95	3.80
农村居民消费结构	Consumption Structure of Rural Residents			
食品消费支出	Food	50.31	36.63	36.34
衣 着	Clothing	8.39	6.65	6.11
居 住	Residence	5.92	21.41	17.76
家庭设备用品及服务	Household facilities,Articles and Services	5.17	5.47	5.11
医疗保健	Health Care	1.78	6.93	8.19
交通和通讯	Transportation and Communication	8.09	4.21	8.19
文化娱乐用品及服务	Recreation,Education and Culture Articles	18.53	14.49	16.15
其它商品及服务	Articles for Daily Use and Others	1.81	4.21	2.15
卫 生	**Health Care**			
卫生技术人员结构	Medical Technical Personnel by Types			
执业（助理）医师	Licensed（Assistant） Doctors	45.42	44.82	41.96
注册护士	Registered Nurses	32.68	34.29	33.14
药 师	Junior Paramedics	8.78	8.31	7.30
技 师	Technicians	5.21	5.21	5.33
其 他	Others	7.91	7.37	12.27

注：2014年为城乡住户调查一体化改革后数据，居民消费结构与往年不可比。

continued 3

(%)

2007	2008	2009	2010	2011	2012	2013	2014
30.72	31.63	31.90	32.47	31.97	32.96	33.91	33.87
1.68	1.55	1.35	1.42	1.29	1.18	1.08	0.97
26.25	25.53	24.68	24.30	23.70	23.36	22.95	23.62
25.55	24.68	23.83	23.10	22.37	21.97	21.49	20.57
36.61	36.40	32.43	31.29	31.29	32.48	32.44	29.21
9.41	10.25	10.98	11.11	12.27	12.17	12.02	9.09
5.91	6.33	7.28	7.56	8.11	7.87	7.80	7.21
8.40	9.67	9.65	9.50	9.00	8.52	7.99	7.32
11.35	10.37	11.33	12.06	12.81	14.26	14.01	14.16
14.52	14.35	14.34	14.66	14.27	14.33	14.17	12.60
10.18	8.81	8.86	9.33	8.26	8.47	7.82	17.89
3.62	3.82	5.13	4.49	4.00	1.91	3.76	2.53
38.15	36.95	35.81	32.54	31.89	33.83	32.96	29.93
6.09	6.52	6.40	6.55	7.20	7.42	7.87	7.44
22.72	19.39	19.47	24.41	23.92	21.91	19.82	21.99
5.66	7.02	6.97	6.53	7.10	7.46	7.76	6.97
7.61	8.05	8.50	8.54	8.65	8.85	8.41	11.07
7.58	7.84	9.83	8.45	9.01	10.19	9.86	10.66
10.44	12.43	11.13	11.20	10.43	10.20	10.56	10.26
1.75	1.80	1.89	1.78	1.80	0.14	2.77	1.68
39.51	38.09	37.34	33.16	35.17	34.46	33.58	32.66
35.09	36.23	39.05	40.01	40.87	41.61	42.13	42.28
6.19	5.74	5.45	5.36	5.10	5.05	4.99	4.88
6.97	6.68	6.49	8.11	5.91	5.91	5.75	5.63
12.24	13.26	11.67	13.36	12.95	12.97	13.55	14.56

1-13 主要年份国民经济和社会发展比例和效益指标

指 标	Item	1995
人口与就业	**Population and Employment**	
人口	**Population**	
出生率(‰)	Birth Rate(‰)	11.95
死亡率(‰)	Death Rate(‰)	4.98
自然增长率(‰)	Natural Growth Rate(‰)	6.79
就业	**Employment**	
就业者负担人口	Dependency Ratio	1.7
三次产业就业者比例	Employment Ratio by Type of Industry	
(以第一产业为100)	(Employment in primary industry=100)	
第一产业	Primary Industry	100
第二产业	Secondary Industry	71.5
第三产业	Tertiary Industry	71.4
城镇登记失业率(%)	Unemployment Rate in Urban Areas(%)	3.1
宏观经济	**Macro Economy**	
国民经济核算	**National Accounting**	
三次产业增加值比例	Ratio of Value-added by Type of Industry	
(以第一产业为100)	(Employment in primary industry=100)	
第一产业	Primary Industry	100
第二产业	Secondary Industry	326.9
第三产业	Tertiary Industry	371.1
全社会劳动生产率(元/人)	Overall Labor Productivity(yuan/person)	8963
第一产业	Primary Industry	2698
第二产业	Secondary Industry	12404
第三产业	Tertiary Industry	14488
人均生产总值(元)	Per Capita GDP(yuan)	5131
固定资产投资	**Investment in Fixed Assets**	
全社会固定资产投资相当于生产总值比例(%)	Proportion of Investment in fixed Assets to GDP(%)	31.3
房屋建筑面积竣工率(%)	Rate of Floor Space of Buildings Completed in Construction(%)	33.4
固定资产交付使用率(%)	Rate of Fixed Assets Completed in Capital Construction and Put into Use(%)	70.7
建设项目建成投产率(%)	Rate of Projects Completed in Capital Construction and Put into Use(%)	43.7
财政	**Finance**	
财政总收入相当于生产总值比例(%)	Proportion of Local Government Revenue to GDP(%)	5.5
一般预算支出相当于生产总值比例(%)	Proportion of Local Government Expenditures to GDP(%)	5.6
利用外资	**Utilization of Foreign Capital**	
外商实际直接投资额相当于利用外资协议金额比例(%)	Proportion of Foreign Capital Actually Used to Total Amount of Foreign Capital for Utilization by Signed Contracts or Agreements (%)	64.4

注：本表财政收入数据2009年及以前为一般预算财政收入和基金收入之和。

Proportions of National Economic and Social Development and Benefit Index in Main Years

2000	2003	2004	2005	2006	2007	2008	2009	2010	2011	2012	2013	2014
13.07	8.48	9.19	9.58	9.98	10.00	10.15	10.08	9.73	9.71	10.13	9.57	10.11
5.96	4.68	5.87	5.16	5.46	5.48	5.57	5.63	5.34	5.38	5.57	5.37	5.47
7.11	3.8	3.32	4.42	4.52	4.52	4.58	4.45	4.39	4.33	4.56	4.20	4.64
1.8	1.8	1.8	1.8	1.8	1.9	1.9	1.9	1.8	1.7	1.7	1.6	1.4
100	100	100	100	100	100	100	100	100	100	100	100	100
73	74.4	78.8	83.8	85.9	93.8	101.9	107.7	124	125	141.3	137.17	144.59
91.7	101.7	100.1	121.3	126.5	133.5	148.6	171	183.3	184.7	206.5	243.33	262.85
3.4	4.5	4.3	4.3	4.3	4.3	4.2	4.3	4.2	3.9	3.5	3.4	3.4
100	100	100	100	100	100	100	100	100	100	100	100	100
620.7	803.2	792.1	818.8	916.6	947.7	948.8	1037.1	1004.4	967.0	962.1	997.1	1023
726.4	963.3	938.8	1071.7	1168.2	1202.5	1192.0	1330.8	1210.1	1163.9	1170.2	1359.7	1437.1
16367	236.5	27069	31837	36730	43252	52422	59832	68965	79349	86410	94233	103281
2960	3501	4174	4747	5191	6148	7921	8830	11452	14530	16578	17789	19915
25443	36914	43199	47853	56073	64851	76899	87452	102992	112851	119979	127374	144703
24024	33502	37040	44024	48938	56870	67031	73674	80267	91908	99315	107722	113188
9484	13341	15294	16406	18890	22463	27794	32411	38343	45475	51166	57464	63794
36.0	50.5	58.7	65.8	72.4	81.4	82.2	91.8	100.3	86.6	97.2	104.3	107.5
42.0	33.8	24.4	28.1	26.1	29.0	16.9	16.0	6.9	10.0	8.7	13.2	11.4
74.0	62.7	42.8	52.8	46.6	49.8	40.5	42.8	38.4	40.4	42.4	37.1	42.5
44.2	39.9	41.5	54.2	47.0	40.6	53.3	72.5	53.9	54.9	56.1	56.1	62.5
7.3	7.7	7.8	6.6	6.5	7.1	10.9	12.2	15.8	16.8	17.2	18.3	18.6
8.0	8.2	8.1	8.1	9.1	9.9	14.5	15.4	11.5	12.8	13.7	14.8	14.9
28.9	26.5	35.2	47.0	45.2	77.5	97.1	203.0	130.9	167.0	68.8	124.3	145.0

1–13 续表1

指　　标	Item	1995
能　源	**Energy**	
单位生产总值能耗降低率(%)	Decreasing Rate of Energy Consumption per Unit GDP(%)	
规模以上工业单位工业增加值能耗降低率(%)	Decreasing Rate of Energy Consumption per Unit Industrial value-added of Industry Above Designated Size(%)	
单位生产总值电耗降低率(%)	Decreasing Rate of Electricity Consumption per Unit GDP(%)	
产　业	**Industries**	
农业	**Agriculture**	
人均耕地面积(公顷)	Per Capita Cultivated Land(hectare)	0.08
农业从业者人均耕地面积(公顷)	Cultivated Land per Agricultural Laborer(hectare)	0.2
每公顷耕地农业机械总动力(千瓦)	Total Power of Agricultural Machinery per Hectare of Cultivated Land(kw)	5.23
每公顷耕地化肥施用量(公斤)	Chemical Fertilizer Consumption per Hectare of Cultivated Land(kg)	536
每公顷耕地生产的农业总产值(元)	Agricultural Output Value per Hectare of Cultivated Land(yuan)	24396
每个农林牧渔及服务业劳动力农产品生产量(公斤)	Output of Farm Products per Farming,Forestry,Animal Husbandry,Fishery and Service Husbandry and Fishery Laborer (kg)	
粮食	Grain	1150
蔬菜	Vegetables	877
禽蛋	Poultry Eggs	93
肉类	Meat	84
水产品	Aquatic Products	6
每公顷播种面积农产品产量(公斤)	Output of Farm Crops per Hectare of Sown Area(kg)	
粮食	Grain	3806
油料	Oil-bearing Crops	1753
蔬菜	Vegetables	34800
工业	**Industrial**	
规模以上工业企业经济效益	**Economic Benefit of Industrial Enterprises above Designated Size**	
总资产贡献率(%)	Ratio of Total Assets to Industrial Output Value (%)	
资产负债率(%)	Assets-Liability Ratio (%)	
流动资产周转次数（次/年）	Rate of Annual Turnover Working Capitals(times/year)	
成本费用利润率(%)	Ratio of Profits to Cost (%)	
产品销售率(%)	Proportion of Industrial Products Sold(%)	
全员劳动生产率（元/人）	Overall Labor Productivity (yuan/person)	
建筑业	**Construction**	
机械装备率(元／人)	Value of Machinery per Laborer(yuan/person)	5990
产值利润率(%)	Ratio of Per-tax Profits to Gross Output Value (%)	3.5
全员劳动生产率(元／人)(按总产值计算)	Overall Labor Productivity(yuan/person) (in terms of gross output value per employee)	37689
邮电通信业	**Post and Communication Services**	
电话普及率(含移动电话）(部/百人)	Access to Telephones, National(include mobilphone) (set/100 persons)	7.9
移动电话普及率(部/百人)	Access to Mobilphones (set/100 persons)	0.48

continued 1

2000	2003	2004	2005	2006	2007	2008	2009	2010	2011	2012	2013	2014
				4.15	5.75	6.65	5.56	2.06	3.56	3.51	3.57	5.89
				3.04	12.56	13.43	10.48	12.18	15.44	10.52	17.69	15.21
				4.48	6.94	6.93	5.33	1.00	4.43	2.92	2.26	
0.07	0.07	0.07	0.07	0.06	0.06	0.06	0.06	0.06	0.06	0.06	0.06	0.06
0.2	0.19	0.19	0.22	0.23	0.25	0.21	0.21	0.22	0.22	0.22	0.23	0.22
6.78	7.54	7.93	8.39	8.63	8.99	10.41	10.12	10.48	11.5	12.1	12.73	13.32
664	725	780	794	819	843	867	891	922	953	987	982	1045
25161	30357	35862	39937	43261	51361	64593	69106	88869	108457	125041	140441	152695
1382	1213	1392	1493	1569	1433	1695	1792	1901	1567	1700	1688	1592
1110	1167	1287	1421	1536	1549	1752	1990	2171	2253	2452	2748	2867
95	89	84	86	92	74	86	96	106	108	115	125	123
101	114	122	132	145	77	91	104	117	124	134	145	147
8	7	7	7	7	9	10	11	10	10	12	13	13
4342	4182	4656	4796	5025	4452	5102	5206	5349	4764	5045	4837	4777
1526	1532	1758	1821	1880	1934	2008	1956	2004	1988	1987	1956	2097
37797	36657	35002	35231	35916	33677	35723	38344	39667	40475	42607	44767	46713
	7.0	6.9	8.4	7.8	10.2	8.6	11.3	12.2	8.6	7.7	8.5	7.4
65	61.3	65.2	65	64.3	64.6	62.6	61.1	57.6	57.7	59.4	59.5	59.7
1.0	1.1	1.2	1.3	1.4	1.6	1.5	1.7	1.7	1.5	1.5	1.5	1.4
4.2	5.7	5.0	3.1	5.5	7.3	4.6	8.1	8.8	5.2	4.5	5.2	5.2
97.1	96.3	97.9	97.5	98.2	96.8	96.1	97.6	97.1	97.4	96.7	95.7	94.9
29496	58801	66752	82815	97561	129706	150641	161289	188483	194105	230032	264324	275288
6805	9453	13240	13332	13502	9079	12026	11928	9461	28669	12216	10339	
3.4	4.1	4.4	4.8	4.5	5.2	6.0	6.3	4.4	4.4	2.8	2.6	2.3
74347	132981	163414	206337	241887	203994	226669	285854	321340	334172	479232	354419	347000
31.2	69.1	88.8	100.0	111.1	117.9	124.7	167.1	199.0	221.3	247.2	288.7	270.3
10.62	33.67	48.29	56.62	66.99	80.02	88.09	132.79	168.00	189.58	210.87	251.59	234.75

1-13 续表2

指　　标	Item	1995
国内贸易	**Domestic Trade**	
人均批发零售和住宿餐饮业消费品零售额(元)	Per Capita Retail Sales of Wholesale,Retail Trade and Accommodation Catering Trade (yuan)	1979
对外经济贸易	**Foreign Trade**	
进出口总额相当于生产总值比例(%)	Proportion of Total Imports & Exports to GDP(%)	34.76
国际旅游	**International Tourism**	
每一来华游客花费(元)	Expenditure per International Tourist in China(yuan)	2511
金融业	**Finance and Insurance**	
金融机构存款相当于生产总值比例(%)	Bank Deposits as Percentage of GDP(%)	108.83
金融机构贷款相当于生产总值比例(%)	Bank Loans as Percentage of GDP(%)	101.26
教育、科技、文化	**Education, Science and Technology and Culture**	
教育	**Education**	
毕业率(%)	Graduation Rate(%)	
小学	Primary Schools	
初中	Junior Schools	
学校教师负担系数	Student-teacher Ratio(in percentage)	
高等学校	Colleges and Universities	6.83
中等学校	Secondary Schools	14.42
小学	Primary Schools	26.22
文化	**Culture (unit)**	
每百万人有艺术表演团体	Number of Troupes per Million Persons	3.39
每百万人有公共图书馆	Number of Public Libraries per Million Persons	2.31
家庭、生活、环境	**Family, People's Livelihood and Environment**	
家庭	**Family**	
城市居民家庭	Urban Households	
平均每户就业面(%)	Percentage of Employees Per Household (%)	55.9
每一就业者负担人数(人)	Persons Supported by Each Laborer (person)	1.79
农村居民家庭	Rural Households	
平均每一劳动力负担人口（人）	Persons Supported by Each Laborer(person)	1.58
卫生	**Health Care**	
每万人医院数（个）	Number of Hospitals per 10 000 Persons(unit)	0.6
每万人医生数(人)	Number of Doctors per 10 000 Persons(person)	29.1
每万人医院床位数(张)	Number of Hospital Beds per 10 000 Persons(unit)	43.6
市政建设	**City Construction**	
城市自来水普及率(%)	Percentage of Households with Access to Tap Water(%)	
城市用气普及率(%)	Percentage of Households with Access to Tap Gas (%)	
人均公园绿地面积(平方米)	Public Green Areas per 10 000 Persons(hectare)	3.8

continued 2

2000	2003	2004	2005	2006	2007	2008	2009	2010	2011	2012	2013	2014
4027	6956	7859	8795	9437	10932	13840	16432	19363	23145	26529	32004	35943
22.25	20.19	23.29	24.79	22.01	22.21	21.97	18.17	21.20	20.56	18.74	22.27	27.89
3445	3584	4212	4324	4353	4242	4544	4614	5037	5116	5192	5298	
206.71	281.61	277.73	283.41	275.92	259.8	264.31	279.84	278.99	267.98	275.87	277.48	274.26
150.51	206.43	186.17	169.91	159.11	152.16	149.22	166.65	203.30	194.07	196.04	201.63	210.76
								100.4	100.2	100.2	99.8	99.6
								99.7	100.6	98.7	99.3	99.9
12.38	19.87	16.69	17.99	17.36	16.97	17.13	17.32	17.41	17.92	18.15	18.05	18.27
17.84	18.52	18.78	18.47	20.51	19.99	18.97	18.27	17.78	16.91	16.43	15.07	14.01
25.75	22.69	21.71	20.38	19.78	18.61	17.99	17.32	17.22	18.06	17.15	17.66	18.94
3.20	3.07	3.03	2.56	2.31	2.16	2.15	2.13	1.53	3.52	2.22	2.10	2.09
2.18	1.95	2.07	2.02	1.82	1.81	1.79	1.78	1.77	1.76	1.75	1.75	1.74
45.73	48.00	48.80	47.44	48.30	47.77	47.87	53.2	53.7	54.8	54.0	54.6	
2.19	2.08	2.05	2.11	2.07	2.09	2.09	1.88	1.86	1.83	1.85	1.83	1.31
1.57	1.56	1.56	1.6	1.59	1.57	1.5	1.5	1.5	1.5	1.5	1.5	1.4
0.57	0.40	0.4	0.59	0.58	0.55	0.52	0.49	0.49	0.43	0.44	0.44	0.44
25.3	20.2	20.4	21.98	21.89	20.79	21.57	22.86	22.14	25.31	26.95	27.81	28.77
38.72	39.40	39.1	37.29	37.49	37.11	39.40	41.38	43.42	43.77	47.45	51.45	54.56
98.95	99.04	99.09	99.00	99.09	100.01	111.22	100.00	98.77	99.95	100.00	100.00	100.00
81.51	91.23	91.20	91.30	92.62	98.60	97.66	98.15	97.02	97.46	98.19	98.68	98.71
5.12	5.35	5.03	5.63	7.59	7.61	7.80	7.90	9.11	9.89	10.22	10.70	11.22

1-14 主要年份平均每天主要社会经济活动

指　　标	Item	1995	2000
一、每天创造的财富	**Daily Production**		
生产总值(万元)	Gross Domestic Product(10 000 yuan)	9050.7	17702.2
第一产业	Primary Industry	1134.3	1223.3
第二产业	Secondary Industry	3707.7	7592.6
工业	Industry	3082.2	5984.7
建筑业	Construction	625.5	1608
第三产业	Tertiary Industry	4208.8	8886.3
#交通运输、仓储和邮政业	Transport, Storage, Post & Telecommunication Services	674	1709.3
住宿和餐饮业	Hotels and Catering Services		
批发和零售业	Wholesale and Retail Trade		
财政总收入(万元)	Total Government Revenue(10 000 yuan)	498.8	1304.0
财政一般预算支出(万元)	Government General Budgetary Expenditures(10 000 yuan)	504.7	1274.1
粮食(吨)	Grain(ton)	4801.0	5532.0
奶类(吨)	Milk(ton)	364	674
蔬菜(吨)	Vegetables(ton)	3660	4442
肉类(吨)	Meat(ton)	350	404
水产品(吨)	Aquatic Products(ton)	23	31
布(万米)	Cloth(10 000 m)	83	77
发电量(万千瓦小时)	Electricity(10 000 kwh)	610	534
钢材(吨)	Steel(ton)	861	274
汽车(辆)	Motor Vehicle(unit)	8	25
二、每天消费量	**Daily National Consumption**		
最终消费(万元)	Final Consumption Expenditure(10 000 yuan)	6565.5	11326.9
社会消费品零售总额(万元)	Total Retail Sales of Consumer Goods (10 000 yuan)	5112.3	9874.5
三、每天其他经济活动	**Other Daily Economic Activities**		
资本形成总额(万元)	Gross Capital Formation(10 000 yuan)	4152.1	7885.5
固定资本形成	Fixed Capital Formation		
存货增加	Changes in Stock		
竣工住宅面积(平方米)	Floor Space of Buildings Completed (sq.m)	6927	14930
货运量(万吨)	Freight Traffic(10 000 tons)	26.3	19.2
客运量(万人次)	Passenger Traffic(10 000 person-times)	24.8	22.1
邮电业务总量(万元)	Business Volume of Postal and Telecommunications Services(10 000 yuan)	209.6	1264.7
进出口总额(万美元)	Total Value of Imports and Exports (USD 10 000)	110.2	475.9
出口额	Exports	82.5	290.6
进口额	Imports	27.7	185.3
外商实际直接投资额(万美元)	Foreign Capital Actually Used(USD 10 000)	51.1	42.8
国际旅游者人数（人次）	Number of Tourists from Abroad(person-time)	1134	1782
四、每天人口变动和婚姻	**Daily Population Changes and Marriages**		
出　生(人)	Births(person)	211	247
死　亡(人)	Deaths(person)	88	113
结　婚(对)	Marriages(couple)	129	129
离　婚(对)	Divorces(couple)	12	14

注：本表财政收入数据2009年及以前为一般预算财政收入和基金收入之和。

Major Social and Economic Activities in Major Years

2005	2006	2007	2008	2009	2010	2011	2012	2013	2014
35998.1	42162.7	50866.6	63510.7	74632.3	88813.4	105824.1	119619.2	134930.7	150483.3
1808.5	1929.9	2260.6	2834.3	3024.1	3837.3	4743.6	5358.6	5492.1	5878.1
14808.2	17689.0	21423.0	26892.6	31363.0	38540.3	45871.5	51554.8	54762.2	60131.0
11506.9	13540.3	16300.0	19764.4	22381.4	27495.1	32592.1	36403.0	37718.9	40767.7
3301.4	4148.8	5123.0	7128.2	8981.6	11045.2	13279.5	15151.8	17596.2	19965.5
19381.4	22543.8	27183.0	33783.8	40245.2	46435.9	55209.0	62705.8	74676.4	84474.2
1816.4	2029.6	2307.1	2716.7	3030.1	3416.2	4044.9	4597.9	5893.4	6454.2
4032.9	4567.7	5356.4	6655.1	8028.8	9256.4	11477.8	13323.8	15773.2	17360.3
1381.9	1431.0	1920.3	2346.6	2576.7	2837.8	3405.2	3754.0	3714.5	3949.3
2300.6	2638.6	3433.6	6417.8	9080.0	13991.5	17805.0	20632.1	24733.3	27936.7
2819.6	3689.0	4771.4	8679.2	11509.0	10181.4	13550.0	16369.6	19994.8	22453.2
5631	5831	5180	5874	5978	6074	4987	5275	5017	4811
1157	1292	1447	1616	1694	1736	1775	1826	1802	1803
5362	5709	5601	6069	6641	6934	7169	7611	8168	8665
499	538	280	316	346	374	396	416	431	444
26	27	34	34	36	33	32	38	39	39
74.0	72.6	76.7	62.3	60.8	65.2	44.8	39.1	38.0	33.0
1316.3	1930.1	1946.3	1964.1	2279.7	2655.9	2603	2725.5	5055	4920
658	1960	2157	1312	3028	3035	506	857	1488	1175
112	282	468	734	1389	1787	1525	1484	1156	1027
21003.3	23861.1	27266.3	32400.3	38441.1	43794.8	50874.2	57341.6		
18371.5	21505.5	25649.6	32235.1	37838.9	44850.4	53862.5	62023.6	75147.7	84764.1
22986.6	28637.5	39766.3	50352.3	62518.1	77682.7	89447.4	103646.6		
20918.4	26404.9	34795.6	45315.3	58878.9	72237.8	83395.6	97509.0		
2068.2	2232.6	4970.7	5037.0	3639.2	5444.9	6051.8	6137.5		
16400	15975	25466	18998	22537	12287	23601	24762	23014	40078
33.0	32.4	41.4	75.5	83.9	94.0	107.5	123.1	137.3	115.2
28.7	30.8	34.2	72.6	78.6	83.0	91.4	99.1	104.9	70.5
3617.7	5116.7	6212.7	7256.4	8189.6	8852.3	5494.8	5923.6	6793.0	8016.4
1068.9	1138.1	1468.9	1928.9	1985.3	2847.3	3452.5	3565.6	4927.5	6833.5
721.8	747.6	951.0	1225.0	912.6	1456.8	1596.3	1999.7	2322.8	3276.7
347.1	390.5	517.9	703.9	1072.6	1390.5	1856.2	1565.9	2604.7	3556.8
156.5	225.9	305.7	314.4	333.9	429.2	549.4	678.9	857.5	1014.5
2125	2376	2740	1732	1844	2306	2746	3160	3318	
210	223	226	232	232	225	226	237	225	238
63	122	124	127	130	124	125	130	126	129
137	184	185	213	241	229	259	246	244	250
35	35	43	43	43	52	53	51	56	60

1-15　各区县国民经济和社会发展主要指标（2014年）

指　标	Item	新城区 Xincheng	碑林区 Beilin
一、年底总人口（常住人口）（万人）	Population at the Year-end Permanent population(10 000 persons)	59.86	62.40
二、生产总值（亿元）	Gross Domestic Product(100 mil. yuan)	467.08	617.90
第一产业	Primary Industry		
第二产业	Secondary Industry	186.67	120.03
#工业	Industry	95.84	13.03
第三产业	Tertiary Industry	280.41	497.87
三、全社会固定资产投资总额（亿元）	Total Investment in Fixed Assets(100 mil. yuan)	400.27	543.43
#城镇	Urban Area	400.27	543.43
#房地产	Real Estate	94.67	102.34
四、财政一般预算收入（亿元）	Local Financial Revenue(100 mil. yuan)	35.58	43.23
财政一般预算支出（亿元）	Local Financial Expenditure(100 mil. yuan)	31.12	28.29
五、农林牧渔及服务业总产值（万元）	Gross Output Value of Farming Forestry Animal Husbandry and Fishery(10 000 yuan)		
主要农产品产量（ 万吨）	Output of Major Farm Products(10 000 tons)		
粮食	Grain		
蔬菜	Vegetables		
瓜果	Melon and Fruit		
肉类(吨)	Meat (Ton)		
奶类(吨)	Milk (Ton)		
六、规模以上工业总产值（亿元）	Gross industrial Output Value(100 mil. yuan)	372.75	27.66
七、建筑业（亿元）	Gross Output Value(100 mil. yuan)	282.23	583.68
房屋建筑施工面积（万平方米）	Floor Space of Buildings under Construction (10 000 sq.m)	1080.63	3363.75
房屋建筑竣工面积（万平方米）	Total Retail Sales of Consumer Goods (100 mil. yuan)	242.68	862.56
八、社会消费品零售总额（亿元）	Floor Space of Buildings Completed(100 mil. yuan)	446.06	445.11
九、城镇居民人均可支配收入（元）	Per Capita Annual Disposable Income of Urban Households (yuan)	37029	37765
农村居民人均纯收入（元）	Per Capita Net Income of Rural Residents(yuan)		
十、医疗机构数（个）	Number of Health Care Institutions(unit)	281	371
卫生技术人员（人）	Number of Medical Technical Personnel (person)	11774	12011
床位数（张）	Number of Beds(unit)	7424	7495

Principal Indicators of National Economy and Social Development by Region (2014)

莲湖区 Lianhu	灞桥区 Baqiao	未央区 Weiyang	雁塔区 Yanta	阎良区 Yanliang	临潼区 Lintong	长安区 Chang'an	蓝田县 Lantian	周至县 Zhouzhi	户　县 Huxian	高陵县 Gaoling
70.68	60.82	82.28	119.74	28.53	67.16	110.59	52.30	57.57	56.60	34.22
539.53	309.73	703.14	1114.46	184.25	221.78	445.43	109.57	98.84	155.92	298.27
	18.14	1.06	1.62	22.21	31.16	33.67	25.90	27.62	27.20	25.96
193.90	141.61	371.00	389.82	105.61	116.26	217.23	35.33	26.09	71.56	219.67
106.52	101.24	266.42	245.07	89.19	101.65	174.18	18.67	17.98	58.31	199.92
345.63	149.98	331.08	723.02	56.43	74.36	194.53	48.34	45.13	57.16	52.64
608.82	413.68	915.51	969.65	261.23	231.56	678.22	164.28	148.80	152.69	415.83
608.82	404.77	904.12	967.41	250.21	219.61	655.51	76.74	103.00	135.94	412.60
175.47	147.58	461.86	580.51	19.10	16.31	93.48	5.01	10.12	16.82	38.60
47.13	47.06	23.67	35.51	12.04	12.14	35.43	3.84	3.52	8.27	13.25
33.91	32.67	22.03	23.98	18.70	29.40	49.42	25.14	28.43	26.92	20.27
	300728	19090	26798	354330	538221	538210	462420	482477	481686	468141
	5.28	0.40		8.10	31.79	33.84	25.06	22.50	29.60	19.04
	28.65	2.53	1.89	76.20	44.52	58.61	16.80	19.81	27.68	39.59
	0.82	0.06		23.75	6.36	8.28	3.75	0.49	5.40	2.84
	7335	1325	750	7205	44665	21704	18801	30179	19975	9947
	66295	6931	950	98354	335356	24316	41570	13293	26785	44166
407.16	300.73	858.40	694.34	300.25	418.75	546.35	46.22	29.10	104.68	854.73
179.81	107.67	538.94	678.95	22.92	11.59	60.76	9.66	8.84	16.47	84.82
1608.47	119.03	1858.88	2320.61	84.06	47.85	182.06	55.09	63.04	145.37	253.35
275.57	18.82	269.05	482.82	19.39	21.07	56.57	20.5	37.97	58.49	171.25
368.62	132.26	423.72	534.30	31.37	64.08	144.94	45.74	30.71	50.97	25.01
37757	35147	36462	38345	37503	29804	32377	23907	24445	27026	28581
	16982	18364		17007	13595	14206	9911	9961	12218	13615
339	478	310	508	159	488	770	594	451	592	213
9810	4130	5701	13560	1931	2578	4775	1550	2617	3454	2114
6326	2944	3573	9245	1418	2309	3575	1142	1398	2780	1436

主要统计指标解释

行政区划 指国家对行政区域的划分。根据有关法规规定，我国的行政区域划分如下：（1）全国分为省、自治区、直辖市；（2）省、自治区分为自治州、县、自治县、市；（3）自治州分为县、自治县、市；（4）县、自治县分为乡、民族乡、镇；（5）直辖市和较大的市分为区、县；（6）国家在必要时设立的特别行政区。

气候 指地球与大气之间长期能量交换与质量交换所形成的一种自然环境状态，它是多种因素综合作用的结果。气候既是人类生活和生产的环境要素之一，又是供给人类生活和生产的重要资源。气温、降水、湿度等气象要素的多年平均值是用来描述一个地区气候状况的主要参数，而各种气象要素某年、某月的平均值（或总量）则可以反映出该时期天气气候状况的重要特征。

自然资源 指人类可以直接从自然界获得，并用于生产和生活的物质资源。自然资源一般可以分成可再生资源和非再生资源两大类。可再生资源指在较短时间内可以再生、可以循环利用的资源，包括土地资源、水资源、气候资源、生物资源和海洋资源等。非再生资源指在使用后不能再生的资源，包括矿产资源和地热能源。

土地资源 土地指陆地的表层部分，它主要由岩石、岩石的风化物和土壤构成。土地资源按利用类型可以分为农用地、建筑用地和未利用地。农用地包括耕地、园地、林地、牧草地和水面。建筑用地包括居民点及工矿用地、交通用地和水利设施用地。未利用地指农用地和建筑用地以外的土地，包括滩涂、荒漠、戈壁、冰川和石山等。

耕地面积 指经过开垦用以种植农作物并经常进行耕耘的土地面积。包括种有作物的土地面积、休闲地、新开荒地和抛荒未满三年的土地面积。

森林面积 指由乔木树种构成，郁闭度0.2以上（含0.2）的林地或冠幅宽度10米以上的林带的面积，即有林地面积。森林面积包括天然起源和人工起源的针叶林面积、阔叶林面积、针阔混交林面积和竹林面积，不包括灌木林地面积和疏林地面积。

林业用地面积 指生长乔木、竹类、灌木、沿海红树林等林木的土地面积，包括有林地、灌木林、疏林地、未成林造林地、迹地、苗圃等。

水资源总量 指评价区内降水形成的地表和地下产水总量，即地表产流量与降水入渗补给地下水量之和，不包括过境水量。

地表水资源量 指评价区内河流、湖泊、冰川等地表水体中可以逐年更新的动态水量，即当地天然河川径流量。

地下水资源量 指评价区内降水和地表水对饱水岩土层的补给量，包括降水入渗补给量和河道、湖库、渠系、渠灌田间等地表水体的入渗补给量。

气温 指空气的温度，我国一般以摄氏度（℃）为单位表示。气象观测的温度表是放在离地面约1.5米处通风良好的百叶箱里测量的，因此，通常说的气温指的是离地面1.5米处百叶箱中的温度。其统计计算方法为：

月平均气温是将全月各日的平均气温相加，除以该月的天数而得。

年平均气温是将12个月的月平均气温累加后除以12而得。

降水量 指从天空降落到地面的液态或固态（经融化后）水，未经蒸发、渗透、流失而在地面上积聚的深度。其统计计算方法为：

月降水量是将全月各日的降水量累加而得。

年降水量是将12个月的月降水量累加而得。

日照时数 指太阳实际照射地面的时间。其统计方法与降水量相同。

平均增长速度 平均增长速度表明社会经济现象在一个较长的时期内逐期平均增长变化的程度，它不能根据各个环比增长速度直接求得，但与平均发展速度之间存在着一定的数量关系：平均增长速度 = 平均发展速度 - 1。

平均发展速度 是一种根据环比发展速度计算的序时平均数,由于各时期对比的基础不同，所以计算平均发展速度不能采用一般的序时平均数的计算方法，计算方法分为水平法和累计法。水平法，又称几何平均法，即将环比发展速度按连乘法用几何平均数公式计算。累计法，也称方程法，根据一段时期内各年发展水平总和与基期水平的关系，列出方程式计算平均发展速度。水平法着重考虑最后一年所达到的发展水平；累计法着重考虑整个时期累计发展水平的总量。

本《年鉴》内所列的平均增长速度，均用“水平法”计算。从某年到某年平均增长速度的年份，均不包括基期年在内。如建国六十年以来的平均增长速度是以1949年为基期计算的，则写为1950-2009年平均增长速度，其余类推。

Explanatory Notes on Main Statistical Indicators

Divisions of Administrative Areas refers to the division of administrative areas by the State. The relative laws stipulate that (1)the whole country is divided into provinces, autonomous regions and municipalities directly under the Central Government;(2)provinces and autonomous regions are further divided into autonomous prefectures, counties, autonomous counties and cities; (3)autonomous prefectures are further divided into counties, autonomous counties and cities; (4)counties and autonomous counties are further divided into townships, ethnic townships and towns; (5)municipalities directly under the Central Government and large cities are divided into districts and counties, (6)the State shall, when necessary, establish special administrative regions.

Climate refers to the natural environmental status formed by the long-term exchange of energy and mass between the earth and the atmosphere, and is the result of interaction of many factors. Climate is both one of the environment factors and also the important resources for living and production activities of the human being. The average values across several years of meteorological factors such as temperature, rainfall and humidity are used as important parameters to describe the climate of a region, while the average values (or total values)of a given year or month of meteorological factors reflect the key characteristics of climate for that period of time.

Natural Resources refer to material resources that could be obtained from the nature by human being and used for production and living. Natural resources in general can be classified as renewable resources and non-renewable resources. Renewable resources refer to resources that could be renewed and recycled during a relatively short period of time, including land resource, water resource, climate resource, biology resource and marine resource. Non-renewable resources include resources that could not be renewed, such as minerals and geothermal resource.

Land Resource Land refers to the surface of the earth, consisting of mainly rocks and its whethering and earth. Land resource can be classified, by its utilization, as land for agriculture, land for construction and unused land. Land for agriculture includes cultivated land, plantation land, forestland, grassland and waters. Land for construction includes land for residential purpose, for manufacturing and mining, for transportation and for water-conservancy projects. Unused land refers to land other than land for agriculture and.construction, including beaches, deserts, Gobi, glaciers and rock mountains.

Area of Cultivated Land refers to area of land reclaimed for the regular cultivation of various farm crops, including crop-cover land, fallow, newly reclaimed land and land laid idle for less than 3 years.

Forest Area refers to the area of trees and bamboo grow with canopy density above 0.2, the area of shrubby tree according to regulations of the government, the area of forest land inside farm land and the area of trees planted by the side of villages, farm houses and along roads and rivers.

Area of Afforested Land refers to area for land for trees bamboo, bushes and mangrove, including forest-covered land, bush-covered land, sparse forest land, land planned for afforestation and nurseries of young trees.

Total Water Resources refers to total volume of water resources measured as run-off for surface water from rainfall and recharge for groundwater in a given area, excluding transit water.

Surface Water Resources refers to total renewable resources which exist in rivers, lakes, glaciers and other collectors from rainfall and are measured as run-off of rivers.

Groundwater Resources refers to replenishment of aquifers with rainfall and surface water.

Temperature refers to the air temperature. China uses centigrade as the unit. The thermometry used for weather observation is put in a breezy shutter, which is 1.5 meters high from the ground. Therefore, the commonly used temperature refers to the temperature in the breezy shutter 1.5 meters away from the ground. The calculation method is as follows:

Monthly average temperature is the summation of average daily temperature of one month divided by the actual days of that particular month.

Annual average temperature is the summation of monthly average of a year divided by 12 months.

Volume of Precipitation refers to the deepness of liquid state or solid state (thawed)water falling from the sky to the ground that has not been evaporated, infiltrated or run off. The calculation method is as follows:

Monthly precipitation is the summation of daily precipitation of a month.

Annual precipitation is the summation of 12 months precipitation of a year.

Sunshine Hours refer to the actual hours of sun irradiating the earth. The calculation method is the same as that of the precipitation.

Average Annual Growth Rate shows the average growth rate of social and economic development during a longer period. It can not be directly calculated by chain based growth rate. The relation is:

Average Annual Growth Rate=Average Speed of Development 1

Average speed of development is the time series average of speed which calculated by chain based.Because the reference bases during the different periods are not same, average speed of development can not be calculated by the general method. Level approach and accumulative approach for calculating average speed of development rate are applied. The "level approach" , or the method of calculating the geometric average, is derived by the formula of geometric average of the chain-based speeds of development, or comparing the level of the last year of the interval with that of the beginning year; the other is called the "accumulative approach" or the "algebraic average" , "equation" method, which is derived by the summation of the actual figure of each year in the interval divided by the figure in the base year. The level approach focuses on the level of the last year, while the accumulative approach emphasizes the aggregate development in the duration.

The average annual growth rates listed in the Yearbook are calculated by the level approach except for the growth rate of investment in fixed assets. The base year is not listed in the duration for which average annual growth rates are computed. For instance, the average annual growth rate of the 60 years since 1949 is shown as the average annual growth rate of 1950-2009 without showing the base year 1949.

2

基本单位

BASIC UNIT

资料整理：张　奇　张　斌
Data management：Zhang Qi　Zhang Bin
数据审核：张利民
Data audit：Zhang Limin

第二部分　基本单位

一、简要说明

本章资料主要包括法人单位、产业活动单位和企业一套表调查单位数等资料,由西安市统计局普查中心提供。2014统计年鉴一套表单位数为快报数，本年统计年鉴一套表单位数为年报数，使用时请注意。

二、主要指标

法人单位数（个）	111034	比上年增长	5.3%
产业活动单位数（个）	127136	比上年增长	10.6%
规模以上工业企业数（个）	1113		
限额以上批发零售住宿餐饮业企业数（个）	1341		
资质内建筑业企业数（个）	539		
房地产开发经营企业数（个）	784		
规模以上服务业企业数（个）	964		

2　BASIC UNIT

Ⅰ.Brief Introduction

This chapter consists of unified data of Enterprises and industrial active unites and investigation unit in “Enterprises of a table”, provided by Xian bureau of statistic’s census center. Data of “Enterprises of a table” in 2014 Statistical Yearbook were Express number, data of “Enterprises of a table” in this Statistical Yearbook is the number of annual reports, please note that when used.

Ⅱ.Major Indicators

		Increase over Preceding Year
Number of Enterprises (unit)	111034	5.3%
Number of Industrial Active Units (unit)	127136	10.6%
Number of Industrial Enterprises above designed size (unit)	1113	
Number of Enterprises about Wholesale、Retail、Accommodation and Catering above designed size (unit)	1341	
Number of Qualified Construction Enterprises (unit)	539	
Number of Real Estate Development Enterprises (unit)	784	
Number of service Enterprises above designed size (unit)	964	

2-1 按登记注册类型分法人单位数（2014年）

Impersonal Entities Grouped by Status of Registion（2014）

单位：个 (unit)

分 组	Classify	法人单位数 Number of Enterprises	企业 Enterprises
总 计	**Total**	**111034**	**94902**
#非公有制经济	Non-public sectors of the economy	90510	89387
按登记注册类型分	**Grouped by Status of Registion**		
（一）内资	Domestic Funded Enterprises	110230	94106
国有	State-owned Enterprises	7115	1675
集体	Collective-owned Enterprises	2686	1530
股份合作	Cooperative Enterprises	317	297
联营	Joint Ownership Enterprises	234	199
国有联营	State Joint Ownership Enterprises	31	25
集体联营	Collective Joint Ownership Enterprises	120	114
国有与集体联营	Joint State-collective Ownership Enterprises	17	11
其他联营	Other Joint Ownership Enterprises	66	49
有限责任公司	Limited Liability Corporations	42884	42759
国有独资公司	State Sole Funded Corporations	256	256
其他有限责任公司	Other Limited Liability Corporations	42628	42503
股份有限公司	Share-holding Corporations Limited	1101	1093
私营	Private Enterprises	43455	43199
私营独资企业	Private-funded Enterprises	10431	10270
私营合伙	Private Partnership Enterprises	1227	1189
私营有限责任公司	Private Limited Liability Corporations	30634	30579
私营股份有限公司	Private Share-holding Corporations Ltd.	1163	1161
其他	Other Domestic Funded Enterprises	12438	3354
（二）港、澳、台商投资企业	Enterprises with Funds from Hong Kong, Macao and Taiwan	252	251
与港、澳、台商合资经营	Joint-venture with Funds from Hong Kong,Macao and Taiwan	96	96
与港、澳、台商合作经营	Cooperative Enterprises with Funds from Hong Kong Macau and Taiwan	12	11
港澳台商独资经营	Enterprises with Sole Investment from Hong Kong Macau and Taiwan	135	135
港澳台商投资股份有限公司	Share-holding Corporations Ltd. with funds from Hong Kong, Macao & Taiwan	8	8
其他港澳台商投资	Other Enterprises with Funds from Hong Kong, Macao and Taiwan	1	1
（三）外商投资	Foreign Funded Enterprises	552	545
中外合资经营	Sino-foreign Joint Ventures	212	211
中外合作经营	Sino-Foreign Cooperation Enterprises	16	15
外资企业	Foreign Owned Enterprises	270	266
外商投资股份有限公司	Limited Company Funded by Foreign Investment	30	30
其他外商投资	Other Foreign Funded Enterprises	24	23

2-2 按国民经济行业分法人单位数（2014年）

Impersonal Entities by Sector（2014）

单位：个 (unit)

分 组	Classify	法人单位数 Number of Enterprises	企业 Enterprises
总 计	**Total**	**111034**	**94902**
（一）农、林、牧、渔业	Agriculture,Forestry,Animal Husbandry and Fishery	2840	2003
农业	Farming	1327	866
林业	Forestry	362	312
畜牧业	Animal Husbandry	871	647
渔业	Fishery	48	39
农、林、牧、渔服务业	Services in Support of Agriculture	232	139
（二）采矿业	Mining	241	241
煤炭开采和洗选业	Mining and Washing of Coal	11	11
石油和天然气开采业	Extraction of Petroleum and Natural Gas	20	20
黑色金属矿采选业	Mining of Ferrous Metal Ores	14	14
有色金属矿采选业	Mining of Non-ferrous Metal Ores	22	22
非金属矿采选业	Mining and Processing of Nonmetal Ores	73	73
开采辅助活动	Mining of Other Ores	77	77
其他采矿业	Manufacturing	24	24
（三）制造业	Processing of Food from Agricultural Products	13651	13651
农副食品加工业	Manufacture of Foods	416	416
食品制造业	Manufacture of Beverages	396	396
酒、饮料和精制茶制造业	Manufacture of Tobacco	126	126
烟草制品业	Manufacture of Textile	2	2
纺织业	Manufacture of Textile Wearing Apparel, Footware and Caps	137	137
纺织服装、服饰业	Manufacture of Leather, Fur, Feather and Related Products	134	134
皮革、毛皮、羽毛及其制品和制鞋业	Processing of Timber,Manufacture of Wood, Bamboo,Rattan its Froducts and Footwear	36	36
木材加工和木、竹、藤、棕、草制品业	Plam and Straw Products and Straw Products	187	187
家具制造业	Manufacture of Furniture	375	375
造纸及纸制品业	Manufacture of Paper and Paper Products	322	322
印刷和记录媒介复制业	Printing,Reproduction of Recording Media	528	528
文教、工美、体育和娱乐用品制造业	Manufacture of Articles For Culture, Education and Sport Activities	193	193

2-2 续表1 continued 1

单位：个 (unit)

分组	Classify	法人单位数 Number of Enterprises	企业 Enterprises
石油加工、炼焦和核燃料加工业	Processing of Petroleum, Coking, Processing of Nuclear Fuel	54	54
化学原料和化学制品制造业	Manufacture of Raw Chemical Materials and Chemical Products	638	638
医药制造业	Manufacture of Medicines	337	337
化学纤维制造业	Manufacture of Chemical Fibers	19	19
橡胶和塑料制品业	Manufacture of Rubber and Manufacture of Plastics	454	454
非金属矿物制品业	Manufacture of Non-metallic Mineral Products	1301	1301
黑色金属冶炼和压延加工业	Smelting and Pressing of Ferrous Metals	245	245
有色金属冶炼和压延加工业	Smelting and Pressing of Non-ferrous Metals	188	188
金属制品业	Manufacture of Metal Products	987	987
通用设备制造业	Manufacture of General Purpose Machinery	1825	1825
专用设备制造业	Manufacture of Special Equipment	1316	1316
汽车制造业	Manufacture of Motor Vehicle	165	165
铁路、船舶、航空航天和其他运输设备制造业	Railways,Shipbuilding,Aerospace and Other Transportation Equipment Manufacturing Industry	289	289
电气机械和器材制造业	Manufacture of Electric Equipment and Machinery	1369	1369
计算机、通信和其他	Manufacture of Communication Equipment,	801	801
电子设备制造业	Computers and other Electronic Equipment	502	502
仪器仪表制造业	Manufacture of Measuring Instruments and Machinery	128	128
其他制造业	Other Manufacturing	47	47
废弃资源综合利用	Recycling and Disposal of Waste	134	134
金属制品、机械和设备修理业	Metal Products,Machinery and Equipment Repair Industry	286	284
（四）电力、燃气及水的生产供应业	Production and Distribution of Electricity,Gas and Water	286	284
电力、热力生产和供应业	Production and Supply of Electric Power and Heat Power	172	171
燃气生产和供应业	Gas mining and supplying industry	43	43
水的生产和供应业	Production and Supply of Water	71	70
（五）建筑业	Construction	7708	7708
房屋建筑业	Construction of Building	1393	1393
土木工程建筑业	Civil Engineering	1419	1419
建筑安装业	Architectural Installation	1450	1450
建筑装饰和其他建筑业	Architectural Decoration and Other Construction	3446	3446
（六）批发和零售业	Wholesale and Retail Trades	34657	34638

2–2 续表2 continued 2

单位：个 (unit)

分 组	Classify	法人单位数 Number of Enterprises	企业 Enterprises
批发业	Wholesale Trade	19915	19911
零售业	Retail Trade	14742	14727
（七）交通运输、仓储和邮政业	Traffic, Transport, Storage and Post	1976	1924
铁路运输业	Transport Via Railway	35	30
道路运输业	Transport Via Road	1084	1051
水上运输业	Water Transport	1	1
航空运输业	Air Transport	57	56
管道运输业	Transport Via Pipeline	8	8
装卸搬运和运输代理服务业	Loading, Unloading, Portage and Other Transport Services	442	440
仓储业	Storage	258	248
邮政业	Post	91	90
（八）住宿和餐饮业	Hotels and Catering Services	2982	2973
住宿业	Hotels	1213	1208
餐饮业	Catering Services	1769	1765
（九）信息传输、软件和信息技术服务业	Information Transmission, Computer Services and Software	4135	4113
电信、广播电视和卫星传输服务	Telecom & Other Information Transmission Services	186	181
互联网和相关服务	internet and relevant services	609	605
软件和信息技术服务	Software Industry	3340	3327
（十）金融业	Financial Intermediation	741	731
货币金融服务	Monetary and Financial Services	173	170
资本市场服务	Capital Market Services	315	313
保险业	Insurance	157	156
其他金融业	Other Financial Intermediation	96	92
（十一）房地产业	Real Estate	6106	6078
房地产业	Real Estate	6106	6078
（十二） 租赁和商务服务业	Leasing and Business Services	10606	10290
租赁业	Leasing	779	776
商务服务业	Business Services	9827	9514
（十三）科学研究和技术服务业	Scientific Research, Technical Sevice	5219	4610
研究与试验发展	Research and Experimental Development	489	400
专业技术服务业	Professional Technical Services	3280	2977

2–2　续表3 continued 3

单位：个　　(unit)

分　组	Classify	法人单位数 Number of Enterprises	企业 Enterprises
科技推广和应用服务业	Services of Science and Technology Exchanges and Promotion	1450	1233
（十四）水利、环境和公共设施管理业	Management of Water Conservancy, Environment and Public Facilities	920	719
水利管理业	Management of Water Conservancy	164	79
生态保护和环境治理业	Environmental Management	97	70
公共设施管理业	Management of Public Facilities	659	570
（十五）居民服务、修理和其他服务业	Services to Households and Other Services	2544	2473
居民服务业	Services to Households	828	772
机动车、电子产品和日用产品修理业	The repair service industry for motor vehicle、electronic	1007	998
其他服务业	Other Services	709	703
（十六）教育	Education	3655	411
教育	Education	3655	411
（十七）卫生和社会工作	Health, Social Security	3209	215
卫生	Health	3003	200
社会工作	Social	206	15
（十八）文化、体育和娱乐业	Culture, Sports and Entertainment	2148	1836
新闻和出版业	Journalism and Publishing Activities	171	125
广播、电视、电影和影视录音制作业	Broadcasting, Movies, Television and Audiovisual Activities	326	307
文化艺术业	Cultural and Art Activities	659	456
体育	Sports Activities	137	103
娱乐业	Entertainment	855	845
（十九）公共管理、社会保障和社会组织	Public Management and Social Organizaion	7410	4
中国共产党机关	Organs of Communist Party of China	159	
国家机构	Government Agencies	2088	
人民政协、民主党派	People's Pc~litical Consultative Conference and Democratic Parties	32	
社会保障	Social Security	66	4
群众团体、社会团体和其他成员组织	Mass organizations、social groups and other members of the organization	1344	
基层群众自治组织	Grass-roots Mass Self-Government Organizations	3721	
（二十）国际组织	International Organizations		
国际组织	International Organizations		

2-3 按行政区划分法人单位数（2014年）

Impersonal Entities by Region（2014）

单位：个 (unit)

区 县	Region	法人单位数 Number of Enterprises	企业 Enterprises
总 计	**Total**	**111034**	**94902**
新城区	Xincheng	7984	7065
碑林区	Beilin	12752	11737
莲湖区	Lianhu	10751	9798
灞桥区	Baqiao	4895	3924
未央区	Weiyang	18259	17262
雁塔区	Yanta	28983	27950
阎良区	Yanliang	2310	1766
临潼区	Lintong	3606	2029
长安区	Chang'an	7021	4877
蓝田县	Lantian	3231	1622
周至县	Zhouzhi	3154	1544
户 县	Huxian	4806	2871
高陵县	Gaoling	3282	2457

2-4 按登记注册类型分产业活动单位数（2014年）

Industrial Active Units by Status of Registion（2014）

单位：个 (unit)

分 组	Classify	产业活动单位数 Number of Industrial Active Units	企业 Enterprises
总计	**Total**	**127136**	**107333**
按登记注册类型分	Grouped by Status of Registion		
（一）内资	Domestic Funded Enterprises	125523	105730
国有	State-owned Enterprises	11126	2991
集体	Collective-owned Enterprises	3522	2029
股份合作	Cooperative Enterprises	622	601
联营	Joint Ownership Enterprises	341	298
国有联营	State Joint Ownership Enterprises	58	50
集体联营	Collective Joint Ownership Enterprises	156	146
国有与集体联营	Joint State-collective Ownership Enterprises	28	20
其他联营	Other Joint Ownership Enterprises	99	82
有限责任公司	Limited Liability Corporations	47612	47470
国有独资公司	State Sole Funded Corporations	307	307
其他有限责任公司	Other Limited Liability Corporations	47305	47163
股份有限公司	Share-holding Corporations Limited	2493	2483
私营	Private Enterprises	46506	46229
私营独资企业	Private-funded Enterprises	11016	10844
私营合伙	Private Partnership Enterprises	1345	1305
私营有限责任公司	Private Limited Liability Corporations	32857	32795
私营股份有限公司	Private Share-holding Corporations Ltd.	1288	1285
其他	Other Enterprises	13301	3629

2-4 续表 continued

单位：个 (unit)

分 组	Classify	产业活动单位数 Number of Industrial Active Units	企业 Enterprises
（二）港、澳、台商投资企业	Enterprises with Funds from Hong Kong,Macao and Taiwan	481	479
与港、澳、台商合资经营	Joint-venture with Funds from Hong Kong,Macao and Taiwan	130	130
与港、澳、台商合作经营	Cooperative Enterprises with Funds from Hong Kong Macau and Taiwan	24	23
港澳台商独资经营	Enterprises with Sole Investment from Hong Kong Macau and Taiwan	306	305
港澳台商投资股份有限公司	Share-holding Corporations Ltd. with funds from Hong Kong, Macao & Taiwan	14	14
其他港澳台商投资	Other Enterprises with Funds from Hong Kong,Macao and Taiwan	7	7
（三）外商投资	Foreign Funded Enterprises	1132	1124
中外合资经营	Sino-foreign Joint Ventures	344	343
中外合作经营	Sino-Foreign Cooperation Enterprises	29	28
外资企业	Foreign Owned Enterprises	569	564
外商投资股份有限公司	Limited Company Funded by Foreign Investment	125	125
其他外商投资	Other Foreign Funded Enterprises	65	64

2-5 按国民经济行业分产业活动单位数（2014年）

Industrial Active Units by Sector（2014）

单位：个 (unit)

分 组	Classify	产业活动单位数 Number of Industrial Active Units	企业 Enterprises
总 计	**Total**	**127136**	**107333**
（一）农、林、牧、渔业	Agriculture,Forestry,Animal Husbandry and Fishery	2867	2022
农业	Farming	1334	873
林业	Forestry	371	314
畜牧业	Animal Husbandry	880	656
渔业	Fishery	48	39
农、林、牧、渔服务业	Services in Support of Agriculture	234	140
（二）采矿业	Mining	262	262
煤炭开采和洗选业	Mining and Washing of Coal	14	14
石油和天然气开采业	Extraction of Petroleum and Natural Gas	25	25
黑色金属矿采选业	Mining of Ferrous Metal Ores	14	14
有色金属矿采选业	Mining of Non-ferrous Metal Ores	22	22
非金属矿采选业	Mining and Processing of Nonmetal Ores	73	73
开采辅助活动	Mining of Other Ores	90	90
其他采矿业	Manufacturing	24	24
（三）制造业	Processing of Food from Agricultural Products	14300	14300
农副食品加工业	Manufacture of Foods	431	431
食品制造业	Manufacture of Beverages	420	420
酒、饮料和精制茶制造业	Manufacture of Tobacco	139	139
烟草制品业	Manufacture of Textile	3	3
纺织业	Manufacture of Textile Wearing Apparel, Footware and Caps	146	146
纺织服装、服饰业	Manufacture of Leather, Fur, Feather and Related Products	143	143
皮革、毛皮、羽毛及其制品和制鞋业	Processing of Timber,Manufacture of Wood, Bamboo,Rattan its Froducts and Footwear	40	40
木材加工和木、竹、藤、棕、草制品业	Plam and Straw Products and Straw Products	198	198
家具制造业	Manufacture of Furniture	395	395
造纸及纸制品业	Manufacture of Paper and Paper Products	329	329
印刷和记录媒介复制业	Printing,Reproduction of Recording Media	549	549
文教、工美、体育和娱乐用品制造业	Manufacture of Articles For Culture, Education and Sport Activities	201	201

2–5 续表1 continued 1

单位：个 (unit)

分组	Classify	产业活动单位数 Number of Industrial Active Units	企业 Enterprises
石油加工、炼焦和核燃料加工业	Processing of Petroleum, Coking, Processing of Nuclear Fuel	57	57
化学原料和化学制品制造业	Manufacture of Raw Chemical Materials and Chemical Products	671	671
医药制造业	Manufacture of Medicines	354	354
化学纤维制造业	Manufacture of Chemical Fibers	19	19
橡胶和塑料制品业	Manufacture of Rubber and Manufacture of Plastics	466	466
非金属矿物制品业	Manufacture of Non-metallic Mineral Products	1362	1362
黑色金属冶炼和压延加工业	Smelting and Pressing of Ferrous Metals	252	252
有色金属冶炼和压延加工业	Smelting and Pressing of Non-ferrous Metals	191	191
金属制品业	Manufacture of Metal Products	1023	1023
通用设备制造业	Manufacture of General Purpose Machinery	1902	1902
专用设备制造业	Manufacture of Special Equipment	1384	1384
汽车制造业	Manufacture of Motor Vehicle	182	182
铁路、船舶、航空航天和其他运输设备制造业	Railways,Shipbuilding,Aerospace and Other Transportation Equipment Manufacturing Industry	302	302
电气机械和器材制造业	Manufacture of Electric Equipment and Machinery	1437	1437
计算机、通信和其他电子设备制造业	Manufacture of Communication Equipment, Computers and other Electronic Equipment	841	841
仪器仪表制造业	Manufacture of Measuring Instruments and Machinery	536	536
其他制造业	Other Manufacturing	134	134
废弃资源综合利用	Recycling and Disposal of Waste	54	54
金属制品、机械和设备修理业	Metal Products,Machinery and Equipment Repair Industry	139	139
（四）电力、燃气及水的生产供应业	Production and Distribution of Electricity,Gas and Water	409	404
电力、热力生产和供应业	Production and Supply of Electric Power and Heat Power	270	266
燃气生产和供应业	Gas mining and supplying industry	56	56
水的生产和供应业	Production and Supply of Water	83	82
（五）建筑业	Construction	8498	8498
房屋建筑业	Construction of Building	1749	1749
土木工程建筑业	Civil Engineering	1560	1560
建筑安装业	Architectural Installation	1548	1548
建筑装饰和其他建筑业	Architectural Decoration and Other Construction	3641	3641
（六）批发和零售业	Wholesale and Retail Trades	39184	39165

2–5 续表2 continued 2

单位：个 (unit)

分 组	Classify	产业活动单位数 Number of Industrial Active Units	企业 Enterprises
批发业	Wholesale Trade	20972	20968
零售业	Retail Trade	18212	18197
（七）交通运输、仓储和邮政业	Traffic, Transport, Storage and Post	2659	2557
铁路运输业	Transport Via Railway	77	65
道路运输业	Transport Via Road	1300	1241
水上运输业	Water Transport	2	2
航空运输业	Air Transport	62	61
管道运输业	Transport Via Pipeline	14	14
装卸搬运和运输代理服务业	Loading, Unloading, Portage and Other Transport Services	554	550
仓储业	Storage	284	274
邮政业	Post	366	350
（八）住宿和餐饮业	Hotels and Catering Services	3919	3906
住宿业	Hotels	1438	1430
餐饮业	Catering Services	2481	2476
（九）信息传输、软件和信息技术服务业	Information Transmission, Computer Services and Software	4644	4607
电信、广播电视和卫星传输服务	Telecom & Other Information Transmission Services	412	399
互联网和相关服务	internet and relevant services	665	660
软件和信息技术服务	Software Industry	3567	3548
（十）金融业	Financial Intermediation	2505	2481
货币金融服务	Monetary and Financial Services	1494	1480
资本市场服务	Capital Market Services	384	382
保险业	Insurance	521	518
其他金融业	Other Financial Intermediation	106	101
（十一）房地产业	Real Estate	6709	6667
房地产业	Real Estate	6709	6667
（十二） 租赁和商务服务业	Leasing and Business Services	11574	11167
租赁业	Leasing	829	826
商务服务业	Business Services	10745	10341
（十三）科学研究和技术服务业	Scientific Research, Technical Sevice	5662	4971
研究与试验发展	Research and Experimental Development	518	426
专业技术服务业	Professional Technical Services	3583	3245

2-5 续表3 continued 3

单位：个 (unit)

分 组	Classify	产业活动单位数 Number of Industrial Active Units	企业 Enterprises
科技推广和应用服务业	Services of Science and Technology Exchanges and Promotion	1561	1300
（十四）水利、环境和公共设施管理业	Management of Water Conservancy, Environment and Public Facilities	1036	762
水利管理业	Management of Water Conservancy	207	83
生态保护和环境治理业	Environmental Management	109	73
公共设施管理业	Management of Public Facilities	720	606
（十五）居民服务、修理和其他服务业	Services to Households and Other Services	2937	2842
居民服务业	Services to Households	1073	999
机动车、电子产品和日用产品修理业	The repair service industry for motor vehicle、electronic	1109	1100
其他服务业	Other Services	755	743
（十六）教育	Education	4419	531
教育	Education	4419	531
（十七）卫生和社会工作	Health, Social Security	3611	245
卫生	Health	3389	229
社会工作	Social	222	16
（十八）文化、体育和娱乐业	Culture, Sports and Entertainment	2356	1942
新闻和出版业	Journalism and Publishing Activities	192	138
广播、电视、电影和影视录音制作业	Broadcasting, Movies, Television and Audiovisual Activities	342	321
文化艺术业	Cultural and Art Activities	767	475
体育	Sports Activities	164	128
娱乐业	Entertainment	891	880
（十九）公共管理、社会保障和社会组织	Public Management and Social Organizaion	9585	4
中国共产党机关	Organs of Communist Party of China	181	
国家机构	Government Agencies	3867	
人民政协、民主党派	People's Pc~litical Consultative Conference and Democratic Parties	44	
社会保障	Social Security	101	4
群众团体、社会团体和其他成员组织	Mass organizations、social groups and other members of the organization	1482	
基层群众自治组织	Grass-roots Mass Self-Government Organizations	3910	
（二十）国际组织	International Organizations		
国际组织	International Organizations		

2-6 按行政区划分产业活动单位数（2014年）

Industrial Active Units by Region（2014）

单位：个 (unit)

区 县	Region	法人单位数 Number of Enterprises	企业 Enterprises
总 计	**Total**	**127136**	**107333**
新城区	Xincheng	9330	8181
碑林区	Beilin	15543	14329
莲湖区	Lianhu	12690	11532
灞桥区	Baqiao	6136	4665
未央区	Weiyang	19901	18701
雁塔区	Yanta	31381	30134
阎良区	Yanliang	2701	2049
临潼区	Lintong	4582	2473
长安区	Chang'an	7804	5524
蓝田县	Lantian	4061	1866
周至县	Zhouzhi	3819	1774
户 县	Huxian	5568	3363
高陵县	Gaoling	3620	2742

2-7 按统计机构分企业一套表调查单位数（2014年）

Number of Survey Units by Statistical Agencies of "One Table" （2014）

单位：个 (unit)

区县、开发区	Region	合计 Total	规模以上工业 Industrial Enterprises above designed size	限额以上批发零售住宿餐饮业 Above wholesale and retail accommodation and catering industry	资质内建筑业 Qualified Construction Enterprises	房地产开发经营企业 Real Estate Development Enterprises	规模以上服务业 Service Enterprises above designed size
全市	**Total**	**4741**	**1113**	**1341**	**539**	**784**	**964**
新城区	Xincheng	277	12	144	33	35	53
碑林区	Beilin	466	12	208	62	77	107
莲湖区	Lianhu	405	30	147	49	69	110
灞桥区	Baqiao	259	106	55	36	33	29
未央区	Weiyang	219	27	72	26	50	44
雁塔区	Yanta	449	39	124	113	69	104
阎良区	Yanliang	127	58	18	18	25	8
临潼区	Lintong	128	48	31	22	9	18
长安区	Chang'an	202	44	71	26	39	22
蓝田县	Lantian	74	32	14	9	14	5
周至县	Zhouzhi	92	36	13	11	22	10
户　县	Huxian	128	60	31	5	22	10
高陵县	Gaoling	151	66	30	7	32	16
高新技术开发区	GaoXin	751	255	150	70	55	221
经济技术开发区	JingKai	537	195	147	38	52	105
曲江新区	Qujiang	169		22	4	75	68
阎良国家航空技术产业基地	Aviation Industry Base	37	25			10	2
国家民用航天产业基地	Aerospace Base	68	22	12	3	25	6
浐灞生态区	Chanba Eco-District	73		13	1	49	10
国际港务区	International Trade &Logistic Park	21	1	3	1	7	9
沣东新城	FengDongXinCheng	108	45	36	5	15	7
其他	other						

注：由于统计口径不同，一套表调查单位数与各专业有差异。

2-8 按行政区划分企业一套表调查单位数（2014年）

Number of Survey Units by Region of "One Table"（2014）

单位：个 (unit)

区 县	Region	合计 Total	规模以上工业 Industrial Enterprises above designed size	限额以上批发零售住宿餐饮业 Above wholesale and retail accommodation and catering industry	资质内建筑业 Qualified Construction Enterprises	房地产开发经营企业 Real Estate Development Enterprises	规模以上服务业 Service Enterprises above designed size
全市	**Total**	**4741**	**1113**	**1341**	**539**	**784**	**964**
新城区	Xincheng	281	11	144	33	40	53
碑林区	Beilin	475	14	211	62	80	108
莲湖区	Lianhu	410	31	147	49	71	112
灞桥区	Baqiao	332	110	65	37	73	47
未央区	Weiyang	820	199	258	70	139	154
雁塔区	Yanta	1254	225	283	185	179	382
阎良区	Yanliang	164	83	18	18	35	10
临潼区	Lintong	129	48	31	22	10	18
长安区	Chang'an	353	127	93	31	68	34
蓝田县	Lantian	75	33	14	9	14	5
周至县	Zhouzhi	93	37	13	11	22	10
户 县	Huxian	139	71	31	5	22	10
高陵县	Gaoling	216	124	33	7	31	21

主要统计指标解释

企业（单位）登记注册类型 是以在工商行政管理机关登记注册的各类企业为划分对象，以工商行政管理部门对企业登记注册的类型为依据，将企业登记注册类型分为内资企业、港澳台商投资企业和外商投资企业三大类。内资企业包括国有企业、集体企业、股份合作企业、联营企业、有限责任公司、股份有限公司、私营公司和其他企业；港澳台商投资企业和外商投资企业分别包括合资经营企业、合作经营企业、独资经营企业和股份有限公司。对不在工商行政管理部门进行登记注册的行政机关、事业单位和社会团体，主要按其经费来源和管理方式进行划分。

国有企业 指企业全部资产归国家所有，并按《中华人民共和国企业法人登记管理条例》规定登记注册的非公司制的经济组织。不包括有限责任公司中的国有独资公司。

集体企业 指企业资产归集体所有，并按《中华人民共和国企业法人登记管理条例》规定登记注册的经济组织。

股份合作企业 指以合作制为基础，由企业职工共同出资入股，吸收一定比例的社会资产投资组建，实行自主经营，自负盈亏，共同劳动，民主管理，按劳分配与按股分红相结合的一种集体经济组织。

联营企业 指两个及两个以上相同或不同所有制性质的企业法人或事业单位法人，按自愿、平等、互利的原则，共同投资组成的经济组织。联营企业包括国有联营企业、集体联营企业、国有与集体联营企业和其他联营企业。

有限责任公司 指根据《中华人民共和国公司登记管理条例》规定登记注册，由两个以上、五十个以下的股东共同出资，每个股东以其所认缴的出资额对公司承担有限责任，公司以其全部资产对其债务承担责任的经济组织。有限责任公司包括国有独资公司以及其他有限责任公司。

股份有限公司 指根据《中华人民共和国公司登记管理条例》规定登记注册，其全部注册资本由等额股份构成并通过发行股票筹集资本，股东以其认购的股份对公司承担有限责任，公司以其全部资产对其债务承担责任的经济组织。

私营企业 指由自然人投资设立或由自然人控股，以雇佣劳动为基础的营利性经济组织。包括按照《公司法》、《合伙企业法》、《私营企业暂行条例》规定登记注册的私营有限责任公司、私营股份有限公司、私营合伙企业和私营独资企业。

其他企业 指上述企业之外的其他内资经济组织。

与港澳台商合资经营企业 指港澳台地区投资者与内地企业依照《中华人民共和国中外合资经营企业法》及有关法律的规定，按合同规定的比例投资设立、分享利润和分担风险的企业。

与港澳台商合作经营企业 指港澳台地区投资者与内地企业依照《中华人民共和国中外合作经营企业法》及有关法律的规定，依照合作合同的约定进行投资或提供条件设立、分配利润和分担风险的企业。

港澳台商独资经营企业 指依照《中华人民共和国外资企业法》及有关法律的规定，在内地由港澳台地区投资者全额投资设立的企业。

港澳台商投资股份有限公司 指根据国家有关规定，经原外经贸部依法批准设立，其中港、澳、台商的股本占公司注册资本的比例达25%以上的股份有限公司。凡其中港、澳、台商的股本占公司注册资本的比例小于25%的，属于内资企业中的股份有限公司。

中外合资经营企业 指外国企业或外国人与中国内地企业依照《中华人民共和国中外合资经营企业法》及有关法律的规定，按合同规定的比例投资设立、分享利润和分担风险的企业。

中外合作经营企业 指外国企业或外国人与中国内地企业依照《中华人民共和国中外合作经营企业法》及有关法律的规定，依照合作合同的约定进行投资或提供条件设立、分配利润和分担风险的企业。

外资企业 指依照《中华人民共和国外资企业法》及有关法律的规定，在中国内地由外国投资者全额投资设立的企业。

外商投资股份有限公司 指根据国家有关规定，经原外经贸部依法批准设立，其中外资的股本占公司注册资本的比例达25%以上的股份有限公司。凡其中外资股本占公司注册资本的比例小于25%的，属于内资企业中的股份有限公司。

行政机关、事业单位和社会团体 参照企业登记注册类型，主要按其经费来源和管理方式划分。具体规定如下：

（1）行政机关：包括国家机关和政党机关，原则上均列为“国有”。但有特殊规定的，如供销社等，则列为“集体”。

（2）事业单位：包括经国家机构编制部门和有关业务主管部门批准成立的各类事业单位，不包括实行企业化管理的事业单位。事业单位的划分办法如下：

①由国家财政预算拨款或列入财政预算外资金管理以及经费主要来源于国有主管部门或国有上级单位的事业单位，列为“国有”。

②经费主要来源于集体单位的事业单位，列为“集体”。

③公民个人（或个人合伙）开办的事业单位，列为“私营”。

④上述以外的其他事业单位，如果其经费来源不明确，按管理方式进行归类。

（3）社会团体：包括经民政部门批准成立以及未纳入社会团体管理条例范围的工会、妇联等各类社会团体。社会团体的划分办法如下：

①未纳入民政部社会团体管理条例范围的工会、妇联、共青团、青联、工商联、科协、侨联等社会团体，国家拨款设立的基金会或基金管理组织以及经费主要来源于国有业务主管部门或国有上级单位的社会团体，列为“国有”。

②经费主要来源于集体单位的社会团体，列为“集体”。

③公民个人（或个人合伙）开办的社会团体，划为“私营”。

④上述以外的其他社会团体，如果其经费来源不明确，改按管理方式进行归类。

Explanatory Notes on Main Statistical Indicators

Registration Status of Enterprises Enterprises are classified into 3 categories, namely domestic-funded enterprises, enterprises with investment from Hong Kong, Macau and Taiwan, and enterprises with foreign investment, according to the registration status of an enterprise in industrial and commercial administration agencies. Domestic-funded enterprises include State- owned enterprises, collective-owned enterprises, cooperative enterprises, joint ownership enterprises, limited liability corporations, share-holding corporations Ltd., private enterprises and other enterprises. Included in the enterprises with investment from Hong Kong, Macau and Taiwan and enterprises with foreign investment are joint-venture enterprises, cooperative enterprises, sole investment enterprises and share-holding corporations Ltd. For government agencies, institutions and social organizations which are not registered in industrial and commercial administration agencies, they are classified mainly by their sources of funding and manner of management.

State–owned Enterprises refer to non-corporation economic units where the entire assets are owned by the State and which have been registered in accordance with the Regulation of the People's Republic of China on the Management of Registration of Corporate Enterprises. Not included from this category are solely State-funded corporations in the limited liability corporations.

Collective–owned Enterprises refer to economic units where the assets are owned collectively and which have been registered in accordance with the Regulation of the People's Republic of China on the Management of Registration of Corporate Enterprises.

Cooperative Enterprises refer to a form of collective economic units (enterprises)where capitals come mainly from employees as their shares, with certain proportion of capital from the outside, where production is organized on the basis of independent operation, independent accounting for profits and losses, joint work, democratic management, and a distribution system that integrates remuneration according to work with dividend according to capital share.

Joint Ownership Enterprises refer to economic units established by two or more corporate enterprises or corporate institutions of the same or different ownership, through joint investment on the basis of voluntary participation, equality, and mutual benefits. They include State joint ownership enterprises; collective joint ownership enterprises; joint State-collective enterprises; and other joint ownership enterprises.

Limited Liability Corporations refer to economic units established with investment from 2-50 investors and registered in accordance with the Regulation of the People's Republic of China on the Management of Registration of Corporations, each investor bearing limited liability to the corporation depending on its share of investment, and the corporation bearing liability to its debt to the maximum of its total assets. Limited liability corporations include solely State-funded limited liability corporations and other limited liability corporations.

Share–holding Corporations Ltd. refer to economic units registered in accordance with the Regulation of the People's Republic of China on the Management of Registration of Corporations, with total registered capital divided into equal shares and raised through issuing stocks. Each investor bears limited liability to the corporation depending on the holding of shares, and the corporation bears liability to its debt to the maximum of its total assets.

Private Enterprises refer to profit-making economic units invested and established by natural persons, or controlled by natural persons using employed labour~ Included in this category are private limited liability corporations, private share-holding corporations Ltd., private partnership enterprises and private-funded enterprises registered in accordance with the Company Law, the Law on Partnership Business and Interim Regulations on Private Enterprises.

Other Domestic–funded Enterprises refer to domestic-funded economic units other than those mentioned above.

Joint Venture Enterprises with Funds from Hong Kong, Macau and Taiwan are enterprises established by investors from Hong Kong, Macau and Taiwan with enterprises in the mainland of China in accordance with the Law of the People's Republic of China on Sino-foreign Equity Joint Ventures and other relevant laws, where the establishment of the investment and the sharing of profits and risks are stipulated under joint venture contracts.

Cooperative Enterprises with Funds from Hong Kong, Macan and Taiwan established by investors from Hong Kong, Macau and Taiwan with enterprises in the mainland of China in accordance with the Law of the People's Republic of China on Sino-foreign Contractual Joint Venture and other relevant laws, where the investment or provision of facilities and the sharing of profits and risks are stipulated under cooperative contracts.

Enterprises with Sole (exclusive)Investment from

Hong Kong, Macau and Taiwan refer to enterprises established in the mainland of China with exclusive investment from investors from Hong Kong, Macau and Taiwan in accordance with the Law of the People's Republic of China on Wholly Foreign-owned Enterprises and other relevant laws.

Share-holding Corporations Ltd. with Investment from Hong Kong, Macau and Taiwan refer to share- holding corporations Ltd. established with the approval from the former Ministry of Foreign Trade and Economic Relations in line with relevant State regulations, where the share of investment from Hong Kong, Macau or Taiwan businessmen exceeds 25% of the total registered capital of the corporation. In case the share of investmentfrom Hong Kong, Macau or Taiwan is less than 25% of thetotal registered capital, the enterprise is to be classified as domestic-funded share-holding corporation Ltd.

Joint Venture Enterprises with Foreign Investment refer to enterprises jointly established byforeign enterprises or foreigners with enterprises in themainland of China in accordance with the Law of thePeople's Republic of China on Sino-foreign Equity JointVentures and other relevant laws, where the sharing ofinvestment, profits and risks is stipulated under contract.

Cooperative Enterprises with Foreign Investment refer to enterprises jointly established by foreign enterprises or foreigners with enterprises in the mainland of China in accordance with the Law of the People's Republic of China on Sino-foreign Contractual Joint Venture and other relevant laws, where the investment or provision of facilities and the sharing of profits and risks are stipulated under cooperative contracts.

Enterprises with Sole (exclusive)Foreign Investment refer to enterprises established in the mainland of China with exclusive investment from foreign investors in accordance with the Law of the People's Republic of China on Wholly Foreign-owned Enterprises and other relevant laws.

Share-holding Corporations Ltd. with Foreign Investment refer to share-holding corporations Ltd. established with the approval from the former Ministry of Foreign Trade and Economic Relations in line with relevant State regulations, where the share of investment from foreign investors exceeds 25% of the total registered capital of the corporation. In case the share of foreign investment is less than 25% ofthe total registered capital, the enterprise is to be classified as domestic-funded share-holding corporation Ltd.

Government Agencies, Institutions and Social Organizations are classified into the following categories by source of funds and manner of management taking reference of thc registration status of enterprises:

(1)Government agencies: include State and party agencies, classified in principle as State-owned. There are exceptions, such as supply and marketing cooperatives which are classified as collective-owned.

(2)Institutions: include institutions of various types established with the approval by organization and staffing departments of the government, but exclude institutions where enterprise management system is introduced. Institutions are further classified as follows:

(a)Institutions for which their main budgets are from government budget appropriations or extra-budget funds, or allocated from the budget of their competent government agencies. Such institutions are classified as state-owned.

(b)Institutions for which their budget mainly come from collective units. Such institutions are classified as collective-owned.

(c)Social institutions established by individual or a group of citizens, which are classified as private.

(d)Institutions other than those mentioned above for which their sources of budget are not clear. Such institutions are classified by the manner of management.

(3)Social organizations: include social organizations established with the approval from the Ministry of Civil Affairs, and organizations that are not covered by social organization management regulations such as trade unions, women's federations etc.. Social organizations are further classified as follows:

(a)Social organizations that are not covered by social organization management regulations of the Ministry of Civil Affairs such as trade unions, women federations, communist youth leagues, youth associations, industrial and commerce associations, scientist associations, overseas Chinese associations, etc., foundations and fund management organizations established with funds from the state, and social organizations whose funds mainly come from the budget of their competent government agencies. Such institutions are classified as State-owned.

(b)Social organizations for which their budget mainly come from collective units. Such institutions are classified as collective-owned.

(c)Social organizations established by individual or a group of citizens, which are classified as private.

(d)Social organizations other than those mentioned above for which their sources of budget are not clear. Such organizations are classified by the manner of management.

3 国民经济核算

NATIONAL ECONOMIC ACCOUNTS

资料整理：吴　羽　徐　枫　段　斐
Data management：Wu Yu Xu Feng Duan Fei
数据审核：连　鹏
Data audit：Lian Peng

第三部分　国民经济核算

一、简要说明

本章资料包括西安生产总值、构成和指数，分区县生产总值等。根据国家统计局的统一要求，2013年数据为第三次经济普查结果，2014年数据是2014年年报最终核实数据，以前年度未经修订；2013、2014年三次产业分类依据国家统计局2012年制定的新《三次产业划分规定》；人均GDP按户籍人口计算，2005年以后按常住人口计算。资料由西安市统计局国民经济核算处提供。

二、主要指标

生产总值（亿元）	5492.64	比上年增长	9.9%
第一产业	214.55	比上年增长	5.1%
第二产业	2194.78	比上年增长	9.3%
第三产业	3083.31	比上年增长	10.7%
人均生产总值（元/人）	63794	比上年增长	9.4%

3 NATIONAL ECONOMIC ACCOUNTS

Ⅰ.Brief Introduction

The data in this chapter consists of Xi'an GDP, composition, index, and sub-county gross production, etc. According to the uniform requirements of National Bureau of Statistics, 2013 data was revised by the Third Economic Census, 2014 data was the Annual Report final verification data, and previous year data was unamended. Three industrial classification based on the new "three industrial division rule" in the year of 2013 and 2014, per capita GDP was calculated on permanent population after 2005 ,had been calculated on register population before 2005.Data in this chapter is provided by National Economics Accounting Division of the Xi'an Bureau of Statistics.

Ⅱ.Major Indicators

		Increase over Preceding Year
Gross Domestic Product(100 mil. yuan)	5492.64	9.9%
Primary Industry	214.55	5.1%
Secondary Industry	2194.78	9.3%
Tertiary Industry	3083.31	10.7%
Per Capita Gross Domestic Product (yuan/person)	63794	9.4%

3-1 主要年份生产总值

Gross Domestic Product in Representative Years

(本表按当年价格计算)　　(Data in the table are calculated at current prices)

单位：亿元　　(100 million yuan)

年份 Year	生产总值 Gross Domestic Product	第一产业 Primary Industry	第二产业 Secondary Industry	第三产业 Tertiary Industry	人均生产总值 (元/人) Per Capita GDP (yuan/person)
1952	3.37	1.59	0.88	0.90	135
1965	12.76	2.62	7.22	2.92	323
1970	17.76	3.13	10.96	3.67	412
1975	21.33	4.14	12.63	4.56	448
1978	25.35	4.83	14.59	5.93	513
1980	31.66	4.73	18.69	8.24	623
1983	35.89	5.22	20.14	10.53	674
1984	44.14	7.45	24.17	12.52	817
1985	57.58	8.76	30.83	17.99	1049
1986	65.78	9.59	33.86	22.33	1178
1987	80.16	10.73	37.69	31.74	1409
1988	99.22	11.47	46.58	41.17	1711
1989	109.38	12.78	48.91	47.69	1861
1990	116.51	13.94	50.15	52.42	1932
1991	136.14	17.17	57.06	61.91	2224
1992	164.85	18.78	69.22	76.85	2662
1993	229.56	22.58	110.88	96.10	3661
1994	289.82	31.68	128.27	129.87	4563
1995	330.35	41.40	135.33	153.62	5131
1996	406.95	46.94	161.63	198.38	6246
1997	488.82	51.33	197.97	239.52	7424
1998	525.85	51.91	216.32	257.62	7906
1999	577.29	45.53	243.35	288.41	8599
2000	646.13	44.65	277.13	324.35	9484
2001	734.86	45.87	312.90	376.09	10628
2002	826.68	47.77	353.58	425.33	11831
2003	946.66	50.72	407.38	488.56	13341
2004	1102.39	60.21	476.92	565.26	15294
2005	1313.93	66.01	540.50	707.42	16406
2006	1538.94	70.44	645.65	822.85	18890
2007	1856.63	82.51	781.94	992.18	22463
2008	2318.14	103.45	981.58	1233.11	27794
2009	2724.08	110.38	1144.75	1468.95	32411
2010	3241.69	140.06	1406.72	1694.91	38343
2011	3862.58	173.14	1674.31	2015.13	45475
2012	4366.10	195.59	1881.75	2288.76	51166
2013	4924.97	200.45	1998.82	2725.70	57464
2014	5492.64	214.55	2194.78	3083.31	63794

注：2005年以后人均GDP按平均常住人口计算。

2013年数据为第三次经济普查结果，以前年度未经修订。

2014年数据是2014年年报最终核实数据。

2013、2014年三次产业分类依据国家统计局2012年制定的新《三次产业划分规定》。(下同)

3-2 主要年份生产总值指数（上年＝100）

Indices of Gross Domestic Product in Representative Years(preceding year = 100)

(本表按可比价格计算) (Data in the table are calculated at constant prices)

年　份	Year	生产总值 Gross Domestic Product	第一产业 Primary Industry	第二产业 Secondary Industry	第三产业 Tertiary Industry	人均生产总值 Per Capita GDP
1952		103.6	92.2	137.5	123.7	
1965		126.1	134.1	133.0	106.7	
1970		122.0	109.4	140.0	100.1	
1975		103.8	92.6	107.1	107.5	
1978		101.7	101.6	99.4	108.2	
1980		111.5	83.3	119.7	116.5	
1985		112.6	107.5	111.8	116.9	
1986		111.4	107.7	108.4	118.8	
1987		113.6	100.8	109.1	126.6	
1988		111.4	81.2	115.5	114.7	
1989		106.7	103.0	104.5	110.8	
1990		105.2	103.0	102.5	109.6	
1991		109.8	118.6	108.6	108.6	108.2
1992		115.6	109.4	118.1	115.0	114.3
1993		123.9	112.5	142.7	108.4	122.3
1994		110.3	98.4	110.6	113.2	108.8
1995		110.0	104.5	112.1	108.6	108.5
1996		114.9	106.8	118.8	111.7	113.5
1997		114.4	109.1	116.7	112.4	113.2
1998		113.3	106.5	117.5	108.8	112.1
1999		112.2	97.4	115.7	110.1	111.2
2000		113.0	103.5	115.1	111.5	111.4
2001		113.1	102.5	115.3	112.6	111.4
2002		113.3	103.1	115.0	113.0	112.1
2003		113.5	101.8	117.5	111.2	111.7
2004		113.5	106.7	115.9	112.0	111.7
2005		114.0	107.5	112.3	116.3	112.2
2006		114.0	107.1	113.7	114.9	112.9
2007		115.6	104.5	115.7	116.4	113.9
2008		116.3	107.6	116.4	116.9	115.3
2009		114.5	106.3	114.0	115.5	113.7
2010		114.5	106.9	118.0	112.5	113.8
2011		113.8	106.7	114.9	113.4	113.2
2012		111.8	106.0	111.8	112.2	111.3
2013		111.1	104.7	113.6	109.7	110.6
2014		109.9	105.1	109.3	110.7	109.4
平均每年增长	**Yearly Average Growth Rates**					
"一五"时期	**The First Five-Year Plan Period**	**15.8**	**5.9**	**37.7**	**16.9**	
"二五"时期	**The Second Five-Year Plan Period**	**2.0**	**-3.7**	**2.5**	**8.4**	
1963--1965年	**Readjust Period**	**14.2**	**16.1**	**23.4**	**0.3**	
"三五"时期	**The Third Five-Year Plan Period**	**7.1**	**0.1**	**11.7**	**5.4**	
"四五"时期	**The Fourth Five-Year Plan Period**	**5.0**	**4.0**	**5.3**	**5.0**	
"五五"时期	**The Fifth Five-Year Plan Period**	**6.0**	**-0.7**	**6.5**	**10.1**	
"六五"时期	**The Sixth Five-Year Plan Period**	**10.7**	**7.9**	**10.4**	**12.9**	
"七五"时期	**The Seventh Five-Year Plan Period**	**9.6**	**-1.3**	**7.9**	**15.9**	
"八五"时期	**The Eighth Five-Year Plan Period**	**13.8**	**8.5**	**17.8**	**10.7**	**12.3**
"九五"时期	**The Ninth Five-Year Plan Period**	**13.6**	**4.6**	**16.8**	**10.9**	**12.3**
"十五"时期	**The Tenth Five-Year Plan Period**	**13.5**	**4.3**	**15.2**	**13.0**	**11.8**
"十一五"时期	**The Eleventh Five-Year Plan Period**	**15.0**	**6.5**	**15.5**	**15.2**	**13.9**

3-3 主要年份生产总值指数（1952年=100）

Indices of Gross Domestic Product in Representative Years(1952= 100)

(本表按可比价格计算) (Data in the table are calculated at constant prices)

年 份 Year	生产总值 Gross Domestic Product	第一产业 Primary Industry	第二产业 Secondary Industry	第三产业 Tertiary Industry
1952	100.0	100.0	100.0	100.0
1965	341.6	173.3	1048.3	329.2
1970	481.6	174.3	1821.0	428.6
1975	614.2	211.9	2362.5	547.9
1978	678.7	231.3	2560.8	643.8
1980	821.4	204.2	3237.2	885.2
1983	988.4	222.5	3846.2	1154.4
1984	1213.6	278.2	4748.8	1388.7
1985	1366.8	299.1	5310.6	1632.4
1986	1523.1	322.3	5756.7	1928.9
1987	1730.0	324.9	6280.6	2441.6
1988	1926.3	263.7	7256.6	2801.2
1989	2054.8	271.6	7583.1	3104.6
1990	2162.5	279.7	7772.7	3403.6
1991	2374.4	331.7	8441.2	3696.3
1992	2744.8	362.9	9969.1	4250.7
1993	3400.8	408.2	14225.9	4607.8
1994	3751.1	401.8	15733.8	5216.0
1995	4126.2	419.9	17637.6	5664.6
1996	4741.0	448.5	20953.5	6327.4
1997	5423.7	489.3	24452.7	7112.0
1998	6145.1	521.1	28731.9	7737.9
1999	6894.8	507.6	33242.8	8519.4
2000	7791.1	525.4	38262.5	9499.1
2001	8811.7	538.5	44116.7	10696.0
2002	9983.7	555.2	50734.2	12086.5
2003	11331.5	265.2	59612.7	13440.2
2004	12861.3	603.1	69091.1	15053.0
2005	14661.9	648.3	77589.3	17506.6
2006	16714.6	694.3	88219.0	20115.1
2007	19322.1	725.5	102069.4	23414.0
2008	22471.6	780.6	118808.8	27371.0
2009	25730.0	829.8	135442.0	31613.5
2010	29460.9	950.1	155081.1	36197.5
2011	33513.2	1013.8	178177.0	41045.6
2012	37469.9	1074.6	199290.7	46062.0
2013	41641.6	1125.1	226469.8	50525.4
2014	45781.1	1182.4	247563.5	55940.2

3-4 主要年份生产总值构成

Composition of Gross Domestic Product in Representative Years

(本表按当年价格计算) (Data in the table are calculated at current prices)

单位:% (%)

年 份	Year	生产总值 Gross Domestic Product	第一产业 Primary Industry	第二产业 Secondary Industry	第三产业 Tertiary Industry
1952		100	47.18	26.11	26.71
1965		100	20.53	56.58	22.89
1970		100	17.62	61.71	20.67
1975		100	19.41	59.21	21.38
1978		100	19.05	57.55	23.40
1980		100	14.94	59.03	26.03
1985		100	15.21	53.54	31.25
1986		100	14.58	51.47	33.95
1987		100	13.39	47.02	39.59
1988		100	11.56	46.95	41.49
1989		100	11.68	44.72	43.60
1990		100	11.96	43.04	45.00
1991		100	12.61	41.91	45.48
1992		100	11.39	41.99	46.62
1993		100	9.84	48.30	41.86
1994		100	10.93	44.26	44.81
1995		100	12.53	40.97	46.50
1996		100	11.53	39.72	48.75
1997		100	10.50	40.50	49.00
1998		100	9.87	41.14	48.99
1999		100	7.89	42.15	49.96
2000		100	6.91	42.89	50.20
2001		100	6.24	42.58	51.18
2002		100	5.78	42.77	51.45
2003		100	5.36	43.03	51.61
2004		100	5.46	43.26	51.28
2005		100	5.02	41.14	53.84
2006		100	4.58	41.95	53.47
2007		100	4.44	42.12	53.44
2008		100	4.46	42.34	53.20
2009		100	4.05	42.02	53.93
2010		100	4.32	43.39	52.29
2011		100	4.48	43.35	52.17
2012		100	4.48	43.10	52.42
2013		100	4.07	40.59	55.34
2014		100	3.91	39.96	56.13
"一五"时期	**The First Five-Year Plan Period**	**100**	**32.88**	**43.92**	**23.20**
"二五"时期	**The Second Five-Year Period**	**100**	**18.08**	**58.63**	**23.29**
1963--1965年	**Readjust Period**	**100**	**19.36**	**55.38**	**25.26**
"三五"时期	**The Third Five-Year Plan Period**	**100**	**18.60**	**57.33**	**24.07**
"四五"时期	**The Fourth Five-Year Plan Period**	**100**	**20.46**	**59.59**	**19.95**
"五五"时期	**The Fifth Five-Year Plan Period**	**100**	**18.41**	**57.69**	**23.90**
"六五"时期	**The Sixth Five-Year Plan Period**	**100**	**16.03**	**55.01**	**28.96**
"七五"时期	**The Seventh Five-Year Plan Period**	**100**	**12.42**	**46.11**	**41.47**
"八五"时期	**The Eighth Five-Year Plan Period**	**100**	**11.44**	**43.52**	**45.04**
"九五"时期	**The Ninth Five-Year Plan Period**	**100**	**9.09**	**41.45**	**49.46**
"十五"时期	**The Tenth Five-Year Plan Period**	**100**	**5.49**	**42.47**	**52.04**
"十一五"时期	**The Eleventh Five-Year Plan Period**	**100**	**4.34**	**42.47**	**53.19**

3-5 各区县生产总值（2014年）

Gross Domestic Product by Region (2014)

单位：亿元 (100 million yuan)

区　县	Region	生产总值 Gross Domestic Product	第一产业 Primary Industry	第二产业 Secondary Industry	第三产业 Tertiary Industry
新城区	Xincheng	467.08		186.67	280.41
碑林区	Beilin	617.90		120.03	497.87
莲湖区	Lianhu	539.53		193.90	345.63
灞桥区	Baqiao	309.73	18.14	141.61	149.98
未央区	Weiyang	703.14	1.06	371.00	331.08
雁塔区	Yanta	1114.46	1.62	389.82	723.02
阎良区	Yanliang	184.25	22.21	105.61	56.43
临潼区	Lintong	221.78	31.16	116.26	74.36
长安区	Chang'an	445.43	33.67	217.23	194.53
蓝田县	Lantian	109.57	25.90	35.33	48.34
周至县	Zhouzhi	98.84	27.62	26.09	45.13
户　县	Huxian	155.92	27.20	71.56	57.16
高陵县	Gaoling	298.27	25.96	219.67	52.64

3–6 各区县生产总值指数（2014年）（上年＝100）

Indices of Gross Domestic Product by Region (2014) (preceding year = 100)

区 县	Region	生产总值 Gross Domestic Product	第一产业 Primary Industry	第二产业 Secondary Industry	第三产业 Tertiary Industry
新城区	Xincheng	109.0		108.5	109.4
碑林区	Beilin	110.8		110.2	111.0
莲湖区	Lianhu	109.0		107.6	110.0
灞桥区	Baqiao	111.1	105.1	111.2	111.8
未央区	Weiyang	110.1	93.9	110.0	110.3
雁塔区	Yanta	110.7	95.1	110.7	110.7
阎良区	Yanliang	109.9	105.5	110.6	110.4
临潼区	Lintong	105.0	105.0	101.9	109.1
长安区	Chang'an	111.3	105.1	114.6	108.9
蓝田县	Lantian	108.8	105.1	109.9	109.5
周至县	Zhouzhi	108.8	105.6	109.7	109.8
户 县	Huxian	107.8	105.0	106.8	110.3
高陵县	Gaoling	112.0	105.7	113.4	107.3

3-7 各区县生产总值构成（2014年）

Composition of Gross Domestic Product by Region (2014)

单位：%　　　　(%)

区县	Region	生产总值 Gross Domestic Product	第一产业 Primary Industry	第二产业 Secondary Industry	第三产业 Tertiary Industry
新城区	Xincheng	100		40.0	60.0
碑林区	Beilin	100		19.4	80.6
莲湖区	Lianhu	100		35.9	64.1
灞桥区	Baqiao	100	5.9	45.7	48.4
未央区	Weiyang	100	0.2	52.8	47.0
雁塔区	Yanta	100	0.1	35.0	64.9
阎良区	Yanliang	100	12.1	57.3	30.6
临潼区	Lintong	100	14.0	52.4	33.6
长安区	Chang'an	100	7.6	48.8	43.6
蓝田县	Lantian	100	23.6	32.2	44.2
周至县	Zhouzhi	100	27.9	26.4	45.7
户　县	Huxian	100	17.4	45.9	36.7
高陵县	Gaoling	100	8.7	73.6	17.7

3-8 分行业增加值

Value added by Industry

单位：亿元　　　　(100 million yuan)

指　标	Item	增加值 Value Added 2013	2014	指数（上年=100） Index 2013	2014
生产总值	**Gross Domestic Product**	**4924.97**	**5492.64**	**111.1**	**109.9**
农、林、牧、渔业	Farming Forestry Animal Husbandry Fishery	217.76	233.61	104.8	105.1
工业	Industry	1376.74	1488.02	114.0	108.4
建筑业	Construction	642.26	728.74	113.9	110.9
批发和零售业	Wholesale and Retail Trades	575.72	633.65	110.4	109.3
交通运输、仓储及邮政业	Transportation,Storage,Post and Telecommunications	215.11	235.58	108.2	106.2
住宿和餐饮业	Accommodation and Catering Trade	135.58	144.15	100.7	102.0
金融业	Financial Intermediation	429.51	534.00	119.0	121.1
房地产业	Real Estate	292.41	326.10	111.9	107.7
其他服务业	Others Services	1039.88	1168.79	106.1	110.2
第一产业	Primary Industry	200.45	214.55	104.7	105.1
第二产业	Secondary Industry	1998.82	2194.78	113.6	109.3
第三产业	Tertiary Industry	2725.70	3083.31	109.7	110.7

3-9 三次产业贡献率、拉动率（2014年）

Share of the Contribution of the Three Strata of Industry to the Increase of the GDP(2014)

(本表按可比价格计算) (Data in the table are calculated at constant prices)

指 标	Item	贡献率（%） Contribution tate（%）	拉动率（百分点） pull rate（percentage）
生产总值	**Gross Domestic Product**	**100.0**	**9.9**
第一产业	Primary Industry	1.7	0.2
第二产业	Secondary Industry	39.3	3.9
第三产业	Tertiary Industry	59.0	5.8

注：2013年、2014年数据根据GDP调整及三次产业划分的变化相应进行了调整。

3-10 主要年份非公有制经济增加值

The Added Value of Non-public-owned Economic in Representative Years

年 份 Year	非公有制经济增加值（亿元） the Added Value of Non-public-owned Economic (100 million yuan)	第一产业 Primary Industry	第二产业 Secondary Industry	第三产业 Tertiary Industry	非公有制经济增加值占GDP比重(%) the Added Value of Non-public-owned Economic Percentage to GDP(%)	第一产业 Primary Industry	第二产业 Secondary Industry	第三产业 Tertiary Industry
2005	568.45	20.86	232.66	314.93	43.26	31.60	43.05	44.52
2006	684.66	26.27	279.06	379.33	44.46	37.29	43.22	46.04
2007	854.26	25.25	365.24	463.77	46.01	30.60	46.71	46.74
2008	1103.96	36.42	468.58	598.96	47.62	35.21	47.74	48.57
2009	1327.49	36.32	542.37	748.80	48.73	32.90	47.38	50.98
2010	1611.28	42.66	665.90	902.72	49.70	30.46	47.34	53.26
2011	1952.78	52.93	814.44	1085.41	50.56	30.57	48.64	53.86
2012	2244.25	59.79	902.29	1282.17	51.40	30.57	47.95	56.02
2013	2569.20	53.72	970.24	1545.24	52.20	26.80	48.50	56.70
2014	2892.90	57.40	1079.60	1755.90	52.70	26.80	49.20	56.90

注：2013年、2014年数据根据GDP调整及三次产业划分的变化相应进行了调整。

主要统计指标解释

生产总值（GDP） 是按市场价格计算的一个地区（或国家）所有常住单位在一定时期内生产活动的最终成果。生产总值有三种表现形态，即价值形态、收入形态和产品形态。从价值形态看，它是所有常住单位在一定时期内生产的全部货物和服务价值超过同期中间投入的全部非固定资产货物和服务价值的差额，即所有常住单位的增加值之和；从收入形态看，它是所有常住单位在一定时期内创造并分配给常住单位和非常住单位的初次收入分配之和；从产品形态看，它是所有常住单位在一定时期内最终使用的货物和服务价值与货物和服务净出口价值之和。在实际核算中，生产总值有三种计算方法，即生产法、收入法和支出法。三种方法分别从不同的方面反映生产总值及其构成。

三次产业 是根据社会生产活动历史发展的顺序对产业结构的划分，产品直接取自自然界的部门称为第一产业，对初级产品进行再加工的部门称为第二产业，为生产和消费提供各种服务的部门称为第三产业。它是世界上较为通用的产业结构分类，但各国的划分不尽一致。

三产业的划分是世界上较为常用的产业结构分类，但各国的划分不尽一致。我国的三次产业划分是：

第一产业：农业（包括农业、林业、畜牧业、渔业和农林牧渔服务业）。

第二产业：工业（包括采矿业，制造业，电力气及水的生产和供应业）和建筑业。

第三产业：除第一、第二产业以外的其他各业。

劳动者报酬 指劳动者因从事生产活动所获得的全部报酬。包括劳动者获得的各种形式的工资、奖金和津贴，既包括货币形式的，也包括实物形式的，还包括劳动者所享受的公费医疗和医药卫生费、上下班交通补贴、单位支付的社会保险费、住房公积金等。

生产税净额 指生产税减生产补贴后的余额。生产税指政府对生产单位从事生产、销售和经营活动以及因从事生产活动使用某些生产要素（如固定资产、土地、劳动力）所征收的各种税、附加费和规费。生产补贴与生产税相反，指政府对生产单位的单方面转移支出，因此视为负生产税，包括政策亏损补贴、价格补贴等。

固定资产折旧 指一定时期内为弥补固定资产损耗按照规定的固定资产折旧率提取的固定资产折旧，或按国民经济核算统一规定的折旧率虚拟计算的固定资产折旧。它反映了固定资产年当期生产中的转移价值。各类企业和企业化管理的事业单位的固定资产折旧是指实际计提的折旧费；不计提折旧的政府机关、非企业化管理的事业单位和居民住房的固定资产折旧是按照统一规定的折旧率和固定资产原值计算的虚拟折旧。原则上，固定资产折旧应按固定资产当期的重置价值计算，但是目前我国尚不具备对全社会固定资产进行重估价的基础，所以暂时只能采用上述办法。

营业盈余 指常住单位创造的增加值扣除劳动者报酬、生产税净额和固定资产折旧后的余额。它相当于企业的营业利润加上生产补贴，但要扣除从利润中开支的工资和福利等。

支出法国内生产总值 是从最终使用的角度反映一个国家（或地区）一定时期内生产活动最终成果的一种方法，包括最终消费支出、资本形成总额及货物和服务净出口三部分。计算公式为：

支出法国内生产总值二最终消费支出+资本形成总额+货物和服务净出口

最终消费支出 指常住单位为满足物质、文化和精神生活的需要，从本国经济领土和国外购买的货物和服务的支出。它不包括非常住单位在本国经济领土内的消费支出。最终消费支出分为居民消费支出和政府消费支出。

居民消费支出 指常住住户在一定时期内对于货物和服务的全部最终消费支出。居民消费支出除了直接以货币形式购买的货物和服务的消费支出外，还包括以其他方式获得的货物和服务的消费支出，即所谓的虚拟消费支出。居民虚拟消费支出包括如下几种类型：单位以实物报酬及实物转移的形式提供给劳动者的货物和服务；住户生产并由本住户消费了的货物和服务，其中的服务仅指住户的自有住房服务和付酬的家庭雇员提供的家庭和个人服务；金融机构提供的金融媒介服务。

政府消费支出 指政府部门为全社会提供的公共服务的消费支出和免费或以较低的价格向居民住户提供的货物和服务的净支出，前者等于政府服务的产出价值减去政府单位所获得的经营收入的价值，后者等于政府部门免费或以较低价格向居民住户提供的货物和服务的市场价值减去向住户收取的价值。

资本形成总额 指常住单位在一定时期内获得减去处置的固定资产和存货的净额，包括固定资本形成总

生产总值（GDP） 是按市场价格计算的一个地区（或国家）所有常住单位在一定时期内生产活动的最终成果。生产总值有三种表现形态，即价值形态、收入形态和产品形态。从价值形态看，它是所有常住单位在一定时期内生产的全部货物和服务价值超过同期中间投入的全部非固定资产货物和服务价值的差额，即所有常住单位的增加值之和；从收入形态看，它是所有常住单位在一定时期内创造并分配给常住单位和非常住单位的初次收入分配之和；从产品形态看，它是所有常住单位在一定时期内最终使用的货物和服务价值与货物和服务净出口价值之和。在实际核算中，生产总值有三种计算方法，即生产法、收入法和支出法。三种方法分别从不同的方面反映生产总值及其构除当期由于价格变动而产生的持有收益。存货增加可以是正值，也可以是负值，正值表示存货上升，负值表示存货下降。存货包括生产单位购进的原材料、燃料和储备物资等存货，以及生产单位生产的产成品、在制品和半成品等存货。

货物和服务净出口 指货物和服务出口减货物和服务进口的差额。出口包括常住单位向非常住单位出售或无偿转让的各种货物和服务的价值；进口包括常住单位从非常住单位购买或无偿得到的各种货物和服务的价值。由于服务活动的提供与使用同时发生，一般把常住单位从非常住单位得到的服务作为进口，非常住单位从常住单位得到的服务作为出口。货物的出口和进口都按离岸价格计算。

Explanatory Notes on Main Statistical Indicators

Gross Domestic Product (GDP) refers to the final products at market prices produced by all resident units in a country (or a region) during a certain period of time. Gross domestic product is expressed in three different perspectives, namely value, income, and products respectively. GDP in its value perspective refers to the total value of all goods and services produced by all resident units during a certain period of time, minus the total value of input of goods and services of the nature of non-fixed assets; in other words, it is the sum of the value-added of all resident units. GDP from the perspective of income includes the primary income created by all resident units and distributed to resident and non-resident units. GDP from the perspective of products refers to the value of all goods and services for final demand by all resident units plus the net exports of goods and services during a given period of time. In the practice of national accounting, gross domestic product is calculated from three approaches, namely production approach, income approach and expenditure approach, which reflect gross domestic product and its composition from different angles.

For a region, it is called as Gross Regional Product(GRP) or regional GDP.

Three Strata of Industry Classification of economic activities into three strata of industry is a common practice in the world, although the grouping varies to some extent from country to country. In China economic activities are categorized into the following three strata of industry:

Primary industry refers to agriculture, forestry, animal husbandry and fishery and services in support of these industries.

Secondary industry refers to mining and quarrying, manufacturing, production and supply of electricity, water and gas, and construction.

Tertiary industry refers to all other economic activities not included in the primary or secondary industries.

Compensation of Employees refers to the total payment of various forms to employees for the productive activities they are engaged in. It includes wages, bonuses and allowances, which the employees earn in cash or in kind. It also includes the free medical services provided to the employees and the medicine expenses, transport subsidies and social insurance, and housing fund paid by the employers.

Net Taxes on Production refers to taxes on production less subsidies on production. The taxes on production refers to the various taxes, extra charges and fees levied on the production units on their production, sale and business activities as well as on the use of some factors of production, such as fixed assets, land and labour in the production activities they are engaged in. In contrast to taxes on production, subsidies on production refer to the unilateral government transfer to the production units and are therefore regarded as negative taxes on production. They include subsidies on the loss due to implementation of government policies, price subsidies, etc.

Depreciation of Fixed Assets refers to the depreciation of fixed assets in a given period, drawn in accordance with the stipulated depreciation rate for the purpose of compensating the wear-and-tear loss of the fixed assets or the depreciation of fixed assets imputed in accordance with the stipulated unified depreciation rate in the national economic accounting system. It reflects the value of transfer of the fixed assets in the production of the current period. The depreciation of fixed assets in various enterprises and institutions managed as enterprises refers to the depreciation expenses actually drawn. In government agencies and institutions not managed as enterprises which do not draw the depreciation expenses, as well as for the houses of residents, the depreciation of fixed assets is the imputed depreciation, which is calculated in accordance with the stipulated unified depreciation rate. In principle, the depreciation of fixed assets should be calculated on the basis of the re-purchased value of the fixed assets. However, currently the conditions in China do not facilitate the revaluation of all the fixed assets. Therefore, only the above-mentioned methods can be adopted at present.

Operating Surplus refers to the balance of the value added created by the resident units after deducting the labourers remuneration, net taxes on production and the depreciation of fixed assets. It is equivalent to the business profit of the enterprises plus subsidies to production, but the wages and welfare expenses paid from the profits should be deducted.

GDP by Expenditure Approach refers to the method of measuring the final results of production activities of a country (region) during a given period from the perspective of final uses. It includes final consumption expenditure, gross capital formation and net export of goods and services. The formula for computation is.:

GDP by expenditure approach = final consumption expenditure + gross capital formation + net export of goods and services

Final Consumption Expenditure refers to the total expenditure of resident units for purchases of goods and services from both the domestic economic territory and abroad to meet the needs of material, cultural and spiritual life. It does not include the expenditure of non-resident units on consumption in the economic territory of the country. The final consumption expenditure is broken down into household consumption expenditure and government consumption expenditure.

Household Consumption Expenditure refers to the total expenditure of resident households on the final consumption of goods and services. In addition to the consumption of goods and services bought by the households directly with money, the household consumption expenditure also includes expenditure on goods and services obtained by the households in other ways, i.e. the so-called imputed consumption expenditure, which includes the following: (a) the goods and services provided to households by employers in the form of payment in kind and transfer in kind; (b) goods and services produced and consumed by the households themselves, in which the services refer to the owner-occupied housing and services offered by payed family employees; (c) financial intermediate services provided by financial institution.

Government Consumption Expenditure refers to the consumption expenditure spent for the provision of public services provided by the government to the whole country and the net expenditure on the goods and services provided by the government to households free of charge or at reduced prices. The former equals to the output value of the government services minus the value of operating income obtained by the government departments. The latter equals to the market value of the goods and services provided by the government free of charge or at reduced prices to the households minus the value received by the government from the households.

Gross Capital Formation refers to the fixed assets acquired less disposals and the net value of inventory, thus including gross fixed capital formation and changes in inventories.

Gross Fixed Capital Formation refers to the value of acquisitions less those disposals of fixed assets during a given period. Fixed assets are the assets produced through production activities with unit value above a specified amount and which could be used for over one year. Natural assets are not included. Gross fixed capital formation can be categorized into total tangible fixed capital formation and total intangible fixed capital formation. Total tangible fixed capital formation includes the value of the construction projects and installation projects completed and the equipment, apparatus and instruments purchased (less those disposed) as well as the value of land improved, the value of draught animals, breeding stock and animals for milk, for wool and for recreational purposes and the newly increased forest with economic value. Total intangible fixed capital formation includes the prospecting of minerals and the acquisition of computer software minus the disposal of them.

Changes in Inventories refers to the market value of the change in the physical volume of inventory of resident units during a given period, i.e. the difference between the values at the beginning and at the end of the period minus the gains due to the change in prices. The changes in inventories can have a positive or a negative value. A positive value indicates an increase in inventory while a negative value indicates a decrease in inventory. The inventory includes raw materials, fuels and reserve materials purchased by the production units as well as the inventory of finished products, semi-finished products and work-in-progress.

Net Export of Goods and Services refers to the exports of goods and services subtracting the imports of goods and services. Exports include the value of various goods and services sold or gratuitously transferred by resident units to non-resident units. Imports include the value of various goods and services purchased or gratuitously acquired resident units from non-resident units. Because the provision of services and the use of them happen simultaneously, the acquisition of services by resident units from abroad is usually treated as import while the acquisition of services by non-resident units in this country is usually treated as export. The exports and imports of goods are calculated at FOB.

4 人口、从业人员与职工工资

POPULATION,EMPLOYMENT AND WAGES

资料整理：王义龙　张　静
Data management：Wang Yilong Zhang Jing
数据审核：冯军魁
Data audit：Feng Junkui

第四部分　人口、从业人员与职工工资

一、简要说明

本章资料包括主要年份人口、分区县户籍和常住人口及变动、从业人员及劳动报酬等。户籍人口数为公安年报数，1991年以前年份市区数未包括临潼、长安。主要数据由西安市统计局人口就业处提供。

二、主要指标

年末户籍人口（万人）	815.29	比上年增长	1.0%
人口自然增长率（‰）	4.64	比上年提高	0.44个千分点
常住人口（万人）	862.75	比上年增长	0.5%
男女性别比（以女性为100）	105.51	比上年下降	0.03个百分点
户籍人口密度（人/平方公里）	807	比上年增加	8人/平方公里
城镇非私营单位在岗职工年平均工资（元）	56491	比上年增长	11.2%

4　POPULATION,EMPLOYMENT AND WAGES

Ⅰ.Brief Introduction

This chapter consists of the data about ragistered population and permanent resident population consequent years, population of all the districts and counties and the correspondent changes, the employed and their wages. The registered population data are from the annual report of the Xi'an Bureau of Public Security, with Lintong, Chang'an not included before 1991. The population data is provided primarily by Population & Employment Office of the Xi'an Bureau of Statistics.

Ⅱ.Major Indicators

		Increase over Preceding Year
Total registered Population of Year-end(10 000 persons)	815.29	1.0%
Natural Growth Rate(‰)	4.64	0.44 Thousands of Higher
Permanent Population(10 000 persons)	862.75	0.5%
Sex Ratio (Female=100)	105.51	-0.03 Percentage Points
Density of Population (person/sq.km)	807	8
Aunual Average Wage of Stuff and Workers in Urban Non-privite Enterprises(yuan)	56491	11.2%

4-1 主要年份人口数、人口密度和人口发展情况

Population, Population Density and Population Development in Representative years

单位：万人 (10 000 persons)

年份 Year	总人口 Total population	市区 Urban	女性人口数 Number of Female	非农业人口数 Non-Agricultural Population	人口密度 (人／平方公里) Density of Population (person/sq.km)	总人口指数（上年为100）Total Population Index (100 for preceding year) 全市 Whole City	市区 Urban
1952	252.92	92.42	118.81	57.61	254	102.6	103.1
1965	400.05	179.88	190.72	136.39	401	102.5	103.4
1970	435.12	188.12	210.47	139.12	436	101.9	101.4
1978	498.10	210.15	241.82	159.98	499	101.7	102.7
1980	511.91	221.19	249.26	172.85	513	101.4	102.6
1985	553.11	245.76	268.40	201.90	554	101.6	102.2
1986	563.97	251.80	273.30	205.92	565	102.0	102.5
1987	574.46	257.69	278.12	210.25	575	101.9	102.3
1988	585.85	264.94	283.68	216.99	587	102.0	102.8
1989	597.36	270.80	289.44	222.54	598	102.0	102.2
1990	608.89	275.69	295.29	226.98	610	101.9	101.8
1991	615.48	419.29	298.13	230.85	617	101.1	152.1
1992	623.20	429.54	301.92	236.45	624	101.3	102.4
1993	630.91	435.41	305.30	240.85	632	101.2	101.4
1994	639.45	442.30	309.17	248.35	641	101.4	101.6
1995	648.21	448.65	313.46	255.71	645	101.4	101.4
1996	654.87	454.68	316.60	261.28	653	101.0	101.3
1997	662.06	461.17	320.18	267.52	663	101.1	101.4
1998	668.22	466.31	323.20	271.75	669	100.9	101.1
1999	674.50	463.56	326.12	276.14	676	100.9	99.4
2000	688.01	483.10	332.83	285.79	689	102.0	104.2
2001	694.84	489.88	336.04	292.62	696	101.0	101.4
2002	702.59	497.38	339.51	300.05	704	101.1	101.5
2003	716.58	510.26	346.26	312.88	718	102.0	102.6
2004	725.01	516.30	350.85	318.50	717	101.2	101.2
2005	741.73	533.21	359.71	333.14	734	102.3	103.3
2006	753.11	540.97	365.74	343.78	745	101.5	101.5
2007	764.25	549.19	371.84	353.85	756	101.5	101.5
2008	772.30	554.73	376.76	363.87	764	101.1	101.0
2009	781.67	561.58	382.39	370.66	773	101.2	101.2
2010	782.73	562.65	383.93	374.64	774	100.1	100.2
2011	791.83	568.77	389.31	391.31	783	101.2	101.1
2012	795.98	572.76	392.04	398.40	788	100.5	100.7
2013	806.93	580.60	398.15	409.82	799	101.4	101.4
2014	815.29	587.16	402.83	418.16	807	101.0	101.1

注：人口部分均为公安年报数据，系户籍人口。1991年以前年份，市区数未包括临潼、长安。行政区划面积自2012年发生变更，调整了2012年和2013年户籍人口密度。

4-2 主要年份人口自然变动情况

Natural Population Movements in Representative Years

单位：万人　　　　　　　　　　　　　　　　　　　　(10 000 persons)

年份 Year	出生 Birth		死亡 Death		自然增长率（‰） Natural Growth Rate (‰)	迁入人口 Immigrant population	迁出人口 Emigrant population
	人数 Population	出生率（‰） Birth Rate (‰)	人数 Population	死亡率（‰） Death Rate (‰)			
1985	8.95	16.30	3.01	5.48	10.82	11.60	8.74
1986	10.14	18.15	2.78	4.97	13.18	11.79	8.39
1987	9.76	17.14	2.83	4.97	12.17	12.58	9.26
1988	9.42	16.24	2.89	4.98	11.26	13.54	8.97
1989	11.78	19.92	3.04	5.13	14.79	12.73	10.15
1990	12.40	20.55	3.45	5.72	14.83	11.82	9.86
1991	8.73	14.25	3.26	5.33	8.92	8.98	6.09
1992	8.98	14.49	3.39	5.48	9.01	13.94	9.54
1993	9.25	14.75	3.37	5.38	9.37	11.50	8.33
1994	8.08	12.71	3.16	4.97	7.74	13.40	8.59
1995	7.69	11.95	3.21	4.98	6.97	14.41	8.85
1996	7.26	11.15	3.41	5.24	5.91	11.94	8.88
1997	6.84	10.38	3.12	4.75	5.63	12.58	8.62
1998	6.40	9.62	3.10	4.66	4.96	10.89	8.36
1999	6.19	9.22	3.88	5.78	3.44	12.58	9.23
2000	8.90	13.07	4.06	5.96	7.11	17.12	9.23
2001	5.11	7.39	2.89	4.19	3.20	15.16	10.83
2002	5.34	7.64	3.08	4.41	3.23	13.90	9.41
2003	6.02	8.48	3.32	4.68	3.80	20.60	9.15
2004	6.63	9.19	4.23	5.87	3.32	15.56	10.19
2005	7.67	9.58	4.13	5.16	4.42	22.61	9.46
2006	8.13	9.98	4.45	5.46	4.52	17.23	11.75
2007	8.27	10.00	4.53	5.48	4.52	19.90	14.01
2008	8.47	10.15	4.65	5.57	4.58	18.49	15.04
2009	8.47	10.08	4.73	5.63	4.45	16.84	13.14
2010	8.23	9.73	4.51	5.34	4.39	14.09	13.50
2011	8.25	9.71	4.57	5.38	4.33	14.21	11.74
2012	8.64	10.13	4.75	5.57	4.56	12.55	13.10
2013	8.20	9.57	4.60	5.37	4.20	10.83	8.60
2014	8.70	10.11	4.71	5.47	4.64	9.10	7.61

注：2004年以前为公安年报数据。迁入人口和迁出人口为公安年报数据。2010年出生、死亡、自然增长率根据第六次人口普查数据推算得出。2005-2009、2011-2014年出生、死亡、自然增长率为人口变动抽样调查数据。

4-3 全市及各区县人口数和户数（2014年）

Population and Households by Region（2014）

单位：万人 （10 000 persons）

区县 Region	总户数（万户）Number of Households (10 000 households)	总人口 Total Population	非农业人口 Non-agriculture	按性别划分Grouped by Sex 男 Male	女 Female	迁入人口(人) Immigrant population (person)	迁出人口(人) Emigrant population (person)
全 市 Total	**250.26**	**815.29**	**418.16**	**412.46**	**402.83**	**91009**	**76110**
新城区 Xincheng	17.24	50.8	50.8	25.77	25.03	4240	1627
碑林区 Beilin	21.38	71.02	71.02	36.18	34.84	12634	16616
莲湖区 Lianhu	22.78	65.75	65.75	33.09	32.66	5619	2571
灞桥区 Baqiao	17.84	53.6	25.6	26.39	27.21	4476	2013
未央区 Weiyang	18.93	58.7	44.59	29.2	29.5	9386	6196
雁塔区 Yanta	26.63	83.25	73.53	41.6	41.65	17845	22887
阎良区 Yanliang	7.93	26.26	9	13.19	13.07	1488	788
临潼区 Lintong	20.68	71.85	12.01	36.33	35.52	2814	1626
长安区 Chang'an	31.35	105.93	21.8	52.75	53.18	9939	4644
蓝田县 Lantian	19.07	65.45	5.77	33.94	31.51	4765	5010
周至县 Zhouzhi	17.86	68.79	6.42	36.24	32.55	5728	4915
户 县 Huxian	18.4	60.98	13.55	31.41	29.57	5597	4070
高陵县 Gaoling	10.17	32.91	18.32	16.37	16.54	6478	3147

注：本表均为公安年报数据。

4-4 全市及各区县常住人口数和人口变动情况（2014年）

Permanent Population and Population Changes by Region（2014）

区 县	Region	常住人口（万人）Permanent Population (10 000 persons)	城镇 Urban	出生率（‰）Birth Rate（‰）	死亡率（‰）Death Rate（‰）	自然增长率（‰）Natural Growth Rate（‰）
全 市	**Total**	**862.75**	**626.44**	**10.11**	**5.47**	**4.64**
新城区	Xincheng	59.86	59.86	6.92	3.39	3.53
碑林区	Beilin	62.40	62.40	7.57	3.86	3.71
莲湖区	Lianhu	70.68	70.68	7.22	3.78	3.44
灞桥区	Baqiao	60.82	57.25	10.26	5.54	4.72
未央区	Weiyang	82.28	76.79	10.64	5.43	5.21
雁塔区	Yanta	119.74	119.74	9.57	4.74	4.83
阎良区	Yanliang	28.53	16.18	9.76	5.63	4.13
临潼区	Lintong	67.16	22.74	10.85	5.73	5.12
长安区	Chang'an	110.59	63.53	11.88	7.03	4.85
蓝田县	Lantian	52.30	15.09	12.18	7.17	5.01
周至县	Zhouzhi	57.57	17.57	12.67	7.14	5.53
户 县	Huxian	56.60	22.99	10.97	6.11	4.86
高陵县	Gaoling	34.22	21.62	10.88	5.80	5.08

注：本表数据均为人口变动抽样调查数据。

4-5 主要年份常住人口数

Permanent Population in Representative Years

单位：万人 (10 000 persons)

年 份 Year	年末常住人口 Permanent population（year-end）	城镇 Urban	农村 Rural
2000	741.14	450.36	290.78
2005	806.81	510.55	296.26
2006	822.52	530.94	291.58
2007	830.54	548.99	281.55
2008	837.52	565.16	272.36
2009	843.46	581.4	262.06
2010	847.41	584.71	262.7
2011	851.34	596.79	254.55
2012	855.29	611.62	243.67
2013	858.81	618.77	240.04
2014	862.75	626.44	236.31

注：2000年常住人口为普查数据。2010年常住人口为年末常住人口数，根据第六次人口普查数据推算得出。2005-2009、2011-2014年常住人口为人口变动抽样调查数据。

4–6 主要年份社会从业人数

Number of Social Laborers in Representative Years

单位：万人 (10 000 persons)

年 份 Year	合计 Total	一、按城乡分 Grouped by Urban area and Rural area					二、按三次产业分 Grouped by Industry		
		1.城镇 Urban	国有经济 State-owned Enterprises	集体经济 Collective Enterprises	其他经济 Others	2.乡村 Village	第一产业 Primary Industry	第二产业 Secondary Industry	第三产业 Tertiary Industry
1985	**296.80**	129.07	96.80	29.07	3.20	167.73	135.89	98.61	62.30
1986	**299.45**	132.82	101.28	28.43	3.11	166.63	127.46	100.61	71.38
1987	**312.16**	138.56	104.58	30.72	3.26	173.60	130.36	107.75	74.05
1988	**327.76**	142.24	106.46	30.73	5.05	185.52	138.87	108.12	80.77
1989	**332.65**	145.65	108.80	30.44	6.41	187.00	142.21	106.40	84.04
1990	**343.06**	147.93	110.95	29.78	7.20	195.13	149.64	106.74	86.68
1991	**347.65**	149.48	111.87	29.80	7.81	198.17	152.24	108.19	87.22
1992	**357.51**	151.67	113.19	29.97	8.51	205.84	154.75	110.22	92.54
1993	**363.70**	155.72	112.98	29.77	12.97	207.98	154.02	114.02	95.66
1994	**364.56**	154.88	113.39	27.97	13.52	209.68	153.51	108.53	102.52
1995	**372.60**	158.80	113.79	25.58	19.43	213.80	153.39	109.67	109.54
1996	**379.29**	164.54	113.29	24.82	26.43	214.75	153.43	109.17	116.69
1997	**385.14**	169.52	112.44	23.52	33.56	215.62	153.23	109.46	122.45
1998	**393.95**	177.20	106.06	21.50	49.64	216.75	153.00	110.45	130.50
1999	**400.43**	180.27	105.08	20.50	54.69	220.16	154.64	110.58	135.21
2000	**389.10**	176.45	103.46	18.40	54.59	212.65	147.03	107.26	134.81
2001	**389.30**	177.94	100.47	17.10	60.37	211.36	145.09	108.96	135.25
2002	**397.16**	181.85	100.54	16.90	64.41	215.31	143.04	111.62	142.50
2003	**404.92**	183.23	94.51	16.78	71.94	221.69	146.67	109.09	149.16
2004	**409.57**	187.53	93.43	15.41	78.69	222.04	141.81	111.70	156.06
2005	**415.83**	192.53	93.27	14.47	84.79	223.30	136.31	114.20	165.32
2006	**422.15**	196.16	84.46	14.41	97.29	225.99	135.10	116.09	170.96
2007	**436.36**	214.27	90.58	11.88	111.81	222.09	133.33	125.06	177.97
2008	**448.05**	224.20	90.17	10.60	123.43	223.85	127.87	130.23	189.95
2009	**462.52**	239.39	90.83	7.63	140.93	223.13	122.13	131.57	208.82
2010	**477.58**	252.54	94.01	5.48	153.05	225.04	117.27	145.40	214.91
2011	**495.99**	265.43	91.62	5.33	168.48	230.56	121.05	151.33	223.61
2012	**514.57**	287.65	95.33	5.10	187.22	226.92	114.92	162.35	237.30
2013	**530.71**	308.04	86.06	7.29	214.69	222.67	110.45	151.50	268.76
2014	**532.92**	316.59	84.83	6.67	225.09	216.33	105.02	151.85	276.05

注：第一产业从业人员中包括城镇农林牧渔及服务业企业人员。

4-7 按国民经济行业分从业人数（2014年）

单位：万人

行 业	Sector	合计 Total
总计	**Total**	**532.92**
（一）农、林、牧、渔业	Agriculture ,Forestry,Animal Husbandry and Fishery	105.02
（二）采矿业	Mining	0.32
（三）制造业	Manufacturing	81.89
（四）电力、燃气及水的生产供应业	Production and Distribution of Electricity,Gas and Water	2.65
（五）建筑业	Construction	66.99
（六）批发和零售业	Wholesale and Retail Trades	75.29
（七）交通运输、仓储和邮政业	Traffic,Transport,Storage and Post	31.67
（八）住宿和餐饮业	Hotels and Catering Services	27.52
（九）信息传输、软件和信息技术服务业	Information Transmission,Software and Information Technology Services	11.55
（十）金融业	Financial Intermediation	7.86
（十一）房地产业	Real Estate	11.86
（十二）租赁和商务服务业	Leasing and Business Services	15.31
（十三）科学研究和技术服务业	Scientific Research and Technical Services	15.00
（十四）水利、环境和公共设施管理业	Management of Water Conservancy, Environment and Public Facilities	3.11
（十五）居民服务、修理和其他服务业	Services to Households, Repairs and Other Services	20.99
（十六）教育	Education	24.04
（十七）卫生和社会工作	Health and Social Work	15.62
（十八）文化、体育和娱乐业	Culture, Sports and Entertainment	3.13
（十九）公共管理、社会保障和社会组织	Public Administration, Social Security and Social Organizations	13.10
（二十）国际组织	International Organizations	

Number of Employed Persons Grouped by Sector（2014）

(10 000 persons)

国有经济 State-owned Enterprises	集体经济 Collective Enterprises	城镇其他经济 Urban Other Enterprises	城镇私营经济及个体劳动者 Urban Private Enterprises and Individual Labors	乡镇劳动者 Villages and Towns Labors
84.83	**6.67**	**107.91**	**117.18**	**216.33**
0.18		0.01	0.99	103.84
		0.05	0.27	
14.68	0.37	29.31	14.67	22.86
0.59	0.03	1.92	0.11	
5.17	4.47	23.35	11.85	22.15
1.29	0.24	11.21	48.13	14.42
11.56	0.02	4.83	1.79	13.47
0.61	0.01	6.07	11.80	9.03
0.08		7.65	2.86	0.96
1.20	0.20	5.35	0.13	0.98
1.38	0.05	5.38	5.05	
1.11	0.91	3.97	4.17	5.15
8.85	0.10	3.77	1.82	0.46
1.61	0.02	1.21	0.27	
0.47	0.09	0.68	10.33	9.42
16.64	0.03	1.57	0.52	5.28
7.07	0.13	0.72	0.47	7.23
1.10		0.86	1.17	
11.24			0.78	1.08

4-8 全部单位从业人员情况（2014年）

单位：人

分 组	Classify	单位从业人员 Employed Persons	女性 Female
总计	**Total**	**1994154**	**705699**
一、按机构类型分组	**Grouped by Organization Type**		
#企业	Enterprises	1564861	509932
机关	Government Units	105734	34931
事业	Public Institutions	306043	152772
二、按国民经济行业分组	**Grouped by Economic Sector**		
（一）农业	Agriculture ,Forestry,Animal Husbandry and Fishery	1883	606
（二）采矿业	Mining	452	68
（三）制造业	Manufacturing	443578	138091
（四）电力、燃气及水的生产供应业	Production and Distribution of Electricity,Gas and Water	25368	7585
（五）建筑业	Construction	329788	42909
（六）批发和零售业	Wholesale and Retail Trades	127362	66279
（七）交通运输、仓储和邮政业	Traffic,Transport,Storage and Post	164100	48672
（八）住宿和餐饮业	Hotels and Catering Services	66927	39118
（九）信息传输、软件和信息技术服务业	Information Transmission,Software and Information Technology Services	77362	31944
（十）金融业	Financial Intermediation	67603	34828
（十一）房地产业	Real Estate	68120	27448
（十二）租赁和商务服务业	Leasing and Business Services	59970	21559
（十三）科学研究和技术服务业	Scientific Research and Technical Services	127143	38425
（十四）水利、环境和公共设施管理业	Management of Water Conservancy, Environment and Public Facilities	28371	11350
（十五）居民服务、修理和其他服务业	Services to Households, Repairs and Other Services	12475	5623
（十六）教育	Education	182468	95146
（十七）卫生和社会工作	Health and Social Work	79173	49678
（十八）文化、体育和娱乐业	Culture, Sports and Entertainment	19641	9200
（十九）公共管理、社会保障和社会组织	Public Administration, Social Security and Social Organizations	112370	37170
（二十）国际组织	International Organizations		

Basic Facts on All Employed Persons（2014）

(persons)

在岗职工合计 Total Fully Employed Staff and Workers	其他从业人员 Other Employed Persons	单位从业人员平均人数 Average Employment	在岗职工 Staff and Workers	其他从业人员 Other Employed Persons
1832191	**161963**	**2110068**	**1936632**	**173436**
1435059	129802	1651194	1512029	139165
92218	13516	108159	94739	13420
287827	18216	333380	312955	20425
1883		1889	1889	
452		620	620	
430412	13166	494314	481157	13157
24134	1234	25971	24828	1143
248182	81606	334715	245001	89714
124511	2851	125696	122728	2968
160533	3567	170876	167574	3302
58139	8788	68004	59347	8657
77214	148	76730	76542	188
59394	8209	78365	68188	10177
66550	1570	66756	65124	1632
58383	1587	60533	59000	1533
122755	4388	142600	135179	7421
24441	3930	28020	24431	3589
12186	289	12025	11743	282
172128	10340	194427	184861	9566
74093	5080	94685	89711	4974
18592	1049	18954	17893	1061
98209	14161	114888	100816	14072

4-9　国有单位从业人员情况（2014年）

单位：人

分　组	Classify	单位从业人员 Employed Persons	女性 Female
总计	**Total**	**848372**	**322247**
一、按机构类型分组	**Grouped by Organization Type**		
#企业	Enterprises	439536	136597
机关	Government units	105734	34931
事业	Public institutions	301448	150150
二、按国民经济行业分组	**Grouped by Economic Sector**		
（一）农业	Agriculture ,Forestry,Animal Husbandry and Fishery	1833	588
（二）采矿业	Mining		
（三）制造业	Manufacturing	146757	45654
（四）电力、燃气及水的生产供应业	Production and Distribution of Electricity,Gas and Water	5928	1697
（五）建筑业	Construction	51748	8541
（六）批发和零售业	Wholesale and Retail Trades	12850	7292
（七）交通运输、仓储和邮政业	Traffic,Transport,Storage and Post	115583	31442
（八）住宿和餐饮业	Hotels and Catering Services	6121	3316
（九）信息传输、软件和信息技术服务业	Information Transmission,Software and Information Technology Services	815	215
（十）金融业	Financial Intermediation	12012	5736
（十一）房地产业	Real Estate	13799	5642
（十二）租赁和商务服务业	Leasing and Business Services	11121	4470
（十三）科学研究和技术服务业	Scientific Research and Technical Services	88464	28426
（十四）水利、环境和公共设施管理业	Management of Water Conservancy, Environment	16083	5969
	and Public Facilities	4729	1759
（十五）居民服务、修理和其他服务业	Services to Households, Repairs and Other Services		
（十六）教育	Education	166407	85960
（十七）卫生和社会工作	Health and Social Work	70722	43714
（十八）文化、体育和娱乐业	Culture, Sports and Entertainment	11030	4656
（十九）公共管理、社会保障和社会组织	Public Administration, Social Security and Social Organizations	112370	37170
（二十）国际组织	International Organizations		

Basic Facts on Persons Employed by State-owned Units（2014）

(persons)

在岗职工合计 Total Fully Employed Staff and Workers	其他从业人员 Other Employed Persons	单位从业人员平均人数 Average Employment	在岗职工 Staff and Workers	其他从业人员 Other Employed Persons
790158	**58214**	**950436**	**891612**	**58824**
412242	27294	511821	486036	25785
92218	13516	108159	94739	13420
284044	17404	328805	309186	19619
1833		1839	1839	
141273	5484	189797	184150	5647
5504	424	6925	6503	422
37332	14416	51977	39045	12932
12566	284	12730	12247	483
113594	1989	123332	121481	1851
5686	435	6315	5871	444
798	17	810	793	17
11652	360	13500	13181	319
13394	405	14051	13671	380
10674	447	11831	11495	336
85474	2990	104722	98673	6049
14053	2030	16195	14244	1951
4694	35	4641	4597	44
157362	9045	179019	170723	8296
65953	4769	86488	81819	4669
10107	923	11376	10464	912
98209	14161	114888	100816	14072

4-10 城镇集体单位从业人员情况（2014年）

单位：人

分 组	Classify	单位从业人员 Employed Persons	女性 Female
总计	**Total**	**66715**	**10409**
一、按机构类型分组	**Grouped by Organization Type**		
#企业	Enterprises	65586	9823
机关	Government units		
事业	Public institutions	1109	569
二、按国民经济行业分组	**Grouped by Economic Sector**		
（一）农业	Agriculture ,Forestry,Animal Husbandry and Fishery		
（二）采矿业	Mining	3728	1187
（三）制造业	Manufacturing	277	63
（四）电力、燃气及水的生产供应业	Production and Distribution of Electricity,Gas and Water	44573	4532
（五）建筑业	Construction	2394	824
（六）批发和零售业	Wholesale and Retail Trades	188	62
（七）交通运输、仓储和邮政业	Traffic,Transport,Storage and Post	140	102
（八）住宿和餐饮业	Hotels and Catering Services	19	9
（九）信息传输、软件和信息技术服务业	Information Transmission,Software and Information Technology Services	2042	1015
（十）金融业	Financial Intermediation	519	186
（十一）房地产业	Real Estate	9149	674
（十二）租赁和商务服务业	Leasing and Business Services	1001	348
（十三）科学研究和技术服务业	Scientific Research and Technical Services	169	78
（十四）水利、环境和公共设施管理业	Management of Water Conservancy, Environment and Public Facilities	908	360
（十五）居民服务、修理和其他服务业	Services to Households, Repairs and Other Services	312	172
（十六）教育	Education	1294	797
（十七）卫生和社会工作	Health and Social Work	2	
（十八）文化、体育和娱乐业	Culture, Sports and Entertainment		
（十九）公共管理、社会保障和社会组织	Public Administration, Social Security and Social Organizations		
（二十）国际组织	International Organizations		

Basic Facts on Persons Employed by Urban Collective-owned Units（2014）

(persons)

		单位从业人员		
在岗职工合计 Total Fully Employed Staff and Workers	其他从业人员 Other Employed Persons	平均人数 Average Employment	在岗职工 Staff and Workers	其他从业人员 Other Employed Persons
64205	**2510**	**65694**	**63255**	**2439**
63316	2270	64567	62368	2199
872	237	1107	870	237
3451	277	3783	3640	143
277		282	239	43
43438	1135	43778	42624	1154
1612	782	2409	1617	792
188		188	188	
140		139	139	
19		19	19	
1990	52	2016	1965	51
483	36	521	487	34
9118	31	8805	8774	31
941	60	1072	1015	57
169		164	164	
789	119	915	799	116
312		313	313	
1276	18	1288	1270	18
2	0	2	2	

4-11 其他经济类型单位从业人员情况（2014年）

单位：人

分　组	Classify	单位从业人员 Employed Persons	女性 Female
总计	**Total**	**1079067**	**373043**
一、按机构类型分组	**Grouped by Organization Type**		
#企业	Enterprises	1059739	363512
机关	Government units		
事业	Public institutions	3486	2053
二、按国民经济行业分组	**Grouped by Economic Sector**		
（一）农业	Agriculture ,Forestry,Animal Husbandry and Fishery	50	18
（二）采矿业	Mining	452	68
（三）制造业	Manufacturing	293093	91250
（四）电力、燃气及水的生产供应业	Production and Distribution of Electricity,Gas and Water	19163	5825
（五）建筑业	Construction	233467	29836
（六）批发和零售业	Wholesale and Retail Trades	112118	58163
（七）交通运输、仓储和邮政业	Traffic,Transport,Storage and Post	48329	17168
（八）住宿和餐饮业	Hotels and Catering Services	60666	35700
（九）信息传输、软件和信息技术服务业	Information Transmission,Software and Information Technology Services	76528	31720
（十）金融业	Financial Intermediation	53549	28077
（十一）房地产业	Real Estate	53802	21620
（十二）租赁和商务服务业	Leasing and Business Services	39700	16415
（十三）科学研究和技术服务业	Scientific Research and Technical Services	37678	9651
（十四）水利、环境和公共设施管理业	Management of Water Conservancy, Environment and Public Facilities	12119	5303
（十五）居民服务、修理和其他服务业	Services to Households, Repairs and Other Services	6838	3504
（十六）教育	Education	15749	9014
（十七）卫生和社会工作	Health and Social Work	7157	5167
（十八）文化、体育和娱乐业	Culture, Sports and Entertainment	8609	4544
（十九）公共管理、社会保障和社会组织	Public Administration, Social Security and Social Organizations		
（二十）国际组织	International Organizations		

Basic Facts on Persons Employed by Other Units（2014）

(persons)

在岗职工合计 Total Fully Employed Staff and Workers	其他从业人员 Other Employed Persons	单位从业人员平均人数 Average Employment	在岗职工 Staff and Workers	其他从业人员 Other Employed Persons
977828	**101239**	**1093938**	**981765**	**112173**
959501	100238	1074806	963625	111181
2911	575	3468	2899	569
50		50	50	
452		620	620	
285688	7405	300734	293367	7367
18353	810	18764	18086	678
167412	66055	238960	163332	75628
110333	1785	110557	108864	1693
46751	1578	47356	45905	1451
52313	8353	61550	53337	8213
76397	131	75901	75730	171
45752	7797	62849	53042	9807
52673	1129	52184	50966	1218
38591	1109	39897	38731	1166
36340	1338	36806	35491	1315
10219	1900	11661	10023	1638
6703	135	6469	6347	122
14454	1295	15095	13825	1270
6864	293	6909	6622	287
8483	126	7576	7427	149

4–12 主要年份单位从业人员数及工资总额

Number of Employed Persons and Remuneration in Representative Years

年 份 year	单位从业人员 （万人） Number of Employed Persons (10 000 persons)	从业人员工资总额 （亿元） Remuneration of Employed Persons (100 million yuan)	城镇非私营单位从业人员年平均工资（元） Aunual Average Wage of Employees in Urban Non-privite Units(yuan)
1978	67.19	4.71	713
1980	91.76	7.31	859
1985	127.04	14.17	1148
1986	132.78	16.87	1311
1987	135.48	19.13	1446
1988	137.56	22.81	1702
1989	139.86	25.64	1873
1990	141.55	29.48	2133
1991	142.86	26.88	2276
1992	144.51	30.80	2545
1993	146.03	43.25	2999
1994	142.37	58.87	4172
1995	141.17	67.23	4763
1996	140.60	75.64	5407
1997	138.89	80.83	5785
1998	138.78	82.85	6900
1999	115.88	90.13	7764
2000	112.45	103.80	9179
2001	113.93	123.12	10786
2002	115.77	138.88	12138
2003	116.68	155.95	13504
2004	118.15	184.63	15473
2005	123.66	215.67	17728
2006	125.10	250.87	20475
2007	129.40	319.23	25012
2008	130.85	379.29	29749
2009	135.64	450.48	34032
2010	140.38	520.88	37870
2011	154.33	658.73	41679
2012	165.59	770.86	44533
2013	198.42	1031.46	49350
2014	199.41	1151.53	54573

注：城镇非私营单位从业人员年平均工资2012年前为城镇非私营单位在岗职工年平均工资。

4-13 全部单位从业人员工资总额（2014年）

Total Wages of All Employed Persons（2014）

单位：万元 （10 000yuan）

分组	Classify	单位从业人员工资总额 Total Wages of Employment	在岗职工工资总额 Total Wages of Employed Staff and Workers
总计	**Total**	**11515262**	**10940160**
一、按机构类型分组	**Grouped by Organization Type**		
#企业	Enterprises	8992044	8487144
机关	Government Units	506829	483876
事业	Public Institutions	1933431	1887101
二、按国民经济行业分组	**Grouped by Economic Sector**		
（一）农业	Agriculture ,Forestry,Animal Husbandry and Fishery	8100	8100
（二）采矿业	Mining	2611	2611
（三）制造业	Manufacturing	2445982	2394769
（四）电力、燃气及水的生产供应业	Production and Distribution of Electricity, Gas and Water	135299	132192
（五）建筑业	Construction	1615852	1247551
（六）批发和零售业	Wholesale and Retail Trades	514281	506780
（七）交通运输、仓储和邮政业	Traffic,Transport,Storage and Post	1011403	1004091
（八）住宿和餐饮业	Hotels and Catering Services	210227	202329
（九）信息传输、软件和信息技术服务业	Information Transmission,Software and Information Technology Services	771521	770573
（十）金融业	Financial Intermediation	740024	716200
（十一）房地产业	Real Estate	321232	316784
（十二）租赁和商务服务业	Leasing and Business Services	283463	279542
（十三）科学研究和技术服务业	Scientific Research and Technical Services	997603	978796
（十四）水利、环境和公共设施管理业	Management of Water Conservancy, Environment and Public Facilities	120580	112929
（十五）居民服务、修理和其他服务业	Services to Households, Repairs and Other Services	39055	38049
（十六）教育	Education	1136445	1111257
（十七）卫生和社会工作	Health and Social Work	513118	496030
（十八）文化、体育和娱乐业	Culture, Sports and Entertainment	108491	106145
（十九）公共管理、社会保障和社会组织	Public Administration, Social Security and Social Organizations	539975	515432
（二十）国际组织	International Organizations		

4-13 续表 continued

单位：万元 (10 000 yuan)

分组	Classify	其他从业人员工资总额 Remuneration of Other Employed Persons	城镇非私营单位从业人员年平均工资（元） Aunual Average Wage of Employees in UrbanNon-privite Units(yuan)
总计	**Total**	**575102**	**54573**
一、按机构类型分组	**Grouped by Organization Type**		
#企业	Enterprises	504900	54458
机关	Government Units	22953	46860
事业	Public Institutions	46330	57995
二、按国民经济行业分组	**Grouped by Economic Sector**		
（一）农业	Agriculture ,Forestry,Animal Husbandry and Fishery		42881
（二）采矿业	Mining		42116
（三）制造业	Manufacturing	51213	49482
（四）电力、燃气及水的生产供应业	Production and Distribution of Electricity, Gas and Water	3107	61252
（五）建筑业	Construction	368301	48275
（六）批发和零售业	Wholesale and Retail Trades	7501	40915
（七）交通运输、仓储和邮政业	Traffic,Transport,Storage and Post	7312	59189
（八）住宿和餐饮业	Hotels and Catering Services	7898	30914
（九）信息传输、软件和信息技术服务业	Information Transmission,Software and Information Technology Services	948	100550
（十）金融业	Financial Intermediation	23824	104433
（十一）房地产业	Real Estate	4448	48120
（十二）租赁和商务服务业	Leasing and Business Services	3921	46828
（十三）科学研究和技术服务业	Scientific Research and Technical Services	18807	69958
（十四）水利、环境和公共设施管理业	Management of Water Conservancy, Environment and Public Facilities	7651	43033
（十五）居民服务、修理和其他服务业	Services to Households, Repairs and Other Services	1006	32478
（十六）教育	Education	25188	58451
（十七）卫生和社会工作	Health and Social Work	17088	59892
（十八）文化、体育和娱乐业	Culture, Sports and Entertainment	2346	57239
（十九）公共管理、社会保障和社会组织	Public Administration, Social Security and Social Organizations	24543	47000
（二十）国际组织	International Organizations		

4-14 国有单位从业人员工资总额（2014年）

Total Wages of Persons Employed by State-owned Units（2014）

单位：万元　　　　(10 000yuan)

分组	Classify	单位从业人员工资总额 Total Wages of Employment	在岗职工工资总额 Total Wages of Employed Staff and Workers
总计	**Total**	**5145453**	**4975064**
一、按机构类型分组	**Grouped by Organization Type**		
#企业	Enterprises	2723772	2620760
机关	Government Units	506829	483876
事业	Public Institutions	1908496	1864073
二、按国民经济行业分组	**Grouped by Economic Sector**		
（一）农业	Agriculture ,Forestry,Animal Husbandry and Fishery	7993	7993
（二）采矿业	Mining		
（三）制造业	Manufacturing	895240	870027
（四）电力、燃气及水的生产供应业	Production and Distribution of Electricity,	31358	30132
	Gas and Water		
（五）建筑业	Construction	249208	191884
（六）批发和零售业	Wholesale and Retail Trades	62293	61106
（七）交通运输、仓储和邮政业	Traffic,Transport,Storage and Post	774781	771193
（八）住宿和餐饮业	Hotels and Catering Services	19349	18484
（九）信息传输、软件和信息技术服务业	Information Transmission,Software and Information	4020	3883
	Technology Services	130318	129003
（十）金融业	Financial Intermediation		
（十一）房地产业	Real Estate	55690	54874
（十二）租赁和商务服务业	Leasing and Business Services	40864	40157
（十三）科学研究和技术服务业	Scientific Research and Technical Services	653569	641318
（十四）水利、环境和公共设施管理业	Management of Water Conservancy, Environment	65009	61488
	and Public Facilities		
（十五）居民服务、修理和其他服务业	Services to Households, Repairs and Other Services	14939	14844
（十六）教育	Education	1067521	1047445
（十七）卫生和社会工作	Health and Social Work	473385	457831
（十八）文化、体育和娱乐业	Culture, Sports and Entertainment	59941	57970
（十九）公共管理、社会保障和社会组织	Public Administration, Social Security and Social	539975	515432
	Organizations		
（二十）国际组织	International Organizations		

4-14 续表 continued

单位：万元 (10 000 yuan)

分 组	Classify	其他从业人员工资总额 Remuneration of Other Employed Persons	城镇非私营单位从业人员年平均工资（元） Aunual Average Wage of Employees in UrbanNon-privite Units(yuan)
总计	**Total**	**170389**	**54138**
一、按机构类型分组	**Grouped by Organization Type**		
#企业	Enterprises	103012	53217
机关	Government Units	22953	46860
事业	Public Institutions	44423	58043
二、按国民经济行业分组	**Grouped by Economic Sector**		
（一）农业	Agriculture ,Forestry,Animal Husbandry and Fishery		43464
（二）采矿业	Mining		
（三）制造业	Manufacturing	25213	47168
（四）电力、燃气及水的生产供应业	Production and Distribution of Electricity, Gas and Water	1226	45282
（五）建筑业	Construction	57324	47946
（六）批发和零售业	Wholesale and Retail Trades	1187	48934
（七）交通运输、仓储和邮政业	Traffic,Transport,Storage and Post	3588	62821
（八）住宿和餐饮业	Hotels and Catering Services	865	30640
（九）信息传输、软件和信息技术服务业	Information Transmission,Software and Information	137	49625
	Technology Services	1315	96532
（十）金融业	Financial Intermediation		
（十一）房地产业	Real Estate	816	39635
（十二）租赁和商务服务业	Leasing and Business Services	707	34540
（十三）科学研究和技术服务业	Scientific Research and Technical Services	12251	62410
（十四）水利、环境和公共设施管理业	Management of Water Conservancy, Environment and Public Facilities	3521	40141
（十五）居民服务、修理和其他服务业	Services to Households, Repairs and Other Services	95	32189
（十六）教育	Education	20076	59632
（十七）卫生和社会工作	Health and Social Work	15554	54734
（十八）文化、体育和娱乐业	Culture, Sports and Entertainment	1971	52690
（十九）公共管理、社会保障和社会组织	Public Administration, Social Security and Social Organizations	24543	47000
（二十）国际组织	International Organizations		

4-15 城镇集体单位从业人员工资总额（2014年）

Total Wages of Persons Employed by Urban Collective-owned Units in Towns and Cities（2014）

单位：万元 （10 000yuan）

分组	Classify	单位从业人员工资总额 Total Wages of Employment	在岗职工工资总额 Total Wages of Employed Staff and Workers
总计	**Total**	**269391**	**262002**
一、按机构类型分组	**Grouped by Organization Type**		
#企业	Enterprises	265133	258141
机关	Government Units		
事业	Public Institutions	4201	3819
二、按国民经济行业分组	**Grouped by Economic Sector**		
（一）农、林、牧、渔业	Agriculture ,Forestry,Animal Husbandry and Fishery		
（二）采矿业	Mining	12301	12066
（三）制造业	Manufacturing	1963	1790
（四）电力、燃气及水的生产供应业	Production and Distribution of Electricity, Gas and Water	187649	183093
（五）建筑业	Construction	6248	4760
（六）批发和零售业	Wholesale and Retail Trades	632	632
（七）交通运输、仓储和邮政业	Traffic,Transport,Storage and Post	514	514
（八）住宿和餐饮业	Hotels and Catering Services	79	79
（九）信息传输、软件和信息技术服务业	Information Transmission,Software and Information Technology Services	14878	14738
（十）金融业	Financial Intermediation	2199	2131
（十一）房地产业	Real Estate	26248	26141
（十二）租赁和商务服务业	Leasing and Business Services	6350	6016
（十三）科学研究和技术服务业	Scientific Research and Technical Services	330	330
（十四）水利、环境和公共设施管理业	Management of Water Conservancy, Environment and Public Facilities	3557	3327
（十五）居民服务、修理和其他服务业	Services to Households, Repairs and Other Services	1933	1933
（十六）教育	Education	4501	4443
（十七）卫生和社会工作	Health and Social Work	9	9
（十八）文化、体育和娱乐业	Culture, Sports and Entertainment		
（十九）公共管理、社会保障和社会组织	Public Administration, Social Security and Social Organizations		
（二十）国际组织	International Organizations		

4-15 续表 continued

单位：万元 (10 000 yuan)

分 组	Classify	其他从业人员工资总额 Remuneration of Other Employed Persons	城镇非私营单位从业人员年平均工资（元） Aunual Average Wage of Employees in UrbanNon-privite Units(yuan)
总计	**Total**	**7389**	**41006**
一、按机构类型分组	**Grouped by Organization Type**		
#企业	Enterprises	6992	41063
机关	Government Units		
事业	Public Institutions	382	37956
二、按国民经济行业分组	**Grouped by Economic Sector**		
（一）农、林、牧、渔业	Agriculture ,Forestry,Animal Husbandry and Fishery		
（二）采矿业	Mining	235	32517
（三）制造业	Manufacturing	173	69592
（四）电力、燃气及水的生产供应业	Production and Distribution of Electricity, Gas and Water	4556	42864
（五）建筑业	Construction	1488	25935
（六）批发和零售业	Wholesale and Retail Trades		33628
（七）交通运输、仓储和邮政业	Traffic,Transport,Storage and Post		36971
（八）住宿和餐饮业	Hotels and Catering Services		41368
（九）信息传输、软件和信息技术服务业	Information Transmission,Software and Information Technology Services	140	73799
（十）金融业	Financial Intermediation	68	42202
（十一）房地产业	Real Estate	107	29809
（十二）租赁和商务服务业	Leasing and Business Services	334	59231
（十三）科学研究和技术服务业	Scientific Research and Technical Services		20104
（十四）水利、环境和公共设施管理业	Management of Water Conservancy, Environment and Public Facilities	230	38877
（十五）居民服务、修理和其他服务业	Services to Households, Repairs and Other Services		61757
（十六）教育	Education	58	34942
（十七）卫生和社会工作	Health and Social Work		45000
（十八）文化、体育和娱乐业	Culture, Sports and Entertainment		
（十九）公共管理、社会保障和社会组织	Public Administration, Social Security and Social Organizations		
（二十）国际组织	International Organizations		

4-16 其他经济类型单位从业人员工资总额（2014年）

Total Wages of Persons Employed by Other Units（2014）

单位：万元 (10 000yuan)

分 组	Classify	单 位 从业人员 工资总额 Total Wages of Employment	在岗职工 工资总额 Total Wages of Employed Staff and Workers
总计	**Total**	**6100421**	**5703097**
一、按机构类型分组	**Grouped by Organization Type**		
#企业	Enterprises	6003139	5608243
机关	Government Units		
事业	Public Institutions	20733	19209
二、按国民经济行业分组	**Grouped by Economic Sector**		
（一）农、林、牧、渔业	Agriculture ,Forestry,Animal Husbandry and Fishery	107	107
（二）采矿业	Mining	2611	2611
（三）制造业	Manufacturing	1538441	1512676
（四）电力、燃气及水的生产供应业	Production and Distribution of Electricity, Gas and Water	101978	100270
（五）建筑业	Construction	1178993	872573
（六）批发和零售业	Wholesale and Retail Trades	445741	440914
（七）交通运输、仓储和邮政业	Traffic,Transport,Storage and Post	235989	232265
（八）住宿和餐饮业	Hotels and Catering Services	190364	183331
（九）信息传输、软件和信息技术服务业	Information Transmission,Software and Information Technology Services	767423	766611
（十）金融业	Financial Intermediation	594829	572460
（十一）房地产业	Real Estate	263344	259779
（十二）租赁和商务服务业	Leasing and Business Services	216351	213245
（十三）科学研究和技术服务业	Scientific Research and Technical Services	337684	331462
（十四）水利、环境和公共设施管理业	Management of Water Conservancy, Environment and Public Facilities	55242	51112
（十五）居民服务、修理和其他服务业	Services to Households, Repairs and Other Services	20559	19879
（十六）教育	Education	66991	61879
（十七）卫生和社会工作	Health and Social Work	35232	33756
（十八）文化、体育和娱乐业	Culture, Sports and Entertainment	48542	48167
（十九）公共管理、社会保障和社会组织	Public Administration, Social Security and Social Organizations		
（二十）国际组织	International Organizations		

4-16 续表 continued

单位：万元　　(10 000 yuan)

分　组	Classify	其他从业人员工资总额 Remuneration of Other Employed Persons	城镇非私营单位从业人员年平均工资（元） Aunual Average Wage of Employees in UrbanNon-privite Units(yuan)
总计	**Total**	**397324**	**55766**
一、按机构类型分组	**Grouped by Organization Type**		
#企业	Enterprises	394896	55853
机关	Government Units		
事业	Public Institutions	1524	59783
二、按国民经济行业分组	**Grouped by Economic Sector**		
（一）农、林、牧、渔业	Agriculture ,Forestry,Animal Husbandry and Fishery		21440
（二）采矿业	Mining		42116
（三）制造业	Manufacturing	25765	51156
（四）电力、燃气及水的生产供应业	Production and Distribution of Electricity, Gas and Water	1708	54348
（五）建筑业	Construction	306420	49339
（六）批发和零售业	Wholesale and Retail Trades	4827	40318
（七）交通运输、仓储和邮政业	Traffic,Transport,Storage and Post	3724	49833
（八）住宿和餐饮业	Hotels and Catering Services	7033	30928
（九）信息传输、软件和信息技术服务业	Information Transmission,Software and Information Technology Services	812	101108
（十）金融业	Financial Intermediation	22369	94644
（十一）房地产业	Real Estate	3565	50464
（十二）租赁和商务服务业	Leasing and Business Services	3106	54228
（十三）科学研究和技术服务业	Scientific Research and Technical Services	6222	91747
（十四）水利、环境和公共设施管理业	Management of Water Conservancy, Environment and Public Facilities	4130	47373
（十五）居民服务、修理和其他服务业	Services to Households, Repairs and Other Services	680	31780
（十六）教育	Education	5112	44379
（十七）卫生和社会工作	Health and Social Work	1476	50995
（十八）文化、体育和娱乐业	Culture, Sports and Entertainment	375	64074
（十九）公共管理、社会保障和社会组织	Public Administration, Social Security and Social Organizations		
（二十）国际组织	International Organizations		

4–17 主要年份城镇登记失业人数及失业率

Registered Unemployed Persons and Unemployment Rate in Urban Area in Representative Years

年 份 year	城镇登记失业人员数（万人） Real Number of Registered Unemployed Persons (10 000 persons)	城镇登记失业率（%） Registered Unemployment in Urban Area (%)
2002		3.70
2003		4.50
2004	8.29	4.30
2005	8.45	4.30
2006	8.74	4.30
2007	8.77	4.30
2008	9.40	4.20
2009	10.02	4.30
2010	10.46	4.20
2011	10.37	3.90
2012	9.60	3.50
2013	10.13	3.40
2014	10.84	3.40

主要统计指标解释

人口数 指一定时点、一定地区范围内的有生命的个人的总和。年度统计的年末人口数，指每年12月31日24时的人口数。

常住人口 指实际经常居住在某地区一定时间（半年以上，含半年）的人口。常住人口包括户口在本辖区人也在本辖区居住的人，户口在本辖区之外但在户口登记地半年以上的人，户口待定（无户口和口袋户口）的人，户口在本辖区但离开本辖区半年以下的人。

城镇人口和乡村人口 城镇人口是指居住在城镇范围内的全部常住人口；乡村人口是除上述人口以外的全部人口。

出生率（又称粗出生率） 指在一定时期内（通常为一年）平均每千人所出生的人数的比率，一般用千分率表示。其计算公式为：

出生率＝年出生人数／年平均人数×1000‰

式中：出生人数指活产婴儿，即胎儿脱离母体时（不管怀孕月数），有过呼吸或其他生命现象。年平均人数指年初、年底人口数的平均数，也可用年中人口数代替。

死亡率（又称粗死亡率） 指在一定时期内（通常为一年）一定地区的死亡人数与同期内平均人数（或期中人数）之比，一般用千分率表示。本资料中的死亡率指年死亡率，其计算公式为：

死亡率＝年死亡人数／年平均人数×1000‰

人口自然增长率 指在一定时期内（通常为一年）人口自然增加数（出生人数减死亡人数）与该时期内平均人数（或期中人数）之比，一般用千分率表示。计算公式为：

人口自然增长率＝（本年出生人数—本年死亡人数）／年平均人数×1000‰。

从业人员 指在16周岁及以上，从事一定社会劳动并取得劳动报酬或经营收入的人员。这一指标反映了一定时期内全部劳动力资源的实际利用情况，是研究我国基本国情国力的重要指标。

单位从业人员 指在各级国家机关、政党机关、社会团体及企业、事业单位中工作，取得工资或其他形式的劳动报酬的全部人员。包括在岗职工、再就业的离退休人员、民办教师以及在各单位中工作的外方人员和港澳台方人员、兼职人员、借用的外单位人员和第二职业者。不包括离开本单位仍保留劳动关系的职工。各单位的就业人员反映了各单位实际参加生产或工作的全部劳动力。

城镇私营和个体就业人员 城镇私营就业人员指在工商管理部门注册登记，其经营地址设在县城关镇（含城关镇）以上的私营企业就业人员；包括私营企业投资者和雇工。城镇个体就业人员指在工商管理部门注册登记，并持有城镇户口或在城镇长期居住，经批准从事个体工商经营的就业人员；包括个体经营者和在个体工商户劳动的家庭帮工和雇工。

国有单位 指资产归国家所有的经济组织。包括按《中华人民共和国企业法人登记管理条例》规定登记注册的非公司制的经济组织，以及中央、地方各级国家机关、事业单位和社会团体。

集体单位 指生产资料归集体所有，并按《中华人民共和国企业法人登记管理条例》规定登记注册的经济组织。

其他单位 包括股份合作单位、联营单位、有限责任公司、股份有限公司、港澳台商投资单位以及外商投资单位等其他登记注册类型单位。

在岗职工 指在本单位工作并由单位支付工资的人员，以及有工作岗位，但由于学习、病伤产假等原因暂未工作，仍由单位支付工资的人员。

职工工资总额 指各单位在一定时期内直接支付给本单位全部职工的劳动报酬总额。工资总额的计算原则应以直接支付给职工的全部劳动报酬为根据。各单位支付给职工的劳动报酬以及其他根据有关规定支付的工资，不论是计入成本的还是不计入成本的，不论是按国家规定列入计征奖金税项目的，还是未列入计征奖金税项目的，不论是以货币形式支付的还是以实物形式支付的，均包括在工资总额内。

职工平均工资 指企业、事业、机关单位的职工在一定时期内平均每人所得的货币工资额。它表明一定时期职工工资收入的高低程度，是反映职工工资水平的主要指标。计算公式为：

职工平均工资＝报告期实际支付的全部职工工资总额/报告期全部职工平均人数

城镇登记失业人员 指有非农业户口，在一定的劳动年龄内，有劳动能力，无业而要求就业，并在当地就业服务机构进行求职登记的人员。

城镇登记失业率 指城镇登记失业人数同城镇从业人数与城镇从业人数与城镇登记失业人数之和的比。计算公式为：

$$\text{城镇登记失业率}=\frac{\text{城镇登记失业人数}}{\text{（城镇单位就业人员–使用的农村劳动力–聘用的离退休人员–聘用的港澳台及外方人员）+不在岗职工+城镇私营业主+城镇个体户主+城镇私营企业及个体就业人员+城镇登记失业人数}}\times 100\%$$

Explanatory Notes on Main Statistical Indicators

The annual statistics on total population is taken at midnight, the 31st of December, not including residents in Taiwan province, Hong Kong SAR and Macao SAR and Chinese national residing abroad.

Permanent population refers to the population of actual habitual residence in a certain area six months or over six months. Permanent popul ation include the accounts in this area which are also living in this area, accounts outside this area but with more than half a year of household registration, accounts to be determined including people without accounts or pockets of accounts, and accounts in the area but leaving this area less than six months.

Urban Population and Rural Population Urban population refers to all people residing in cities and towns, while rural population refers to population other than urban population.

Birth Rate (or Crude Birth Rate) refers to the ratio of the number of births to the average population (or mid-period population) during a certain period of time (usually one year), expressed in ‰. Birth ratc in the chapter refers to annual birth rate. The following formula is used:

$$\text{Birth Rate}=\frac{\text{Number of Births}}{\text{Annual Average Population}}\times 1000‰$$

Number of births in the formula refers to live births, i.e. when a baby has breathed or showed any vital phenomena regardless of the length of pregnancy.

Annual average population is the average of the number of population at the beginning of the year and that at the end of the year. Sometimes it is substituted by the mid-year population.

Death Rate (or Crude Death Rate) refers to the ratio of the number of deaths to the average population (or mid-period population) during a certain period of time (usually one year), expressed in ‰. Death rate in the chapter refers to annual death rate. The following formula is used:

$$\text{DeathRate}=\frac{\text{Number of Deaths}}{\text{Annual Average Population}}\times 1000‰$$

Natural Growth Rate of Population refers to the ratio of natural increase in population (number of births minus number of deaths) in a certain period of time (usually one year) to the average population (or mid-period population) of the same period, expressed in ‰. The following formula is applied:

Natural Growth Rate of Population =(Number of Births-Number of Deaths)/Annual Average Population× 1000‰

Employed Persons refer to the ones aged 16 and over who are engaged in gainful employment and thus receive remuneration payment or earn business income. This indicator reflects the actual utilization of total labour force during a certain period of time and is often used for the research on China's economic situation and national power.

Persons Employed in Various Units refer to all the persons working in government agencies of various levels, political and party organizations, social organizations, enterprises and institutions, and receiving wages or other forms of payment. They include fully-employed staff and workers, re-employed retirees, teachers in the schools run by the local people, foreigners and Chinese compatriots from Hong Kong, Macao, and Taiwan working in various units, part-time employees, employees of other units working temporarily at current posts, and employees holding the second job, but do not include persons who have left their working units while keeping their labour contract (employment relation) unchanged. This indicator reflects the total number of laborers actually engaged in production or other operations in various units.

Persons Employed in Private Enterprises and Self- Employed Individuals in Urban Areas Persons employed in private enterprises refer to the persons employed in the private enterprises which have been registered at the departments of industrial and commercial administration for which the business operation are situated at a county town (i.e. a town where the county government is located), or at urban areas with administrative hierarchy higher than a county town. The self-employed individuals in urban areas refer to persons who hold the certificates of residence in urban areas or have resided in the urban areas for a long time and have been registered at the departments of industrial and commercial administration and approved to be engaged in individual industrial or commercial business, including self-employed persons as well as helpers and hired labourers who work in individual households.

State-owned Units refer to economic units whose assets are owned by the state, including non-corporation units registered according to Regulation of the People's Republic of China on the Registration of Enterprises and

Corporations, state organs, institutions and social organizations at the central-level and local levels.

Collective-owned Units refer to economic units registered according to Regulation of the People's Republic of China on the Registration of Enterprises and Corporations where the means of production are collectively owned.

Units of Other Types of Ownership refer to units registered with other types of ownership, including cooperative units, joint ownership units, limited liability corporations, share holding corporations, units funded by entrepreneurs from Hong Kong, Macao, and Taiwan, and foreign- funded units.

Employed Staff and Workers refer to persons who work in, and receive wages from their working units, including persons who have their work posts but are temporarily absent from work for reasons of study or on sick, injury or maternal leave and still receive wages from their working units.

Total Wage Bill refers to the total remuneration payment to employed persons in various units during a certain period of time. The calculation of total wage bill is based on the total remuneration payment to employed persons . Therefore, all the wages and salaries and other payments to employed persons are included in the total wage bill regardless of sources, reckoning the cost of production or not, category, listing as items of premium taxation or not, and forms, paying in cash or in kind.

Average Wage refers to the average wage in money terms per person during a certain period of time for employed persons in enterprises, institutions, and government agencies, which reflects the general level of wage income during a certain period of time and is calculated as follows:

$$\text{AverageWage}=\frac{\text{TotalWage Billof Employed Personsat Reference Time}}{\text{Average Number of Persons Employedat Reference Time}}$$

Registered Unemployed Persons in Urban Areas refer to the persons with non-agricultural household registration at certain working ages (16 years old to retirement age), who are capable of working, unemployed and willing to work, and have been registered at the local employment service agencies to apply for a job.

Registered Unemployment Rate in Urban Areas refers to the ratio of the number of the registered unemployed persons to the sum of the number of persons employed in various units (minus the employed rural labour force, re-employed retirees, and Hong Kong, Macao, Taiwan or foreign employees), laid-off staff and workers in urban units, owners of private enterprises in urban areas, owners of self-employed individuals in urban areas, employees of private enterprises in urban areas, employee of self-employed individuals in urban areas, and the registered unemployed persons in urban areas. The formula is as follows:

$$\text{Registered Unemployment rate in urban areas}=\frac{\text{numberof registered urban unemployed persons}}{\text{number of persons employed in urbanunits-employed rurallabour force re-employed retirees - HongKong, Macao,Taiwan or foreign employees + laid-off staff and workers+owners of urban private Enterprises+ owners of urbanself-employed Individuals + employees ofurbanprivate Enterprises+employees of urbanself- employed Individuals+ registered unemployed persons in urbanareas}}\times 100\%$$

5 固定资产投资

INVESTMENT IN FIXED ASSETS

资料整理：令润翠　康　敏
Data management：Ling Runcui Kang Min
数据审核：黄小丹
Data audit：Huang Xiaodan

第五部分　固定资产投资

一、简要说明

本章资料主要包括全社会固定资产投资、城镇投资、房地产开发投资、城乡集体固定资产投资和城乡私人建房投资以及分区县情况，由西安市统计局固定资产投资处提供。

二、主要指标

全社会固定资产投资（亿元）	5903.98	比上年增长	15.0%
#国有经济单位	1916.31	比上年增长	8.2%
集体经济单位	203.35	比上年下降	7.5%
#城镇投资	5682.42	比上年增长	14.1%
#房地产开发	1761.88	比上年增长	10.4%
全市新增固定资产（亿元）	2476.12	比上年增长	32.1%
全市竣工住宅面积（万平方米）	1462.86	比上年增长	74.1%

5　INVESTMENT IN FIXED ASSETS

Ⅰ.Brief Introduction

This chapter consists of primarily the data on fixed asset investment, investment of urban units, real estate development investment, urban and rural area collective fixed asset investment, urban and rural area private housing investment and the classified data of the districts and the counties on real estate development investment, provided by Fixed Asset Investment Division of the Xi'an Bureau of Statistics.

Ⅱ.Major Indicators

		Increase over Preceding Year
Investment Fulfilled In Fixed Assets(100 mil. Yuan)	5903.98	15.0%
State-owned Enterprises	1916.31	8.2%
Collective-owned Enterprises	203.35	-7.5%
Investment of Urban Units	5682.42	14.1%
Real Estate Development	1761.88	10.4%
Investment Fulfilled Newly Increased FixedAssets(100 mil. yuan)	2476.12	32.1%
Total Floor Space of Building Completed(10 000 sq.m)	1462.86	74.1%

5-1 主要年份按城乡分全社会固定资产投资

Total Investment in Fixed Assets in the Whole Country by Rural and Urban Areas in Representative Years

单位：亿元　　　　　　　　　　　　　　　　　　　　　　　　(100 million yuan)

年 份 Year	全社会固定资产投资合计 Total	城镇 Urban Area	房地产开发 Real Estate	农村 Rural Area
1979	4.08	3.01		1.07
1980	6.12	4.48		1.64
1981	5.59	4.56		1.03
1982	9.49	8.02		1.47
1983	10.46	9.17		1.29
1984	12.89	10.69		2.20
1985	18.44	14.44		4.00
1986	22.15	18.54		3.61
1987	27.05	23.15		3.90
1988	29.14	24.43		4.71
1989	28.30	23.85		4.45
1990	26.39	23.10	0.91	3.29
1991	30.76	25.55	2.01	5.21
1992	38.48	32.85	3.32	5.63
1993	75.06	66.65	7.39	8.41
1994	85.57	73.47	12.02	12.10
1995	103.42	88.50	21.65	14.92
1996	114.38	96.98	24.66	17.40
1997	116.90	95.17	24.68	21.73
1998	154.80	138.68	38.21	16.12
1999	197.31	172.64	44.30	24.67
2000	232.37	203.01	51.85	29.36
2001	287.72	256.95	67.42	30.77
2002	338.15	307.24	79.37	30.91
2003	478.10	445.74	124.82	32.36
2004	646.69	612.03	169.67	34.66
2005	835.10	776.33	225.23	58.77
2006	1066.62	971.84	285.76	94.78
2007	1435.33	1340.59	387.33	94.74
2008	1906.36	1786.60	540.26	119.76
2009	2500.13	2367.58	696.34	132.55
2010	3250.56	3104.92	842.34	145.64
2011	3346.26	3207.97	996.81	138.29
2012	4243.43	4107.54	1281.90	135.89
2013	5134.56	4982.25	1595.64	152.31
2014	5903.98	5682.42	1761.88	221.56

5-2 主要年份按经济成分划分全社会固定资产投资

Total Investment in Fixed Assets in the Whole Country by Registion Stares in Representative Years

单位：亿元 (100 million yuan)

年份 Year	合计 Total	国有经济 State-owned	集体经济 Collective-owned	个体经济 Self-employed Individual	其他经济 Others
1985	18.44	13.96	1.36	3.12	
1986	22.15	18.05	0.97	3.13	
1987	27.05	22.18	1.50	3.37	
1988	29.14	23.72	1.86	3.56	
1989	28.30	23.22	1.46	3.62	
1990	26.39	22.21	1.44	2.74	
1991	30.76	24.42	2.26	4.08	
1992	38.48	32.04	1.45	4.99	
1993	75.06	59.66	3.03	6.55	5.82
1994	85.57	64.71	4.14	10.09	6.63
1995	103.42	69.08	9.78	11.13	13.43
1996	114.38	80.66	8.73	12.50	12.49
1997	116.90	77.46	10.21	15.11	14.12
1998	154.80	113.07	7.89	10.59	23.25
1999	197.31	136.50	13.62	16.22	30.97
2000	232.37	159.60	14.65	24.40	33.72
2001	287.72	175.58	14.67	38.57	58.90
2002	338.15	200.06	13.70	44.68	79.71
2003	478.10	264.83	22.33	73.43	117.51
2004	646.69	329.14	40.06	48.95	228.54
2005	835.10	373.70	59.23	79.04	323.13
2006	1066.62	401.14	110.68	107.33	447.47
2007	1435.33	476.78	207.08	183.09	568.38
2008	1906.36	694.89	246.89	50.43	914.15
2009	2500.13	932.91	289.91	97.86	1179.45
2010	3250.56	1348.76	326.44	54.73	1520.63
2011	3346.26	1204.80	258.15	74.64	1808.67
2012	4243.43	1661.22	194.71	82.72	2304.78
2013	5134.56	1770.84	219.88	84.43	3059.41
2014	5903.98	1916.31	203.35	83.28	3701.04

注：集体经济：包括城镇集体和农村集体。

个体经济：包括私营个体投资及城镇工矿区私人建房和农村私人建房。

5-3 主要年份按产业分全市固定资产投资

Total Investment in Fixed Assets in the Whole City by Three Strata of Industry in Representative Years

单位：亿元 (100 million yuan)

年 份 Year	合计 Total	第一产业 Primary Industry	第二产业 Secondary Industry	工业 Industry	第三产业 Tertisry Industry
1979	3.01	0.06	1.24	1.20	1.71
1980	4.48	0.06	2.09	1.99	2.33
1981	4.56	0.11	2.10	1.83	2.35
1982	8.02	0.04	4.07	3.63	3.91
1983	9.17	0.11	4.97	4.41	4.09
1984	10.69	0.19	4.56	3.99	5.94
1985	14.44	0.18	7.22	6.45	7.04
1986	18.54	0.16	8.98	8.37	9.40
1987	23.15	0.19	11.81	11.26	11.15
1988	24.43	0.15	11.95	11.20	12.33
1989	23.85	0.13	11.94	11.50	11.78
1990	23.10	0.25	11.03	10.59	11.82
1991	25.55	0.27	12.48	11.95	12.80
1992	32.85	0.10	15.60	14.73	17.15
1993	66.65	0.07	24.50	22.44	42.08
1994	73.47	0.03	27.04	25.85	46.40
1995	88.50	0.14	28.80	27.71	59.56
1996	96.98	0.13	25.96	24.24	70.89
1997	95.17	0.24	23.65	21.66	71.28
1998	138.68	0.48	35.33	29.86	102.87
1999	172.64	0.94	39.88	36.40	131.82
2000	203.01	0.76	57.21	54.37	145.04
2001	256.95	0.86	63.31	61.28	192.78
2002	307.24	4.29	74.34	68.45	228.61
2003	445.74	3.34	83.25	78.41	359.15
2004	612.03	3.38	97.69	95.67	510.96
2005	776.33	5.26	144.25	140.44	626.82
2006	971.84	10.04	213.43	206.48	748.37
2007	1340.59	10.20	297.53	286.61	1032.86
2008	1786.60	23.75	369.74	356.12	1393.11
2009	2367.58	24.46	458.44	442.70	1884.68
2010	3104.92	39.83	556.10	498.62	2508.99
2011	3207.97	43.10	474.73	390.30	2690.14
2012	4165.99	99.34	671.92	578.17	3394.73
2013	5055.23	73.15	983.09	868.57	3998.99
2014	5824.53	75.15	1261.70	1205.53	4487.68

注：全市固定资产投资不含农户投资。

5-4 全市固定资产投资（2014年）

Total Investment in Fixed Assets in the Whole City （2014）

单位：万元 (10 000 yuan)

指 标	Item	合计 Total	房地产开发 Real Estate
一、本年完成投资（万元）	**Investment Completed This Year(10 000 yuan)**	**58245332**	**17618818**
#住宅	Residential Buildings	14540130	13344332
（一）按登记注册类型分	**Grouped by Registion Status**		
内资	Domestic Funded Enterprises	53446678	16348152
国有	State-owned Enterprises	18317010	716959
集体	Collective-owned Enterprises	1812777	5940
股份合作	Cooperative Enterprises	211997	124194
联营	Joint Ownership Enterprises	113244	
国有联营	State Joint Ownership Enterprises	44626	
集体联营	Collective Joint Ownership Enterprises	8680	
国有与集体联营	Joint State-collective Ownership Enterprises	7722	
其他联营	Other Joint Ownership Enterprises	52216	
有限责任公司	Limited Liability Corporations	18554236	9784447
国有独资公司	State-funded Corporations	801494	635749
其他有限责任公司	Other Limited Liability Corporations	17752742	9148698
股份有限公司	Stock Limited Corporation	880373	393965
私营	Private Enterprises	10514617	5322647
私营独资	Private -funded Enterprises	690420	94234
私营合伙	Private Limited Liability Corporations	124538	
私营有限责任公司	Private Limited Liability Corporations	9403966	5046541
私营股份有限公司	Private Share Holding Corporations	295693	181872
其他	Other	3042424	
港澳台商投资	Enterprises Funded by Hong Kong, Macao and Taiwan	1128681	707312
与港澳台合资经营	Joint-venture Enterprises	363158	53534
与港澳台合作经营	Cooperative Enterprises	19526	19526
港澳台独资	Wholly Funded from Hong Kong,Macao and Taiwan	683442	634252
港澳台投资股份有限公司	Share-holding Corporations Ltd.	57455	
其他港澳台投资		5100	

5-4 续表1 continued 1

单位：万元 (10 000 yuan)

指　标	Item	合计 Total	房地产开发 Real Estate
外商投资	Foreign Owned Enterprises	3669973	563354
中外合资经营	Joint-venture Enterprises	445190	106849
中外合作经营	Cooperation Enterprises	96602	96602
外资企业	Foreign Funded Enterprises	2687477	359903
外商投资股份有限公司	Share-holding Corporations Ltd. With Foreign Funds	376813	
其他外商投资	Foreign Investment	63891	
（二）按隶属关系分	**Grouped by Jurisdiction of Management**		
中央	Central	3694095	791696
省属	Provincial	4017587	719799
市属	Municipal	50533650	16107323
（三）按建设性质分	**Grouped by Type of Construction**		
新建	New Construction	29798357	
扩建	Expansion	1102377	
改建和技术改造	Reconstruction	2605272	
（四）按构成分	**Grouped by Composition**		
1. 建筑工程	Construction Projects	40585016	13022563
2. 安装工程	Installment Projects	4116168	1881597
3. 设备、工器具购置	Purchasing of Equipment and Instruments	8847403	150426
4. 其他费用	Others	4696745	2564232

5-4 续表2 continued 2

单位：万元 (10 000 yuan)

指 标	Item	合计 Total	房地产开发 Real Estate
二、构成(%)	**Proportion (%)**		
（一）按登记注册类型分组	**Grouped by Status**		
#国有经济	State-owned	32.9	7.7
集体经济	Collective-owned	4.6	4.3
（二）按隶属关系分组	**Grouped by Jurisdiction of Management**		
中央	Central	6.3	4.5
省属	Provincial	6.9	4.1
市属	Municipal	86.8	91.4
（三）按建设性质分	**Grouped by Type of Construction**		
新建	New Construction	51.2	
扩建	Expansion	1.9	
改建和技术改造	Reconstruction	4.5	
（四）按构成分	**Grouped by Composition of Funds**		
1. 建筑工程	Construction Projects	69.7	73.9
2. 安装工程	Installation Projects	7.1	10.7
3. 设备、工器具购置	Purchasing of the Equipment and Instruments	15.2	0.9
4. 其他	Others	8.1	14.6
三、本年新增固定资产（万元）	**Newly Increase in Fixed Assets(10 000 yuan)**	24761197	5314364
四、房屋面积（万平方米）	**Floor Space (10 000 sq.m)**		
本年施工房屋面积	Floor Space of Buildings Under Construction This Year	**16249.30**	**12422.10**
住宅	Residential Buildings	10577.51	9727.60
本年竣工房屋面积	Floor Space of Buildings Completed This Year	1856.70	1533.70
住宅	Residential Buildings	1462.86	1307.64
五、竣工房屋价值（万元）	**Value of the Building Completed (10 000 yuan)**	**4427413**	**4427413**
住宅	Residential Buildings	3682519	3682519

5-5 按国民经济行业分全市固定资产投资（2014年）

Investment in Fixed Assets in the Whole City by Sector（2014）

单位：万元 (10 000 yuan)

行 业	Sector	2014
本年完成固定资产投资（万元）	**Grouped by Sector (10 000 yuan)**	**58245332**
（一）农、林、牧、渔业	Agriculture,Forestry,Animal Husbandry and Fishery	860369
（二）采矿业	Mining	15000
（三）制造业	Manufacturing	10123892
农副食品加工业	Processing of Food from Agricultural Products	117120
食品制造业	Manufacture of Foods	179636
酒、饮料和精制茶制造业	Wine, soft drinks and refined tea industry	104740
烟草制品业	Tobacco Processing	34882
纺织业	Textile Industry	49799
纺织服装、服饰业	Textile, apparel industry	14219
皮革、毛皮、羽毛及其制品和制鞋业	Leather, Fur, Feather (eiderdown) and Their Products Industry	5500
木材加工和木、竹、藤、棕、草制品业	Timber Processing,Bamboo,Cane,Palm Fiber and Straw Products	18300
家具制造业	Furniture Manufacturing	89435
造纸及纸制品业	Papermaking and Paper products	40552
印刷和记录媒介复制业	Printing,Record Medium Reproduction	95658
文教、工美、体育和娱乐用品制造业	Culture, education, Craft art, sports and entertainment goods manufacturing industry	12500
石油加工、炼焦和核燃料加工业	Petroleum Refining, Ccoke Making and Nuclear Fuel Processing Industry	304991
化学原料和化学制品制造业	Raw Chemical Materials and Chemical Products	305323
医药制造业	Medical and Pharmaceutical Products	261832
化学纤维制造业	Chemical Fiber	5000
橡胶和塑料制品业	Rubber and plastic products industry	44522
非金属矿物制品业	Nonmetal Mineral Products	249402
黑色金属冶炼和压延加工业	Smelting and Pressing of Ferrous Metals	145575
有色金属冶炼和压延加工业	Smelting and Pressing of Nonferrou Metals	235163
金属制品业	Metal Products	381029

5-5 续表1 continued 1

单位：万元 (10 000 yuan)

行 业	Sector	2014
通用设备制造业	General Equipment Manufacturing Industry	803773
专用设备制造业	Special Purpose Equipment	705086
汽车制造业	Automotive Manufacturing	678300
铁路、船舶、航空航天和其他运输设备制造业	Railroad, Marine, Aerospace and other Transportation Equipment Manufacturing	1228508
电气机械和器材制造业	Electric Equipment and Machinery	925130
计算机、通信和其他电子设备制造业	Communication Equipment, Computer and Other Electronic Equipment Manufacturing Industry	2486728
仪器仪表制造业	Instrument Manufacturing Industry	524334
其他制造业	Other Manufacturing	72655
废弃资源综合利用	Comprehensive Utilization of waste Resources	
金属制品、机械和设备修理业	Metal Products, Machinery and Equipment Repair Industry	4200
（四）电力、燃气及水的生产供应业	Production & Supply of Electricity,Gas & Water	1920639
（五）建筑业	Construction	561710
（六）批发和零售业	Wholesale and Retail Trades	1848277
（七）交通运输、仓储和邮政业	Transport, Storage and Post	3361532
（八）住宿和餐饮业	Hotels and Catering Services	906183
（九）信息传输、软件和信息技术服务业	Information Transmission,Computer Service and Software	684737
（十）金融业	Financial Intermediation	230185
（十一）房地产业	Real Estate	27858519
（十二） 租赁和商务服务业	Leasing and Business Services	1193581
（十三）科学研究和技术服务业	Scientific Research,Technical Service and Geologic Prospecting	1814791
（十四）水利、环境和公共设施管理业	Management of Water Conservancy, Environment and Public Facilities	4118303
（十五）居民服务、修理和其他服务业	Services to Households, repairs and other services	223700
（十六）教育	Education	836501
（十七）卫生和社会工作	Health and social work	963977
（十八）文化、体育和娱乐业	Culture, Sports and Entertainment	357129
（十九）公共管理、社会保障和社会组织	Public administration, social security and social organizations	366307
（二十）国际组织	International Organizations	

5-6 主要年份按资金来源及建设性质分全市固定资产投资

Total Investment in Fixed Assets in the Whole City by Sources of Funds and Type of Construction in Representative Years

单位：万元 (10 000 yuan)

指标	Item	1995	2001	2002	2003	2004	2005	2006
一. 投资总额(万元)	**Total Investment (10 000 yuan)**	**884994**	**2569496**	**3072442**	**4457381**	**6120324**	**7763283**	**9718418**
（一）按资金来源分	Grouped by Funds Source							
1. 国家预算内投资	State Budgetary Funds	69185	256403	355960	365263	436496	728885	677145
2. 国内贷款	Domestic Loans	216565	672379	666146	1219234	1565246	1257175	1631689
3. 债券	Bonds	873	6753	766	3278			
4. 利用外资	Utilization of Foreign Funds	80792	54907	15192	47509	47401	40583	165390
5. 自筹资金	Self-raising Funds	385047	1121502	1392915	1733132	2629720	4001700	5538393
6. 其他资金	Others	132532	457552	641463	1088965	1441461	1734940	1705801
（二）按构成分	Grouped by Composition of Funds							
1. 建筑安装工程	Construction and Installation Projects	527220	1698777	2119151	3067309	4127677	5086664	6486233
2. 设备、工器具购置	Purchasing of Equipment and Instruments	233730	452602	552251	577240	708988	1021079	1409589
3. 其它费用	Others	124044	418117	401040	812832	1283659	1655540	1822596
（三）按建设性质分	Grouped by Type of Construction							
#新建	New Construction	210926	723957	874392	1294032	1874116	2907551	3511432
扩建	Expansion	180210	581138	868603	1102914	1169537	1208430	1101740
改建	Reconstruction	157457	344879	343184	447944	670229	782953	1099304
二. 房屋施工面积（万平方米）	**Floor Space Under Construction （10 000sq.m）**	**1070.58**	**1767.13**	**2396.89**	**2716.18**	**3177.36**	**4030.38**	**4589.39**

5-6 续表1 continued 1

单位：万元　　(10 000 yuan)

指标	Item	2007	2008	2009	2010	2011	2012	2013	2014
一. 投资总额(万元)	**Total Investment (10 000 yuan)**	**13405920**	**17865977**	**23675759**	**31049184**	**32079666**	**41659924**	**50552171**	**58245332**
(一) 按资金来源分	Grouped by Funds Source								
1. 国家预算内投资	State Budgetary Funds	670592	1555809	2562756	1649563	1480412	1851860	1439721	1622413
2. 国内贷款	Domestic Loans	1619218	2162957	3301919	4288663	3546561	4023452	4146647	5592450
3. 债券	Bonds							11356	
4. 利用外资	Utilization of Foreign Funds	183422	261325	144124	126802	89047	135147	182153	789982
5. 自筹资金	Self-raising Funds	8565573	12771844	15776565	18279153	19400468	28680236	36446760	41430249
6. 其他资金	Others	2367115	1114042	1890395	6705003	7563178	6969229	8325534	8810238
(二) 按构成分	Grouped by Composition of Funds								
1. 建筑安装工程	Construction and Installation Projects	9165668	12864657	16337466	21690205	25553161	34268466	41672647	44701184
2. 设备、工器具购置	Purchasing of Equipment and Instruments	1858720	2024631	2619783	3094336	1911180	3311375	4861642	8847403
3. 其它费用	Others	2381532	2976689	4718510	6264643	4615325	4080083	4017882	4696745
(三) 按建设性质分	Grouped by Type of Construction								
#新建	New Construction	5123975	6356716	8567540	14292899	16077747	21651399	26063028	29798357
扩建	Expansion	994841	2118013	3054929	2649749	1956527	1685922	1232264	1102377
改建	Reconstruction	1548130	1921664	2738799	2620997	2155112	2810903	3183300	2605272
二. 房屋施工面积（万平方米）	**Floor Space Under Construction (10 000sq.m)**	**5759.28**	**6570.94**	**9571.25**	**11166.19**	**12353.11**	**14093.91**	**14749.84**	**16249.30**

5-7 主要年份市属固定资产投资

Investment In Fixed Assets of Municipal Units in Representative Years

单位：万元 (10 000 yuan)

指 标	Item	1995	2000	2001	2002	2003	2004	2005	2006
一、投资总额	**Total Investment**	**432451**	**1263023**	**1539717**	**1848833**	**2978747**	**4355271**	**5788693**	**7835681**
#房地产开发	Real Estate	171291	473787	566557	702233	1114809	1492693	2062940	2641871
按经济类型分	Grouped by Type of Enterprises								
国有经济	State-owned Enterprises	258545	890546	894700	1006245	1586057	1884624	2198836	2591184
集体经济	Collective-owned Enterprises	5720	52893	62895	63877	142849	257226	258327	363909
其他经济	Others	168186	319584	582122	778711	1249841	2213421	3331530	4880588
二、新增固定资产	**Newly Increased Fixed Assets**	**273324**	**953173**	**1159980**	**1295389**	**1812099**	**1962795**	**3011104**	**3495179**
三、房屋竣工面积	**Floor Space of the Building**	**202.52**	**509.48**	**535.98**	**537.44**	**631.89**	**606.23**	**767.70**	**914.80**
（万平方米）	**Completed(10 000sq.m)**								
#住宅	Residential Buildings	143.30	373.51	396.01	331.45	387.82	388.79	436.43	432.43

5-7 续表1 continued 1

单位：万元 (10 000 yuan)

指 标	Item	2007	2008	2009	2010	2011	2012	2013	2014
一、投资总额	**Total Investment**	**10555849**	**14648360**	**19063075**	**25474854**	**26820029**	**35875223**	**44187825**	**50533650**
#房地产开发	Real Estate	3515719	4938202	6575526	8020893	9001953	11655613	14410956	16107323
按经济类型分	Grouped by Type of Enterprises								
国有经济	State-owned Enterprises	2972840	4480627	6527566	9306901	8750285	12264895	12847731	12835067
集体经济	Collective-owned Enterprises	1366567	1646111	1614290	2253851	1897980	1932578	2148977	1927394
其他经济	Others	6216442	8521622	10921219	13914102	16171764	21677750	29191117	35771189
二、新增固定资产	**Newly Increased Fixed Assets**	**5279938**	**6488364**	**8380033**	**10423906**	**10663882**	**15376910**	**16019776**	**21603094**
三、房屋竣工面积	**Floor Space of the Building**	**1343.88**	**987.05**	**1359.46**	**668.49**	**1002.82**	**1450.29**	**975.03**	**1591.28**
（万平方米）	**Completed(10 000sq.m)**								
#住宅	Residential Buildings	734.05	602.69	727.41	448.46	531.38	1069.61	760.87	1262.20

5-8 市属固定资产投资（2014年）

Investment in Fixed Assets of Municipal Units（2014）

单位：万元 (10 000 yuan)

指　标	Item	城镇 Urban Area	房地产开发 Real Estate
一、本年完成投资	**Investment Completed This Year**	**50533650**	**16107323**
#住宅	Residential Buildings	13055424	12160503
（一）按登记注册类型分	**Grouped by Registion Status**		
内资	Domestic Funded Enterprises	45737900	14836657
国有	State-owned Enterprises	12283743	563443
集体	Collective-owned Enterprises	1725008	5940
股份合作	Cooperative Enterprises	193706	114006
联营	Joint Ownership Enterprises	113244	
国有联营	State Joint Ownership Enterprises	44626	
集体联营	Collective Joint Ownership Enterprises	8680	
国有与集体联营	Joint State-collective Ownership Enterprises	7722	
其他联营	Other Joint Ownership Enterprises	52216	
有限责任公司	Limited Liability Corporations	17045366	8442193
国有独资公司	State-funded Corporations	506698	386601
其他有限责任公司	Other Limited Liability Corporations	16538668	8055592
股份有限公司	Stock Limited Corporation	859888	388428
私营	Private Enterprises	10514617	5322647
私营独资	Private -funded Enterprises	690420	94234
私营合伙	Private Limited Liability Corporations	124538	
私营有限责任公司	Private Limited Liability Corporations	9403966	5046541
私营股份有限公司	Private Share Holding Corporations	295693	181872
其他	Other	3002328	
港澳台商投资	Enterprises Funded by Hong Kong, Macao and Taiwan	1128681	707312
与港澳台合资经营	Joint-venture Enterprises	363158	53534
与港澳台合作经营	Cooperative Enterprises	19526	19526
港澳台独资	Wholly Funded from Hong Kong,Macao and Taiwan	683442	634252
港澳台投资股份有限公司	Share-holding Corporations Ltd.	57455	
其他港澳台投资	Investment From Hongkong,Macao,Taiwan	5100	
外商投资	Foreign Owned Enterprises	3667069	563354
中外合资经营	Joint-venture Enterprises	442286	106849
中外合作经营	Cooperation Enterprises	96602	96602
外资企业	Foreign Funded Enterprises	2687477	359903

5-8 续表1 continued 1

单位：万元 (10 000 yuan)

指 标	Item	城镇 Urban Area	房地产开发 Real Estate
外商投资股份有限公司	Share-holding Corporations Ltd. With Foreign Funds	376813	
其他外商投资	Foreign Investment	63891	
（二）按建设性质分	**Grouped by Type of Construction**		
新建	New Construction	26670408	
扩建	Expansion	1082527	
改建和技术改造	Reconstruction	2247377	
（三）按构成分	**Grouped by Composition**		
建筑工程	Construction Projects	36624888	12022690
安装工程	Installment Projects	3468111	1745807
设备、工器具购置	Purchasing of Equipment and Instruments	6258493	144416
其他费用	Others	4182158	2194410
二、本年完成投资额构成(%)	**the Constitution of Compeleted Investment this year (%)**		
（一）按登记注册类型分组	**Grouped by Status**		
# 国有经济	State-owned	25.4	5.9
集体经济	Collective-owned	4.6	3.1
（二）按建设性质分	**Grouped by Type of Construction**		
新建	New Construction	52.8	
扩建	Expansion	2.1	
改建和技术改造	Reconstruction	4.4	
（三）按构成分	**Grouped by Composition of Funds**		
建筑工程	Construction Projects	72.5	74.6
安装工程	Installation Projects	6.9	10.8
设备、工器具购置	Purchasing of the Equipment and Instruments	12.4	0.9
其他	Others	8.3	13.6
三、本年新增固定资产（万元）	**Newly Increase in Fixed Assets**	**21603094**	**4909588**
四、房屋面积（万平方米）	**Floor Space (10 000 sq.m)**		
本年施工房屋面积	Floor Space of Buildings Under Construction This Year	14740.51	11398.35
#住宅	Residential Buildings	9592.26	8898.89
本年竣工房屋面积	Floor Space of Buildings Completed This Year	1591.28	1380.97
#住宅	Residential Buildings	1262.2	1175.02
五、竣工房屋价值（万元）	**Value of the Building Completed**	**4033261**	**4033261**
#住宅	Residential Buildings	3352644	3352644

5-9 按国民经济行业分市属固定资产投资（2014年）

Investment in Fixed Assets of Municipal Units by Sector （2014）

单位：万元 （10 000 yuan)

行 业	Sector	2014
本年完成固定资产投资	**Grouped by Sector**	**50533650**
（一）农、林、牧、渔业	Agriculture,Forestry,Animal Husbandry and Fishery	850158
（二）采矿业	Mining	15000
（三）制造业	Manufacturing	8956017
农副食品加工业	Processing of Food from Agricultural Products	117120
食品制造业	Manufacture of Foods	179636
酒、饮料和精制茶制造业	Wine, soft drinks and refined tea industry	104740
烟草制品业	Tobacco Processing	34882
纺织业	Textile Industry	49799
纺织服装、服饰业	Textile, apparel industry	14219
皮革、毛皮、羽毛及其制品和制鞋业	Leather, Fur, Feather (eiderdown) and Their Products Industry	5500
木材加工和木、竹、藤、棕、草制品业	Timber Processing,Bamboo,Cane,Palm Fiber and Straw Products	18300
家具制造业	Furniture Manufacturing	89435
造纸及纸制品业	Papermaking and Paper products	40552
印刷和记录媒介复制业	Printing,Record Medium Reproduction	32675
文教、工美、体育和娱乐用品制造业	Culture, education, Craft art, sports and entertainment goods manufacturing industry	12500
石油加工、炼焦和核燃料加工业	Petroleum Refining, Ccoke Making and Nuclear Fuel Processing Industry	298623
化学原料和化学制品制造业	Raw Chemical Materials and Chemical Products	269941
医药制造业	Medical and Pharmaceutical Products	258928
化学纤维制造业	Chemical Fiber	5000
橡胶和塑料制品业	Rubber and plastic products industry	44522
非金属矿物制品业	Nonmetal Mineral Products	239602
黑色金属冶炼和压延加工业	Smelting and Pressing of Ferrous Metals	145575
有色金属冶炼和压延加工业	Smelting and Pressing of Nonferrou Metals	235163
金属制品业	Metal Products	356329

5-9 续表1 continued 1

行　业	Sector	2014
通用设备制造业	General Equipment Manufacturing Industry	673822
专用设备制造业	Special Purpose Equipment	588158
汽车制造业	Automotive Manufacturing	663454
铁路、船舶、航空航天和其他运输设备制造业	Railroad, Marine, Aerospace and other Transportation Equipment Manufacturing	686660
电气机械和器材制造业	Electric Equipment and Machinery	885919
计算机、通信和其他电子设备制造业	Communication Equipment, Computer and Other Electronic Equipment Manufacturing Industry	2350876
仪器仪表制造业	Instrument Manufacturing Industry	477232
其他制造业	Other Manufacturing	72655
废弃资源综合利用	Comprehensive Utilization of waste Resources	
金属制品、机械和设备修理业	Metal Products, Machinery and Equipment Repair Industry	4200
（四）电力、燃气及水的生产供应业	Production & Supply of Electricity,Gas & Water	886002
（五）建筑业	Construction	260499
（六）批发和零售业	Wholesale and Retail Trades	1757316
（七）交通运输、仓储和邮政业	Transport, Storage and Post	2565117
（八）住宿和餐饮业	Hotels and Catering Services	884063
（九）信息传输、软件和信息技术服务业	Information Transmission,Computer Service and Software	446620
（十）金融业	Financial Intermediation	60933
（十一）房地产业	Real Estate	25615625
（十二） 租赁和商务服务业	Leasing and Business Services	1124072
（十三）科学研究和技术服务业	Scientific Research,Technical Service and Geologic Prospecting	1251498
（十四）水利、环境和公共设施管理业	Management of Water Conservancy, Environment and Public Facilities	3836602
（十五）居民服务、修理和其他服务业	Services to Households, repairs and other services	208000
（十六）教育	Education	601153
（十七）卫生和社会工作	Health and social work	534774
（十八）文化、体育和娱乐业	Culture, Sports and Entertainment	345579
（十九）公共管理、社会保障和社会组织	Public administration, social security and social organizations	334622
（二十）国际组织	International Organizations	

5-10 按资金来源及建设性质分市属固定资产投资（2014年）

Investment in Fixed Assets of Municipal Units by Sources of Funds and Type of Construction（2014）

单位：万元 (10 000 yuan)

指　标	Item	2014
投资总额	**Total Investment**	**50533650**
一、按资金来源分	**Grouped by Funds Sources**	
1. 国家预算内资金	State Budgetary Funds	1543692
2. 国内贷款	Domestic Loans	4385490
3. 债券	Bonds	
4. 利用外资	Utilization of Foreign Funds	782675
5. 自筹资金	Self-raising Funds	35926246
6. 其他资金	Others	7895547
二、按建设性质分	**Grouped by Type of Construction**	
#新建	New Construction	26670408
扩建	Expansion	1082527
改建	Reconstruction	2247377
三、按构成分	**Grouped by Composition of Funds**	
1. 建筑工程	Construction Project	36624888
2. 安装工程	Installation Projects	3468111
3. 设备、工器具购置	Purchasing of Equipment and Instruments	6258493
4. 其他费用	Others	4182158
四、房屋施工面积（万平方米）	**Floor Space of Buildings Under Construction (10 000 sq.m)**	**14742**

5-11 全市固定资产投资资金来源（2014年）

Source of Funds for Total Fixed Assets Investment of Whole City（2014）

单位：万元 (10 000 yuan)

指 标	Item	城镇 Urban Area	房地产开发 Real Estate
一、本年资金来源合计	**Total of Sources of Funds This Year**	**68844659**	**25143005**
1. 上年末结余资金	Balance of Last Year	9269553	5409624
2. 本年资金来源小计	Subtotal Funds This Year	59575106	19733381
(1) 国家预算资金	State Budgetary Funds	1659454	
(2) 国内贷款	Domestic Loans	5720129	3155906
(3) 债券	Bonds		
(4) 利用外资	Utilization of Foreign Funds	808018	
(5) 自筹资金	Self-raising Funds	42376125	8867486
(6) 其他资金来源	Others	9011380	7709989
二、本年各项应付款合计	**Total Sums of Money to be Paid This Year**	**5155927**	**4351954**

5-12 全市固定资产投资效果（2014年）

Achievements of Total Assets Investment of Whole City（2014）

指 标	Item	城镇 Urban Area	房地产开发 Real Estate
一、建设项目投产率（%）	**Rate of Projects Put Into use(%)**	**62.5**	
施工项目个数（个）	Number of Constructing Projects (unit)	2225	
本年投产项目个数（个）	Number of Projects Put into Use (unit)	1390	
二、固定资产交付使用率（%）	**Rate of Fixed Assets Put into Use(%)**	**42.5**	**30.2**
本年新增固定资产（亿元）	Newly Increased Fixed Assets This Year(100 million yuan)	2476.12	531.44
本年完成投资（亿元）	Investment Completed This Year (100 million yuan)	5824.53	1761.88
三、建设周期（年）	**Construction Period (year)**	**3.3**	**5.4**
计划总投资（亿元）	Total Planned Investment(100 million yuan)	19469.41	9464.21
本年完成投资（亿元）	Investment Completed This Year (100 million yuan)	5824.53	1761.88
四、房屋建筑面积竣工率（%）	**Completion Rate of Buildings (%)**	**11.4**	**12.3**
本年施工房屋面积（万平方米）	Floor Space of the Constructing Buildings This Year (10 000 sq.m)	16249.3	12422.1
本年竣工房屋面积（万平方米）	Floor Space of the Buildings Completed This Year (10 000 sq.m)	1856.7	1533.7

5-13 分区县、开发区全社会固定资产投资额（2014年）

Investment Fulfilled in Fixed Assets by Region and Development Zone（2014）

单位：亿元 (100 million yuan)

区县、开发区	Region	全社会固定资产投资 Investment Fulfilled In Fixed Assets	城镇投资 Urban Area	房地产 Real Estate	农村集体 Rural Collective-owned Units	农村私人建房 Private Housing in Country
区县	**Region**	**5903.98**	**5682.42**	**1761.88**	**142.11**	**79.45**
新城区	Xincheng	400.27	400.27	94.67		
碑林区	Beilin	543.43	543.43	102.34		
莲湖区	Lianhu	608.82	608.82	175.47		
灞桥区	Baqiao	413.68	404.77	147.58	3.13	5.78
未央区	Weiyang	915.51	904.12	461.86	7.55	3.84
雁塔区	Yanta	969.65	967.41	580.51		2.24
阎良区	Yanliang	261.23	250.21	19.10	7.72	3.30
临潼区	Lintong	231.56	219.61	16.31	0.79	11.17
长安区	Chang'an	678.22	655.51	93.48	5.95	16.76
蓝田县	Lantian	164.28	76.74	5.01	77.06	10.48
周至县	Zhouzhi	148.80	103.00	10.12	33.42	12.38
户　县	Huxian	152.69	135.94	16.82	6.49	10.26
高陵县	Gaoling	415.83	412.60	38.60		3.23
开发区	**Development Zones**	**2667.29**	**2667.29**	**962.36**		
高新区	GaoXin	660.77	660.77	112.64		
经开区	JingKai	597.50	597.50	200.74		
曲江新区	Qujiang	566.35	566.35	339.86		
浐灞生态区	Chanba Eco-District	321.46	321.46	187.63		
航空基地	Aviation Industry Base	88.35	88.35	12.52		
航天基地	Aerospace Base	122.80	122.80	51.38		
国际港务区	International Trade&Logistic Park	120.81	120.81	12.31		
沣东新城	FengDongXinCheng	189.24	189.24	45.28		

5-14 主要年份全市新增固定资产及房屋竣工面积

Value of Newly Added Fixed Assets and Floor Spaces Completed of Municipal Units in Representative Years

年 份 Year	新增固定资产（亿元） Newly Increased Fixed Assets (100 million yuan)	房屋竣工面积（万平方米） Floor Space of Buildings Completed (10 000sq.m)	住宅 Residential Buildings
1978	4.96	99.10	40.76
1980	4.64	164.87	100.15
1985	8.62	222.42	129.07
1986	13.40	272.95	155.91
1987	16.72	241.48	119.21
1988	16.82	211.83	102.43
1989	16.58	178.45	87.77
1990	20.30	211.88	111.05
1991	17.86	185.34	95.84
1992	22.33	204.75	112.66
1993	41.70	257.90	144.88
1994	55.37	282.91	184.49
1995	62.58	357.67	252.84
1996	60.04	332.18	249.52
1997	62.88	374.46	286.54
1998	80.23	382.80	275.63
1999	118.92	681.04	550.83
2000	150.16	714.83	544.95
2001	167.77	692.56	502.26
2002	198.97	773.28	486.13
2003	279.44	917.96	578.06
2004	261.95	776.59	498.33
2005	409.72	1131.41	598.61
2006	453.01	1199.45	583.10
2007	667.97	1672.16	929.50
2008	725.17	1113.31	693.42
2009	1013.44	1529.13	822.62
2010	1193.05	775.16	521.08
2011	1297.35	1231.91	861.44
2012	1765.05	1626.25	1189.04
2013	1875.00	1118.69	840.02
2014	2476.12	1856.70	1462.86

5-15 全市按国民经济行业分房屋建筑面积（2014年）

单位：平方米 (sq.m)

行业	Sector	本年施工房屋面积 Floor Space of Buildings Under Construction This Year	住宅 Residential Residence
总　计	**Total**	**162493028**	**105775132**
（一）农、林、牧、渔业	Agriculture, Forestry, Animal Husbandry and Fishery	28750	2210
（二）采矿业	Mining		
（三）制造业	Manufacturing	10657526	40484
（四）电力、燃气及水的生产供应业	Generation and Supply of Electricity, Production and Supply of Gas and Water	27308	615
（五）建筑业	Construction		
（六）批发和零售业	Wholesale and Retail Trades	1216043	25851
（七）交通运输、仓储和邮政业	Transportation, Storage and Post	268964	15850
（八）住宿和餐饮业	Hotels and Catering Services	366079	
（九）信息传输、软件和信息技术服务业	Information Transmission, Computer Service and Software	753008	
（十）金融业	Financial Intermediation	232000	
（十一）房地产业	Real Estate	143560414	105248712
（十二） 租赁和商务服务业	Leasing and Business Services	929479	
（十三）科学研究和技术服务业	Scientific Research and Technical Service	680151	
（十四）水利、环境和公共设施管理业	Management of Water Conservancy, Environment and Public Facilities	162666	28276
（十五）居民服务、修理和其他服务业	Services to Households, repairs and other services	40900	
（十六）教育	Education	2182730	413134
（十七）卫生和社会工作	Health and social work	1073658	
（十八）文化、体育和娱乐业	Culture, Sports and Entertainment	129831	
（十九）公共管理、社会保障和社会组织	Public administration, social security and social organizations	183521	
（二十）国际组织	International Organizations		

Floors Space of Buildings Construction of Municipal Units by Sector（2014）

单位：平方米 (sq.m)

本年竣工房屋面积 Floor Space of Buildings Completed This Year	住宅 Residential Residence	本年竣工房屋价值（万元） Value of Buildings Completed (10 000 yuan)	住宅 Residential Residence
18566951	**14628631**	**4427413**	**3682519**
22600	2060		
510458	27484		
60	15		
317263			
18290	15850		
161600			
17100775	14574922	4427413	3682519
24000			
8300	8300		
223155			
148680			
22000			
9770			

5-16 分区县、开发区新增固定资产及房屋施工、竣工面积（2014年）

区县、开发区	Region	新增固定资产（亿元）Increased Fixed Assets (100 million yuan)	本年施工房屋面积（万平方米）Floor Space of Buildings Under Construction (10 000sq.m)	住宅 Residenctial Buildings
区县	**Region**	**2426.23**	**16249.30**	**10577.51**
新城区	Xincheng	173.47	627.77	475.20
碑林区	Beilin	408.57	1506.86	1152.58
莲湖区	Lianhu	290.85	1423.38	1168.21
灞桥区	Baqiao	94.80	1161.39	832.14
未央区	Weiyang	325.81	4028.87	2735.57
雁塔区	Yanta	280.85	3568.12	2399.84
阎良区	Yanliang	121.96	313.85	141.05
临潼区	Lintong	131.32	336.90	120.16
长安区	Chang'an	155.51	1394.22	773.84
蓝田县	Lantian	157.75	81.20	69.99
周至县	Zhouzhi	76.60	160.81	115.38
户　县	Huxian	49.81	412.27	160.56
高陵县	Gaoling	158.91	1233.68	432.97
开发区	**Development Zones**	**621.02**	**6308.85**	**3796.44**
高新区	GaoXin	99.62	1207.67	503.49
经开区	JingKai	156.73	1082.36	771.97
曲江新区	Qujiang	201.36	1512.58	1129.75
浐灞生态区	Chanba Eco-District	60.58	1173.54	679.62
航空基地	Aviation Industry Base	4.27	78.61	38.79
航天基地	Aerospace Base	66.90	776.41	404.04
国际港务区	International Trade&Logistic Park	13.23	73.51	71.30
沣东新城	FengDong Xincheng	18.32	404.17	197.48

Newly Added Fixed Assets and Floor Space of Constructing and Completed Buildings by Region and Development Zone（2014）

本年竣工房屋面积（万平方米） Floor Space of Buildings Completed(10 000 sq.m)	住 宅 Residenctial Buildings	本年竣工房屋价值（亿元） Value of Buildings Completed (100 million yuan)	住宅 Residenctial Buildings	商品房销售面积（万平方米） Floor Space of Houses Sales(sq.m) Houses(10 000sq.m)	商品房销售额（亿元） Sales Income of Commercial Houses(100 million yuan)
1856.70	**1462.86**	**442.74**	**368.25**	**1707.71**	**1100.71**
56.87	53.97	15.21	14.82	25.21	16.46
508.77	426.02	118.71	98.92	233.07	152.14
143.20	95.75	30.12	22.53	123.03	84.21
98.58	84.81	38.99	32.10	213.22	123.19
503.16	416.51	103.88	89.12	412.13	254.33
207.19	166.17	58.56	47.52	446.59	336.55
36.14	33.83	11.03	10.34	16.67	7.21
81.08	17.71			15.99	6.97
63.85	51.47	26.67	22.31	108.90	71.58
0.83	0.83			9.40	3.54
16.33	4.87	7.10	1.26	11.72	7.01
72.98	50.30	17.53	16.23	15.11	7.58
67.71	60.63	14.94	13.09	76.67	29.93
376.66	**316.00**	**128.14**	**106.97**	**821.99**	**567.26**
49.55	40.97	22.68	18.17	95.12	77.73
109.89	94.07	27.88	22.68	218.93	128.12
117.66	98.56	37.41	31.27	220.71	179.96
51.16	43.08	22.56	19.54	203.25	131.09
3.40	3.40	1.30	1.30	3.68	1.45
45.00	35.93	16.31	14.00	51.53	29.04
				2.24	1.94
				26.53	17.92

5-17 全市按行业分施工项目（2014年）

行　业	Sector	本年新增固定资产（万元）Increased Fixed Assets This Year(10 000 yuan)
总计	**Total**	**24761197**
（一）农、林、牧、渔业	Agriculture, Forestry, Animal Husbandry and Fishery	629720
（二）采矿业	Mining	24000
（三）制造业	Manufacturing	3254133
（四）电力、燃气及水的生产供应业	Generation and Supply of Electricity, Production and Supply of Gas and Water	711276
（五）建筑业	Construction	512380
（六）批发和零售业	Wholesale and Retail Trades	964681
（七）交通运输、仓储和邮政业	Transportation, Storage and Post	777302
（八）住宿和餐饮业	Hotels and Catering Services	659033
（九）信息传输、软件和信息技术服务业	Information Transmission, Computer Service and Software	404787
（十）金融业	Financial Intermediation	14691
（十一）房地产业	Real Estate	10829257
（十二） 租赁和商务服务业	Leasing and Business Services	565659
（十三）科学研究和技术服务业	Scientific Research and Technical Service	669359
（十四）水利、环境和公共设施管理业	Management of Water Conservancy, Environment and Public Facilities	2793740
（十五）居民服务、修理和其他服务业	Services to Households, repairs and other services	100469
（十六）教育	Education	586032
（十七）卫生和社会工作	Health and social work	602067
（十八）文化、体育和娱乐业	Culture, Sports and Entertainment	185385
（十九）公共管理、社会保障和社会组织	Public administration, social security and social organizations	477226
（二十）国际组织	International Organizations	

Construction Project Grouped by Sector in the Whole City（2014）

施工项目个数（个） Number of Constructing Projects (unit)	本年新开工 Newly Started This Year	本年投产项目个数（个） Projects put into Use (unit)
2225	**1270**	**1390**
170	138	142
2	1	1
496	270	273
80	52	55
9	8	9
143	96	91
130	77	76
83	61	69
41	21	19
11	2	4
351	124	174
43	26	25
44	25	22
386	239	267
31	23	27
102	50	65
30	16	18
38	22	25
35	19	28

5-18 主要年份房地产开发投资主要指标

单位：万平方米

指　标	Item	1997	1998	1999	2000
本年完成投资额（亿元）	Investment Completed This Year(100 million yuan)	24.68	38.21	44.30	51.85
本年房屋施工面积	Floor Space of Buildings Under Construction This Year	451.47	678.87	793.46	763.18
#住宅	Residential Buildings	331.16	552.37	649.53	619.85
本年房屋竣工面积	Floor Space of Buildings Completed This Year	135.62	156.17	377.79	321.10
#住宅	Residential Buildings	120.33	133.33	352.28	295.55
本年房屋竣工价值（亿元）	Value of Floor Space of Buildings Completed(100million yuan)	11.96	14.36	38.22	26.94
#住宅	Residential Buildings	9.63	11.00	33.02	22.97
商品房销售面积	Floor Space of Commercialized Buildings sold	78.45	117.11	296.97	212.92
#住宅	Residential Buildings	72.69	108.61	284.95	200.77
商品房销售额（亿元）	Total Sales of Commercialized Buildings(100 million yuan)	12.81	17.74	35.19	32.52
#住宅	Residential Buildings	11.39	15.46	32.35	29.46
商品房预售面积	Floor Space of Commercialized Buildings Presold	26.35	252.02	30.25	253.03
#住宅	Residential Buildings	23.27	246.77	27.34	253.03
商品房空置面积	Floor Space of Vacant Commercialized Buildings	58.71	32.52	62.38	36.41
#住宅	Residential Buildings	50.26	22.81	52.32	24.02
商品房出租面积	Floor Space of Commercialized Buildings Recenting	25.69	1.04	1.88	1.17
#住宅	Residential Buildings	22.87	0.01	0.15	0.02
本年新增固定资产（亿元）	Newly Increased Fixed Assets This Year(100 million yuan)	14.36	19.93	43.10	38.38

Main Indicators of Investment in Real Estate Development in Representative Years

(10 000 sq.m)

2001	2002	2003	2004	2005	2006	2007	2008	2009	2010	2011	2012	2013	2014
67.42	79.37	124.82	169.67	225.23	285.76	387.33	540.26	696.34	842.34	996.81	1281.90	1595.64	1761.88
743.78	1172.58	1343.12	1633.68	2174.29	2383.56	2915.95	3632.87	5708.63	6697.39	8247.69	9947.89	10454.27	12422.10
580.43	964.68	943.61	1204.01	1783.36	1890.27	2376.82	3079.13	4901.59	5777.71	7108.27	8294.92	8461.71	9727.60
316.24	329.71	339.67	380.84	361.62	399.64	483.30	443.96	542.81	463.65	631.03	1063.70	795.35	1533.70
269.61	290.30	289.56	308.06	316.52	342.15	422.47	412.46	453.49	412.44	564.59	903.82	663.20	1307.64
37.20	36.93	54.73	73.75	80.58	82.02	101.13	106.50	168.08	145.62	213.29	310.57	279.63	442.74
28.62	30.46	44.01	55.58	68.11	65.80	77.13	96.02	137.42	128.69	185.31	260.04	222.64	368.25
225.35	252.90	252.74	305.47	497.34	621.50	833.92	760.72	1256.02	1587.81	1778.02	1538.91	1662.75	1707.71
192.20	237.04	230.28	279.90	476.39	584.06	782.91	715.76	1202.12	1523.24	1674.85	1383.84	1522.50	1525.95
47.22	51.35	54.29	81.35	171.29	206.15	281.79	296.44	488.55	707.00	1091.31	1017.74	1112.87	1100.71
35.53	45.46	44.25	71.27	158.03	179.47	251.74	268.92	450.71	661.27	973.71	858.53	976.19	928.74
67.44	61.02	52.35	17.60	300.07	428.20	491.07	569.22	1125.44	1510.20	3105.76	2627.73	1787.89	842.98
65.20	55.73	49.12	159.10	287.13	408.11	457.54	541.20	1095.17	1452.20	2826.79	2340.69	1597.82	727.31
50.82	57.14	63.85	108.52	123.59	112.49	45.42	55.40	40.68	34.32	59.76	102.58	74.59	187.13
34.18	44.70	52.34	72.76	99.17	85.89	38.62	35.40	28.73	26.23	45.41	83.78	61.24	143.21
9.19	15.75	10.56	11.18	17.32	8.53	10.84	34.94	38.23	28.60	8.01	15.16	15.57	7.15
0.10	1.13	5.43	5.78	4.09	3.74	5.36	4.53	6.55	0.70	3.25	4.03	0.73	0.07
50.77	48.43	62.13	83.36	92.78	100.22	143.17	124.02	195.71	168.20	25.53	358.03	334.41	531.44

5-19 分区县、开发区房地产开发主要指标（2014年）

单位：万元

区县、开发区	Region	企业（单位）个数（个）Number of Enterprises (Unit)	本年完成投资 Investment Completed This Yea	本年新增固定资产 Increased Fixed Assets This Year
区县	**Region**			
新城区	Xincheng	42	946727	379224
碑林区	Beilin	79	1023449	1262750
莲湖区	Lianhu	71	1754668	331527
灞桥区	Baqiao	67	1475793	390123
未央区	Weiyang	143	4618596	1351090
雁塔区	Yanta	180	5805110	742322
阎良区	Yanliang	35	191014	110283
临潼区	Lintong	10	163130	21804
长安区	Chang'an	68	934844	277708
蓝田县	Lantian	14	50118	121
周至县	Zhouzhi	22	101200	89709
户　县	Huxian	22	168172	197054
高陵县	Gaoling	31	385997	160649
开发区	**Development Zones**			
高新区	GaoXin	55	1126371	276796
经开区	JingKai	52	2007401	377276
曲江新区	Qujiang	75	3398637	403106
浐灞生态区	Chanba Eco-District	49	1876292	225745
航空基地	Aviation Industry Base	10	125216	13024
航天基地	Aerospace Base	25	513751	174075
国际港务区	International Trade&Logistic Park	7	123129	
沣东新城	FengDongXinCheng	15	452849	200

Main Indicators of Real Estate Development by Region and Development Zone（2014）

(10 000 yuan)

房屋施工面积（平方米）Floor Space of Buildings Under Constmction(sq.m)	住宅 Residenctial Buildings	房屋竣工面积（平方米）Floor Space of Buildings Completed(sq.m)	住宅 Residenctial Buildings	竣工房屋价值 Value of Buildings Completed	住宅 Residenctial Buildings
5949115	4700998	568725	539709	152072	148227
13315487	10565897	4620220	3792722	1187145	989224
12329730	10486274	627006	522492	301211	225303
9850310	8321385	985813	848125	389883	321042
30226138	22595640	4196314	3702857	1038752	891237
31997047	23814246	2005039	1661664	585601	475197
2071712	1410515	361382	338256	110283	103367
1014468	837391				
9485767	7565468	638495	514657	266699	223107
712962	668319				
1415142	1153848	117803	48677	71042	12614
1096145	993874	539106	500939	175294	162277
4757006	4162168	677143	606339	149431	130924
9403299	5034857	495525	409659	226759	181679
10803652	7719741	1098927	940718	278846	226810
14993148	11297519	1176628	985582	374069	312718
8231292	6796159	511621	430762	225586	195424
766090	387942	33970	33970	13024	13024
4868178	3867427	449962	359282	163066	140030
735132	713002				
2297194	1974833				

5-20 房地产开发投资主要指标（2014年）

Main Indicators of Investment in Real Estate Development（2014）

单位：万元 (10 000 yuan)

指标	Item	全市合计 Total	#国有 State-owned	市区 Urban	市属 Municipal
一、企业（单位）个数（个）	**Number of Enterprises(unit)**	**784**	**39**	**695**	**727**
二、本年完成投资	**Investment Completed This Year**	**17618818**	**1352708**	**16913331**	**16107323**
按工程用途分	Grouped by Function				
住宅	Residential Buildings	13344332	1102170	12732733	12160503
#别墅、高档公寓	Villas and Top-Grade Apartments	348915	62461	305721	348915
办公楼	Office Buildings	840013	40763	839385	778648
商业营业用房	Houses for Business Use	2101737	68089	2018779	2009074
其他	Others	1332736	141686	1322434	1159098
三、本年新增固定资产	**Increased Fixed Assets This Year**	**5314364**	**261854**	**4866831**	**4909588**
四、房屋施工面积（万平方米）	**Floor Space of Buildings Under Construction (10 000 sq.m)**	**12422.10**	**954.78**	**11623.98**	**11398.35**
#住宅	Residential Buildings	9727.60	767.65	9029.78	8898.89
五、本年房屋竣工面积（万平方米）	**Floor Space of Buildings Completed (10 000 sq.m)**	**1533.70**	**106.64**	**1400.30**	**1380.97**
#住宅	Residential Buildings	1307.64	93.88	1192.05	1175.02
六、本年房屋竣工价值（亿元）	**Value of Buildings Completed (100 million yuan)**	**442.74**	**25.69**	**403.16**	**403.33**
#住宅	Residential Buildings	368.25	22.62	337.67	335.26
七、本年商品房屋销售面积（万平方米）	**Floor Space of Commercialized Buildings Sold (10 000 sq.m)**	**1707.71**	**124.79**	**1594.80**	**1577.53**
本年商品房销售额（亿元）	Sales Income of Commercialized Buildings (100 million yuan)	1100.71	74.05	1052.65	1023.13

5-21　商品房销售情况（2014年）

Sales of Commercial Houses（2014）

指　标	Item	全市合计 Total	#国有 State-owned	市区 Urban	市属 Municipal
商品房销售面积（平方米）	**Floor Space of Commercialized Buildings Sold(sq.m)**	**17077090**	**1247879**	**15948044**	**15775326**
现房销售面积	**Floor Space of Completed Apartment Sales**	**1487684**	**35704**	**1356520**	**1426791**
期房销售面积	**Floor Space of Forward Delivery Housing Sales**	**15589406**	**1212175**	**14591524**	**14348535**
住宅	Residential Buildings	15259483	1015091	14231466	14053628
#别墅、高档公寓	Villas and High-grade Apartments	396271	108150	384898	396271
办公楼	Office Buildings	458300	11528	458300	445568
商业营业用房	Houses for Business Use	819227	74714	728198	770708
其他	Others	540080	146546	530080	505422
本年商品房销售额（万元）	**Real estate sales this year(10 000 Yuan)**	**11007099**	**740515**	**10526476**	**10231260**
现房销售额	**Floor Space of Completed Apartment Sales**	**874709**	**24106**	**799047**	**842865**
期房销售额	**Floor Space of Forward Delivery Housing Sales**	**10132390**	**716409**	**9727429**	**9388395**
住宅	Residential Buildings	9287428	584888	8895065	8621513
#别墅高档公寓	Villas and High-grade Apartments	406194	80308	385956	389501
办公楼	Office Buildings	428372	17058	428372	440260
商业营业用房	Houses for Business Use	1025376	112389	939116	678858
其他	Others	265923	26180	263923	447291
待售面积（平方米）	**Area for Sale(sq.m)**	**1871267**	**41173**	**1700692**	**1795865**
#待售一年以上（一—三年）	Being Idle for One Year	755022	21386	707756	715798
待售三年以上（含三年）	Being Idle for Three Year	54378	5987	54378	48391
住宅	Residence	1432134	35721	1290841	1362184
#别墅高档公寓	Villas and High-grade Apartments	6278			6278
办公楼	Office Buildings	2341		2341	2341
商业营业用房	Houses for Business Use	241095	2945	213508	238150
其他	Others	195697	2507	194002	193190
房屋出租面积（平方米）	**Rental area(sq.m)**	**71465**		**64647**	**66242**
住宅	Residential Buildings	686			686
办公楼	Office Buildings	1394		1394	1394
商业营业用房	Houses for Business Use	24003		22871	20307
其他	Others	45382		40382	43855

5-22 房地产开发投资资金来源（2014年）

Source of Funds for Investment in Real Estate Development（2014）

单位：万元 (10 000 yuan)

指 标	Item	全市合计 Total	#国有 State-owned	市区 Urban	市属 Municipal
一. 本年资金来源合计	**Total**	**25143005**	**1686066**	**24234438**	**23067208**
1. 上年末结余资金	Balance of Last Year	5409624	462351	5170263	4907587
2. 本年资金来源小计	Total Funds This Year	19733381	1223715	19064175	18159621
(1) 国内贷款	Domestic Loans	3155906	79929	3112020	2916121
#银行贷款	Bank Loan	2363244	61919	2325761	2172244
非银行金融机构贷款	Loans from financial Institutions except Bank	792662	18010	786259	743877
(2) 利用外资	Utilization of Foreign Funds				
#外商直接投资	Foreign Direct Investment				
(3) 自筹资金	Self-raising Funds	8867486	515748	8548027	8358385
#自有资金	Funds at the disposal of Enterprises	3040483	243621	2902240	2781986
(4) 其他资金	Others	7709989	628038	7404128	6885115
#定金及预收款	Earnest Money and Advance payment	4857698	489050	4717299	4381241
个人按揭贷款	Personal Mortgage loan	2054131	115872	1909682	1883822
二. 本年各项应付款合计（万元）	**Total Sums of Money to be Paid This Year**	**4351954**	**356287**	**4123995**	**4027132**
#工程款	Project Fund	2377892	192395	2193403	2228158

5-23 房地产开发经营情况（2014年）

Running of Real Estate Development（2014）

单位：万元　　(10 000 yuan)

指　标	Item	全市合计 Total	#国有 State-owned	市区 Urban	市属 Municipal
一、资产负债情况	**Assets and Liabilities**				
1. 资产总计	Total Assets	61563303	4540554	59671714	56597709
2. 负债总计	Total Liabilities	51725577	3416212	50050908	47387432
3. 所有者权益合计	Total Creditor's Equity	9837726	1124341	9620806	9210277
#实收资本	Held Capital	7216254	524516	7001838	6754265
二、损益及分配情况	**Profit or Loss and the Distribution**				
1. 主营业务收入	Revenue from Principal Business	10609512	1022947	10185207	10010608
土地转让收入	Revenue of Land Transferred	9253	1464	8949	7289
商品房屋销售收入	Revenue of Commercial Houses Sold	10166073	754422	9743020	9615753
房屋出租收入	Revenue of Houses Leased	88848	15056	87977	86827
其他收入	Other Revenue	345338	252005	345261	300740
2. 主营业务成本	Cost of Principal Business	7460757	731351	7152954	7019416
3. 主营业务税金及附加	Taxes and Other Charges on Principal Business	943001	68821	912815	902094
4. 其他业务利润	Other Business Profit	22250	14085	22361	9157
5. 销售费用	Sales Expenditures	378053	21109	355096	347887
6. 管理费用	Management Cost	424724	29544	404047	393655
#税金	Tax	25534	3412	24713	23018
7. 财务费用	Fiscal Expenditure	141400	8120	136366	131426
#利息支出	Interest Exchange	98605	6781	95052	90644
8. 营业利润	Operating Profit	1164844	176083	1133201	1103397
投资收益	Investment Revenue				
营业外收入	Non-business Revenue	14200	1562	13874	12843
营业外支出	Non-business Expenditures	51202	391	50406	48063
9. 利润总额	Total Profit	1127841	177254	1096670	1068177
10. 应付职工薪酬	Salary Payable	318449	49138	303288	289323

主要统计指标解释

全社会固定资产投资 是以货币形式表现的在一定时期内全社会建造和购置固定资产的工作量以及与此有关的费用的总称。该指标是反映固定资产投资规模、结构和发展速度的综合性指标，又是观察工程进度和考核投资效果的重要依据。全社会固定资产投资按登记注册类型可分为国有、集体、联营、股份制、私营和个体、港澳台商、外商、其他等。

城镇固定资产投资 指城镇各种登记注册类型的企业、事业、行政单位及个体户进行的计划总投资500万元及500万元以上的建设项目投资和房地产开发投资。县城及以上区域内发生的投资，县及县以上各级政府及主管部门直接领导、管理的建设项目和企业事业单位的投资均为城镇固定资产投资。

房地产开发投资 指各种登记注册类型的房地产开发公司、商品房建设公司及其他房地产开发法人单位和附属于其他法人单位实际从事房地产开发或经营活动的单位统一开发的包括统代建、拆迁还建的住宅、厂房、仓库、饭店、宾馆、度假村、写字楼、办公楼等房屋建筑物和配套的服务设施，土地开发工程（如道路、给水、排水、供电、供热、通讯、平整场地等基础设施工程）的投资；不包括单纯的土地交易活动。

农村投资 包括在农村区域范围内进行固定资产投资活动的企业、事业、行政单位及农户投资。

固定资产投资的资金来源 根据固定资产投资的资金来源不同，分为国家预算资金、国内贷款、利用外资、自筹资金和其他资金。

（1）国家预算资金：包括一般预算、政府性基金预算、国有资本经营预算和社保基金预算等资金。

（2）国内贷款：指报告期固定资产投资单位向银行及非银行金融机构借入的用于固定资产投资的各种国内借款，包括银行利用自有资金及吸收的存款发放的贷款、上级主管部门拨入的国内贷款、国家专项贷款、地方财政专项资金安排的贷款、国内储备贷款、周转贷款等。

（3）利用外资：指报告期收到的用于固定资产建造和购置的境外资金（包括设备、材料、技术在内）。包括对外借款（外国政府、国际金融组织贷款、出口信贷、外国银行商业贷款、对外发行债券和股票）、外商直接投资及外商其他投资。不包括我国自有外汇资金（国家外汇、地方外汇、留成外汇、调剂外汇和中国银行自有资金发行的外汇贷款等）。计算利用外资时，需要折算成人民币，折算中所使用的外汇汇率按现汇计算，即按使用外汇时的汇率计算。

（4）自筹资金：指固定资产投资单位报告期收到的，由各地区、各部门及企、事业单位筹集用于固定资产投资的预算外资金，包括中央各部门、各级地方和企、事业单位的自筹资金。

（5）其他资金：指在报告期收到的除以上各种资金之外其他用于固定资产投资的资金，包括企业或金融机构通过发行各种债券筹集到的资金、社会集资、个人资金、无偿捐赠的资金及其他单位拨人的资金等。

固定资产投资按国民经济行业分 根据现有企业、事业、行政单位和建设项目建成投产后的主要产品种类或主要用途及社会经济活动性质来确定国民经济行业。一般情况下，一个建设项目或一个企业、事业单位只能属于一种国民经济行业。

固定资产投资按隶属关系分 是按建设单位或企业、事业、行政单位的主管上级机关确定的。

（1）中央：是指中共中央、人大常委会和国务院各部、委、局、总公司以及直属机构直接领导的建设项目和企业、事业、行政单位。这些单位的固定资产投资计划由国务院各部门直接编制和下达，建设中所需物资、主要设备以及建设中的问题都由中央有关部门安排和解决。

（2）地方：是由省（自治区、直辖市）、地区（州、盟、省辖市）、县（旗、县级市）三级政府及业务主管部门直接领导和管理的建设项目、企业、事业、行政单位。地方项目还包括不隶属以上各级政府及主管部门的建设项目和企业、事业单位，如外商投资企业和无主管部门的企业等。

固定资产投资按建设性质分 根据整个建设项目情况来确定。建设项目的性质一般分为新建、扩建、改建和技术改造、单纯建造生活设施、迁建、恢复、单纯购置。房地产开发单位、农户投资不划分建设性质。

（1）新建：一般指从无到有开始建设的企业、事业和行政单位或建设项目。有的单位原有基础很小，经过建设后新增的固定资产价值超过该企、事业、行政单位原有固定资产价值（原值）三倍以上的也应作为新建。

（2）扩建：指在厂内或其他地点，为扩大原有产品的生产能力（或效益）或增加新的产品生产能力，而增建主要的生产车间（或主要工程）、分厂、独立的生产线。行政、事业单位在原单位增建业务用房（如学校增建教学用房、医院增建门诊部、病房等）也作为扩建。

现有企、事业单位为扩大原有主要产品生产能力或增加新的产品生产能力，增建一个或几个主要生产车间（或主要工程）、分厂，同时进行一些更新改造工程的，也应作为扩建。

（3）改建和技术改造：指现有企业、事业单位，对原有设施进行技术改造或更新（包括相应配套的辅助性生产、生活福利设施）的建设项目。现有企业、事业单位为适应市场变化的需要，而改变企业的主要产品种类（如军工企业转产民用品等）的建设项目，应作为改建。原有产品生产作业线由于各工序（车间）之间能力不平衡，为填平补齐充分发挥原有生产能力而增建不增加本企业主要产品设计能力的车间，也应作为改建。技术改造是指企业、事业单位在现有基础上，用先进的技术代替落后的技术，用先进的工艺和装备代替落后的工艺和装备，以改变企业落后的技术经济面貌，实现以内涵为主的扩大再生产，达到提高产品质量、促进产品更新换代、节约能源、降低消耗、扩大生产规模、全面提高社会经济效益的目的。技术改造具体包括以下内容：机器设备和工具的更新改造；生产工艺改革、节约能源和原材料的改造；厂房建筑和公共设施的改造；劳动条件和生产环境的改造等。

固定资产投资按构成分 固定资产投资活动按其工作内容和实现方式分为建筑安装工程，设备工具器具购置和其他费用三个部分。

（1）建筑安装工程（建筑安装工作量）：指各种房屋、建筑物的建造工程和各种设备、装置的安装工程。包括各种房屋建造工程；各种用途设备基础和各种工业窑炉的砌筑工程及金属结构工程；为施工而进行的各种准备工作和临时工程以及完工后的清理工作等；铁路、道路的铺设，矿井的开凿及石油管道的架设等；水利工程；防空地下建筑等特殊工程；列入房屋丁程预算内的暖气、卫生、通风、照明、煤气等设备的价值及装设油饰工程；列入建筑工程预算内的各种管道（蒸汽、压缩空气、石油、给排水等管道）、电力、电讯电缆导线等的敷设工程；以及各种机械设备的安装下程；为测定安装工程质量，对设备进行的试运工作；房地产开发单位进行的商品房屋开发建设工程、土地开发工程。

在建筑安装工程中，不包括被安装设备本身的价值。

（2）设备工具器具购置：指建设单位或企、事业单位购置或自制的，达到固定资产标准的设备、工具、器具的价值。新建单位及扩建单位的新建车间，按照设计或计划要求购置或自制的全部设备、工具、器具，不论是否达到固定资产标准均计入“设备工具器具购置”中。

（3）其他费用：指在固定资产建造和购置过程中发生的，除上述几项内容以外的各种应分摊计入固定资产的费用。

施工项目 指报告期内所有施工的建设项目个数，包括本年新开工的项目和以前年度开工在本年继续施工的建设项目。凡是报告期内施过工的建设项目，不论施工时间长短，均作为施工项目统计。施工项目个数可以反映一定时期固定资产投资的实际规模，与同期全部建成投产项目个数相比，可以从建设速度的角度反映固定资产投资的效果。

全部建成投产项目 指报告期内按设计文件规定的全部生产能力（或效益）建成投产，经验收合格交付使用的建设项目。

新增生产能力（或工程效益） 指通过固定资产投资活动而增加的设计能力（或工程效益）。主要指标包括建设规模、本年施工规模、自开始建设累计新增生产能力（或工程效益）、本年新增生产能力（或工程效益）等。

建设规模 指建设项目或工程设计文件中规定的全部设计能力（或工程效益）。包括已经建成投产和尚未建成投产的工程的生产能力（或工程效益）。

本年施工规模 指报告期内施工的单项工程的设计能力（或工程效益），即全部建设规模中在本年正式施工的部分。

自开始建设累计新增生产能力（或工程效益） 指自开始建设至本年底止建成投产的全部单项工程累计的新增生产能力（或工程效益）。

本年新增生产能力（或工程效益） 指在本年度内按照新增生产能力（或工程效益）的计算条件和标准，实际建成投入生产或交付使用的生产能力（或工程效益）。

施工房屋面积 指报告期内施工的全部房屋（包括地下室、半地下室以及配套房屋）建筑面积。包括本期新开工的面积和上期开工跨入本期继续施工的房屋面积，以及上期已停建在本期恢复施工的房屋面积。本期竣工和本期施工后又停缓建的房屋，其建筑面积仍计入本期房屋施工面积中。

竣工房屋面积 指在报告期内房屋建筑按照设计要求已经全部完工，达到住人和使用条件，经验收鉴定合格（或达到竣工验收标准），可正式移交使用单位的各栋房屋建筑面积的总和。

新增固定资产 指报告期内交付使用的固定资产价值。包括本年内建成投入生产或交付使用的工程投资和达到固定资产标准的设备、工具、器具的投资及有关应摊入的费用。该指标是表示固定资产投资成果的价值指标，也是反映建设进度，计算固定资产投资效果的重要指标。

项目建成投产率 指一定时期内全部建成投产项目个数与同期施工项目个数的比率。该指标是从建设单位建设速度的角度反映投资效果的指标。

固定资产交付使用率 指一定时期新增固定资产与同期完成投资额的比率。该指标是反映固定资产动用速度，衡量建设过程中宏观投资效果的综合指标。由于新增固定资产是较长时期内形成的结果，而投资额则是当年完成的，因此，该指标一般适宜于反映较长时期内固定资产的动用情况。

商品房销售面积 指报告期内出售商品房屋的合同总面积（即双方签署的正式买卖合同中所确定的建筑面积）。由现房销售建筑面积和期房销售建筑面积两部分组成。

商品房销售额 指报告期内出售商品房屋的合同总价款（即双方签署的正式买卖合同中所确定的合同总价）。该指标与商品房销售面积同口径，由现房销售额和期房销售额两部分组成。

经济适用房 指根据经济适用房计划安排建设的政策性住宅。经济是指房屋建筑造价和销售价格低于一般商品住宅；适用是指适合中低收入家庭购买使用。经济适用房主要是由地方政府统一下达投资计划，房地产公司开发，对外销售；用地一般采用行政划拨或招标投标方式，免收土地出让金；对各种经批准的收费减半征收，开发利润不超过3%；销售价格实行政府指导价。该指标可以分析房地产投资结构，反映中低收入家庭商品住宅的供求平衡情况。

Explanatory Notes on Main Statistical Indicators

Total Investment in Fixed Assets in the Whole Country refers to the volume of activities in construction and purchases of fixed assets of the whole country and related fees, expressed in monetary terms during the reference period. It is a comprehensive indicator which shows the size, structure and growth of the investment in fixed assets, providing a basis for observing the progress of construction projects and evaluating results of investment. Total investment in fixed assets in the whole country includes, by type of ownership, the investment by State-owned units, collective-owned units, joint ownership units, share-holding units, private units individuals as well as investments by entrepreneurs from Hong Kong, Macao and Taiwan, foreign investors and others.

Urban Investment in Fixed Assets refers to construction projects involving a total planned investment of 5000 000 yuan and over by enterprises of various types of ownership, institutions, administrative units and individuals in urban areas, investment in real estate development. In other words, all investments that take place in county towns and urban areas, investment in construction projects under the direct leadership and management of government agencies at and above county levels and investments by enterprises and institutions at and above county levels are covered in urban investment in fixed assets.

Investment in Real Estate Development refers to investment by real estate development companies, commercialized buildings construction companies and other real estate development units of various types of ownership in the construction of buildings, such as residential buildings, factory buildings, warehouses, hotels, guesthouses, holiday villages, office buildings, and the complementary service facilities and land development projects, such as roads, water supply, water drainage, power supply, heating supply, telecommunications, land leveling and other infrastructural projects. It does not include activities in pure land transactions.

Investment in Rural Areas refers to investment in fixed assets by enterprises, institutions, administrative units and households in rural areas.

Sources of Funds for Investment in Fixed Assets are categorized as funds from the State budget, domestic loans, foreign investment, self-raised funds, and others, depending on the sources of investment.

(1) Fund from the State budget consists of budgetary appropriation and loans from the State budget. More specifically, it includes, from the budget of the central government, capital construction fund (operation fund and non-operational fund), special expenses, loans from repayment, discount fund, expenses on innovation and trial production of new products, expenses on urban construction, expenses on temporary construction from business departments, development fund for less developed areas, as well as local budgetary fund transferred from the central budget.

(2) Domestic loans refer to loans of various forms borrowed by investing units from banks and non-bank financial institutions during the reference period for the purpose of investment in fixed assets, including loans issued by banks from their self-owned funds and deposit, loans appropriated by higher authorities, special loans by government, loans arranged by local government from special funds, domestic reserve loan, and working loan.

(3) Foreign investment refers to overseas funds received during the reference period for the construction and purchase of investment in fixed assets (covering equipment, materials and technology), including foreign borrowings (loans from foreign governments and international financial institutions, export credit, commercial loans from foreign banks, issue of bonds and stocks overseas), foreign direct investment and other foreign investments. Excluded from this category is capital in foreign exchanges owned by China (foreign exchanges owned by the central and local governments, foreign exchanges retained by enterprises, foreign exchanges by enterprises through the regulating mechanism, loans in foreign exchanges issued by the Bank of China with its own fund, etc). In calculating the utilization of foreign capital, foreign currencies are converted into Chinese Renminbi applying the current exchange rate when the foreign capitals are actually used.

(4) Self-raised funds refer to extra-budgetary funds for investment in fixed assets received during the reference period by investing units from central government ministries, local governments, enterprises and institutions, including their self-raised funds.

(5) Others refer to funds for investment in fixed assets received from sources other than those listed above, including capital raised through issuing bonds by

enterprises or financial institutions, funds raised from individuals and through donations, and funds transferred from other units.

Investment in Fixed Assets by Sector The classification of construction projects by sector is determined by enterprises, institutions, administrative units and the major products or the purpose of the projects of existing enterprises, institutional and administrative units when they are put into production or use, and by the nature of their social economic activities. In general, one project or one enterprise or institution can only be classified into one sector.

Investment in Fixed Assets by Jurisdiction of Management refers to the classification of investment by the competent authorities under which investment is made by construction units, enterprises, institutions or administrative units.

(1) Central investment refers to the investment in projects or by enterprises, institutions or administrative units which are under the direct leadership and management of the State Council and of the national commissions, ministries, agencies and State-owned large corporations. Various ministries and departments of the State Council prepare and implement plans for investment in fixed assets by those departments, and arrange and ensure the supply of materials and key equipment required for the projects.

(2) Local investment refers to the investment in projects or by enterprises, institutions or administrative units which are under the direct leadership and management of departments under the provincial, prefecture and county governments. Also included are projects by foreign-invested enterprises and enterprises without competent managing authorities.

Investment in Fixed Assets by Type of Construction Construction projects in general can be classified, by the type of construction, into new construction, expansion, reconstruction and technical transformation, purely construction of living facilities, moving, restoration and purely purchasing. However, investment by type of construction is not applied to investment by real-estate development units and investment by rural households.

(1) New construction in general refers to construction projects, which start from scratch, of enterprises, institutions, administrative agencies. In case the size of the existing unit is quite small, and the value of newly added fixed assets is more than three times of the original value, the expansion will be considered as new construction.

(2) Expansion refers to construction of new major production workshop, branch factory or independent production line within a factory or in other locations, for the purpose of increasing the production capacity (or improving efficiency) or adding new production capacity. Newly constructed accommodation for the operation of institutions and administrative organizations (such as newly constructed buildings for teaching in schools, buildings for clinics or wards in hospitals, etc.) are also classified as expansion.

Also included in expansion are investments by existing enterprises or institutions in building major production line(s) or branch factory(ies) along with some work on innovation, for the purpose of expanding the production capacity of original products or producing new products.

(3) Reconstruction and technical transformation refers to construction projects by existing enterprises or institutions in innovation or technical transformation of the old facilities (including auxiliary production equipment and welfare facilities). Also considered as reconstruction is the construction of new workshops by the existing enterprises or institutions to change the variety of products to meet the market demand (such as the production of civil products by defence industries), or to bring the designed production capacity into full play through a more balanced production process on production lines. Technical transformation refers to replacement of old technology or equipment by new technology or equipment, in order to expand the reproduction through improvement of technology contents in production, to improve product quality, to promote new products to save energy,to reduce consumption, to expand the production scale and to improve overall social-economic efficiency. Contents of technical transformation include: updating of machinery, equipment and tools; reforming production process by using energy or materials saving technology; construction of factory workshops and transformation of public facilities; improvement of working conditions and environment, etc.

Investment in Fixed Assets by Structure By their

contents and the mode of implementation, investment activities are classified into 3 categories, i.e. construction and installation, purchase of equipment and instrument, and other expenses.

(1) Construction and installation (work volume of construction and installation) refers to the construction of houses and buildings and the installation of various kinds of equipment and instruments. They include construction of houses; equipment foundations, industrial kilns and stoves, and metal structure work; preparation works and temporary works for project construction, and clearing up works post project construction; pavement of railways and roads, drilling of mines and putting up of oil pipes; construction of water conservancy; construction of underground air-raid shelters and construction of other special projects; value of equipment for heating, sanitation, ventilation, lighting, gas, painting, etc. that are covered by the budget of housing projects; laying out of various pipelines (for steam, compressed air, petroleum, tap water and sewage) and wiring and cabling for electric power and for communications; installation of various machinery and equipment; testing operation for pre- testing the quality of installation projects, and land and other development work conducted by real estate developers for commercialized housing.

The value of equipment installed is itself not included in the value of construction and installation projects.

(2) Purchase of equipment and instruments refers to the total value of equipment, tools, and instruments purchased or self-produced which come up to the cut-off point for fixed assets by the construction units or investing enterprises or institutions. Equipment, tools and instruments purchased or self-produced for new workshops by newly established or expanded units are categorized as "purchase of equipment and instruments" no matter whether they come up to the cut-off point for fixed assets.

(3) Other expenses refer to expenses arising during the construction or purchase of fixed assets other than those mentioned above.

Projects under Construction refer to number of all projects with construction activities newly started in current year or left-over from the previous year in the reference period. All projects that have construction activities undertaken during the reference period are reported as projects under construction irrespective of the length of construction work. The number of projects under construction can reflect the actual size of investment in fixed assets during a given period, and when compared with the number of projects completed and put into use during the same period, it demonstrates the results of investment in fixed assets from the angle of the speed of the construction.

Projects Completed and Put into Use refer to projects have been completed in accordance with the design documents, resulting in forming production capacity (efficiency) and have been checked and accepted after relevant tests, and have been formally delivered for use.

Newly Increased Production Capacity (or Project Efficiency) refers to the increase in design capacity (or project efficiency) through investment in fixed assets. The main indicators include: construction scale, scale of projects under construction in current year, the accumulated newly increased production capacity (project efficiency) since the start of the projects and the newly increased production capacity (project efficiency) of current year.

Construction Scale refers to the total designed production capacity (project efficiency) of the construction projects in accordance with the design document, including those have been put into operation and those that have not been completed.

Scale of Projects under Construction in Current Year refers to the designed production capacity (project efficiency) of a single project under construction in the reference period, i.e. the part of the total scale of project which is officially under construction in current year.

The Accumulated Newly Increased Production Capacity (project efficiency) since the Start of the Projects refers to the accumulated newly increased production capacity of all the single projects which have been put into use from the beginning of the projects till the end of current year.

The Newly Increased Production Capacity (project efficiency) of Current Year refers to the production capacity (project efficiency) that has been completed and put into operation in current year according to the calculation conditions and standards on newly increased production capacity (project efficiency).

Floor Space of Buildings under Construction refers to the total floor space of all the buildings (including basement, semi-basement and auxiliary buildings), including the effective area and the area occupied by the structure. This indicator is one of the important indicators in physical terms to reflect the scale and accomplishment of the construction industry and also an important basis for monitoring the progress, Calculating the cost, analyzing the efficiency and studying the supply of building materials in relation to the construction projects.

Floor Space Completed refers to the floor space of all buildings completed in the reference period, which have been appraised and accepted (or come up to the designed standards) and have been transferred to owner units.

Newly Increased Fixed Assets refer to the value of fixed that has been put into use, including investment in projects that have been completed and put into operation in current year and the investment in equipment, tools and appliance that meet the standard of fixed assets and fees that should be apportioned. This is an indicator that demonstrates the results of investment in fixed assets in monetary terms, and an important indicator to reflect the speed of construction and to calculate the efficiency of investment.

Rate of Construction Projects Completed and Put into Use refers to the ratio of the number of construction projects completed and put into use in a certain period of time to the number of projects under construction in the same period. This reflects the investment efficiency from the perspective of the speed of projects construction.

Rate of Projects of Fixed Assets Completed and Put into Operation refers to the ratio of the newly increased fixed assets to the total investment made in the same period. This is a comprehensive indicator reflecting the speed of the employment of fixed assets and the investment efficiency at the macro-level. As the newly increase fixed assets is the result of a long period while the investment is completed in the current year, this indicator is expected to be used to reflect the employment of fixed assets over a long period of time.

6 财　政

GOVERNMENT FINANCE

资料整理：刘　婷
Data management：Liu Ting
数据审核：陈　英
Data audit：Chen Ying

第六部分　财政

一、简要说明

本章资料主要包括地方财政收入、支出总额构成及分区县情况，由西安市统计局综合处根据西安市财政局提供资料整理。

二、主要指标

财政总收入（亿元）	1019.69	比上年增长	13.0%
一般预算收入（亿元）	583.79	比上年增长	16.3%
一般预算支出（亿元）	819.54	比上年增长	12.3%

6　GOVERNMENT FINANCE

Ⅰ.Brief Introduction

This chapter consists of primarily data on regional revenue, expenditure of the municipal government, regional revenue and expenditure of the districts and the counties. The data are provided by the Xi'an Bureau of Finance and are compiled by Integration division of the Xi'an Bureau of Statistics.

Ⅱ.Major Indicators

		Increase over Preceding Year
Total Government Revenue(100 mil. Yuan)	1019.69	13.0%
General Budgetary Revenue(100 mil. Yuan)	583.79	16.3%
Ordinary Budgetary Expenditures(100 mil. Yuan)	819.54	12.3%

6-1 主要年份地方财政一般预算收入及支出

General Revenue Local Government Revenue and Expenditure in Representative Years

单位：亿元 （100 million yuan）

年 份 Year	地方财政一般预算收入 General Budgetary Revenue of Local Government	地方财政一般预算支出 General Budgetary Expenditure of Local Government
2000	46.80	52.00
2001	51.45	57.30
2002	54.50	63.80
2003	72.90	76.60
2004	75.30	87.30
2005	72.92	97.61
2006	85.89	119.22
2007	112.92	161.25
2008	145.61	226.99
2009	181.40	276.85
2010	241.86	371.62
2011	318.55	494.58
2012	396.96	597.49
2013	501.98	729.81
2014	583.79	819.54

注：本表数据来源于市财政局。

6-2 财政收入（2014年）

Government Revenue（2014）

单位：万元 （10 000 yuan）

指　标	Item	2014
财政总收入	**Total Government Revenue**	**10196913**
#一般预算收入	**General Budgetary Revenue**	**5837888**
一、税收收入	**Total Tax Revenue**	**4233880**
1. 国内增值税	Value-added Tax	296724
2. 改征增值税	Levying VAT	225390
3. 营业税	Business Tax	1179103
4. 企业所得税	Corporate Income Tax	367706
5. 企业所得税退税	Return for Corporate Income Tax	
6. 个人所得税	Individual Income Tax	139933
7. 资源税	Resource Tax	533
8. 城市维护建设税	City Maintenance and Construction Tax	298257
9. 房产税	House Property Tax	154842
10. 印花税	stamp tax	102949
11. 城镇土地使用税	Urban Land Use Tax	81534
12. 土地增值税	Land Appreciation Tax	389433
13. 车船税	Tax on the Use of Vehicles and Ships	64661
14. 耕地占用税	Farm Land Occupatian Tax	404421
15. 契税	Deed Tax	528394
二、非税收入	**Total Non-tax Revenue**	**1604008**
1. 专项收入	Special Program Receipts	144961
2. 行政性收费收入	Charge of Adminnistrative and Institutional Units	629610
3. 罚没收入	Penalty Receipts	95673
4. 国有资本经营收入	State-owned Assets Profit	252466
5. 国有资源（资产）有偿使用收入	Revenue for the use of State-owned Assets (Resources)	481078
6. 其他收入	Other Revenue	220
政府性基金收入	**Governmental Fund Revenue**	**5084154**

注：本表数据来源于市财政局。

6-3 财政支出（2014年）

Government Expenditures（2014）

单位：万元 （10 000 yuan）

指　　标	Item	2014
一、政府性基金支出	**Governmental Fund Revenue Expenditure**	**5005000**
二、一般预算支出	**General Budget Expenditure**	**8195366**
1.一般公共服务支出	Expenditure for General Public Services	643262
2.国防支出	Expenditure for National Defense	6620
3.公共安全支出	Expenditure for Public Security	385886
4.教育支出	Expenditure for Education	1115171
5.科学技术支出	Expenditure for Science and Technology	134866
6.文化体育与传媒支出	Expenditure for Cultural, sports and the media	160224
7.社会保障和就业支出	Expenditure for Social Safety Net and Employment Effort	879890
8.医疗卫生与计划生育支出	Medical 、 Health and Family Planning Expenditure	589512
9.节能环保支出	Expenditure for Energy Saving and Environment Protection	222421
10.城乡社区支出	Expenditure for Urban and Rural Community Aaffairs	2089604
11.农林水支出	Expenditure for Agriculture, Forestry and Water Conservancy	487646
12.交通运输支出	Expenditure for Transportation	354435
13.资源勘探信息等支出	Expenditure for Exploration of the Power of Information	316835
14.商业服务业等支出	Expenditure for Business Services	127121
15.金融支出	Expenditure for Finance	37978
16.国土海洋气象等支出	Land and Marine Meteorological and Other Expenses	39758
17.住房保障支出	Expenditure for Housing Support	490227
18.粮油物资储备支出	Expenditure for Grain and Oil Stockpiles	18817
19.国债还本付息支出	Expenditure for National Debt and Interest(10 000yuan)	74209
20.其它支出	Other Expenditure	20884

注：本表数据来源于市财政局。

6-4 各区县、开发区财政收入（2014年）

单位：万元

区县、开发区	Region	一般预算收入 General Budgetary Revenue	税收收入 Tax Revenue	增值税 Value Added Tax	营业税 Business Revenue	企业所得税 Corporate Income Tax
合计	**Total**	**5837888**	**4233880**	**522114**	**1179103**	**367706**
市本级合计	**Sum of city level**	**788396**	**544179**	**69798**	**26284**	**55323**
区、县合计	**Region**	**3206746**	**2251319**	**289512**	**797996**	**177839**
新城区	Xincheng	355811	181796	20580	69906	34892
碑林区	Beilin	432276	286217	60784	93356	41186
莲湖区	Lianhu	471313	282996	51632	111483	20021
雁塔区	Yanta	470617	358484	56859	128078	31321
灞桥区	Baqiao	236711	199189	11301	83113	6555
未央区	Weiyang	355092	271244	30268	113656	18045
阎良区	Yanliang	120355	92284	7998	14872	3036
临潼区	Lintong	121441	107307	10366	21069	3639
长安区	Chang'an	354267	249191	13196	87201	11317
蓝田县	Lantian	38387	24483	1713	9485	455
周至县	Zhouzhi	35218	26124	2781	11212	302
户　县	Huxian	82748	67899	10920	21981	3336
高陵县	Gaoling	132510	104105	11114	32584	3734
开发区合计	**Sum of Development Zones**	**1842746**	**1438382**	**162804**	**354823**	**134544**
高新区	GaoXin	882799	636501	108919	115662	74536
经开区	JingKai	364520	284775	41754	84922	22545
曲江新区	Qujiang	350425	319538	3758	92550	30087
浐灞生态区	Chanba Eco-District	128329	94969	2302	28807	3410
航天基地	Aerospace Base	39229	32579	1859	10145	1771
航空基地	Aviation Industry Base	8553	7881	546	2413	202
国际港务区	International Trade&Logistic Park	30074	27915	460	8299	719
沣东新城	FengDongXinCheng	38817	34224	3206	12025	1274

注：本表数据来源于市财政局。

Public revenue by Region and Development Zone（2014）

（10 000 yuan）

一般预算收入 General Budgetary Revenue					
税收收入 Tax Revenue					
个 人 所得税 Individual Income Tax	资源税 Resource Tax	城市维护建设税 City Maintenance and Construction Tax	耕地占用税 Farm Land Occupation Tax	契税 Deed Tax	其他各项税收收入 Other Tax Revenue
139933	**533**	**298257**	**404421**	**528394**	**793419**
29131		**44834**		**237522**	**81287**
63371	**531**	**155900**	**356748**	**61650**	**347772**
7052	1	14222	800		34343
17038		23289			50564
8555	1	25609	77		65618
12584		24666	54984		49992
1823		12508	56987		26902
6816	1	24497	26873		51088
2885		4222	32236	18209	8826
1579	1	5553	53948	3212	7940
2715	12	8794	85496	19128	21332
172	247	1139	7762	774	2736
174	217	1043	5927	1773	2695
783	46	4729	12053	5956	8095
1195	5	5629	19605	12598	17641
47431	**2**	**97523**	**47673**	**229222**	**364360**
35835		50773	47400	52448	150928
7346	2	26269		37768	64169
2052		10340		85261	95490
598		3534		31925	24393
767		1666		8188	8183
119		730		1439	2432
116		947		8662	8712
598		3264	273	3531	10053

6-4 续表

单位：万元

区县、开发区	Region	一般预算收入 General Budgetary Revenue		
		非税收入 Non-tax Revenue	专项收入 Special Program Receipts	行政事业性收费收入 Charge of Adiministrative and Institutional Units
合计	**Total**	**1604008**	**144961**	**629610**
市本级合计	**Sum of city level**	**244217**	**35205**	**112524**
区、县合计	**Region**	**955427**	**67668**	**489535**
新城区	Xincheng	174015	6040	5855
碑林区	Beilin	146059	10036	129721
莲湖区	Lianhu	188317	11048	164261
雁塔区	Yanta	112133	10604	95938
灞桥区	Baqiao	37522	5378	3518
未央区	Weiyang	83848	8957	3298
阎良区	Yanliang	28071	1808	22454
临潼区	Lintong	14134	2386	2471
长安区	Chang'an	105076	3583	28363
蓝田县	Lantian	13904	1256	7789
周至县	Zhouzhi	9094	683	3808
户　县	Huxian	14849	2847	5037
高陵县	Gaoling	28405	3042	17022
开发区合计	**Sum of Development Zones**	**404364**	**42088**	**27551**
高新区	GaoXin	246298	21774	11294
经开区	JingKai	79745	10494	478
曲江新区	Qujiang	30887	4284	783
浐灞生态区	Chanba Eco-District	33360	1481	10035
航天基地	Aerospace Base	6650	713	3161
航空基地	Aviation Industry Base	672	313	305
国际港务区	International Trade&Logistic Park	2159	407	1338
沣东新城	FengDongXinCheng	4593	2622	157

continued

(10 000 yuan)

罚没收入 Penalty Receipts	国有资本经营收入 State-owned Assets Profit	国有资源(资产)有偿使用收入 The Revenues of the Compensation for the Use of State-owned Resoures(Assants)	其他收入 Other Income	政府性基金收入 Governmental Fund Revenue
95673	**252466**	**481078**	**220**	**5084154**
44393	**2546**	**49549**		**1126474**
43342	**530**	**354132**	**220**	**940881**
4885		157235		2162
2894		3408		3727
3152		9856		205705
3698		1892	1	3052
1226		27318	82	12813
3326		68267		24883
989	530	2290		4044
3680		5545	52	58522
5580		67550		293211
2222		2552	85	33880
3313		1290		43261
3252		3713		60938
5125		3216		79373
7938	**249390**	**77397**		**3016799**
2121	201600	9509		478581
2520	3263	62990		507084
1074	23667	1079		888992
556	18500	2788		328017
268	2360	148		236771
49		5		49876
362		52		195673
988		826		331805

6-5 各区县、开发区财政支出（2014年）

单位：万元

区县、开发区	Region	一般预算支出 Ordinary Budgetary Expenditures	一般公共服务支出 General Public Services	国防支出 Expenditure for National Defense	公共安全支出 Expenditure for Public Safety
合计	**Total**	**8195366**	**643262**	**6620**	**385886**
市本级合计	**Sum of city level**	**3126626**	**172153**	**4185**	**160699**
区、县合计	**Region**	**3702745**	**341003**	**2415**	**201211**
新城区	Xincheng	311201	31137	125	20547
碑林区	Beilin	282868	32557	440	20948
莲湖区	Lianhu	339115	39802	453	20283
雁塔区	Yanta	326731	27956	240	25195
灞桥区	Baqiao	220305	18095	177	14422
未央区	Weiyang	239836	22775	301	19084
阎良区	Yanliang	186987	25673		8952
临潼区	Lintong	293966	26907		13259
长安区	Chang'an	494189	41723	251	19838
蓝田县	Lantian	251369	13663	157	8789
周至县	Zhouzhi	284284	15216	70	8756
户　县	Huxian	269178	21957	106	11758
高陵县	Gaoling	202716	23542	95	9380
开发区合计	**Sum of Development Zones**	**1365995**	**130106**	**20**	**23976**
高新区	GaoXin	582182	31999	20	6768
经开区	JingKai	248466	26150		4519
曲江新区	Qujiang	253294	32302		1460
浐灞生态区	Chanba Eco-District	119492	18193		2950
航天基地	Aerospace Base	42523	5440		1810
航空基地	Aviation Industry Base	13150	5138		
国际港务区	International Trade&Logistic Park	33329	3464		
沣东新城	FengDongXinCheng	73559	7420		6469

注：本表数据来源于市财政局。

Expenditure by Region and Development Zone（2014）

（10 000 yuan）

教育支出 Expenditure for Education	科学技术支出 Expenditure for Science and Technology	文化体育与传媒支出 Expenditure for Culture,Sport and Media	社会保障和就业支出 Expenditure for Social Safety Net and Employment Effort	医疗卫生与计划生育支出 Medical 、Health and Family Planning Expenditure	节能环保支出 Expenditure for Energy Saving and Environment Protection
1115171	**134866**	**160224**	**879890**	**589512**	**222421**
227075	**47284**	**62399**	**395686**	**216327**	**140060**
818107	**23051**	**34431**	**470891**	**359225**	**61207**
57077	1599	346	30675	9715	175
50926	2709	1328	49947	12585	1959
74456	2526	743	43434	16012	467
59011	2457	933	34609	19840	6218
65626	1674	1407	31224	25700	15852
55403	1926	5830	25152	17328	3578
38053	1216	1878	20179	21493	1235
72735	1771	4372	37314	38819	8838
105137	2949	4049	59251	61933	1450
59005	424	3338	39290	35676	2805
74165	379	2915	38400	35438	8078
65462	1683	4560	38165	31636	4563
41051	1738	2732	23251	33050	5989
69989	**64531**	**63394**	**13313**	**13960**	**21154**
7149	58136	2765	1334	197	9186
13122	3895	200	690		3026
15867		57678		70	3760
4914					1053
2250	2500	975	37	3000	1529
568					450
1100		1700			1246
25019		76	11252	10693	904

6-5 续表1

单位：万元

区县、开发区	Region	一般预算支出 Ordinary Budgetary Expenditures 城乡社区支出 Expenditure for Urban and Rural Community Affairs	农林水支出 Expenditure for Agriculture, Forestry and Water Conservancy	交通运输支出 Expenditure for Industry,Commerce and Banking	资源勘探电力信息等支出 Expenditure for Exploration of the Power of Information
合计	**Total**	**2089604**	**487646**	**354435**	**316835**
市本级合计	**Sum of city level**	**567948**	**135810**	**300090**	**150599**
区、县合计	**Region**	**832697**	**341685**	**53753**	**23694**
新城区	Xincheng	151865	251	616	273
碑林区	Beilin	102449	258	598	313
莲湖区	Lianhu	126429	123	483	4138
雁塔区	Yanta	139499	3091	914	657
灞桥区	Baqiao	9502	20574	2426	493
未央区	Weiyang	68961	6017	2265	344
阎良区	Yanliang	36543	19215	2857	2247
临潼区	Lintong	31947	40983	3526	4760
长安区	Chang'an	98958	56770	18542	609
蓝田县	Lantian	18811	51978	4426	2445
周至县	Zhouzhi	8919	71265	3327	3598
户　县	Huxian	17742	47147	7667	3115
高陵县	Gaoling	21072	24013	6106	702
开发区合计	**Sum of Development Zones**	**688959**	**10151**	**592**	**142542**
高新区	GaoXin	341756	468		109388
经开区	JingKai	156770	187	136	25184
曲江新区	Qujiang	109744	3592		882
浐灞生态区	Chanba Eco-District	52358	578	272	25
航天基地	Aerospace Base	18879	242	156	5586
航空基地	Aviation Industry Base	2822			1472
国际港务区	International Trade&Logistic Park	500			
沣东新城	FengDongXinCheng	6130	5084	28	5

continued 1

(10 000 yuan)

商业服务业等支出 Expenditure for Business Services:	金融支出 Expenditure for Finance	国土海洋 气象等支出 Land and Marine Meteorological and Other Expenses	住房保障支出 Expenditure for Housing Support	粮油物资 储备支出 Expenditure for Grain and Oil Stockpiles
127121	**37978**	**39758**	**490227**	**18817**
71662	**35921**	**5083**	**341074**	**13556**
13530	**195**	**27312**	**78114**	**5261**
432	100	577	4771	15
2039		739	2978	17
1162	95	646	7805	15
467		2537	3030	12
458		738	6161	160
1434		6519	2813	25
246		2364	4039	505
833		1380	6168	239
1478		3079	17127	739
569		1744	6010	1899
1950		1403	3722	504
2061		1597	8547	737
401		3989	4943	394
41929	**1862**	**7363**	**71039**	
766	227	1039	10859	
981			12835	
3575	138	980	23200	
16083	1497	4594	16945	
9		110		
		300	2400	
20513			4800	
2		340		

6-5 续表2 continued 2

单位：万元 （10 000 yuan）

区县、开发区	Region	一般预算支出 Ordinary Budgetary Expenditures		政府性基金支出 Governmental Fund Revenue
		国债还本付息支出 Expenditure for National Debt and Interst	其他支出 Other Expenditure	
合计	**Total**	**74209**	**20884**	**5005000**
市本级合计	**Sum of city level**	**64764**	**14251**	**1198795**
区、县合计	**Region**	**9306**	**5657**	**1053831**
新城区	Xincheng	905		29909
碑林区	Beilin	78		14116
莲湖区	Lianhu	43		201926
雁塔区	Yanta	1	64	38850
灞桥区	Baqiao	5616		118146
未央区	Weiyang	81		27811
阎良区	Yanliang	117	175	11293
临潼区	Lintong	115		85230
长安区	Chang'an	96	210	243685
蓝田县	Lantian	140	200	49013
周至县	Zhouzhi	1727	4452	72122
户　县	Huxian	222	453	64753
高陵县	Gaoling	165	103	96977
开发区合计	**Sum of Development Zones**	**139**	**976**	**2752374**
高新区	GaoXin		125	429373
经开区	JingKai		771	467920
曲江新区	Qujiang	46		830867
浐灞生态区	Chanba Eco-District		30	304351
航天基地	Aerospace Base			214992
航空基地	Aviation Industry Base			52027
国际港务区	International Trade&Logistic Park	6		176600
沣东新城	FengDongXinCheng	87	50	276244

主要统计指标解释

财政收入 指国家财政参与社会产品分配所取得的收入，是实现国家职能的财力保证。主要包括：

（1）税收收入：包括增值税、消费税、营业税、企业所得税、企业所得税退税、个人所得税、资源税、城市维护建设税、房产税、印花税、城镇土地使用税、土地增值税、车船税、船舶吨税、车辆购置税、关税、耕地占用税、契税、烟叶税等。

（2）非税收入：包括专项收入、行政事业性收费、罚没收入、国有资本经营收入、国有资源（资产）有偿使用收入和其他收入。

财政支出 指国家财政将筹集起来的资金进行分配使用，以满足经济建设和各项事业的需要。主要包括：

（1）一般公共服务支出：指政府提供基本公共管理与服务的支出，包括人大事务、政协事务、政府办公厅（室）及相关机构事务、发展与改革事务、统计信息事务、财政事务、税收事务、审计事务、海关事务、人力资源事务、纪检监察事务、商贸事务、知识产权事务、工商行政管理事务、质量技术监督与检验检疫事务、民族事务、宗教事务、港澳台侨事务、档案事务、民主党派及工商联事务、群众团体事务、共产党事务等。

（2）外交支出：指政府外交事务支出，包括外交管理事务、驻外机构、对外援助、国际组织、对外合作与交流、对外宣传、边界勘界联检等方面的支出。

（3）国防支出：指政府用于国防方面的支出，包括用于现役部队、国防科研事业、专项工程、国防动员等方面的支出。

（4）公共安全支出：指政府维护社会公共安全方面的支出，包括武装警察、公安、国家安全、检察、法院、司法、监狱、劳教、国家保密、缉私警察等。

（5）教育支出：指政府教育事务支出，包括教育管理、学前教育、普通教育、职业教育、成人教育、广播电视教育、留学教育、特殊教育、进修及培训、教育费附加安排的支出等。

（6）科学技术支出：指用于科学技术方面的支出，包括科学技术管理事务、基础研究、应用研究、技术研究与开发、科技条件与服务、社会科学、科学技术普及、科技交流与合作、科技重大专项等。

（7）文化体育与传媒支出：指政府在文化、文物、体育、广播影视、新闻出版等方面的支出。

（8）社会保障和就业支出：指政府在社会保障与就业方面的支出，包括人力资源和社会保障管理事务、民政管理事务、财政对社会保险基金的补助、补充全国社会保障基金、行政事业单位离退休、企业改革补助、就业补助、抚恤、退役安置、社会福利、残疾人事业、城市居民最低生活保障、其他城市生活救助、自然灾害生活救助、红十字事业、农村最低生活保障、其他农村生活救助、补充道路交通事故社会救助基金等。

（9）医疗卫生和计划生育支出：指政府医疗卫生方面的支出，包括医疗卫生管理事务、公立医院、基层医疗卫生机构、公共卫生、医疗保障、中医药、食品和药品监督管理、人口与计划生育事务等。

（10）节能环保支出：指政府节能环保支出，包括环境保护管理事务、环境监测与监察、污染治理、自然生态保护、天然林保护工程、退耕还林、风沙荒漠治理、退牧还草、已垦草原退耕、能源节约利用、污染减排、可再生能源和资源综合利用等支出。

（11）城乡社区支出：指政府城乡社区事务支出，包括城乡社区管理事务、城乡社区规划与管理、城乡社区公共设施、城乡社区环境卫生、建设市场管理与监督等。

（12）农林水支出：指政府用于农林水事务支出，包括农业、林业、水利、南水北调、扶贫、农业综合开发、农业综合改革、促进金融支农等。

（13）交通运输支出：指政府交通运输和邮政业方面的支出，包括公路水路运输、铁路运输、民用航空运输、石油价格改革对交通运输的补贴、邮政业、车辆购置税等。

（14）资源勘探电力信息支出：指政府用于资源勘探、制造业、建筑业、电力信息等方面的支出，包括资源勘探开发、制造业、建筑业、电力监管、工业和信息产业监管、安全生产监管、国有资产监管、支持中小企业发展和管理等。

（15）商业服务业支出：指政府用于商业服务业方面的支出，包括商业流通事务、旅游业管理与服务、涉外发展服务等。

（16）金融支出：指政府用于金融方面的支出，包括金融部门行政、金融部门监管、金融发展、金融调控等。

（17）援助其他地区支出：指用于援助方政府安排并管理的对其他地区各类援助、捐赠等资金支出。

（18）国土海洋气象支出：指政府用于国土资源、海洋、测绘、地震、气象等公益服务事业方面的支出。

（19）住房保障支出：指政府用于住房方面的支出，包括保障性安居工程、住房改革、城乡社区住宅等。

（20）粮油物资储备支出：指政府用于粮油物资储备方面的支出，包括粮油事务、物资事务、能源储备、粮油储备、重要商品储备等。

（21）国债还本付息支出：指国债还本、付息、发行等方面的支出。

（22）其他支出：指不能划分到上述功能科目的其它政府支出。

中央财政收入和地方财政收入 指按现行分税制财政体制划分的中央本级收入和地方本级收入。属于中央财政的收入包括关税，进口货物增值税和消费税，出口货物退增值税和消费税，消费税，铁道部门、各银行总行、各保险公司总公司等集中交纳的营业税和城市维护建设税，增值税75%部分，纳入共享范围的企业所得税60%部分，未纳入共享范围的中央企业所得税、中央企业上交的利润，个人所得税60%部分，车辆购置税，船舶吨税，证券交易印花税97%部分，海洋石油资源税，中央非税收入等。属于地方财政的收入包括营业税（不含铁道部门、各银行总行、各保险公司总公司集中交纳的营业税），地方企业上交利润，城市维护建设税（不含铁道部门、各银行总行、各保险公司总公司集中交纳的部分），房产税，城镇土地使用税，土地增值税，车船税，耕地占用税，契税，烟叶税，印花税，增值税25%部分，纳入共享范围的企业所得税40%部分，个人所得税40%部分，证券交易印花税3%部分，海洋石油资源税以外的其他资源税，地方非税收入等。

中央财政支出和地方财政支出 指根据政府在经济和社会活动中的不同职责，划分中央和地方政府的责权，按照政府的责权划分确定的支出。中央财政支出包括一般公共服务，外交支出，国防支出，公共安全支出，以及中央政府调整国民经济结构、协调地区发展、实施宏观调控的支出等。地方财政支出包括一般公共服务，公共安全支出，地方统筹的各项社会事业支出等。

Explanatory Notes on Main Statistical Indicators

Government Revenue refers to income for the government finance through participating in the distribution of social products. It is the financial guarantee to ensure government functioning. The contents of government revenue include the following main items:

(1)Tax revenue, including business tax, corporate income tax, corporate income tax refund ,individual income tax, resource tax, city maintenance and construct tax, house property tax, stamp tax, urban land use tax, land appreciation tax, tax on vehicles and boat operation, ship tonnage tax, vehicle purchase tax, tariffs, farm land occupation tax, deed tax, and tobacco leaf tax, etc.

(2) Non-tax revenue, including special program receipts, charge of administrative and institutional units, penalty receipts ,state-owned capital operating income,State-owned resources (assets) compensation for the use of incomeand others non-tax receipts.

Government Expenditure refers to the distribution and use of the funds which the government finance has raised, so as to meet the needs of economic construction and various causes. It includes the following main items:

(1) Expenditure for general public services: It refers to the spending on the basic public management and services which provided by governments, including the expense on affairs of People' s Congress, affairs of People' s Political Consultative Conference, affairs of government general office and relative institutions, affairs of development and reform, affairs of statistics, affairs of finance, affairs of taxation, affairs of audit, affairs of customs, affairs of human resources and social security, affairs of discipline inspection and supervision, affairs of population and family planning, affairs of commerce and trade, affairs of intellectual property, affairs of administration for industry and commerce, affairs of land and resources, affairs of oceanic administration, affairs of surveying and mapping, affairs of earthquake, ethnic affairs, religious affairs, affairs of Hong Kong, Macao, Taiwan, and Overseas Chinese, affairs of archives administration, affairs of Chinese Communist Party, affairs of democratic parties and federation of industry and commerce, affairs of mass organization, and affairs of lottery, etc.

(2) Expenditure for foreign affairs: It refers to the spending of government on foreign affairs, including the expense on administration of foreign affairs, missions overseas, external assistance, international organizations, foreign cooperation and communication, surveying and joint inspection on borderline, etc.

(3) Expenditure for national defense: It refers to the spending of government on national defense, including the expense on active force, scientific research on national defense, special projects, mobilization of national defense, etc.

(4) Expenditure for public security: It refers to the spending of government on maintaining social and public security, including the expense on armed police force, public security, state security, prosecution, courts, justice, prison, labor education and rehabilitation, protection of state secrecy, anti-smuggling police, etc.

(5) Expenditure for education: It refers to the spending of government on education, including the expense on the administration of education, pre-primary education, regular vocational school education, adult education,radio and television education, student abroad education, special education, education and training,education surtax arrangementsspending, etc.

(6) Expenditure for science and technology: It refers to the spending of government on science and technology (S&T), including the expense on the administration of S&T, basic research, applied research, research and development, conditions and services of S&T, popularization of social science, science and technology, exchanges and cooperation of S&T, etc.

(7) Expenditure for culture, sport and media: It refers to the spending of government on culture, cultural heritage, sports, radio, film, television, press and publication, etc.

(8) Expenditure for social safety net and employment effort: It refers to the spending of government on social safety net and employment, including the expense on administration of social safety net and employment, civil affairs, budgetary subsidy on the social insurance funds, subsidy on National Social Security Fund, retirees of administrative units and institutions, subsidy on enterprise reform, subsidy on

employment effort, pension, placement of ex-serviceman, social welfare, the handicapped undertakings, the system of cost of living allowances for urban residents, other urban social relief, rural social relief, living relief of natural disasters, affairs of Red Cross Society, etc.

(9)Expenditure for medical and health careand birth controlplanning expenditures: It refers to government spending on health care, including health management services, public hospitals, primary health care institutions, public health, health care, the pharmaceutical, food and drug supervision and management, population and family planning affairs.

(10) Expenditure for energy saving: It refers to the government energy-saving and environmental protection expenditures, including environmental management services, environmental monitoring and surveillance, pollution control, ecological protection, natural forest protection project, forest, desert sand control, pasture, grassland of cultivated farmland, energy conservation and utilization expenditure pollution reduction, renewable energy and comprehensive utilization of resources, etc.

(11) Expenditure for urban and rural community affairs: It refers to the spending of government on urban and rural community affairs, including the expense on administration of urban and rural community, planning and management of urban and rural community, public facilities of urban and rural community, housing of urban and rural community, sanitation of urban and rural community, management and supervision on the construction market, etc.

(12) Expenditure for agriculture, forestry and water conservancy: It refers to the spending of government on agriculture, forestry and water conservancy, including the expense on agriculture, forestry, water conservancy, South-to-North Water Diversion Project, poverty alleviation, agricultural comprehensive development, comprehensive agricultural reform, promoting financial support for agriculture, etc.

(13) Expenditure for transportation: It refers to the spending of government on transportation and postal services, including the expense on road transport, sea transport, rail transport, civil aviation transportation, oil price reform subsidies for transportation, postal services, vehicle purchase tax, etc.

(14) Expenditure for exploration of the power of information: It refers to the spending on exploration, manufacturing, construction, electricity and other aspects of information, including resource exploration and development, manufacturing, construction, electricity regulation, industry and information industry regulation, safety supervision, the state-owned assets supervision and support of small and medium enterprise development and management, etc.

(15) Expenditure for business services: It refers to government spending on commercial aspects of services, including commercial distribution business, tourism management and services, foreign development services, etc.

(16) Expenditure forfinancial: It refers to government spending on financial aspects, including administrative of financial sector, financial sector supervision, financial development, financial control, etc.

(17) Expenditure forassistance to other parts: It refers to the various types of assistance to other regions, financial donations, donors, government expenditure and management arrangements, etc.

(18) Expenditure for Land and Marine Meteorology expenditure: It refers to government spending on land resources, marine, mapping, seismic, weather and other aspects of public service undertakings, etc.

(19) Expenditure for housing security: It refers to government spending on housing, including affordable housing projects, housing reform, urban and rural communities housing, etc.

(20) Expenditure for Grain and Oil stockpiles: It refers to government spending on supplies of grain and oil reserves, including grain and oil services, supplies services, energy reserves, grain and oil reserves, reserves of other important commodities, etc.

(21) Expenditure for Treasury debt service: It refers to the national debt principal, interest expenses, and other aspects of the issue, etc.

(22) Other expenditure:It refers to other government spending cannot be divided into the above functions subjects.

Revenue of the Central Government and Revenue of the Local Governments refers to the revenue collected by the Central Government and that by the local governments as defined by the decentralized taxation system. In accordance with this system, the revenue of the Central Government includes tariff, VAT and consumption tax from imports, VAT and consumption tax rebate for exports, consumption tax, business tax and city maintenance and construct tax from the Ministry of Railways, head offices of banks, head offices of insurance company, which are handed over to the government in a centralized way, 75% of the value added tax, 60% the share part of the corporate income tax, unshared part of corporate income tax of the central enterprises, profit handed in by the central enterprises, 60% of individual income tax, vehicle purchase tax, ship tonnage tax, 97% of stamp tax on securities transactions, resource tax on the offshore petroleum resources. The revenue of the local governments includes business tax (excluding the part of the Ministry of Railways, head offices of banks, head offices of insurance company, which are handed over to the government in a centralized way), profit handed in by the local enterprises, city maintenance and construct tax (excluding the part of the Ministry of Railways, head offices of banks, head offices of insurance company, which are handed over to the government in a centralized way), house property tax, urban land use tax, land appreciation tax, tax on vehicles and boat operation, farm land occupation tax, deed tax, and tobacco leaf tax, stamp tax, 25% of the value added tax, 40% the share part of the corporate income tax, 40% of individual income tax, 3% of stamp tax on securities transactions, resource tax other than the tax on offshore petroleum resources, local non-tax revenue, etc.

Expenditure of the Central Government and Expenditure of the Local Governments according to the different functions of the Central Government and local governments in economic and social activities, the rights of affairs administration are demarcated between those of the Central Government and those of local governments; and the classification of the expenditure between the Central Government and local governments are made on the basis of the classification of the rights of affairs administration between them. The expenditure of the Central Government includes the expenditure for general public services, expenditure for foreign affairs, expenditure for public security, and the expenditure of the Central Government for adjusting the national economic structure; coordinating the development among different regions; and exercising macroeconomic regulation. The expenditure of the local governments includes mainly the expenditure for general public services, expenditure for public security, and expenditures for social development which are planned by local governments, etc.

7 物价指数

PRICE INDICES

资料整理：周　文　李海瑞　王　茹
Data management：Zhou Wen Li Hairui Wang Ru
数据审核：刘　青　祝立新　党　军　雷麦鸽
Data audit：Liu Qing Zhu Lixin Dang Jun Lei Maige

第七部分　物价指数

一、简要说明

本章资料主要包括居民消费、商品零售、工业生产者出厂、工业生产者购进、房地产销售以及固定资产投资等价格指数，由国家统计局西安调查队提供。

二、主要指标

商品零售价格总指数（上年=100）	100.7	比上年下降	1.0个百分点
居民消费价格总指数（上年=100）	101.4	比上年下降	1.3个百分点

7　PRICE INDICES

Ⅰ.Brief Introduction

This chapter consists of primarily data on consumer price indices, retail price indices, producer price indices for industrial products,purchasing price indices for industrial products,real estate selling, fixed asset investment,provided by Fixed Asset NBS Survey Office in Xi'an.

Ⅱ.Major Indicators

		Increase over Preceding Year
Retail Price Index(the price preceding year=100)	100.7	-1.0 percentage points
Consumer Price Index(the price preceding year=100)	101.4	-1.3 percentage points

7-1 主要年份各种价格指数

Price Indices in Representative Years

(以上年价格为100)

(the price of preceding year= 100)

年　份 Year	居民消费价格指数 Consumer Price Index	商品零售价格指数 Retail Price Index	工业生产者出厂价格指数 Producer Price Indiees (PPI) for Industrial Producers	工业生产者购进价格指数 Industrial Purchasing Indices （IPI）for Industrial Producers	固定资产投资价格指数 Price Index for Investment in Fixed Assets
1980	108.7	109.3			
1981	102.4	102.7			
1982	100.9	101.0			
1983	102.6	102.0			
1984	104.7	104.8			
1985	109.7	109.3			
1986	108.5	107.4			
1987	110.6	111.4			
1988	122.8	123.2			
1989	118.3	117.8			
1990	102.5	100.9			
1991	109.4	108.3			
1992	112.2	112.4			
1993	117.2	112.8	102.5	104.3	
1994	128.5	126.2	132.2	115.0	
1995	117.0	114.6	110.8	113.1	
1996	110.9	107.9	100.7	103.8	
1997	106.0	101.5	98.6	102.5	
1998	97.9	95.5	94.4	97.5	
1999	96.8	97.4	97.5	96.9	100.8
2000	100.2	98.7	99.4	102.4	102.1
2001	99.9	98.9	99.3	101.0	101.3
2002	98.6	98.5	98.2	98.4	101.2
2003	100.5	100.0	101.5	105.3	102.4
2004	102.3	101.9	102.7	110.4	103.3
2005	100.3	99.7	103.9	109.6	102.4
2006	101.6	101.5	103.2	106.1	102.0
2007	104.7	103.7	101.9	106.2	103.5
2008	106.0	105.4	103.7	108.5	110.5
2009	99.7	99.5	99.9	100.7	97.9
2010	103.5	102.7	102.3	106.3	103.8
2011	105.6	104.4	102.5	108.8	105.4
2012	102.8	102.3	100.5	97.2	101.9
2013	102.7	101.7	99.5	97.2	100.8
2014	101.4	100.7	99.5	99.5	100.8

注：本表数据来源国家统计局西安调查队。

7-2 居民消费价格指数（2014年）

Residents Consumer Price Indices (2014)

(以上年价格为100) (the price of preceding year=100)

指　标	Item	2014
居民价格消费总指数	**Consumer Price Index**	**101.4**
非食品价格指数	Non-foodstuff Price Index	100.7
服务项目价格指数	Price Index of Service	101.6
工业品价格指数	Ex-factory Price Indices of Industrial Products	100.0
扣除食品烟酒和能源价格指数	Price Index with Food,Tobacco,Liquor and Energy Excluded	100.8
扣除鲜菜鲜果总指数	Price Index with Fresh Vegetables and Fruits Excluded	101.4
消费品价格指数	Price Index of Consumer Goods	101.4
一、食品	**Food**	**102.9**
1. 粮食	Grain	103.2
2. 淀粉及制品	Starches and Processed Products	95.1
3. 干豆类及豆制品	Beans and Bean Products	112.6
4. 油脂	Oil or Fat	92.6
5. 肉禽及其制品	Meat,Poultry and Processed Products	99.5
6. 蛋	Eggs	111.1
7. 水产品	Aquatic Products	103.6
8. 菜	Vegetables	93.1
9. 调味品	Flavouring	102.4
10. 糖	Carbohydrate	104.9
11. 茶及饮料	Tea and Beverages	103.0
12. 干鲜瓜果	Dried and Fresh Melons and Fruits	113.9
13. 糕点饼干面包	Cake,Biscuit and Bread	104.2
14. 液体乳及乳制品	Milk and Its Product	114.0
15. 在外用膳食品	Dining Out	103.0
16. 其他食品	Other Food	100.3
二、烟酒	**Tobacco and Liquor**	**98.4**
1. 烟草	Tobacco	99.8
2. 酒	Liquor	95.7
三、衣着	**Clothing**	**101.1**
1. 服装	Garments	101.1
2. 衣着材料	Clothing Material	100.0
3. 鞋袜帽	Footgear and Hats	100.7
4. 衣着加工服务费	Clothing Manufacturing Services	106.2

注：本表数据来源国家统计局西安调查队。

7-2 续表 continued

(以上年价格为100) (the price of preceding year= 100)

指　标	Item	2014
四、家庭设备用品及维修服务	**Household facilities,Articles and Services**	**101.9**
1. 耐用消费品	Durable Consumer Goods	99.9
2. 室内装饰品	Interior Decorations	98.6
3. 床上用品	Bed Articles	101.1
4. 家庭日用杂品	Daily Use Household Articles	100.6
5. 家庭服务及加工维修服务	Household Service and Maintenance Renovation	114.3
五、医疗保健和个人用品	**Health Care and Personal Articles**	**102.8**
1. 医疗保健	Health Care	104.5
(1)医疗器具及用品	Medical Instrument Articles	104.5
(2)中药材及中成药	Traditional Chinese Medicine	111.1
(3)西药	Western Medicine	101.6
(4)保健器具及用品	Health Care Appliances and Articles	102.5
(5)医疗保健服务	Health Care Services	100.0
2. 个人用品及服务	Personal Articles and Services	99.3
六、交通和通信	**Transportation and Communication**	**100.2**
1. 交通	Transportation	101.9
(1)交通工具	Transportation Facility	99.7
(2)车用燃料及零配件	Fuels and Parts	98.7
(3)车辆使用及维修费	Fees for Vehicles Use and Maintenance	105.3
(4)市区公共交通费	Incity Traffic Fare	100.0
(5)城市间交通费	Intercity Traffic Fare	105.1
2. 通信	Communication	98.4
(1)通信工具	Telecommunication Facility	81.4
(2)通信服务	Telecommunication Service	100.0
七、娱乐教育文化用品及服务	**Recreation,Education and Culture Articles**	**100.1**
1. 文娱用耐用消费品及服务	Durable Consumer Goods for Cultural and Recreational Use and Services	95.1
2. 教育	Education	101.5
3. 文化娱乐用品	Cultural and Recreational Articles	103.1
4. 旅游	Touring	95.1
八、居住	**Residence**	**99.8**
1. 建房及装修材料	Building and Building Decoration Materials	93.6
2. 住房租金	Rental Housing	102.6
3. 自有住房	Private Housing	103.7
4. 水、电、燃料	Water, Electricity and Fuels	99.8

7-3 商品零售价格指数（2014年）

Retail Price Indices (2014)

（以上年价格为100） (the price of preceding year= 100)

指　标	Item	2014
商品零售价格总指数	**Retail Price Indices**	**100.7**
一、食品	**Food**	**103.0**
1. 粮食	Grain	102.6
2. 淀粉及制品	Starches and Processed Products	95.1
3. 干豆类及豆制品	Beans and Bean Products	111.9
4. 油脂	Oil or Fat	92.6
5. 肉禽及其制品	Meat,Poultry and Processed Products	99.7
6. 蛋	Eggs	111.1
7. 水产品	Aquatic Products	103.0
8. 菜	Vegetables	93.0
9. 调味品	Flavouring	102.1
10. 糖	Carbohydrate	104.2
11. 干鲜瓜果	Dried and Fresh Melons and Fruits	113.8
12. 糕点饼干面包	Cake,Biscuit and Bread	103.6
13. 液体乳及乳制品	Milk and Its Product	114.4
14. 在外用膳食品	Dining Out	103.0
15. 其他食品	Other Food and Manufacturing Services	100.3
二、饮料、烟酒	**Beverages,Tobacco and Liquor**	**100.4**
1. 茶及饮料	Tea and Beverages	103.7
2. 烟草	Tobacco	99.7
3. 酒	Liquor	95.7
三、服装、鞋帽	**Garments,Shoes and Hats**	**100.9**
1. 服装	Garments	100.9
2. 鞋袜帽	Footgear and Hats	101.1
3. 其他	Others	91.9
四、纺织品	**Textiles**	**101.1**
1. 衣着材料	Cotton Cloth	100.0
2. 床上用品	Blend Cloth	101.6
五、家用电器及音像器材	**Household Appliances,Music and Video Equipment**	**98.7**
1. 家庭设备	Household facility	100.9
2. 文娱用耐用消费品	Durable Consumer Goods on Cultural and Recreational Use	94.7
3. 专业音像器材	Music and Video Equipment	100.0

注：本表数据来源国家统计局西安调查队。

7-3 续表 continued

(以上年价格为100) (the price of preceding year= 100)

指 标	Item	2014
六、文化办公用品	**Cultural and Office Appliances**	**97.9**
七、日用品	**Articles for Daily Use**	**100.4**
1. 日用百货	General Merchandise for Daily Use	99.0
2. 日用杂品	Miscellaneous for Daily Use	101.3
3. 洗涤用品	Daily Use Articles For Washing	101.6
4. 其他日用品	Other Daily Articles	100.2
八、体育娱乐用品	**Sports and Recreation Articles**	**98.8**
1. 体育用品	Sports Goods	99.1
2. 娱乐用品	Receration Goods	98.6
九、交通、通信用品	**Transportation and Communication Goods**	**98.8**
1. 交通运输机械	Transportation Machinery	100.2
2. 通信器材	Communication Machinery	87.5
十、家具	**Furniture**	**98.2**
十一、化妆品	**Cosmetics**	**101.5**
十二、金银珠宝	**Gold,Silver and Jewelry**	**91.2**
十三、中西药品及医疗保健用品	**Traditional Chinese and Western Medicines And Health Care Articles**	**104.5**
1. 医疗器具及用品	Medical Apparatus and Article	104.5
2. 中药材及中成药	Traditional Chinese Medicinal Materials and Medicines	112.2
3. 西药	Western Medicine	101.4
4. 保健器具及用品	Health Care Apparatus and Article	102.0
十四、书报杂志及电子出版物	**Books,Newspapers,Magazines and Electronic Publications**	**104.1**
1. 教材及参考书	Teaching Materials and Reference Books	102.7
2. 书报杂志	Books, Newspapers and Magazines	107.9
3. 电子音像制品	Electronic Audio-video Products	101.2
十五、燃料	**Fuel**	**98.5**
1、煤炭及制品	Coal and Its Products	94.7
2、石油及制品	Oil and Its Products	98.9
十六、建筑材料及五金电料	**Building Materials and Hardware**	**94.2**
1. 建筑装潢材料	Building Decoration Materials	93.1
2. 五金电料	Hardware	98.6

7-4 主要年份工业生产者出厂价格指数

(上年价格=100)

类　别	Classify	1997	1998	1999	2000	2001
全部工业品	**industrial products**	**98.6**	**94.4**	**97.5**	**99.4**	**99.3**
按轻重工业分	Grouped by Light Industry and Heavy Industry					
轻工业	Light Industry	98.2	91.1	95.9	97.8	99.6
以农产品为原料	Using Farm Products as Raw Materials	99.2	89.5	95.2	99.2	99.0
以非农产品为原料	Using Non-farm Products as Raw Materials	96.8	93.4	97.0	95.5	100.6
重工业	Heavy Industry	99.0	97.3	98.9	100.8	99.2
采掘	Mining & Quarrying		104.1	101.5	97.5	94.8
原料	Raw Materials	101.0	100.7	102.3	107.7	101.1
加工	Processing	97.9	95.6	98.0	98.4	98.5
按生产生活资料分	by means of production and livelihood					
生产资料	Means of Production	99.6	96.6	98.3	100.5	99.1
采掘	Mining & Quarrying		104.1	101.5	97.5	94.8
原料	Raw Materials	100.9	100.6	100.2	106.4	101.1
加工	Processing	98.9	94.7	97.6	98.7	98.5
生活资料	Consumer Goods	97.0	91.4	96.5	97.3	99.9
食品	Food	108.2	97.8	95.8	94.4	99.6
衣着	Clothing	93.0	83.9	95.2	101.6	99.4
一般日用品	Articles for Daily Use	91.6	95.1	97.6	96.9	101.9
耐用消费品	Durable Consumer Goods	99.7	95.4	98.0	95.9	97.0
按工业部门分	Grouped by Industrial Sector					
1. 冶金工业	Metallurgical Industry	99.2	97.5	91.2	98.2	97.2
2. 电力工业	Power Industry	111.3	111.2	109.3	109.6	102.4
3. 煤炭及炼焦工业	Coal and Coking Industry	98.9	98.5	96.3	100.5	110.3
4. 石油工业	Petroleum Industry			107.1	134.2	96.6
5. 化学工业	Chemical Industry	91.8	92.9	96.6	96.7	100.5
6. 机械工业	Machine Manufacturing Industry	98.8	94.6	98.1	98.0	98.3
7. 建筑材料工业	Building Materials Industry	98.2	99.3	96.7	98.5	100.6
8. 森林工业	Timber Industry	107.6	104.5	97.9	98.9	98.1
9. 食品工业	Food Industry	106.8	95.3	95.5	94.3	99.8
10. 纺织工业	Textiles Industry	94.3	82.6	93.7	103.4	97.5
11. 缝纫工业	Tailoring Industry	100.1	97.3	99.1	103.5	100.0
12. 皮革工业	Leather Industry	91.2	96.8	98.0	99.2	101.0
13. 造纸工业	Paper Industry			95.3	96.7	102.3
14. 文教艺术用品工业	Cultural,Educational & Handicrafts Articles			96.7	96.4	101.1
15. 其它工业	Other Industry	109.5	109.2	98.9	104.8	107.1

注：本表数据来源国家统计局西安调查队。

Producer Price Indices (PPI) for Industrial Producers in Representative Years

(the price of preceding year= 100)

2002	2003	2004	2005	2006	2007	2008	2009	2010	2011	2012	2013	2014
98.2	**101.5**	**102.7**	**103.9**	**103.2**	**101.9**	**103.7**	**99.9**	**102.3**	**102.5**	**100.5**	**99.5**	**99.5**
98.4	101.3	103.4	99.9	100.2	101.8	103.7	100.6	102.5	107.0	100.4	100.7	100.9
98.4	104.5	108.7	97.3	100.1	103.3	106.0	98.9	104.0	109.3	100.3	101.0	100.8
98.6	99.9	100.8	101.2	100.2	100.8	102.1	101.8	101.4	100.9	100.5	99.9	101.3
98.2	101.6	101.9	107.9	105.5	101.9	103.8	99.3	102.2	101.6	100.5	99.2	99.2
101.3	103.4	140.5	107.9	100.6	111.6	122.3	90.0	150.2	102.6	101.8	100.6	100.6
101.3	111.2	109.0	114.2	111.8	104.9	110.8	99.5	108.9	111.2	108.6	95.1	97.6
97.7	100.1	100.6	106.7	104.2	101.2	101.9	99.4	100.8	100.1	99.2	99.9	99.5
98.0	101.8	102.7	105.3	104.2	101.3	103.4	99.3	102.2	101.9	100.3	99.2	99.5
101.3	103.4	140.5	107.9	100.6	111.6	122.3	90.0	150.2	102.6	101.8	100.6	100.6
101.0	108.1	106.6	111.3	111.6	104.8	110.2	99.7	109.0	111.3	108.7	95.2	97.7
97.4	100.9	102.0	104.3	103.0	100.6	102.0	99.3	101.0	100.3	98.9	99.9	99.7
99.1	100.5	102.5	100.4	100.4	103.5	104.7	101.4	102.5	104.5	100.8	100.4	99.7
101.2	101.0	103.6	100.3	100.4	105.3	106.6	100.3	103.3	109.5	101.6	100.9	101.2
100.8	99.4	102.7	102.0	103.3	104.6	105.1	102.7	101.2	111.9	99.4	100.4	99.1
97.9	101.2	101.2	101.3	100.8	100.1	102.7	102.6	101.2	101.5	101.5	99.1	101.3
98.1	97.2	98.3	99.1	99.4	100.7	100.7	103.9	101.9	99.5	99.0	100.9	95.9
98.7	103.8	107.1	103.9	106.5	103.2	104.8	92.0	105.8	116.3	100.7	97.5	97.5
100.0	103.2	104.1	110.6	107.9	105.5	110.0	109.0	101.2	104.7	111.2	100.6	99.4
106.7	136.8	131.4	97.1	95.4	106.8	104.8	101.7	110.6	109.3	101.5	100.0	100.0
100.7	118.6	110.5	121.7	117.6	104.8	115.6	96.7	114.2	108.4	108.2	89.7	97.2
99.2	100.2	100.8	103.2	100.8	101.1	104.1	102.6	100.8	104.2	100.3	99.6	100.9
97.6	99.8	100.6	104.9	103.4	101.0	101.7	99.9	100.9	99.5	99.0	100.0	99.4
99.6	99.7	100.0	98.6	98.9	98.9	101.8	101.9	99.9	100.6	99.6	99.3	99.1
98.9	100.1	100.2	101.6	101.6	101.1	101.1	101.1	101.7	105.2	103.2	103.4	101.6
101.1	102.8	107.5	98.3	99.0	106.1	109.3	98.3	104.3	110.1	101.7	101.0	101.3
94.9	117.3	119.1	89.9	102.4	98.4	99.7	97.5	108.9	107.2	88.7	103.9	99.3
101.1	100.2	103.6	100.8	103.5	104.6	105.1	102.6	101.3	113.4	99.4	100.4	99.0
101.8	98.7	99.6	101.2	100.0	99.0	99.6	99.7	99.6	98.0	99.9	99.9	100.0
95.0	96.9	100.2	101.2	100.0	100.1	104.5	98.4	100.4	103.4	99.2	98.4	98.1
103.4	97.5	96.5	98.1	100.1	99.1	99.2	102.2	99.9	100.7	106.0	97.5	100.0
99.4	103.3	105.0	103.4	105.7	111.4	104.3	99.7	100.5	104.3	101.2	99.6	100.0

7-5 主要年份工业生产者购进价格指数

Industrial Purchasing Indices (IPI) for Industrial Producers in Representative Years

(上年价格=100) (the price of preceding year= 100)

指 标	Item	2000	2001	2002	2003	2004	2005	2006
全部原材料	**raw materials**	**102.4**	**101.0**	**98.4**	**105.3**	**110.4**	**109.6**	**106.1**
(一)燃料、动力类	Fuel and Power	105.0	101.8	100.9	105.7	109.4	123.5	112.6
(二)黑色金属材料类	Ferrous Metals	102.7	102.1	98.5	107.4	117.4	107.6	99.2
#钢材	Steel	103.4	102.4	97.9	106.0	114.8	107.5	98.5
(三)有色金属材料和电线类	Non-ferrous Metals and Electric Wires	105.2	95.5	96.8	105.8	114.1	107.8	116.5
(四)化工原料类	Raw Chemical Materials	104.6	102.5	97.9	102.4	106.3	106.1	101.6
(五)木材及纸浆类	Timber and Paper Pulp	101.2	102.8	99.4	101.2	100.3	108.2	111.7
(六)建筑材料及非金属矿类	Building Materials and Non-metal ores	100.3	99.7	98.6	99.6	110.4	99.3	100.7
(七)其它工业原材料及半成品类	Other Industrial Raw Materials and Semi-Products	98.8	100.8	98.9	102.5	111.2	106.1	104.3
(八)农副产品类	Agricultural Products	100.4	102.8	98.2	113.7	112.7	100.9	107.2
(九)纺织原料类	Textile Materials	98.0	96.8	90.6	103.4	103.9	97.6	101.5

注：本表数据来源国家统计局西安调查队。

7-5 续表 continued

(上年价格=100) (the price of preceding year= 100)

指 标	Item	2007	2008	2009	2010	2011	2012	2013	2014
全部原材料	**raw materials**	**106.2**	**108.5**	**100.7**	**106.3**	**108.8**	**97.2**	**97.2**	**99.5**
(一)燃料、动力类	Fuel and Power	107.0	109.8	105.1	108.6	113.5	102.3	96.8	98.2
(二)黑色金属材料类	Ferrous Metals	104.8	111.3	99.2	103.1	102.9	93.4	98.0	97.9
#钢材	Steel	104.9	111.7	98.7	103.5	102.9	93.3	98.0	97.9
(三)有色金属材料和电线类	Non-ferrous Metals and Electric Wires	110.7	99.1	93.9	113.6	118.9	93.0	94.5	96.6
(四)化工原料类	Raw Chemical Materials	105.6	111.4	95.0	103.9	108.1	87.7	90.8	104.6
(五)木材及纸浆类	Timber and Paper Pulp	105.9	106.5	102.6	101.1	105.4	100.9	99.2	100.7
(六)建筑材料及非金属矿类	Building Materials and Non-metal ores	104.0	104.8	106.8	102.1	102.9	97.4	102.2	101.1
(七)其它工业原材料及半成品类	Other Industrial Raw Materials and Semi-Products	108.8	110.6	101.4	108.1	109.4	100.3	98.9	100.9
(八)农副产品类	Agricultural Products	107.2	108.9	99.6	106.5	107.4	103.4	100.5	98.8
(九)纺织原料类	Textile Materials	100.5	99.8	97.6	104.6	107.0	89.1	97.6	99.3

7-6 住宅销售价格指数（2014年）

Selling Price Indices of Residential Buildings（2014）

(上年价格=100) (the price of preceding year= 100)

指 标	Item	2014
新建住宅	**Newly built residential buildings**	**103.7**
一、保障性住房	guaranteed house	
二、新建商品住宅	New commodity residential house	104.1
（一）90平方米及以下	90 square meters and less	104.2
（二）90-144平方米	90-144 square metre	103.5
（三）144平方米以上	144 square meters and more	105.1
二手住宅	**used/second hand residential buildings**	**99.8**
一、90平方米及以下	90 square meters and the following	99.7
二、90-144平方米	90-144 square metre	99.8
三、144平方米以上	144 square meters	100.1

注：本表数据来源国家统计局西安调查队。

7-7 主要年份固定资产投资价格指数

Price Indices for Investment in Fixed Assets in Representative Years

(上年价格=100) (the price of preceding year= 100)

指 标	Item	2000	2004	2005	2006	2007	2008	2009	2010	2011	2012	2013	2014
固定资产投资价格指数	**Price Indices for Investment in Fixed Assets**	**102.1**	**103.3**	**102.4**	**102**	**103.5**	**110.5**	**97.9**	**103.8**	**105.4**	**101.9**	**100.8**	**100.8**
建筑安装、装饰工程	Construction,Installation and Decoration	103.9	104.6	102.3	102.6	104.9	114.9	97.1	105.5	107.2	102.6	101.0	100.8
设备、工器具购置	Purchase of Equipment and Instruments	97.9	100.5	104.5	100.8	100.7	101.0	98.6	100.0	100.6	99.1	99.5	99.9
其他费用	Others	100.0	100.6	100.5	100.5	100.6	101.9	100.9	100.8	102.8	102.7	101.9	101.8

注：本表数据来源国家统计局西安调查队。

主要统计指标解释

居民消费价格指数 是反映一定时期内城乡居民所购买的生活消费品和服务项目价格变动趋势和程度的相对数，是对城市居民消费价格指数和农村居民消费价格指数进行综合汇总计算的结果。通过该指数可以观察和分析消费品的零售价格和服务项目价格变动对城乡居民实际生活费支出的影响程度。

商品零售价格指数 是反映一定时期内城乡商品零售价格变动趋势和程度的相对数。商品零售价格的变动与国家的财政收入、市场供需的平衡、消费与积累的比例关系有关。因此，该指数可以从一个侧面对上述经济活动进行观察和分析。

工业生产者出厂价格指数 是反映一定时期内全部工业产品出厂价格总水平的变动趋势和程度的相对数，包括工业企业售给本企业以外所有单位的各种产品和直接售给居民用于生活消费的产品。该指数可以观察出厂价格变动对工业总产值及增加值的影响。

工业生产者购进价格指数 是反映工业企业作为生产投入，而从市场和能源、原材料生产企业购买原材料、燃料和动力产品价格的变动趋势和程度的统计指标，是扣除工业企业物质消耗成本中的价格变动影响的重要依据。

固定资产投资价格指数 是反映一定时期内固定资产投资品及取费项目的价格变动趋势和程度的相对数。固定资产投资额是由建筑安装工程投资完成额、设备工器具购置投资完成额和其他费用投资完成额三部分组成的。编制固定资产投资价格指数应首先分别编制上述三部分投资的价格指数，然后采用加权算术平均法求出固定资产投资价格总指数。

该指数可以准确地反映固定资产投资中涉及的各类投资品和取费项目价格变动趋势和变动幅度，消除按现价计算的固定资产投资指标中的价格变动因素，真实地反映固定资产投资的规模、速度、结构和效益，为国家科学地制定、检查固定资产投资计划并提高宏观调控水平，为完善国民经济核算体系提供科学的、可靠的依据。

Explanatory Notes on Main Statistical Indicators

Consumer Price Indices reflect the trend and degree of changes in prices of consumer goods and services purchased by urban and rural households during a given period. They are obtained by combining Consumer Price Indices of Urban Household and Consumer Price Indices of Rural Household. The Indices enable the observation and analysis of the degree of impact of the changes in the prices of retailed goods and services on the actual living expenses of urban and rural residents.

Retail Price Indices reflect the trend and degree of change in retail prices of commodities during a given period. The change in retail prices of commodities is related to government revenue, the equilibrium of market supply and demand, and the ratio of consumption to accumulation. Therefore, the retail price indices are useful from an oblique perspective for observing and analyzing the changes of the above economic activities.

Producer Price Indices (PPI) for Industrial Producers reflect the trend and degree of changes in general ex-factory prices of all manufactured goods during a given period, including sales of manufactured goods by an industrial enterprise to all units outside the enterprise, as well as sales of consumer goods to residents. It can be used to analyze the impact of ex-factory prices on gross output value and value-added of the industrial sector.

Industrial Purchasing Indices (IPI) for Industrial Producers reflect changes in the level and degree of prices paid by industrial enterprises when they purchase production input such as raw materials, fuels and power from the market or from other energy or raw materials producing enterprises. These indices provide an important basis for measuring the material consumption of industrial enterprises after removing the influence of price changes.

Price Indices for Investment in Fixed Assets reflect the trend and degree of changes in prices of investment goods and projects in fixed assets during a given period. The investment in fixed assets consists of three components, namely the investment in construction and installation, the investment in purchases of equipment and instrument, and the investment in other items. Price indices for investment in fixed assets are calculated as the weighted arithmetic mean of the price indices for the three components of investment in fixed assets.

Removing the factor of price change in the aggregates of investment at current prices, this indicator shows the changes in the prices of commodities and fees involved in the investment of fixed assets, and can be used to observe the actual size, growth, structure, and efficiency of investment in fixed assets and provides reliable and scientific data for government planning, management, decision-making, and further improving the current national accounting system.

8 人民生活

PEOPLE´S LIVELIHOOD

资料整理：安海军　赵兰莉　严孟飞
Data management：An Haijun　Zhao Lanli　Yan Mengfei
数据审核：冯军魁
Data audit：Feng Junkui

第八部分　人民生活

一、简要说明

本章资料反映我市城乡常住居民生活现状及变化情况，2014年数据为实施城乡住户调查一体化改革后的全市居民生活主要数据，表8-1和表8-3为老口径数据，使用时请注意。本章资料由西安市统计局人口就业处提供。

二、主要指标

全体居民人均可支配收入（元）	25599		
城镇常住居民人均可支配收入（元）	30715	比上年增长	9.1%
城镇常住居民人均消费支出（元）	20893		
农村常住居民人均可支配收入（元）	12898	比上年增长	11.9%
农村常住居民人均消费支出（元）	8780		

8 PEOPLE'S LIVELIHOOD

Ⅰ.Brief Introduction

Data in this chapter reflected the city's urban and rural residents living condition and changes in circumstances. Data reflected the implementation of the city's residents in 2014 integrated household survey reformed life. Data in sheet 8-1 and 8-3 were former statistical standard which readers must pay attention to. The data come from Population & Employment Division of the Xi'an Bureau of Statistics.

Ⅱ.Major Indicators

Indicator	Value	Increase over Preceding Year
Per Capita disposable Income of all Residents(yuan)	25599	
Per Capita disposable Income of Urban Residents (yuan)	30715	9.1%
Per Capita Consumption Expenditure of Urban Residents (yuan)	20893	
Per Capita disposable Income of Rural Residents	12898	11.9%
Per Capita Consumption Expenditure of Rural Residents(yuan)	8780	

8-1 主要年份城乡居民人均收入及恩格尔系数

Per Capita Annual Income and Engel's Coefficient of Urban and Rural Households in Representative Years

年 份 Year	城镇居民家庭人均可支配收入 Per Capita Annual Disposable Income of Urban Households		农村居民家庭人均纯收入 Per Capita Annual Net Income of Rural Households		城镇居民家庭 恩格尔系数 （%） Engel's Coefficient of Urban Households	农村居民家庭 恩格尔系数 （%） Engel's Coefficient of Rural Households
	绝对数 （元） Absoulte number (yuan)	指数 （1980年=100） Index (preceding year= 100)	绝对数 （元） Absoulte number (yuan)	指数 （1978年=100） Index (preceding year= 100)		
1978			140	100.0		
1979						
1980	414	100.0	190	135.7	53.3	53.3
1981	446	107.7	207	147.9	52.9	53.7
1982	479	115.6	254	181.4	55.1	56.7
1983	509	122.9	245	175.0	55.1	58.4
1984	540	130.3	299	213.6	54.9	51.7
1985	719	173.5	351	250.7	49.5	48.5
1986	911	219.8	390	278.6	49.9	47.9
1987	1034	249.7	434	310.0	50.6	50.3
1988	1142	275.6	482	344.3	44.9	47.5
1989	1344	324.3	530	378.6	51.7	48.2
1990	1518	366.5	610	435.7	53.1	49.5
1991	1619	390.9	707	505.0	51.6	46.7
1992	1992	481.0	783	559.3	52.5	50.9
1993	2661	642.5	870	621.4	46.4	46.0
1994	3517	849.1	1078	770.0	45.2	50.1
1995	4153	1002.5	1353	966.4	44.7	50.3
1996	5023	1212.6	1586	1132.9	42.6	49.9
1997	5344	1290.1	1846	1318.6	40.7	49.2
1998	5670	1368.7	2052	1465.7	39.8	42.4
1999	5999	1448.3	2203	1573.6	36.3	39.1
2000	6364	1536.5	2344	1674.3	36.5	36.6
2001	6705	1618.8	2490	1778.6	34.8	33.9
2002	7184	1734.3	2641	1886.4	34.4	31.1
2003	7748	1870.7	2838	2027.1	34.8	37.6
2004	8544	2062.8	3143	2245.0	36.1	35.7
2005	9628	2324.5	3460	2471.4	37.0	36.3
2006	10905	2632.9	3808	2720.0	34.4	36.8
2007	12662	3057.0	4399	3142.1	36.6	38.2
2008	15207	3671.4	5212	3722.9	36.4	37.0
2009	18963	4578.2	6275	4482.3	32.4	35.8
2010	22244	5370.4	7750	5535.7	31.3	32.5
2011	25981	6272.6	9788	6991.4	31.3	31.9
2012	29982	7238.5	11442	8172.9	32.5	33.8
2013	33100	7991.3	12930	9235.7	32.5	33.0
2014	36100	8718.5	14462	10334.7	32.3	34.2

注：2014年实施城乡住户一体化调查后，统计口径发生变化，新老口径存在差异。本表为老口径数据。

8-2 主要年份城乡居民人民币储蓄存款

Savings Deposit of Urban and Rural Households in Representative Years

单位：亿元 (100 million yuan)

年 份 Year	年末余额 Balance at Ycar-end	指数（上年＝100） Index(preccding year=100)
1978	3.72	
1979	4.85	130.4
1980	5.48	113.0
1981	6.36	116.1
1982	7.76	122.0
1983	10.02	129.1
1984	14.70	146.7
1985	16.70	113.6
1986	23.10	138.3
1987	32.13	139.1
1988	32.51	101.2
1989	45.78	140.8
1990	62.23	135.9
1991	78.64	126.4
1992	96.09	122.2
1993	124.61	129.7
1994	174.19	139.8
1995	230.63	132.4
1996	394.02	170.8
1997	358.78	91.1
1998	499.68	139.3
1999	586.40	117.4
2000	675.83	115.3
2001	800.86	118.5
2002	988.04	123.4
2003	1210.56	122.5
2004	1432.86	118.4
2005	1716.76	119.8
2006	1950.53	113.6
2007	2002.38	102.7
2008	2513.70	125.5
2009	3084.20	122.7
2010	3641.09	118.1
2011	4155.65	114.1
2012	4787.03	115.2
2013	5357.05	111.9
2014	5698.15	106.4

注：本表数据来源于人民银行西安营管部。

8-3　各区县城乡居民人均收入

Per Capita Income of Urban and Rural Households by Region

区　县	Region	城镇居民人均可支配收入 Per Capita Disposable Income of Urban Households			农村居民人均纯收入 Per Capita net Income of Rural Households		
		绝对数（元）Absoulte number(yuan)		2014指数（上年＝100）	绝对数（元）Absoulte number(yuan)		2014指数（上年＝100）
		2013	2014	Index(preceding year=100)（2014）	2013	2014	Index(preceding year=100)（2014）
全　市	**Total**	**33100**	**36100**	**109.1**	**12930**	**14462**	**111.9**
新城区	Xincheng	33816	37029	109.5			
碑林区	Beilin	34520	37765	109.4			
莲湖区	Lianhu	34450	37757	109.6			
灞桥区	Baqiao	31952	35147	110.0	15203	16982	111.7
未央区	Weiyang	33268	36462	109.6	16455	18364	111.6
雁塔区	Yanta	35341	38345	108.5	16724		
阎良区	Yanliang	34375	37503	109.1	15212	17007	111.8
临潼区	Lintong	27318	29804	109.1	12160	13595	111.8
长安区	Chang'an	29460	32377	109.9	12695	14206	111.9
蓝田县	Lantian	21953	23907	108.9	8833	9911	112.2
周至县	Zhouzhi	22243	24445	109.9	8870	9961	112.3
户　县	Huxian	24817	27026	108.9	10899	12218	112.1
高陵县	Gaoling	26030	28581	109.8	12167	13615	111.9

注：2014年实施城乡住户一体化调查后，统计口径发生变化，新老口径存在差异。本表为老口径数据。

8-4 全市居民家庭基本情况（2014）

Basic Conditions of All Households（2014）

指标名称	Item	全市居民 All Households	城镇住户 Urban Households	农村住户 Rural Households
调查户数（户）	Number of Households Surveyed (household)	2378	1752	626
调查户人口（人）	Residents Surveyed(person)			
平均每户常住人口	Average Household Size	3.04	2.86	3.54
平均每户劳动力人数	Average Number of Employed Persons	2.26	2.18	2.46
平均每劳动力负担人口	Average Number of Persons Supported by a Laborer	1.35	1.31	1.44
人均可支配收入（元）	Annual Per Capita Disposable Income(yuan）	25599.26	30714.66	12898.11
工资性收入	Wages Income	15976.74	19754.71	6596.31
经营净收入	Household Business Income	2533.72	2095.77	3621.14
财产净收入	Property Income	1988.47	2646.92	353.57
转移净收入	Transfer Income	5100.33	6217.26	2327.09
人均消费支出（元）	Annual Per Capita Consumption Expenditure (yuan)	17394.33	20892.89	8707.64
食品烟酒	Food,Tobacco and Alcohol	5098.76	6102.53	2606.48
衣着	Clothing	1539.17	1898.24	647.62
居住	Residence	3214.63	3738.22	1914.60
生活用品及服务	Living Articles and Services	1248.82	1507.16	607.37
交通通信	Transport and Communication Services	2374.77	2957.51	927.85
教育文化娱乐	Recreation, Education and Culture Services	2133.03	2632.18	893.68
医疗保健	Medical and Health Care Services	1366.47	1528.72	963.64
其他用品和服务	Other Commodities and Services	418.68	528.33	146.40

8-5 全市居民家庭人均可支配收入（2014年）

Per Capita Annual Disposable Income of All Households（2014）

单位：元 (yuan)

指标名称	Item	总平均 Total
可支配收入	Disposable income	25599.26
一、工资性收入	Wage income	15976.74
（一）工资	Wage	15141.40
（二）实物福利	Benefits in kind	108.25
（三）其他	Others	727.09
二、经营净收入	Net Income from Business	2533.72
（一）第一产业经营净收入	Net Income from Primary Industry Business	513.28
（二）第二产业经营净收入	Net Income from Secondary Industry Business	197.58
（三）第三产业经营净收入	Net Income from Tertiary Industry Business	1822.86
三、财产净收入	Net Income from Properties	1988.47
#利息净收入	Net interest	98.76
红利收入	Bonus	138.67
转让承包土地经营权租金净收入	Net Rental from Transfer of Contracted Land Management Rights	25.44
出租房屋财产性收入	The Property Income by Renting House	814.90
出租机械、专利、版权等资产的收入	The Income by Renting Assets like Mechanical, Patents, Copyright ect.	32.38
四、转移净收入	Net Income from Transfer	5100.33
（一）转移性收入	Net Income from Transfer	6256.99
（二）转移性支出	Transfer Expenditure	1156.66

8-6 全市居民家庭年人均消费支出（2014年）

Per Capita Living Expenditure of All Households（2014）

单位：元 （yuan）

指标名称	Item	总平均 Total
消费支出	**Total Living Expenditure**	**17394.33**
一、食品烟酒	**Food,Tobacco and Alcohol**	**5098.76**
1.食品	food	3311.25
2.烟酒	Alcohol and tobacco	464.98
3.饮料	Drink	108.42
4.饮食服务	Catering Services	1214.11
二、衣着	**Clothing**	**1539.17**
衣类	Garments	1190.16
鞋类	Footwear	349.01
三、居住	**Residence**	**3214.63**
#租赁房房租	Rental Housing Rent	268.25
住房维修及管理	Housing Repair and Management	287.07
水电燃料及其他	Water,Electric Power Fuel and Others	927.72
四、生活用品及服务	**Living Articles and Services**	**1248.82**
家具及室内装饰品	Furniture and External Decorations	204.51
家用器具	Household Appliances	331.32
家用纺织品	Household textile	119.75
家庭日用杂品	Household Articles of Daily Use	346.85
个人用品	Personal Items	213.68
家庭服务	Household Services	32.71
五、交通通信	**Transportation and Communications**	**2374.77**
交通	Transportation	1580.85
通信	Communications	793.92
六、教育文化娱乐	**Recreation, Education and Culture Services**	**2133.03**
教育	Education	1090.74
文化娱乐	Recreation	1042.29
七、医疗保健	**Medicine and Medical Services**	**1366.47**
医疗器具及药品	Medical Instruments and Medicines	533.90
医疗服务	Medical Services	832.57
八、其他用品和服务	**Others**	**418.68**

8-7 全市居民家庭人均购买主要商品数量（2014年）

Per Capita Annual Purchases of Major Commodities of All Households(2014)

单位：千克

(kg)

指标名称	Item	总平均 Total
面粉	Flour	22.93
大米	Rice	17.66
薯类	Potato	10.27
豆类	Beans	8.35
食用植物油	Edible vegetable oil	11.07
鲜菜	Fresh vegetables	80.26
猪肉	Pork	9.47
牛肉	Beef	1.46
羊肉	Lamb	0.35
鸡	Chicken	2.00
鱼类	Fish	2.66
虾类	Shrimp	0.49
鲜蛋	Eggs	7.77
鲜奶	Milk	11.83
酸奶	Yogurt	3.96
奶粉	Milk	0.76
鲜瓜果	Fresh fruit	47.38
糕点	Cake	4.11
茶叶	Tea	0.33
卷烟（盒）	Cigarettes (box)	22.99
啤酒	Beer	3.69
白酒	Liquor	0.82
果酒	Wine	0.30
鞋(双)	Footwear (pair)	2.70
水（吨）	Water (tons)	19.91
电（度）	Electricity （kwh）	540.66
煤炭	Coal	47.08
管道天燃气（立方米）	Gas pipeline (cu.m)	49.72
罐装液化石油气	Bottled liquefied petroleum gas	4.39

8-8 全市居民家庭每百户年末耐用品拥有情况（2014年）

Ownership of Major Durable Consumer Goods Per 100 All Households(2014)

指标名称	Item	2014
家用汽车（辆）	Automobile (unit)	25.7
摩托车（辆）	Motorcycles (unit)	22.2
助力车（台）	Strength-aid Cycle (unit)	38.5
洗衣机（台）	washing machine (unit)	97.4
电冰箱（柜）	Refrigerator (unit)	91.2
微波炉（台）	Microwave Oven (unit)	46.5
彩色电视机（台）	Color TV Set (unit)	116.9
#接入有线电视（台）	Cable TV Set(unit)	76.0
空调（台）	Air conditioning(unit)	120.1
热水器（台）	Water heaters(unit)	79.8
#太阳能热水器（台）	Solar water heaters (unit)	37.5
消毒碗柜（台）	Sterilizing Cupboard (unit)	4.8
洗碗机（台）	Dishwasher (unit)	1.0
排油烟机（台）	Exhauster (unit)	65.9
固定电话（线）	Ordinary Telephone (unit)	52.1
移动电话（部）	Mobile phones (unit)	233.9
#接入互联网（部）	Access to the Internet(unit)	84.3
计算机（台）	Computer (a)	64.4
#接入互联网（台）	Access to the Internet(unit)	52.2
摄像机（台）	Pickup Camera (unit)	7.2
照相机（台）	Camera (unit)	38.0
中高档乐器（架）	High-end Instruments (unit)	3.2
健身器材（台）	Setting-up Apparatus (unit)	3.0
组合音响（套）	Music Center (unit)	6.6

8-9 按收入五等份分组的城镇常住居民人均可支配收入（2014年）

Per capita Annual Disposable Income of Urban Households by Income percentile(2014)

单位：元 (yuan)

指标名称	Item	总平均 Total	低收入户 Low income households	中低收入户 Lower Middle income households
可支配收入	Disposable income	30714.66	15108.47	23184.25
一、工资性收入	Wage income	19754.71	11227.94	14850.14
（一）工资	Wage	18758.21	10934.31	14468.04
（二）实物福利	Benefits in kind	125.65	95.33	97.37
（三）其他	Others	870.85	198.30	284.73
二、经营净收入	Net Income from Business	2095.77	809.99	1192.42
（一）第一产业经营净收入	Net Income from Primary Industry Business	36.00	126.60	24.00
（二）第二产业经营净收入	Net Income from Secondary Industry Business	110.19	7.18	73.88
（三）第三产业经营净收入	Net Income from Tertiary Industry Business	1949.58	676.21	1094.54
三、财产净收入	Net Income from Properties	2646.92	1452.72	2559.87
#利息净收入	Net interest	131.93	-54.33	122.92
红利收入	Bonus	181.65	59.53	267.96
出租房屋财产性收入	The Property Income by Renting House	1093.30	771.01	1231.39
出租机械、专利、版权等资产的收入	The Income by Renting Assets like Mechanical, Patents, Copyright ect.Patents, Copyright ect.	7.41	1.39	-0.08
四、转移净收入	Net Income from Transfer	6217.26	1617.82	4581.82
（一）转移性收入	Net Income from Transfer	7730.12	2489.26	5814.37
（二）转移性支出	Transfer Expenditure	1512.86	871.44	1232.55

8-9 续表 continued

指标名称	Item	中等收入户 Middle income households	中高收入户 Upper Middle income households	高收入户 High income households
可支配收入	Disposable income	30016.05	37658.07	56304.18
一、工资性收入	Wage income	18913.01	23579.06	35264.72
（一）工资	Wage	17924.61	22418.50	32624.01
（二）实物福利	Benefits in kind	92.14	86.65	282.60
（三）其他	Others	896.26	1073.91	2358.11
二、经营净收入	Net Income from Business	1798.59	2171.93	5351.11
（一）第一产业经营净收入	Net Income from Primary Industry Business	1.20	1.53	-1.50
（二）第二产业经营净收入	Net Income from Secondary Industry Business	58.62	0.53	471.80
（三）第三产业经营净收入	Net Income from Tertiary Industry Business	1738.77	2169.87	4880.81
三、财产净收入	Net Income from Properties	2342.09	2743.76	4675.67
#利息净收入	Net interest	89.32	54.12	531.58
红利收入	Bonus	166.71	124.73	312.68
出租房屋财产性收入	The Property Income by Renting House	794.88	1019.89	1766.66
出租机械、专利、版权等资产的收入	The Income by Renting Assets like Mechanical, Patents, Copyright ect.Patents, Copyright ect.	12.83	-0.33	27.72
四、转移净收入	Net Income from Transfer	6962.36	9163.32	11012.68
（一）转移性收入	Net Income from Transfer	8533.53	10884.99	13520.22
（二）转移性支出	Transfer Expenditure	1571.17	1721.67	2507.54

8-10 城镇常住居民人均消费支出（2014年）

Per Capita Living Expenditure of Urban Households (2014)

单位：元 (yuan)

指标名称	Item	总平均 Total
消费支出	**Total Living Expenditure**	**20892.89**
一、食品烟酒	**Food,Tobacco and Alcohol**	**6102.53**
1.食品	food	3881.21
2.烟酒	Alcohol and tobacco	531.86
3.饮料	Drink	133.46
4.饮食服务	Catering Services	1556.00
二、衣着	**Clothing**	**1898.24**
衣类	Garments	1469.39
鞋类	Footwear	428.85
三、居住	**Residence**	**3738.22**
#租赁房房租	Rental Housing Rent	326.80
住房维修及管理	Housing Repair and Management	304.33
水电燃料及其他	Water,Electric Power Fuel and Others	1114.02
四、生活用品及服务	**Living Articles and Services**	**1507.16**
家具及室内装饰品	Furniture and External Decorations	244.27
家用器具	Household Appliances	403.48
家用纺织品	Household textile	137.94
家庭日用杂品	Household Articles of Daily Use	402.64
个人用品	Personal Items	278.13
家庭服务	Household Services	40.70
五、交通通信	**Transportation and Communications**	**2957.51**
交通	Transportation	1993.14
通信	Communications	964.37
六、教育文化娱乐	**Recreation, Education and Culture Services**	**2632.18**
教育	Education	1253.61
文化娱乐	Recreation	1378.57
#健身器材	Fitness Equipment	7.86
体育及户外用品	Sports and outdoor products	17.89
体育健身活动	Sports fitness activity	45.09
七、医疗保健	**Medicine and Medical Services**	**1528.72**
医疗器具及药品	Medical Instruments and Medicines	632.63
医疗服务	Medical Services	896.09
八、其他用品和服务	**Others**	**528.33**

8-11 城镇常住居民家庭人均购买主要商品数量（2014年）

Per Capita Annual Purchases of Major Commodities of Urban Households (2014)

单位：千克 (kg)

指标名称	Item	总平均 Total
面粉	Flour	23.79
大米	Rice	20.05
薯类	Potato	11.85
豆类	Beans	9.14
食用植物油	Edible vegetable oil	11.10
鲜菜	Fresh vegetables	89.34
猪肉	Pork	10.53
牛肉	Beef	1.95
羊肉	Lamb	0.47
鸡	Chicken	2.55
鱼类	Fish	3.39
虾类	Shrimp	0.66
鲜蛋	Eggs	8.77
鲜奶	Milk	15.28
酸奶	Yogurt	4.65
奶粉	Milk	0.64
鲜瓜果	Fresh fruit	55.06
糕点	Cake	4.84
茶叶	Tea	0.38
卷烟（盒）	Cigarettes (box)	21.35
啤酒	Beer	3.83
白酒	Liquor	0.88
果酒	Wine	0.26
鞋(双)	Footwear (pair)	2.90
水（吨）	Water (tons)	25.18
电（度）	Electricity （kwh）	608.19
煤炭	Coal	33.42
管道天燃气（立方米）	Gas pipeline (cu.m)	68.75
罐装液化石油气	Bottled liquefied petroleum gas	4.05

8-12 城镇常住居民家庭每百户耐用品拥有情况（2014年）

Ownership of Major Durable Consumer Goods Per 100 Urban Households(2014)

指标名称	Item	2014
家用汽车（辆）	Automobile (unit)	27.9
摩托车（辆）	Motorcycles (unit)	11.8
助力车（台）	Strength-aid Cycle (unit)	30.9
洗衣机（台）	washing machine (unit)	97.6
电冰箱（柜）	Refrigerator (unit)	95.4
微波炉（台）	Microwave Oven (unit)	55.9
彩色电视机（台）	Color TV Set (unit)	113.9
空调（台）	Air conditioning(unit)	136.9
热水器（台）	Water heaters(unit)	85.4
#太阳能热水器（台）	Solar water heaters (unit)	34.2
消毒碗柜（台）	Sterilizing Cupboard (unit)	6.1
洗碗机（台）	Dishwasher (unit)	1.2
排油烟机（台）	Exhauster (unit)	79.8
固定电话（线）	Ordinary Telephone (unit)	56.3
移动电话（部)	Mobile phones (unit)	224.0
计算机（台）	Computer (a)	75.0
摄像机（台）	Pickup Camera (unit)	9.3
照相机（台）	Camera (unit)	47.4
中高档乐器（架）	High-end Instruments (unit)	3.9
健身器材（台）	Setting-up Apparatus (unit)	3.6
组合音响（套）	Music Center (unit)	6.4

8-13 城镇常住居民家庭居住情况（2014年）

Housing Conditions of Urban Households (2014)

指标名称	Item	2014
调查户数（户）	**Number of Households Surveyed (household)**	**1752**
平均每户居住人口（人）	**Average Number of Resident Population (person)**	**2.86**
人均现住房建筑面积（平方米/人）	**The Average Floor Area Per Person (sq.m / person)**	**32.06**
一、按居住空间样式分（%）	**by Living space style（%）**	**100**
单栋楼房	Single building Room	6.73
单栋平房	Single-storey House	4.79
单元房	Apartment	81.00
筒子楼或连片平房	Tube-shaped Apartment or Lace Single-storey Houses	7.37
其他	Other	0.11
二、按主要建筑材料分（%）	**by main construction materials（%）**	**100**
钢筋混凝土	Reinforced concrete soil	25.19
砖混材料	Brick and concrete material	74.24
砖瓦砖土	Tile and brick earth	0.46
其他	Others	0.11
三、按房屋来源分（%）	**by Source of Housing（%）**	**100**
租赁住房	Rental housing	11.35
自建住房	Self-establish Housing	12.65
购买商品房	Commercial Residential Housing	31.66
购买房改住房	Private Housing through Housing Reform	34.90
购买保障性住房	Indemnificatory Housing	2.34
拆迁安置房	Resettlement Housing	4.24
继承或获赠住房	Inheriting and Donation Housing	0.51
其他	Others	2.35
四、住房外道路为硬化路面的户比重（%）	**proportion of households which outer road is Hardened road（%）**	**99.14**
五、按住宅有管道供水情况分（%）	**By Piped Water Supply Condition（%）**	**100**
管道供水入户	Pipe water into People's Homes	98.40
管道供水至公共取水点	Pipe water to Public Watering Points	0.92
没有管道设施	No Pipeline Facilities	0.68
六、按住户主要饮水来源情况分（%）	**By Source of main Drinking Water（%）**	**100**
经过净化处理的自来水	Purified Tap Water	88.48
受保护的井水和泉水	Protected Wells and Springs	8.44
不受保护的井水和泉水	Unprotected Wells and Springs	1.31
江河湖泊水	Rivers and Lakes Water	0.29
其他饮用水来源	Others	1.48
七、按住宅内厕所类型分（%）	**By Household Lavatory Type (%)**	**100**
水冲式卫生厕所	Sanitary Water Closet	92.11
水冲式非卫生厕所	Insanitary Water Closet	0.70
卫生旱厕	Sanitary Latrine	2.91
普通旱厕	Latrine	3.94
无厕所	No Lavatory	0.34
八、按主要炊用能源状况分（%）	**By Cooking Fuel Condition（%）**	**100**
天然气、煤气、液化石油气	Pipeline Natural Gas，Pipeline Gas，Pipeline Liquified Petroleum Gas	75.01
煤炭	Coal	3.14
电	Electricity	20.31
沼气	Methane	0.16
其他	Others	1.38

8-14 按收入五等份分组的农村常住居民家庭人均可支配收入（2014年）

Per capita Annual Disposable Income of Rural Households by Income percentile(2014)

单位：元 (yuan)

指标名称	Item	总平均 Total	低收入户 Low income households	中低收入户 Lower Middle income households
可支配收入	Disposable income	12898.11	5083.43	9163.86
一、工资性收入	Wage income	6596.31	2800.20	5312.71
（一）工资	Wage	6161.09	2373.27	4909.80
（二）实物福利	Benefits in kind	65.05	0.66	4.81
（三）其他	Others	370.17	426.27	398.10
二、经营净收入	Net Income from Business	3621.14	1596.90	2538.35
（一）第一产业经营净收入	Net Income from Primary Industry Business	1698.38	1395.10	1779.92
（二）第二产业经营净收入	Net Income from Secondary Industry Business	414.55	15.27	17.80
（三）第三产业经营净收入	Net Income from Tertiary Industry Business	1508.21	186.53	740.63
三、财产净收入	Net Income from Properties	353.57	43.26	74.13
#利息净收入	Net interest	16.41	-12.82	-10.62
红利收入	Bonus	31.93	2.34	3.72
转让承包土地经营权租金净收入	Net Rental from Transfer of Contracted Land Management Rights	47.89	30.64	58.54
出租房屋财产性收入	The Property Income by Renting House	123.65		16.54
出租机械、专利、版权等资产的收入	The Income by Renting Assets like Mechanical, Patents, Copyright ect.Patents, Copyright ect.	94.37		0.74
四、转移净收入	Net Income from Transfer	2327.09	643.07	1238.67
（一）转移性收入	Net Income from Transfer	2599.33	927.67	1412.60
（二）转移性支出	Transfer Expenditure	272.24	284.60	173.93

8-14 续表 continued

指标名称	Item	中等收入户 Middle income households	中高收入户 Upper Middle income households	高收入户 High income households
可支配收入	Disposable income	12963.01	16549.49	24591.40
一、工资性收入	Wage income	6782.36	8124.59	11653.60
（一）工资	Wage	6514.46	7623.19	11050.56
（二）实物福利	Benefits in kind	26.37	254.70	75.99
（三）其他	Others	241.53	246.70	527.05
二、经营净收入	Net Income from Business	3139.81	4851.52	7050.13
（一）第一产业经营净收入	Net Income from Primary Industry Business	1294.19	2428.71	1673.41
（二）第二产业经营净收入	Net Income from Secondary Industry Business	22.75	1705.12	559.28
（三）第三产业经营净收入	Net Income from Tertiary Industry Business	1822.87	717.69	4817.44
三、财产净收入	Net Income from Properties	259.52	332.37	1274.38
#利息净收入	Net interest	-4.60	26.25	104.90
红利收入	Bonus	7.06	46.38	121.91
转让承包土地经营权租金净收入	Net Rental from Transfer of Contracted Land Management Rights	30.53	55.05	68.38
出租房屋财产性收入	The Property Income by Renting House	107.66	90.85	487.01
出租机械、专利、版权等资产的收入	The Income by Renting Assets like Mechanical, Patents, Copyright ect.Patents, Copyright ect.	29.38	109.76	402.83
四、转移净收入	Net Income from Transfer	2781.32	3241.01	4613.29
（一）转移性收入	Net Income from Transfer	2948.31	3532.72	5095.33
（二）转移性支出	Transfer Expenditure	166.99	291.71	482.04

8-15 农村常住居民家庭人均消费支出（2014年）

Per Capita Living Expenditure of Rual Households by Income Percentile(2014)

单位：元 (yuan)

指标名称	Item	总平均 Total
消费支出	**Total Living Expenditure**	**8707.64**
一、食品烟酒	**Food,Tobacco and Alcohol**	**2606.48**
1.食品	food	1896.09
2.烟酒	Alcohol and tobacco	298.93
3.饮料	Drink	46.24
4.饮食服务	Catering Services	365.22
二、衣着	**Clothing**	**647.62**
衣类	Garments	496.84
鞋类	Footwear	150.78
三、居住	**Residence**	**1914.60**
#租赁房房租	Rental Housing Rent	122.89
住房维修及管理	Housing Repair and Management	244.23
水电燃料及其他	Water,Electric Power Fuel and Others	465.17
四、生活用品及服务	**Living Articles and Services**	**607.37**
家具及室内装饰品	Furniture and External Decorations	105.77
家用器具	Household Appliances	152.16
家用纺织品	Household textile	74.58
家庭日用杂品	Household Articles of Daily Use	208.34
个人用品	Personal Items	53.65
家庭服务	Household Services	12.87
五、交通通信	**Transportation and Communications**	**927.85**
交通	Transportation	557.14
通信	Communications	370.71
六、教育文化娱乐	**Recreation, Education and Culture Services**	**893.68**
教育	Education	686.36
文化娱乐	Recreation	207.32
七、医疗保健	**Medicine and Medical Services**	**963.64**
医疗器具及药品	Medical Instruments and Medicines	288.75
医疗服务	Medical Services	674.89
八、其他用品和服务	**Others**	**146.40**

8-16 农村常住居民家庭人均购买主要商品数量（2014年）

Per Capita Annual Purchases of Major Commoditiesof Rural Households by Income Percentile(2014)

单位：千克　　　　　　　　　　　　　　　　　　　　(kg)

指标名称	Item	总平均 Total
面粉	Flour	20.79
大米	Rice	11.71
薯类	Potato	6.32
豆类	Beans	6.39
食用植物油	Edible vegetable oil	10.99
鲜菜	Fresh vegetables	57.71
猪肉	Pork	6.82
牛肉	Beef	0.23
羊肉	Lamb	0.08
鸡	Chicken	0.63
鱼类	Fish	0.83
虾类	Shrimp	0.06
鲜蛋	Eggs	5.28
鲜奶	Milk	3.28
酸奶	Yogurt	2.24
奶粉	Milk	1.06
鲜瓜果	Fresh fruit	28.31
糕点	Cake	2.29
茶叶	Tea	0.19
卷烟（盒）	Cigarettes (box)	27.09
啤酒	Beer	3.36
白酒	Liquor	0.66
果酒	Wine	0.41
鞋(双)	Footwear (pair)	2.18
水（吨）	Water (tons)	6.85
电（度）	Electricity （kwh）	372.97
煤炭	Coal	81.00
管道天燃气（立方米）	Gas pipeline (cu.m)	2.49
罐装液化石油气	Bottled liquefied petroleum gas	5.22

8-17 农村常住居民家庭平均每百户耐用品拥有情况（2014年）

Ownership of Major Durable Consumer Goods Per 100 Rural Households by Income Percentile(2014)

指标名称	Item	2014
家用汽车（辆）	Automobile (unit)	19.5
摩托车（辆）	Motorcycles (unit)	51.6
助力车（台）	Strength-aid Cycle (unit)	59.8
洗衣机（台）	washing machine (unit)	96.8
电冰箱（柜）	Refrigerator (unit)	79.3
微波炉（台）	Microwave Oven (unit)	20.2
彩色电视机（台）	Color TV Set (unit)	125.3
空调（台）	Air conditioning(unit)	73.2
热水器（台）	Water heaters(unit)	64.2
#太阳能热水器（台）	Solar water heaters (unit)	46.8
消毒碗柜（台）	Sterilizing Cupboard (unit)	1.4
洗碗机（台）	Dishwasher (unit)	0.3
排油烟机（台）	Exhauster (unit)	26.9
固定电话（线）	Ordinary Telephone (unit)	40.4
移动电话（部)	Mobile phones (unit)	261.6
计算机（台）	Computer (a)	34.6
#接入互联网（台）	Access to the Internet(unit)	24.9
摄像机（台）	Pickup Camera (unit)	1.4
照相机（台）	Camera (unit)	11.5
中高档乐器（架）	High-end Instruments (unit)	1.4
健身器材（台）	Setting-up Apparatus (unit)	1.1
组合音响（套）	Music Center (unit)	7.1

8-18 农村常住居民家庭居住情况（2014年）

Housing Conditions of Urban Households (2014)

指标名称	Item	2014
调查户数（户）	**Number of Households Surveyed (household)**	**626**
平均每户居住人口（人）	**Average Number of Resident Population (person)**	**3.54**
人均现住房建筑面积（平方米/人）	**The Average Floor Area Per Person (sq.m / person)**	**48.83**
一、按居住空间样式分（%）	**by Living space style（%）**	**100**
单栋楼房	Single building Room	42.47
单栋平房	Single-storey House	44.07
单元房	Apartment	11.86
筒子楼或连片平房	Tube-shaped Apartment or Lace Single-storey Houses	0.32
其他	Other	1.28
二、按主要建筑材料分（%）	**by main construction materials（%）**	**100**
钢筋混凝土	Reinforced concrete soil	21.85
砖混材料	Brick and concrete material	67.93
砖瓦砖土	Tile and brick earth	8.79
竹草土坯	Bamboo grass mud	1.27
其他	Others	0.16
三、按房屋来源分（%）	**by Source of Housing（%）**	**100**
租赁住房	Rental housing	4.11
自建住房	Self-establish Housing	84.34
购买商品房	Commercial Residential Housing	2.64
购买房改住房	Private Housing through Housing Reform	1.12
购买保障性住房	Indemnificatory Housing	1.44
拆迁安置房	Resettlement Housing	6.03
继承或获赠住房	Inheriting and Donation Housing	
其他	Others	0.32
四、住房外道路为硬化路面的户比重（%）	**proportion of households which outer road is Hardened road（%）**	**94.30**
五、按住宅有管道供水情况分（%）	**By Piped Water Supply Condition （%）**	**100**
管道供水入户	Pipe water into People's Homes	90.25
管道供水至公共取水点	Pipe water to Public Watering Points	0.48
没有管道设施	No Pipeline Facilities	9.27
六、按住户主要饮水来源情况分（%）	**By Source of main Drinking Water （%）**	**100**
经过净化处理的自来水	Purified Tap Water	66.88
受保护的井水和泉水	Protected Wells and Springs	21.53
不受保护的井水和泉水	Unprotected Wells and Springs	11.02
江河湖泊水	Rivers and Lakes Water	0.57
其他饮用水来源	Others	
七、按住宅内厕所类型分（%）	**By Household Lavatory Type (%)**	**100**
水冲式卫生厕所	Sanitary Water Closet	39.79
水冲式非卫生厕所	Insanitary Water Closet	5.91
卫生旱厕	Sanitary Latrine	18.13
普通旱厕	Latrine	35.05
无厕所	No Lavatory	1.12
八、按主要炊用能源状况分（%）	**By Cooking Fuel Condition （%）**	**100**
天然气、煤气、液化石油气	Pipeline Natural Gas，Pipeline Gas，Pipeline Liquified Petroleum Gas	33.35
煤炭	Coal	3.79
电	Electricity	34.43
沼气	Methane	0.32
其他	Others	28.11

主要统计指标解释

住户 指居住在一个住宅内，共同分享生活开支或收入的一群人。居住在同一房间内、不共同分享生活开支的人群，每个人都视为一个住户。住家保姆、住家家庭帮工视为单独的住户。

常住居民 指住户成员中，经常在家居住、或者调查期内居住时间超过一半的人员，以及本住户供养的学生。常住居民是住户收支的调查对象。

整、半劳动力 整劳动力是指男子18周岁到50周岁，女子18周岁到45周岁；半劳动力是指男子16周岁到17周岁，51周岁到60周岁；女子16周岁到17周岁，46周岁到55周岁，同时具有劳动能力的人。虽然在劳动年龄之内，但已丧失劳动能力的人，不应算为劳动力；超过劳动年龄，但能经常参加劳动，计入半劳动力数内。常住人口中的职工，若这些职工为劳动力，就包括在本户的整半劳动力中。

居民人均可支配收入 指调查期内居民家庭成员人均获得的、可用于最终消费支出和储蓄的总和，即居民可以用来自由支配的收入，既包括现金收入，也包括实物收入。全体居民可支配收入可以体现各地区城乡一体的居民收入及生活水平变化情况。按照收入的来源，可支配收入包含四项，分别为：工资性收入、经营净收入、财产净收入、转移净收入。

工资性收入 指就业人员通过各种途径得到的全部劳动报酬和各种福利，包括受雇于单位或个人、从事各种自由职业、兼职和零星劳动得到的全部劳动报酬和福利。

经营净收入 指住户或住户成员从事生产经营活动所获得的净收入，是全部经营收入中扣除经营费用、生产性固定资产折旧和生产税净额（生产税减去生产补贴）之后得到的净收入。计算公式为：

经营净收入＝经营收入－经营费用－生产性固定资产折旧－生产税净额（生产税–生产补贴）

财产净收入 指住户或住户成员将其所拥有的金融资产和自然资源交由其他机构单位、住户或个人支配而获得的回报并扣除相关的费用之后得到的净收入。计算公式为：

财产净收入＝财产性收入－财产性支出

转移净收入 指国家、单位、社会团体对住户的各种经常性转移支付和住户之间的经常性收入转移。包括政府、非行政事业单位、社会团体对居民转移的养老金或退休金、社会救济和补助、政策性生活补贴、救灾款、经常性捐赠和赔偿以及报销医疗费等；住户之间的赡养收入、经常性捐赠和赔偿以及农村地区（村委会）在外（含国外）工作的本住户非常住成员寄回带回的收入等。计算公式为：

转移净收入=转移性收入–转移性支出

居民收入五等份分组 指将所有调查户按人均收入水平从低到高顺序排列，平均分为五个等份，处于最高20%的收入群体为高收入组，依此类推依次为中高收入组、中等收入组、中低收入组、低收入组。

居民人均生活消费支出 指住户用于满足家庭日常生活消费需要的全部支出，包括用于消费品的支出和用于服务性消费的支出。根据用途不同，消费支出可划分为食品烟酒、衣着、居住、生活用品及服务、交通通信、教育文化娱乐、医疗保健、其他用品及服务八大类。

城镇居民人均可支配收入（老口径） 指城镇家庭总收入扣除交纳的个人所得税和个人交纳的各项社会保障支出之后，按照城镇居民家庭人口平均的收入水平。其中家庭总收入是指该家庭中生活在一起的所有家庭人员从各种渠道得到的所有收入之和。计算公式为：

可支配收入=家庭总收入–交纳个人所得税–个人交纳的社会保障支出–记账补贴

农村居民人均纯收入（老口径） 指农村住户当年从各个来源得到的家庭总收入扣除有关费用性支出后，最终归农村居民所有的收入总和，按照农村住户人口平均的纯收入水平。计算公式为：

纯收入＝总收入–家庭经营费用支出–税费支出–生产性固定资产折旧–赠送农村内部亲友

Explanatory Notes on Main Statistical Indicators

Households refer to persons living and sharing economically together in one house. When people don't share living expenses, every single person are deemed to be one household. Live-in Nanny and family helpers are deemed to be one household.

Usual Resident Population refers to persons staying at home regularly or for over half of time in survey period and students provided by the household. Usual resident population is the respondent of household living expenses.

Full/Semi Labour Force Full labour force refers to persons capable of work, aged 18-50 for males and 18-45 for females. Semi labour force refers to persons capable of work, aged 16-17 and 51-60 for males and 16-17 and 46-55 for females. Persons at their working ages but not capable of work are not to be included as labour force. Persons not at working ages but participating regularly in work are included in semi labour force. For staff and workers who are usual residents, are included as full or semi labour force of the household if they are in the labour force.

Disposable Income of Residents refers to the actual income at the disposal of members of the households which can be used for final consumption and savings in survey period, residents can use that at their disposal. It includes cash income and physical income. This income demonstrates the situation about incomes of both rural and urban residents and living standard in various regions. According to the source of income, disposable income include wage income, net business income, net property income and net transferability income.

Wages Income refers to the work reward and all benefits received in various ways by the members of rural households,include the work reward and all benefits received from employed by other units or individuals,liberal professions, part-time job and sporadic labor.

Net Business Income refers to the net income received by households engaged in manufacturing & managing activities.This equals to total business income minus operating costs, depreciation for productive plant assets and net product tax(production taxes minus production subsidies).The following formula is used:

Net business income=business income-operating costs-depreciation for productive plant assets- net product tax(production taxes-production subsidies)

Net Property Income refers to the income received as returns by owners of financial assets or nature sources by providing nature sources to other institutional units,households and individuals. The following formula is used:

Net property income = property income - property expenditure

Net Transferability Income refers to various current transfers of nation, units and social organizations pay to households and recurring revenue transfer between households. This income includes pension transferred from government, the non administrative institutions and social organizations to households, social assistance, policy living allowance, disaster relief funds, regular donation and compensation, recoverable medical cost; alimony income, regular donation and compensation, income from the ones who are not resident in rural areas between the households.The following formula is used:

Net transferability income = transfer income - transfer expenditure

Five Equal Groups of Resident Income According to income per head, all investigative households are arranged from low to high. Divided five groups equally, the maximum 20% of the income groups is high-income groups, and so on, there are middle and upper-income groups, middle-income groups, medium-low-income groups and low-income groups.

Consumption Expenditure of Households refers to total expenditure of households for consumption in daily life, including expenditure on the eight categories of food; clothing; housing; household appliances and services; health care and medical services; transport and communications; recreation, education and cultural services; and miscellaneous goods and services.

The per capita disposable income(the old range) This equals to total income minus income tax, personal contribution to social security and subsidy for keeping diaries in being a sample household. The following formula is used:

Disposable income = total household income - income tax - personal contribution to social security - subsidy for keeping diaries for a sampled household

The Average Per Capita Net Income of Rural Residents(the old range) refers to the total income of rural households from all sources minus all corresponding expenses. The formula for calculation is as follows:

Net income = total income - household operation expenses - taxes and fees paid - taxes and fees depreciation of fixed assets for production - gifts to non-rural relatives.

9 城市公用事业

URBAN PUBLIC UTILITIES

资料整理：郝　静
Data management：Hao Jing
数据审核：王金桂
Data audit：Wang Jingui

第九部分　城市公用事业

一、简要说明

本章资料主要包括城市供水、供燃气、供热、公共交通、市政设施、市政设施水平、城市规模及用地状况、园林绿地、环境卫生等情况，由西安市统计局社会科技处根据西安市建委、市交通局及地铁办提供的数据整理。

二、主要指标

人均公园绿地面积（平方米）	11.22	比上年同口径增长	4.9%
人均城市道路面积（平方米）	18.00	比上年同口径增长	0.8%
用水普及率（%）	100	比上年同口径增加	持平
燃气普及率（%）	98.71	比上年同口径提高	0.03个百分点

9　URBAN PUBLIC UTILITIES

Ⅰ.Brief Introduction

Data in this chapter reflects basic condition of urban public utilities of Xi'an City. Data on public utilities primarily consist of urban water supply, gas sales, urban heating, public transportation, municipal facilities, level of municipal construction, scale of the city, condition of land utilization, parks, greenbelt and environmental sanitation. Data in this chapter is compiled by Social Science & Technology Division of Xi'an Bureau of Statistics according to the data provided by Committee of Urban Construction of Xi'an, Xi'an Burean of Transportation and Xi'an Metro office.

Ⅱ.Major Indicators

		Increase over Preceding Year
Per Capita Public Green Areas (sq.m)	11.22	4.9%
Per Captia Area of Roads (sq.m)	18.00	0.8%
Water-Consuming Popularization (%)	100	essentially on a par with last year's
Gas-Consuming Popularization (%)	98.71	0.03 percentage points

9-1 城市供水

Urban Water Supply

指 标	Item	2009	2010	2011	2012	2013	2014
年末水厂个数（个）	Number of Water Factory at Year-end (units)	9	9	15	15	15	16
供水综合生产能力（万立方米/日）	Total Volume of Water Supply (10 000 cu.m/day)	190.00	197.40	197.40	200.33	195.52	196.50
# 地下水	Groundwater	55.30	55.80	54.80	57.04	51.35	51.33
年末供水管道总长度（公里）	Length of Water Supply Pipelines at Year-end (kms)	1985	2416	2721	3207.73	3385.33	3499.97
全年供水总量（万立方米）	Total Annual Volume of Water Supply (10 000 cu.m)	38307	41089	38934	45791.77	51372.07	53798.99
#全年售水量	Annual Volume of Water Sales	32859	35099	33139	39734.86	44701.26	46755.71
#生产运营用水	For Productive Use	6414	6267	5484	5334.28	6272.62	15680.53
居民家庭用水	For Residential Use	18513	20944	19945	24703.73	26138.73	28497.40
用水人口（万人）	Population with Access to Tap Water (10 000 persons)	357.60	410.90	394.10	406.32	444.35	452.57

注：本表数据来源于市建委和市水务局。
2009年部门统计制度变化，年末供水管道总长度和用水人口数调整。
2010年后数据为全市口径，2009年以前数据为市区口径。

9-2 城市供燃气

Gas Supply in Urban Area

指 标	Item	2009	2010	2011	2012	2013	2014
一、天然气	**Natural Gas**						
管道长度（公里）	Total Length of Gas Pipelines (km)	3932	4488	4500	5075.19	6163.39	6892.25
供气总量（万立方米）	Total Gas Supply(10 000 cu.m)	95885	109052	120330	142262.84	153488.90	186259.15
#销售气量	Volume of Gas Sales	91336	104055	114955	136530.93	147592.97	179536.78
#家庭用量	Residential Households	15473	20989	22868	27760.63	36671.17	59057.38
用气人口（万人）	Population with Access to Gas (10 000 persons)	285	333	356	371.54	410.56	425.72
二、液化石油气	**Liquefied Petroleum Gas**						
供气总量（吨）	Total Gas Supply (tons)	74913	11469	5920	4529.7	6047.9	5299.7
#销售气量	Volume of Gas Sales		11441	5891	4482	5986	5244
#家庭用量	Residential Households	46275	7376	4352	4254	4945	4281
用气人口（万人）	Population with Access to Gas (10 000 persons)	50.50	31.20	28.60	27.44	27.92	21.00

注：本表数据来源于市建委。
2010年后数据为全市口径，2009年以前数据为市区口径。

9-3 城市供热

Heating in Urban Area

指　标	Item	2009	2010	2011	2012	2013	2014
供热能力	Heating Capacity						
蒸气（吨/小时）	Steam (tons/hour)	2118	2235	2075	3073	4283	2893
热水（兆瓦）	Hot Water (megawatts)	11467	3531	4570	5402	12691	13967
供热总量(万吉焦)	Volume Supplied (10 000 gigajoules)						
蒸气	Steam	1541	1674	1421	1616.98	1667.88	1743.87
热水	Hot Water	1220	2570	2901	2443.57	2990.38	3726.89
管道长度（公里）	Length of Pipelines (km)						
蒸气	Steam	209	180	167	187.07	204.33	231.04
热水	Hot Water	289	361	500	516.18	608.12	663.20
供热面积（万平方米）	Heated Area (10 000sq.m)	5178	6094	6524	8512.84	10980.27	13492.55
#住宅	Residential Buildings	4325	5009	5226	7328.16	9874.54	11828.59

注：本表数据来源于市建委。
2010年后数据为全市口径，2009年以前数据为市区口径。

9-4 城市公共交通

Urban Public Traffic

指　标	Item	2009	2010	2011	2012	2013	2014
运营车辆（辆）	Operating Vehicles (units)	7039	7107	7462	7695	8128	7769
标准运营车辆（标台）	Standard Vehicles (units)	7833	8139	8598	8926	9371	9050
公交客运总量（万人次）	Total of Bus Passenger(10 000 person-times)	161782	162400	175234	175241	174051	170960
公交客运收入（万元）	Bus Passenger Transport Income (10 000 yuan)		129397	141505	135505	146417	140914
出租汽车数（辆）	Number of Taxis (units)	12786	12786	13839	14139	14139	14159
地铁运营线路长度（公里）	Length of Subway Lines in Operation(km)				19.87	44.68	50.94
地铁客运量（万人次）	Total of Subway Passenger(10 000 person-times)				5911.64	12189.61	29953.07

注：本表数据来源于市交通局和地铁办。

9–5 市政设施

Municipal Facilities

指 标	Item	2010	2011	2012	2013	2014
一、道路长度（公里）	**Length of Roads (km)**	**2662**	**2755**	**3119.3**	**3387.43**	**3461.18**
二、道路面积（万平方米）	**Area of Roads (10 000 sq.m)**	**5965**	**6259**	**7126.56**	**7931.80**	**8144.22**
三、人行道面积（万平方米）	**Area of Sidewalks (10 000 sq.m)**	**1834**	**1867**	**2105.31**	**2259.29**	**2310.46**
四、桥梁数（座）	**Number of Bridges (units)**	**347**	**402**	**422**	**432**	**437**
#立交桥	Overpasses	71	91	97	97	105
五、路灯盏数（盏）	**Number of Street Lights (units)**	**291754**	**311991**	**329881**	**333393**	**337991**
六、排水管道长度（公里）	**Length of Drainage Pipelines (km)**	**3765**	**4043**	**4435.92**	**4629.70**	**4839.49**
七、污水年排放量（万立方米）	**Annual Discharge Volume of Sewage (10 000 cu.m)**	**34706**	**36673**	**40302.7**	**46186**	**51673**
八、污水处理厂处理能力（万立方米/日）	**Daily Disposal Capacity of Sewage (10 000 cu.m/day)**	**106.5**	**111.6**	**128.1**	**153.1**	**153.1**
九、污水年处理量（万立方米）	**Yearly Disposal Capacity of Sewage Disposal Plant (10 000 cu.m)**	**25088**	**31512**	**35463**	**41898**	**47907**
十、防洪堤长度（公里）	**Length of Flood Control Dikes (km)**	**168**	**168**	**188**		

注：本表数据来源于市建委。
2010年后数据为全市口径，2009年以前数据为市区口径。

9–6 城市设施水平

Urban Municipal Facilities

指 标	Item	2010	2011	2012	2013	2014
一、人均日生活用水量（升）	**Per Capita Daily Consumption of Tap Water For Residential Use (liters)**	**186.2**	**185.2**	**220.96**	**225.78**	**178.45**
二、用水普及率(%)	**Water-Consuming Popularization (%)**	**98.8**	**100**	**100**	**100**	**100**
三、每万人拥有公共交通车辆（标台）	**Number of Public Transport Vehicles Per 10 000 Population (units)**	**13.9**	**14.4**	**14.6**	**15.1**	**14.4**
四、燃气普及率(%)	**Gas-Consuming Popularization (%)**	**97**	**97.5**	**98.19**	**98.68**	**98.71**
五、人均城市道路面积（平方米）	**Per Captia Area of Roads (sq.m)**	**15.4**	**15.9**	**17.54**	**17.85**	**18.00**
六、建成区排水管道密度（公里/平方公里）	**Density of Drainage Pipelines in Developed Areas (km/sq.km)**	**9.5**	**9.7**	**9.83**	**9.17**	**9.27**
七、污水处理率(%)	**Rate of Sewerage Disposal (%)**	**84**	**85.9**	**89.51**	**90.72**	**92.71**
八、园林绿化	**Afforestation and Parks and Gardens**					
人均公园绿地面积（平方米）	Per Capita Public Green Areas (sq.m)	9.1	9.9	10.22	10.70	11.22
建城区绿地率（%）	Rate of Green Areas in Developed Areas (%)	29.2	30.9	31.20	32.32	32.60
九、生活垃圾无害化处理率(%)	**Rate of No Harm Disposal of Garbage (%)**	**93.9**	**93.7**	**94.93**	**93.95**	**93.48**

注：本表数据来源于市建委。
2010年后数据为全市口径，2009年以前数据为市区口。
每万人拥有公共交通车辆计算数据口径调整，故与往年年鉴数据不可比。

9–7 城市规模及用地情况

City Scale and Land Use

单位：平方公里 (sq.km)

指 标	Item	2010	2011	2012	2013	2014
建成区面积	Area of the Constructed Regions	395	415	451.38	504.68	521.91
城市建设用地	Land use for Construction	336	349	376.39	489.03	507.66

注：本表数据来源于市建委。

2010年后数据为全市口径，2009年以前数据为市区口径。

9–8 城市园林绿化

Urban Parks,Gardens and Green Areas in Cities

指 标	Item	2010	2011	2012	2013	2014
一、公园个数（个）	**Number of Parks (units)**	**68**	**66**	**72**	**81**	**85**
二、公园面积（公顷）	**Area of Parks (hectares)**	**1335**	**1478**	**1529**	**2406**	**2484**
三、园林绿地面积（公顷）	**Total Area of Parks,Gardens and Green Areas (hectares)**	**12140**	**13680**	**15196**	**17751**	**18914**
#公园绿地面积	Public Green Areas	3526	3898	4154	4756	5076
四、年末绿化覆盖面积（公顷）	**Coverage Space of Green Areas at year-end (hectares)**	**15646**	**17325**	**19017**	**21865**	**23217**
五、建成区绿化覆盖率（%）	**Coverage of Green Areas in Developed Areas (%)**	**37.50**	**38.96**	**39.53**	**40.29**	**40.76**

注：本表数据来源于市建委。

2006年统计制度变化，"公共绿地面积"改为"公园绿地面积"。

2010年数据为全市口径，2009年以前数据为市区口径。

9–9 城市环境卫生

Urban Environment Sanitation

指　标	Item	2010	2011	2012	2013	2014
清扫面积（万平方米）	Area Under Cleaning Program (10 000 sq.m)	6290	6411	6952	8725	10110
清运生活垃圾（万吨）	Volume of Residential Garbage Disposal (10 000 tons)	237	265	287.32	290.76	359.37
清运粪便（万吨）	Volume of Excrement and Urine Disposal (10 000 tons)	3	4	2.99	2.96	2.90
公共厕所（座）	Number of Public Lavatories (units)	1257	1493	1594	1770	2151
市容环卫专用车辆（辆）	Special Vehicles of Environmental Sanitation (units)	1042	1200	1279	1639	1990

注：本表数据来源于市建委。
2010年后数据为全市口径，2009年以前数据为市区口径。

9–10 市区及县供水（2014年）

Urban Water Supply (2014)

指　标	Item	西安 Xi'an	市区 City	蓝田 Lantian	周至 ZhouZhi	户县 Huxian	高陵 GaoLing
年末水厂个数（个）	Number of Water Factory at Year-end (units)	16	12	1	1	1	1
供水综合生产能力（万立方米/日）	Total Volume of Water Supply (10 000 cu.m/day)	189.9	183.5	0.6	0.8	2.5	2.5
#地下水	Groundwater	47.95	47.75		0.20		
年末供水管道总长度（公里）	Length of Water Supply Pipelines at Year-end (km)	3403.33	3036.87	60.46	43	90	173
全年供水总量（万立方米）	Total Annual Volume of Water Supply (10 000 cu.m)	52243.28	50714.64	218.64	331	735	244
#销售水量	Volume of Water Sales	45200	43828.36	196.64	292	664	219
#生产运营用水	For Productive Use	15344.66	15187.91	24.85	3.90	121	7
居民家庭用水	For Residential Use	27819.32	26770.68	137.64	253	483	175
用水人口（万人）	Population with Access to Tap Water (10 000 persons)	441.90	397.91	8.23	6.57	16.03	13.16

注：本表数据来源于市建委及市水务局。
2009年部门统计制度变化，年末供水管道总长度和用水人口数调整。

9-11 市区及县供燃气（2014年）

Gas Supply in Urban Area (2014)

指　标	Item	西安 Xi'an	市区 Urban	蓝田 Lantian	周至 ZhouZhi	户县 Huxian	高陵 GaoLing
一、天然气	**Natural Gas**						
管道长度（公里）	Total Length of Gas Pipelines (km)	6892.25	6603.76	51.30	34.00	69.00	134.19
供气总量（万立方米）	Total Gas Supply(10 000 cu.m)	186259.15	178124.90	706.50	652.00	1610.29	5165.46
#销售气量	Volume of Gas Sales	179536.78	171616.32	705	650	1600	4965.46
#家庭用量	Residential Households	59057.38	54177.38	650	630	1390	2210
用气人口（万人）	Population with Access to Gas (10 000 persons)	425.72	397.36	4.44	1.22	9.40	13.30
二、液化石油气	**Liquefied Petroleum Gas**						
供气总量（吨）	Total Gas Supply (tons)	5300	1885	1069	1161	965	220
#销售气量	Volume of Gas Sales	5244	1875	1069	1160	940	200
#家庭用量	Residential Households	4281	1097	884	1160	940	200
用气人口（万人）	Population with Access to Gas (10 000 persons)	21	1	6	6	7	1

注：本表数据来源于市建委。

9-12 市区及县供热（2014年）

Heating in Urban Area (2014)

指　标	Item	西安 Xi'an	市区 Urban	蓝田 Lantian	周至 ZhouZhi	户县 Huxian	高陵 GaoLing
供热能力	Heating Capacity						
蒸气（吨/小时）	Steam (tons/hour)	2893.00	2663			230	
热水（兆瓦）	Hot Water (megawatts)	13967.00	6774				7193
供热总量(万吉焦）	Volume Supplied(10 000 gigajoules)						
蒸气	Steam	1743.87	1706.31			37.56	
热水	Hot Water	3726.89	3472.89				254.00
管道长度（公里）	Length of Pipelines (km)						
蒸气	Steam	231.04	214.04			17.00	
热水	Hot Water	663.20	633.00				30.20
供热面积（万平方米）	Heated Area (10 000sq.m)	13492.55	13072.28			56.00	364.27
#住宅	Residential Buildings	11828.59	11422.59			56.00	350.00

注：本表数据来源于市建委。

9-13 市区及县市政设施（2014年）

Municipal Facilities in Urban Area (2014)

指标	Item	西安 Xi'an	市区 Urban	蓝田 Lantian	周至 ZhouZhi	户县 Huxian	高陵 GaoLing
一、道路长度（公里）	**Length of Roads (km)**	**3461.18**	**3145.73**	**71.60**	**38.50**	**120.86**	**84.49**
二、道路面积（万平方米）	**Area of Roads (10 000 sq.m)**	**8144.22**	**7199.75**	**127.06**	**83.60**	**462.13**	**271.68**
三、人行道面积（万平方米）	**Area of Sidewalks (10 000 sq.m)**	**2310.46**	**2035.33**	**54.82**	**33.10**	**97.62**	**89.59**
四、桥梁数（座）	**Number of Bridges (units)**	**437**	**417**	**11**	**3**	**3**	**3**
#立交桥	Crossroads	105	100			3	2
五、路灯盏数（盏）	**Number of Street Lights (units)**	**337991**	**314339**	**1576**	**4595**	**8681**	**8800**
六、排水管道长度（公里）	**Length of Drainage Pipelines (km)**	**4839.49**	**4373.41**	**80.28**	**43.00**	**148.00**	**194.80**
七、污水年排放量（万立方米）	**Annual Discharge Volume of Sewage (10 000 cu.m)**	**51673**	**49261**	**460**	**390**	**1315**	**247**
八、污水处理厂处理能力（万立方米/日）	**Daily Disposal Capacity of Sewage (10 000 cu.m/day)**	**153.1**	**146.5**	**1.5**	**1.1**	**3.0**	**1.0**
九、污水年处理量（万立方米）	**Yearly Disposal Capacity of Sewage Disposal Plant (10 000 cu.m)**	**47907**	**46059**	**352**	**298**	**1010**	**188**

注：本表数据来源于市建委。

9-14 市区及县市政设施水平(2014年）

Urban Municipal Facilities in Urban Area (2014)

指标	Item	西安 Xi'an	市区 Urban	蓝田 Lantian	周至 ZhouZhi	户县 Huxian	高陵 GaoLing
一、人均日生活用水量（升）	**Per Capita Daily Consumption of Tap Water For Residential Use (liters)**	**178.45**	**187.4**	**93.7**	**163.46**	**165.4**	**47.36**
二、用水普及率(%)	**Water-Consuming Popularization (%)**	**100**	**100**	**100**	**100**	**100**	**100**
三、每万人拥有公共交通车辆（标台）	**Number of Public Transport Vehicles Per 10 000 Population (units)**	**14.4**					
四、燃气普及率（%）	**Gas-Consuming Popularization (%)**	**98.71**	**100.00**	**68.01**	**98.90**	**97.74**	**96.75**
五、人均城市道路面积（平方米）	**Per Captia Area of Roads (sq.m)**	**18.00**	**18.07**	**8.28**	**11.45**	**27.54**	**18.38**
六、建成区排水管道密度（公里/平方公里）	**Density of Drainage Pipelines (km/sq.km)**	**9.27**	**9.94**	**6.68**	**4.30**	**5.94**	**5.57**
七、污水处理率(%)	**Rate of Sewerage Disposal (%)**	**92.71**	**93.50**	**76.52**	**76.41**	**76.81**	**76.11**
八、园林绿化	**Afforestation and Parks and Gardens**						
人均公园绿地面积（平方米）	Per Capita Public Green Areas (sq.m)	11.22	11.60	4.31	14.66	9.63	8.12
建城区绿地率（%）	Rate of Green Areas in Developed Areas(%)	32.60	33.90	29.18	19.40	35.85	18.96
九、生活垃圾无害化处理率(%)	**Rate of No Harm Disposal of Garbage (%)**	**93.48**	**99.87**		**100**		**100**

注：本表数据来源于市建委。

主要统计指标解释

建成区面积 城市行政区内实际已成片开发建设、市政公用设施和公共设施基本具备的区域。对核心城市，它包括集中连片的部分以及分散的若干个已经成片建设起来，市政公用设施和公共设施基本具备的地区；对一城多镇来说，它包括由几个连片开发建设起来的，市政公用设施和公共设施基本具备的地区组成。因此建成区范围，一般是指建成区外轮廓线所能包括的地区，也就是这个城市实际建设用地所达到的范围。

供水综合生产能力 指按供水设施取水、净化、送水、出厂输水干管等环节设计能力计算的综合生产能力。包括在原设计能力的基础上，经挖、革、改增加的生产能力。计算时，以四个环节中最薄弱的环节为主确定能力。

供水管道长度 指从送水泵至用户水表之间所有管道的长度。不包括新安装尚未使用、水厂内以及用户建筑物内的管道。在同一条街道埋设两条或两条以上管道时，应按每条管道的长度计算。

供水总量 指报告期供水企业（单位）供出的全部水量。包括有效供水量和漏损水量。

用水普及率 指报告期末城区内用水人口与总人口的比率。计算公式:

$$用水普及率=\frac{城区用水人口（含暂住人口）}{城区人口+城区暂住人口}\times100\%$$

供气管道长度 指报告期末从气源厂压缩机的出口或门站出口至各类用户引入管之间的全部已经通气投入使用的管道长度。不包括煤气生产厂、输配站、液化气储存站、灌瓶站、储配站、气化站、混气站、供应站等厂（站）内的管道。

供气总量 指报告期燃气企业（单位）向用户供应的燃气数量。包括销售量和损失量。

燃气普及率 指报告期末城区内使用燃气的人口与总人口的比率。计算公式：

$$燃气普及率=\frac{城区用气人口（含暂住人口）}{城区人口+城区暂住人口}\times100\%$$

供热能力 指供热企业（单位）向城市热用户输送热能的设计能力。不是热电厂的生产能力。

供热总量 指在报告期供热企业（单位）向城市热用户输送全部蒸汽和热水的总热量。

供热管道长度 指从各类热源到热用户建筑物接入口之间的全部蒸汽和热水的管道长度。不包括各类热源厂内部的管道长度。

供热面积 指供热企业（单位）向城市各类房屋建筑物、构筑物及其附属设施供热的全部建筑面积。

道路长度 指道路长度和与道路相通的桥梁、隧道的长度，按车行道中心线计算。

道路面积 指道路实际铺装面积和与道路相通的广场、桥梁、隧道的铺装面积（统计时，将人行道面积单独统计）。

人行道面积按道路两侧面积相加计算，包括步行街和广场，不含人车混行的道路。

排水管道长度 指所有排水总管、干管、支管、检查井及连接井进出口等长度之和。计算时按单管计算，即在同一条街道上如有两条或两条以上并排的排水管道时，应按每条排水管道的长度相加计算。

绿化覆盖面积 指城市中的乔木、灌木、草坪等所有植被的垂直投影面积。包括公园绿地、防护绿地、生产绿地、附属绿地、其他绿地的绿化种植覆盖面积、屋顶绿化覆盖面积以及零散树木的覆盖面积，不含各类绿地中的水域面积以及没有被植被覆盖的面积（硬化道路、无屋顶绿化的建筑物等）。乔木树冠下重迭的灌木和草本植物不重复计算。

人均城市道路面积 指报告期末城区内平均每人拥有的城市道路面积。计算公式：

$$人均城市道路面积=\frac{城区道路面积}{城区人口+城区暂住人口}$$

建成区排水管道密度 指报告期末建成区排水管道分布的疏密程度，计算公式：

$$排水管道密度=\frac{排水管道长度}{建成区面积}$$

污水处理率 指报告期内污水处理总量与污水排放总量的比率。计算公式：

$$污水处理率=\frac{污水处理总量}{污水排放总量}\times100\%$$

人均公园绿地面积 指报告期末城区内平均每人拥有的公园绿地面积。计算公式：

$$人均公园绿地面积=\frac{城区公园绿地面积}{城区人口+城区暂住人口}$$

建成区绿地率 指报告期末建成区内绿地面积与建成区面积的比率。计算公式：

$$建成区绿地率\frac{建成区绿地面积}{建成区面积}\times100\%$$

Explanatory Notes on Main Statistical Indicators

Area of the Constructed Regions refers to developed and built city administrative area where basic municipal utilities and public facilities complete constructed. To core city, it includes part of contiguous centralized and a number of decentralized part where basic municipal utilities and public facilities complete constructed. To a multi-city town, it consists of several contiguous developed and build area where municipal utilities and public facilities with basic composition. Therefore, the range of built-up area, generally refers to the built-up areas in the contour line, which is the actual construction site of the city achieved range.

Production Capacity of Water Supply refers to the designed overall production capacity of water facilities, covering the four segments of water collection, purification, conveyance, and out flow through trunk pipelines. Increased capacity through transformation and innovation projects is included as well. The capacity is determined mainly on the weakest of the above-mentioned four segments.

Length of Water Supply Pipelines at Year-end refers to the total length of all the pipelines between the water pumps and the user water meters, excluding pipelines newly installed but not used yet, pipeline in the water factory, and pipeline in the user's buildings.

Volume of Water Supply refers to the total volume of water supplied by water-works(units) during the reference period, including both the effective water supply and loss during the water supply.

Coverage Rate of Urban Population with Access to Tap Water refers to the ratio of the urban population with access to tap water to the total urban population . The formula is :

$$\text{Coverage of urban population with access to tap water} = \frac{\text{Urban population with access to tap water}}{\text{Urban population}} \times 100\%$$

Length of Gas Pipeline refers to the total length of pipelines in use between the outlet of the compressor of gas-work of outlet gas stations and the leading pipe of users , excluding pipelines within gasworks , delivery stations ,LPG storage stations ,refilling stations, gas-mixing stations and supply stations.

Volume of Gas Supply refers to the total volume of gas provided to users by gas-producing enterprises (units) in a year ,including the volume sold and the volume lost .

Coverage Rate of Urban Population with Access to Gas refers to the ratio of the urban population with access to gas to the total urban population at the end of the reference period. The formula is :

$$\text{Coverage rate of urban population with access to gas} = \frac{\text{Urban population with access to gas}}{\text{Urban population}} \times 100\%$$

City Heating capacity in Urban Areas refers to the designed capacity of heating enterprises (units) in supplying heating energy to urban users during the reference period .

City Quantity of Heat Supplied in Urban Areas refers to the total quantity of heat from steam and hot water urban users by heating enterprises (units) during the reference period .

City Length of Urban Heating Pipelines refers to the total length of steam or hot water pipelines for sources of heat to the leading pipelines of the building of the users ,excluding internal pipelines in heat generating enterprises

Heated Area refers to the total structure area of heat supplied to urban constructions, structures and ancillary facilities by heating enterprises (units) during the reference period .

Length of Paved Roads refers to the length of roads with paved surface including bridges and tunnels connected with roads. Length of the roads is measured by the central lines .

Area of Paved Roads refers to the actual pavement area of roads and the actual pavement area of squares, bridges and tunnels connecting to the roads (the area of sidewalk pavements is calculated separately).

The area of sidewalk pavements is the sum of area of roads on sides of road, including pedestrian streets and squares, excluding roads for both pedestrians and vehicles .

Length of exhaust pipelines refers to the total length of all main drain piles ,trunk pipes ,branch pipes

,access manholes ,and connector well entrances and exits ,and so on . The whole length is calculated as of single pipes. Namely ,if there are two or more drain pipes parallel on a street ,the length of every pipe shall be summed .

Total area of green land refers to vertical projection area of all vegetation including trees, shrubs, lawns. Including parks, protective green space, production green space, green subsidiaries, green plants covering area, covering an area other green spaces, green roofs and covering area of scattered trees, excluding kinds of water area in kinds of green area and the area not covered by vegetation(hardened road, building of no green roof). shrubs and herbaceous plants overlap under the canopy of trees do not double counting.

Per Capita Area of Paved Roads refers to the area of urban roads per capita at the end of the reporting period. The formula is :

$$\text{Per capita area of paved roads} = \frac{\text{Area of urban roads}}{\text{Urban population+temporary resident population}}$$

Density of Drainage Pipelines refers to density of drainage pipelines in developed areas at the end of the reporting period .The formula is :

$$\text{Density of drainage pipelines} = \frac{\text{Length of drainage pipelines}}{\text{Ares of developed areas}}$$

Rate of Sewerage Disposal refers to the ratio of waste water disposed with the total discharge of waste water in the reporting period .The formula is:

$$\text{Rate of Sewerage Disposal} = \frac{\text{Waste Water Disposed}}{\text{Total Discharge of Waste Water}} \times 100\%$$

Per Capita Area of Public Green refers to the area of public green areas per capita at end of the reporting period .The formula is :

$$\text{Per capita area of public green} = \frac{\text{Area of public green areas}}{\text{Urban population+temporary resident population}}$$

Coverage of Green Areas in Developed Areas refers to the ratio of green areas in built-up areas with the area of developed areas at the end of reporting period . The formula is:

$$\text{Coverage of green land in developed areas} = \frac{\text{Area of green land in developed aresa}}{\text{Area of developed areas}} \times 100\%$$

10 环境保护

ENVIRONMENT PROTECTION

资料整理：李　炜
Data management：Li Wei
数据审核：陈　英
Data audit：Chen Ying

第十部分　环境保护

一、简要说明

本章资料反映环境保护、工业污染排放及处理利用情况、危险废物集中处置情况、生活及其他污染情况和工业污染治理项目建设情况，由西安市统计局综合处根据西安市环保局提供的数据资料整理。

二、主要指标

工业用水重复利用率（%）	68.88	比上年提高	0.57个百分点
工业固体废物综合利用率（%）	92.43	比上年下降	3.0个百分点
全年环境空气达到二级以上天数（天）	211	比上年增加	73天

10 ENVIRONMENT PROTECTION

Ⅰ.Brief Introduction

This chapter contain information that reflect environment protection, discharge and treatment of industrial pollutant, centralized treatment of dangerous wastes, domestic pollution and other pollution, construction of projects of industrial pollution treatment. Data in this chapter is compiled by General Division of the Xi'an Bureau of Statistics according to the reported data from Environment Protection Administration department of the municipal government.

Ⅱ.Major Indicators

		Increase over Preceding Year
Percentage of Industrial Water Recycled (%)	68.88	0.57 percentage points
Percentage of Industrial Solid Waste Utilized (%)	92.43	−3.0 percentage points
Days of Air Quality up to the secondarylevels（day）	211	73

10-1 城市环境保护（2014年）

Urban Environmental Protection (2014)

指 标	Item	2014
一、饮用水环境	**Potable Water Environment**	
全市饮用水水质达标率(%)	Compliance Rate of the City's Potable Water Quality (%)	100
二、大气环境	**Atmospheric Environment**	
1、可吸入颗粒物浓度年平均值(毫克/立方米)	Annual Average Concentration of Particulate Matters(mg/cu.m)	0.147
二氧化硫浓度年平均值	Annual Average Concentration of Sulphur Dioxide	0.032
二氧化氮浓度年平均值	Annual Average Concentration of Nitrogen Dioxide	0.047
2、全年环境空气质量达标天数(天)	Days of Air Quality up to the Standards(days)	211
全年环境空气质量达标率(%)	Annual compliance rate of Ambient Air Quality(%)	57.81
三、声环境	**Voice**	
1、功能区噪声平均值(dB(A))	Average Noise Value of Functional Districts(dB(A))	
0类区	Class 0	45.0
1类区	Class 1	58.0
2类区	Class 2	58.0
3类区	Class 3	65.0
4类区	Class 4	70.0
2、道路交通噪声平均值(dB(A))	Average Noise Value of Road Traffic(dB(A))	55.2
3、区域噪声平均值(dB(A))	Average Noise Value of Region(dB(A))	68.0
四、环境污染治理	**Environmental pollution treatment**	
当年完成环保验收项目环境保护投资（亿元）	Year Completed Investment in Environmental Protection Projects of Environmental acceptance(100 million yuan)	12.99

注：本表数据来源于市环保局。

10-2 主要年份工业“三废”排放及处理利用情况

指　标	Item	2000	2006	2007
一、工业废水排放量（万吨）	**Volume of Waste Water Discharge (10 000 tons)**	**9145**	**16389**	**19069**
工业废水处理量（万吨）	Volume of Industrial Wastewater Disposal (10 000 tons)			
废水治理设施数（套）	Number of Facilities for Treatment of Waste Water (sets)			
二、工业废气排放量（亿立方米）	**Total Volume of Industrial Waste Gas Emission (100 million cu.m)**	**275.97**	**642.51**	**1149.41**
废气治理设施数（套）	Number of Facilities for Treatment of Waste Gas(sets)		466	846
三、工业固体废物产生量（万吨）	**Volume of Industrial Solid Wastes Produced (10 000 tons)**	**107**	**161**	**193**
工业固体废物处置量（万吨）	Volume of Industrial Solid Wastes Treated (10 000 tons)	20	5	6
工业固体废物综合利用量（万吨）	Volume of Industrial Solid Waste Utilized (10 000 tons) in a Comprehensive Way	63	143	171
工业固体废物综合利用率（%）	Percentage of Volume of Industrial Solid Waste Utilized in a Comprehensive Way(%)	58.88	89.07	88.48
四、工业锅炉（台/蒸吨）	**Industrial Boilers (units/tons)**			

注：本表数据来源于市环保局。

2010年全国统一进行了污染源普查动态更新调查工作，“十二五”的环境统计体系与污染源普查体系相衔接，与“十一五”环境统计口径不同。

Discharge and Treatrment of Waste Gas, Water & Solid Wastes in Repersentative Years

2008	2009	2010	2011	2012	2013	2014
18304	**13168**	**13840**	**13148**	**10223.73**	**8972.97**	**6339.85**
		10673.52	12632.38	9089.04	6798.71	5818.27
		267	314	312	295	305
1519.18	**737.24**	**791.56**	**1018.46**	**1043.31**	**844.11**	**901.23**
920	852	816	745	649	661	740
220	**246**	**267.29**	**279**	**259.14**	**255.78**	**252.66**
5	4.85	3.56	6	9.24	9.68	17.54
215	241	262	271	248.58	244.08	233.52
97.78	97.83	98.05	97.3	95.92	95.43	92.43
		503/8785	**576/13466**	**567/14565**	**520/14177**	**519/17717**

10-3 工业污染排放及处理利用情况（2014年）

Discharge and Treatment of Industrial Pollution (2014)

指 标	Item	2014
一、被调查企业基本情况	**Basic condition of Enterprises investigated**	
1. 企业数（个）	Number of Enterprises (units)	491
2. 工业总产值（亿元）（当年价格）	Gross Industry Output Value (100 millian yuan)	2249.80
3. 工业锅炉数（台/蒸吨）	Industrial Boilers (units/tons)	519/17717
4. 工业炉窑数（座）	Number of Industrial Grates (items)	207
二、工业废水	**Industrial Waste Water**	
1. 工业用水总量（万吨）	Total Volume of Industrial Water (10 000 tons)	36994.88
新鲜水量	Volume of Fresh Water	11513.40
重复用水量	Volume of Water Recycled	25481.48
2. 工业用水重复利用率（%）	Percentage of Industrial Water Recycled (%)	68.88
3. 废水治理设施数（套）	Number of Facilities for Treatment of Waste Water (sets)	305
4. 废水治理设施处理能力（万吨/日）	Disposal Capacity of Facilities for Treatment of Waste Water (10 000 tons/day)	25.16
5. 废水治理设施运行费用（万元）	Operating Expense of Facilities for Treatment of Waste Water (10 000 yuan)	10216
6. 工业废水排放量（万吨）	Volume of Industrial Waste Water Discharged (10 000 tons)	6339.85
三、工业废气	**Industrial Waste Gas**	
1. 煤炭消费量（万吨）	Total Coal Consumption (10 000 tons)	793.70
2. 燃料油消费量（不含车船用）（万吨）	Fuel Oil Consumption (10 000 tons)	0.50
3. 天然气消费量（亿立方米）	Natural Gas Consumption (100 millian cu.m)	2.55
4. 工业废气排放总量（亿立方米）	Total Volume of Industrial Waste Gas Emission (100 millian cu.m)	901.23
5. 废气治理设施数（套）	Number of Facilities for Treatment of Waste Gas (sets)	740
6. 废气治理设施处理能力（万立方米/时）	Disposal Capacity of Facilities for Treatment of Waste Gas (10 000 cu.m./h)	4497.76
7. 废气治理设施设备运行费用（万元）	Operating Expense of Facilities for Treatment of Waste gas(10 000 yuan)	40420.60
8. 二氧化硫去除量（吨）	Volume of Sulphur Dioxide Removed (tons)	161751.55
9. 二氧化硫排放量（吨）	Volume of Sulphur Dioxide Emission (tons)	62604.03
10. 氮氧化物生产量（吨）	Production of nitrogen oxides(tons)	46410.11
11. 氮氧化物排放量（吨）	Nitrogen oxide emissions(tons)	31823.37
12. 烟（粉）尘生产量（吨）	Tobacco (powder) dust production(tons)	1668076.68
13. 烟（粉）尘排放量（吨）	The smoke (powder) dust emissions(tons)	21985.40
四、工业固体废物	**Industrial Solid Waste**	
1. 工业固体废物产生量（万吨）	Volume of Industrial Solid Waste Produced (10 000tons)	252.66
2. 工业固体废物综合利用量（万吨）	Volume of Industrial Solid Waste Utilized (10 000tons)	233.52
3. 工业固体废物综合利用率（%）	Percentage of Industrial Solid Waste Utilized (%)	92.43
4. 工业固体废物贮存量（万吨）	Volume of Industrial Solid Waste Accumulated (10 000tons)	1.61
5. 工业固体废物处置量（万吨）	Volume of Industrial Solid Waste Treated (10 000tons)	17.54
6. 工业固体废物倾倒丢弃量（吨）	Volume of Industrial Solid Waste Discharged (tons)	43

注：本表数据来源于市环保局。

10-4 城市污水排放及处理情况（2014年）

Discharge and Treatment of City Sewage(2014)

指　标	Item	2014
一、污水处理厂数（座）	**Number of Sewage Treatment Works(units)**	**35**
污水处理厂处理能力（万吨/日）	Daily Disposal Capacity of Sewage(10 000 tons/day)	195.06
二、污水处理	**Sewgae Disposal**	
污水实际处理量（万吨）	Volume of Sewgae Disposal(10 000 tons)	43827.67
生活污水处理量	Volume of Domestic Sewgae Disposal	42891.43
工业污水处理量	Volume of Industrial Sewage Disposal	936.24
三、再生水	**Recycled water**	
生产量（万吨）	Production(10 000 tons)	918.29
利用量（万吨）	Utilization(10 000 tons)	798.42
四、化学需氧量去除量（吨）	**Volume of COD Removed (tons)**	**143109.50**
五、氨氮去除量（吨）	**Volume of Ammonia and Nitrogen Removed(tons)**	**13376.70**
六、总磷去除量（吨）	**Volume of Total Phosphorus Removed(tons)**	**1592.50**
七、污泥生产量（万吨）	**Volume of Sludge Produced(10 000 tons)**	**32.37**
八、污泥处置量（万吨）	**Volume of Sludge Disposal(10 000 tons)**	**32.37**
九、污泥倾倒丢弃量（吨）	**Dumping sludge discards (tons)**	
十、本年运行费用（万元）	**Operating Expense(10 000 yuan)**	**38817.64**

注：本表数据来源于市环保局。

10-5 危险废物（医疗废物）集中处理情况(2014年)

Condition of Collected Dangerous Wastes Treated (2014)

指 标	Item	2014
一、危险废物集中处理（置）厂数（个）	**Number of Colleted Dangerous Wastes Treated Plants(items)**	**3**
二、医疗废物集中处理（置）厂数（个）	**The number of Manufacturing Plants of Medical waste treatment (units)**	**1**
三、危险废物设计处置能力（吨/日）	**Design hazardous waste disposal capacity (tons / day)**	**467.40**
四、实际处置危险废物量（吨）	**The actual amount of hazardous waste disposal (tons)**	**97455.50**
五、危险废物综合利用量（吨）	**Volume of Dangerous Wastes Utilized in a Comprehensive Way (tons)**	**150**
六、焚烧残渣流向（千克）	**Flow Direction of Residuum after Burning (kg)**	
1. 焚烧残渣量	Volume of Residuum after Burning	390029.60
2. 焚烧残渣安全填进处理量	Secure landfill disposal incineration residues	390029.60
3. 焚烧飞灰生产量	Fly ash production	67605.10
4. 焚烧飞灰安全填进处理量	Fly ash landfill disposal safety	67605.10
七、当年运行费用（万元）	**Operating Expenses in Current year(10 000 yuan)**	**6898.29**

注：本表数据来源于市环保局。

10-6 生活及其他污染情况(2014年)

Domestic Pollution and Other conditions (2014)

指 标	Item	2014
一、基本情况	**Basic Condition**	
1. 生活天然气消费量（万立方米）	Volume of Living natural gas consumption (10 000 cu.m)	160707.95
2. 生活用水总量（万吨）	Volume of Living water (10 000 tons)	50303.13
二、污染排放情况	**Discharge of Pollutant**	
1. 城镇生活污水排放量（万吨）	Volume of Urban Domestic Sewage Discharged(10 000 tons)	44769.79
2. 生活污水处理量（万吨）	Volume of Domestic Sewgae Disposal(10 000 tons)	42531.30
3. 生活CDD生产量（吨）	Volume of Life CDD production (tons)	158854.11
4. 生活CDD排放量（吨）	Volume of Life CDD emissions (tons)	61592.52
5. 生活氨氮生产量（吨）	Volume of Ammonia and Nitrogen in Urban Domestic Sewage Produced (tons)	20334.37
6. 生活氨氮排放量（吨）	Volume of Ammonia and Nitrogen in Urban Domestic Sewage Discharged (tons)	10385.69
7. 二氧化硫排放量（吨）	Volume of Domestic and Other Sulphur Dioxide Emission (tons)	29805.75
8. 氨氮化物排放量（吨）	Volume of Ammonia and Nitrogen in Urban Domestic Sewage Discharged (tons)	11698.29
9. 烟尘排放量（吨）	Volume of Soot Emission (tons)	15131.20

注：本表数据来源于市环保局。

10-7 工业污染治理项目建设情况（2014年）

Condition of Anti-Industrial-Pollution Projects (2014)

指 标	Item	2014
一、工业企业数（个）	**Number of Industrial Enterprises (units)**	**26**
二、老工业污染源项目治理本年施工总数（个）	**The total number of construction projects of Old industrial pollution sources control this year(units)**	**20**
#工业废水治理项目	Treatment of Waste Water	3
工业废气治理项目	Treatment of Waste Gas	11
工业固体废物治理项目	Treatmen of Solid Wastes	
三、老工业污染源项目治理本年竣工总数（个）	**The Total Number of Old Industrial Pollution Control Projects Completed this year(units)**	**24**
#工业废水治理项目	Treatment of Waste Water	3
工业废气治理项目	Treatment of Waste Gas	16
工业固体废物治理项目	Treatmen of Solid Wastes	
四、老工业污染源治理项目本年完成投资（万元）	**Investment completed in Old industrial pollution control projects this Year(10 000 yuan)**	**46821.79**
#废水治理项目	Treatment of Waste Water	1315.00
废气治理项目	Treatment of Waste Gas	34298.79
固体废物治理项目	Treatmen of Solid Wastes	
五、老工业污染源治理项目本年投资来源（万元）	**Source of Investment in Old industrial pollution control projects this Year(10 000 yuan)**	
#排污费补助	Pollution Charges Subsidies	2900.00
政府其他补助	Other Government Subsidies	9987.45
企业自筹	Self-raising Funds	33934.34
#银行贷款	Lonans	700.00
六、"三同时"项目竣工验收数（个）	**number of "Three simultaneous" project completion and acceptance (a)**	**4**
七、"三同时"竣工验收项目实际环保投资（万元）	**"Three simultaneous" actual environmental investment completed and accepted (10 000 yuan)**	**8120.24**
八、"三同时"项目废水治理新增处理能力（万吨/日）	**"Three simultaneous"Add processing capacity of wastewater treatment (10 000 tons / day)**	**0.046**
九、"三同时"项目废气治理新增处理能力（万立方米/时）	**"Three simultaneous"Add processing capacity of Exhaust treatment (10 000 cu.m/h)**	**11.33**

注：本表数据来源于市环保局。

"三同时"指建设项目中防治污染的措施，必须与主体工程同时设计，同时施工，同时投产使用。

10-8 各区县、开发区环境保护基本情况（2014年）

区县、开发区	Region	本年完成环保验收项目环保投资额（万元）Investment Completed in accepted Environmental projects this year (10 000 yuan)	工业二氧化硫排放量（吨）Volume of Industrial Sulphur Dioxide Discharged (tons)
全　市	**Total**	**130915.8**	**62604.03**
新城区	Xincheng	2887.0	87.03
碑林区	Beilin	87.0	1822.27
莲湖区	Lianhu	11315.9	4441.85
灞桥区	Baqiao	3316.0	8835.33
未央区	Weiyang	1898.5	876.16
雁塔区	Yanta	23898.1	1201.01
阎良区	Yanliang	599.6	2377.28
临潼区	Lintong	3873.6	1059.18
长安区	Chang'an	3086.7	2879.25
蓝田县	Lantian	1377.0	519.38
周至县	Zhouzhi	1810.0	251.39
户　县	Huxian	2650.0	7897.51
高陵县	Gaoling	2328.4	751.69
高新开发区	Gaoxinkaifaqu	18633.0	1222.30
经济开发区	Jingjikaifaqu	7652.0	2774.07
航天基地	Hangtianjidi	448.0	603.46
沣东新城	Fendongxincheng	699.0	25004.87

注：本表数据来源于市环保局。

环境统计中污水处理厂个数包含部分大学园区及部分大型小区的污水处理厂。

Condition of Environment Protection by Regions (2014)

工业化学需氧量排放量 （吨） Volume of COD Removed (tons)	垃圾处理站数 （座） Number of Rubbish Disposal Works (units)	污水处理厂数 （个） Number of Sewage Treatment Works (units)
20137.42	**3**	**35**
312.85		
6.49		
674.72		2
1142.59	1	3
1938.13		5
102.79		3
126.15	1	1
503.31		3
137.18		7
31.95		3
116.99		1
5217.78		3
121.35	1	1
1802.39		1
860.75		1
335.06		
6706.94		1

主要统计指标解释

工业用水 指工矿企业在生产过程中用于制造、加工、冷却、空调、净化、洗涤等方面的用水，按新水取用量计，不包括企业内部的重复利用水量。

工业废水排放量 指经过企业厂区所有排放口排到企业外部的工业废水量。包括生产废水、外排的直接冷却水、超标排放的矿井地下水和与工业废水混排的厂区生活污水，不包括外排的间接冷却水（清污不分流的间接冷却水应计算在内）。

直接排入海的 指经企业位于海边的排放口，直接排入海的废水量。直接排放指废水经过工厂的排污口直接排入海，而未经过城市下水道或其他中间体，也不受其他水体的影响。

工业废水排放达标量 指报告期内废水中各项污染物指标都达到国家或地方排放标准的外排工业废水量，包括未经处理外排达标的，经废水处理设施处理后达标排放的，以及经污水处理厂处理后达标排放的。

生活污水排放量 指城镇居民每年排放的生活污水。用人均系数法测算。测算公式为：

$$\text{生活污水排放量} = \text{城镇生活污水排放系数} \times \text{市镇非农业人口} \times 365$$

生活污水中化学需氧量（COD）排放量 指城镇居民每年排放的生活污水中的COD的量。用人均系数法测算。测算公式为：

$$\text{城镇生活污水中COD产生系数} = \text{城镇牛活污水中COD排放量} \times \text{市镇非农业人口} \times 365$$

化学需氧量（COD） 指用化学氧化剂氧化水中有机污染物时所需的氧量。COD值越高，表示水中有机污染物污染越重。

工业废气排放量 指报告期内企业厂区内燃料燃烧和生产工艺过程中产生的各种排入大气的含有污染物的气体的总量，以标准状态（273K，101325Pa）计算。测算公式为：

$$\text{工业废气排放量} = \text{燃料燃烧过程中废气排放量} + \text{生产工艺过程中废气排放量}$$

生活及其他SO_2排放量 以生活及其他煤炭消费量和其含硫量为基础，根据以下公式计算：

$$\text{生活及其他}SO_2\text{排放量} = \text{生活及其他煤炭消费量} \times \text{含硫量} \times 0.8 \times 2$$

工业SO_2排放量 指报告期内企业在燃料燃烧和生产工艺过程中排入大气的SO_2总量，计算公式为：

$$\text{工业}SO_2\text{排放量} = \text{燃料燃烧过程中}SO_2\text{排放量} + \text{生产工艺过程中}SO_2\text{排放量}$$

工业烟尘排放量 指企业厂区内燃料燃烧过程中产生的烟气中夹带的颗粒物排放量。

生活及其他烟尘排放量 指除工业生产活动以外的所有社会、经济活动及公共设施的经营活动中燃烧所排放的烟尘纯重量。以生活及其他煤炭消费量为基础进行测算。

工业粉尘排放量 指企业在生产工艺过程中排放的能在空气中悬浮一定时间的固体颗粒物排放量。如钢铁企业的耐火材料粉尘、焦化企业的筛焦系统粉尘、烧结机的粉尘、石灰窑的粉尘、建材企业的水泥粉尘等。不包括电厂排入大气的烟尘。

工业固体废物产生量 指报告期内企业在生产过程中产生的固体状、半固体状和高浓度液体状废弃物的总量，包括危险废物、冶炼废渣、粉煤灰、炉渣、煤矸石、尾矿、放射性废物和其他废物等；不包括矿山开采的剥离废石和掘进废石（煤矸石和呈酸性或碱性的废石除外）。酸性或碱性废石指采掘的废石其流经水、雨淋水的pH值小于4或pH值大于10.5者。

危险废物 指列入国家危险废物名录或根据国家规定的危险废物鉴别标准和鉴别方法认定的，具有爆炸性、易燃性、易氧化性、毒性、腐蚀性、易传染疾病等危险特性之一的废物。

工业固体废物综合利用量 指报告期内企业通过回收、加工、循环、交换等方式，从固体废物中提取或者使其转化为可以利用的资源、能源和其他原材料的固体废物量（包括当年利用往年的工业固体废物贮存量），如用作农业肥料、生产建筑材料、筑路等。综合利用量由原产生固体废物的单位统计。

工业固体废物综合利用率 指工业固体废物综合利用量占丁业固体废物产生量（包括综合利用往年贮存量）的百分率。计算公式为：

$$\text{工业固体废物综合利用率}=\frac{\text{工业固体废物综合利用量}}{\text{工业固体废物产生量}+\text{综合利用往年贮存量}}\times 100\%$$

工业固体废物贮存量 指报告期内企业以综合利用或处置为目的，将固体废物暂时贮存或堆存在专设的贮存设施或专设的集中堆存场所内的数量。专设的固体废物贮存场所或贮存设施必须有防扩散、防流失、防渗漏、防止污染大气、水体的措施。

工业固体废物处置量 指报告期内企业将固体废物焚烧或者最终置于符合环境保护规定要求的场所，并不再回取的工业固体废物量（包括当年处置往年的工业固体废物贮存量）。处置方式有填埋（其中危险废物应安全填埋）、焚烧、专业贮存场（库）封场处理、深层灌注、回填矿井及海洋处置（经海洋管理部门同意投海处置）等。

工业固体废物排放量 指报告期内企业将所产生的固体废物排到固体废物污染防治设施、场所以外的数量，不包括矿山开采的剥离废石和掘进废石（煤矸石和呈酸性或碱性的废石除外）。

"三废"综合利用产品产值 指报告期内利用"三废"作为主要原料生产的产品价值（现行价）；已经销售或准备销售的应计算产品价值，留作生产自用的不应计算产品价值。

生活垃圾清运量 指报告期内收集和运送到各生活垃圾处理厂（场）和生活垃圾最终消纳点的生活垃圾数量。生活垃圾指城市日常生活或为城市日常生活提供服务的活动中产生的固体废物以及法律行政规定的视为城市生活垃圾的固体废物。包括：居民生活垃圾、商业垃圾、集市贸易市场垃圾、街道清扫垃圾、公共场所垃圾和机关、学校、厂矿等单位的生活垃圾。

生活垃圾无害化处理率 指报告期生活垃圾无害化处理量与生活垃圾产生量的比率。在统计上，由于生活垃圾产生量不易取得，可用清运量代替。计算公式为：

$$\text{生活垃圾无害化处理率}=\frac{\text{生活垃圾无害化处理量}}{\text{生活垃圾产生量}}\times 100\%$$

Explanatory Notes on Main Statistical Indicators

Water Use by Industry refers to new withdrawals of water, excluding reuse of water within enterprises.

Waste Water Discharged by Industry refers to the volume of waste water discharged by industrial enterprises through all their outlets, including waste water from production process, directly cooled water, groundwater from mining wells which does not meet discharge standards and sewage from households mixed with waste water produced by industrial activities, but excluding indirectly cooled water discharged (It should be included if the discharge is not separated from waste water).

Waste Water Directly Discharged into Sea refers to the volume of waste water directly discharged into sea through outlets of enterprises situated by sea without going through municipal sewerage networks or any other intermediates or being affected by any other water bodies.

Industrial Waste Water Meeting Discharge Standards refers to volume of industrial waste water discharge which, with or without treatment, reaches national or local standards with regard to all pollutants.

Urban Non-industrial Waste Water Discharge refers to annual discharge of non-industrial waste water by urban households. It is estimated by per capita coefficient using the formula:

Urban non-industrial waste water discharge = urban non-industrial waste water discharge coefficient × urban non-alagricultur population × 365

Volume of Chemical Oxygen Demand (COD) Generated by Urban Non-industrial Waster Water refers to chemical oxygen demand generated through the annual discharge of non-industrial waste water by urban households. It is estimated as:

Volume of chemical oxygen demand (cod) generated by urban non-industrial waster water = Coefficient of COD generated through urban non-industrial waste water × urban non-agricultural population × 365

Chemical Oxygen Demand (COD) refers to the amount of oxygen required when chemical oxidants are used to oxidize organic pollutants in water. A higher value of COD corresponds to more serious pollution by organic pollutants.

Industrial Waste Air Emission refers to the discharge into atmosphere of waste air containing pollutants generated from fuel burning and production processes in enterprises within a given period of time. It is calculated at standard status (273K, 101325Pa) as:

Industrial waste air emission = tnoissimehrough fuel burning + tnoissimehrough production process

SO_2 Emission through Non-industrial and Other Activities is calculated on the basis of consumption of coal by households and other activities and the sulphur content of coal with the following formula:

SO_2 emission through non-industrial and other activities = of coalby households andother activities × sulphur content × 0.8 × 2

SO_2 Emission through Industrial Activities refers to volume of sulphur dioxide emission from fuel burning and production process by enterprises during a given period of time. It is calculated as:

SO_2 emission through industrial activities = SO_2emIssIon from fuel burning + SO_2 emission from production process

Industrial Soot Emission refers to the volume of soot in smoke emitted in the process of fuel burning in the premises of enterprises.

Soot Emission by Consumption and Others refers to the net volume of soot emitted by fuel burning from all social and economic activities and operations of public facilities other than industrial activities. It is calculated on the basis of coal consumption by households and others.

Industrial Dust Emission refers to volume of dust emitted by production process of enterprises and suspended in the air for a given period of time, including dust from refractory material of iron and steel works, dust from coke-screening systems and sintering machines of coke plants, dust from lime kilns and dust from cement production in building material enterprises, but excluding soot and dust emitted from power plants.

Industrial Solid Wastes Produced refers to total volume of solid, semi-solid and high concentration liquid residues produced by industrial enterprises from production process in a given period of time, including hazardous wastes, slag, coal ash, gangue, tailings, radioactive residues and other wastes, but excluding stones stripped or dug out in mining - gangue and acid or alkaline stones not included (a stone is acid or alkaline according to the pH value of the water being below 4 or above 10.5 when the stone is in, or soaked by water).

Hazardous Wastes refers to those included in the national hazardous wastes catalogue or specified as any one of the following properties in the national hazardous wastes identification standards: explosive, ignitable, oxidizable, toxic, corrosive or liable to cause infectious diseases or lead to other dangers.

Industrial Solid Wastes Utilized refers to volume of solid wastes from which useful materials can be extracted or which can be converted into usable resources, energy or other materials by means of reclamation, processing, recycling and exchange (including utilizing in the year the stocks of industrial solid wastes of the previous year). Examples of such utilizations include fertilizers, building materials and road materials. The information shall be collected by the producing units of the wastes.

Rate of Utilization of Industrial Solid Wastes refers to the percentage of industrial solid wastes utilized over industrial solid wastes produced (including stocks of the previous years). It is calculated as:

$$\text{Rate of utilization of industrial solid wastes} = \frac{\text{volume of industrial solid wastes utilized}}{\text{industrial solid wastes produced} + \text{stock of previous years}} \times 100\%$$

Stock of Industrial Solid Wastes refers to the volume of solid wastes placed in special facilities or special sites for purposes of utilization or disposal. The sites or facilities should take measures against dispersion, loss, seepage, and air and water contamination.

Industrial Solid Wastes Disposed refers to the quantity of industrial solid wastes which are burnt or placed ultimately in the sites meeting the requirements for environmental protection and not salvaged or recycled (including disposition in the year of those wastes of previous years). The disposition includes landfill (Safe landfills should be conducted for hazardous wastes), incineration, containment spaces, deep underground disposal, backfill in mining pits and disposal at sea.

Industrial Solid Wastes Discharged refers to the volume of industrial solid wastes discharged by producing enterprises to disposal facilities or to other sites. The wastes exclude stones stripped or dug from mining (gangue and acid or alkaline waste stones not included).

Output Value of Products Made from Waste Gas, Waste Water and Solid Wastes refers to the current value of products with waste gas, waste water and solid wastes as main materials of production. Products sold and ready to sell shall be included while those produced for own use shall not be included.

Consumption Wastes Transported refers to volume of consumption wastes collected and transported to disposal factories or sites. Consumption wastes are solid wastes produced from urban households or from service activities for urban households, and solid wastes regarded by laws and regulations as urban consumption wastes, including those from households, commercial activities, markets, cleaning of streets, public sites, offices, schools, factories, mining units and other sources.

Ratio of Consumption Wastes Treated refers to consumption wastes treated over that produced. In practical statistics, as it is difficult to estimate, the volume of consumption wastes produced is replaced with that transported. It is calculated as:

$$\text{Ratio of consumption wastes treated} = \frac{\text{consumption wastes treated}}{\text{consumption wastes produced}} \times 100\%$$

11 农 业

AGRICULTURE

资料整理：张喜兰　马秋娟　薛　丰
Data management：Zhang Xilan　Ma Qiujuan　Xue Feng
数据审核：王明珠
Data audit：Wang Mingzhu

第十一部分　农业

一、简要说明

本章资料主要包括农村基本情况、农业生产条件与生产情况、耕地、农林牧渔及服务业产值、主要农产品产量以及各区县农业生产和农村经济效益主要指标，由西安市统计局农村处提供。

二、主要指标

年末耕地面积（万亩）	360.73	比上年下降	1.5%
农林牧渔及服务业总产值（亿元）	367.21	比上年增长	5.1%
农作物播种面积（万亩）	684.28	比上年下降	1.6%
粮食产量（万吨）	175.61	比上年下降	4.1%

11　AGRICULTURE

Ⅰ.Brief Introduction

Data in this chapter reflects basic condition of agriculture production of Xi'an city. It is primarily consist of basic condition of rural area, condition of agriculture production, plow land, production value of farming, forestry, animal husbandry and fishery, gross yield of primary produce and primary indicators of agriculture production and rural area economic performance. The data are provided and compiled by Rural Area Division of the Xi'an Bureau of Statistics.

Ⅱ.Major Indicators

		Increase over Preceding Year
Cultivated Area Year-end(10 000 mu)	360.73	-1.5%
Gross Output Value of Farming, Forestry, Animal Husbandry, Fishery and Service(100 mil. Yuan)	367.21	5.1%
Sown Area of Crops(10 000 mu)	684.28	-1.6%
Grain Output(10 000 tons)	175.61	-4.1%

11-1 主要年份耕地面积

Area of Cultivated Land in Representatives Years

单位：万亩 (10 000 mu)

年 份 Year	年末实有耕地面积 Cultivated Area Year-end	水田 Paddy Field	水浇地 Irrigable Land
1970	554.09	18.20	297.05
1975	538.35	20.34	349.13
1978	530.96	16.70	370.46
1980	526.29	17.45	372.96
1985	508.88	17.63	328.10
1990	495.32	17.97	311.91
1991	492.09	17.03	309.17
1992	485.30	16.44	298.19
1993	479.04	14.36	304.49
1994	471.44	13.98	299.58
1995	463.97	17.04	278.01
1996	451.50	14.21	283.76
1997	456.62	11.90	290.49
1998	455.15	11.18	282.23
1999	450.74	11.31	281.96
2000	443.37	10.26	284.04
2001	431.69	9.00	274.73
2002	424.46	7.98	275.96
2003	413.84	6.65	263.75
2004	404.87	6.59	254.04
2005	400.17	5.55	254.04
2006	395.79	5.33	263.75
2007	391.77	4.80	255.95
2008	390.77	4.64	255.36
2009	387.89	4.39	260.71
2010	383.32	4.03	257.43
2011	377.10	3.80	253.46
2012	369.91	3.32	248.97
2013	366.23	5.33	263.75
2014	360.73	2.42	237.26

11–2 各区县耕地面积（2014年）

单位：亩

区 县	Region	年末实有耕地面积 Cultivated Area Year-end	水田 Paddy Field	旱地 Dry Land	水浇地 Irrigable Land
合 计	**Total**	**3607328**	**24208**	**3583120**	**2372576**
新城区	Xincheng				
碑林区	Beilin				
莲湖区	Lianhu				
灞桥区	Baqiao	138618		138618	89616
未央区	Weiyang	15701		15701	7918
雁塔区	Yanta	6511		6511	5000
阎良区	Yanliang	234476		234476	225670
临潼区	Lintong	697381		697381	527238
长安区	Chang'an	629695	21848	607847	332507
蓝田县	Lantian	596000	700	595300	96500
周至县	Zhouzhi	499042	940	498102	361057
户 县	Huxian	563019	720	562299	500185
高陵县	Gaoling	226885		226885	226885

Area of Cultivated Land by Region (2014)

(mu)

当年增加的耕地面积 Area of Newly Increased Cultivated Land	新开荒地面积 Area of Newly Reclamation of Wasteland	当年减少的耕地面积 Decrease in Cultivated Area in the Year	国家基建占地 Capital Construction	退耕改果、茶、桑面积 Area for Change into Fruit, Tea and Mulberry	退耕造林面积 Area for Change into Woods
8380	**5061**	**73083**	**28218**	**39142**	**3137**
		8979	6398	1684	479
		5089	3436		
		962	615	181	
112		5991	4335	1507	
65	28	19104	8289	9467	1348
985	850	4542	2032	2000	510
7146	4183	20201	1881	17320	800
72		7143	160	6983	
		1072	1072		

11-3 主要年份农业机械拥有量（年末数）

指标	Item	2006	2007	2008
农用机械总动力（千瓦）	Total Power of Agricultural Machinery(kw)	2277584	2348856	2712616
大中型拖拉机（台）	Large and Medium Tractors(unit)	8963	10431	11092
小型拖拉机（台）	Mini-tractors(unit)	23437	21555	19036
大中型拖拉机配套农具（台）	Number of Large and Medium Tractor Towing Farm Machinery(unit)	18724	23487	25125
小型拖拉机配套农具（台）	Mini-Tractor Towing Farm Machinery (unit)	30439	28780	26984
农用排灌柴油机（台）	Agricultural Diesel Engines(unit)	3547	2709	2670
农用排灌电动机（台）	Agricultural Motors(unit)	76614	84416	85349
农用水泵（台）	Agricultural Water Pump(unit)	73039	80722	80462
节水灌溉类机械（套）	Equipment in Water-saving Irrigation(set)	2656	1991	1728
联合收割机（台）	Combine Harvesters(unit)	5026	5294	5390
自走式机动割晒机（台）	Self-propelled Motorized Swather(unit)	1342	4918	2174
机动脱粒机（台）	Motorized Huller (unit)	5806	11585	23781
农用运输车（辆）	Agricultucal Transporter(unit)	50395	49576	54860

Possession of Agricultural Machinery

in Representative Years（Number of year-end）

2009	2010	2011	2012	2013	2014
2616053	2677334	2890247	2983979	3108354	3203302
11479	14675	12585	12987	12927	9946
18406	14194	13008	11471	8971	7538
26575	29215	36209	32166	32662	31451
29039	24393	29624	27869	25853	21806
2691	3309	2639	2891	2509	2409
83243	79462	87461	87056	86216	85244
80174	77367	75426	80982	80575	79849
1799	1710	1733	2106	2218	2562
6155	6718	7854	8502	9114	7815
1220	208	187			
11960	13231	13407	14493	14700	14749
50671	51665	51838	51850	51710	51410

11-4 各区县农业机械拥有量（2014年）

指标	Item	西安市 Xi' an	灞桥区 Baqiao	未央区 Weiyang
农用机械总动力（千瓦）	Total Power of Agricultural Machinery(kw)	3203302	181659	47814
大中型拖拉机（台）	Large and Medium Tractors(unit)	9946	96	132
小型拖拉机（台）	Mini-tractors(unit)	7538	25	8
大中型拖拉机配套农具（台）	Number of Large and Medium Tractor Towing Farm Machinery(unit)	31451	882	455
小型拖拉机配套农具（台）	Mini-Tractor Towing Farm Machinery (unit)	21806	50	7
农用排灌柴油机（台）	Agricultural Diesel Engines(unit)	2409		
农用排灌电动机（台）	Agricultural Motors(unit)	85244	3188	1050
农用水泵（台）	Agricultural Water Pump(unit)	79849	2927	875
节水灌溉类机械（套）	Equipment in Water-saving Irrigation(set)	2562	55	120
联合收割机（台）	Combine Harvesters(unit)	7815	83	34
自走式机动割晒机（台）	Self-propelled Motorized Swather(unit)			
机动脱粒机（台）	Motorized Huller (unit)	14749	50	10
农用运输车（辆）	Agricultucal Transporter(unit)	51410	3681	480

Possession of Agricultural Machinery by Region（2014）

雁塔区 Yanta	阎良区 Yanliang	临潼区 Lintong	长安区 Chang'an	蓝田县 Lantian	周至县 Zhouzhi	户　县 Huxian	高陵县 Gaoling
92415	190369	608868	545161	309780	453137	495146	278953
35	940	1960	1448	1078	1287	1697	1273
10	326	640	933	824	3385	1260	127
70	2350	7396	4441	2297	2083	6077	5400
30	652	3668	2073	4052	7146	3446	682
		73	1309	682	289	56	
520	5902	16973	22645	3147	15324	12735	3760
500	5746	16460	16923	2486	17437	12735	3760
	515	142	1246	63	272	149	
16	657	1815	1383	349	340	2611	527
	1385	4948	981	2025	2431	2374	545
725	2244	14007	7782	4508	8337	3778	5868

11-5 主要年份农业机械化、化肥、水利、水电情况

指标	Item	2000	2007	2008
一、农业机械化水平（万亩）	**Statistics on Agricultural Machinery (10 000 mu)**			
当年机械耕地面积（实际）	Area Ploughed by Tractors	366.81	361.62	404.42
当年机械播种面积（作业）	Seeded Area by Tractors	482.74	521.36	539.81
当年机械收获面积（作业）	Harvest Area by Tractors	272.83	296.06	313.11
二、农用化肥施用量（吨）	**Use of Agricultural Fertilizers and Insecticides(ton)**			
1. 按实物量计算合计	Practicality Consumption	697243	762401	767980
氮肥	Nitrogenous Fertilizer	392366	408847	413397
磷肥	Phosphate Fertilizer	155480	160932	157145
钾肥	Potash Fertilizer	31841	34284	34149
复合肥	Compound Fertilizer	78620	124784	132481
2. 按折纯法计算合计	Standard Consumption	196343	220251	225949
氮肥	Nitrogenous Fertilizer	102982	109484	112000
磷肥	Phosphate Fertilizer	18658	19311	18855
钾肥	Potash Fertilizer	15921	17141	17077
复合肥	Compound Fertilizer	39313	62398	66247
三、农用塑料薄膜使用量（公斤）	**Plastic Sheet for Agricultural Use(kg)**	**1622198**	**2096169**	**2122310**
四、农用柴油使用量（吨）	**Diesel Oil for Agricultural Use (ton)**	**52706**	**50137**	**51097**
五、农药使用量（公斤）	**Pesticide (kg)**	**1559333**	**1444867**	**1465819**
六、农村水利化情况（万亩）	**Irrigation and Water Conservancy (10 000 mu)**			
有效灌溉面积	Effective Irrigation Area	335.97	276.28	274.48
旱涝保收面积	Stable-Harvesting Arable Land	294.06	247.99	249.31
机电排灌面积	Electrical Irrigation Area	249.11	210.51	211.01
七、农村电气化情况	**Rural electrization**			
乡村及村以下办水电站（个）	Hydropower Station in Rural Areas(unit)	67	76	76
装机容量（千瓦）	Installed Power Generation Capacity(kw)	7236	24827	24827
发电量（万千瓦小时）	Generating Capacity (10 000 kwh)	1137.95	10085	10477
已配套机电井（眼）	Electricity Powered Well(unit)	50289	45783	47032

Agricultural Machinery,Chemical Fertilizers,Water Conservancy, Hydropower in Representative Years

2009	2010	2011	2012	2013	2014
413.7	367.32	427.03	425.4	425.21	549.07
544.86	548.28	507.55	529.99	523.15	509.58
342.82	403.5	413.93	428.28	443.57	466.21
776319	781072	785885	807900	794361	820315
414481	397975	398395	414339	401140	412544
153825	152943	151005	151967	152565	156662
33069	37715	38195	43356	39630	42504
142137	158062	163797	198238	201026	208605
230299	235532	239497	243281	239701	251217
112275	108868	110412	113662	109497	116055
18457	18315	18026	18061	18023	18505
16534	17997	18095	21267	18973	20110
71042	78811	81764	90291	93208	96547
2141969	**2450496**	**2533372**	**2683201**	**2678745**	**2657870**
51346	**61917**	**61637**	**57451**	**62563**	**74935**
1325459	**1243105**	**1242773**	**1252490**	**1210060**	**1220638**
273.17	281.28	262.32	267.84	240.22	248.34
247.6	234.15	214.62	211.31	196.96	189.69
213.42	224.6	200.36	198.66	229.29	230.58
75	44	44	46	46	48
25047	22325	22325	78848	80433	80633
10678	7268	7268	26447	19613	25526.08
46790	44310	40345	33959		

11-6 各区县农业机械化、化肥、水利、水电情况（2014年）

指标	Item	西安市 Xi'an	灞桥区 Baqiao	未央区 Weiyang
一、农业机械化水平（万亩）	**Statistics on Agricultural Machinery (10 000 mu)**			
当年机械耕地面积（实际）	Area Ploughed by Tractors	549.07	18.10	4.24
当年机械播种面积（作业）	Seeded Area by Tractors	509.58	17.10	0.80
当年机械收获面积（作业）	Harvest Area by Tractors	466.21	16.10	1.45
二、农用化肥施用量（吨）	**Use of Agricultural Fertilizers and Insecticides(ton)**			
1. 按实物量计算合计	Practicality Consumption	820315	20863	4348
氮肥	Nitrogenous Fertilizer	412544	8006	2637
磷肥	Phosphate Fertilizer	156662	699	428
钾肥	Potash Fertilizer	42504	2312	13
复合肥	Compound Fertilizer	208605	9846	1270
2.按折纯法计算合计	Standard Consumption	251217	8616	1524
氮肥	Nitrogenous Fertilizer	116055	3684	954
磷肥	Phosphate Fertilizer	18505	85	38
钾肥	Potash Fertilizer	20110	1155	6
复合肥	Compound Fertilizer	96547	3692	526
三、农用塑料薄膜使用量（公斤）	**Plastic Sheet for Agricultural Use(kg)**	**2657870**	**189930**	**18130**
四、农用柴油使用量（吨）	**Diesel Oil for Agricultural Use (ton)**	**74935**	**601**	**708**
五、农药使用量（公斤）	**Pesticide (kg)**	**1220638**	**30148**	**5088**
六、农村水利化情况（万亩）	**Irrigation and Water Conservancy (10 000 mu)**			
有效灌溉面积	Effective Irrigation Area	248.34	9.92	1.90
旱涝保收面积	Stable-Harvesting Arable Land	189.69		1.91
机电排灌面积	Electrical Irrigation Area	230.58	10.17	3.17
七、农村电气化情况	**Rural electrization**			
乡村及村以下办水电站（个）	Hydropower Station in Rural Areas(unit)	48		
装机容量（千瓦）	Installed Power Generation Capacity(kw)	80633		
发电量（万千瓦小时）	Generating Capacity (10 000 kwh)	25526.08		
已配套机电井（眼）	Electricity Powered Well(unit)			

Agricultural Machinery,Chemical Fertilizers,Water Conservancy, Hydropower by Region （2014）

雁塔区 Yanta	阎良区 Yanliang	临潼区 Lintong	长安区 Chang'an	蓝田县 Lantian	周至县 Zhouzhi	户　县 Huxian	高陵县 Gaoling
	26.78	98.00	112.77	58.76	97.09	90.05	43.28
	22.33	97.03	102.60	67.00	76.07	86.60	40.05
	28.99	91.55	101.66	44.50	56.90	86.60	38.46
411	66878	150770	127047	122345	148827	112921	65905
210	30283	80236	72382	64760	62400	66372	25258
30	13816	44233	24324	25810	16105	17244	13973
75	5665	2839	6365	8288	9044	5229	2674
96	17114	23462	23976	23487	61278	24076	24000
115	24039	39641	29920	46013	47017	33755	20577
27	11551	21183	11830	28156	15328	17780	5562
3	1581	5308	2919	2895	1930	2069	1677
37	2764	1419	3183	3616	4242	2350	1338
48	8143	11731	11988	11346	25517	11556	12000
	1116840	**223560**	**180000**	**183610**	**98780**	**601010**	**46010**
60	**2925**	**15236**	**13453**	**10105**	**3385**	**10502**	**17960**
15	**187351**	**319525**	**126492**	**74375**	**165172**	**63310**	**249162**
	21.69	53.36	32.65	11.43	49.17	45.66	22.56
	22.55	46.56	19.71		30.70	47.77	20.49
0.63	20.30	45.57	26.54	9.05	46.17	47.23	21.75
			7	6	28	7	
			5625	14270	56118	4620	
			1555.08	2265.00	20525.00	1181.00	

11-7 主要年份农林牧渔及服务业总产值及指数

Gross Output Value of Farming,Forestry,Animal Husbandry,Fishery, Service and Related Indices in Representative Years

单位：万元 (10 000 yuan)

年份 Year	农林牧渔及服务总产值（现价） Gross Output Value (At current prices)	农业 Farming	林业 Forestry	牧业 Animal Husbandry	渔业 Fishery	农林牧渔服务业 Service of Farming, Forestry, Animal Husbandry and Fishery	指数（上年=100）（可比价） Indices(preceding year= 100) (At cinstant prices)
1970	40617	35965	713	3896	43		111.2
1975	55322	47378	1509	6403	32		93.9
1978	65423	56519	1444	7427	33		104.7
1980	65322	54004	1177	10106	35		85.0
1985	134933	105888	2559	26186	300		106.4
1990	262073	191088	3134	65840	2011		102.5
1991	295620	208324	3362	81070	2864		108.6
1992	321155	219160	4225	94045	3725		108.6
1993	387068	261959	5031	115810	4268		112.8
1994	565056	359609	7819	192140	5488		102.4
1995	754597	513348	7185	228598	5466		106.8
1996	786003	552726	7573	219214	6490		102.1
1997	836201	585973	9226	233623	7379		110.3
1998	853279	625465	8146	212045	7623		107.5
1999	739905	530029	8883	194552	6441		100.7
2000	743712	514845	8482	212612	7773		104.3
2001	767511	527160	8427	223861	8063		102.8
2002	797444	539978	11378	238761	7327		103.0
2003	837857	551398	10550	269610	6299		101.5
2004	967946	580798	12773	314517	6728	53130	108.4
2005	1065437	657262	13086	329856	7340	57893	107.7
2006	1141484	686748	15188	346626	7017	85905	107.2
2007	1341450	798163	15845	410213	9051	108178	105.3
2008	1682725	956549	19031	564095	11084	131966	107.8
2009	1787032	1061756	22663	546191	11830	144592	106.5
2010	2270994	1438934	26787	629376	12830	163067	107.4
2011	2726608	1729295	34453	754593	14856	193411	106.6
2012	3083562	1933149	62291	820392	19877	247853	106.0
2013	3428905	2173363	80199	863902	22773	288668	104.9
2014	3672101	2363649	86889	879515	24030	318018	105.1

11-8 主要年份农林牧渔及服务业总产值指数

Related Indices of Gross Output Value of Farming,Forestry,Animal Husbandry,Fishery and Service in Representative Years

年 份 Year	农林牧渔及服务业总产值指数（上年=100）（可比价） Indices(preceding year= 100) (At constant prices)	农业 Farming	林业 Forestry	牧业 Animal Husbandry	渔业 Fishery	农林牧渔服务业 Service of Farming, Forestry, Animal Husbandry and Fishery
2005	107.7	108.0	98.7	107.3	112.6	107.9
2006	107.2	106.0	102.5	109.3	104.5	109.4
2007	105.3	106.4	101.3	102.4	106.3	108.7
2008	107.8	107.9	112.2	106.0	100.5	113.7
2009	106.5	105.4	121.3	106.8	107.4	110.2
2010	107.4	108.7	115.2	104.3	92.7	108.9
2011	106.6	108.2	105.7	102.9	102.1	107.7
2012	106.0	105.6	143.0	104.8	113.4	108.5
2013	104.9	104.3	131.3	104.0	110.1	105.9
2014	105.1	105.8	105.7	103.2	106.0	105.9

11-9 主要年份农林牧渔及服务业总产值构成

Gross Output Value and Its Composition of Farming, Forestry, Animal Husbandry,Fishery and Service at Current Price in Representative Years

年 份 Year	农林牧渔及服务业总产值(%) Service of Farming, Forestry, Animal Husbandry and Fishery(%)	农业 Farming	林业 Forestry	牧业 Animal Husbandry	渔业 Fishery	农林牧渔服务业 Service of Farming, Forestry, Animal Husbandry and Fishery
2005	100	61.7	1.2	31.0	0.7	5.4
2006	100	60.9	1.3	31.5	0.6	5.7
2007	100	59.5	1.2	30.6	0.7	8.0
2008	100	56.9	1.1	33.5	0.7	7.8
2009	100	59.4	1.3	30.5	0.7	8.1
2010	100	63.3	1.2	27.7	0.6	7.2
2011	100	63.4	1.3	27.7	0.5	7.1
2012	100	62.7	2.0	26.6	0.7	8.0
2013	100	63.4	2.3	25.2	0.7	8.4
2014	100	64.4	2.4	24.0	0.7	8.5

11-10 各区县农林牧渔及服务业总产值（2014年）

Gross Output Value of Farming, Forestry, Animal Husbandry, Fishery and Service by Region（2014）

单位：万元 (10 000 yuan)

区 县	Region	农林牧渔及服务业总产值 Gross Output Value	农业 Farming	林业 Forestry	牧业 Animal Husbandry	渔业 Fishery	农林牧渔服务业 Service of Farming, Forestry, Animal Husbandry and Fishery
合 计	**Total**	**3672101**	**2363649**	**86889**	**879515**	**24030**	**318018**
新城区	Xincheng						
碑林区	Beilin						
莲湖区	Lianhu						
灞桥区	Baqiao	300728	222560	3023	43247	3179	28719
未央区	Weiyang	19090	10621	8	5241	1720	1500
雁塔区	Yanta	26798	17925	266	4718		3889
阎良区	Yanliang	354330	262674	690	60918	330	29718
临潼区	Lintong	538221	284427	8634	192762	4075	48323
长安区	Chang'an	538210	370372	5886	112489	5974	43489
蓝田县	Lantian	462420	276660	21678	123039	4810	36233
周至县	Zhouzhi	482477	332958	39065	75081	931	34442
户 县	Huxian	481686	317386	4182	105969	1374	52775
高陵县	Gaoling	468141	268066	3457	156051	1637	38930

11-11 各区县农林牧渔及服务业总产值指数和构成（2014年）

Gross Output Value and Its Composition of Farming, Forestry, Animal Husbandry,Fishery and Service at Current Price by Region（2014）

单位：% (%)

区 县	Region	农林牧渔及服务业总产值 Gross Output Value	农业 Farming	林业 Forestry	牧业 Animal Husbandry	渔业 Fishery	农林牧渔服务业 Service of Farming, Forestry, Animal Husbandry and Fishery
全市指数	**Total**	**105.1**	**105.8**	**105.7**	**103.2**	**106.0**	**105.9**
新城区	Xincheng						
碑林区	Beilin						
莲湖区	Lianhu						
灞桥区	Baqiao	105.2	105.6	140.8	101.3	100.8	106.4
未央区	Weiyang	93.9	92.4	166.7	93.8	104.9	93.7
雁塔区	Yanta	95.2	91.1	186.9	109.2	0.0	96.2
阎良区	Yanliang	105.5	105.6	101.4	104.9	78.0	106.7
临潼区	Lintong	105.0	106.0	103.6	103.2	128.2	105.4
长安区	Chang'an	105.1	105.1	155.0	103.6	97.6	106.0
蓝田县	Lantian	105.2	106.2	91.7	104.9	118.8	106.0
周至县	Zhouzhi	105.7	106.2	99.0	106.4	112.9	107.1
户 县	Huxian	105.1	105.1	163.7	103.2	109.1	106.2
高陵县	Gaoling	105.9	109.2	262.9	100.1	68.7	106.4
全市构成	**Total**	100	64.4	2.4	24.0	0.7	8.5
新城区	Xincheng						
碑林区	Beilin						
莲湖区	Lianhu						
灞桥区	Baqiao	100	74.0	1.0	14.4	1.1	9.5
未央区	Weiyang	100	55.6		27.5	9.0	7.9
雁塔区	Yanta	100	66.9	1.0	17.6		14.5
阎良区	Yanliang	100	74.1	0.2	17.2	0.1	8.4
临潼区	Lintong	100	52.8	1.6	35.8	0.8	9.0
长安区	Chang'an	100	68.8	1.1	20.9	1.1	8.1
蓝田县	Lantian	100	59.8	4.7	26.6	1.0	7.9
周至县	Zhouzhi	100	69.0	8.1	15.6	0.2	7.1
户 县	Huxian	100	65.9	0.9	22.0	0.3	11.0
高陵县	Gaoling	100	57.3	0.7	33.3	0.3	8.3

11-12 主要年份农林牧渔及服务业增加值

Value-Added of Farming, Forestry, Animal Husbandry, Fishery and Service in Representative Years

单位：万元 (10 000 yuan)

年 份 Year	农林牧渔及服务业增加值 Farming,Forestry, Animal Husbandry, Fishery and Service	农业 Farming	林业 Forestry	牧业 Animal Husbandry	渔业 Fishery	农林牧渔服务业 Service of Farming, Forestry, Animal Husbandry and Fishery
1995	413981	329662	4413	76746	3160	
1996						
1997						
1998						
1999						
2000	446481	336777	4323	101353	4028	
2001	458720	342427	4258	108096	3939	
2002	477691	351358	6419	116591	3323	
2003	458378	312849	5473	137236	2820	
2004	582009	393349	6811	164572	2919	14358
2005	660148	444320	6888	169701	3373	35866
2006	704427	465823	8556	177431	3227	49390
2007	825053	538794	8420	210930	4467	62442
2008	1034471	639071	10592	301305	5598	77905
2009	1103793	698043	11958	303594	5913	84285
2010	1400575	935489	14362	349204	6503	95017
2011	1731398	1161249	18807	428169	7679	115494
2012	1955931	1297824	33973	465476	10115	148543
2013	2177588	1459093	43740	490162	11589	173004
2014	2336074	1586842	47388	499021	12229	190594

11-13 主要年份农林牧渔及服务业增加值指数

Indices of Value-Added of Farming, Forestry, Animal Husbandry, Fishery and Service in Representative Years

年 份 Year	农林牧渔及服务业增加值指数（上年=100）（可比价） Farming,Forestry,Animal Husbandry,Fishery and Service	农业 Farming	林业 Forestry	牧业 Animal Husbandry	渔业 Fishery	农林牧渔服务业 Service of Farming, Forestry, Animal Husbandry and Fishery
2008	107.6	107.6	112.0	105.8	100.0	114.0
2009	106.3	103.6	114.6	111.2	106.3	108.8
2010	106.9	107.9	108.7	104.3	94.0	108.9
2011	106.7	108.1	106.1	102.8	102.7	108.1
2012	106.0	105.6	142.8	104.8	113.4	108.5
2013	104.8	104.3	131.3	104.0	110.1	105.9
2014	105.2	105.8	104.1	103.2	106.0	105.9

11-14 各区县农林牧渔及服务业增加值（2014年）

Value-Added of Farming, Forestry, Animal Husbandry, Fishery and Service by Region（2014）

单位：万元 (10 000 yuan)

年 份 Year	Region	农林牧渔及服务业增加值 Farming,Forestry, Animal Husbandry, Fishery and Service	农业 Farming	林业 Forestry	牧业 Animal Husbandry	渔业 Fishery	农林牧渔服务业 Service of Farming, Forestry, Animal Husbandry and Fishery
合 计	**Total**	**2336074**	**1586842**	**47388**	**499021**	**12229**	**190594**
新城区	Xincheng						
碑林区	Beilin						
莲湖区	Lianhu						
灞桥区	Baqiao	197505	152297	1823	26000	1271	16114
未央区	Weiyang	11590	6801	1	3124	687	977
雁塔区	Yanta	19290	12893	188	3096		3113
阎良区	Yanliang	240604	180800	353	40827	162	18462
临潼区	Lintong	342404	190639	4815	113753	2442	30755
长安区	Chang'an	362858	282206	3310	47279	3855	26208
蓝田县	Lantian	280332	173184	12557	71220	2097	21274
周至县	Zhouzhi	295943	215852	20122	39805	493	19671
户 县	Huxian	299470	203215	2310	65720	728	27497
高陵县	Gaoling	286078	168955	1909	88197	494	26523

11-15 各区县农林牧渔及服务业增加值指数（2014年）

Indices of Value-Added of Farming, Forestry, Animal Husbandry, Fishery and Service by Region（2014）

（上年=100）（可比价） (preceding year = 100) (At constant prices)

区 县 Region	农林牧渔及服务业增加值指数 Farming,Forestry,Animal Husbandry,Fishery and Service	农业 Farming	林业 Forestry	牧业 Animal Husbandry	渔业 Fishery	农林牧渔服务业 Service of Farming, Forestry, Animal Husbandry and Fishery
合 计 Total	**105.2**	**105.8**	**104.1**	**103.2**	**106.0**	**105.9**
新城区 Xincheng						
碑林区 Beilin						
莲湖区 Lianhu						
灞桥区 Baqiao	105.2	106.0	136.5	99.8	99.6	105.9
未央区 Weiyang	93.9	95.0	100.0	93.1	86.3	94.0
雁塔区 Yanta	95.2	91.7	182.3	108.1		96.0
阎良区 Yanliang	105.5	105.9	98.2	103.4	76.7	106.2
临潼区 Lintong	105.0	106.8	100.8	102.1	127.1	105.3
长安区 Chang'an	105.2	105.3	151.0	102.6	96.8	105.6
蓝田县 Lantian	105.2	105.0	91.1	107.8	119.9	106.0
周至县 Zhouzhi	105.7	105.8	97.5	108.9	117.3	107.0
户 县 Huxian	105.1	105.8	159.2	102.0	108.0	105.8
高陵县 Gaoling	105.9	108.3	255.3	100.4	92.7	107.9

11-16 主要年份农作物播种面积

Sown Areas of Farm Crops In Representative Years

单位：万亩 （10 000mu）

年 份 Year	总播种面积 Total Sown Area	粮食 Grain Crops	小麦 Wheat	玉米 Corn	棉花 Cotton	油料 Oil-bearing Crops	蔬菜 Vegetables
1980	835.43	706.35	324.17	273.14	81.23	10.01	24.02
1985	795.41	704.36	378.20	271.14	21.02	8.01	45.03
1990	816.41	731.42	387.20	282.14	15.02	12.00	51.03
1991	820.41	731.37	389.19	283.14	19.01	13.01	47.03
1992	820.65	715.50	384.60	273.60	26.70	16.20	54.60
1993	821.63	713.49	380.40	273.69	17.66	14.84	63.90
1994	821.10	719.00	375.90	272.40	19.70	13.80	59.90
1995	784.74	690.63	370.41	259.55	11.07	18.57	57.59
1996	797.40	709.00	366.30	286.80	7.70	18.80	55.50
1997	755.78	670.83	367.71	248.79	4.50	15.53	59.36
1998	789.99	705.03	370.17	285.45	3.56	14.69	60.95
1999	793.08	709.95	371.94	294.00	2.85	12.74	60.68
2000	784.94	697.55	369.89	283.70	2.48	13.46	64.35
2001	763.16	678.05	359.19	278.57	2.91	11.87	61.77
2002	751.10	655.59	350.64	271.95	2.63	11.40	67.71
2003	737.06	632.55	336.05	261.89	3.38	11.04	69.44
2004	753.83	630.63	311.52	286.50	4.94	9.74	77.55
2005	757.91	642.75	325.10	287.87	5.40	9.51	83.33
2006	769.49	648.00	313.23	307.89	6.09	8.58	87.03
2007	762.38	637.05	306.98	304.13	6.93	7.41	91.07
2008	756.06	630.31	319.39	286.69	6.35	8.59	93.02
2009	757.11	628.69	318.36	285.20	6.45	8.59	94.83
2010	751.74	621.71	317.18	279.93	6.26	8.98	95.71
2011	704.17	573.13	306.39	243.06	5.97	8.83	96.97
2012	701.33	572.50	305.34	242.20	5.00	7.70	97.82
2013	695.53	567.87	298.93	245.64	2.57	7.67	99.89
2014	684.28	551.46	290.53	238.65	0.37	7.01	101.56

注：2011年农作物播种面积为陕西省统计局依据(国统字办[2011]68号)文件调整数。

11-17 各区县主要农作物播种面积（2014年）

Sown Areas of Major Farm Crops by Region (2014)

单位：万亩 (10 000 mu)

区 县	Region	总播种面积 Total Sown Area	粮食 Grain Crops	小麦 Wheat	玉米 Corn	棉花 Cotton	油料 Oil-bearing Crops	蔬菜 Vegetables	瓜果类 Fruits Class
合　计	**Total**	**684.28**	**551.46**	**290.53**	**238.65**	**0.37**	**7.01**	**101.56**	**20.44**
新城区	Xincheng								
碑林区	Beilin								
莲湖区	Lianhu								
灞桥区	Baqiao	26.28	18.11	11.15	6.54	0.07	0.33	7.30	0.46
未央区	Weiyang	3.07	1.43	1.16	0.27			1.61	0.03
雁塔区	Yanta	0.54						0.54	
阎良区	Yanliang	45.64	21.25	11.24	9.99	0.06	0.08	17.52	6.73
临潼区	Lintong	126.35	103.48	57.08	42.04		1.04	14.89	6.90
长安区	Chang'an	131.24	104.94	53.85	49.63	0.01	1.54	22.28	2.35
蓝田县	Lantian	110.00	95.75	50.27	32.70	0.23	2.17	9.36	1.58
周至县	Zhouzhi	89.80	77.01	39.37	35.82		1.40	9.06	0.18
户　县	Huxian	100.01	88.19	45.31	41.82		0.45	9.26	1.90
高陵县	Gaoling	51.35	41.30	21.10	19.84			9.74	0.31

11-18 主要年份农作物产品产量

Yield of Major Farm Crops in Representative Years

单位：万吨　　　　(10 000 ton)

年份 Year	粮食作物 Grain Crops	夏粮 Summer Grain	小麦 Wheat	秋粮 Autumn Grain	稻谷 Rice	玉米 Corn	棉花 Cotton	油料 Oil-bearing Crops	油菜籽 Rapeseeds	蔬菜 Vegetables
1978	132.8	64.2	58.2	68.7	5.1	55.8	2.85	0.09	0.07	45.66
1980	114.4	56.6	52.2	57.8	4.7	47.7	1.97	0.54	0.50	40.13
1981	116.1	78.7	74.3	37.4	3.4	31.5	1.36	0.76	0.75	34.06
1982	148.9	85.6	82.2	63.3	4.9	55.5	2.88	0.51	0.49	53.71
1983	148.1	81.8	79.6	66.3	4.8	58.5	0.85	0.36	0.34	46.99
1984	157.6	82.4	81.0	75.2	5.0	66.5	1.49	0.46	0.29	75.47
1985	150.1	76.1	74.8	74.0	5.1	65.1	0.49	0.75	0.39	86.44
1986	162.4	91.7	90.1	70.7	4.8	61.8	0.44	1.25	0.82	85.84
1987	171.2	87.0	85.2	84.2	5.0	74.3	0.47	1.57	1.22	95.16
1988	158.0	86.8	84.6	71.1	3.8	61.4	0.42	0.89	0.51	113.50
1989	173.6	93.5	91.2	80.2	4.7	70.4	0.55	1.33	0.94	129.32
1990	172.4	91.7	89.7	80.8	5.5	70.4	0.70	1.35	0.94	119.32
1991	178.8	91.1	89.2	87.7	5.0	77.5	0.97	1.20	0.74	117.41
1992	183.4	101.7	99.6	81.7	4.7	72.3	0.74	1.49	0.87	128.12
1993	190.0	101.1	99.0	88.9	4.9	78.6	0.75	1.40	1.00	145.80
1994	157.4	86.9	84.9	70.5	4.5	61.4	0.65	1.08	0.78	135.26
1995	175.3	99.8	97.4	75.5	3.4	67.8	0.29	2.17	1.90	133.60
1996	187.5	80.1	78.4	107.4	3.4	95.6	0.24	1.83	1.55	138.01
1997	190.5	114.3	112.3	76.3	3.5	69.4	0.17	1.86	1.65	142.11
1998	212.7	104.4	104.0	108.3	3.2	99.1	0.14	1.67	1.36	148.87
1999	204.4	95.5	94.4	108.9	2.9	99.7	0.15	1.30	1.00	153.24
2000	201.9	92.6	91.6	109.3	3.1	100.5	0.14	1.34	0.95	162.14
2001	197.1	98.1	97.2	98.9	2.7	91.3	0.17	1.23	0.90	152.80
2002	192.4	94.5	93.5	97.9	2.1	91.6	0.18	1.22	0.84	169.74
2003	176.3	98.2	96.7	78.2	1.6	72.3	0.22	1.13	0.70	169.67
2004	195.8	97.8	96.0	98.0	1.7	91.6	0.40	1.14	0.84	180.96
2005	205.5	100.0	99.1	105.5	1.6	99.3	0.45	1.16	0.89	195.70
2006	193.5	86.0	85.4	107.4	1.4	101.2	0.48	1.08	0.87	189.30
2007	189.1	77.3	76.7	111.8	1.5	105.6	0.59	0.96	0.77	204.30
2008	214.4	105.9	105.6	108.5	0.9	103.0	0.62	1.15	0.95	221.53
2009	218.2	103.0	102.1	115.2	0.9	109.5	0.63	1.12	0.93	242.41
2010	221.7	106.6	105.8	115.1	0.8	108.9	0.60	1.20	1.00	253.10
2011	182.04	90.54	89.68	91.49	0.67	85.30	0.56	1.17	0.95	261.66
2012	192.55	95.73	94.92	96.82	0.57	89.29	0.47	1.02	0.88	277.80
2013	183.12	83.59	82.77	99.52	0.39	91.83	0.25	1.00	0.87	298.12
2014	175.61	88.05	87.35	87.56	0.25	83.30	0.03	0.98	0.80	316.28

注：2011年农作物产品产量为陕西省统计局依据(国统字办[2011]70号)文件调整数。

11-19 各区县主要农作物产品产量（2014年）

Yield of Major Farm Crops by Region (2014)

单位：万吨 (10 000 ton)

区 县	Region	粮食作物 Grain Crops	夏粮 Summer Grain	小麦 Wheat	秋粮 Autumn Grain	稻谷 Rice	玉米 Corn
合 计	**Total**	**175.61**	**88.05**	**87.35**	**87.56**	**0.25**	**83.30**
新城区	Xincheng						
碑林区	Beilin						
莲湖区	Lianhu						
灞桥区	Baqiao	5.28	3.01	3.01	2.27		2.17
未央区	Weiyang	0.40	0.31	0.31	0.09		0.09
雁塔区	Yanta						
阎良区	Yanliang	8.10	4.31	4.31	3.79		3.78
临潼区	Lintong	31.79	16.78	16.78	15.01		13.66
长安区	Chang'an	33.84	15.79	15.79	18.05	0.21	17.53
蓝田县	Lantian	25.06	13.05	12.82	12.01		9.98
周至县	Zhouzhi	22.50	11.21	10.99	11.29	0.04	11.13
户 县	Huxian	29.60	14.74	14.50	14.86		14.84
高陵县	Gaoling	19.04	8.85	8.84	10.19		10.12

11-19 续表 continued

单位：万吨 (10 000 ton)

区 县	Region	棉花 Cotton	油料 Oil-bearing Crops	油菜籽 Rapeseeds	蔬菜 Vegetables	瓜果类 Fruits Class
合 计	**Total**	**0.03**	**0.98**	**0.80**	**316.28**	**51.75**
新城区	Xincheng					
碑林区	Beilin					
莲湖区	Lianhu					
灞桥区	Baqiao		0.04	0.04	28.65	0.82
未央区	Weiyang				2.53	0.06
雁塔区	Yanta				1.89	
阎良区	Yanliang	0.01	0.01	0.01	76.20	23.75
临潼区	Lintong		0.14	0.11	44.52	6.36
长安区	Chang'an		0.26	0.23	58.61	8.28
蓝田县	Lantian	0.02	0.23	0.23	16.80	3.75
周至县	Zhouzhi		0.22	0.12	19.81	0.49
户 县	Huxian		0.08	0.06	27.68	5.40
高陵县	Gaoling				39.59	2.84

11-20 主要年份农作物单位面积产量

Yield of Farm Crops Per Unit Area in Representative Years

单位：公斤/亩　　(kg/mu)

年份 Year	粮食作物 Grain Crops	夏粮 Summer Grain	小麦 Wheat	秋粮 Autumn Grain	玉米 Corn	棉花 Cotton	油料 Oil-bearing Crops	油菜籽 Rapeseeds	蔬菜 Vegetables
1990	236	232	232	241	249	46	103	101	2349
1995	254	263	263	243	261	27	117	128	2320
1996	265	214	214	321	333	32	86	100	2489
1997	284	305	306	257	279	38	76	129	2395
1998	302	278	279	328	347	40	114	121	2443
1999	288	253	254	327	339	52	102	106	2526
2000	289	247	248	338	354	55	102	112	2520
2001	291	270	271	314	328	60	104	113	2474
2002	293	266	267	326	337	70	107	115	2507
2003	279	287	288	269	276	67	102	110	2444
2004	310	308	308	313	320	81	117	129	2333
2005	320	304	305	336	345	84	121	132	2349
2006	299	273	273	323	329	80	125	135	2175
2007	297	250	250	341	347	85	129	132	2245
2008	340	330	331	350	359	97	134	137	2382
2009	347	320	321	375	384	97	131	131	2556
2010	357	333	334	381	389	94	130	131	2644
2011	318	293	293	347	351	95	133	134	2698
2012	336	310	311	367	369	94	132	130	2840
2013	322	277	277	374	374	96	130	125	2985
2014	318	301	301	339	349	89	140	130	3114

注：2011年农作物单产为陕西省统计局依据(国统字办[2011]72号)文件调整数。

11-21 各区县主要农作物单位面积产量（2014年）

The Output of Main Crops Per Unit Area by Region (2014)

单位：公斤/亩　　(kg/mu)

区县	Region	粮食作物 Grain Crops	夏粮 Summer Grain	小麦 Wheat	秋粮 Autumn Grain	玉米 Corn
合　计	**Total**	**318**	**301**	**301**	**339**	**349**
新城区	Xincheng					
碑林区	Beilin					
莲湖区	Lianhu					
灞桥区	Baqiao	292	270	270	327	332
未央区	Weiyang	280	269	269	326	326
雁塔区	Yanta					
阎良区	Yanliang	381	384	384	378	378
临潼区	Lintong	307	294	294	323	325
长安区	Chang'an	322	293	293	353	353
蓝田县	Lantian	262	255	255	269	305
周至县	Zhouzhi	292	279	279	306	311
户　县	Huxian	336	320	320	353	355
高陵县	Gaoling	461	419	419	505	510

11-21 续表 continued

单位：公斤/亩 (kg/mu)

区 县	Region	棉花 Cotton	油料 Oil-bearing Crops	油菜籽 Rapeseeds	蔬菜 Vegetables	瓜果类 Fruits Class
合 计	**Total**	**89**	**140**	**130**	**3114**	**2532**
新城区	Xincheng					
碑林区	Beilin					
莲湖区	Lianhu					
灞桥区	Baqiao	66	131	131	3927	1788
未央区	Weiyang				1567	1952
雁塔区	Yanta				3530	
阎良区	Yanliang	101	126	124	4349	3534
临潼区	Lintong		132	117	2991	921
长安区	Chang'an	80	167	161	2631	3521
蓝田县	Lantian	93	108	110	1794	2375
周至县	Zhouzhi		154	120	2185	2675
户 县	Huxian	100	184	188	2989	2843
高陵县	Gaoling				4066	9159

11-22 设施农业生产情况（2014年）
Agricultural Production Facilities (2014)

指 标	Item	种植面积（亩） planting area (mu)	产量（吨） output(ton)
一、蔬菜	**Vegetables**	**256430**	**1343361**
其中：芹菜	Celery	77795	405971
油菜	Rape	2755	6907
菠菜	Spinach	14879	38611
黄瓜	Cucumber	22667	111748
西红柿	Tomato	25320	113747
辣椒	Chilli	12013	42166
二、瓜果类	**Fruits class**	105195	376754
其中：草莓	Strawberry	6086	8333
三、花卉苗木	**Flower seedling wood**	13674	
四、食用菌	**Edible Fungi**	2674	10029
五、其他	**Others**	24728	

11-23 主要年份林业生产情况

Statistics on Forestry in Representative Years

指　标	Item	2000	2008	2009	2010	2011	2012	2013	2014
一、营林情况	**Afforestation**								
当年造林面积合计（万亩）	Build Forestry Areas(10 000 mu)	27.47	8.76	15.60	16.10	10.42	9.08	12.29	14.70
封山育林面积（万亩）	Hill-closeure for Afforestation Areas (10 000 mu)	18.78	30.19	37.40	55.10	41.30	41.90	44.40	42.99
零星四旁植树（万株）	Planting(10 000 plants)	731.0	952.0	931.0	509.2	536.7	579.2	588.3	621.0
育苗面积（万亩）	Raise Seedlings Areas(10 000 mu)	2.05	4.72	3.41	11.95	9.93	11.64	17.37	17.73
#本年新育	New Seedling of Current Year	1.69	2.19	1.86	1.75	1.93	1.98	6.10	2.70
二、主要林产品产量（吨）	**Main Forestry Product(ton)**								
生漆	Lacquer	11	6	5	10	4			
核桃	Walnuts	997	4589	4306	7875	13235	15253	18033	16531
板栗	Chinese Chestnut	744	2728	3122	7736	8229	7654	4379	6922
花椒	Pepper	140	842	689	1420	889	879	319	371
三、村及村以下采伐木材（万立方米）	**Timber Harvested at or below** Village Level (10 000 cu.m)	1.62	1.23	0.97	3.30	1.39	1.04	0.88	

注：2009年迹地更新面积改为更新造林面积；
2010年起，根据统计制度要求，林业统计数据取自林业部门。

11-24 各区县林业生产情况（2014年）

Statistics On Forestry by Region (2014)

区　县	Region	当年造林面积（亩）Build Forestry Areasin in The Year(mu)	零星植树（万株）Planting (10 000 plants)	育苗面积（亩）Raise Seedlings Areas(mu)	核桃产量（吨）Output of Walnuts (ton)	板栗产量（吨）Output of Chinese Chestnut (ton)
合　计	**Total**	**146970**	**621**	**177255**	**16531**	**6922**
新城区	Xincheng					
碑林区	Beilin					
莲湖区	Lianhu					
灞桥区	Baqiao	7590		3000		
未央区	Weiyang					
雁塔区	Yanta		90		180	
阎良区	Yanliang	3000	30	510		
临潼区	Lintong	10875	72	495		
长安区	Chang'an	5100	142	14685	1381	123
蓝田县	Lantian	73395	82	23520	5800	5000
周至县	Zhouzhi	30015	80	126000	8840	1775
户　县	Huxian	15000	95	5550	330	24
高陵县	Gaoling	1995	30	3495		

11-25 主要年份果业生产情况

Statistics on Fruits in Representative Years

指标	Item	2000	2005	2010	2011	2012	2013	2014
果园面积合计（万亩）	**Areas of Orchards (10 000 mu)**	**47.86**	**55.55**	**74.95**	**74.27**	**76.83**	**78.06**	**81.23**
苹果园	Apple Orchards	12.15	5.96	3.55	1.53	1.44	1.28	1.22
梨园	Pears Orchards	5.79	3.01	2.27	1.66	1.65	1.68	1.61
葡萄园	Grapes Orchards	1.89	3.02	4.83	4.91	5.46	6.70	9.39
桃园	Peach Orchards	3.47	8.66	7.68	6.87	6.78	6.49	6.14
猕猴桃园	Chinese Goosebeery Orchards	16.83	4.33	34.92	36.97	41.36	41.99	42.16
杏园	Apricot Orchards	0.62	2.50	3.62	3.60	3.59	3.52	3.99
柿子园	Presimmons Orchards	1.96	2.69	3.16	2.83	2.91	2.78	2.59
石榴园	Pomegranate Orchards			3.43	3.38	3.61	3.57	3.59
水果产量（吨）	**Output of Fruits (ton)**	**343551**	**512869**	**847821**	**911361**	**932054**	**951851**	**996570**
苹果	Apple	89416	53387	39130	34313	28675	25212	26047
梨	Pears	65459	57059	55122	48026	47463	47618	48757
葡萄	Grapes	16647	30951	64885	69003	75516	92380	99889
桃	Peach	27010	89755	142051	137683	125857	122186	125147
猕猴桃	Chinese Goosebeery	96640	137853	296023	357066	386336	395847	410614
杏	Apricot			48544	34340	57772	55330	61145
柿子	Persimmon			35287	31625	41211	41712	43705
石榴	Pomegranate			40211	34340	32329	30642	32793

11-26 各区县果业生产情况（2014年）

Area and Output of Fruits by Region (2014)

区　县	Region	果园面积（万亩） Area of Orchards(10 000 mu)	水果产量（吨） Output of Fruits(ton)
合　计	**Total**	**81.23**	**996570**
新城区	Xincheng		
碑林区	Beilin		
莲湖区	Lianhu		
灞桥区	Baqiao	7.38	103857
未央区	Weiyang	0.07	1327
雁塔区	Yanta	0.02	2329
阎良区	Yanliang	2.72	67520
临潼区	Lintong	5.32	55304
长安区	Chang'an	5.57	79109
蓝田县	Lantian	9.28	130439
周至县	Zhouzhi	40.33	404056
户　县	Huxian	7.50	94895
高陵县	Gaoling	3.04	57734

11-27 主要年份畜牧业生产情况

Statistics on Livestock Husbandry in Representative Years

指标	Item	2000	2005	2010	2011	2012	2013	2014
一、大牲畜年末总头数（头）	**Large Animals In Stock at Year-end (head)**	**260742**	**322521**	**216043**	**212351**	**211852**	**211791**	**217257**
# 役畜	Draught Animals	98130	90717	42243	32877	31866	31510	26760
1. 牛	Cattle	256073	320773	215072	211334	210819	210743	216326
# 能繁殖母畜	Female Animals of Reprductive Ability	136626	176445	144012	142977			
# 当年生仔畜	Newborn Livestock in the Year	69015	72163	40052	36093			
#肉牛	Farm Cattle			65447	62127	60233	60165	64478
#奶牛	Dairy Cattle	48164	96498	118747	117149	119888	120836	126174
2. 马	Horses	736	559	456	496	533	549	513
3. 驴	Donkeys	476	175	67	71	46	52	59
4. 骡	Mules	3457	1014	448	450	454	447	359
二、猪年末头数（头）	**Hogs in Stock Year-end (head)**	**1284592**	**1472869**	**943183**	**943987**	**966018**	**965683**	**950124**
# 能繁殖的母猪	Female Hogs of Reprductive Ability	93775	123543	106610	101332	103926	103967	99989
三、羊年末只数（只）	**Sheeps and Goats in Stock at Year-end(head)**	**421103**	**532471**	**294539**	**295995**	**284596**	**273747**	**279207**
1. 山羊	Goats	397121	520354	288738	288346	278738	267382	271722
# 奶山羊	Milch Goats	266525	358733	246442	245118	234643	222546	224901
2. 绵羊	Sheeps	23982	12117	5801	7649	5858	6365	7485
四、家禽年末存栏（万只）	**Poultry in Stock at Year-end (10 000 heads)**	**1623.81**	**1372.56**	**1034.20**	**1153.76**	**1176.73**	**1172.61**	**1161.16**
五、年末养蜂箱数（箱）	**Honey (box)**	**20408**	**24287**	**22984**	**17567**	**17161**	**17415**	**20663**

11-28 各区县畜牧业生产情况（2014年）

Statistics On Livestock, Animal Husbandry by Region（2014）

区　县	Region	大牲畜年末头数（头） Large Animals In Stock at Year-end (head)	役畜 Draught Animals	牛（头） Cattle (head)	奶牛 Dairy Cattle	马（匹） Horses (head)	驴（头） Donkeys (head)
合　计	**Total**	**217257**	**26760**	**216326**	**126174**	**513**	**59**
新城区	Xincheng						
碑林区	Beilin						
莲湖区	Lianhu						
灞桥区	Baqiao	13276	146	13258	12942	18	
未央区	Weiyang	6185		6185	5489		
雁塔区	Yanta	219		219	219		
阎良区	Yanliang	19247		19247	17853		
临潼区	Lintong	73253	7685	73253	65568		
长安区	Chang'an	11375	624	10831	4331	281	
蓝田县	Lantian	38355	8388	38355	2989		
周至县	Zhouzhi	33327	9641	33217	2800	75	
户　县	Huxian	9713	46	9713	5321		
高陵县	Gaoling	12307	230	12048	8662	139	59

11-28　续表　continued

区　县	Region	骡（头） Mutes (head)	猪（头） Swine (head)	能繁殖的母猪 breeding sows	羊（只） Sheep and Goats (head)	山羊 Goats	奶山羊 Milch Goats	家禽（万只） Poultry (10 000 heads)	蜂（箱） Honey (box)
合　计	**Total**	**359**	**950124**	**99989**	**279207**	**271722**	**224901**	**1161.16**	**20663**
新城区	Xincheng								
碑林区	Beilin								
莲湖区	Lianhu								
灞桥区	Baqiao		49193	6037	11803	11803	11317	44.76	330
未央区	Weiyang		21760	1174	1568	1568	1383	5.60	
雁塔区	Yanta		4000	200				2.70	
阎良区	Yanliang		38302	4391	55514	55514	55514	61.52	631
临潼区	Lintong		237626	21156	82232	82232	82232	265.00	1623
长安区	Chang'an	263	116606	10881	16639	13424	4634	286.58	4458
蓝田县	Lantian		80049	8816	72306	72306	46831	127.00	2718
周至县	Zhouzhi	35	200498	24797	13039	12882	2377	97.50	6500
户　县	Huxian		151580	15504	7205	7205	6832	130.50	4403
高陵县	Gaoling	61	50510	7033	18901	14788	13781	140.00	

11-29 主要年份畜产品和水产品产量

Output of Livestock Products and Aquatic Products in Representative Years

单位：吨 (ton)

年 份 Year	肉类总产量 Output of Meat	猪 肉 Pork	牛 肉 Beef	羊 肉 Mutton	禽 肉 Poultry
1990	63273	50646	4667	1931	5885
1991	72268	55086	5623	2162	9062
1992	88994	68134	6468	2460	11290
1993	93420	71274	7249	2220	12174
1994	106691	79433	8298	2350	15681
1995	127815	86513	11251	3731	23948
1996	91468	63750	5402	2578	19324
1997	106597	75381	6672	3468	20596
1998	134152	98974	8788	4710	21424
1999	130124	93859	9827	4147	21963
2000	147571	106137	12066	4766	23760
2001	157277	113353	11900	5153	20540
2002	161092	118634	11516	5394	20515
2003	165860	122759	13241	5180	19682
2004	171545	126404	13641	5874	18493
2005	182046	136503	14031	6106	18803
2006	108634	81199	8267	2841	13417
2007	102191	73254	8589	3111	14075
2008	115352	84654	9840	3335	16060
2009	126182	94490	10142	3677	17190
2010	136501	102296	10854	3875	18338
2011	144631	104816	11860	3645	19390
2012	151711	110506	12079	3697	20046
2013	157449	114288	12143	4036	20817
2014	161886	118627	12288	4198	20887

注：2010年起，根据统计制度要求，水产品产量及养殖面积统计数据取自水务部门。

11-29 续表 continued

单位：吨 (ton)

年 份 Year	奶类产量 Output of Milk	牛 奶 Cow Milk	禽 蛋 Poultry Eggs	蜂蜜（公斤） Honey(kg)	水产品 Output of Aquatic Products	养殖面积（万亩） Water Raise Areas (10 000 mu)
1990	82017	50528	55938	1035392	4259	2.55
1991	91006	57700	90558	1022797	4949	2.63
1992	100080	63586	104970	739275	6015	2.80
1993	111070	73897	125244	662049	7132	2.97
1994	145412	99025	146503	547808	7900	3.10
1995	132909	85753	141227	535891	8517	3.21
1996	133372	86103	138044	613290	8910	3.51
1997	150964	98078	156066	713918	10054	3.46
1998	174099	119719	142519	537304	10480	3.40
1999	209144	145191	135981	541613	11061	3.38
2000	245913	176155	138305	460598	11384	3.35
2001	255437	179977	132303	479839	12480	3.17
2002	288009	202826	134336	497530	12017	3.31
2003	336296	245407	128833	537805	9967	2.48
2004	384319	289564	117597	449765	9721	2.46
2005	422229	327961	118115	421052	9370	2.38
2006	471438	374813	97816	414271	11937	1.60
2007	528037	428462	98140	401761	12402	1.38
2008	589697	475681	108515	503031	12487	1.40
2009	618186	498394	116685	528731	13044	1.52
2010	633663	509178	123793	436759	11850	2.24
2011	647978	509777	125639	217632	11800	2.20
2012	666439	513337	129970	213174	14010	2.95
2013	657748	512796	135382	219344	14200	2.33
2014	658016	514587	135191	250464	14218	2.31

11-30 各区县主要畜产品和水产品产量（2014年）

Output of Major Livestock Products and Aquatic Products by Region（2014）

单位：吨 (ton)

区 县	Region	肉类总产量 Output of Meat	猪 肉 Pork	牛 肉 Beef	羊 肉 Mutton	禽 肉 Poultry
合 计	**Total**	**161886**	**118627**	**12288**	**4198**	**20887**
新城区	Xincheng					
碑林区	Beilin					
莲湖区	Lianhu					
灞桥区	Baqiao	7335	5579	766	144	830
未央区	Weiyang	1325	1194	78	17	36
雁塔区	Yanta	750	680	13		57
阎良区	Yanliang	7205	4836	652	672	969
临潼区	Lintong	44665	32232	3534	1612	4506
长安区	Chang'an	21704	15108	645	251	5307
蓝田县	Lantian	18801	10529	3452	1066	2907
周至县	Zhouzhi	30179	25223	2004	200	1733
户 县	Huxian	19975	16439	642	78	2350
高陵县	Gaoling	9947	6807	502	158	2192

11-30 续表 continued

单位：吨 (ton)

区 县	Region	奶类产量 Output of Milk	牛 奶 Cow Milk	禽 蛋 Poultry Eggs	蜂蜜（公斤） Honey(kg)	水产品 Output of Aquatic Products	养殖面积（亩） Water Raise Areas (mu)
合 计	**Total**	**658016**	**514587**	**135191**	**250464**	**14218**	**23100**
新城区	Xincheng						
碑林区	Beilin						
莲湖区	Lianhu						
灞桥区	Baqiao	66295	58521	5648	8300	700	1800
未央区	Weiyang	6931	6912	103		1805	3585
雁塔区	Yanta	950	950	260		50	15
阎良区	Yanliang	98354	71267	7025	17293	225	165
临潼区	Lintong	335356	279562	33652	43862	3305	4965
长安区	Chang'an	24316	19290	40492	77562	4950	5640
蓝田县	Lantian	41570	11836	6491	22263	1300	3660
周至县	Zhouzhi	13293	11490	10275	60320	500	2310
户 县	Huxian	26785	22506	14857	20864	1153	780
高陵县	Gaoling	44166	32253	16388		230	180

11-31 农业科技、教育情况（2014年）

Agricultural Science and Technology Education（2014）

指标	Item	2014
农业研究开发机构（个）	Agricultural research and development institutions (unit)	245
农业科技人员（人）	Agricultural scientific and technical personnel(persons)	3781
农业科研成果（个）	Agricultural scientific research achievements (unit)	15
农民技能培训人数（万人）	The number of peasants skills training(10 000 persons)	19
良种推广面积（万亩）	Thoroughbred promotion area (10 000 mu)	
农业信息站（个）	information station of Agricultural (unit)	3104

11-32 主要年份农产品人均占有量

Per Capita Output of Major Farm Products in Representative Years

单位：公斤/人　　(kg/ person)

年份 rear	粮食 Grain	棉花 Cotton	油料 Oil-bearing Crops	猪牛羊肉 Pork Beef and Mutton	禽蛋 Poultry Eggs	奶类 Milk	水果 Fruits	蔬菜 Vegetables
1978	266.7	5.7	0.2	5.4	0.9	3.3	6.8	91.7
1979	288.6	5.2	0.6	6.7	1.0	4.0	5.1	97.3
1980	223.5	3.8	1.1	5.9	1.2	4.1	6.9	78.4
1981	222.9	2.6	1.5	6.6	1.7	4.7	5.8	65.4
1982	281.5	5.5	1.0	4.9	2.7	5.6	5.9	101.6
1983	276.6	1.6	0.7	4.9	3.2	6.5	5.0	87.8
1984	289.4	2.7	0.8	4.8	6.2	8.7	4.8	138.6
1985	271.4	0.9	1.4	6.8	5.7	10.2	7.6	156.3
1986	288.0	0.8	2.2	7.8	6.4	12.1	9.6	152.2
1987	298.0	0.8	2.7	7.3	6.8	13.8	10.6	165.6
1988	269.7	0.7	1.5	8.0	8.9	15.6	11.1	193.7
1989	290.7	0.9	2.2	8.4	7.6	13.1	10.2	216.5
1990	298.7	1.2	2.1	9.4	9.2	14.2	11.5	196.0
1991	290.6	1.6	2.0	10.2	14.7	14.8	11.7	190.8
1992	294.3	1.2	2.4	12.4	16.8	16.2	17.3	205.6
1993	301.2	1.2	2.2	12.8	19.9	17.6	25.9	231.1
1994	246.1	1.0	1.7	14.1	22.9	22.7	28.0	211.5
1995	270.4	0.5	3.4	15.7	21.8	20.5	37.5	206.1
1996	286.3	0.4	3.2	11.0	21.1	20.4	43.9	210.8
1997	287.8	0.3	2.8	12.9	23.6	22.8	43.3	214.7
1998	318.3	0.2	2.5	16.8	21.3	26.1	50.0	222.8
1999	303.0	0.2	1.9	16.0	20.2	31.0	52.7	227.2
2000	293.5	0.2	1.9	17.9	20.1	35.7	49.9	235.7
2001	283.7	0.2	1.8	18.8	19.0	36.8	48.8	219.9
2002	273.8	0.3	1.7	19.3	19.1	41.0	53.5	241.6
2003	246.0	0.3	1.6	19.7	18.0	46.9	53.6	236.8
2004	270.1	0.6	1.6	20.1	16.2	53.0	63.9	249.6
2005	277.1	0.6	1.6	21.1	15.9	56.9	69.1	263.8
2006	256.9	0.6	1.4	12.3	13.0	62.6	73.5	251.4
2007	247.4	0.8	1.3	11.1	12.8	69.1	79.2	267.3
2008	256.0	0.7	1.4	11.7	13.0	70.4	85.6	264.5
2009	258.7	0.7	1.3	12.8	13.8	73.3	93.6	287.4
2010	261.8	0.7	1.4	13.8	14.6	74.8	100.1	298.9
2011	213.8	0.7	1.4	14.1	14.8	76.1	107.1	318.9
2012	225.6	0.6	1.2	14.8	15.2	78.1	109.2	325.6
2013	213.2	0.3	1.2	15.2	15.8	76.6	110.8	347.1
2014	204.0	0.0	1.1	15.7	15.7	76.3	115.8	367.5

11-33 主要年份农村经济效益指标

Main Indicators of Rural Economic Benefit in Representative Years

年份 Year	每一劳动力创造的 Average Labor Force Production 农林牧渔及服务业总产值（元） Gross Output Value of Farming,Forestry, Animal Husbandry, Fishery and Service (yuan)	粮食（公斤） Grain Crops(kg)	棉花（公斤） Cotton (kg)	油料（公斤） Oil-bearing Crops(kg)	每亩耕地种植业总产值（元） Output of Each Unit of Area Planting(yuan)	每百元物耗生产的总产值（元） Output per 100-Yuan of Material Consumed(yuan)
1978	504.7	1024.6	22.0	0.7	104.3	
1979	549.0	1096.5	19.8	2.3	116.0	
1980	483.1	846.1	14.5	4.0	99.2	
1981	502.8	840.5	9.9	5.5	105.4	
1982	631.5	1058.9	20.5	3.6	139.3	
1983	606.5	1053.2	6.1	2.6	124.1	
1984	850.7	1154.2	10.9	3.4	163.6	
1985	1020.1	1134.6	3.7	5.6	183.1	
1986	1132.2	1236.4	3.4	9.5	204.6	
1987	1280.3	1277.2	3.5	11.7	231.5	
1988	1558.4	1148.0	3.0	6.5	273.2	
1989	1605.3	1231.9	3.9	9.5	295.0	
1990	1766.3	1279.1	5.2	10.0	343.4	233.3
1991	1958.8	1326.6	7.2	8.9	380.4	238.4
1992	2093.7	1360.7	5.5	11.1	451.6	241.8
1993	2528.9	1409.7	5.6	10.4	546.8	240.1
1994	3705.0	1167.8	4.8	8.0	762.8	227.6
1995	4953.0	1300.6	2.2	16.1	1106.5	225.9
1996	5154.8	1391.2	1.8	13.6	1224.2	234.5
1997	5493.0	1413.4	1.3	13.8	1283.3	239.2
1998	5615.9	1578.1	1.0	12.4	1374.3	247.0
1999	4826.5	1516.6	1.1	9.7	1175.9	251.7
2000	5091.5	1498.0	1.0	9.9	1161.1	250.2
2001	5328.5	1462.4	1.3	9.1	1221.1	248.6
2002	5617.4	1427.5	1.3	9.1	1272.0	265.9
2003	5761.2	1308.1	1.6	8.4	1332.4	254.3
2004	6885.4	1452.7	3.0	8.5	1434.6	261.7
2005	7737.9	1524.7	3.3	8.6	1642.3	262.9
2006	8415.5	1435.7	3.6	8.0	1756.9	263.1
2007	10165.6	1403.0	4.4	7.1	2037.3	259.8
2008	13306.4	1695.4	4.9	9.1	2447.9	259.6
2009	14674.3	1791.7	5.1	9.2	2737.9	261.6
2010	19480.7	1901.3	5.1	10.0	3753.4	260.9
2011	23474.6	1567.2	4.9	10.1	4585.8	274.0
2012	27219.4	1699.6	4.2	10.1	5175.7	273.5
2013	31608.7	1688.0	2.3	9.2	5934.5	274.0
2014	33292.2	1605.0	0.3	8.9	6552.4	274.9

主要统计指标解释

农林牧渔业总产值 指以货币表现的农、林、牧、渔业全部产品和对农林牧渔业生产活动进行的各种支持性服务活动的价值总量，它反映一定时期内农林牧渔业生产总规模和总成果。1957年以前的农林牧渔业总产值中包括了厩肥和农民自给性手工业（如农民自制衣服、鞋、袜，自己从事粮食初步加工等）。1958年及以后，林业中增加了村及村以下竹木采伐产值；牧业中取消了厩肥产值；副业中取消了农民自给性手工业产值，增加了村及村以下办的工业产值；渔业中增加了海洋捕捞水产品产值。1980年及以后，在副业中增加了农民家庭兼营工业商品部分的产值。从1984年起村及村以下工业产值划归工业。从1993年起取消副业，将野生动物的捕猎划入牧业，野生植物采集和农民家庭兼营商品性工业划归农业。从2003年起，执行新的国民经济行业分类标准，农林牧渔业总产值中包括了农林牧渔服务业产值。林业中增加了森林采运业产值。农业中取消了家庭兼营商品性工业产值，将野生林产品的采集划归林业。第一次农业普查以后，由于畜牧业产品年报数据与普查数据之间存在一定的差距，根据农业普查结果对畜牧业年报数据进行了修正，对畜牧业产值进行了相应修正。

农林牧渔业总产值的计算方法通常是按农、林、牧、渔业产品及其副产品的产量分别乘以各自单位产品价格求得；少数生产周期较长，当年没有产品或产品产量不易统计的，则采用间接方法匡算其产值；然后将四业产品产值及农林牧渔服务业产值相加即为农林牧渔业总产值。

粮食产量 指全社会的产量。包括国有经济经营的、集体统一经营的和农民家庭经营的粮食产量，还包括工矿企业办的农场和其他生产单位的产量。粮食除包括稻谷、小麦、玉米、高粱、谷子及其他杂粮外，还包括薯类和豆类。其产量计算方法，豆类按去豆荚后的干豆计算；薯类（包括甘薯和马铃薯，不包括芋头和木薯）1963年以前按每4公斤鲜薯折1公斤粮食计算，从 1964年开始改为按5公斤鲜薯折1公斤粮食计算。城市郊区作为蔬菜的薯类（如马铃薯等）按鲜品计算，并且不作粮食统计。其他粮食一律按脱粒后的原粮计算。1989年以前全国粮食产量数据主要靠全面报表取得，1989年开始使用抽样调查数据。

棉花产量 指全社会的产量。包括春播棉和夏播棉。产量按皮棉计算。不包括木棉。

油料产量 指全部油料作物的生产量。包括花生、油菜籽、芝麻、向日葵籽、胡麻籽（亚麻籽）和其他油料。不包括大豆、木本油料和野生油料。花生以带壳干花生计算。

水产品产量 指人工养殖的水产品和天然生长的水产品的捕捞量。包括海水的鱼类、虾蟹类、贝类和藻类以及内陆水域的鱼类、虾蟹类和贝类，不包括淡水生植物。水产品产量是通过各级水产和统计部门逐级上报取得数据。1995年及以前，贝类中牡蛎按鲜肉计算；蚶、蛤、蛏按5斤鲜品折1斤计算。1996年以后则统一按鲜品计算。

猪、牛、羊肉产量 指当年出栏并已屠宰、除去头蹄下水后带骨肉（即胴体重）的重量。包括全社会范围内的产量。1996年前为各级逐级上报数据。1996年第一次农业普查以后，由于畜牧业产品年报数据与普查数据之间存在一定的差距，根据普查结果对畜牧业年报数据进行了修正。1999年以后，国家统计局在部分地区开展了猪、牛、羊、禽等主要畜禽品种的抽样调查，并用抽样数据作为国家定案数据使用。未开展抽样调查的地区和品种，仍使用各级统计部门逐级上报数据。2007年，根据第二次农业普查结果，对2000-2006年畜牧业年报数据进行了修正。2008年，建立了主要畜禽监测调查制度，猪、牛、羊、禽等主要畜牧业数据均以抽样调查数为法定数据。

期初（末）畜禽存栏头（只）数 指报告期初（末）农村各种合作经济组织和国营农场、农民个人、机关、团体、学校、工矿企业、部队等单位以及城镇居民饲养的大牲畜、猪、羊、家禽等畜禽的存栏数。

常用耕地 是指耕地总资源中专门种植农作物并经常进行耕种、能够正常收获的土地。包括当年实际耕种的熟地；弃耕、休闲不满三年，随时可以复耕的地；开荒利用三年以上的地。不包括临时种植农作物的坡度在25度以上的陡坡地；在河套、湖畔、库区临时开发的成片或零星土地；也不包括已列为国家和省（区、市）退耕计划但临时耕种的土地。

农作物播种面积 指实际播种或移植有农作物的面积。凡是实际种植有农作物的面积，不论种植在耕地上还是种植在非耕地上，均包括在农作物播种面积中。在播种季节基本结束后，因遭灾而重新改种和补种的农作物面积，也包括在内。它是反映我国耕地面积利用情况的一个重要指标。目前，农作物播种面积主要包括粮食、棉花、油料、糖料、麻类、烟叶、蔬菜和瓜类、药材和其他农作物九大类。

有效灌溉面积 指具有一定的水源，地块比较平整，灌溉工程或设备已经配套，在一般年景下，当年能够进行正常灌溉的耕地面积。在一般情况下，有效灌溉面积应等于灌溉工程或设备已经配备，能够进行正常灌溉的水田和水浇地面积之和。它是反映我国耕地抗旱能力的一个重要指标。

农用化肥施用量 指本年内实际用于农业生产的化肥数量，包括氮肥、磷肥、钾肥和复合肥。化肥施用量要求按折纯量计算数量。折纯量是指把氮肥、磷肥、钾肥分别按含氮、含五氧化二磷、含氧化钾的百分之百成份进行折算后的数量。复合肥按其所含主要成分折算。公式为：

折纯量=实物量×某种化肥有效成份含量的百分比

农业机械总动力 指主要用于农、林、牧、渔业的各种动力机械的动力总和。包括耕作机械、排灌机械、收获机械、农用运输机械、植物保护机械、牧业机械、林业机械、渔业机械和其他农业机械【内燃机按引擎马力折成瓦（特）计算、电动机按功率折成瓦（特）计算】。不包括专门用于乡、镇、村、组办工业、基本建设、非农业运输、科学试验和教学等非农业生产方面用的动力机械与作业机械。这个指标的统计数据主要来源于农机部门。

Explanatory Notes on Main Statistical Indicators

Gross Output Value of Agriculture, Forestry, Animal Husbandry and Fishery refers to the total value of products of agriculture, forestry, animal husbandry and fishery, and total value of services in support of agriculture, forestry, animal husbandry and fishery activities. It reflects the total scale and results of agricultural production during a given period. Prior to 1957, China's gross agricultural output value included barnyard manure and handicraft products for self- consumption (clothes, shoes, stockings, and initial grain processing undertaken by peasants). Since 1958, cutting and felling of bamboo and trees by villages and other cooperative organizations under villages have been included in forestry; value of barnyard manure has been excluded from animal husbandry; self consumed handicrafts have not been included from sideline occupations, while the output value of industries run by villages and cooperative organizations under village has been included in sideline occupations; and the output value of fish catches by motor fishing boats has been added to fishery. Since 1980, the value of handicraft products made for sale by individuals in households has been added to sideline occupations. Since 1984, industries run by villages and under villages have been included in the sector of industry. Since 1993, the subdivision of sideline occupations has been cancelled, and the hunting of wild animals has been classified into animal husbandry, and the gathering of wild plants and commodity industry run by rural household have been included in farming. A new industrial classification of economic activities was introduced in 2003. Under the new classification, value of services to agriculture, forestry, animal husbandry and fishery is included in the gross output value of agriculture, value of wood felling and transport is included in forestry, value of industrial output by rural households is not included in agriculture, and the collection of wild forest products is taken from agriculture and included in forestry. The First Agriculture Census of China revealed some discrepancy between the production of animal products from the annual reports and that from the census. According to the result of the First Agriculture census, efforts were made to adjust the output value of animal husbandry to make the figures from the annual reports consistent with the census data.

Gross output value of agrieulture is obtained by multiplying the output of each product or by-product by its price, resulting in the output value of each single item. For a small number of products, annual output of which is not available or difficult to get due to the long production (growing) process involved, the output value is estimated through an indirect approach. The sum of output values of all products of agriculture, forestry, animal husbandry and fishery and services in support to those industries is then equal to the gross output value of agriculture.

Grain Output refers to the total output in the whole country including grains produced by State farms, collective units, rural households, as well as by farms affiliated to industrial and mining enterprises and other production units. Grain includes rice, wheat, corn, sorghum, millet and other miscellaneous grains as well as tubers and beans. Output of beans refers to dry beans without pods. The output of tubers (sweet potatoes and potatoes, not including taros and cassava) are converted into that of grain at the ratio 4:1, i.e. 4 kilograms of fresh tubers were equivalent to 1 kilogram of grain up to 1963. Since 1964 the ratio for conversion has been 5:1. Tubers supplied as vegetables (such as potatoes) in cities and suburbs are calculated as fresh vegetables and their output is not included in the output of grain. Output of all other grains refers to husked grain. Data on grain production before 1989 were obtained through the Comprehensive Statistical Reporting System. Since 1989, data from sample surveys are used.

Cotton Output refers to cotton production in the whole country including cotton planted in spring and in autumn. Output is measured as the weight of ginned cotton. Ceiba is not included.

Output of Oil–bearing Crops refers to the total production of oil-bearing crops of various kinds, including peanuts (dry, in shell), rapeseeds, sesame, sunflower seeds, flax seeds, and other oil-bearing crops. Soybeans, oil-bearing woody plants, and wild oil-bearing crops are not included.

Output of Aquatic Products refers to catches of both artificially cultured and naturally grown aquatic products, including fish, shrimps, crabs and shellfish in sea and inland water as well as seaweed. Freshwater plants are not included. Data on output of aquatic products are reported by aquatic product and statistical agencies level by level. Before 1995, among the shellfish, oyster was counted as fresh meat; 5 kilograms of ark shell, clams and frogs are equivalent to 1 kilogram of fresh aquatic products; they have all been counted as flesh aquatic products since 1996.

Output of Pork, Beef, and Mutton refers to the meat of slaughtered hogs, cattle, sheep and goats with head, feet, and offal taken away. Data refers to the production of the whole country. The First Agricultural Census of China in 1996 revealed some discrepancy between the production of animal products from the annual reports and that from the census. Efforts were made to adjust the output value of animal husbandry to make the figures from the annual reports consistent with the census data. Since 1999, the NBS conducted sample surveys for the major animal husbandry products, such as hogs, cattle, sheep and goats and fowls, and the data from sample surveys are used as national finalized data. Those products, which are not covered by the sample survey, are still reported by statistical agencies level by level. In 2007. the data on animal husbandry from 2000 to 2006 were revised according to the results of the Second Agriculture Census of China. In 2008, A Monitoring and Survey Program was set up on main livestock, the data on the main livestock such as hog, cattle, sheep and poultry became the official data based on the sampling survey.

Number of Livestock or Poultry in Stock at Beginning (or End) of Period refers to the total number of large animals, pigs, sheep, fowls, etc. raised by rural cooperative organizations, State farms, rural individuals, government agencies, schools, industrial and mining enterprises, army, and urban residents at the beginning (or end) of the reference period.

Regularly Cultivated Land refers to farmland among the total land resources which is exclusively used for farming and is under regular cultivation with harvest in normal years. Included are currently cultivated land, land that has been abandoned or put in idle for less than 3 years and could be re-used for cultivation at any time, and new-claimed land that has been put into cultivation for more than 3 years. Excluded under this category are steep slope land over 25 degrees under temporary cultivation, land (large or small plots) that is claimed along river bends, lake sides or banks of reservoirs, as well as land that has been designated under the "Green for Grain" programmes of the state and provincial governments but is still temporarily under cultivation.

Sown Area of Crops refers to area of transplanted with crops regardless of being land sown or in cultivated area or non-cultivated area. Area of land re-sown due to lso included. This is an important indicator that can reflect the utilization condition of the cultivated land in China. At present, the sown area of crops mainly include the following 9 categories of crops: grain, cotton, oil-bearing crops, sugar crops, flax crops, tobacco, vegetables and melons, medicinal materials and other farm crops.natural disasters is also included. This is an important indicator that can reflect the utilization condition of the cultivated land in China. At present, the sown area of crops mainly include the following 9 categories of crops: grain, cotton, oil-bearing crops, sugar crops, flax crops, tobacco, vegetables and melons, medicinal materials and other farm crops.

Irrigated Area refers to area of land that are effectively irrigated, i.e. relatively level land, where there are water sources or complete sets of irrigation facilities to lift and move adequate water for irrigation purpose under normal conditions. Under normal situations, irrigated area is the sum of watered fields and irrigated fields where irrigation systems or equipment have been installed for regular irrigation purpose. This important indicator reflects drought resistance capacity of the cultivated land in China.

Consumption of Chemical Fertilizers in Agriculture refers to the quantity of chemical fertilizers applied in agriculture in the year, including nitrogenous fertilizer, phosphate fertilizer, potash fertilizer, and compound fertilizer. The consumption of chemical fertilizers is calculated in terms of volume of effective components by means of converting the gross weight of the respective fertilizers into weight containing effective component (e.g. nitrogen content in nitrogenous fertilizer, phosphorous pentoxide contents in phosphate fertilizer, and potassium oxide contents in potash fertilizer). Compound fertilizer is converted in regard to its major components. The formula is:

Volume of effective component= physical quantity × effective component of certain chemical fertilizer (%)

Total Power of Agricultural Machinery refers to total mechanical power of machinery used in agriculture, forestry, animal husbandry and fishery, including machinery for ploughing, irrigation and drainage, harvesting, transport, plant protection, animal husbandry, forestry and fishery and other agricultural machineries. (For the power of internal combustion engines, it is converted from its horsepower into watts while for electric motors the output power is converted into watts.) Machinery employed for non-agricultural purposes, such as the machines used in township-run and village-run industry, construction, non-agricultural transport, scientific experiments and teaching, are not included. Data are mainly from agricultural machinery agencies.

12 工　业

INDUSTRY

资料整理：赵　晖　王凤玲　赵　博　陈小兵　李　玫　王　玥
Data management：Zhao Hui Wang Fengling Zhao Bo Chen Xiaobing Li Mei Wang Yue
数据审核：马　琰
Data audit：Ma Yan

第十二部分　工业

一、简要说明

本章资料包括规模以上工业企业单位数、总产值、主要经济指标等，由西安市统计局工业处提供。

二、主要指标

规模以上工业企业单位数（个）	1146	比上年增长	8.5%
规模以上工业增加值（亿元）	1304.12	比上年增长	9.4%

12

12　INDUSTRY

Ⅰ.Brief Introduction

Data in this chapter includes number of industrial enterprises above designated size and gross product, primary economic. Data in this chapter are provided and compiled by Industry Division of the Xi'an Bureau of Statistics.

Ⅱ.Major Indicators

		Increase over Preceding Year
Number of Industrial Enterprises Above Designated Size(item)	1146	8.5%
Value Added of Industry Above Designated Size(100 million yuan)	1304.12	9.4%

12-1 主要年份全部工业总产值

Gross Output Value of Industry In Representative Years

单位：万元　　(10 000 yuan)

年份 Year	全部工业总产值 Gross Industrial Output Value	工业总产值指数（上年=100） Index of Gross Industry Output Value (Preceding Year=100)	国有经济 State-owned Enterprises	集体经济 Collective-owned Enterprises	其他经济类型 Enterprises of Other Ownership
1952	23512	139.6	9917	464	13131
1962	120833	86.8	102103	17599	1131
1965	200416	132.1	183164	17252	
1970	333386	143.5	305303	28083	
1975	385509	106.1	332982	52527	
1978	483262	116.9	405376	77886	
1979	517483	106.6	438850	78633	
1980	531755	101.8	440139	91577	39
1981	524587	98.6	433740	90675	172
1982	549200	107.1	450308	98516	456
1983	603507	112.2	493773	108923	811
1984	674963	112.8	520593	153056	1314
1985	853196	120.4	632702	218893	1601
1986	976326	112.1	706380	267282	2664
1987	1142220	114.2	809186	328701	4341
1988	1429811	116.0	1012268	416217	1326
1989	1653472	106.1	1160877	486754	5814
1990	1771310	107.4	1196777	548605	25928
1991	2002727	110.0	1325242	604495	72990
1992	2300472	112.5	1488541	561369	250562
1993	3045988	121.7	1748145	1071122	226721
1994	3891584	120.6	1960533	1581321	349730
1995	4058952	108.7	2071755	1663536	323661
1996	5338510	133.4	2132140	2836176	370194
1997	5794532	121.8	1915536	2005610	1873386
1998	6738224	117.3	2593405	2077273	2067546
1999	7151528	117.1	2128243	2174220	2849065
2000	6394812	115.3	2749778	2094680	1550354
2001	7361510	116.4	3098431	2380910	1882169
2002	8379363	115.8	3472067	2312923	2594373
2003	9750800	115.1	4149015	1501372	4100413
2004	11853224	118.4	5414952	875412	5562860
2005	13085580	106.3	5916553	674900	6494127
2006	15573516	119.0	7527607	514810	7531099
2007	19798593	122.1	10179303	365329	9253961
2008	23881446	120.6	12479652	441987	10959807
2009	28270652	118.3	14440321	388777	13441554
2010	35628753	126.0	18353877	435206	16839669
2011	40933178	114.9	20654524	377199	19901455
2012	46560824	113.8	24303736	376427	21880661
2013	50426416	108.3	25358096	325004	24743316
2014	56606272	112.3	27352693	332712	28920867

注：2013年数据为全国第三次经济普查数据，以前年份未做调整。

12-1 续表 continued

单位：万元 (10 000 yuan)

年份 Year	轻工业 Light Industry	重工业 Heavy Industry	大型工业 Large-size Industry Enterprises	中型工业 Medium-size Industry Enterprises	小型工业 Small-size Industry Enterprises
1952	20800	2712			
1962	68221	52618			
1965	98631	101785			
1970	124467	208919			
1975	167285	218224	145262	130592	109655
1978	220480	262782	168397	121813	193052
1979	243043	274440	189877	133759	193847
1980	283475	248280	193092	130053	208610
1981	309199	215388	178130	140810	205639
1982	303249	246031	213015	128597	207668
1983	315785	287722	245053	127164	231290
1984	321678	353285	241842	143165	289956
1985	401748	451448	333820	147488	371888
1986	458270	518056	401037	150644	424609
1987	516776	625452	472958	171698	497572
1988	699593	730210	615946	210089	603776
1989	712743	940729	696368	258414	698690
1990	787857	983453	716421	279098	775791
1991	897676	1105051	888052	303151	844524
1992	967104	1333368			
1993	1121957	1924031	1258137	384255	1403596
1994	1578875	2312709	1479613	390233	2021738
1995	1636219	2432733	1575030	371156	2112766
1996	2347887	2990623	1693985	358913	3285612
1997	2700085	3094447	1675521	274888	3844123
1998	3232681	3505543	1821556	308424	4608244
1999	3488547	3662981	1744637	337795	5069096
2000	3121419	3273393	2320973	328494	3745345
2001	3518054	3843456	2656010	368497	4337003
2002	3935764	4443599	3038828	398834	4941701
2003	4028859	5721941	2662073	2027256	5061471
2004	4211592	7641632	3595150	3237701	5020373
2005	4078417	9007163	4640325	3228553	5216702
2006	4510970	11062546	5970535	3414468	6188513
2007	7331719	12466874	8351303	4171131	7276159
2008	6010865	17870581	10472686	5005676	8403084
2009	6636464	21634188	12309192	6186395	9775065
2010	7841869	27786884	15002737	8537140	12088876
2011	8992547	31940631	16844272	6207660	17881246
2012	10218288	36342536	22563292	6243799	17753733
2013	9297919	41128497	17390620	7271086	25764710
2014	10369659	46236614	24880136	8754767	22971370

12-2 主要年份规模以上工业企业主要经济指标

Main Economic Indicators of all Industrial Enterprises above Designated Size in Representative Years

单位：亿元 (100 million yuan)

年 份 Year	企业单位数（个） Number of Enterprises (unit)	工业总产值（当年价） Gross Industrial Output Value (At Current Prices)	工业增加值（现价） Value-added of Industry	从业人员年平均人数（万人） Annual Average Employed Persons (10 000 persons)	资产合计 Total Assets
1998	793	350.38	99.20	51.71	810.56
1999	770	366.59	106.56	45.64	853.90
2000	816	417.97	130.18	43.25	958.05
2001	785	482.61	149.06	40.12	1054.36
2002	771	544.78	170.39	38.48	1065.76
2003	735	638.66	202.74	36.55	1195.69
2004	1066	830.06	254.17	38.08	1333.91
2005	902	981.02	314.01	37.92	1503.85
2006	904	1187.74	370.11	37.94	1651.67
2007	937	1577.05	499.96	38.55	1940.52
2008	1032	2007.85	605.25	40.17	2426.13
2009	1131	2468.27	700.13	43.42	2913.56
2010	1126	3130.15	862.28	47.11	3592.13
2011	891	3552.21	1012.58	50.42	3975.38
2012	970	4066.31	1132.44	49.23	4775.92
2013	1056	4436.57	1194.88	44.27	5127.69
2014	1146	4961.12	1304.12	49.53	6048.34

12-2 续表 continued

年 份 Year	负债合计 Total Liabilities	所有者权益合计 Owners' Equities	主营业务收入 Revenue from Principal Business	利润总额 Total Profits	利税总额 Total Pre-tax Profits
1998	548.68	261.88	346.84	-1.26	14.82
1999	577.94	275.96	346.26	8.26	27.30
2000	622.46	323.72	420.42	16.11	36.29
2001	657.88	384.65	451.62	17.97	40.84
2002	643.78	412.27	541.64	25.43	51.31
2003	733.04	460.97	645.53	33.82	64.99
2004	869.30	464.60	812.46	38.57	74.23
2005	977.42	508.82	980.97	28.72	67.25
2006	1062.11	578.33	1183.51	61.46	110.23
2007	1254.01	686.51	1561.25	106.22	168.54
2008	1518.86	907.27	1928.05	84.89	168.63
2009	1779.38	1130.76	2384.52	177.20	280.68
2010	2069.29	1515.65	3011.19	245.37	373.56
2011	2295.49	1678.19	3381.27	172.94	312.78
2012	2835.55	1926.72	3758.56	167.77	320.57
2013	3049.36	2071.72	4171.21	211.26	392.14
2014	3607.62	2436.06	4493.69	226.17	401.20

注：2013年数据为全国第三次经济普查数据，以前年份未做调整。

12-3 各区县、开发区规模以上工业企业工业总产值（2014年）

Gross Output Value of Industrial Enterprises above Designated Size by Region and Development Zone (2014)

单位：亿元 (100 million yuan)

区县、开发区	Regin	单位数（个）Name of Enterprises (unit)	工业总产值 Gross Industrial Output Value	国有经济 State-owned Enterprises	集体经济 Collective-owned Enterprises	其他经济类型 Enterprises of Other Ownership
新城区	Xincheng	15	372.75	145.95		226.80
碑林区	Beilin	14	27.66			27.66
莲湖区	Lianhu	35	407.16	206.35		200.81
灞桥区	Baqiao	112	300.73	25.86	10.58	264.29
未央区	Weiyang	201	858.40	97.43	1.32	759.65
雁塔区	Yanta	237	694.34	127.24		567.10
阎良区	Yanliang	85	300.25	7.90	2.86	289.49
临潼区	Lintong	48	418.75	7.39		411.36
长安区	Chang'an	131	546.35	76.54	0.41	469.40
蓝田县	Lantian	35	46.22	8.64	0.75	36.83
周至县	Zhouzhi	37	29.10		0.57	28.53
户县	Huxian	72	104.68	15.16	0.69	88.83
高陵县	Gaoling	124	854.73	0.41		854.32
在总计中：	**Sum of Development Zones**					
高新区	GaoXin	255	937.72	76.45		861.27
经济开发区	JingKai	195	1352.68	16.68		1336.00
航空基地	Aviation Industry Base	25	18.30			18.30
航天基地	Aerospace Base	22	108.58	28.46		80.12
沣东新城	FengDongXinCheng	45	126.54	79.88	0.70	45.96

12-3 续表 continued

单位：亿元 (100 million yuan)

区县、开发区	Regin	轻工业 Light Industry	重工业 Heavy Industry	大型工业 Large-size Industry Enterprises	中型工业 Medium-size Industry Enterprises	小型工业 Small-size Industry Enterprises
新城区	Xincheng	72.25	300.50	345.11	17.88	9.76
碑林区	Beilin	11.70	15.96	7.25	13.22	7.19
莲湖区	Lianhu	44.93	362.23	375.92	20.87	10.37
灞桥区	Baqiao	52.22	248.51	47.23	24.12	229.38
未央区	Weiyang	199.14	659.26	293.34	152.68	412.38
雁塔区	Yanta	96.00	598.34	288.19	223.61	182.54
阎良区	Yanliang	62.92	237.33	154.11	23.97	122.17
临潼区	Lintong	173.32	245.43	116.91	89.29	212.55
长安区	Chang'an	61.13	485.22	378.29	71.40	96.66
蓝田县	Lantian	18.81	27.41	7.31	13.28	25.63
周至县	Zhouzhi	18.99	10.11		0.66	28.44
户县	Huxian	56.14	48.54	33.09	24.16	47.43
高陵县	Gaoling	42.70	812.03	441.26	200.34	213.13
在总计中：	**Sum of Development Zones**					
高新区	GaoXin	111.25	826.47	480.15	257.48	200.09
经济开发区	JingKai	191.45	1161.23	587.78	290.46	474.44
航空基地	Aviation Industry Base	1.86	16.44		3.30	15.00
航天基地	Aerospace Base	27.34	81.24	87.78	7.88	12.92
沣东新城	FengDongXinCheng	7.87	118.67	97.24	9.99	19.31

12-4 规模以上工业企业主要工业产品产量（2014年）

Output of Major Industrial Products of Enterprises above Designated Size(2014)

产品名称	Name of Products	2014	比上年增长（%） Increase over Preceding Year (%)
铁矿石成品矿(万吨)	Iron Orc(10 000 ton)	3.90	19.7
自来水生产量(亿立方米)	Tap Water Production (100 million cu.m)	4.30	5.2
大米(万吨)	Rice (10 000 ton)	3.95	-13.1
小麦粉(万吨)	Wheat Flour (10 000 tons)	140.49	6.4
精制食用植物油(万吨)	Edible Vegetable Oil (10 000 ton)	21.47	9.2
鲜、冷藏肉（万吨）	Fresh/Frozen Meat(10 000 ton)	4.41	18.5
饲料	Mixed Feed(10 000 ton)	116.86	11.7
配合饲料	Compound feed	26.01	22.2
混合饲料	Mixed feed	88.90	8.7
方便面(万吨)	instant Noodle(10 000 ton)	8.51	-1.2
乳制品(万吨)	Dairy Products (10 000 ton)	111.01	-16.7
液体乳(万吨)	Milk	97.74	-19.7
固体及半固体乳制品	Solid and semi-solid dairy products	13.27	15.2
饮料酒(万千升)	Beverage Wine (10 000 kiloliter)	44.73	1.6
白酒（折65度，商品量）	Liquor (as 65 degree, amount of goods)	0.07	4.6
啤酒	Beer	44.66	1.5
软饮料(万吨)	Soft Beverage (10 000 ton)	204.93	-18.4
碳酸饮料类（汽水）（万吨）	Carbonated Beverage	49.02	-4.5
果汁和蔬菜汁饮料	Juice and Fruit Beverage	45.22	15.9
包装饮用水类	Canned Drinking Water	12.62	23.8
纱(万吨)	Yarn (10 000 ton)	2.24	-14.7
1. 棉纱	Cotton Yarn	0.38	-34.2
2. 棉混纺纱	Blend Fabric	0.40	-9.1
3. 化学纤维纱	Pure Chemical-Fibre Yarn	1.46	-9.3
布(亿米)	Cloth (100 million m)	1.12	-19.7
1. 棉布	Cotton Cloth	0.34	-30.8
2. 棉混纺布	Blend Fabric	0.19	-12.8
3. 化学纤维布	Pure Chemical-Fibre Cloth	0.59	-14.2
服装（万件）	Garment (10 000 units)	749.11	1.4
梭织服装	Shuttle-Woven Garment	749.11	2.2
鞋(万双)	shoes(10000 pairs)	183.53	-10.6
皮革鞋靴（万双）	Leather Shoes (10 000 pairs)	183.53	-10.6
人造板（万立方米）	Artificial Board (10 000 cu.m)	49.47	6.7
纤维板	Fibre Board	49.47	6.7
家具（件）	Furniture (unit)	272109.00	-41.7

12-4 续表1 continued1

产品名称	Name of Products	2014	比上年增长（%） Increase over Preceding Year (%)
木质家具	Wooden Furniture	116425.00	34.1
金属家具	Metal furniture	45910.00	-28.3
软体家具	Soft Furniture (inc.: Sofa ,Mattress etc.)	92053.00	-10.0
机制纸及纸板（外购原纸加工除外）（万吨）	Machine Made Paper(not including processing of procured base paper)(10 000 ton)	11.24	-35.7
纸制品（万吨）	Paper-Made Products (10 000 ton)	10.85	21.2
瓦楞纸箱	Corrugated Paper	7.94	6.6
单色印刷（万令）	Monochrom Printed products(10 000 reams)	162.25	-6.9
多色印刷品（万对开色令）	Colored Printed products(10 000 reams)	1022.57	26.7
化学农药原药（折有效成分100%）(万吨)	Chemical Pesticide(100% effective content)(10 000 ton)	0.80	101.8
涂料（万吨）	Construction Paint(10 000 ton)	1.29	-19.0
合成洗涤剂（万吨）	Synthetic Detergents (10 000 ton)	11.59	-1.1
合成洗衣粉（万吨）	Washing Power	2.64	-16.9
液体洗涤剂	Liquid detergent	7.00	1.5
化学原料药（万吨）	Chemical Medicine (10 000 ton)	0.02	-41.5
中成药（万吨）	Traditional Chinese Medicine (10 000 ton)	0.46	-2.4
化学纤维（万吨）	Chemical Fiber	2.94	3.6
人造纤维（纤维素纤维）（万吨）	Man-made Fiber	2.44	3.6
塑料制品（万吨）	Plastic Product (10 000 ton)	15.02	5.2
水泥（万吨）	Cement (10 000 ton)	412.69	5.5
硅酸盐水泥熟料（万吨）	Portland Cement Clinker (10 000 ton)	147.33	-13.3
窑外分解窑水泥熟料（万吨）	Outside Decomposition of Kiln Cement Clinker	1.65	-63.7
水泥混凝土电杆（万根）	Cement Pole(10 000 unit)	3.40	-13.0
商品混凝土(万立方米)	Ready-mixed Concrete (10 000 cu.m)	2789.14	10.9
沥青和改性沥青防水卷材（万平方米）	Asphalt and Modified Bitumen Membrane(10 000 sq.m)	2517.12	38.4
钢化玻璃(万平方米)	Toughened Glass(10 000 sq.m)	140.13	216.0
日用玻璃制品（万吨）	Glassware(10 000 ton)	0.87	37.3
钢材（万吨）	Rolled-steel Final Products (10 000 ton)	42.87	2.3
盘条（线材）	Wire Rod	16.03	-0.9
无缝钢管	Seamless Steel Pipe	0.45	-53.8
焊接钢管	Welded Steel Pipes	0.64	-38.6
其他钢材	Other steel	25.75	8.6
铁合金（万吨）	Ferroalloy (10 000 ton)	1.10	-4.6
铝材(万吨)	Aluminum Material (10 000 ton)	4.02	43.3
黄金（千克）	Gold (kg)	262.00	-1.5
单晶硅（千克）	Monocrystalline Silicon (kg)	2973121.00	20.4
工业锅炉（蒸发量吨）	industrial Boiler steam(ton)	2459.68	-22.2
发动机（万千瓦）	Engine (10 000 kw)	330.51	-2.4
汽车发动机（万千瓦）	Motor Engine	330.51	-2.4

12-4 续表2 continued2

产品名称	Name of Products	2014	比上年增长（%） Increase over Preceding Year (%)
金属切削机床(万台)	Metal-cutting Machines (10 000 unit)	0.61	77.3
泵(万台)	Pump (Liquid pump)(10 000 unit)	3.57	236.1
风机（万台）	Fan(10 000 unit)	0.59	226.0
气体压缩机（万台）	Gas Compressor(10 000 unit)	41.04	-5.3
阀门（万吨）	Valves (10 000 ton)	0.26	276.1
铸铁件（万吨）	iron Castings (10 000 ton)	1.04	-7.3
铸钢件（万吨）	Steel Castings (10 000 ton)	5.90	114.9
锻件（万吨）	Forgings (10 000 ton)	1.44	36.1
矿山专用设备（万吨）	Mining Equipment (10 000 ton)	9.27	854.5
炼油、化工生产专用设备（万吨）	Oil Refining and Chemical industry Machine(10 000 ton)	0.51	-62.3
金属冶炼设备（吨）	Metal Smelting Equipments(ton)	10588.10	16.6
金属轧制设备（吨）	Metal-rolling Machine(ton)	1717.00	-75.5
印刷专用设备（吨）	Printing Equipment(ton)	167.00	0.0
环境污染防治设备(台/套)	Special Equipment for Environment Protection	132.00	48.3
大气污染防治设备	Equipment for Preventing Atmospheric Pollution	123.00	38.2
固体废弃物处理设备	Solid waste disposal facilities	9.00	0.0
铁路货车（辆）	Freight(unit)	2398.00	-16.3
汽车（万辆）	Motor Vehicle(10 000unit)	37.47	-11.2
基本型乘用车（轿车）（万辆）	Basic Passenger Vehicles (10 000Cars)	26.71	-15.8
1升<排量≤1.6升	1.0L- 1.6L Gas Displacement(1.6L included)	26.63	-15.2
1.6升<排量≤2.0升	1.6L-2.0L Gas Displacement(2.0L included)	0.07	-59.7
客车	Passenger Vehicles	0.12	-57.8
大型客车（车长>10）	Buses	0.06	-11.5
轻型客车（车长<7）	Large(40seats and above)	0.06	-72.0
载货汽车	Trucks	10.65	4.4
改装汽车（万辆）	Refit Trucks (10 000 ton)unit)	1.45	1.2
电动机（万千瓦）	Electric motor(Ten thousand kilowatts)	846.55	35.5
直流电动机	DC motors	52.97	9.1
交流电动机	Alternating Current Motor(10 000kw)	792.42	37.8
变压器（万千伏安）	Transformer(10 000KVA)	14793.29	28.0
高压开关板（面）	High-voltage Switch Panel(unit)	24635.00	42.3
低压开关板（万面）	Low-voltage Switch Panel(10 000 unit)	26743.00	68.8
电力电缆(万千米)	Electric Power Cables(10 000 km)	2.09	12.7
通信及电子网络用电缆(万对千米)	Communication Cables(10 000 pair km)	3.08	4.1
光缆(光纤通讯电缆)（万芯千米）	Cable (Optical Communication Cable) (10 000 Core.km)	513.96	29.2
绝缘制品(吨)	Insulating Products(ton)	8186.24	10.3
电子元件（亿只）	Electronic Components(100 million units)	2.48	3.0
工业自动化调节仪表与控制系统（万台、套）	Automatization meter and system (10 000 unit)	9.60	-36.8
电工仪器仪表（万台）	Electrical instrumentation (10 000 sets)	2.85	77.7

12-4 续表3 continued3

产品名称	Name of Products	2014	比上年增长（%） Increase over Preceding Year (%)
分析仪器及装置（万台、套）	Analysis instruments and Apparatus(10 000 sets)	3.03	-20.6
化学试剂（万吨）	Chemicals Reagents(10000 ton)	34.03	-9.2
水泥混凝土排水管（千米）	Cement concrete drain (kilometers)	1810.98	11.5
十种有色金属（吨）	Ten kinds of nonferrous metals (tonnes)	137730.00	131.3
锌	Zinc	42570.00	150.3
镍	Nickel	95160.00	123.6
金属切削工具（万件）	Metal cutting tool (ten thousand sets)	39.00	-23.5
起重机（吨）	Crane (tons)	1074.00	-6.3
金属密封件（万件）	Metal seal (ten thousand sets)	2.43	-24.5
减速机（台）	Reducer (a)	6020.00	-13.3
石油钻井设备（台/套）	Oil drilling equipment (units / sets)	2937.00	18.2
水泥专用设备（吨）	Cement equipment (tons)	3761.68	-27.7
模具（套）	Molds (sets)	27467.00	54.0
机械化农业及园艺机具（台）	Mechanization of agriculture and horticulture machinery (Tai)	20109.00	17.3
种植施肥机械	Fertilizer application	109.00	-70.9
电动自行车（辆）	Electric bicycle (cars)	597766.00	36.2
互感器（台）	Transformers (a)	4586.00	-7.0
电力电容器（千乏）	Power capacitors (kvar)	20366400.00	-15.2
高压开关设备（11万伏以上）（台）	High Voltage Switchgear (above 110,000 volts) (a)	15866.00	19.5
安全、自动化监控设备（台/套）	Security, automated monitoring equipment (units / sets)	15772.00	
灯具及照明装置（套/台/个）	Lamps and lighting equipment (sets / a)	36242.00	-36.5
移动通信手持机（手机）（台）	Mobile handset (phone) (a)	290885.00	
半导体分立器件（万只）	Discrete semiconductor devices (ten thousand)	428805.16	-27.1
光电子器件（万只/片）	Optoelectronic devices (million / tablet)	4527.50	46.0
印刷电路板（平方米）	Printed circuit board (meters)	331367.00	49.1
工业仪表（台/个）	Industrial Instrumentation (a)	21443.00	-60.7
试验机（台）	Tester (Tai)	2573.00	
环境监测专用仪器仪表（台）	Special instrumentation for environmental monitoring (a)	135613.00	106.9
汽车仪器仪表（台）	Automotive instrument (Tai)	95.15	-0.9
原油加工量（万吨）	Crude Oil Processing (10 000 ton)	148.05	-30.5
汽油（万吨）	Petrol(10 000 ton)	35.41	-27.8
柴油（万吨）	Diesel(10 000 ton)	40.43	-35.4
燃料油（万吨）	Fuel Oil(10 000 ton)	0.27	-94.7
液化石油气（万吨）	Liquefied Petroleum Gas (10 000 ton)	7.34	-19.1
石油焦（万吨）	Petroleum Coke (10 000 ton)	6.67	-89.9
石油沥青（万吨）	Petroleum Pitch (10 000 ton)	42.76	515.3
发电量（亿千瓦小时）	Power generation(One hundred million kilowatt-hours)	179.58	-2.5
火力发电量（亿千瓦小时）	Thermal power generation(One hundred million kilowatt-hours	161.05	-0.6
水力发电量（亿千瓦小时）	Hydropower(One hundred million kilowatt-hours)	16.18	-18.8
风力发电量（亿千瓦小时）	Wind power generation(One hundred million kilowatt-hours)	2.35	6.7

12-5 规模以上工业企业分行业工业增加值(2014年)

Value Added of Industrial Enterprises above Designated Size by Sector (2014)

单位:亿元 (100 million yuan)

行　业	Sector	2013	2014
总计	**Total**	**1194.88**	**1304.12**
按工业行业大类分	**Grouped by Sector**		
煤炭开采和洗选业	Mining and Washing of Coal		
石油和天然气开采业	Extraction of Petroleum and Natural Gas		
黑色金属矿采选业	Mining and Processing of Ferrous Metal Ores	0.09	0.11
有色金属矿采选业	Mining and Processing of Non-ferrous Metal Ores		
非金属矿采选业	Mining and Processing of Nonmetal Ores		
开采辅助活动	Mining Auxiliary Activities	16.87	9.09
其他采矿业	Mining of Other Ores		
农副食品加工业	Processing of Food from Agricultural Porducts	48.88	46.61
食品制造业	Manufacture of Foods	41.65	45.04
酒、饮料和精制茶制造业	Manufacture of Alcohol,Beverages and Tea	31.29	30.84
烟草制品业	Manufacture of Tobacco	0.69	0.80
纺织业	Manufacture of Textile	5.13	3.32
纺织服装、服饰业	Textile, Garments industry	4.21	5.08
皮革、毛皮、羽毛及其制品和制鞋业	Manufacture of Leather, Fur, Feather and Related Products	1.08	1.10
木材加工和木、竹、藤、棕、草制品业	Processing of Timber, Manufacture of Wood,Plam and Straw Products	4.46	4.90
家具制造业	Manufacture of Furniture	1.75	2.00
造纸及纸制品业	Manufacture of Paper and Paper Products	4.50	5.48
印刷和记录媒介复制	Printing,Reproduction of Recording Media	22.42	24.92
文教、工美、体育和娱乐用品制造业	Manufacture of Articles For Cultural,Educational and Sports Activities	6.96	24.40
石油加工业、炼焦和核燃料加工业	Processing of Petroleum, Cokeing,Processing of Nuclear and Nuclear Fuel	47.63	40.58
化学原料及化学制品制造业	Manufacture of Raw Chemical Materials and Chemical Products	49.30	59.55
医药制造业	Manufacture of Medicines	50.66	61.77
化学纤维制造业	Manufacture of Chemical Fibers	2.97	3.14
橡胶和塑料制品业	Manufacture of Rubber and Plastics	16.36	16.18
非金属矿物制品业	Manufacture of Non-metallic Mineral Products	50.10	55.76
黑色金属冶炼和压延加工业	Smelting and Pressing of Ferrous Metals	19.10	11.86
有色金属冶炼和压延加工业	Smelting and Pressing of Non-ferrous Metals	22.94	29.29
金属制品业	Manufacture of Metal Products	36.20	41.39
通用设备制造业	Manufacture of General Purpose Machinery	47.28	36.46
专用设备制造业	Manufacture of Special Equipment	73.88	84.03
汽车制造业	Manufacture of Motor Vehicle	168.35	168.84
铁路、船舶、航空航天和其他运输设备制造业	Railways, Shipbuilding,Aerospace and Other Transportation Equipment Manufacturing Industry	139.79	125.72
电气机械和器材制造业	Manufacture of Electric Equipment and Machinery	92.18	114.04
计算机、通讯和其他电子设备制造业	Manufacture of Communication Equipment, Computers and other Electronic Equipment	34.38	93.78
仪器仪表制造业	Manufacture of Measuring Instruments and Machinery	44.52	57.63
其他制造业	Manufacture of Other Manufacturing	3.77	3.54
废弃资源综合利用业	Recycling and Disposal of Waste		
金属制品、机械和设备修理业	Metal Products,Machinery and Equipment Repair Industry	0.64	0.54
电力、热力的生产和供应业	Production and Supply of Electric Power and Heat Power	89.39	76.90
燃气生产和供应业	Gas Mining and Supplying Industry	10.88	14.29
水的生产和供应业	Production and Supply of Water	4.59	5.14

注：2013年数据为第三次全国经济普查数据。

12-6 各区县、开发区规模以上工业企业主要经济指标（2014年）

Main Economic Indicators of All Industrial Enterprises above Designated Size by Region and Development Zone (2014)

区县、开发区	Region	企业单位数（个）Number of Enterprises (unit)	从业人员年平均人数（万人）Annual Average Employers (10 000 persons)	资产合计（亿元）Total Assets (100 mill yuan)	负债合计 Total Liabilites
新城区	Xingcheng	15	4.22	498.26	331.57
碑林区	Beilin	14	0.60	65.89	39.10
莲湖区	Lianhu	35	6.12	768.49	333.11
灞桥区	Baqiao	112	3.07	211.03	117.43
未央区	Weiyang	201	8.09	735.99	446.56
雁塔区	Yanta	237	8.50	1215.51	790.27
阎良区	Yanliang	85	3.46	495.57	305.63
临潼区	Lintong	48	1.51	266.00	143.98
长安区	Chang'an	131	6.77	991.98	574.06
蓝田县	Lantian	35	0.55	63.40	38.19
周至县	Zhouzhi	37	0.37	19.30	7.88
户县	Huxian	72	1.55	120.04	70.48
高陵县	Gaoling	124	4.84	596.88	409.36
在总计中：	Among of Tltal:				
高新区	GaoXin	255	11.46	1723.29	1053.69
经济开发区	JingKai	195	8.88	940.58	619.92
航空基地	Aviation Industry Base	25	0.28	35.06	17.35
航天基地	Aerospace Base	22	0.74	167.97	99.78
沣东新城	Fengdongxincheng	45	1.35	84.59	56.11

12-6 续表1 continued1

单位：亿元 (100 million yuan)

区县、开发区	Region	所有者权益合计 Total Owners' Equities	主营业务收入 Revenue from Principal Business	利润总额 Total Profits	利税总额 Total Pre-tax Profits
新城区	Xingcheng	166.69	368.01	11.94	30.23
碑林区	Beilin	26.78	28.67	2.92	4.65
莲湖区	Lianhu	435.69	395.14	23.37	41.90
灞桥区	Baqiao	91.65	262.83	29.03	40.05
未央区	Weiyang	289.28	831.55	37.55	85.49
雁塔区	Yanta	425.23	675.60	43.71	74.26
阎良区	Yanliang	188.68	302.64	2.90	5.91
临潼区	Lintong	120.97	317.25	7.76	14.23
长安区	Chang'an	417.85	492.00	23.04	35.17
蓝田县	Lantian	25.03	37.44	1.47	2.21
周至县	Zhouzhi	11.13	24.03	1.29	1.91
户县	Huxian	49.56	100.06	4.01	9.08
高陵县	Gaoling	187.52	648.47	37.18	56.11
在总计中：	Among of Tltal:				
高新区	GaoXin	669.59	876.43	52.35	88.27
经济开发区	JingKai	320.61	1112.85	89.31	139.82
航空基地	Aviation Industry Base	17.71	13.10	0.44	0.68
航天基地	Aerospace Base	68.19	93.87	5.24	7.27
沣东新城	Fengdongxincheng	28.37	131.41	-3.25	10.48

12-7 主要年份规模以上工业企业经济效益指标（2014年）

Indicators of Economic Benefit of Industrial Enterprises above Designated Size in Representative Years(2014)

年 份 Year	总资产贡献率 (%) Ratio of Total Assets to Industrial Output Value (%)	资产负债率 (%) Assets-Liability Ratio (%)	流动资产周转次数 (次/年) Rate of Annual Turnover Working Capitals (times/year)	成本费用利润率 (%) Ratio of Profits to Cost (%)	全员劳动生产率 (元/人·年) Overall Labor Productivity (yuan/person稞ear)	产品销售率 (%) Proportion of Industrial Products Sold (%)
1998		67.7	0.9	-266.1	19185	95.3
1999		67.7	0.9	2.5	22878	95.9
2000		65.0	1.0	4.2	29496	97.1
2001	5.8	62.4	0.9	4.1	38267	96.7
2002	6.2	60.4	1.1	5.1	46940	96.7
2003	7.0	61.3	1.1	5.7	58801	96.3
2004	6.9	65.2	1.2	5.0	66752	97.9
2005	8.4	65.0	1.3	3.1	82815	97.5
2006	7.8	64.3	1.4	5.5	97561	98.2
2007	10.2	64.6	1.6	7.3	129706	96.8
2008	8.6	62.6	1.5	4.6	150641	96.1
2009	11.3	61.1	1.7	8.1	161289	97.6
2010	12.2	57.6	1.7	8.8	188483	97.1
2011	8.6	57.7	1.5	5.2	194105	97.4
2012	7.7	59.4	1.5	4.5	230032	96.7
2013	8.5	59.5	1.5	5.2	264324	95.7
2014	7.4	59.7	1.4	5.2	275288	94.9

12-8 规模以上工业企业主要经济指标（2014年）

单位：万元

分组	Classify	企业单位数（个） Number of Enterprises (unit)	亏损企业 Loss Making Enterprises	工业总产值（当年价格） Gross Industrial Output Value (At Current Prices)
总计	**Total**	**1146**	**226**	**49611217.8**
#市区	Urban	878	163	38812086.8
#亏损企业	Deficit Enterprises	226	226	7224053.1
按隶属关系分	**Grouped by Jurisdiction of Management**			
中央企业	Central Enterprises	85	16	12450012.3
省属企业	Provincial Enterprises	73	21	8484267.8
市属企业	Municipal Enterprises	988	189	28676937.7
按登记注册类型分组	**Grouped by Registion Status**			
内资企业	Domestic Investment Enterprises	1025	189	40979348.7
国有	State-owned Enterprises	45	6	7188683.4
集体	Collective-owned Enterprises	13		171825.6
股份合作	Share-holding Corperative	9		165201.7
联营	Joint Ownership Enterprises			
国有联营	State Joint Ownership Enterprises			
集体联营	Collective Joint Ownership Enterprises			
国有与集体联营	Joint State-collective Ownership Enterprises			
其他联营	Other Joint Ownership Enterprises			
有限责任公司	Limited Liability Corporations	576	120	25430459.5
国有独资公司	State Sole Funded Enterprises	37	11	4148308.2
其他有限责任公司	Other Limited Liability Corporation	539	109	21282151.3
股份有限公司	Share-holding Corperation Ltd.	79	12	3351577.8
私营	Private Enterprises	302	51	4667700.7
私营独资	Private-funded Enterprises	12		185274.3
私营合伙	Private Partnership Enterprises	1		3551.9
私营有限责任公司	Private Limited Liability Corporations	274	50	4222498.3
私营股份有限公司	Private Share Holding Corporations	15	1	256376.2
其他	Other Domestic Funded Enterprises	1		3900.0
港澳台商投资	Enterprises with Funds from Hong Kong,Macao and Taiwan	25	9	882458.1
外商投资	Foreign Funded Enterprises	96	28	7749411.0
按轻重工业分	**Grouped by Light Industry and Heavy Industry**			
轻工业	Light Industry	300	56	9102567.0
重工业	Heavy Industry	846	170	40508650.8

Main Economic Indicators of All Industrial Enterprises above Designated Size (2014)

(10 000yuan)

工业销售产值（当年价）Value of Industry Products Sales (At Current Prices)	出口交货值 Export Delivery Value	从业人员年平均人数（人）Annual Average Employers (person)	资产总计 Total Assets	流动资产合计 Total Working Capitals	固定资产合计 Total Fixed Assets	固定资产原价 Origing Value of Fixed Assets	累计折旧 Accumulative Total Depreciation
47087524.2	**3494766.7**	**496495.0**	**60483423.1**	**31778991.2**	**19760762.4**	**29231574.9**	**11182327.6**
36964864.3	3093259.3	420665.0	52141866.6	27014685.5	17833421.9	26521711.5	10167350.5
7087339.5	330342.4	105353.0	11252767.1	6379781.3	2680271.3	3995778.3	1509753.5
12219262.2	580196.9	189585.0	24495957.1	12105161.3	9149861.9	13746967.6	5709399.7
8096464.5	356464.9	67262.0	8074644.7	4853031.2	1475501.9	2260625.5	880028.2
26771797.5	2558104.9	239648.0	27912821.3	14820798.7	9135398.6	13223981.8	4592899.7
39228366.5	2292464.2	418103.0	49857412.1	28032981.0	14460203.5	22315559.8	9330802.6
7131176.4	139801.3	87343.0	11313415.9	5670997.2	3634326.0	5842307.1	2533185.1
161110.0		2671.0	102960.7	57920.7	37567.0	52566.0	21672.7
164622.0		1890.0	258561.4	196443.8	19008.8	35961.6	17062.2
24223027.1	1248078.1	253411.0	30606136.4	17422933.0	8926187.2	13242089.0	5291345.9
3965987.3	348203.3	69779.0	10067323.7	4534106.5	4319487.6	6334955.2	2533524.8
20257039.8	899874.8	183632.0	20538812.7	12888826.5	4606699.6	6907133.8	2757821.1
2815149.5	440581.2	35736.0	4636517.8	2919540.3	1153169.5	1975434.9	931119.9
4729418.5	464003.6	36923.0	2936671.0	1763489.5	688452.6	1165352.6	536060.6
179307.2		1058.0	74014.6	22034.2	47444.4	58002.0	10980.1
3551.9		95.0	2970.7	2320.0	650.7	862.7	212.0
4295012.5	463996.7	33812.0	2616799.1	1613577.3	616518.4	1070821.4	512665.6
251546.9	6.9	1958.0	242886.6	125558.0	23839.1	35666.5	12202.9
3863.0		129.0	3148.9	1656.5	1492.4	1848.6	356.2
792310.6	71684.4	6529.0	554600.9	287958.4	150418.0	242494.6	106532.9
7066847.1	1130618.1	71863.0	10071410.1	3458051.8	5150140.9	6673520.5	1744992.1
8757093.7	626053.8	80626.0	6249906.0	3642749.2	1678068.0	3317870.0	1793304.7
38330430.5	2868712.9	415869.0	54233517.1	28136242.0	18082694.4	25913704.9	9389022.9

12-8 续表1

单位：万元

分组	Classify	负债合计 Total Liabilites	流动负债合计 Total Working Liabilities	非流动负债 Non-Working Liabilities
总计	**Total**	**36076191.0**	**27029706.1**	**5421454.3**
#市区	Urban	30566105.7	22428526.4	4847212.6
#亏损企业	Deficit Enterprises	7580289.1	6336617.6	1023326.0
按隶属关系分	**Grouped by Jurisdiction of Management**			
中央企业	Central Enterprises	14640534.3	9364755.6	2512921.6
省属企业	Provincial Enterprises	5346101.1	4546671.1	557374.6
市属企业	Municipal Enterprises	16089555.6	13118279.4	2351158.1
按登记注册类型分组	**Grouped by Registion Status**			
内资企业	Domestic Investment Enterprises	29844345.4	22122374.6	4335738.2
国有	State-owned Enterprises	6286996.8	4663126.6	1573643.9
集体	Collective-owned Enterprises	61180.8	48615.5	766.3
股份合作	Share-holding Corperative	215537.8	180679.5	34473.6
联营	Joint Ownership Enterprises			
国有联营	State Joint Ownership Enterprises			
集体联营	Collective Joint Ownership Enterprises			
国有与集体联营	Joint State-collective Ownership Enterprises			
其他联营	Other Joint Ownership Enterprises			
有限责任公司	Limited Liability Corporations	19201569.1	14088483.6	2102470.0
国有独资公司	State Sole Funded Enterprises	6328375.1	2990478.3	612557.7
其他有限责任公司	Other Limited Liability Corporation	12873194.0	11098005.3	1489912.3
股份有限公司	Share-holding Corperation Ltd.	2441660.8	1899494.2	479690.7
私营	Private Enterprises	1634635.8	1239250.9	144653.7
私营独资	Private-funded Enterprises	22320.1	10991.2	7043.8
私营合伙	Private Partnership Enterprises	2216.1	249.1	1967.0
私营有限责任公司	Private Limited Liability Corporations	1528043.2	1169965.1	123137.7
私营股份有限公司	Private Share Holding Corporations	82056.4	58045.5	12505.2
其他	Other Domestic Funded Enterprises	2764.3	2724.3	40.0
港澳台商投资	Enterprises with Funds from Hong Kong,Macao and Taiwan	322634.5	221913.8	48915.0
外商投资	Foreign Funded Enterprises	5909211.1	4685417.7	1036801.1
按轻重工业分	**Grouped by Light Industry and Heavy Industry**			
轻工业	Light Industry	3487895.3	2931892.5	399728.9
重工业	Heavy Industry	32588295.7	24097813.6	5021725.4

continued1

(10 000yuan)

所有者权益合计 Total Owners' Equities	实收资本 Total Capital Hold	营业收入 Total Revenue	主营业务收入 Revenue from Principal Business	营业成本 Total Cost	主营业务成本 Cost of Principal Business	营业税金及附加 Taxs and Other Changes	主营业务税金及附加 Taxes and Other Charges on Principal Business
24360628.5	**11207334.0**	**45662035.3**	**44836936.2**	**38753771.9**	**38111768.6**	**338267.9**	**333160.7**
21533861.2	9542603.3	37056312.5	36413326.7	31245648.4	30747487.1	312389.6	307495.8
3673431.4	2576211.8	6641289.2	6528558.1	6102788.3	6038448.0	164064.9	163668.2
9839962.4	3469284.0	13837144.9	13650259.5	11943117.3	11798739.5	170966.0	168612.3
2734692.5	1294325.6	7157612.6	6882329.7	6063752.2	5843819.9	24989.2	24533.8
11785973.6	6443724.4	24667277.8	24304347.0	20746902.4	20469209.2	142312.7	140014.6
19966970.3	8076984.9	38337181.0	37709187.5	32818426.0	32327234.8	271604.3	266750.3
5010971.7	1413979.0	7108450.5	6872064.8	6080014.4	5882308.0	135214.2	133854.3
41061.7	12661.9	180002.7	179612.6	152162.1	151961.8	630.0	630.0
43023.4	19326.2	102782.8	102254.0	92168.3	91878.3	280.0	280.0
11388057.9	4998655.5	23813825.4	23480687.8	20548482.7	20291209.5	104250.5	100937.6
3738948.6	1423907.7	4788852.2	4704818.3	4010918.2	3951439.7	32012.8	29671.9
7649109.3	3574747.8	19024973.2	18775869.5	16537564.5	16339769.8	72237.7	71265.7
2194700.7	993983.4	2736900.6	2707168.6	2143714.2	2122355.3	15009.2	14887.8
1288770.3	638178.9	4391356.0	4363536.7	3798407.6	3784045.2	16202.1	16142.3
50299.3	53810.2	178935.7	178530.4	159719.2	158493.8	473.3	473.2
754.6	600.0	3551.9	3551.9	2989.3	2989.3	10.2	10.2
1076886.3	513961.4	3956596.2	3930266.3	3427634.0	3415235.9	14285.5	14225.8
160830.1	69807.3	252272.2	251188.1	208065.1	207326.2	1433.1	1433.1
384.6	200.0	3863.0	3863.0	3476.7	3476.7	18.3	18.3
231466.4	225943.2	799139.7	778271.4	703912.7	699300.9	1567.3	1567.3
4162191.8	2904405.9	6525714.6	6349477.3	5231433.2	5085232.9	65096.3	64843.1
2740243.6	1354884.3	8122876.2	8045648.4	6450748.7	6373098.5	45890.1	45082.5
21620384.9	9852449.7	37539159.1	36791287.8	32303023.2	31738670.1	292377.8	288078.2

12-8 续表2

单位：万元

分组	Classify	销售费用 Expenses for Sales	管理费用 Expenses for Management	财务费用 Financial cost
总计	**Total**	**1614290.1**	**2572651.0**	**496967.3**
#市区	Urban	1368759.3	2216240.9	428770.7
#亏损企业	Deficit Enterprises	195431.3	421936.7	110210.6
按隶属关系分	**Grouped by Jurisdiction of Management**			
中央企业	Central Enterprises	260352.2	936407.1	248166.1
省属企业	Provincial Enterprises	352011.8	354263.8	58472.8
市属企业	Municipal Enterprises	1001926.1	1281980.1	190328.4
按登记注册类型分组	**Grouped by Registion Status**			
内资企业	Domestic Investment Enterprises	1149786.0	2128921.4	443550.1
国有	State-owned Enterprises	167737.1	465752.4	86180.5
集体	Collective-owned Enterprises	3900.7	6227.2	378.4
股份合作	Share-holding Corperative	5153.5	5526.3	2985.2
联营	Joint Ownership Enterprises			
国有联营	State Joint Ownership Enterprises			
集体联营	Collective Joint Ownership Enterprises			
国有与集体联营	Joint State-collective Ownership Enterprises			
其他联营	Other Joint Ownership Enterprises			
有限责任公司	Limited Liability Corporations	666781.3	1290491.3	269873.5
国有独资公司	State Sole Funded Enterprises	88894.4	347128.2	118617.5
其他有限责任公司	Other Limited Liability Corporation	577886.9	943363.1	151256.0
股份有限公司	Share-holding Corperation Ltd.	158750.7	201176.8	49522.0
私营	Private Enterprises	147437.9	159643.3	34463.0
私营独资	Private-funded Enterprises	1166.8	1261.2	450.9
私营合伙	Private Partnership Enterprises	294.1	161.5	75.1
私营有限责任公司	Private Limited Liability Corporations	133467.9	141937.4	31451.6
私营股份有限公司	Private Share Holding Corporations	12509.1	16283.2	2485.4
其他	Other Domestic Funded Enterprises	24.8	104.1	147.5
港澳台商投资	Enterprises with Funds from Hong Kong,Macao and Taiwan	31258.5	26860.3	3184.4
外商投资	Foreign Funded Enterprises	433245.6	416869.3	50232.8
按轻重工业分	**Grouped by Light Industry and Heavy Industry**			
轻工业	Light Industry	744891.7	412465.4	59015.2
重工业	Heavy Industry	869398.4	2160185.6	437952.1

continued 2

(10 000yuan)

营业利润 Operating Profit	利润总额 Total Profits	亏损企业亏损额 Total Loss of Deficit Enterprises	利税总额 Total Pre-tax Profits	应付职工薪酬 Salary Payable	本年应交增值税 Value Added Tax Payable
1882560.8	**2261732.6**	**303786.3**	**4012039.1**	**3631499.4**	**1412038.6**
1481412.0	1814429.2	263672.5	3305289.8	3273340.4	1178471.0
-370864.8	-303786.3	303786.3	-38336.4	637227.2	101385.0
360680.8	449241.2	97490.3	1032528.5	1753041.6	412321.3
278229.9	311076.4	49963.9	571261.2	444645.9	235195.6
1243650.1	1501415.0	156332.1	2408249.4	1433811.9	764521.7
1510086.0	1728526.4	222424.4	3086010.9	3039919.7	1085880.2
229684.6	281588.1	53312.1	629217.5	816181.3	212415.2
17407.8	16807.7		21619.2	8593.2	4181.5
-3207.5	2410.1		8604.7	5581.7	5914.6
884808.1	1011471.8	121646.2	1769488.4	1801330.9	653766.1
191205.1	239168.2	29236.0	493148.6	538276.9	221967.6
693603.0	772303.6	92410.2	1276339.8	1263054.0	431798.5
149909.9	171162.1	37985.7	271669.1	255959.8	85497.8
231391.5	244995.0	9480.4	385192.1	151963.8	123995.0
15678.2	15678.2		21927.6	5594.1	5776.1
21.7	21.7		134.0	378.8	102.1
206226.6	218371.5	9306.4	347227.3	137475.8	114570.3
9465.0	10923.6	174.0	15903.2	8515.1	3546.5
91.6	91.6		219.9	309.0	110.0
18564.8	19362.3	26247.1	60470.5	52936.8	39540.9
353910.0	513843.9	55114.8	865557.7	538642.9	286617.5
441731.3	475648.7	24778.3	870000.9	558305.2	348462.1
1440829.5	1786083.9	279008.0	3142038.2	3073194.2	1063576.5

12-8 续表3

单位：万元

分 组	Classify	企业单位数（个） Number of Enterprises (unit)	亏损企业 Loss Making Enterprises	工业总产值（当年价格） Gross Industrial Output Value (At Current Prices)
按企业规模分	**Grouped by Size of Enterprises**			
大型企业	Large-size	61	7	24880136.3
中型企业	Medium-size	161	32	8875553.2
小型企业	Small-size	924	187	15855528.3
微型企业	Microenterprise			
按经济组织类型分组	**Grouped by Economic Type of Orgnization**			
独资企业	Appropratorship	116	22	10001812.5
合作、合伙企业	Partnership	13		179383.1
股份有限公司	Corporaton	97	13	3927585.5
有限责任公司	Limited Liability Company	920	191	35502436.7
按控股情况分	**Grouped by Cast strand**			
国有控股	State owned shares	235	54	26366390.7
集体控股	Collective shares	38	3	1334604.3
私人控股	Private holdings	724	129	14914379.4
港澳台控股	Hong Kong and Macao Holdings	21	9	840560.3
外商投资	Foreign Investment	66	19	5020346.2
其他	Others	62	12	1134936.9
按工业行业大类分	**Grouped by Sector**			
煤炭开采和洗选业	Mining and Washing of Coal			
石油和天然气开采业	Extraction of Petroleum and Natural Gas			
黑色金属矿采选业	Mining and Processing of Ferrous Metal Ores	1		3800.0
有色金属矿采选业	Mining and Processing of Non-ferrous Metal Ores			
非金属矿采选业	Mining and Processing of Nonmetal Ores			
开采辅助活动	Mining Auxiliary Activities	3	1	154770.9
其他采矿业	Mining of other Ores			
农副食品加工业	Processing of Food from Agricultural Porducts	55	14	2207419.0
食品制造业	Manufacture of Foods	37	3	1588297.9
酒、饮料和精制茶制造业	Manufacture of Alcohol,Beverages and Tea	17	6	820676.7
烟草制品业	Manufacture of Tobacco	1		9862.6
纺织业	Manufacture of Textile	9	2	115659.7
纺织服装、服饰业	Textile, apparel industry	7	1	155602.0
皮革、毛皮、羽毛及其制品和制鞋业	Manufacture of Leather, Fur, Feather and Related Products, and Shoes	2	1	41432.5
木材加工和木、竹、藤、	Processing of Timber, Manufacture of Wood,Plam	7	2	157797.5

continued 3

(10 000yuan)

工业销售产值（当年价）Value of Industry Products Sales (At Current Prices)	出口交货值 Export Delivery Value	从业人员年平均人数（人）Annual Average Employers (person)	资产总计 Total Assets	流动资产合计 Total Working Capitals	固定资产合计 Total Fixed Assets	固定资产原价 Origing Value of Fixed Assets	累计折旧 Accumulative Total Depreciation
23972256.4	2056669.8	296345.0	39819215.9	19015018.7	14961802.3	21670921.0	7913200.7
7923774.6	626836.8	94355.0	9492142.6	5742091.5	2348340.7	3581942.0	1507242.0
15191493.2	811260.1	105795.0	11172064.6	7021881.0	2450619.4	3978711.9	1761884.9
9653245.0	1018313.3	111263.0	16980205.9	6904732.9	7539764.4	10557908.6	3382190.6
178399.3	927.2	2269.0	272692.2	204611.8	24682.3	39674.9	18212.6
3318713.7	606429.4	39676.0	5270340.5	3236819.0	1334324.3	2485667.2	1260572.9
33937166.2	1869096.8	343287.0	37960184.5	21432827.5	10861991.4	16148324.2	6521351.5
25297515.7	1300469.0	296186.0	38860268.4	21263294.3	11997425.5	18059145.9	7374187.4
1277550.9	314919.4	10586.0	1283679.9	740456.2	386964.9	792176.8	425861.3
14326397.6	688338.7	136861.0	11367080.8	6587582.2	2664606.7	4209547.7	1792858.3
772373.9	71470.3	5311.0	361873.4	146746.7	132960.8	209561.5	91057.0
4378905.8	1052831.2	33484.0	7273954.0	2179635.1	4260684.2	5500473.5	1342161.5
1034780.3	66738.1	14067.0	1336566.6	861276.7	318120.3	460669.5	156202.1
3800.0		85.0	2136.8	1673.9	335.2	1036.1	701.3
156020.9		11363.0	226490.3	114819.5	102466.8	170878.1	68106.6
2185278.4	7226.0	8920.0	840151.5	488160.7	201423.2	491497.8	297681.8
1495951.6	374.0	12689.0	657248.8	322750.5	220196.3	394059.1	189904.1
907892.3	168012.4	7798.0	1013530.2	505175.0	342200.8	820679.0	478965.1
10288.6		297.0	22262.6	9238.7	3763.8	6743.4	2979.6
95633.4	6083.4	5838.0	130827.8	87253.6	25929.0	63856.6	37927.6
130758.5	152.9	2280.0	132218.5	106022.4	17097.2	22454.6	5867.6
41787.3		1020.0	53798.7	31481.3	3079.6	5972.1	2892.5
139073.7		871.0	163631.5	72092.7	55021.6	87806.8	45430.4

12-8 续表4

单位：万元

分组	Classify	负债合计 Total Liabilites	流动负债合计 Total Working Liabilities	非流动负债 Non-Working Liabilities
按企业规模分	**Grouped by Size of Enterprises**			
大型企业	Large-size	24078604.6	17346912.3	3962163.9
中型企业	Medium-size	5516337.9	4251876.9	912455.8
小型企业	Small-size	6481248.5	5430916.9	546834.6
微型企业	Microenterprise			
按经济组织类型分组	**Grouped by Economic Type of Orgnization**			
独资企业	Appropratorship	9486464.6	7099873.5	2319536.7
合作、合伙企业	Partnership	225118.5	187393.5	36880.6
股份有限公司	Corporaton	2774941.1	2136531.7	564427.8
有限责任公司	Limited Liability Company	23589666.8	17605907.4	2500609.2
按控股情况分	**Grouped by Cast strand**			
国有控股	State owned shares	23813239.1	17375785.9	3630176.4
集体控股	Collective shares	692130.1	590909.8	88449.5
私人控股	Private holdings	6417047.4	5008654.8	797089.4
港澳台控股	Hong Kong and Macao Holdings	223584.9	180177.0	14246.1
外商投资	Foreign Investment	4167926.2	3173349.5	831122.4
其他	Others	762263.3	700829.1	60370.5
按工业行业大类分	**Grouped by Sector**			
煤炭开采和洗选业	Mining and Washing of Coal			
石油和天然气开采业	Extraction of Petroleum and Natural Gas			
黑色金属矿采选业	Mining and Processing of Ferrous Metal Ores	3937.7	1170.3	2767.4
有色金属矿采选业	Mining and Processing of Non-ferrous Metal Ores			
非金属矿采选业	Mining and Processing of Nonmetal Ores			
开采辅助活动	Mining Auxiliary Activities	157601.3	82358.9	75242.4
其他采矿业	Mining of other Ores			
农副食品加工业	Processing of Food from Agricultural Porducts	634042.7	536346.9	44308.7
食品制造业	Manufacture of Foods	271066.7	250627.5	17740.0
酒、饮料和精制茶制造业	Manufacture of Alcohol,Beverages and Tea	602095.3	513714.9	81796.4
烟草制品业	Manufacture of Tobacco	14125.6	14125.6	0.0
纺织业	Manufacture of Textile	78361.9	67538.8	4362.9
纺织服装、服饰业	Textile, apparel industry	87354.9	62115.8	23599.1
皮革、毛皮、羽毛及其制品和制鞋业	Manufacture of Leather, Fur, Feather and Related Products, and Shoes	23079.2	18590.8	4488.4
木材加工和木、竹、藤、	Processing of Timber, Manufacture of Wood,Plam	97916.7	44915.2	53001.5

continued 4

(10 000yuan)

所有者权益合计 Total Owners' Equities	实收资本 Total Capital Hold	营业收入 Total Revenue	主营业务收入 Revenue from Principal Business	营业成本 Total Cost	主营业务成本 Cost of Principal Business	营业税金及附加 Taxs and Other Changes	主营业务税金及附加 Taxes and Other Charges on Principal Business
15725154.7	6226222.6	24092336.5	23604470.2	20527797.4	20132980.7	255633.0	252698.9
3975647.7	1916380.6	7432864.8	7205664.0	5985202.1	5808906.8	33034.8	31443.9
4659826.1	3064730.8	14136834.0	14026802.0	12240772.4	12169881.1	49600.1	49017.9
7476178.2	3622557.9	9721872.6	9454418.2	8165274.6	7918816.5	145715.9	144355.8
47572.5	23034.2	116470.1	115941.3	104068.3	103778.3	310.1	310.1
2495242.9	1092868.7	3151651.0	3118675.0	2503603.3	2461558.6	17531.7	17334.4
14341634.9	6468873.2	32672041.6	32147901.7	27980825.7	27627615.2	174710.2	171160.4
15031566.8	5927128.2	25329091.3	24754520.3	21908950.0	21475505.5	221787.4	217209.3
590831.5	315479.1	1217936.4	1195911.1	993130.1	976398.3	4212.2	4212.2
4920275.9	2014462.9	13154875.2	13023819.2	11224084.5	11135428.1	87272.9	87097.9
137788.5	194491.9	757883.2	737463.0	678401.0	674091.4	1246.9	1246.9
3106023.8	2381421.9	4178532.9	4120424.1	3142999.3	3060548.5	18740.1	18494.7
574142.0	374350.0	1023716.3	1004798.5	806207.0	789796.8	5008.4	4899.7
-1800.9	600.0	3016.0	3016.0	2457.7	2457.7	103.4	103.4
68889.0	14982.7	298590.0	295809.0	277192.1	273363.4	1070.0	1068.8
190778.1	101903.9	1919947.5	1906881.5	1764967.2	1761620.8	2501.1	2478.4
383676.6	164695.4	1376775.7	1355426.6	1117729.0	1097972.9	4464.0	4464.0
411431.2	274188.4	817725.8	802510.9	623968.5	590875.0	14396.1	14314.5
8137.0	1514.7	11230.3	10978.8	5282.5	5216.2	118.6	118.6
52465.8	30942.9	104683.1	104682.1	87456.4	87456.4	507.5	506.6
44863.5	19700.0	141280.4	141075.3	112677.0	112408.2	2722.6	2719.0
30719.4	12500.0	41778.0	41778.0	36498.0	36018.3	200.8	200.8
65714.7	18640.0	119959.6	119796.9	111447.2	111124.6	378.0	377.8

12-8 续表5

单位：万元

分　组	Classify	销售费用 Expenses for Sales	管理费用 Expenses for Management	财务费用 Financial cost
按企业规模分	**Grouped by Size of Enterprises**			
大型企业	Large-size	809030.4	1486318.6	326793.5
中型企业	Medium-size	382628.0	480124.5	78800.1
小型企业	Small-size	422631.7	606207.9	91373.7
微型企业	Microenterprise			
按经济组织类型分组	**Grouped by Economic Type of Orgnization**			
独资企业	Appropratorship	315255.1	707540.5	102679.4
合作、合伙企业	Partnership	5698.7	6274.5	3293.9
股份有限公司	Corporaton	179697.0	227913.7	63966.8
有限责任公司	Limited Liability Company	1113639.3	1630922.3	327027.2
按控股情况分	**Grouped by Cast strand**			
国有控股	State owned shares	583076.2	1532073.8	314271.7
集体控股	Collective shares	55817.2	63059.6	13617.4
私人控股	Private holdings	534304.1	572781.3	116720.0
港澳台控股	Hong Kong and Macao Holdings	29358.2	18617.5	2173.6
外商投资	Foreign Investment	350513.5	318388.3	37403.7
其他	Others	61220.9	67730.5	12780.9
按工业行业大类分	**Grouped by Sector**			
煤炭开采和洗选业	Mining and Washing of Coal			
石油和天然气开采业	Extraction of Petroleum and Natural Gas			
黑色金属矿采选业	Mining and Processing of Ferrous Metal Ores	25.2	423.1	132.8
有色金属矿采选业	Mining and Processing of Non-ferrous Metal Ores			
非金属矿采选业	Mining and Processing of Nonmetal Ores			
开采辅助活动	Mining Auxiliary Activities	3549.6	3593.3	374.4
其他采矿业	Mining of other Ores			
农副食品加工业	Processing of Food from Agricultural Porducts	54446.2	41278.6	12994.3
食品制造业	Manufacture of Foods	139697.6	47106.4	-1655.1
酒、饮料和精制茶制造业	Manufacture of Alcohol,Beverages and Tea	104397.2	33748.0	9068.5
烟草制品业	Manufacture of Tobacco	165.5	2026.3	-15.2
纺织业	Manufacture of Textile	1987.7	7045.2	310.2
纺织服装、服饰业	Textile, apparel industry	5373.8	5680.4	2482.5
皮革、毛皮、羽毛及其制品和制鞋业	Manufacture of Leather, Fur, Feather and Related Products, and Shoes	1132.1	1868.8	272.6
木材加工和木、竹、藤、	Processing of Timber, Manufacture of Wood,Plam	1645.6	3866.6	1507.0

continued 5

(10 000yuan)

营业利润 Operating Profit	利润总额 Total Profits	亏损企业亏损额 Total Loss of Deficit Enterprises	利税总额 Total Pre-tax Profits	应付职工薪酬 Salary Payable	本年应交增值税 Value Added Tax Payable
750225.2	1025536.0	102395.5	2026870.2	2434783.3	745701.2
451674.2	509806.5	83198.1	799417.4	607325.6	256576.1
680661.4	726390.1	118192.7	1185751.5	589390.5	409761.3
336906.3	481741.7	93725.0	901343.9	994879.4	273886.3
-3058.5	2649.2		9151.3	6852.5	6192.0
156583.1	188165.9	38159.7	305546.8	281529.3	99849.2
1392129.9	1589175.8	171901.6	2795997.1	2348238.2	1032111.1
802278.4	972662.9	185494.8	1891859.8	2492723.3	697409.5
84146.5	86878.0	1243.7	124960.9	76135.8	33870.7
579312.2	674414.9	51808.6	1119110.2	637269.7	357422.4
14254.7	15084.5	26247.1	54306.8	47787.8	37975.4
333160.7	435989.4	26237.0	690399.8	295449.7	235670.3
69408.3	76702.9	12755.1	131401.6	82133.1	49690.3
41.4	41.4		212.6	163.4	67.8
10915.1	10355.6	3249.2	12763.3	34497.9	1337.7
21891.2	31755.6	3642.9	65169.0	55630.4	30912.3
70503.6	72434.8	1631.1	109427.1	108689.0	32528.3
51530.5	60513.5	11097.4	119984.4	69108.0	45074.8
3650.2	3647.8		4704.2	2956.8	937.8
7123.5	8757.0	1027.7	13383.0	14787.3	4118.5
12869.1	12960.3	24.2	19711.7	7354.9	4028.8
2606.9	2657.2	102.9	3364.3	5476.5	506.3
1861.3	3828.2	424.6	10104.3	5212.9	5898.1

12-8 续表6

单位：万元

分 组	Classify	企业单位数（个）Number of Enterprises (unit)	亏损企业 Loss Making Enterprises	工业总产值（当年价格）Gross Industrial Output Value (At Current Prices)
棕、草制品业	and Straw Products			
家具制造业	Manufacture of Furniture	10	1	66283.8
造纸及纸制品业	Manufacture of Paper and Paper Products	19	3	172232.2
印刷和记录媒介复制	Printing,Reproduction of Recording Media	22	3	592549.9
文教、工美、体育和娱乐用品制造业	Manufacture of Articles For Cultural,Educational and Sports Activities	9	3	508202.2
石油加工业、炼焦和核燃料加工业	Processing of Petroleum, Cokeing,Processing of Nuclear and Nuclear Fuel	8	1	2383561.6
化学原料及化学制品制造业	Manufacture of Raw Chemical Materials and Chemical Products	67	10	1974067.7
医药制造业	Manufacture of Medicines	49	8	1776348.2
化学纤维制造业	Manufacture of Chemical Fibers	4	1	105725.6
橡胶和塑料制品业	Manufacture of Rubber and Plastics	28	2	715563.8
非金属矿物制品业	Manufacture of Non-metallic Mineral Products	99	26	1993273.0
黑色金属冶炼和压延加工业	Smelting and Pressing of Ferrous Metals	20	5	547682.1
有色金属冶炼和压延加工业	Smelting and Pressing of Non-ferrous Metals	41	12	1852560.1
金属制品业	Manufacture of Metal Products	58	9	1508015.9
通用设备制造业	Manufacture of General Purpose Machinery	78	9	1656586.5
专用设备制造业	Manufacture of Special Equipment	108	27	2699662.7
汽车制造业	Manufacture of Motor Vehicle	48	13	9059950.7
铁路、船舶、航空航天和其他运输设备制造业	Railways,Shipbuilding,Aerospace and Other Transportation Equipment Manufacturing Industry	60	7	4611056.1
电气机械和器材制造业	Manufacture of Electric Equipment and Machinery	125	19	4951079.1
计算机、通讯和其他电子设备制造业	Manufacture of Communication Equipment, Computers and other Electronic Equipment	67	14	2584954.3
仪器仪表制造业	Manufacture of Measuring Instruments and Machinery	47	9	1649418.8
其他制造业	Manufacture of Other Manufacturing	7	3	49141.0
废弃资源综合利用业	Recycling and Disposal of Waste			
金属制品、机械和设备修理业	Metal Products,Machinery and Equipment Repair Industry	4	1	15831.4
电力、热力的生产和供应业	Production and Supply of Electric Power and Heat Power	15	7	2357431.6
燃气生产和供应业	Gas Mining and Supplying Industry	10	2	431621.9
水的生产和供应业	Production and Supply of Water	4	1	93098.8

continued 6

(10 000yuan)

工业销售产值（当年价） Value of Industry Products Sales (At Current Prices)	出口交货值 Export Delivery Value	从业人员年平均人数（人） Annual Average Employers (person)	资产总计 Total Assets	流动资产合计 Total Working Capitals	固定资产合计 Total Fixed Assets	固定资产原价 Origing Value of Fixed Assets	累计折旧 Accumulative Total Depreciation
59634.5		1398.0	56479.2	34561.2	13301.4	19420.3	11671.4
169828.0		2463.0	118244.4	56743.7	23847.3	33307.4	13610.3
569496.7	633.2	7456.0	611802.2	291225.2	243394.6	425656.1	207819.7
507756.5	425460.2	824.0	185726.2	175836.6	9110.1	14801.6	5691.5
2366842.4		6032.0	566742.4	274171.7	291145.4	354985.1	125332.1
1891961.4	401690.3	20736.0	2458029.6	1391610.2	779199.3	1400425.0	651360.5
1616913.5	13011.3	16404.0	1500341.6	981879.2	290337.1	472386.0	232325.1
105169.9		688.0	83547.3	41865.6	26710.9	71863.0	45152.1
631191.7	4495.5	7480.0	961120.9	602696.8	208382.1	282597.5	99070.3
1628596.0	1262.1	13467.0	1080757.4	641813.3	359876.7	613365.9	285194.3
383085.1	5041.1	3237.0	280488.9	145175.6	95191.2	143296.2	52117.4
1648397.8	115406.2	10465.0	1667629.2	925736.0	393565.4	580394.9	228420.3
1475338.3	82051.6	24250.0	2072112.3	1150905.8	717135.4	907108.7	365461.2
1612213.8	113778.5	18670.0	3142521.9	2359765.4	386938.0	594924.4	229967.6
2406595.3	171492.8	30358.0	3996993.9	2569042.0	746647.9	1082300.9	415244.0
8627705.5	344165.9	77239.0	6691842.6	3676876.3	1589420.4	2221388.7	773618.1
4429652.1	581664.2	75350.0	9549287.1	5506458.4	2106197.8	2970265.9	1305747.6
4814989.6	145343.1	44669.0	6055936.1	4209374.6	1136369.6	1818254.0	706985.7
2499901.3	834087.5	30258.0	6749217.3	2158335.3	3858024.4	4620027.9	830463.3
1538391.7	73094.5	23082.0	2292376.1	1416830.6	557426.8	822434.9	380369.6
48108.9	240.0	924.0	78599.7	52605.3	13759.3	20608.6	7882.0
15546.4		409.0	24273.0	20689.3	2296.3	3676.3	1380.0
2349303.3		22066.0	6000787.2	903269.3	4586218.3	7133998.8	2827054.1
431321.0		4356.0	808576.2	357522.8	248430.3	315085.7	86898.6
93098.8		3053.0	207693.7	95332.7	106322.9	244017.5	163034.2

12-8 续表7

单位：万元

分组	Classify	负债合计 Total Liabilites	流动负债合计 Total Working Liabilities	非流动负债 Non-Working Liabilities
棕、草制品业	and Straw Products			
家具制造业	Manufacture of Furniture	29686.4	27454.9	2066.6
造纸及纸制品业	Manufacture of Paper and Paper Products	69800.9	54527.3	13891.3
印刷和记录媒介复制	Printing,Reproduction of Recording Media	227590.8	183905.4	16842.0
文教、工美、体育和娱乐用品制造业	Manufacture of Articles For Cultural,Educational and Sports Activities	174064.9	170404.2	0.0
石油加工业、炼焦和核燃料加工业	Processing of Petroleum, Cokeing,Processing of Nuclear and Nuclear Fuel	419480.2	390784.0	28370.1
化学原料及化学制品制造业	Manufacture of Raw Chemical Materials and Chemical Products	1414902.7	1066120.0	325574.7
医药制造业	Manufacture of Medicines	753743.5	694358.9	32503.5
化学纤维制造业	Manufacture of Chemical Fibers	15200.6	14742.6	458.0
橡胶和塑料制品业	Manufacture of Rubber and Plastics	723396.0	596701.7	121550.2
非金属矿物制品业	Manufacture of Non-metallic Mineral Products	647012.2	537369.6	53434.4
黑色金属冶炼和压延加工业	Smelting and Pressing of Ferrous Metals	195682.2	137539.8	10239.4
有色金属冶炼和压延加工业	Smelting and Pressing of Non-ferrous Metals	873208.1	716781.7	153785.0
金属制品业	Manufacture of Metal Products	1238657.3	893746.8	301979.2
通用设备制造业	Manufacture of General Purpose Machinery	1699216.4	1555554.1	108976.6
专用设备制造业	Manufacture of Special Equipment	1810275.3	1600726.8	171350.6
汽车制造业	Manufacture of Motor Vehicle	4386967.6	3841819.8	379793.1
铁路、船舶、航空航天和其他运输设备制造业	Railways,Shipbuilding,Aerospace and Other Transportation Equipment Manufacturing Industry	5438476.0	4356083.6	1044928.0
电气机械和器材制造业	Manufacture of Electric Equipment and Machinery	2939456.3	2480127.5	371104.4
计算机、通讯和其他电子设备制造业	Manufacture of Communication Equipment, Computers and other Electronic Equipment	4117567.8	3087290.0	976041.3
仪器仪表制造业	Manufacture of Measuring Instruments and Machinery	1161963.9	961868.8	104751.8
其他制造业	Manufacture of Other Manufacturing	47585.5	47205.5	13.0
废弃资源综合利用业	Recycling and Disposal of Waste			
金属制品、机械和设备修理业	Metal Products,Machinery and Equipment Repair Industry	14946.6	14145.5	801.1
电力、热力的生产和供应业	Production and Supply of Electric Power and Heat Power	5095153.6	1494505.3	838324.4
燃气生产和供应业	Gas Mining and Supplying Industry	497861.1	431172.0	25921.3
水的生产和供应业	Production and Supply of Water	114713.1	83265.6	31447.5

continued 7

(10 000yuan)

所有者权益合计 Total Owners' Equities	实收资本 Total Capital Hold	营业收入 Total Revenue	主营业务收入 Revenue from Principal Business	营业成本 Total Cost	主营业务成本 Cost of Principal Business	营业税金及附加 Taxs and Other Changes	主营业务税金及附加 Taxes and Other Charges on Principal Business
26792.8	14450.0	60340.1	60078.6	48098.3	47912.7	477.8	477.8
48443.4	21370.6	141428.4	141004.1	124317.3	124099.4	370.1	370.1
384202.1	208268.5	532548.1	527178.2	406754.9	403876.4	3213.0	3213.0
11661.3	8122.6	463156.7	463156.7	457676.9	457676.9	107.7	107.7
147261.9	354690.6	1717183.3	1714898.1	1601225.9	1599697.4	102731.8	102683.1
1027006.6	551269.3	1854226.7	1822204.8	1558938.7	1521308.8	7232.3	7173.7
742681.1	248475.0	1560130.3	1558465.0	904299.4	903982.1	12298.6	12298.6
68346.7	54300.0	104815.3	104815.3	86133.1	86133.1	468.4	468.4
237724.6	138359.8	631198.3	624126.2	517453.4	510552.0	3236.3	3092.2
431928.7	256286.4	1574575.1	1561296.8	1353245.3	1344811.4	8628.7	8617.8
91111.3	42913.9	434377.3	429163.8	388848.7	384385.8	1819.7	1816.8
794420.1	365652.3	1560232.0	1444210.8	1388032.9	1285974.2	2416.4	2396.1
829187.1	434228.1	1429100.9	1415547.5	1208876.7	1199636.2	5833.9	5808.5
1443291.0	291599.1	1489535.4	1481194.6	1212571.6	1207555.7	8403.2	8341.4
2186715.3	1073544.4	2286514.9	2244168.8	1804125.6	1777871.8	11453.9	11311.5
2300874.2	843819.4	7257355.2	7037943.5	6488676.5	6344115.9	58334.7	58313.0
4107898.2	1250381.6	5295831.3	5251306.4	4532045.1	4495965.9	20795.3	19995.6
3116472.9	900718.1	4482741.8	4364695.8	3726210.2	3640173.7	21927.2	21817.6
2629654.1	2081127.5	2619655.8	2588584.9	2193741.9	2147709.9	5569.1	5014.8
1130411.2	543564.8	1442492.0	1424487.2	1124711.7	1114887.7	9657.7	8152.2
31014.2	22128.0	47817.8	47090.2	38673.4	38457.4	257.6	257.6
9326.3	4654.5	23070.8	23063.7	16354.2	16354.2	150.4	150.4
905633.5	596725.0	3259834.7	3242917.5	2995463.2	2990955.7	21602.5	20977.4
310714.9	214430.6	450546.9	391084.9	348420.5	312121.8	3620.4	3453.2
92980.6	46585.9	108339.8	92297.7	89200.9	77039.0	1199.1	500.3

12-8 续表8

单位：万元

分组	Classify	销售费用 Expenses for Sales	管理费用 Expenses for Management	财务费用 Financial cost
棕、草制品业	and Straw Products			
家具制造业	Manufacture of Furniture	4351.1	3948.8	568.2
造纸及纸制品业	Manufacture of Paper and Paper Products	3393.2	4762.4	1084.3
印刷和记录媒介复制	Printing,Reproduction of Recording Media	10602.4	49482.0	1378.7
文教、工美、体育和娱乐用品制造业	Manufacture of Articles For Cultural,Educational and Sports Activities	802.0	1236.4	226.2
石油加工业、炼焦和核燃料加工业	Processing of Petroleum, Cokeing,Processing of Nuclear and Nuclear Fuel	11672.2	28512.3	8747.5
化学原料及化学制品制造业	Manufacture of Raw Chemical Materials and Chemical Products	56114.3	135833.5	25288.7
医药制造业	Manufacture of Medicines	366681.3	149646.0	18318.3
化学纤维制造业	Manufacture of Chemical Fibers	385.9	3655.2	39.6
橡胶和塑料制品业	Manufacture of Rubber and Plastics	25707.5	33496.3	13702.7
非金属矿物制品业	Manufacture of Non-metallic Mineral Products	34810.0	63730.2	8116.7
黑色金属冶炼和压延加工业	Smelting and Pressing of Ferrous Metals	5710.6	13902.9	6337.4
有色金属冶炼和压延加工业	Smelting and Pressing of Non-ferrous Metals	13485.5	45386.3	24777.9
金属制品业	Manufacture of Metal Products	26412.7	99749.8	18365.9
通用设备制造业	Manufacture of General Purpose Machinery	51204.3	147187.1	-1906.5
专用设备制造业	Manufacture of Special Equipment	94214.4	186720.7	11609.6
汽车制造业	Manufacture of Motor Vehicle	182345.7	254517.9	37953.5
铁路、船舶、航空航天和其他运输设备制造业	Railways,Shipbuilding,Aerospace and Other Transportation Equipment Manufacturing Industry	100304.5	399072.3	57153.5
电气机械和器材制造业	Manufacture of Electric Equipment and Machinery	195088.9	301933.4	23112.2
计算机、通讯和其他电子设备制造业	Manufacture of Communication Equipment, Computers and other Electronic Equipment	43819.4	291012.7	31204.1
仪器仪表制造业	Manufacture of Measuring Instruments and Machinery	31939.6	137423.3	10788.4
其他制造业	Manufacture of Other Manufacturing	2534.2	4924.3	1748.1
废弃资源综合利用业	Recycling and Disposal of Waste			
金属制品、机械和设备修理业	Metal Products,Machinery and Equipment Repair Industry	1398.0	3565.2	35.5
电力、热力的生产和供应业	Production and Supply of Electric Power and Heat Power	5896.0	28796.5	170077.7
燃气生产和供应业	Gas Mining and Supplying Industry	28916.6	26458.2	2321.2
水的生产和供应业	Production and Supply of Water	4079.3	11060.6	445.9

continued 8

(10 000yuan)

营业利润 Operating Profit	利润总额 Total Profits	亏损企业亏损额 Total Loss of Deficit Enterprises	利税总额 Total Pre-tax Profits	应付职工薪酬 Salary Payable	本年应交增值税 Value Added Tax Payable
2352.3	2677.5	21.1	4234.3	4572.4	1079.0
9523.7	10262.1	563.7	14359.3	8344.7	3727.1
63343.6	64779.1	427.9	100137.6	71540.8	32145.5
3107.5	3231.8	140.6	27164.2	2921.3	23824.7
-35781.5	-36014.8	47401.0	126941.3	31503.0	60224.3
72850.2	83919.0	22710.7	122085.3	167424.5	30934.0
129433.6	133842.3	2715.9	279701.1	135607.4	133560.2
14133.0	15006.3	181.0	20963.0	5749.5	5488.3
43216.4	49967.6	486.0	75574.7	41498.1	22370.8
101206.2	103864.6	7615.5	165315.0	60905.8	52821.7
13087.0	13784.1	13242.9	29824.6	18034.9	14220.8
81007.3	89863.4	13847.6	128866.5	60465.4	36586.7
68484.8	76678.9	4673.3	110722.5	171081.5	28209.7
79292.4	101192.1	4268.4	152202.7	110202.6	42607.4
135815.2	158670.8	51973.0	249493.9	207741.2	79369.2
232349.1	311346.7	34142.0	541126.4	375610.5	171445.0
186935.2	210626.2	15559.7	326592.2	727249.8	95170.7
211468.6	225083.8	12982.7	437902.4	362114.3	190891.4
60946.2	161311.2	26100.8	192406.4	229310.8	25526.1
119405.0	142121.2	4495.8	201332.7	241241.8	49553.8
-100.0	1198.3	703.2	2980.8	4535.1	1524.9
1209.6	1256.2	143.2	2598.1	2899.7	1191.5
59816.6	82022.6	16348.8	273507.6	226153.4	169882.5
44405.1	45153.8	1749.5	58921.4	38121.4	10147.2
2060.9	2936.4	92.0	8261.2	22792.4	4125.7

12-9 规模以上国有及国有控股工业企业主要经济指标（2014年）

单位：万元

分 组	Classify	企业单位数（个） Number of Enterprises (unit)	亏损企业 Loss Making Enterprises	工业总产值（当年价格） Gross Industrial Output Value (At Current Prices)
总计	**Total**	235	54	26366390.7
#市区	Urban	192	46	19620352.6
#亏损企业	Deficit Enterprises	54	54	3581824.4
按隶属关系分	**Grouped by Jurisdiction of Management**			
中央企业	Central Enterprises	83	15	12410328.6
省属企业	Provincial Enterprises	46	14	6822275.4
市属企业	Municipal Enterprises	106	25	7133786.7
按轻重工业分	**Grouped by Light Industry and Heavy Industry**			
轻工业	Light Industry	32	8	1117978.5
重工业	Heavy Industry	203	46	25248412.2
按企业规模分	Grouped by Size of Enterprises			
大型企业	Large-size	43	6	18659836.6
中型企业	Medium-size	69	19	3447385.1
小型企业	Small-size	123	29	4259169.0
微型企业	Microenterprise			
按工业行业大类分	**Grouped by Sector**			
煤炭开采和洗选业	Mining and Washing of Coal			
石油和天然气开采业	Extraction of Petroleum and Natural Gas			
黑色金属矿采选业	Mining and Processing of Ferrous Metal Ores			
有色金属矿采选业	Mining and Processing of Non-ferrous Metal Ores			
非金属矿采选业	Mining and Processing of Nonmetal Ores			
开采辅助活动	Mining Auxiliary Activities	1		110554.6
其他采矿业	Mining of Other Ores			
农副食品加工业	Processing of Food from Agricultural Porducts	3	1	41218.5
食品制造业	Manufacture of Foods	4		323287.1
酒、饮料和精制茶制造业	Manufacture of Alcohol,Beverages and Tea	1		110189.7
烟草制品业	Manufacture of Tobacco	1		9862.6
纺织业	Manufacture of Textile	2	1	43707.7
纺织服装、服饰业	Textile, apparel industry			
皮革、毛皮、羽毛及其制品和制鞋业	Leather fur feathers and its products and footwear	1		37557.7
木材加工和木、竹、藤、棕、草制品业	Processing of Timber, Manufacture of Wood,Plato and Straw Products			

Economic Indicators of all State-owned and State-holding Share Industrial Enterprises above Designated Size (2014)

(10 000 yuan)

工业销售产值（当年价） Value of Industry Products Sales (At Current Prices)	出口交货值 Export Delivery Value	从业人员年平均人数（人） Annual Average Employers (person)	资产总计 Total Assets	流动资产合计 Total Working Capitals	固定资产合计 Total Fixed Assets	固定资产原价 Origing Value of Fixed Assets	累计折旧 Accumulative Total Depreciation
25297515.7	1300469.0	296186.0	38860268.4	21263294.3	11997425.5	18059145.9	7374187.4
18999906.3	959915.7	250298.0	33221280.6	18053007.9	10695222.2	16192047.9	6656669.5
3475707.6	212158.3	53026.0	7491644.6	4605430.9	1531213.8	2435619.7	958025.4
12179578.5	573749.6	188841.0	24459313.6	12082848.2	9138821.5	13725738.2	5699210.7
6563288.6	347655.8	58850.0	6846477.0	4138001.1	1333775.8	2005637.9	741791.6
6554648.6	379063.6	48495.0	7554477.8	5042445.0	1524828.2	2327769.8	933185.1
1266593.0	14827.4	19214.0	1176249.4	641819.1	403071.7	854413.3	499848.5
24030922.7	1285641.6	276972.0	37684019.0	20621475.2	11594353.8	17204732.6	6874338.9
18160495.8	926147.8	231967.0	30596077.7	16054511.3	10081293.8	15212143.0	6162489.3
3133775.7	290001.1	45780.0	5052083.6	3193837.6	1356859.9	2035468.0	896832.2
4003244.2	84320.1	18439.0	3212107.1	2014945.4	559271.8	811534.9	314865.9
111804.6		10356.0	130368.9	59679.1	67823.5	119394.1	51265.8
38923.5	7226.0	946.0	40040.5	27726.4	10975.7	28119.5	17143.9
316259.9		1521.0	44313.5	28288.9	15052.7	33752.7	18779.8
266264.3		1422.0	182131.6	111095.2	21607.9	58885.8	37447.6
10288.6		297.0	22262.6	9238.7	3763.8	6743.4	2979.6
42609.2	6079.3	5034.0	59600.1	42404.2	13055.9	47940.2	34884.3
37873.3		881.0	46323.6	24122.7	3016.7	5769.9	2753.2

12-9 续表1

单位：万元

分 组	Classify	负债合计 Total Liabilites	流动负债合计 Total Working Liabilities	非流动负债 Non-Working Liabilities
总计	**Total**	23813239.1	17375785.9	3630176.4
#市区	Urban	19996868.0	14023918.0	3172174.8
#亏损企业	Deficit Enterprises	4902006.0	4123844.5	770749.7
按隶属关系分	**Grouped by Jurisdiction of Management**			
中央企业	Central Enterprises	14621670.2	9346798.6	2512014.5
省属企业	Provincial Enterprises	4512359.1	3996666.7	496725.5
市属企业	Municipal Enterprises	4679209.8	4032320.6	621436.4
按轻重工业分	**Grouped by Light Industry and Heavy Industry**			
轻工业	Light Industry	503722.4	439638.8	64060.7
重工业	Heavy Industry	23309516.7	16936147.1	3566115.7
按企业规模分	Grouped by Size of Enterprises			
大型企业	Large-size	18723933.9	13125360.8	2836265.9
中型企业	Medium-size	3190928.7	2560265.5	628224.9
小型企业	Small-size	1898376.5	1690159.6	165685.6
微型企业	Microenterprise			
按工业行业大类分	**Grouped by Sector**			
煤炭开采和洗选业	Mining and Washing of Coal			
石油和天然气开采业	Extraction of Petroleum and Natural Gas			
黑色金属矿采选业	Mining and Processing of Ferrous Metal Ores			
有色金属矿采选业	Mining and Processing of Non-ferrous Metal Ores			
非金属矿采选业	Mining and Processing of Nonmetal Ores			
开采辅助活动	Mining Auxiliary Activities	125993.8	50751.4	75242.4
其他采矿业	Mining of Other Ores			
农副食品加工业	Processing of Food from Agricultural Porducts	60486.8	60486.8	0.0
食品制造业	Manufacture of Foods	15449.0	15443.7	5.3
酒、饮料和精制茶制造业	Manufacture of Alcohol,Beverages and Tea	64060.0	62374.6	1685.4
烟草制品业	Manufacture of Tobacco	14125.6	14125.6	0.0
纺织业	Manufacture of Textile	46876.2	44573.3	2302.9
纺织服装、服饰业	Textile, apparel industry			
皮革、毛皮、羽毛及其制品和制鞋业	Leather fur feathers and its products and footwear	21955.6	17467.2	4488.4
木材加工和木、竹、藤、棕、草制品业	Processing of Timber, Manufacture of Wood,Plato and Straw Products			

continued 1

(10 000 yuan)

所有者权益合计 Total Owners' Equities	实收资本 Total Capital Hold	营业收入 Total Revenue	主营业务收入 Revenue from Principal Business	营业成本 Total Cost	主营业务成本 Cost of Principal Business	营业税金及附加 Taxs and Other Changes	主营业务税金及附加 Taxes and Other Charges on Principal Business
15031566.8	5927128.2	25329091.3	24754520.3	21908950.0	21475505.5	221787.4	217209.3
13208950.7	4832417.4	20008910.0	19575394.8	17126583.5	16795369.6	207717.1	203159.6
2589638.0	1722640.0	3597294.7	3561967.4	3252790.5	3228834.3	116084.1	115806.7
9822183.1	3454332.5	13797453.3	13610575.8	11906919.9	11762644.5	170783.9	168430.2
2334117.4	1133292.2	5729077.7	5473777.0	5076917.2	4867419.5	17996.8	17541.4
2875266.3	1339503.5	5802560.3	5670167.5	4925112.9	4845441.5	33006.7	31237.7
672517.5	458862.7	1280982.2	1256989.0	1022506.7	1005075.4	15636.1	14937.3
14359049.3	5468265.5	24048109.1	23497531.3	20886443.3	20470430.1	206151.3	202272.0
11856687.6	3836412.5	18816249.7	18421842.3	16203635.5	15904947.9	199460.8	196665.3
1861153.8	1108518.1	3169609.0	3016284.4	2669288.2	2545730.7	12943.3	11668.6
1313725.4	982197.6	3343232.6	3316393.6	3036026.3	3024826.9	9383.3	8875.4
4375.1	1800.0	256956.6	255219.8	246431.0	243007.4	42.0	40.8
-20446.3	2152.7	36575.1	36095.5	26846.8	26540.4	135.2	135.2
28864.5	15590.5	319788.1	317217.8	261628.7	259663.6	428.7	428.7
118071.6	118071.6	266264.8	265939.8	211076.5	210742.2	10069.8	10069.8
8137.0	1514.7	11230.3	10978.8	5282.5	5216.2	118.6	118.6
12723.8	7746.2	42965.6	42965.6	39267.7	39267.7	344.1	344.1
24367.9	6000.0	37873.3	37873.3	33224.3	32744.6	179.5	179.5

12-9 续表2

单位：万元

分 组	Classify	销售费用 Expenses for Sales	管理费用 Expenses for Management	财务费用 Financial cost
总计	**Total**	583076.2	1532073.8	314271.7
#市区	Urban	470469.3	1325907.8	271957.1
#亏损企业	Deficit Enterprises	93991.7	286248.2	55960.1
按隶属关系分	**Grouped by Jurisdiction of Management**			
中央企业	Central Enterprises	259977.2	933409.5	247833.3
省属企业	Provincial Enterprises	160746.2	285680.1	41743.1
市属企业	Municipal Enterprises	162352.8	312984.2	24695.3
按轻重工业分	**Grouped by Light Industry and Heavy Industry**			
轻工业	Light Industry	61098.2	91650.8	-1969.9
重工业	Heavy Industry	521978.0	1440423.0	316241.6
按企业规模分	Grouped by Size of Enterprises			
大型企业	Large-size	435369.4	1178643.9	259980.5
中型企业	Medium-size	107690.1	236087.2	33714.4
小型企业	Small-size	40016.7	117342.7	20576.8
微型企业	Microenterprise			
按工业行业大类分	**Grouped by Sector**			
煤炭开采和洗选业	Mining and Washing of Coal			
石油和天然气开采业	Extraction of Petroleum and Natural Gas			
黑色金属矿采选业	Mining and Processing of Ferrous Metal Ores			
有色金属矿采选业	Mining and Processing of Non-ferrous Metal Ores			
非金属矿采选业	Mining and Processing of Nonmetal Ores			
开采辅助活动	Mining Auxiliary Activities	102.7	570.2	-3.6
其他采矿业	Mining of Other Ores			
农副食品加工业	Processing of Food from Agricultural Porducts	3804.9	3098.6	249.3
食品制造业	Manufacture of Foods	27942.1	18122.4	4.6
酒、饮料和精制茶制造业	Manufacture of Alcohol,Beverages and Tea	11285.7	4058.9	-3467.0
烟草制品业	Manufacture of Tobacco	165.5	2026.3	-15.2
纺织业	Manufacture of Textile	689.7	5077.0	-89.5
纺织服装、服饰业	Textile, apparel industry			
皮革、毛皮、羽毛及其制品和制鞋业	Leather fur feathers and its products and footwear	896.0	1520.2	144.7
木材加工和木、竹、藤、棕、草制品业	Processing of Timber, Manufacture of Wood,Plato and Straw Products			

continued 2

(10 000 yuan)

营业利润 Operating Profit	利润总额 Total Profits	亏损企业亏损额 Total Loss of Deficit Enterprises	利税总额 Total Pre-tax Profits	应付职工薪酬 Salary Payable	本年应交增值税 Value Added Tax Payable
802278.4	972662.9	185494.8	1891859.8	2492723.3	697409.5
645049.1	781457.9	162179.4	1564778.4	2256707.7	575603.4
-192177.6	-185494.8	185494.8	-11757.0	398277.5	57653.7
361048.0	449508.2	96726.4	1031121.3	1746104.7	410829.2
121419.1	153354.8	40573.2	282187.7	343189.8	110836.1
319811.3	369799.9	48195.2	578550.8	403428.8	175744.2
105277.0	112970.7	2323.7	175706.1	171493.5	47099.3
697001.4	859692.2	183171.1	1716153.7	2321229.8	650310.2
595268.2	711207.3	89744.7	1425384.8	2016026.6	514716.7
85175.3	120602.8	72304.8	237621.5	344388.3	104075.4
121834.9	140852.8	23445.3	228853.5	132308.4	78617.4
8143.7	7331.3		7720.9	31747.6	347.6
2460.0	2438.5	431.6	3694.3	4031.8	1120.6
11660.8	11983.1		16257.2	43954.8	3845.4
34548.2	34896.9		55216.5	15584.0	10249.8
3650.2	3647.8		4704.2	2956.8	937.8
-2576.0	-766.0	966.4	985.7	12688.6	1407.6
2709.8	2760.1		3300.9	5016.1	361.3

12-9 续表3

单位：万元

分 组	Classify	企业单位数（个） Number of Enterprises (unit)	亏损企业 Loss Making Enterprises	工业总产值（当年价格） Gross Industrial Output Value (At Current Prices)
家具制造业	Manufacture of Furniture			
造纸及纸制品业	Manufacture of Paper and Paper Products			
印刷和记录媒介复制	Printing,Reproduction of Recording Media	3	1	220708.3
文教、工美、体育和娱乐用品制造业	Manufacture of Articles For Cultural,Educational and Sports Activities			
石油加工业、炼焦和业核燃料加工	Processing of Petroleum, Cokeing,Processing of Nuclear and Nuclear Fuel	1	1	2088152.0
化学原料及化学制品制造业	Manufacture of Raw Chemical Materials and Chemical Products	15	2	642121.3
医药制造业	Manufacture of Medicines	2		30566.7
化学纤维制造业	Manufacture of Chemical Fibers	2	1	99512.8
橡胶和塑料制品业	Manufacture of Rubber and Plastics	3		319828.2
非金属矿物制品业	Manufacture of Non-metallic Mineral Products	8	1	168215.4
黑色金属冶炼和压延加工业	Smelting and Pressing of Ferrous Metals	2	1	330559.4
有色金属冶炼和压延加工业	Smelting and Pressing of Non-ferrous Metals	17	6	864283.6
金属制品业	Manufacture of Metal Products	14		1044375.4
通用设备制造业	Manufacture of General Purpose Machinery	15	1	1075520.9
专用设备制造业	Manufacture of Special Equipment	22	9	1278102.3
汽车制造业	Manufacture of Motor Vehicle	15	3	6087750.0
铁路、船舶、航空航天和其他运输设备制造业	Railways,Shipbuilding,Aerospace and Other Transportation Equipment Manufacturing Industry	30	4	4021775.2
电气机械和器材制造业	Manufacture of Electric Equipment and Machinery	23	7	2874065.5
计算机、通讯和其他电子设备制造业	Manufacture of Communication Equipment, Computers and other Electronic Equipment	19	7	702639.0
仪器仪表制造业	Manufacture of Measuring Instruments and Machinery	11	2	1130549.6
其他制造业	Manufacture of Other Manufacturing	2	1	21357.9
废弃资源综合利用业	Recycling and Disposal of Waste			
金属制品、机械和设备修理业	Metal Products,Machinery and Equipment Repair Industry	1		2291.7
电力、热力的生产和供应业	Production and Supply of Electric Power and Heat Power	9	4	2273117.4
燃气生产和供应业	Gas Mining and Supplying Industry	4		321421.4
水的生产和供应业	Production and Supply of Water	4	1	93098.8

continued 3

(10 000 yuan)

工业销售产值（当年价） Value of Industry Products Sales (At Current Prices)	出口交货值 Export Delivery Value	从业人员年平均人数（人） Annual Average Employers (person)	资产总计 Total Assets	流动资产合计 Total Working Capitals	固定资产合计 Total Fixed Assets	固定资产原价 Origing Value of Fixed Assets	累计折旧 Accumulative Total Depreciation
225319.4		2990.0	306838.2	142791.6	158013.9	283738.7	144459.0
2070098.0		1653.0	384280.0	217176.2	167103.8	240837.7	97323.6
607835.5	63682.5	12944.0	932765.8	472648.4	325862.1	561766.0	255461.8
33462.5		856.0	66054.5	38162.5	10998.7	16399.4	5400.7
98128.2		383.0	74540.7	37805.6	25674.4	70141.1	44466.7
309352.1	3568.3	4291.0	758393.9	482270.7	137314.9	180388.9	59547.8
162347.4	1262.1	1924.0	185349.3	121203.2	48036.1	53429.2	16968.3
168538.8	3288.1	1116.0	108347.2	70679.2	30596.4	49523.5	18927.1
735901.4	39502.4	4353.0	711027.0	457364.7	203874.6	249402.5	86367.5
1031703.2	78998.7	19445.0	1677641.8	968353.2	593797.9	750323.0	322592.7
1063104.1	53036.3	10923.0	2541906.3	1958376.8	269491.9	429159.9	159550.5
1065557.4	71521.1	13785.0	2427411.3	1598061.4	334565.5	461982.7	190363.2
5691079.0	296820.0	40561.0	4446730.9	2787998.9	907885.0	1328754.7	458123.5
3851844.3	547447.3	70662.0	9128981.3	5232779.2	2032393.3	2830889.3	1235783.8
2886923.3	87789.4	29512.0	4623392.3	3229931.2	886309.7	1435154.8	551977.9
719752.5	33425.5	15136.0	1832627.1	1109979.8	433554.0	590172.8	204403.0
1042369.3	6582.0	17012.0	1682599.0	989004.7	503281.4	739955.7	347279.2
21297.8	240.0	291.0	12676.1	9709.4	2450.3	3903.9	1453.6
2291.7		54.0	2667.2	2587.5	79.7	154.3	74.6
2272408.3		21237.0	5626049.3	699287.6	4473944.3	6983277.6	2782133.2
321079.3		3548.0	597254.7	239234.6	210578.5	255167.1	63241.3
93098.8		3053.0	207693.7	95332.7	106322.9	244017.5	163034.2

12-9 续表4

单位：万元

分组	Classify	负债合计 Total Liabilites	流动负债合计 Total Working Liabilities	非流动负债 Non-Working Liabilities
家具制造业	Manufacture of Furniture			
造纸及纸制品业	Manufacture of Paper and Paper Products			
印刷和记录媒介复制	Printing,Reproduction of Recording Media	39620.6	39607.0	13.6
文教、工美、体育和娱乐用品制造业	Manufacture of Articles For Cultural,Educational and Sports Activities			
石油加工业、炼焦和业核燃料加工	Processing of Petroleum, Cokeing,Processing of Nuclear and Nuclear Fuel	307008.4	294037.7	12970.7
化学原料及化学制品制造业	Manufacture of Raw Chemical Materials and Chemical Products	520618.6	440098.8	79599.3
医药制造业	Manufacture of Medicines	25181.6	25055.7	125.9
化学纤维制造业	Manufacture of Chemical Fibers	10464.4	10006.4	458.0
橡胶和塑料制品业	Manufacture of Rubber and Plastics	619632.9	510769.8	108863.1
非金属矿物制品业	Manufacture of Non-metallic Mineral Products	88631.4	78963.8	9526.9
黑色金属冶炼和压延加工业	Smelting and Pressing of Ferrous Metals	74898.9	65583.9	9315.1
有色金属冶炼和压延加工业	Smelting and Pressing of Non-ferrous Metals	415021.7	354762.4	60259.3
金属制品业	Manufacture of Metal Products	1049273.5	728518.8	284905.1
通用设备制造业	Manufacture of General Purpose Machinery	1385382.8	1298472.1	85350.2
专用设备制造业	Manufacture of Special Equipment	1103839.1	1023760.7	59634.1
汽车制造业	Manufacture of Motor Vehicle	2892144.6	2665694.4	225886.1
铁路、船舶、航空航天和其他运输设备制造业	Railways,Shipbuilding,Aerospace and Other Transportation Equipment Manufacturing Industry	5227545.5	4177961.3	1033060.4
电气机械和器材制造业	Manufacture of Electric Equipment and Machinery	2174691.3	1883911.8	290563.4
计算机、通讯和其他电子设备制造业	Manufacture of Communication Equipment, Computers and other Electronic Equipment	1367574.1	1034527.7	325726.6
仪器仪表制造业	Manufacture of Measuring Instruments and Machinery	852332.3	759842.8	92489.5
其他制造业	Manufacture of Other Manufacturing	6278.0	6278.0	
废弃资源综合利用业	Recycling and Disposal of Waste			
金属制品、机械和设备修理业	Metal Products,Machinery and Equipment Repair Industry	2130.8	2130.8	
电力、热力的生产和供应业	Production and Supply of Electric Power and Heat Power	4804304.7	1261132.8	819434.4
燃气生产和供应业	Gas Mining and Supplying Industry	383003.8	366181.0	16822.8
水的生产和供应业	Production and Supply of Water	114713.1	83265.6	31447.5

continued 4

(10 000 yuan)

所有者权益合计 Total Owners' Equities	实收资本 Total Capital Hold	营业收入 Total Revenue	主营业务收入 Revenue from Principal Business	营业成本 Total Cost	主营业务成本 Cost of Principal Business	营业税金及附加 Taxs and Other Changes	主营业务税金及附加 Taxes and Other Charges on Principal Business
267208.5	155362.3	227511.1	225196.1	172811.4	171509.7	1887.7	1887.7
77271.5	308302.4	1472657.5	1472657.5	1386719.8	1386719.8	101513.6	101513.6
396699.9	158370.1	600466.9	579538.4	496532.4	481684.9	4021.5	3982.5
40872.9	10642.2	31429.3	31348.2	19659.9	19659.9	184.0	184.0
64076.3	50800.0	98141.2	98141.2	80085.7	80085.7	362.1	362.1
138760.9	83387.8	332239.2	325228.7	282859.9	276005.6	2263.8	2119.7
96717.7	74281.5	169561.2	168468.0	154385.2	154384.2	899.7	899.7
33448.3	18763.5	167659.5	164263.9	157342.0	154522.6	378.8	375.9
296004.7	228410.4	637810.6	524948.4	570077.5	470735.3	1046.0	1046.0
628368.2	289834.0	982739.6	971018.5	828333.2	820554.3	3173.8	3172.4
1156523.5	125541.4	1010450.8	1003478.1	808620.8	804302.6	5982.0	5953.4
1323572.0	668524.2	958520.2	947791.6	791080.3	786124.8	5414.9	5409.1
1554586.3	592269.0	4867819.7	4728120.3	4338651.8	4231555.3	14218.2	14197.6
3901431.9	1150209.4	4747230.0	4702878.6	4095783.8	4059752.4	18939.1	18139.4
2448700.6	460255.7	2575346.4	2481279.5	2114097.0	2037714.2	16125.7	16027.1
465052.9	209193.9	827099.8	817612.7	685312.7	679371.2	2165.9	1617.2
830266.6	429953.0	992243.0	977015.5	802993.6	794617.0	6613.8	5130.2
6398.1	4000.0	20873.2	20687.4	18908.4	18860.9	80.1	80.1
536.4	200.0	2291.7	2290.8	1620.8	1620.8	22.8	22.8
821744.6	551511.2	3148028.5	3131131.2	2889488.0	2884980.5	20775.2	20237.3
214250.8	157854.6	378978.3	322837.4	300627.4	266522.7	3201.7	3034.5
92980.6	46585.9	108339.8	92297.7	89200.9	77039.0	1199.1	500.3

12-9 续表5

单位：万元

分 组	Classify	销售费用 Expenses for Sales	管理费用 Expenses for Management	财务费用 Financial cost
家具制造业	Manufacture of Furniture			
造纸及纸制品业	Manufacture of Paper and Paper Products			
印刷和记录媒介复制	Printing,Reproduction of Recording Media	3367.6	33188.6	-921.2
文教、工美、体育和娱乐用品制造业	Manufacture of Articles For Cultural,Educational and Sports Activities			
石油加工业、炼焦和业核燃料加工	Processing of Petroleum, Cokeing,Processing of Nuclear and Nuclear Fuel	4873.3	18377.5	7083.5
化学原料及化学制品制造业	Manufacture of Raw Chemical Materials and Chemical Products	16992.6	72873.4	7768.0
医药制造业	Manufacture of Medicines	2872.9	3891.5	-30.3
化学纤维制造业	Manufacture of Chemical Fibers	329.6	2873.2	-180.8
橡胶和塑料制品业	Manufacture of Rubber and Plastics	12085.3	14749.8	9053.6
非金属矿物制品业	Manufacture of Non-metallic Mineral Products	1217.1	5627.3	1489.3
黑色金属冶炼和压延加工业	Smelting and Pressing of Ferrous Metals	2135.9	5314.5	1931.3
有色金属冶炼和压延加工业	Smelting and Pressing of Non-ferrous Metals	5106.5	28061.0	10931.0
金属制品业	Manufacture of Metal Products	16397.9	79612.4	15394.3
通用设备制造业	Manufacture of General Purpose Machinery	30662.9	116400.2	-6615.7
专用设备制造业	Manufacture of Special Equipment	33054.9	87655.5	-3335.3
汽车制造业	Manufacture of Motor Vehicle	135090.1	185719.7	22983.3
铁路、船舶、航空航天和其他运输设备制造业	Railways,Shipbuilding,Aerospace and Other Transportation Equipment Manufacturing Industry	83400.9	370128.9	55390.2
电气机械和器材制造业	Manufacture of Electric Equipment and Machinery	135368.4	218653.9	8977.6
计算机、通讯和其他电子设备制造业	Manufacture of Communication Equipment, Computers and other Electronic Equipment	21606.9	96637.0	18664.4
仪器仪表制造业	Manufacture of Measuring Instruments and Machinery	6036.0	100462.4	5937.3
其他制造业	Manufacture of Other Manufacturing	383.7	629.9	130.0
废弃资源综合利用业	Recycling and Disposal of Waste			
金属制品、机械和设备修理业	Metal Products,Machinery and Equipment Repair Industry	115.7	318.5	
电力、热力的生产和供应业	Production and Supply of Electric Power and Heat Power	1368.7	24153.0	167014.9
燃气生产和供应业	Gas Mining and Supplying Industry	21643.4	21211.4	-4662.9
水的生产和供应业	Production and Supply of Water	4079.3	11060.6	445.9

continued 5

(10 000 yuan)

营业利润 Operating Profit	利润总额 Total Profits	亏损企业亏损额 Total Loss of Deficit Enterprises	利税总额 Total Pre-tax Profits	应付职工薪酬 Salary Payable	本年应交增值税 Value Added Tax Payable
17427.0	17373.3	171.0	34503.6	48723.0	15242.6
-45911.9	-46051.1	47401.0	73781.0	13385.2	18318.5
11047.5	18192.7	16084.8	36186.6	96895.9	13972.4
16249.9	19543.3		21342.7	4335.6	1615.4
14671.4	14839.7	181.0	19762.9	4558.8	4561.1
10382.0	16956.1		29795.3	27172.2	10575.4
5907.2	6207.6	190.2	10397.0	9971.5	3289.7
-919.5	-930.5	2934.0	9002.2	8898.5	9553.9
18716.4	25428.4	10899.8	50454.6	33060.6	23980.2
40483.8	48361.6		69009.6	145848.9	17474.2
62426.0	82610.6	129.4	119427.8	75645.4	30835.2
34575.8	49662.9	25702.1	92739.3	117164.0	37661.5
152104.2	175408.0	20131.2	292046.8	213385.9	102420.6
125798.4	148369.8	14585.3	233161.0	699874.1	65852.1
96773.3	106470.3	8410.9	216964.0	275210.8	94368.0
8655.9	16208.2	22937.5	31236.6	121851.0	12862.5
62703.2	82187.0	1715.5	122799.9	198085.9	33999.1
740.1	741.5	66.1	1329.0	1587.6	507.4
213.9	230.9		444.0	519.1	190.3
67024.1	84791.6	12465.0	274881.8	222678.8	169315.0
40552.1	40832.9		52453.2	35098.4	8418.6
2060.9	2936.4	92.0	8261.2	22792.4	4125.7

12-10 规模以上股份制工业企业主要经济指标（2014年）

单位：万元

分 组	Classify	企业单位数（个） Number of Enterprises (unit)	亏损企业 Loss Making Enterprises	工业总产值（当年价格） Gross Industrial Output Value (At Current Prices)
总计	**Total**	**618**	**121**	**24633729.1**
#市区	Urban	480	79	16631000.7
#亏损企业	Deficit Enterprises	121	121	3727187.5
按隶属关系分	**Grouped by Jurisdiction of Management**			
中央企业	Central Enterprises	37	7	4038054.0
省属企业	Provincial Enterprises	50	15	5809487.1
市属企业	Municipal Enterprises	531	99	14786188.0
按轻重工业分	**Grouped by Light Industry and Heavy Industry**			
轻工业	Light Industry	161	32	4121385.7
重工业	Heavy Industry	457	89	20512343.4
按企业规模分	**Grouped by Size of Enterprises**			
大型企业	Large-size	23	3	10062010.6
中型企业	Medium-size	91	15	4702475.4
小型企业	Small-size	504	103	9869243.1
微型企业	microenterprise			
按工业行业大类分	**Grouped by Sector**			
煤炭开采和洗选业	Mining and Washing of Coal			
石油和天然气开采业	Extraction of Petroleum and Natural Gas			
黑色金属矿采选业	Mining and Processing of Ferrous Metal Ores	1		3800.0
有色金属矿采选业	Mining and Processing of Non-ferrous Metal Ores			
非金属矿采选业	Mining and Processing of Nonmetal Ores			
开采辅助活动	Mining Auxiliary Activities	2	1	20000.7
其他采矿业	Mining of Other Ores			
农副食品加工业	Processing of Food from Agricultural Porducts	32	9	1405481.9
食品制造业	Manufacture of Foods	18	3	318711.4
酒、饮料和精制茶制造业	Manufacture of Alcohol,Beverages and Tea	7	1	188852.5
烟草制品业	Manufacture of Tobacco			
纺织业	Manufacture of Textile	6		70220.9
纺织服装、服饰业	Textile, apparel industry	4		121390.3
皮革、毛皮、羽毛及其制品和制鞋业	Leather fur feathers and its products and footwear	1	1	3874.8
木材加工和木、竹、藤、棕、草制品业	Processing of Timber,Manufacture of Wood,Plam and Straw Products	4	1	145437.4
家具制造业	Manufacture of Furniture	4	1	33846.9

Main Indicators of Share-holding Corporation Industrial Enterprises above Designated Size (2014)

(10 000 yuan)

工业销售产值（当年价） Value of Industry Products Sales (At Current Prices)	出口交货值 Export Delivery Value	从业人员年平均人数（人） Annual Average Employers (person)	资产总计 Total Assets	流动资产合计 Total Working Capitals	固定资产合计 Total Fixed Assets	固定资产原价 Origing Value of Fixed Assets	累计折旧 Accumulative Total Depreciation
23072189.3	**1340456.0**	**219368**	**25175330.5**	**15808366.8**	**5759869.1**	**8882568.7**	**3688941.0**
15635266.5	955010.6	165506	19473591.7	12152162.7	4581348.1	7317410.0	3188881.2
3583762.9	234721.9	45682	6646199.8	4411159.7	1320070.8	2069810.9	800724.5
3893505.4	349233.4	66065	8870988.2	5411121.4	2287000.7	3335977.0	1387724.2
5514038.1	349492.3	46027	4962657.7	3122030.8	982879.8	1411349.8	477311.5
13664645.8	641730.3	107276	11341684.6	7275214.6	2489988.6	4135241.9	1823905.3
4012552.4	17989.3	36914	2797753.9	1631020.9	717917.0	1295453.3	641717.6
19059636.9	1322466.7	182454	22377576.6	14177345.9	5041952.1	7587115.4	3047223.4
9675156.1	950392.6	108748	13527872.2	8142704.1	3176491.6	4847765.7	1950681.3
4075427.5	192916.9	50272	5125183.1	3408274.9	1166940.4	1696629.1	687357.5
9321605.7	197146.5	60348	6522275.2	4257387.8	1416437.1	2338173.9	1050902.2
3800.0		85	2136.8	1673.9	335.2	1036.1	701.3
19385.9		360	46114.5	23834.3	21315.5	27571.1	6255.7
1389861.4	7226.0	3815	380128.4	191647.2	94279.3	282794.1	192799.9
298524.0	374.0	4789	159801.4	67828.4	69965.6	96757.3	30323.3
343793.9		2318	224354.4	138967.5	31173.3	75705.8	44900.6
57550.7	654.3	889	65413.8	44913.1	11872.6	16186.3	4313.7
96517.1		1663	113188.6	96447.5	9095.4	12028.6	3443.4
3914.0		139	7475.1	7358.6	62.9	202.2	139.3
128237.0		706	156788.5	66652.1	54093.3	85924.4	44476.3
29398.9		538	28182.0	14542.1	5893.6	2754.2	1354.5

12-10 续表1

单位：万元

分组	Classify	负债合计 Total Liabilites	流动负债合计 Total Working Liabilities	非流动负债 Non-Working Liabilities
总计	**Total**	**15314854.8**	**12997499.5**	**1969603.0**
#市区	Urban	11323458.2	9388959.1	1631231.8
#亏损企业	Deficit Enterprises	4459443.4	3772422.6	560829.9
按隶属关系分	**Grouped by Jurisdiction of Management**			
中央企业	Central Enterprises	5201867.5	4307283.6	872060.5
省属企业	Provincial Enterprises	3709486.6	3325956.2	333169.1
市属企业	Municipal Enterprises	6403500.7	5364259.7	764373.4
按轻重工业分	**Grouped by Light Industry and Heavy Industry**			
轻工业	Light Industry	1372114.3	1091444.9	184040.6
重工业	Heavy Industry	13942740.5	11906054.6	1785562.4
按企业规模分	**Grouped by Size of Enterprises**			
大型企业	Large-size	8493084.6	7174093.5	1318990.7
中型企业	Medium-size	2830743.4	2428939.3	316351.2
小型企业	Small-size	3991026.8	3394466.7	334261.1
微型企业	microenterprise			
按工业行业大类分	**Grouped by Sector**			
煤炭开采和洗选业	Mining and Washing of Coal			
石油和天然气开采业	Extraction of Petroleum and Natural Gas			
黑色金属矿采选业	Mining and Processing of Ferrous Metal Ores	3937.7	1170.3	2767.4
有色金属矿采选业	Mining and Processing of Non-ferrous Metal Ores			
非金属矿采选业	Mining and Processing of Nonmetal Ores			
开采辅助活动	Mining Auxiliary Activities	26458.6	26458.6	
其他采矿业	Mining of Other Ores			
农副食品加工业	Processing of Food from Agricultural Porducts	290343.8	234756.5	2660.0
食品制造业	Manufacture of Foods	62773.5	51554.2	8520.1
酒、饮料和精制茶制造业	Manufacture of Alcohol,Beverages and Tea	93225.2	84463.6	2177.6
烟草制品业	Manufacture of Tobacco			
纺织业	Manufacture of Textile	28349.2	19829.0	2060.0
纺织服装、服饰业	Textile, apparel industry	76741.1	55101.1	20000.0
皮革、毛皮、羽毛及其制品和制鞋业	Leather fur feathers and its products and footwear	1123.6	1123.6	
木材加工和木、竹、藤、棕、草制品业	Processing of Timber,Manufacture of Wood,Plam and Straw Products	93785.7	40784.2	53001.5
家具制造业	Manufacture of Furniture	14706.3	12681.7	1859.7

continued 1

(10 000 yuan)

所有者权益合计 Total Owners' Equities	实收资本 Total Capital Hold	营业收入 Total Revenue	主营业务收入 Revenue from Principal Business	营业成本 Total Cost	主营业务成本 Cost of Principal Business	营业税金及附加 Taxes and Other Changes	主营业务税金及附加 Taxes and Other Charges on Principal Business
9843810.0	**4568731.2**	**21761873.8**	**21483038.1**	**18681278.7**	**18462125.1**	**87246.9**	**86153.5**
8133470.0	3569992.0	15479616.9	15355319.2	13107521.1	13016098.8	69863.5	68817.4
2192182.7	1086674.9	3597460.0	3568458.1	3271218.4	3253043.3	15454.9	15088.5
3669107.6	1334233.7	4615443.7	4578700.8	4034062.6	4004075.9	21333.1	21239.4
1259320.1	833132.7	4622453.1	4497166.9	4150522.0	4058395.4	12153.9	11903.7
4915382.3	2401364.8	12523977.0	12407170.4	10496694.1	10399653.8	53759.9	53010.4
1407768.1	761816.4	3725297.4	3714440.7	2921934.8	2913631.6	26324.1	26288.5
8436041.9	3806914.8	18036576.4	17768597.4	15759343.9	15548493.5	60922.8	59865.0
5034778.3	2053353.1	9546580.1	9395570.2	8366541.6	8252462.4	42358.4	42059.1
2294283.3	1028993.6	3824415.9	3753984.7	3073174.1	3018343.1	15738.5	15464.7
2514748.4	1486384.5	8390877.8	8333483.2	7241563.0	7191319.6	29150.0	28629.7
-1800.9	600.0	3016.0	3016.0	2457.7	2457.7	103.4	103.4
19655.9	11800.0	16803.0	16697.8	14229.4	14116.9	283.7	283.7
74455.1	56767.0	1182904.0	1181593.1	1103317.0	1101248.1	1115.4	1097.3
95527.7	49798.7	259834.3	259317.1	204384.3	203855.5	1102.5	1102.5
131128.6	128122.8	342736.2	342280.9	253982.4	253596.1	10482.4	10476.7
37064.5	19808.0	62611.0	62610.0	48315.9	48315.9	178.7	177.8
36447.4	14400.0	107348.1	107143.0	85030.2	84761.4	2430.7	2427.1
6351.5	6500.0	3904.7	3904.7	3273.7	3273.7	21.3	21.3
63002.8	17030.0	109122.9	108960.2	101425.7	101103.1	359.1	358.9
13475.7	7650.0	32818.3	32558.2	25597.3	25411.7	279.0	279.0

12-10 续表2

单位：万元

分组	Classify	销售费用 Expenses for Sales	管理费用 Expenses for Management	财务费用 Financial cost
总计	**Total**	**736637.6**	**1144539.9**	**200778.0**
#市区	Urban	546546.5	894072.6	159187.9
#亏损企业	Deficit Enterprises	118565.3	253206.5	63320.9
按隶属关系分	**Grouped by Jurisdiction of Management**			
中央企业	Central Enterprises	92423.3	351893.6	55929.5
省属企业	Provincial Enterprises	141452.9	204311.0	37820.2
市属企业	Municipal Enterprises	502761.4	588335.3	107028.3
按轻重工业分	**Grouped by Light Industry and Heavy Industry**			
轻工业	Light Industry	320410.2	232962.8	21893.5
重工业	Heavy Industry	416227.4	911577.1	178884.5
按企业规模分	**Grouped by Size of Enterprises**			
大型企业	Large-size	215999.8	508427.7	104032.1
中型企业	Medium-size	254273.0	269149.9	40861.0
小型企业	Small-size	266364.8	366962.3	55884.9
微型企业	microenterprise			
按工业行业大类分	**Grouped by Sector**			
煤炭开采和洗选业	Mining and Washing of Coal			
石油和天然气开采业	Extraction of Petroleum and Natural Gas			
黑色金属矿采选业	Mining and Processing of Ferrous Metal Ores	25.2	423.1	132.8
有色金属矿采选业	Mining and Processing of Non-ferrous Metal Ores			
非金属矿采选业	Mining and Processing of Nonmetal Ores			
开采辅助活动	Mining Auxiliary Activities	3429.4	806.3	374.7
其他采矿业	Mining of Other Ores			
农副食品加工业	Processing of Food from Agricultural Porducts	22861.3	26265.1	5103.0
食品制造业	Manufacture of Foods	29392.5	12388.9	1459.7
酒、饮料和精制茶制造业	Manufacture of Alcohol,Beverages and Tea	31922.6	11571.1	-3015.9
烟草制品业	Manufacture of Tobacco			
纺织业	Manufacture of Textile	1709.2	2351.7	409.8
纺织服装、服饰业	Textile, apparel industry	4612.1	4851.5	2337.2
皮革、毛皮、羽毛及其制品和制鞋业	Leather fur feathers and its products and footwear	236.1	348.6	127.9
木材加工和木、竹、藤、棕、草制品业	Processing of Timber,Manufacture of Wood,Plam and Straw Products	1356.7	3484.8	1475.6
家具制造业	Manufacture of Furniture	2864.4	2869.1	440.4

continued 2

(10 000 yuan)

营业利润 Operating Profit	利润总额 Total Profits	亏损企业亏损额 Total Loss of Deficit Enterprises	利税总额 Total Pre-tax Profits	应付职工薪酬 Salary Payable	本年应交增值税 Value Added Tax Payable
843512.9	**943465.7**	**130395.9**	**1548008.9**	**1519013.8**	**517296.3**
648594.6	707934.7	111088.5	1157131.3	1276899.5	379333.1
-137661.2	-130395.9	130395.9	-70946.6	339262.2	43994.4
72247.7	95227.0	24186.1	193685.9	644577.2	77125.8
53398.0	79820.4	44950.6	167505.1	240531.6	75530.8
717867.2	768418.3	61259.2	1186817.9	633905.0	364639.7
212412.3	226352.4	9872.9	370900.6	235074.1	118224.1
631100.6	717113.3	120523.0	1177108.3	1283939.7	399072.2
288404.4	325889.1	23945.5	532058.6	869656.5	163811.1
151689.6	181068.9	55235.3	318963.1	313263.9	122155.7
403418.9	436507.7	51215.1	696987.2	336093.4	231329.5
41.4	41.4		212.6	163.4	67.8
-2400.7	-2311.5	3249.2	-1680.2	2810.0	347.6
12125.7	14677.7	3264.0	18616.0	34205.3	2822.9
11955.9	12309.4	1631.1	19267.3	25962.8	5855.4
39100.7	39594.0	689.8	65460.1	19051.7	15383.7
9645.7	9784.4		12718.4	2571.0	2755.3
8611.4	8719.8		13871.9	4461.5	2721.4
-102.9	-102.9	102.9	63.4	460.4	145.0
1767.1	3734.0	315.5	9846.4	4740.2	5753.3
224.5	514.1	21.1	1351.9	1862.2	558.8

12-10 续表3

单位：万元

分组	Classify	企业单位数（个） Number of Enterprises (unit)	亏损企业 Loss Making Enterprises	工业总产值（当年价格） Gross Industrial Output Value (At Current Prices)
造纸及纸制品业	Manufacture of Paper and Paper Products	10	2	72381.3
印刷和记录媒介复制	Printing,Reproduction of Recording Media	13	2	396436.8
文教、工美、体育和娱乐用品制造业	Manufacture of Articles For Cultural,Educational and Sports Activities	2	1	5038.3
石油加工业、炼焦和核燃料加工业	Processing of Petroleum, Cokeing,Processing of Nuclear and Nuclear Fuel	4		1305882.4
化学原料及化学制品制造业	Manufacture of Raw Chemical Materials and Chemical Products	33	2	1327119.4
医药制造业	Manufacture of Medicines	35	4	984225.1
化学纤维制造业	Manufacture of Chemical Fibers	3	1	12356.8
橡胶和塑料制品业	Manufacture of Rubber and Plastics	13	1	339412.2
非金属矿物制品业	Manufacture of Non-metallic Mineral Products	60	18	1208194.3
黑色金属冶炼和压延加工业	Smelting and Pressing of Ferrous Metals	6	2	278798.1
有色金属冶炼和压延加工业	Smelting and Pressing of Non-ferrous Metals	27	9	1554104.5
金属制品业	Manufacture of Metal Products	24	4	447636.7
通用设备制造业	Manufacture of General Purpose Machinery	46	4	764951.1
专用设备制造业	Manufacture of Special Equipment	59	12	1479521.8
汽车制造业	Manufacture of Motor Vehicle	31	9	5525600.4
铁路、船舶、航空航天和其他运输设备制造业	Railways,Shipbuilding,Aerospace and Other Transportation Equipment Manufacturing Industry	30	4	3291738.9
电气机械和器材制造业	Manufacture of Electric Equipment and Machinery	56	6	1784674.5
计算机、通讯和其他电子设备制造业	Manufacture of Communication Equipment, Computers and other Electronic Equipment	37	8	813787.2
仪器仪表制造业	Manufacture of Measuring Instruments and Machinery	27	5	298312.4
其他制造业	Manufacture of Other Manufacturing	5	2	27783.1
废弃资源综合利用业	Recycling and Disposal of Waste			
金属制品、机械和设备修理业	Metal Products,Machinery and Equipment Repair Industry	2	1	4628.7
电力、热力的生产和供应业	Production and Supply of Electric Power and Heat Power	8	5	247617.6
燃气生产和供应业	Gas Mining and Supplying Industry	6	1	144822.8
水的生产和供应业	Production and Supply of Water	2	1	7087.9

continued 3

(10 000 yuan)

工业销售产值（当年价） Value of Industry Products Sales (At Current Prices)	出口交货值 Export Delivery Value	从业人员年平均人数（人） Annual Average Employers (person)	资产总计 Total Assets	流动资产合计 Total Working Capitals	固定资产合计 Total Fixed Assets	固定资产原价 Origing Value of Fixed Assets	累计折旧 Accumulative Total Depreciation
71259.6		1435	38642.4	23788.6	11579.5	14741.9	6162.5
399703.2		5016	484311.8	235846.4	211390.2	377534.7	185461.0
4930.8		112	1586.0	925.9	419.7	601.8	182.1
1307217.2		544	173457.2	146386.9	27069.6	35830.1	15383.9
1269730.9	303343.5	7383	1432211.0	907994.3	341632.8	804294.4	477989.5
840275.0	9735.0	9591	815155.5	522881.5	152382.1	227638.8	94528.1
13185.7		427	34584.5	8038.6	12053.0	13299.4	1246.4
293300.2	2560.0	2302	199224.9	128605.9	62794.9	71594.9	27452.7
1114700.9	1262.1	8770	664128.5	406457.6	215579.2	383979.1	190571.7
126317.9		1217	86859.2	35907.8	28255.5	48520.1	22392.6
1368591.3	67469.1	9101	1525286.4	839406.5	357088.6	477562.1	150236.9
418593.8	927.7	3911	262275.4	131542.3	72088.1	132836.6	63256.2
718750.5	36359.9	9649	1146475.4	884368.0	169017.3	213270.8	64201.4
1343427.3	106465.3	18417	2358702.5	1619658.7	495239.1	692001.4	259191.0
5184237.5	294212.2	35611	3619554.7	2314258.1	642377.2	908695.0	296074.1
3168157.9	338059.1	55627	6924401.2	4249429.9	1619851.0	2317520.8	953164.3
1702762.3	51521.9	10827	1329080.8	1035580.0	190845.7	272697.0	94792.3
639823.0	87380.2	14653	1456820.4	940947.8	358474.2	505401.6	150497.7
286337.1	32905.7	4998	366594.0	290496.3	34763.9	51277.5	18927.9
26811.1		633	65923.6	42895.9	11309.0	16704.7	6428.4
4343.7		119	6964.7	4579.2	1834.0	2341.0	507.0
246908.5		2037	657142.0	203352.3	362950.9	600044.5	245281.7
144753.1		1475	316229.7	173135.2	64994.1	86100.7	26976.7
7087.9		211	26135.2	8018.4	17792.8	27119.7	9326.9

12-10 续表4

单位：万元

分组	Classify	负债合计 Total Liabilites	流动负债合计 Total Working Liabilities	非流动负债 Non-Working Liabilities
造纸及纸制品业	Manufacture of Paper and Paper Products	19366.3	18046.5	166.0
印刷和记录媒介复制	Printing,Reproduction of Recording Media	143597.8	132334.3	2393.3
文教、工美、体育和娱乐用品制造业	Manufacture of Articles For Cultural,Educational and Sports Activities	88.2	88.2	
石油加工业、炼焦和核燃料加工业	Processing of Petroleum, Cokeing,Processing of Nuclear and Nuclear Fuel	128542.2	115026.8	13189.3
化学原料及化学制品制造业	Manufacture of Raw Chemical Materials and Chemical Products	850505.6	660461.7	188984.5
医药制造业	Manufacture of Medicines	346432.2	300043.5	31883.9
化学纤维制造业	Manufacture of Chemical Fibers	5796.6	5338.6	458.0
橡胶和塑料制品业	Manufacture of Rubber and Plastics	102800.5	81555.3	17680.7
非金属矿物制品业	Manufacture of Non-metallic Mineral Products	389815.3	329697.8	41170.3
黑色金属冶炼和压延加工业	Smelting and Pressing of Ferrous Metals	62435.7	18458.0	
有色金属冶炼和压延加工业	Smelting and Pressing of Non-ferrous Metals	795977.1	658882.1	137095.0
金属制品业	Manufacture of Metal Products	169099.8	130952.6	15555.5
通用设备制造业	Manufacture of General Purpose Machinery	672108.6	582343.0	61357.7
专用设备制造业	Manufacture of Special Equipment	1130578.5	1026571.3	94620.9
汽车制造业	Manufacture of Motor Vehicle	2710966.1	2482343.0	222016.6
铁路、船舶、航空航天和其他运输设备制造业	Railways,Shipbuilding,Aerospace and Other Transportation Equipment Manufacturing Industry	4267602.3	3591439.2	669169.4
电气机械和器材制造业	Manufacture of Electric Equipment and Machinery	847600.7	804297.8	38342.3
计算机、通讯和其他电子设备制造业	Manufacture of Communication Equipment, Computers and other Electronic Equipment	973846.5	786340.4	136310.7
仪器仪表制造业	Manufacture of Measuring Instruments and Machinery	187507.7	168987.6	4924.0
其他制造业	Manufacture of Other Manufacturing	41307.5	40927.5	13.0
废弃资源综合利用业	Recycling and Disposal of Waste			
金属制品、机械和设备修理业	Metal Products,Machinery and Equipment Repair Industry	5529.9	4728.8	801.1
电力、热力的生产和供应业	Production and Supply of Electric Power and Heat Power	594667.8	395473.3	199194.5
燃气生产和供应业	Gas Mining and Supplying Industry	159211.6	118313.8	130.0
水的生产和供应业	Production and Supply of Water	18025.6	16925.6	1100.0

continued 4

(10 000 yuan)

所有者权益合计 Total Owners' Equities	实收资本 Total Capital Hold	营业收入 Total Revenue	主营业务收入 Revenue from Principal Business	营业成本 Total Cost	主营业务成本 Cost of Principal Business	营业税金及附加 Taxs and Other Changes	主营业务税金及附加 Taxes and Other Charges on Principal Business
19276.0	11930.0	70480.2	70333.8	62371.8	62371.8	199.8	199.8
340704.8	186218.2	400900.4	397293.5	310695.0	309022.9	2724.2	2724.2
1497.8	1400.0	4930.8	4930.8	4024.8	4024.8	12.3	12.3
44914.9	25535.7	716905.9	715928.4	706199.8	705970.8	271.6	271.6
581034.4	336852.2	1191903.0	1178907.9	1019841.3	996488.2	2788.5	2768.9
467691.8	149417.0	786006.7	785144.1	444380.3	444370.0	6193.8	6193.8
28787.9	29500.0	12818.3	12818.3	11778.2	11778.2	106.3	106.3
96424.3	34443.0	303246.3	302792.2	239110.4	238810.3	883.4	883.4
274312.5	172461.5	1073454.9	1064373.5	923420.0	916162.0	6405.6	6405.6
30728.1	6800.0	191261.1	188640.1	171080.5	168513.0	1180.5	1180.5
729308.3	320192.6	1269125.3	1247194.5	1124974.7	1112293.0	2019.0	1998.7
93175.2	70429.6	392790.7	391007.9	334009.5	333201.3	1764.0	1762.4
474357.3	175893.3	707666.6	704575.5	602875.1	601487.9	2986.0	2924.3
1228121.0	523418.4	1313933.9	1282272.1	1084555.2	1063418.4	5511.5	5499.5
908587.8	551977.5	4320981.4	4204211.5	3902454.4	3816064.5	10514.7	10513.6
2653886.5	877150.0	3844530.5	3817583.8	3355668.7	3328908.1	15860.6	15851.7
481475.9	269157.2	1626035.7	1614109.8	1397073.2	1385190.5	4964.5	4908.0
481478.9	230586.3	704948.2	687601.4	583875.1	568306.8	2214.0	1939.9
179085.8	99280.8	296678.3	292485.2	220667.2	218852.9	2056.1	1957.5
24616.1	18128.0	26944.6	26402.8	19765.0	19596.5	177.5	177.5
1434.8	1200.0	4311.7	4310.8	3140.9	3140.9	51.0	51.0
62474.1	50890.8	249217.6	243563.9	223705.8	223437.4	1251.6	915.6
157017.9	107352.6	125239.0	122415.0	88427.6	87641.3	708.0	540.8
8109.6	6040.0	6464.2	6060.3	5170.6	4933.5	46.2	38.9

12-10 续表5

单位：万元

分 组	Classify	销售费用 Expenses for Sales	管理费用 Expenses for Management	财务费用 Financial cost
造纸及纸制品业	Manufacture of Paper and Paper Products	2184.9	2782.1	788.4
印刷和记录媒介复制	Printing,Reproduction of Recording Media	7636.7	42967.1	-1125.2
文教、工美、体育和娱乐用品制造业	Manufacture of Articles For Cultural,Educational and Sports Activities	139.0	298.4	27.6
石油加工业、炼焦和核燃料加工业	Processing of Petroleum, Cokeing,Processing of Nuclear and Nuclear Fuel	3735.6	3671.4	972.2
化学原料及化学制品制造业	Manufacture of Raw Chemical Materials and Chemical Products	34939.3	59291.3	14696.0
医药制造业	Manufacture of Medicines	186982.6	88276.9	4149.1
化学纤维制造业	Manufacture of Chemical Fibers	183.8	1431.6	208.7
橡胶和塑料制品业	Manufacture of Rubber and Plastics	13135.1	20692.2	4098.3
非金属矿物制品业	Manufacture of Non-metallic Mineral Products	16651.1	35441.5	5020.1
黑色金属冶炼和压延加工业	Smelting and Pressing of Ferrous Metals	1107.1	4443.3	2967.1
有色金属冶炼和压延加工业	Smelting and Pressing of Non-ferrous Metals	9344.5	36127.2	21805.7
金属制品业	Manufacture of Metal Products	5700.0	14800.7	2889.2
通用设备制造业	Manufacture of General Purpose Machinery	21837.7	44851.0	3127.6
专用设备制造业	Manufacture of Special Equipment	57439.2	105721.1	1313.0
汽车制造业	Manufacture of Motor Vehicle	102227.3	151090.5	26165.0
铁路、船舶、航空航天和其他运输设备制造业	Railways,Shipbuilding,Aerospace and Other Transportation Equipment Manufacturing Industry	72078.6	285542.4	49859.5
电气机械和器材制造业	Manufacture of Electric Equipment and Machinery	48109.1	59119.4	10278.9
计算机、通讯和其他电子设备制造业	Manufacture of Communication Equipment, Computers and other Electronic Equipment	23523.7	71136.9	14081.9
仪器仪表制造业	Manufacture of Measuring Instruments and Machinery	13983.0	31920.5	2996.5
其他制造业	Manufacture of Other Manufacturing	2150.5	4294.4	1618.1
废弃资源综合利用业	Recycling and Disposal of Waste			
金属制品、机械和设备修理业	Metal Products,Machinery and Equipment Repair Industry	145.2	900.1	3.8
电力、热力的生产和供应业	Production and Supply of Electric Power and Heat Power	468.1	6558.1	19036.0
燃气生产和供应业	Gas Mining and Supplying Industry	14433.2	6543.4	6356.4
水的生产和供应业	Production and Supply of Water	92.8	1278.2	598.9

continued 5

(10 000 yuan)

营业利润 Operating Profit	利润总额 Total Profits	亏损企业亏损额 Total Loss of Deficit Enterprises	利税总额 Total Pre-tax Profits	应付职工薪酬 Salary Payable	本年应交增值税 Value Added Tax Payable
2171.9	2229.4	494.5	3137.1	4576.6	707.9
39594.7	40698.4	256.9	68009.4	62545.1	24586.8
428.7	428.7	7.0	553.7	510.5	112.7
2055.2	2026.1		4275.8	1148.9	1978.1
60008.7	64804.8	140.8	84524.0	65878.8	16930.7
66812.0	71616.8	934.6	124637.6	46827.3	46827.0
-890.4	-14.4	181.0	1019.1	2157.1	927.2
31830.7	33851.3	292.8	47076.3	13798.7	12341.6
87367.4	85818.0	5477.3	125565.8	40402.7	33342.2
10341.6	10915.7	8544.1	15351.1	5360.6	3254.9
69874.8	77760.3	12246.7	110905.5	50877.9	31126.2
31588.8	32299.0	724.8	45897.2	22235.9	11834.2
31581.4	36459.2	2355.6	55307.2	54601.3	15862.0
37473.9	54561.8	21178.4	111775.8	122236.5	51702.5
110592.3	134086.9	13697.7	218921.4	161707.5	74319.8
61792.6	69563.8	14585.3	129425.3	537953.7	44000.9
84153.6	88083.8	4658.1	164851.4	65966.9	71803.1
6467.9	11972.3	21553.2	31609.4	100399.7	17423.1
24093.5	26583.9	1904.9	37395.3	36521.1	8755.3
-840.1	456.8	637.1	1651.8	2947.5	1017.5
70.7	87.7	143.2	423.0	835.1	284.3
-1654.4	3043.0	9726.5	12740.7	14651.5	8446.1
8358.1	9158.1	1289.8	12885.9	7532.7	3019.8
-729.5	13.9	92.0	341.3	1051.7	281.2

12-11 规模以上外商及港澳台商投资工业企业主要经济指标（2014年）

单位：万元

分 组	Classify	企业单位数（个） Number of Enterprises (unit)	亏损企业 Loss Making Enterprises	工业总产值（当年价格） Gross Industrial Output Value (At Current Prices)
总计	**Total**	**121**	**37**	**8631869.1**
#市区	Urban	109	35	7552164.9
#亏损企业	Deficit Enterprises	37	37	1970130.1
按隶属关系分	**Grouped by Jurisdiction of Management**			
中央企业	Central Enterprises	4	2	142643.6
省属企业	Provincial Enterprises	8	1	1351022.4
市属企业	Municipal Enterprises	109	34	7138203.1
按登记注册类型分组	**Grouped by Type of Registration**			
港澳台商投资	Enterprises with Funds from Hong Kong, Macao &Taiwan	25	9	882458.1
与港澳台商合资经营	Cooperative Enterprises	14	5	615281.7
与港澳台商合作经营	Joint-venture Enterprises			
港澳台商独资	Enterprises with Sole Investment	10	4	223576.1
港澳台商投资股份有限公司	Share-holding Corporations Ltd. With their Investment	1		43600.3
其他港澳台投资	Other			
外商投资	Foreign Funded Enterprises	96	28	7749411.0
中外合资经营	Joint-venture Enterprises	56	16	5234197.2
中外合作经营	Cooperation Enterprises	1		3768.3
外资企业	Foreign Funded Enterprises	36	12	2232453.1
外商投资股份有限公司	Share-holding Corporations Ltd. With Foreign Funds	2		276031.2
其他外商投资	Other	1		2961.2
按轻重工业分	**Grouped by Light Industry and Heavy Industry**			
轻工业	Light Industry	35	10	2579157.1
重工业	Heavy Industry	86	27	6052712.0
按企业规模分	**Grouped by Size of Enterprises**			
大型企业	Large-size	12	1	4749422.6
中型企业	Medium-size	24	5	2046018.5
小型企业	Small-size	85	31	1836428.0
微型企业	microenterprise			
按工业行业大类分	**Grouped by Sector**			
煤炭开采和洗选业	Mining and Washing of Coal			
石油和天然气开采业	Extraction of Petroleum and Natural Gas			
黑色金属矿采选业	Mining and Processing of Ferrous Metal Ores			
有色金属矿采选业	Mining and Processing of Non-ferrous Metal Ores			
非金属矿采选业	Mining and Processing of Nonmetal Ores			
开采辅助活动	Mining Auxiliary Activities			
其他采矿业	Mining of Other Ores			

Economic Indicators of Foreign Fund Industrial Enterprises above Designated Size (2014)

(10 000 yuan)

工业销售产值（当年价） Value of Industry Products Sales (At Current Prices)	出口交货值 Export Delivery Value	从业人员年平均人数（人） Annual Average Employers (person)	资产总计 Total Assets	流动资产合计 Total Working Capitals	固定资产合计 Total Fixed Assets	固定资产原价 Origing Value of Fixed Assets	累计折旧 Accumulative Total Depreciation
7859157.7	**1202302.5**	**78392**	**10626011.0**	**3746010.2**	**5300558.9**	**6916015.1**	**1851525.0**
6840913.9	1198798.0	75672	10112034.0	3573853.0	5176437.6	6710358.2	1752592.2
1974344.8	82919.6	37014	2230041.0	826400.1	851538.8	1076494.5	335044.3
140201.5	6447.3	1153	130029.7	73812.5	33547.1	87641.8	54359.8
1292896.2	938.5	5506	882002.0	528408.9	79975.1	148581.1	90887.4
6426060.0	1194916.7	71733	9613979.3	3143788.8	5187036.7	6679792.2	1706277.8
792310.6	71684.4	6529	554600.9	287958.4	150418.0	242494.6	106532.9
539057.8	7103.8	2452	332277.4	201479.1	44336.3	79196.8	39541.0
209768.5	63962.1	3175	179777.9	68201.1	96218.1	143605.5	57163.2
43484.3	618.5	902	42545.6	18278.2	9863.6	19692.3	9828.7
7066847.1	1130618.1	71863	10071410.1	3458051.8	5150140.9	6673520.5	1744992.1
4880068.8	149918.2	53612	4404971.6	2194838.1	1274949.5	1756217.0	677799.0
3741.9	927.2	129	4214.1	3212.1	1002.0	1002.0	582.2
1971882.9	814549.9	17016	5310036.8	1085579.7	3724208.9	4461428.0	759189.5
208533.0	165222.8	1080	348390.5	173442.5	147452.1	454873.5	307421.4
2620.5		26	3797.1	979.4	2528.4		
2437087.7	184895.3	18630	1942682.2	1107509.1	573895.5	1217865.2	688340.8
5422070.0	1017407.2	59762	8683328.8	2638501.1	4726663.4	5698149.9	1163184.2
4424107.1	834453.0	54054	7762500.4	2130136.4	4528942.8	5730443.0	1373538.4
1953641.7	218104.6	13735	1469442.3	814835.0	354178.1	570099.6	240600.3
1481408.9	149744.9	10603.0	1394068.3	801038.8	417438.0	615472.5	237386.3

12-11 续表1

单位：万元

分组	Classify	负债合计 Total Liabilites	流动负债合计 Total Working Liabilities	非流动负债 Non-Working Liabilities
总计	**Total**	**6231845.6**	**4907331.5**	**1085716.1**
#市区	Urban	5862191.7	4717888.8	1082190.2
#亏损企业	Deficit Enterprises	1499965.0	1278028.9	199700.1
按隶属关系分	**Grouped by Jurisdiction of Management**			
中央企业	Central Enterprises	32787.8	31880.7	907.1
省属企业	Provincial Enterprises	615495.6	396208.4	40851.4
市属企业	Municipal Enterprises	5583562.2	4479242.4	1043957.6
按登记注册类型分组	**Grouped by Type of Registration**			
港澳台商投资	Enterprises with Funds from Hong Kong, Macao &Taiwan	322634.5	221913.8	48915.0
与港澳台商合资经营	Cooperative Enterprises	179132.6	90649.7	36762.5
与港澳台商合作经营	Joint-venture Enterprises			
港澳台商独资	Enterprises with Sole Investment	127354.4	115946.4	11322.7
港澳台商投资股份有限公司	Share-holding Corporations Ltd. With their Investment	16147.5	15317.7	829.8
其他港澳台投资	Other			
外商投资	Foreign Funded Enterprises	5909211.1	4685417.7	1036801.1
中外合资经营	Joint-venture Enterprises	2680921.9	2256809.0	238239.0
中外合作经营	Cooperation Enterprises	2761.2	2761.2	
外资企业	Foreign Funded Enterprises	2988612.5	2261193.8	726760.0
外商投资股份有限公司	Share-holding Corporations Ltd. With Foreign Funds	235076.4	163674.3	71402.1
其他外商投资	Other	1839.1	979.4	400.0
按轻重工业分	**Grouped by Light Industry and Heavy Industry**			
轻工业	Light Industry	1084326.3	973069.2	81920.5
重工业	Heavy Industry	5147519.3	3934262.3	1003795.6
按企业规模分	**Grouped by Size of Enterprises**			
大型企业	Large-size	4669966.9	3778156.3	884589.5
中型企业	Medium-size	802031.8	527174.7	95173.4
小型企业	Small-size	759846.9	602000.5	105953.2
微型企业	microenterprise			
按工业行业大类分	**Grouped by Sector**			
煤炭开采和洗选业	Mining and Washing of Coal			
石油和天然气开采业	Extraction of Petroleum and Natural Gas			
黑色金属矿采选业	Mining and Processing of Ferrous Metal Ores			
有色金属矿采选业	Mining and Processing of Non-ferrous Metal Ores			
非金属矿采选业	Mining and Processing of Nonmetal Ores			
开采辅助活动	Mining Auxiliary Activities			
其他采矿业	Mining of Other Ores			

continued 1

(10 000 yuan)

所有者权益合计 Total Owners' Equities	实收资本 Total Capital Hold	营业收入 Total Revenue	主营业务收入 Revenue from Principal Business	营业成本 Total Cost	主营业务成本 Cost of Principal Business	营业税金及附加 Taxs and Other Changes	主营业务税金及附加 Taxes and Other Charges on Principal Business
4393658.2	**3130349.1**	**7324854.3**	**7127748.7**	**5935345.9**	**5784533.8**	**66663.6**	**66410.4**
4249335.2	3023228.0	6502674.5	6322637.0	5283039.7	5140364.3	64922.9	64790.4
729573.0	562914.5	1565305.4	1492870.5	1484853.7	1448310.2	44122.1	44122.0
97241.8	84251.5	140234.8	140214.3	117548.1	117436.2	553.7	553.7
266506.2	78907.9	1167764.5	1149708.6	772279.4	763233.3	5798.1	5798.1
4029910.2	2967189.7	6016855.0	5837825.8	5045518.4	4903864.3	60311.8	60058.6
231466.4	225943.2	799139.7	778271.4	703912.7	699300.9	1567.3	1567.3
152644.8	91136.0	561514.6	545179.1	515934.5	515516.7	513.5	513.5
52423.5	127307.2	206067.5	202595.4	163548.9	160267.7	858.7	858.7
26398.1	7500.0	31557.6	30496.9	24429.3	23516.5	195.1	195.1
4162191.8	2904405.9	6525714.6	6349477.3	5231433.2	5085232.9	65096.3	64843.1
1724045.9	865120.3	4340105.4	4191768.5	3488774.5	3405653.1	55660.7	55483.5
1452.9	1108.0	3741.9	3741.9	3190.2	3190.2	1.6	1.6
2321422.0	2014799.6	2048416.2	2021615.0	1609830.0	1565785.2	8539.7	8539.6
113314.0	21578.0	130920.6	129821.4	127394.7	108360.6	894.3	818.4
1957.0	1800.0	2530.5	2530.5	2243.8	2243.8		
858351.7	387027.3	2294643.8	2259837.0	1672017.4	1621163.0	13233.8	13157.9
3535306.5	2743321.8	5030210.5	4867911.7	4263328.5	4163370.8	53429.8	53252.5
3092533.2	2092529.6	4008784.0	3870217.1	3228935.6	3103579.5	53061.7	52937.1
667410.2	390441.8	1787458.7	1755220.3	1403712.6	1386052.0	8501.8	8376.0
633714.8	647377.7	1528611.6	1502311.3	1302697.7	1294902.3	5100.1	5097.3

12-11 续表2

单位：万元

分 组	Classify	销售费用 Expenses for Sales	管理费用 Expenses for Management	财务费用 Financial cost
总计	**Total**	**464504.1**	**443729.6**	**53417.2**
#市区	Urban	458463.1	415241.2	50926.0
#亏损企业	Deficit Enterprises	56499.3	75704.8	22840.7
按隶属关系分	**Grouped by Jurisdiction of Management**			
中央企业	Central Enterprises	2044.1	8530.6	107.1
省属企业	Provincial Enterprises	161421.1	54081.6	12221.5
市属企业	Municipal Enterprises	301038.9	381117.4	41088.6
按登记注册类型分组	**Grouped by Type of Registration**			
港澳台商投资	Enterprises with Funds from Hong Kong, Macao &Taiwan	31258.5	26860.3	3184.4
与港澳台商合资经营	Cooperative Enterprises	3937.1	13649.3	1479.3
与港澳台商合作经营	Joint-venture Enterprises			
港澳台商独资	Enterprises with Sole Investment	25397.0	12101.6	1046.6
港澳台商投资股份有限公司	Share-holding Corporations Ltd. With their Investment	1924.4	1109.4	658.5
其他港澳台投资	Other			
外商投资	Foreign Funded Enterprises	433245.6	416869.3	50232.8
中外合资经营	Joint-venture Enterprises	309453.0	184844.3	24222.8
中外合作经营	Cooperation Enterprises	98.8	352.4	2.5
外资企业	Foreign Funded Enterprises	117053.5	222198.1	14623.0
外商投资股份有限公司	Share-holding Corporations Ltd. With Foreign Funds	6512.8	9344.3	11300.9
其他外商投资	Other	127.5	130.2	83.6
按轻重工业分	**Grouped by Light Industry and Heavy Industry**			
轻工业	Light Industry	355048.8	109060.6	22054.3
重工业	Heavy Industry	109455.3	334669.0	31362.9
按企业规模分	**Grouped by Size of Enterprises**			
大型企业	Large-size	346137.0	273918.4	34028.4
中型企业	Medium-size	67360.5	92048.2	6804.5
小型企业	Small-size	51006.6	77763.0	12584.3
微型企业	microenterprise			
按工业行业大类分	**Grouped by Sector**			
煤炭开采和洗选业	Mining and Washing of Coal			
石油和天然气开采业	Extraction of Petroleum and Natural Gas			
黑色金属矿采选业	Mining and Processing of Ferrous Metal Ores			
有色金属矿采选业	Mining and Processing of Non-ferrous Metal Ores			
非金属矿采选业	Mining and Processing of Nonmetal Ores			
开采辅助活动	Mining Auxiliary Activities			
其他采矿业	Mining of Other Ores			

continued 2

(10 000 yuan)

营业利润 Operating Profit	利润总额 Total Profits	亏损企业亏损额 Total Loss of Deficit Enterprises	利税总额 Total Pre-tax Profits	应付职工薪酬 Salary Payable	本年应交增值税 Value Added Tax Payable
372474.8	**533206.2**	**81361.9**	**926028.2**	**591579.7**	**326158.4**
230728.2	388543.1	80958.7	734567.9	575926.1	281101.9
-135994.6	-81361.9	81361.9	-9235.8	180368.7	28004.0
11477.3	11817.3	3700.3	18424.2	14768.0	6053.2
161208.9	160800.7	1141.5	283421.4	88486.3	116822.6
199788.6	360588.2	76520.1	624182.6	488325.4	203282.6
18564.8	19362.3	26247.1	60470.5	52936.8	39540.9
26221.7	26529.2	3280.6	55316.7	16829.7	28274.0
-11396.4	-11163.4	22966.5	-657.4	32631.3	9647.3
3739.5	3996.5		5811.2	3475.8	1619.6
353910.0	513843.9	55114.8	865557.7	538642.9	286617.5
274873.5	332803.3	37668.4	623964.7	392601.8	235500.7
96.4	96.4		163.3	487.0	65.3
85532.1	178831.1	17446.4	229237.0	131879.5	41866.2
-6531.3	2083.7		12163.3	13578.6	9185.3
-60.7	29.4		29.4	96.0	
142621.3	153010.7	11768.3	313303.5	217821.6	147059.0
229853.5	380195.5	69593.6	612724.7	373758.1	179099.4
93981.2	247113.4	12650.8	497246.5	370004.7	197071.4
219160.2	222331.3	12616.9	297197.7	131818.0	66364.6
59333.4	63761.5	56094.2	131584.0	89757.0	62722.4

12-11 续表3

单位：万元

分 组	Classify	企业单位数（个） Number of Enterprises (unit)	亏损企业 Loss Making Enterprises	工业总产值（当年价格） Gross Industrial Output Value (At Current Prices)
农副食品加工业	Processing of Food from Agricultural Porducts	3		17502.8
食品制造业	Manufacture of Foods	5		1027030.2
酒、饮料和精制茶制造业	Manufacture of Alcohol,Beverages and Tea	8	5	627104.2
烟草制品业	Manufacture of Tobacco			
纺织业	Manufacture of Textile	1	1	8470.9
纺织服装、服饰业	Textile, apparel industry			
皮革、毛皮、羽毛及其制品和制鞋业	Leather fur feathers and its products and footwear			
木材加工和木、竹、藤、棕、草制品业	Processing of Timber,Manufacture of Wood,Plam and Straw Products			
家具制造业	Manufacture of Furniture			
造纸及纸制品业	Manufacture of Paper and Paper Products	2		40698.8
印刷和记录媒介复制	Printing,Reproduction of Recording Media	1		43600.3
文教、工美、体育和娱乐用品制造业	Manufacture of Articles For Cultural,Educational and Sports Activities	2	1	9409.8
石油加工业、炼焦和核燃料加工业	Processing of Petroleum, Cokeing,Processing of Nuclear and Nuclear Fuel	2		276642.8
化学原料及化学制品制造业	Manufacture of Raw Chemical Materials and Chemical Products	9	6	108610.3
医药制造业	Manufacture of Medicines	5	1	629148.8
化学纤维制造业	Manufacture of Chemical Fibers	1		93368.8
橡胶和塑料制品业	Manufacture of Rubber and Plastics	3		21955.0
非金属矿物制品业	Manufacture of Non-metallic Mineral Products	4	1	371168.0
黑色金属冶炼和压延加工业	Smelting and Pressing of Ferrous Metals	2	1	14278.8
有色金属冶炼和压延加工业	Smelting and Pressing of Non-ferrous Metals	5	2	102371.5
金属制品业	Manufacture of Metal Products	4	2	33777.1
通用设备制造业	Manufacture of General Purpose Machinery	5	1	111740.9
专用设备制造业	Manufacture of Special Equipment	9	3	428501.3
汽车制造业	Manufacture of Motor Vehicle	6	2	2402721.5
铁路、船舶、航空航天和其他运输设备制造业	Railways,Shipbuilding,Aerospace and Other Transportation Equipment Manufacturing Industry	9	1	205048.5
电气机械和器材制造业	Manufacture of Electric Equipment and Machinery	17	5	704947.4
计算机、通讯和其他电子设备制造业	Manufacture of Communication Equipment, Computers and other Electronic Equipment	10	3	984811.3
仪器仪表制造业	Manufacture of Measuring Instruments and Machinery	4	1	102894.2
其他制造业	Manufacture of Other Manufacturing	1	1	4209.0
废弃资源综合利用业	Recycling and Disposal of Waste			
金属制品、机械和设备修理业	Metal Products,Machinery and Equipment Repair Industry	2		11202.7
电力、热力的生产和供应业	Production and Supply of Electric Power and Heat Power			
燃气生产和供应业	Gas Mining and Supplying Industry	1		250654.2
水的生产和供应业	Production and Supply of Water			

continued 3

(10 000 yuan)

工业销售产值（当年价） Value of Industry Products Sales (At Current Prices)	出口交货值 Export Delivery Value	从业人员年平均人数（人） Annual Average Employers (person)	资产总计 Total Assets	流动资产合计 Total Working Capitals	固定资产合计 Total Fixed Assets	固定资产原价 Origing Value of Fixed Assets	累计折旧 Accumulative Total Depreciation
16655.0		581	14979.5	9942.9	4191.3	5233.3	3570.4
974171.6		4727	385428.9	211497.9	110430.0	184413.6	82376.0
559538.4	168012.4	5359	787289.4	365828.2	309520.4	743064.7	433663.1
857.0		105	11323.8	4730.0	1509.2	1973.5	464.3
39880.7		297	27226.7	12459.5	4003.7	8443.7	4440.0
43484.3	618.5	902	42545.6	18278.2	9863.6	19692.3	9828.7
9409.8	9409.8	215	7871.0	6046.1	1800.3	2315.9	515.6
276642.8		4088	155249.0	33572.9	121017.1	109611.2	26493.0
104055.7	22150.1	448	232098.5	62428.6	157442.1	167870.2	18505.7
621296.8	3276.3	5441	526559.6	386368.0	88356.4	156003.8	93262.3
91984.2		261	48962.8	33827.0	14657.9	58563.6	43905.7
18531.2	927.2	410	33243.8	20088.8	12500.5	19460.8	8957.7
113365.8		771	122269.1	38347.7	71335.8	105646.0	40336.7
16096.6	876.9	229	10154.6	6042.1	3501.3	7729.0	3238.0
84981.5	47937.1	405	55847.3	40730.6	5816.3	16270.6	10454.3
35804.4	2989.2	731	63891.1	13399.5	45477.6	57829.0	12351.4
98565.9	19555.7	1433	138175.7	99228.5	19288.6	49857.9	33006.7
393478.8	64185.1	3241	337077.6	223176.3	88219.0	138197.5	58115.6
2381689.9	47036.1	32366	1962049.5	673349.1	637207.3	767182.5	234903.2
203354.0	31951.4	1438	290895.0	258068.4	29093.1	45139.3	27128.5
631736.1	6105.5	3657	464685.7	301593.6	75427.5	133929.1	59433.2
783679.7	743664.4	7254	4284185.0	610970.9	3311779.0	3870722.8	576400.9
94070.9	33606.8	1162	154491.0	121676.6	23794.9	37186.6	14821.7
4200.9		117	5480.5	2933.2	2030.9	3422.6	1391.7
11202.7		290	17308.3	16110.1	462.3	1335.3	873.0
250423.0		2464	446722.0	175315.5	151832.8	204920.3	53087.6

12-11 续表4

单位：万元

分组	Classify	负债合计 Total Liabilites	流动负债合计 Total Working Liabilities	非流动负债 Non-Working Liabilities
农副食品加工业	Processing of Food from Agricultural Porducts	7722.4	6862.7	400.0
食品制造业	Manufacture of Foods	156914.7	156350.3	564.4
酒、饮料和精制茶制造业	Manufacture of Alcohol,Beverages and Tea	507977.4	428358.6	79618.8
烟草制品业	Manufacture of Tobacco			
纺织业	Manufacture of Textile	4805.4	4805.4	
纺织服装、服饰业	Textile, apparel industry			
皮革、毛皮、羽毛及其制品和制鞋业	Leather fur feathers and its products and footwear			
木材加工和木、竹、藤、棕、草制品业	Processing of Timber,Manufacture of Wood,Plam and Straw Products			
家具制造业	Manufacture of Furniture			
造纸及纸制品业	Manufacture of Paper and Paper Products	11646.1	11646.1	
印刷和记录媒介复制	Printing,Reproduction of Recording Media	16147.5	15317.7	829.8
文教、工美、体育和娱乐用品制造业	Manufacture of Articles For Cultural,Educational and Sports Activities	5454.0	5368.8	
石油加工业、炼焦和核燃料加工业	Processing of Petroleum, Cokeing,Processing of Nuclear and Nuclear Fuel	93689.3	78651.6	15037.7
化学原料及化学制品制造业	Manufacture of Raw Chemical Materials and Chemical Products	159868.7	64499.4	73798.7
医药制造业	Manufacture of Medicines	311133.1	304659.5	-747.5
化学纤维制造业	Manufacture of Chemical Fibers	9404.0	9404.0	
橡胶和塑料制品业	Manufacture of Rubber and Plastics	19468.5	19431.9	14.6
非金属矿物制品业	Manufacture of Non-metallic Mineral Products	82866.8	80398.9	2467.8
黑色金属冶炼和压延加工业	Smelting and Pressing of Ferrous Metals	27237.5	27237.5	
有色金属冶炼和压延加工业	Smelting and Pressing of Non-ferrous Metals	21601.8	14143.5	7458.2
金属制品业	Manufacture of Metal Products	38691.6	35014.8	3676.8
通用设备制造业	Manufacture of General Purpose Machinery	34825.6	34578.9	148.0
专用设备制造业	Manufacture of Special Equipment	144585.3	127863.3	10177.9
汽车制造业	Manufacture of Motor Vehicle	1359764.9	1063024.9	148169.3
铁路、船舶、航空航天和其他运输设备制造业	Railways,Shipbuilding,Aerospace and Other Transportation Equipment Manufacturing Industry	149534.3	112331.0	37203.2
电气机械和器材制造业	Manufacture of Electric Equipment and Machinery	245605.5	147934.2	45370.9
计算机、通讯和其他电子设备制造业	Manufacture of Communication Equipment, Computers and other Electronic Equipment	2438081.8	1799635.4	638446.4
仪器仪表制造业	Manufacture of Measuring Instruments and Machinery	64669.4	55705.9	7038.3
其他制造业	Manufacture of Other Manufacturing	2677.7	2677.7	
废弃资源综合利用业	Recycling and Disposal of Waste			
金属制品、机械和设备修理业	Metal Products,Machinery and Equipment Repair Industry	9416.7	9416.7	
电力、热力的生产和供应业	Production and Supply of Electric Power and Heat Power			
燃气生产和供应业	Gas Mining and Supplying Industry	308055.6	292012.8	16042.8
水的生产和供应业	Production and Supply of Water			

continued 4

(10 000 yuan)

所有者权益合计 Total Owners' Equities	实收资本 Total Capital Hold	营业收入 Total Revenue	主营业务收入 Revenue from Principal Business	营业成本 Total Cost	主营业务成本 Cost of Principal Business	营业税金及附加 Taxs and Other Changes	主营业务税金及附加 Taxes and Other Charges on Principal Business
7256.1	3691.8	16403.6	15966.3	12888.8	12586.7	148.3	148.3
228514.0	88817.5	911980.1	894589.0	735423.3	718971.8	2591.5	2591.5
279309.0	145865.6	470369.5	455609.9	366034.6	333327.4	3892.0	3816.1
6518.4	6528.7	4469.3	4469.3	4266.9	4266.9		
15580.6	5540.1	40056.4	39911.3	33585.6	33458.9	105.5	105.5
26398.1	7500.0	31557.6	30496.9	24429.3	23516.5	195.1	195.1
2417.1	2851.3	11636.5	11636.5	11397.1	11397.1		
61559.7	39840.6	223246.9	221939.2	196553.4	195253.9	1058.4	1009.7
72227.8	85642.2	96836.3	96103.9	85804.6	85788.9	685.1	685.1
215426.4	78871.1	661767.9	660965.2	364879.5	364572.5	5478.4	5478.4
39558.8	24800.0	91997.0	91997.0	74354.9	74354.9	362.1	362.1
13775.3	11788.0	14170.0	14108.4	10299.5	10252.4	57.3	57.3
39402.2	26254.7	109361.1	109331.1	99951.7	99939.0	720.1	720.1
-17082.8	9399.4	16223.1	15370.5	14513.1	13636.3	64.0	64.0
34245.5	27394.9	95852.2	95682.8	85568.2	85456.5	53.5	53.5
25199.5	25779.8	38077.2	37924.9	30950.9	30950.9	166.8	166.8
103350.1	53250.2	115375.1	115220.5	98998.6	98953.1	219.4	219.4
192492.3	134107.2	427332.4	424079.4	333199.2	331189.0	2268.1	2144.7
602284.5	229235.7	1825348.2	1747844.8	1658610.8	1622350.7	41295.5	41295.5
141360.4	58903.6	203126.0	202836.0	139581.4	139538.8	1883.1	1883.1
219080.1	205538.4	715206.2	698620.3	626962.7	626502.2	1470.4	1470.3
1845603.0	1727041.5	779135.3	772204.1	603020.8	577690.2	456.4	456.4
89821.4	26452.3	99028.0	98075.4	62961.2	62861.2	849.9	844.8
2802.8	1800.0	3728.4	3590.5	3408.9	3408.9	34.3	34.3
7891.5	3454.5	18759.1	18752.9	13213.3	13213.3	99.4	99.4
138666.4	100000.0	303810.9	250422.6	244487.6	211095.8	2509.0	2509.0

12-11 续表5

单位：万元

分 组	Classify	销售费用 Expenses for Sales	管理费用 Expenses for Management	财务费用 Financial cost
农副食品加工业	Processing of Food from Agricultural Porducts	467.7	1261.5	45.0
食品制造业	Manufacture of Foods	102092.6	26562.7	-3789.3
酒、饮料和精制茶制造业	Manufacture of Alcohol,Beverages and Tea	72225.1	22039.3	12011.2
烟草制品业	Manufacture of Tobacco			
纺织业	Manufacture of Textile	27.4	282.7	-19.2
纺织服装、服饰业	Textile, apparel industry			
皮革、毛皮、羽毛及其制品和制鞋业	Leather fur feathers and its products and footwear			
木材加工和木、竹、藤、棕、草制品业	Processing of Timber,Manufacture of Wood,Plam and Straw Products			
家具制造业	Manufacture of Furniture			
造纸及纸制品业	Manufacture of Paper and Paper Products	595.9	883.7	-46.7
印刷和记录媒介复制	Printing,Reproduction of Recording Media	1924.4	1109.4	658.5
文教、工美、体育和娱乐用品制造业	Manufacture of Articles For Cultural,Educational and Sports Activities	100.1	257.2	12.5
石油加工业、炼焦和核燃料加工业	Processing of Petroleum, Cokeing,Processing of Nuclear and Nuclear Fuel	6368.8	8552.1	1222.2
化学原料及化学制品制造业	Manufacture of Raw Chemical Materials and Chemical Products	2967.7	6076.5	3659.5
医药制造业	Manufacture of Medicines	174563.9	50663.5	12393.6
化学纤维制造业	Manufacture of Chemical Fibers	202.1	2223.6	-169.1
橡胶和塑料制品业	Manufacture of Rubber and Plastics	525.5	1349.2	690.7
非金属矿物制品业	Manufacture of Non-metallic Mineral Products	442.4	14879.2	418.8
黑色金属冶炼和压延加工业	Smelting and Pressing of Ferrous Metals	630.6	1102.9	1031.7
有色金属冶炼和压延加工业	Smelting and Pressing of Non-ferrous Metals	2050.8	2965.3	1306.1
金属制品业	Manufacture of Metal Products	1761.3	4899.9	1305.0
通用设备制造业	Manufacture of General Purpose Machinery	5545.0	5428.3	156.3
专用设备制造业	Manufacture of Special Equipment	10008.6	28453.1	3043.6
汽车制造业	Manufacture of Motor Vehicle	33835.1	49760.9	12802.3
铁路、船舶、航空航天和其他运输设备制造业	Railways,Shipbuilding,Aerospace and Other Transportation Equipment Manufacturing Industry	8303.5	12840.7	-1078.4
电气机械和器材制造业	Manufacture of Electric Equipment and Machinery	15583.7	26447.3	2979.9
计算机、通讯和其他电子设备制造业	Manufacture of Communication Equipment, Computers and other Electronic Equipment	2010.7	150154.5	7931.0
仪器仪表制造业	Manufacture of Measuring Instruments and Machinery	7567.9	6972.0	1250.8
其他制造业	Manufacture of Other Manufacturing	136.2	203.4	21.7
废弃资源综合利用业	Recycling and Disposal of Waste			
金属制品、机械和设备修理业	Metal Products,Machinery and Equipment Repair Industry	1252.8	2665.1	31.7
电力、热力的生产和供应业	Production and Supply of Electric Power and Heat Power			
燃气生产和供应业	Gas Mining and Supplying Industry	13314.3	15695.6	-4452.2
水的生产和供应业	Production and Supply of Water			

continued 5

(10 000 yuan)

营业利润 Operating Profit	利润总额 Total Profits	亏损企业亏损额 Total Loss of Deficit Enterprises	利税总额 Total Pre-tax Profits	应付职工薪酬 Salary Payable	本年应交增值税 Value Added Tax Payable
1544.2	1612.5		2831.5	1411.2	1070.7
49379.4	50963.7		75995.9	70188.9	22440.7
12243.2	20732.9	10407.6	54300.9	49747.2	29676.0
-88.5	-61.3	61.3	-61.3	437.9	
6936.3	7329.8		9960.7	1761.0	2525.4
3739.5	3996.5		5811.2	3475.8	1619.6
-130.4	-52.4	56.7	229.8	1032.0	282.2
9418.7	9354.0		51616.5	17047.7	41204.1
-2370.7	-2579.4	6582.7	-1636.0	5225.1	258.3
52350.9	51829.4	1141.5	141706.0	84127.8	84398.2
15023.4	15020.7		19943.9	3592.4	4561.1
1247.8	1281.0		1875.7	1535.3	537.4
-1175.8	84.9	919.2	6715.1	3879.9	5910.1
-4190.1	-4139.1	4385.2	-3772.6	989.9	302.5
3773.5	4069.3	1599.5	7073.5	3544.3	2950.7
-997.6	-931.7	3679.4	-73.4	4714.4	691.5
5012.4	5806.4	245.4	7860.3	9256.2	1834.5
36737.2	38605.8	23108.5	51347.3	24682.4	10473.4
29587.9	84632.1	19944.1	182125.5	143425.7	56197.9
39826.1	40244.8	853.1	56392.7	17841.8	14264.8
42277.8	43223.4	5501.0	77858.6	35045.7	33164.8
15596.6	105380.5	2007.9	106644.2	65417.7	807.3
19396.2	19323.8	802.7	23602.2	11863.1	3428.5
-66.1	-66.1	66.1	98.2	376.5	130.0
1138.9	1168.5		2175.1	2064.6	907.2
36264.0	36376.2		45406.7	28895.2	6521.5

12-12 规模以上大中型工业企业主要经济指标（2014年）

单位：万元

分组	Classify	企业单位数（个）Number of Enterprises (unit)	亏损企业 Loss Making Enterprises	工业总产值（当年价格）Gross Industrial Output Value (At Current Prices)
总计	**Total**	**222**	**39**	**33755689.5**
#市区	Urban	188	35	26102969.0
#亏损企业	Deficit Enterprises	39	39	5518054.9
按隶属关系分	**Grouped by Jurisdiction of Management**			
中央企业	Central Enterprises	45	9	11562037.8
省属企业	Provincial Enterprises	31	9	7893366.1
市属企业	Municipal Enterprises	146	21	14300285.6
按登记注册类型分组	**Grouped by Registion Status**			
国有	State-owned Enterprises	27	4	6960469.0
集体	Collective-owned Enterprises	1		7036.0
股份合作	Share-holding Corperative	1		129600.5
联营	Joint Ownership Enterprises			
国有联营	State Joint Ownership Enterprises			
集体联营	Collective Joint Ownership Enterprises			
国有与集体联营	Joint State-collective Ownership Enterprises			
其他联营	Other Joint Ownership Enterprises			
有限责任公司	Limited Liability Corporations	102	20	16263105.8
国有独资公司	State Sole Funded Enterprises	25	8	3916782.6
其他有限责任公司	Other Limited Liability Corporation	77	12	12346323.2
股份有限公司	Share-holding Corperation Ltd.	37	6	2567741.2
私营	Private Enterprises	18	3	1032295.9
私营独资	Private-funded Enterprises			
私营合伙	Private Partnership Enterprises			
私营有限责任公司	Private Limited Liability Corporations	16	3	898499.2
私营股份有限公司	Private Share Holding Corporations	2		133796.7
其他	Other Domestic Funded Enterprises			
港澳台商投资	Enterprises with Funds from Hong Kong,Macao and Taiwan	5		235925.6
外商投资	Foreign Funded Enterprises	31	6	6559515.5
按轻重工业分	**Grouped by Light Industry and Heavy Industry**			
轻工业	Light Industry	52	8	4875357.4
重工业	Heavy Industry	170	31	28880332.1
按企业规模分	**Grouped by Size of Enterprises**			
大型企业	Large-size	61	7	24880136.3

Economic Indicators of Large and Medium-sized Industrial Enterprises above Designated Size (2014)

(10 000 yuan)

工业销售产值（当年价）Value of Industry Products Sales (At Current Prices)	出口交货值 Export Delivery Value	从业人员年平均人数（人）Annual Average Employers (person)	资产总计 Total Assets	流动资产合计 Total Working Capitals	固定资产合计 Total Fixed Assets	固定资产原价 Origing Value of Fixed Assets	累计折旧 Accumulative Total Depreciation
31896031.0	**2683506.6**	**390700.0**	**49311358.5**	**24757110.2**	**17310143.0**	**25252863.0**	**9420442.7**
24761263.4	2371031.6	338683.0	43673703.2	21667648.5	15865984.9	23181997.3	8634220.0
5465285.6	272090.6	85133.0	8279482.6	4791740.8	2047593.1	3117649.9	1214646.8
11344955.7	565089.2	183461.0	23572196.3	11428483.4	9020149.0	13485441.4	5563322.3
7535607.1	347886.5	60636.0	6910688.4	4243003.0	1376196.1	2116567.5	816747.5
13015468.2	1770530.9	146603.0	18828473.8	9085623.8	6913797.9	9650854.1	3040372.9
6894908.3	139480.3	83972.0	10955705.7	5405927.5	3579989.4	5762522.4	2500975.4
7082.9		1154.0	4552.5	3679.3	873.2	1773.7	900.5
130599.7		1011.0	214725.0	165355.0	10056.5	17271.6	7215.1
15435139.0	1092494.9	198405.0	24416475.9	13542519.0	7677380.2	11135693.3	4325896.4
3730703.9	347963.3	68033.0	9428682.7	4256867.5	4305366.5	6308655.9	2521346.5
11704435.1	744531.6	130372.0	14987793.2	9285651.5	3372013.7	4827037.4	1804549.9
2046148.5	398777.9	28648.0	3665262.1	2265327.5	971418.3	1717357.4	833488.9
1004403.8	195.9	9721.0	822694.6	429330.5	187304.5	317702.0	137827.7
870816.5	195.9	9086.0	686902.5	376279.8	177504.8	305041.6	134967.0
133587.3		635.0	135792.1	53050.7	9799.7	12660.4	2860.7
211074.3	51504.7	3842.0	309605.5	177246.6	82456.2	138408.4	59572.7
6166674.5	1001052.9	63947.0	8922337.2	2767724.8	4800664.7	6162134.2	1554566.0
4718399.7	182997.2	49783.0	3823542.9	2283519.9	1073452.8	2162024.8	1180691.9
27177631.3	2500509.4	340917.0	45487815.6	22473590.3	16236690.2	23090838.2	8239750.8
23972256.4	2056669.8	296345.0	39819215.9	19015018.7	14961802.3	21670921.0	7913200.7

12-12 续表1

单位：万元

分 组	Classify	负债合计 Total Liabilites	流动负债合计 Total Working Liabilities	非流动负债 Non-Working Liabilities
总计	**Total**	**29594942.5**	**21598789.2**	**4874619.7**
#市区	Urban	25642148.2	18370382.6	4378340.0
#亏损企业	Deficit Enterprises	5644020.9	4747411.2	853472.3
按隶属关系分	**Grouped by Jurisdiction of Management**			
中央企业	Central Enterprises	14143067.6	8921972.1	2480761.7
省属企业	Provincial Enterprises	4688914.1	3991397.4	519080.7
市属企业	Municipal Enterprises	10762960.8	8685419.7	1874777.3
按登记注册类型分组	**Grouped by Registion Status**			
国有	State-owned Enterprises	6079488.7	4476232.5	1566288.1
集体	Collective-owned Enterprises	2723.5	2723.5	
股份合作	Share-holding Corperative	196023.0	163594.8	32428.2
联营	Joint Ownership Enterprises			
国有联营	State Joint Ownership Enterprises			
集体联营	Collective Joint Ownership Enterprises			
国有与集体联营	Joint State-collective Ownership Enterprises			
其他联营	Other Joint Ownership Enterprises			
有限责任公司	Limited Liability Corporations	15427093.4	10873598.0	1783611.6
国有独资公司	State Sole Funded Enterprises	6084950.3	2753667.4	605943.8
其他有限责任公司	Other Limited Liability Corporation	9342143.1	8119930.6	1177667.8
股份有限公司	Share-holding Corperation Ltd.	1981684.9	1483102.2	457674.1
私营	Private Enterprises	435930.3	294207.2	54854.8
私营独资	Private-funded Enterprises			
私营合伙	Private Partnership Enterprises			
私营有限责任公司	Private Limited Liability Corporations	408743.1	267489.8	54385.0
私营股份有限公司	Private Share Holding Corporations	27187.2	26717.4	469.8
其他	Other Domestic Funded Enterprises			
港澳台商投资	Enterprises with Funds from Hong Kong,Macao and Taiwan	178563.0	116303.1	39616.0
外商投资	Foreign Funded Enterprises	5293435.7	4189027.9	940146.9
按轻重工业分	**Grouped by Light Industry and Heavy Industry**			
轻工业	Light Industry	2093100.2	1770256.3	315262.6
重工业	Heavy Industry	27501842.3	19828532.9	4559357.1
按企业规模分	**Grouped by Size of Enterprises**			
大型企业	Large-size	24078604.6	17346912.3	3962163.9

continued 1

(10 000 yuan)

所有者权益合计 Total Owners' Equities	实收资本 Total Capital Hold	营业收入 Total Revenue	主营业务收入 Revenue from Principal Business	营业成本 Total Cost	主营业务成本 Cost of Principal Business	营业税金及附加 Taxs and Other Changes	主营业务税金及附加 Taxes and Other Charges on Principal Business
19700802.4	**8142603.2**	**31525201.3**	**30810134.2**	**26512999.5**	**25941887.5**	**288667.8**	**284142.8**
18015941.6	7339418.1	25570037.4	25007443.4	21264759.4	20797589.8	271450.3	267091.9
2635461.5	1441621.1	5131506.5	5039629.7	4724260.7	4668244.3	158954.4	158933.2
9413672.4	3186788.8	12928219.1	12748261.0	11155035.2	11013008.1	167791.6	165522.9
2221619.3	853362.8	6552114.8	6287431.2	5539854.5	5328344.9	22486.9	22034.3
8065510.7	4102451.6	12044867.4	11774442.0	9818109.8	9600534.5	98389.3	96585.6
4860769.8	1370414.5	6839262.3	6604548.9	5861903.1	5665271.3	133870.3	132513.2
1829.0	1021.6	7064.6	7064.6	6112.3	6112.3	57.0	57.0
18701.9	7125.6	71761.3	71761.3	67402.2	67402.2	42.3	42.3
8989372.5	3418657.4	15958359.2	15678817.8	13704308.2	13493844.2	77790.0	74989.6
3343732.4	1092091.5	4551706.1	4469325.2	3797010.1	3738356.5	31262.7	28921.8
5645640.1	2326565.9	11406653.1	11209492.6	9907298.1	9755487.7	46527.3	46067.8
1683421.5	755780.8	1964342.9	1940062.3	1532417.6	1515317.8	11569.6	11456.0
386764.3	106631.9	888168.3	882441.9	708207.9	704308.2	3775.1	3771.6
278159.4	63282.7	755489.8	750837.5	599941.2	596766.4	2974.0	2970.5
108604.9	43349.2	132678.5	131604.4	108266.7	107541.8	801.1	801.1
131042.4	63874.7	213277.2	208531.0	159843.5	155347.4	1171.8	1171.8
3628901.0	2419096.7	5582965.5	5416906.4	4472804.7	4334284.1	60391.7	60141.3
1730277.8	763575.5	4433929.0	4374805.9	3361565.6	3292642.5	34398.6	33627.7
17970524.6	7379027.7	27091272.3	26435328.3	23151433.9	22649245.0	254269.2	250515.1
15725154.7	6226222.6	24092336.5	23604470.2	20527797.4	20132980.7	255633.0	252698.9

12-12 续表2

单位：万元

分组	Classify	销售费用 Expenses for Sales	管理费用 Expenses for Management	财务费用 Financial cost
总计	**Total**	**1191658.4**	**1966443.1**	**405593.6**
#市区	Urban	1051478.9	1744970.5	356472.0
#亏损企业	Deficit Enterprises	131135.3	312912.5	71775.3
按隶属关系分	**Grouped by Jurisdiction of Management**			
中央企业	Central Enterprises	248995.0	890114.2	245097.8
省属企业	Provincial Enterprises	330668.1	316285.4	51697.3
市属企业	Municipal Enterprises	611995.3	760043.5	108798.5
按登记注册类型分组	**Grouped by Registion Status**			
国有	State-owned Enterprises	164455.5	443583.4	86505.7
集体	Collective-owned Enterprises	26.6	870.8	11.9
股份合作	Share-holding Corperative	4037.7	2627.7	2579.5
联营	Joint Ownership Enterprises			
国有联营	State Joint Ownership Enterprises			
集体联营	Collective Joint Ownership Enterprises			
国有与集体联营	Joint State-collective Ownership Enterprises			
其他联营	Other Joint Ownership Enterprises			
有限责任公司	Limited Liability Corporations	422808.0	960685.0	218807.6
国有独资公司	State Sole Funded Enterprises	85045.5	333960.6	118706.9
其他有限责任公司	Other Limited Liability Corporation	337762.5	626724.4	100100.7
股份有限公司	Share-holding Corperation Ltd.	132510.3	150853.2	44792.4
私营	Private Enterprises	54322.8	41856.4	12063.6
私营独资	Private-funded Enterprises			
私营合伙	Private Partnership Enterprises			
私营有限责任公司	Private Limited Liability Corporations	45989.2	30924.0	11428.4
私营股份有限公司	Private Share Holding Corporations	8333.6	10932.4	635.2
其他	Other Domestic Funded Enterprises			
港澳台商投资	Enterprises with Funds from Hong Kong,Macao and Taiwan	23938.0	13697.6	1943.5
外商投资	Foreign Funded Enterprises	389559.5	352269.0	38889.4
按轻重工业分	**Grouped by Light Industry and Heavy Industry**			
轻工业	Light Industry	541445.9	239870.7	34025.2
重工业	Heavy Industry	650212.5	1726572.4	371568.4
按企业规模分	**Grouped by Size of Enterprises**			
大型企业	Large-size	809030.4	1486318.6	326793.5

continued 2

(10 000 yuan)

营业利润 Operating Profit	利润总额 Total Profits	亏损企业亏损额 Total Loss of Deficit Enterprises	利税总额 Total Pre-tax Profits	应付职工薪酬 Salary Payable	本年应交增值税 Value Added Tax Payable
1201899.4	**1535342.5**	**185593.6**	**2826287.6**	**3042108.9**	**1002277.3**
916484.6	1211445.9	167611.6	2327084.8	2788120.0	844188.6
-242725.3	-185593.6	185593.6	47962.7	532587.6	74601.9
305769.6	391765.1	91999.8	940486.1	1695664.0	380929.4
265167.8	294454.7	36135.0	536195.6	405956.4	219254.0
630962.0	849122.7	57458.8	1349605.9	940488.5	402093.9
203533.8	254639.2	52329.0	596784.0	788139.1	208274.5
16.3	49.4		402.2	2250.3	295.8
-4928.1	506.8		4987.7	3044.7	4438.6
551686.6	649869.1	73257.2	1165524.9	1500066.0	437865.8
185873.9	233303.5	28225.7	475755.9	526326.0	211189.7
365812.7	416565.6	45031.5	689769.0	973740.0	226676.1
74281.3	90392.4	34149.3	161252.7	209180.4	59290.7
64168.1	70440.9	590.4	102891.9	37605.7	28675.9
61611.4	66941.0	590.4	97799.9	36064.0	27884.9
2556.7	3499.9		5092.0	1541.7	791.0
13139.4	13474.6		25447.5	32423.7	10801.1
300002.0	455970.1	25267.7	768996.7	469399.0	252634.9
245807.0	266502.8	8655.7	524850.1	397424.1	223948.7
956092.4	1268839.7	176937.9	2301437.5	2644684.8	778328.6
750225.2	1025536.0	102395.5	2026870.2	2434783.3	745701.2

12-12 续表3

单位：万元

分组	Classify	企业单位数（个）Number of Enterprises (unit)	亏损企业 Loss Making Enterprises	工业总产值（当年价格）Gross Industrial Output Value (At Current Prices)
中型企业	Medium-size	161	32	8875553.2
小型企业	Small-size			
微型企业	Microenterprise			
按经济组织类型分组	**Grouped by Economic Type of Orgnization**			
独资企业	Appropratorship	43	6	9063213.9
合作、合伙企业	Partnership	1		129600.5
股份有限公司	Corporaton	41	6	3012609.8
有限责任公司	Limited Liability Company	137	27	21550265.3
按控股情况分	**Grouped by Cast strand**			
国有控股	State owned shares	111	25	22228008.1
集体控股	Collective shares	9	1	831258.9
私人控股	Private holdings	65	9	5744215.5
港澳台控股	Hong Kong and Macao Holdings	3		194956.7
外商投资	Foreign Investment	24	4	4169662.9
其他	Others	10		587587.4
按工业行业大类分	**Grouped by Sector**			
煤炭开采和洗选业	Mining and Washing of Coal			
石油和天然气开采业	Extraction of Petroleum and Natural Gas			
黑色金属矿采选业	Mining and Processing of Ferrous Metal Ores			
有色金属矿采选业	Mining and Processing of Non-ferrous Metal Ores			
非金属矿采选业	Mining and Processing of Nonmetal Ores			
开采辅助活动	Mining Auxiliary Activities	1		134770.2
其他采矿业	Mining of other Ores			
农副食品加工业	Processing of Food from Agricultural Porducts	6	2	934730.1
食品制造业	Manufacture of Foods	11	1	1144868.3
酒、饮料和精制茶制造业	Manufacture of Alcohol,Beverages and Tea	6	2	718253.2
烟草制品业	Manufacture of Tobacco			
纺织业	Manufacture of Textile	1	1	34546.1
纺织服装、服饰业	Textile, apparel industry	1		55121.0
皮革、毛皮、羽毛及其制品和制鞋业	Manufacture of Leather, Fur, Feather and Related Products, and Shoes	1		37557.7
木材加工和木、竹、藤、棕、草制品业	Processing of Timber, Manufacture of Wood,Plam and Straw Products	1		116933.7
家具制造业	Manufacture of Furniture	1		12422.4

continued 3

(10 000 yuan)

工业销售产值（当年价）Value of Industry Products Sales (At Current Prices)	出口交货值 Export Delivery Value	从业人员年平均人数（人）Annual Average Employers (person)	资产总计 Total Assets	流动资产合计 Total Working Capitals	固定资产合计 Total Fixed Assets	固定资产原价 Origing Value of Fixed Assets	累计折旧 Accumulative Total Depreciation
7923774.6	626836.8	94355.0	9492142.6	5742091.5	2348340.7	3581942.0	1507242.0
8748850.5	925725.3	101876.0	15988834.1	6393593.6	7155914.4	10073449.0	3260578.4
130599.7		1011.0	214725.0	165355.0	10056.5	17271.6	7215.1
2423193.5	564619.2	31190.0	4179002.0	2497837.9	1138338.1	2204025.2	1153236.9
20593387.3	1193162.1	256623.0	28928797.4	15700323.7	9005834.0	12958117.2	4999412.3
21255507.7	1216148.9	277461.0	35574780.8	19152859.9	11458501.9	17284007.3	7075369.5
796363.6	314629.1	6616.0	970528.6	569079.0	289463.6	633230.5	354241.3
5338122.6	117161.4	67445.0	5601651.9	2902526.9	1356247.5	1881174.5	652855.6
192154.2	51290.6	2846.0	151114.6	61660.2	70287.8	112124.9	45457.6
3796243.2	953892.8	28461.0	6503815.4	1745377.9	3987070.4	5140715.3	1238589.9
517639.7	30383.8	7871.0	509467.2	325606.3	148571.8	201610.5	53928.8
136635.0		11003.0	180375.8	90985.2	81151.3	143307.0	61850.9
933076.3	7226.0	4231.0	479195.2	341149.4	76267.6	152816.2	76548.6
1089318.3		9242.0	473216.6	254835.4	158123.3	249280.7	97062.8
807537.4	165222.8	6246.0	884201.0	425709.8	325261.3	783501.8	458528.9
34839.9	5429.1	4829.0	52459.2	36074.3	12452.4	45533.9	33081.5
33123.5		1277.0	86617.4	76185.7	3520.6	5381.3	1860.8
37873.3		881.0	46323.6	24122.7	3016.7	5769.9	2753.2
100955.4		495.0	144369.4	62017.7	46340.1	64530.3	30717.7
12854.2		345.0	15245.1	11113.9	4131.2	13500.5	9369.3

12-12 续表4

单位：万元

分 组	Classify	负债合计 Total Liabilites	流动负债合计 Total Working Liabilities	非流动负债 Non-Working Liabilities
中型企业	Medium-size	5516337.9	4251876.9	912455.8
小型企业	Small-size			
微型企业	Microenterprise			
按经济组织类型分组	**Grouped by Economic Type of Orgnization**			
独资企业	Appropratorship	8887673.1	6629629.6	2221075.3
合作、合伙企业	Partnership	196023.0	163594.8	32428.2
股份有限公司	Corporaton	2252935.6	1681651.2	530375.8
有限责任公司	Limited Liability Company	18258310.8	13123913.6	2090740.4
按控股情况分	**Grouped by Cast strand**			
国有控股	State owned shares	21875579.0	15633077.0	3477756.6
集体控股	Collective shares	519057.1	436155.9	82901.0
私人控股	Private holdings	3115267.2	2374342.2	546472.9
港澳台控股	Hong Kong and Macao Holdings	82916.3	77616.3	5300.0
外商投资	Foreign Investment	3722858.6	2821783.2	738739.6
其他	Others	279264.3	255814.6	23449.6
按工业行业大类分	**Grouped by Sector**			
煤炭开采和洗选业	Mining and Washing of Coal			
石油和天然气开采业	Extraction of Petroleum and Natural Gas			
黑色金属矿采选业	Mining and Processing of Ferrous Metal Ores			
有色金属矿采选业	Mining and Processing of Non-ferrous Metal Ores			
非金属矿采选业	Mining and Processing of Nonmetal Ores			
开采辅助活动	Mining Auxiliary Activities	131142.7	55900.3	75242.4
其他采矿业	Mining of other Ores			
农副食品加工业	Processing of Food from Agricultural Porducts	430044.6	391805.9	38238.6
食品制造业	Manufacture of Foods	184815.2	178648.1	5807.1
酒、饮料和精制茶制造业	Manufacture of Alcohol,Beverages and Tea	507445.5	427505.2	79940.3
烟草制品业	Manufacture of Tobacco			
纺织业	Manufacture of Textile	43745.6	41442.7	2302.9
纺织服装、服饰业	Textile, apparel industry	70609.8	50609.8	20000.0
皮革、毛皮、羽毛及其制品和制鞋业	Manufacture of Leather, Fur, Feather and Related Products, and Shoes	21955.6	17467.2	4488.4
木材加工和木、竹、藤、棕、草制品业	Processing of Timber, Manufacture of Wood,Plam and Straw Products	88804.9	36048.0	52756.9
家具制造业	Manufacture of Furniture	12219.1	12219.1	0.0

continued 4

(10 000 yuan)

所有者权益合计 Total Owners' Equities	实收资本 Total Capital Hold	营业收入 Total Revenue	主营业务收入 Revenue from Principal Business	营业成本 Total Cost	主营业务成本 Cost of Principal Business	营业税金及附加 Taxs and Other Changes	主营业务税金及附加 Taxes and Other Charges on Principal Business
3975647.7	1916380.6	7432864.8	7205664.0	5985202.1	5808906.8	33034.8	31443.9
7085713.4	3288262.5	8704196.2	8442200.7	7301112.9	7058800.0	142155.4	140798.3
18701.9	7125.6	71761.3	71761.3	67402.2	67402.2	42.3	42.3
1925910.7	825208.0	2250940.0	2223425.4	1786014.3	1748242.7	13425.0	13235.5
10670476.4	4022007.1	20498303.8	20072746.8	17358470.1	17067442.6	133045.1	130066.7
13683744.5	4949397.8	21949368.5	21401336.8	18849268.1	18426843.8	212763.4	208532.7
451471.5	260316.2	719893.7	708638.5	596024.5	588273.4	2232.8	2232.8
2486229.0	671554.5	4644077.1	4556197.0	3918496.7	3871816.4	54779.4	54733.5
68198.2	51222.0	180687.6	176378.7	139477.8	135283.8	869.1	869.1
2780956.4	2063542.7	3543168.2	3494053.3	2640968.3	2565874.2	15530.6	15285.3
230202.8	146570.0	488006.2	473529.9	368764.1	353795.9	2492.5	2489.4
49233.1	3182.7	281787.0	279111.2	262962.7	259246.5	786.3	785.1
49150.5	32278.3	774677.3	773952.6	731232.6	730774.4	1294.6	1291.1
288401.1	106280.9	1067482.8	1046473.2	847862.0	828290.7	3504.5	3504.5
376755.5	206168.1	721241.2	706199.8	564443.4	531413.4	13937.3	13861.4
8713.6	4556.2	35217.1	35217.1	32624.5	32624.5	325.3	325.3
16007.5	7500.0	43303.8	43147.5	29349.5	29241.8	2243.5	2243.5
24367.9	6000.0	37873.3	37873.3	33224.3	32744.6	179.5	179.5
55564.5	12500.0	81308.7	81270.1	76946.0	76946.0	293.3	293.3
3026.0	2200.0	11791.5	11791.5	10727.0	10727.0	37.3	37.3

12-12 续表5

单位：万元

分　组	Classify	销售费用 Expenses for Sales	管理费用 Expenses for Management	财务费用 Financial cost
中型企业	Medium-size	382628.0	480124.5	78800.1
小型企业	Small-size			
微型企业	Microenterprise			
按经济组织类型分组	**Grouped by Economic Type of Orgnization**			
独资企业	Appropratorship	292248.1	651379.2	93384.8
合作、合伙企业	Partnership	4037.7	2627.7	2579.5
股份有限公司	Corporaton	149043.2	170979.7	57361.4
有限责任公司	Limited Liability Company	746329.4	1141456.5	252267.9
按控股情况分	**Grouped by Cast strand**			
国有控股	State owned shares	543071.1	1411616.3	295514.1
集体控股	Collective shares	32752.1	36038.4	11363.7
私人控股	Private holdings	244588.6	208956.4	63360.5
港澳台控股	Hong Kong and Macao Holdings	23235.8	7739.6	818.2
外商投资	Foreign Investment	316272.9	272809.1	29341.0
其他	Others	31737.9	29283.3	5196.1
按工业行业大类分	**Grouped by Sector**			
煤炭开采和洗选业	Mining and Washing of Coal			
石油和天然气开采业	Extraction of Petroleum and Natural Gas			
黑色金属矿采选业	Mining and Processing of Ferrous Metal Ores			
有色金属矿采选业	Mining and Processing of Non-ferrous Metal Ores			
非金属矿采选业	Mining and Processing of Nonmetal Ores			
开采辅助活动	Mining Auxiliary Activities	120.2	2787.0	-0.3
其他采矿业	Mining of other Ores			
农副食品加工业	Processing of Food from Agricultural Porducts	28167.9	11264.0	8346.8
食品制造业	Manufacture of Foods	128294.0	36147.2	-3205.2
酒、饮料和精制茶制造业	Manufacture of Alcohol,Beverages and Tea	79595.3	23519.0	6324.0
烟草制品业	Manufacture of Tobacco			
纺织业	Manufacture of Textile	251.1	4296.0	-80.4
纺织服装、服饰业	Textile, apparel industry	4095.1	4183.2	2103.9
皮革、毛皮、羽毛及其制品和制鞋业	Manufacture of Leather, Fur, Feather and Related Products, and Shoes	896.0	1520.2	144.7
木材加工和木、竹、藤、棕、草制品业	Processing of Timber, Manufacture of Wood,Plam and Straw Products	1158.1	2064.9	1437.9
家具制造业	Manufacture of Furniture	0.0	631.2	82.1

continued 5

(10 000 yuan)

营业利润 Operating Profit	利润总额 Total Profits	亏损企业亏损额 Total Loss of Deficit Enterprises	利税总额 Total Pre-tax Profits	应付职工薪酬 Salary Payable	本年应交增值税 Value Added Tax Payable
451674.2	509806.5	83198.1	799417.4	607325.6	256576.1
289546.3	432623.7	54315.4	823853.6	928176.5	249074.5
-4928.1	506.8		4987.7	3044.7	4438.6
73563.6	99475.6	34149.3	183417.9	227053.3	70517.3
843717.6	1002736.4	97128.9	1814028.4	1883834.4	678246.9
668746.2	820928.3	162049.5	1653967.4	2355820.2	620275.7
36800.2	40860.4	180.4	61405.8	57464.5	18312.6
141254.4	215804.4	18040.1	383810.7	306721.3	113226.9
9045.7	9399.4		19504.1	27711.5	9235.6
296573.0	397569.0	5323.6	624380.3	251756.5	211280.7
49479.9	50781.0		83219.3	42634.9	29945.8
13315.8	12667.1		14443.5	31687.9	990.1
-5897.8	1622.6	1876.5	17802.9	17405.6	14885.7
54657.3	56428.3	1191.8	87137.1	92328.9	27204.3
52805.4	61555.9	4481.5	115167.7	62279.3	39674.5
-2452.0	-966.4	966.4	692.8	11748.9	1333.9
727.1	835.5		4123.5	3243.1	1044.5
2709.8	2760.1		3300.9	5016.1	361.3
151.7	2248.7		7714.6	2052.6	5172.6
313.9	313.9		638.0	935.4	286.8

12-12 续表6

单位：万元

分组	Classify	企业单位数（个）Number of Enterprises (unit)	亏损企业 Loss Making Enterprises	工业总产值（当年价格）Gross Industrial Output Value (At Current Prices)
造纸及纸制品业	Manufacture of Paper and Paper Products			
印刷和记录媒介复制	Printing,Reproduction of Recording Media	7	1	371576.5
文教、工美、体育和娱乐用品制造业	Manufacture of Articles For Cultural,Educational and Sports Activities			
石油加工业、炼焦和核燃料加工业	Processing of Petroleum, Cokeing,Processing of Nuclear and Nuclear Fuel	2	1	1039154.4
化学原料及化学制品制造业	Manufacture of Raw Chemical Materials and Chemical Products	9	2	963595.7
医药制造业	Manufacture of Medicines	12		1216641.5
化学纤维制造业	Manufacture of Chemical Fibers			
橡胶和塑料制品业	Manufacture of Rubber and Plastics	3		373183.3
非金属矿物制品业	Manufacture of Non-metallic Mineral Products	7	1	292059.9
黑色金属冶炼和压延加工业	Smelting and Pressing of Ferrous Metals	2	2	213375.6
有色金属冶炼和压延加工业	Smelting and Pressing of Non-ferrous Metals	8	2	1258402.2
金属制品业	Manufacture of Metal Products	8		840205.6
通用设备制造业	Manufacture of General Purpose Machinery	8		1038648.3
专用设备制造业	Manufacture of Special Equipment	25	7	1746725.0
汽车制造业	Manufacture of Motor Vehicle	18	5	8585663.9
铁路、船舶、航空航天和其他运输设备制造业	Railways,Shipbuilding,Aerospace and Other Transportation Equipment Manufacturing Industry	20	2	3910279.5
电气机械和器材制造业	Manufacture of Electric Equipment and Machinery	18	2	2697019.6
计算机、通讯和其他电子设备制造业	Manufacture of Communication Equipment, Computers and other Electronic Equipment	23	4	2022245.8
仪器仪表制造业	Manufacture of Measuring Instruments and Machinery	11	1	1357785.4
其他制造业	Manufacture of Other Manufacturing			
废弃资源综合利用业	Recycling and Disposal of Waste			
金属制品、机械和设备修理业	Metal Products,Machinery and Equipment Repair Industry			
电力、热力的生产和供应业	Production and Supply of Electric Power and Heat Power	6	2	2222675.5
燃气生产和供应业	Gas Mining and Supplying Industry	5	1	336788.8
水的生产和供应业	Production and Supply of Water	1		80460.3

continued 6

(10 000 yuan)

工业销售产值（当年价）Value of Industry Products Sales (At Current Prices)	出口交货值 Export Delivery Value	从业人员年平均人数（人）Annual Average Employers (person)	资产总计 Total Assets	流动资产合计 Total Working Capitals	固定资产合计 Total Fixed Assets	固定资产原价 Origing Value of Fixed Assets	累计折旧 Accumulative Total Depreciation
364655.1	618.5	5213.0	433405.0	218467.6	188185.7	331641.3	168161.3
1021100.4		5400.0	378849.0	118581.6	260267.4	312863.5	107465.1
926103.5	307585.2	15972.0	1550403.6	813534.5	530162.8	1027310.7	503741.9
1085552.8	3218.7	10944.0	960179.5	650867.6	187745.4	299467.4	149304.0
345038.8	3568.3	4545.0	770601.7	489765.3	143448.5	192391.8	61142.0
270956.6		2718.0	219537.5	114296.9	78860.7	144728.5	65936.4
50273.9	3288.1	1394.0	78915.3	39970.4	32795.2	49471.9	16676.7
1081763.7	54992.3	7017.0	1182682.0	573100.9	307884.8	402185.6	127035.5
833686.2	78124.0	19025.0	1648217.3	942628.0	567130.0	715812.4	308802.7
1022673.5	69549.4	11641.0	2572461.8	1964421.9	289212.9	465977.1	185445.9
1501514.5	130219.1	20724.0	2676730.5	1810541.2	573745.0	818639.5	311069.9
8167292.3	342618.1	73439.0	6331315.1	3425076.2	1505918.3	2059798.8	683143.1
3725499.6	530871.1	70654.0	8864452.5	5063591.9	1946132.7	2739443.4	1224964.7
2695598.5	132970.2	34018.0	4813877.9	3275660.7	975659.3	1587118.9	614613.7
1715740.4	796164.4	23719.0	6212861.0	1762284.9	3799039.5	4521985.3	787358.2
1262280.3	51841.3	18372.0	1866442.3	1103521.5	502656.1	747232.9	355017.2
2222675.5		20785.0	5503354.4	673731.5	4411930.7	6894271.5	2755140.6
336951.8		3928.0	731938.7	317115.4	223731.5	277817.2	74328.9
80460.3		2643.0	153130.1	77758.1	75372.0	201083.7	149321.2

12-12 续表7

单位：万元

分　组	Classify	负债合计 Total Liabilites	流动负债合计 Total Working Liabilities	非流动负债 Non-Working Liabilities
造纸及纸制品业	Manufacture of Paper and Paper Products			
印刷和记录媒介复制	Printing,Reproduction of Recording Media	113846.8	99170.0	14676.7
文教、工美、体育和娱乐用品制造业	Manufacture of Articles For Cultural,Educational and Sports Activities			
石油加工业、炼焦和核燃料加工业	Processing of Petroleum, Cokeing,Processing of Nuclear and Nuclear Fuel	286823.3	271642.5	15180.8
化学原料及化学制品制造业	Manufacture of Raw Chemical Materials and Chemical Products	835397.9	606655.8	228669.8
医药制造业	Manufacture of Medicines	447572.5	426828.0	13523.4
化学纤维制造业	Manufacture of Chemical Fibers			
橡胶和塑料制品业	Manufacture of Rubber and Plastics	622141.4	512229.1	109912.3
非金属矿物制品业	Manufacture of Non-metallic Mineral Products	131293.1	129136.9	2015.6
黑色金属冶炼和压延加工业	Smelting and Pressing of Ferrous Metals	53683.5	44368.5	9315.1
有色金属冶炼和压延加工业	Smelting and Pressing of Non-ferrous Metals	586752.6	460906.5	125846.1
金属制品业	Manufacture of Metal Products	989869.0	712712.9	277155.9
通用设备制造业	Manufacture of General Purpose Machinery	1373682.6	1289416.6	82736.4
专用设备制造业	Manufacture of Special Equipment	1177533.4	1032353.0	118192.1
汽车制造业	Manufacture of Motor Vehicle	4212406.2	3689689.2	374146.3
铁路、船舶、航空航天和其他运输设备制造业	Railways,Shipbuilding,Aerospace and Other Transportation Equipment Manufacturing Industry	5077889.2	4047552.6	999866.0
电气机械和器材制造业	Manufacture of Electric Equipment and Machinery	2179210.6	1822617.2	333949.5
计算机、通讯和其他电子设备制造业	Manufacture of Communication Equipment, Computers and other Electronic Equipment	3837310.4	2844261.5	954637.4
仪器仪表制造业	Manufacture of Measuring Instruments and Machinery	960913.6	784199.7	96094.5
其他制造业	Manufacture of Other Manufacturing			
废弃资源综合利用业	Recycling and Disposal of Waste			
金属制品、机械和设备修理业	Metal Products,Machinery and Equipment Repair Industry			
电力、热力的生产和供应业	Production and Supply of Electric Power and Heat Power	4667246.2	1148958.6	794550.1
燃气生产和供应业	Gas Mining and Supplying Industry	465338.4	407747.8	16822.8
水的生产和供应业	Production and Supply of Water	85248.8	56696.5	28552.3

continued 7

(10 000 yuan)

所有者权益合计 Total Owners' Equities	实收资本 Total Capital Hold	营业收入 Total Revenue	主营业务收入 Revenue from Principal Business	营业成本 Total Cost	主营业务成本 Cost of Principal Business	营业税金及附加 Taxs and Other Changes	主营业务税金及附加 Taxes and Other Charges on Principal Business
319549.1	176297.5	334047.1	330265.9	255034.1	252698.1	2347.2	2347.2
92025.6	319314.3	962039.7	960732.4	859249.2	857949.7	102452.9	102404.2
699558.6	335431.8	931910.0	908122.4	750151.5	736750.1	4607.8	4568.8
512451.8	146728.5	1074005.2	1072528.1	595850.8	595541.4	8699.8	8699.8
148460.3	83856.8	369728.7	362848.3	306896.9	300103.7	2264.9	2120.8
88244.4	34498.1	263208.5	256129.5	233429.0	226427.0	1315.5	1315.5
25231.8	12263.5	49125.6	45724.1	41658.4	38839.0	156.0	153.1
595928.9	219202.4	1014750.5	903524.6	901600.2	800792.4	1166.0	1155.1
658348.3	274785.0	811400.5	798856.5	680881.8	672378.0	2286.9	2285.5
1198779.2	139484.5	958380.8	952214.5	762104.8	757924.8	5768.2	5714.3
1499196.9	573269.8	1389826.6	1363925.6	1047525.5	1034489.0	8217.2	8093.4
2118909.0	740946.5	6786703.7	6575639.7	6094110.0	5957233.5	55360.4	55339.8
3786563.2	1089322.7	4623903.9	4581208.4	3993600.9	3958103.6	18826.5	18026.8
2634667.0	512769.1	2350765.2	2253327.7	1811360.5	1730094.1	16536.2	16441.2
2375550.3	1906963.7	1793753.8	1768757.5	1445491.0	1403476.0	3605.8	3056.0
905528.6	427837.0	1149700.3	1136839.6	898679.8	891343.7	7566.3	6159.5
836108.2	539511.2	3109095.2	3097831.7	2853009.3	2848770.2	20473.8	20184.7
266600.2	190454.6	402302.0	346161.1	313085.9	278981.2	3291.4	3124.2
67881.3	39000.0	95871.3	80460.3	79907.9	67983.1	1123.4	431.9

12-12 续表8

单位：万元

分　组	Classify	销售费用 Expenses for Sales	管理费用 Expenses for Management	财务费用 Financial cost
造纸及纸制品业	Manufacture of Paper and Paper Products			
印刷和记录媒介复制	Printing,Reproduction of Recording Media	7023.9	37230.0	649.1
文教、工美、体育和娱乐用品制造业	Manufacture of Articles For Cultural,Educational and Sports Activities			
石油加工业、炼焦和核燃料加工业	Processing of Petroleum, Cokeing,Processing of Nuclear and Nuclear Fuel	7823.2	23060.9	7494.0
化学原料及化学制品制造业	Manufacture of Raw Chemical Materials and Chemical Products	32262.7	94903.5	19347.6
医药制造业	Manufacture of Medicines	267489.4	96728.5	13350.2
化学纤维制造业	Manufacture of Chemical Fibers			
橡胶和塑料制品业	Manufacture of Rubber and Plastics	15884.1	15243.1	9948.6
非金属矿物制品业	Manufacture of Non-metallic Mineral Products	13443.4	18203.3	777.7
黑色金属冶炼和压延加工业	Smelting and Pressing of Ferrous Metals	1703.9	5667.3	1030.0
有色金属冶炼和压延加工业	Smelting and Pressing of Non-ferrous Metals	4838.6	25567.1	17727.1
金属制品业	Manufacture of Metal Products	15985.5	76264.6	13547.2
通用设备制造业	Manufacture of General Purpose Machinery	35135.4	110379.2	-6258.4
专用设备制造业	Manufacture of Special Equipment	70682.4	131739.5	6432.4
汽车制造业	Manufacture of Motor Vehicle	166248.5	227937.4	37433.6
铁路、船舶、航空航天和其他运输设备制造业	Railways,Shipbuilding,Aerospace and Other Transportation Equipment Manufacturing Industry	81480.4	360190.1	54183.2
电气机械和器材制造业	Manufacture of Electric Equipment and Machinery	149136.3	247166.0	15088.8
计算机、通讯和其他电子设备制造业	Manufacture of Communication Equipment, Computers and other Electronic Equipment	31624.9	248000.9	27958.4
仪器仪表制造业	Manufacture of Measuring Instruments and Machinery	17775.0	108180.5	7552.6
其他制造业	Manufacture of Other Manufacturing			
废弃资源综合利用业	Recycling and Disposal of Waste			
金属制品、机械和设备修理业	Metal Products,Machinery and Equipment Repair Industry			
电力、热力的生产和供应业	Production and Supply of Electric Power and Heat Power	1368.4	21471.8	162432.6
燃气生产和供应业	Gas Mining and Supplying Industry	25609.6	23063.3	1889.0
水的生产和供应业	Production and Supply of Water	3565.1	9033.4	-143.6

continued 8

(10 000 yuan)

营业利润 Operating Profit	利润总额 Total Profits	亏损企业亏损额 Total Loss of Deficit Enterprises	利税总额 Total Pre-tax Profits	应付职工薪酬 Salary Payable	本年应交增值税 Value Added Tax Payable
38310.5	38602.5	21.9	62377.1	56492.5	21427.4
-38042.2	-38246.2	47401.0	122401.3	29955.6	58194.6
35972.9	45760.8	16084.8	70661.6	136901.6	20293.0
90048.0	90239.8		205868.0	110501.8	106928.4
18588.3	25232.2		40187.1	29463.8	12690.0
7386.1	11437.9	296.7	23755.4	14200.6	11002.0
-2335.1	-2339.7	3061.8	-1257.3	9238.2	926.4
62368.4	67889.2	8389.4	85982.4	39352.6	16927.2
22038.6	29368.2		41659.3	141540.8	10004.2
58797.2	78222.6		114539.3	75635.6	30548.5
98293.1	118336.0	25075.0	171994.3	158446.3	45441.1
187482.1	265768.5	32962.4	478380.1	356486.6	157251.2
119205.5	141465.9	14381.3	226414.9	685720.2	66122.5
129436.9	137895.2	661.7	269841.2	296913.8	115409.8
42485.9	138334.4	19499.9	159634.7	187009.6	17694.5
102479.4	121813.2	1329.4	171096.8	211473.7	41717.3
72134.7	86515.5	6622.3	273269.3	218459.8	166280.0
38957.6	39543.1	1289.8	51701.5	36722.0	8867.0
1960.3	2037.7		6759.6	20896.0	3598.5

12-13 规模以上高技术产业工业企业主要经济指标（2014年）

单位：万元

行业	Sector	企业单位数（个）Number of Enterprises (unit)	亏损企业 Loss Making Enterprises
总计	**Total**	**222**	**38**
一、医药制造业	**Pharmaceutical Manufacturing**	**49**	**8**
（一）化学药品制造	Chemical manufacturing	18	4
化学药品原料药制造	Chemical raw materials Medicine manufacturing	4	2
化学药品制剂制造	Chemical preparations manufacturing	14	2
（二）中药饮片加工	Chinese medicine Pieces processing	2	1
（三）中成药生产	Chinese medicine production	21	3
（四）兽用药品制造	Veterinary pharmaceutical manufacturing	1	
（五）生物药品制造	Biopharmaceutical manufacturing	5	
（六）卫生材料及医药用品制造	Sanitary materials and medical supplies manufacturing	2	
二、航空航天器制造业	**Aerospace & aviation industry**	**40**	**6**
（一）飞机制造	Aircraft Manufacturing	12	1
（二）航天器制造	Spacecraft Manufacturing	4	
（三）航空、航天相关设备制造	Aviation and aerospace-related equipment manufacturing	20	4
（四）其他航空航天器制造	Other aerospace manufacturing	2	
（五）航空航天器修理	Aerospace vehicle repair	2	1
三、电子及通讯设备制造业	**Electronic and communication equipment manufacturing**	**75**	**14**
（一）电子工业专用设备制造	Electronic equipment manufacturing	5	
（二）光纤、光缆制造	Optical fiber, cable manufacturing	2	
（三）锂离子电池制造	Lithium-ion battery manufacturing	2	
（四）通信设备制造	Communications equipment manufacturing	16	6
通信系统设备制造	Communications system equipment	14	6
通信终端设备制造	Communication Terminal Equipment	2	
（五）广播电视设备制造	Broadcasting and TV Equipment	3	2
广播电视节目制作及发射设备制造	Radio and television program production and transmission equipment		
广播电视接收设备及器材制造	Radio and television reception apparatus and equipment manufacturing	1	
应用电视设备及其他广播电视设备制造	Application television equipment and other radio and television equipment manufacturing	2	2
（六）雷达及配套设备制造	Radar and ancillary equipment manufacturers	3	
（七）视听设备制造	Audiovisual equipment manufacturing		
电视机制造	TV manufacturing		
音响设备制造	Audio Equipment manufacturing		
影视录放设备制造	Video recording equipment manufacturing		
（八）电子器件制造	Electronic device manufacturing	22	4
电子真空器件制造	Electronic vacuum device manufacturing	1	
半导体分立器件制造	Discrete semiconductor device manufacturing	8	
集成电路制造	Semiconductor Manufacturing	7	2
光电子器件及其他电子器件制造	Optoelectronic devices and other electronic device manufacturing	6	2
（九）电子元件制造	Electronics Manufacturing	16	2
电子元件及组件制造	Electronic components and component manufacturing	14	2
印刷电路板制造	Printed circuit board manufacturing	2	
（十）其他电子设备制造	Other electronic equipment manufacturing	6	

Economic Indicators of High Technology Industry

Industrial Enterprises above Designated Size (2014)

(10 000 yuan)

工业总产值（当年价格） Gross Industrial Output Value (At Current Prices)	工业销售产值（当年价） Value of Industry Products Sales (At Current Prices)	出口交货值 Export Delivery Value	从业人员年平均人数（人） Annual Average Employers (person)	资产总计 Total Assets	流动资产合计 Total Working Capitals	固定资产合计 Total Fixed Assets	固定资产原价 Origing Value of Fixed Assets	累计折旧 Accumulative Total Depreciation
10610729.2	**10077662.3**	**1825822.0**	**140685.0**	**20270336.3**	**10000789.3**	**7033282.1**	**9424631.4**	**3017815.0**
1776348.2	**1616913.5**	**13011.3**	**16404.0**	**1500341.6**	**981879.2**	**290337.1**	**472386.0**	**232325.1**
948067.2	900413.6	3218.7	8965.0	743633.6	520046.1	142761.5	228591.6	118372.4
21136.8	18151.5		720.0	37514.1	23017.1	10301.0	14721.0	4847.8
926930.4	882262.1	3218.7	8245.0	706119.5	497029.0	132460.5	213870.6	113524.6
9735.0	9735.0	9735.0	11.0	11711.2	11537.9	0.8	1.3	0.5
458738.7	415088.1	57.6	4540.0	403679.4	256785.4	61705.1	95479.0	39126.5
26613.1	26613.1		856.0	98483.9	81365.3	14945.6	5545.4	2682.1
297773.1	233660.0		1610.0	229155.6	105579.7	65806.6	136523.7	70673.0
35421.1	31403.7		422.0	13677.9	6564.8	5117.5	6245.0	1470.6
3880592.8	**3720451.2**	**580101.1**	**65009.0**	**8690503.6**	**4881989.2**	**1961560.5**	**2793188.4**	**1216287.1**
2957996.9	2818410.2	563658.8	53176.0	7120585.4	4120260.5	1550314.3	2158270.6	890671.9
373842.6	370318.6	1232.0	6609.0	919716.5	433174.5	236461.3	293067.9	150404.6
488528.1	474598.6	15210.3	4599.0	572787.1	265764.5	164287.2	333957.5	172473.4
49328.6	46512.2		485.0	60128.8	48537.0	8547.8	5147.3	1942.0
10896.6	10611.6		140.0	17285.8	14252.7	1949.9	2745.1	795.2
2765425.2	**2667606.1**	**859754.4**	**33340.0**	**6971041.5**	**2280180.6**	**3944198.2**	**4743710.0**	**868061.7**
102212.5	98840.0	24072.7	2151.0	138404.8	61349.7	64411.6	83535.4	19213.8
63781.6	55784.7	312.1	506.0	42157.4	32197.3	8353.4	24488.2	16134.9
19720.8	18324.1	1282.1	600.0	51202.3	35439.6	14477.8	17606.7	3128.9
445823.9	682918.3	16395.3	4102.0	501397.5	400928.2	69826.0	70856.7	33093.9
176110.2	171526.5	16395.3	4000.0	450837.2	350571.9	69622.1	70652.6	33059.7
269713.7	511391.8		102.0	50560.3	50356.3	203.9	204.1	34.2
20288.8	19023.1	3705.6	451.0	37261.1	24141.7	3588.2	6139.1	2550.9
4601.9	4601.9	537.4	103.0	11495.8	10211.5	785.6	1946.6	1161.0
15686.9	14421.2	3168.2	348.0	25765.3	13930.2	2802.6	4192.5	1389.9
365065.1	312515.9	16864.5	5432.0	846348.8	502838.3	243179.5	323913.0	95874.2
1330922.1	1052060.0	731505.8	10836.0	4651559.6	789799.6	3428506.1	4033428.5	620824.9
78756.1	39853.0	6305.1	1140.0	38322.2	30076.0	5500.7	10120.3	4649.6
245542.1	220376.5	102856.6	2520.0	267408.0	139963.1	76251.8	123401.1	48561.9
863306.7	652034.2	621073.7	5623.0	4283725.9	591977.6	3321427.5	3866738.2	559443.7
143317.2	139796.3	1270.4	1553.0	62103.5	27782.9	25326.1	33168.9	8169.7
396660.6	407091.0	65543.5	8644.0	656857.6	398409.8	105373.7	176161.5	74724.1
338165.5	349563.1	14871.4	7759.0	598163.0	382279.1	63062.6	124769.0	62230.8
58495.1	57527.9	50672.1	885.0	58694.6	16130.7	42311.1	51392.5	12493.3
20949.8	21049.0	72.8	618.0	45852.4	35076.4	6481.9	7580.9	2516.1

12-13 续表2

单位：万元

行业	Sector	负债合计 Total Liabilites	流动负债合计 Total Working Liabilities
总计	**Total**	**11571285.0**	**9180964.1**
一、医药制造业	**Pharmaceutical Manufacturing**	**753743.5**	**694358.9**
（一）化学药品制造	Chemical manufacturing	388862.7	369080.0
化学药品原料药制造	Chemical raw materials Medicine manufacturing	16191.6	15908.5
化学药品制剂制造	Chemical preparations manufacturing	372671.1	353171.5
（二）中药饮片加工	Chinese medicine Pieces processing	10722.3	720.8
（三）中成药生产	Chinese medicine production	272835.7	246544.6
（四）兽用药品制造	Veterinary pharmaceutical manufacturing	26135.9	25885.9
（五）生物药品制造	Biopharmaceutical manufacturing	50293.0	48623.7
（六）卫生材料及医药用品制造	Sanitary materials and medical supplies manufacturing	4893.9	3503.9
二、航空航天器制造业	**Aerospace & aviation industry**	**4990362.7**	**3993135.3**
（一）飞机制造	Aircraft Manufacturing	4122869.1	3388369.3
（二）航天器制造	Spacecraft Manufacturing	449612.8	272312.8
（三）航空、航天相关设备制造	Aviation and aerospace-related equipment manufacturing	383201.1	299574.6
（四）其他航空航天器制造	Other aerospace manufacturing	24120.2	23120.2
（五）航空航天器修理	Aerospace vehicle repair	10559.5	9758.4
三、电子及通讯设备制造业	**Electronic and communication equipment manufacturing**	**4233355.8**	**3168936.1**
（一）电子工业专用设备制造	Electronic equipment manufacturing	55000.7	38747.7
（二）光纤、光缆制造	Optical fiber, cable manufacturing	22849.9	22849.9
（三）锂离子电池制造	Lithium-ion battery manufacturing	40684.3	22795.4
（四）通信设备制造	Communications equipment manufacturing	329384.1	225175.6
通信系统设备制造	Communications system equipment	317490.1	214426.5
通信终端设备制造	Communication Terminal Equipment	11894.0	10749.1
（五）广播电视设备制造	Broadcasting and TV Equipment	29640.1	29249.9
广播电视节目制作及发射设备制造	Radio and television program production and transmission equipment		
广播电视接收设备及器材制造	Radio and television reception apparatus and equipment manufacturing	9121.3	8731.1
应用电视设备及其他广播电视设备制造	Application television equipment and other radio and television equipment manufacturing	20518.8	20518.8
（六）雷达及配套设备制造	Radar and ancillary equipment manufacturers	559804.7	483643.3
（七）视听设备制造	Audiovisual equipment manufacturing		
电视机制造	TV manufacturing		
音响设备制造	Audio Equipment manufacturing		
影视录放设备制造	Video recording equipment manufacturing		
（八）电子器件制造	Electronic device manufacturing	2638113.5	1965733.7
电子真空器件制造	Electronic vacuum device manufacturing	16963.5	15988.8
半导体分立器件制造	Discrete semiconductor device manufacturing	142919.1	109940.8
集成电路制造	Semiconductor Manufacturing	2457743.5	1823677.6
光电子器件及其他电子器件制造	Optoelectronic devices and other electronic device manufacturing	20487.4	16126.5
（九）电子元件制造	Electronics Manufacturing	539068.0	362546.5
电子元件及组件制造	Electronic components and component manufacturing	499344.9	326311.2
印刷电路板制造	Printed circuit board manufacturing	39723.1	36235.3
（十）其他电子设备制造	Other electronic equipment manufacturing	18810.5	18194.1

continued 2

(10 000 yuan)

非流动负债 Non-Working Liabilities	所有者权益合计 Total Owners' Equities	实收资本 Total Capital Hold	营业收入 Total Revenue	主营业务收入 Revenue from Principal Business	营业成本 Total Cost	主营业务成本 Cost of Principal Business	营业税金及附加 Taxs and Other Changes	主营业务税金及附加 Taxes and Other Charges on Principal Business
2188395.1	**8690259.1**	**4234813.7**	**10757055.8**	**10662630.4**	**8656167.9**	**8564674.4**	**45590.3**	**42736.6**
32503.5	**742681.1**	**248475.0**	**1560130.3**	**1558465.0**	**904299.4**	**903982.1**	**12298.6**	**12298.6**
3610.3	354770.7	129285.9	930806.9	929474.2	533415.8	533115.1	6942.5	6942.5
283.0	21322.4	18000.0	22145.0	21981.6	15193.8	15193.8	131.7	131.7
3327.3	333448.3	111285.9	908661.9	907492.6	518222.0	517921.3	6810.8	6810.8
	112.8	500.0	22803.8	22803.8	21643.1	21643.1	22.1	22.1
26059.0	127957.9	62358.3	377154.4	376989.4	202111.9	202104.0	3193.1	3193.1
250.0	72348.0	4200.0	26613.1	26613.1	14001.4	14001.4	449.3	449.3
1194.2	178707.7	48630.8	173230.1	173062.5	106512.4	106503.7	1604.3	1604.3
1390.0	8784.0	3500.0	29522.0	29522.0	26614.8	26614.8	87.3	87.3
973709.8	**3697228.2**	**1036365.0**	**4496985.3**	**4459588.1**	**3913918.2**	**3882889.3**	**16684.9**	**15894.1**
717975.9	2997712.5	867615.4	3621997.5	3594515.2	3180429.3	3154878.0	13944.1	13181.1
177300.0	470103.7	31987.0	385828.7	377345.6	316818.4	311624.4	973.7	945.9
76632.8	186677.2	122122.6	435777.5	434368.4	381775.9	381492.3	1304.2	1304.2
1000.0	36008.6	10640.0	42802.0	42779.3	26880.5	26880.5	399.6	399.6
801.1	6726.2	4000.0	10579.6	10579.6	8014.1	8014.1	63.3	63.3
1010160.3	**2735690.4**	**2167675.8**	**2769666.2**	**2735598.0**	**2307605.4**	**2260950.8**	**5893.8**	**5336.4**
16253.0	83404.1	59471.0	89830.8	86981.6	61908.8	61336.9	139.4	136.3
	19307.5	23825.3	49698.5	49633.8	40880.8	40831.4	220.9	220.9
17866.0	10518.0	7852.0	15725.1	15639.2	13471.9	13470.6	9.9	9.9
89586.3	172013.2	153728.0	717584.4	710697.5	666454.5	663773.9	1637.0	1363.6
89586.3	133347.0	120728.0	206192.6	199305.7	163381.0	160700.4	963.0	689.6
	38666.2	33000.0	511391.8	511391.8	503073.5	503073.5	674.0	674.0
390.1	7620.9	8000.0	24618.4	24608.5	21484.7	21432.8	70.4	70.4
390.1	2374.5	2000.0	4601.9	4601.9	3846.8	3846.8	55.3	55.3
	5246.4	6000.0	20016.5	20006.6	17637.9	17586.0	15.1	15.1
76161.3	286544.1	57164.5	389201.2	386376.4	326317.0	324248.4	250.3	5.0
669477.6	2012946.0	1758125.4	1081067.5	1066558.1	849688.5	813988.7	1765.1	1760.6
974.6	21358.7	6270.0	43554.2	41909.1	31019.4	29726.4	628.0	628.0
32978.2	124488.9	47693.9	233555.8	221588.1	205249.9	193198.6	250.6	250.6
634065.9	1825482.3	1674861.5	656397.1	655692.8	492438.4	470082.9	110.2	110.2
1458.9	41616.1	29300.0	147560.4	147368.1	120980.8	120980.8	776.3	771.8
139974.1	116294.9	77359.6	376745.9	370003.9	310091.8	304910.7	1644.8	1613.7
136486.3	97323.5	46555.2	316035.7	312541.9	254054.0	251041.7	1563.8	1532.7
3487.8	18971.4	30804.4	60710.2	57462.0	56037.8	53869.0	81.0	81.0
451.9	27041.7	22150.0	25194.4	25099.0	17307.4	16957.4	156.0	156.0

12-13 续表3

单位：万元

行　业	Sector	销售费用 Expenses for Sales	管理费用 Expenses for Management
总计	**Total**	**531694.9**	**952364.8**
一、医药制造业	**Pharmaceutical Manufacturing**	**366681.3**	**149646.0**
（一）化学药品制造	Chemical manufacturing	209520.0	91110.9
化学药品原料药制造	Chemical raw materials Medicine manufacturing	2240.2	3804.5
化学药品制剂制造	Chemical preparations manufacturing	207279.8	87306.4
（二）中药饮片加工	Chinese medicine Pieces processing	560.4	283.5
（三）中成药生产	Chinese medicine production	116920.1	37663.8
（四）兽用药品制造	Veterinary pharmaceutical manufacturing	1565.4	856.5
（五）生物药品制造	Biopharmaceutical manufacturing	37374.5	19070.6
（六）卫生材料及医药用品制造	Sanitary materials and medical supplies manufacturing	740.9	660.7
二、航空航天器制造业	**Aerospace & aviation industry**	**75936.8**	**336516.2**
（一）飞机制造	Aircraft Manufacturing	65957.9	274787.1
（二）航天器制造	Spacecraft Manufacturing	3131.5	35160.5
（三）航空、航天相关设备制造	Aviation and aerospace-related equipment manufacturing	5106.0	19650.5
（四）其他航空航天器制造	Other aerospace manufacturing	1474.0	5076.9
（五）航空航天器修理	Aerospace vehicle repair	267.4	1841.2
三、电子及通讯设备制造业	**Electronic and communication equipment manufacturing**	**48992.8**	**302523.0**
（一）电子工业专用设备制造	Electronic equipment manufacturing	3013.8	9586.6
（二）光纤、光缆制造	Optical fiber, cable manufacturing	2263.6	2961.3
（三）锂离子电池制造	Lithium-ion battery manufacturing	195.7	803.1
（四）通信设备制造	Communications equipment manufacturing	11153.1	30196.7
通信系统设备制造	Communications system equipment	11023.7	29342.0
通信终端设备制造	Communication Terminal Equipment	129.4	854.7
（五）广播电视设备制造	Broadcasting and TV Equipment	1851.1	1770.8
广播电视节目制作及发射设备制造	Radio and television program production and transmission equipment		
广播电视接收设备及器材制造	Radio and television reception apparatus and equipment manufacturing	192.3	384.4
应用电视设备及其他广播电视设备制造	Application television equipment and other radio and television equipment manufacturing	1658.8	1386.4
（六）雷达及配套设备制造	Radar and ancillary equipment manufacturers	4546.4	36012.9
（七）视听设备制造	Audiovisual equipment manufacturing		
电视机制造	TV manufacturing		
音响设备制造	Audio Equipment manufacturing		
影视录放设备制造	Video recording equipment manufacturing		
（八）电子器件制造	Electronic device manufacturing	13997.7	178572.2
电子真空器件制造	Electronic vacuum device manufacturing	1584.6	3662.3
半导体分立器件制造	Discrete semiconductor device manufacturing	4206.3	12460.1
集成电路制造	Semiconductor Manufacturing	1064.2	149218.1
光电子器件及其他电子器件制造	Optoelectronic devices and other electronic device manufacturing	7142.6	13231.7
（九）电子元件制造	Electronics Manufacturing	10565.7	38392.5
电子元件及组件制造	Electronic components and component manufacturing	10049.3	36974.8
印刷电路板制造	Printed circuit board manufacturing	516.4	1417.7
（十）其他电子设备制造	Other electronic equipment manufacturing	1405.7	4226.9

continued 3

(10 000 yuan)

财务费用 Financial cost	营业利润 Operating Profit	利润总额 Total Profits	亏损企业亏损额 Total Loss of Deficit Enterprises	利税总额 Total Pre-tax Profits	应付职工薪酬 Salary Payable	本年应交增值税 Value Added Tax Payable
127304.4	**464549.1**	**617197.7**	**49379.4**	**940788.7**	**1299361.4**	**278068.7**
18318.3	**129433.6**	**133842.3**	**2715.9**	**279701.1**	**135607.4**	**133560.2**
14264.6	74260.8	74037.2	298.1	177968.6	99201.6	96988.9
666.4	108.4	172.3	256.0	1549.3	3207.2	1245.3
13598.2	74152.4	73864.9	42.1	176419.3	95994.4	95743.6
162.1	132.6	132.6	6.4	312.6	65.4	157.9
3891.8	13332.2	14067.4	2411.4	44046.3	21915.5	26785.8
104.8	9635.7	9777.2		10721.6	133.8	495.1
-322.3	31330.9	34980.7		45179.8	13094.7	8594.8
217.3	741.4	847.2		1472.2	1196.4	537.7
56603.2	**107341.1**	**127376.0**	**15581.6**	**200112.4**	**638238.2**	**56051.5**
45948.8	47615.3	60740.9	10006.0	110309.2	531148.9	35624.2
2682.9	37862.1	43874.7		46339.9	68527.0	1491.5
7575.1	12941.8	13702.9	5432.4	30148.3	32785.5	15141.2
367.0	8582.5	8703.8		12434.7	4737.6	3331.3
29.4	339.4	353.7	143.2	880.3	1039.2	463.3
32884.3	**72373.6**	**174807.2**	**26100.8**	**212807.2**	**243796.3**	**32106.2**
1036.3	8233.0	10220.5		14658.5	11669.6	4298.6
274.8	2969.7	3054.9		4990.3	3570.5	1714.5
505.4	711.1	917.1		1872.1	871.7	945.1
4361.1	9617.8	13766.5	12429.6	19289.3	31768.8	3885.8
4364.1	2954.6	7103.3	12429.6	10502.7	30746.5	2436.4
-3.0	6663.2	6663.2		8786.6	1022.3	1449.4
496.2	-1054.8	-831.3	1046.7	-345.6	2131.8	415.3
-5.6	128.7	215.4		559.9	471.1	289.2
501.8	-1183.5	-1046.7	1046.7	-905.5	1660.7	126.1
2544.1	21802.3	22870.2		29778.2	59400.3	6657.7
13196.4	23211.2	115370.8	8713.5	121511.5	82123.1	4375.6
70.7	5926.3	6278.0		9045.0	5608.6	2139.0
2321.0	9643.1	11287.9		12954.0	14663.9	1415.5
9757.1	3260.4	93079.4	8257.5	93681.1	56318.4	491.5
1047.6	4381.4	4725.5	456.0	5831.4	5532.2	329.6
10145.5	5098.7	7560.5	3911.0	18199.6	47584.4	8994.3
9917.0	2670.6	5085.5	3911.0	15611.7	40655.0	8962.4
228.5	2428.1	2475.0		2587.9	6929.4	31.9
324.5	1784.6	1878.0		2853.3	4676.1	819.3

12-13 续表4

单位：万元

行　业	Sector	企业单位数（个）Number of Enterprises (unit)	亏损企业 Loss Making Enterprises
四、计算机及办公设备制造业	**Computer and office equipment manufacturing**	**1**	
（一）计算机整机制造	Computer machine manufacturing		
（二）计算机零部件制造	Computer parts manufacturing		
（三）计算机外围设备制造	Computer peripheral equipment manufacturing	1	
（四）其他计算机制造	Other computer manufacturing		
（五）办公设备制造	Office Equipment manufacturing		
复印和胶印设备制造	Photocopying and offset printing equipment manufacturing		
计算器及货币专用设备制造	Calculator and money and special equipment manufacturing		
五、医疗设备及仪器仪表制造业	**Medical equipment and instrumentation manufacturing**	**54**	**10**
（一）医疗仪器设备及器械制造	Medical equipment and device manufacturing	7	1
医疗诊断、监护及治疗设备制造	Medical diagnosis, monitoring and treatment equipment manufacturing	2	1
口腔科用设备及器具制造	Stomatology manufacture equipment and appliances		
医疗实验室及医用消毒设备和器具制造	Medical laboratory and medical sterilization equipment and equipment manufacturing		
医疗、外科及兽医用器械制造	Medical, surgical and veterinary instruments manufacturing		
机械治疗及病房护理设备制造	Mechanical treatment and ward care equipment manufacturing	1	
假肢、人工器官及植（介）入器械制造	Prostheses, artificial organs and implantable(interventional) device manufacturing	1	
其他治疗设备及器械制造	Other treatment equipment and equipment manufacturing	3	
（二）仪器仪表制造	Instruments manufacturing	47	9
工业自动控制系统装置制造	Manufacture of industrial automation control system devices manufacturing	9	3
电工仪器仪表制造	Electrical Instruments manufacturing	5	3
绘图、计算及测量仪器制造	Drawings, calculation and measurement equipment manufacturing	1	
实验分析仪器制造	Experimental analysis equipment manufacturing	2	1
试验机制造	Testing Machine Manufacturing		
供应用仪表及其他通用仪器制造	Supply of manufacturing devices and other general instrument Manufacturing	3	
环境检测专用仪器仪表制造	Environmental testing special Instruments Manufacturing	3	
运输设备及生产用计数仪表制造	Transport equipment and manufacturing with the counting instrument manufacturing		
导航、气象及海洋专用仪器制造	Navigation, meteorological and oceanographic special equipment manufacturing	2	
农林牧渔专用仪器仪表制造	Agriculture, forestry, animal husbandry and fishery special Instruments manufacturing	1	
地质勘探和地震专用仪器制造	Geological exploration and seismic special equipment manufacturing	8	1
教学专用仪器制造	Teaching special equipment manufacturing		
核子及核辐射测量仪器制造	Nucleon and nuclear radiation measuring instruments manufacturing	1	
电子测量仪器制造	Electronic Measuring Instruments Manufacturing	1	
其他专用仪器制造	Other special equipment manufacturing	3	
光学仪器制造	Optical Instruments Manufacturing	3	
其他仪器仪表制造业	Other instrumentation manufacturing	5	1
六、信息化学品制造业	**Information chemicals manufacturing**	**3**	
（一）信息化学品制造	Information Chemical Manufacturing	3	

continued 4

(10 000 yuan)

工业总产值（当年价格） Gross Industrial Output Value (At Current Prices)	工业销售产值（当年价） Value of Industry Products Sales (At Current Prices)	出口交货值 Export Delivery Value	从业人员年平均人数（人） Annual Average Employers (person)	资产总计 Total Assets	流动资产合计 Total Working Capitals	固定资产合计 Total Fixed Assets	固定资产原价 Origing Value of Fixed Assets	累计折旧 Accumulative Total Depreciation
5244.0	**5244.0**		**175.0**	**9940.3**	**7141.3**	**1069.0**	**1948.2**	**879.2**
5244.0	5244.0		175.0	9940.3	7141.3	1069.0	1948.2	879.2
1667320.9	**1556823.9**	**73094.5**	**23858.0**	**2341854.9**	**1453804.8**	**567047.7**	**836236.5**	**384550.3**
17902.1	18432.2		776.0	49478.8	36974.2	9620.9	13801.6	4180.7
2548.1	3507.7		264.0	26956.3	18194.9	6431.9	8021.2	1589.3
3210.9	2906.6		158.0	6307.8	4267.4	1578.7	2815.0	1236.3
5600.0	5600.0		48.0	3735.2	3191.3	543.9	856.5	312.6
6543.1	6417.9		306.0	12479.5	11320.6	1066.4	2108.9	1042.5
1649418.8	1538391.7	73094.5	23082.0	2292376.1	1416830.6	557426.8	822434.9	380369.6
198400.1	192909.3	4027.5	1801.0	229356.3	100674.5	11670.2	32119.7	19746.7
19490.9	17946.3	1710.9	613.0	54382.5	36568.3	991.0	3295.7	2304.7
8033.9	9009.7	176.5	235.0	23546.5	20152.4	1582.6	2494.8	912.2
8610.3	8523.5		379.0	11103.7	8576.1	727.5	1190.3	462.8
35654.5	31073.8		681.0	33172.1	28900.9	2820.5	4911.9	2091.4
110097.4	110101.7	29579.3	775.0	79285.8	72036.6	6737.0	15064.9	9757.9
40967.5	40967.5		927.0	28285.0	26803.9	1459.6	3773.1	2313.5
16893.9	18733.0		105.0	9755.7	6720.4	2757.6	2939.5	905.0
577735.7	489173.1	10402.8	6609.0	711709.7	447771.5	165569.9	320776.8	156801.5
15027.0	17757.0		732.0	62151.5	35048.8	27102.7	9932.2	5654.0
3573.6	3054.6		118.0	5529.4	4656.5	761.7	1622.5	866.0
38971.3	37835.2	20542.0	554.0	57852.8	50371.4	1875.9	3737.1	1942.2
534784.9	517159.2	6655.5	8857.0	938860.6	542837.5	322045.0	406965.3	172623.6
41177.8	44147.8		696.0	47384.5	35711.8	11325.6	13611.1	3988.1
515798.1	**510623.6**	**299826.7**	**1865.0**	**756620.4**	**395760.2**	**269035.6**	**577128.3**	**315677.6**
515798.1	510623.6	299826.7	1865.0	756620.4	395760.2	269035.6	577128.3	315677.6

12-13 续表5

单位：万元

行业	Sector	负债合计 Total Liabilites	流动负债合计 Total Working Liabilities
四、计算机及办公设备制造业	**Computer and office equipment manufacturing**	**2746.9**	**2746.9**
（一）计算机整机制造	Computer machine manufacturing		
（二）计算机零部件制造	Computer parts manufacturing		
（三）计算机外围设备制造	Computer peripheral equipment manufacturing	2746.9	2746.9
（四）其他计算机制造	Other computer manufacturing		
（五）办公设备制造	Office Equipment manufacturing		
复印和胶印设备制造	Photocopying and offset printing equipment manufacturing		
计算器及货币专用设备制造	Calculator and money and special equipment manufacturing		
五、医疗设备及仪器仪表制造业	**Medical equipment and instrumentation manufacturing**	**1182378.9**	**979418.8**
（一）医疗仪器设备及器械制造	Medical equipment and device manufacturing	20415.0	17550.0
医疗诊断、监护及治疗设备制造	Medical diagnosis, monitoring and treatment equipment manufacturing	13614.5	12504.5
口腔科用设备及器具制造	Stomatology manufacture equipment and appliances		
医疗实验室及医用消毒设备和器具制造	Medical laboratory and medical sterilization equipment and equipment manufacturing		
医疗、外科及兽医用器械制造	Medical, surgical and veterinary instruments manufacturing		
机械治疗及病房护理设备制造	Mechanical treatment and ward care equipment manufacturing	1437.4	437.4
假肢、人工器官及植（介）入器械制造	Prostheses, artificial organs and implantable(interventional) device manufacturing	831.9	586.9
其他治疗设备及器械制造	Other treatment equipment and equipment manufacturing	4531.2	4021.2
（二）仪器仪表制造	Instruments manufacturing	1161963.9	961868.8
工业自动控制系统装置制造	Manufacture of industrial automation control system devices manufacturing	178244.6	94903.6
电工仪器仪表制造	Electrical Instruments manufacturing	18487.5	10860.9
绘图、计算及测量仪器制造	Drawings, calculation and measurement equipment manufacturing	10945.6	8147.5
实验分析仪器制造	Experimental analysis equipment manufacturing	8338.8	8338.8
试验机制造	Testing Machine Manufacturing		
供应用仪表及其他通用仪器制造	Supply of manufacturing devices and other general instrument Manufacturing	13547.5	13547.5
环境检测专用仪器仪表制造	Environmental testing special Instruments Manufacturing	16181.0	16181.0
运输设备及生产用计数仪表制造	Transport equipment and manufacturing with the counting instrument manufacturing		
导航、气象及海洋专用仪器制造	Navigation, meteorological and oceanographic special equipment manufacturing	13632.3	13632.3
农林牧渔专用仪器仪表制造	Agriculture, forestry, animal husbandry and fishery special Instruments manufacturing	2247.4	2247.4
地质勘探和地震专用仪器制造	Geological exploration and seismic special equipment manufacturing	267929.4	255972.0
教学专用仪器制造	Teaching special equipment manufacturing		
核子及核辐射测量仪器制造	Nucleon and nuclear radiation measuring instruments manufacturing	35050.6	34875.1
电子测量仪器制造	Electronic Measuring Instruments Manufacturing	2188.1	1188.1
其他专用仪器制造	Other special equipment manufacturing	24673.3	16637.5
光学仪器制造	Optical Instruments Manufacturing	549257.2	464106.5
其他仪器仪表制造业	Other instrumentation manufacturing	21240.6	21230.6
六、信息化学品制造业	**Information chemicals manufacturing**	**408663.2**	**342334.1**
（一）信息化学品制造	Information Chemical Manufacturing	408663.2	342334.1

continued 5

(10 000 yuan)

非流动负债 Non-Working Liabilities	所有者权益合计 Total Owners' Equities	实收资本 Total Capital Hold	营业收入 Total Revenue	主营业务收入 Revenue from Principal Business	营业成本 Total Cost	主营业务成本 Cost of Principal Business	营业税金及附加 Taxs and Other Changes	主营业务税金及附加 Taxes and Other Charges on Principal Business
	7193.3	**4600.0**	**5244.0**	**5241.5**	**2398.0**	**2398.0**	**45.5**	**45.5**
	7193.3	4600.0	5244.0	5241.5	2398.0	2398.0	45.5	45.5
106506.8	**1159474.9**	**555583.4**	**1474357.4**	**1456087.8**	**1143432.8**	**1131957.3**	**9890.6**	**8385.1**
1755.0	29063.7	12018.6	31865.4	31600.6	18721.1	17069.6	232.9	232.9
	13341.8	6598.6	10396.9	10163.7	7215.6	7107.0	24.8	24.8
1000.0	4870.4	1000.0	2906.7	2906.7	2711.0	1192.4	38.3	38.3
245.0	2903.2	1020.0	4438.5	4438.5	1963.1	1963.1	36.8	36.8
510.0	7948.3	3400.0	14123.3	14091.7	6831.4	6807.1	133.0	133.0
104751.8	1130411.2	543564.8	1442492.0	1424487.2	1124711.7	1114887.7	9657.7	8152.2
5605.1	51111.3	46078.0	128835.3	128556.7	93974.0	93868.3	789.7	787.0
726.0	35895.0	11150.1	19988.6	19714.8	15713.1	15457.0	234.4	234.4
366.0	12600.9	5900.0	9009.7	7928.5	6073.1	5366.1	80.2	76.2
	2764.9	8800.0	9028.4	8839.0	6859.7	6408.5	31.6	31.6
	19624.5	10500.0	32867.5	32867.5	23373.8	23373.8	232.3	232.3
	63104.7	17066.5	110680.0	110101.3	85492.5	85492.5	815.9	815.9
	14652.7	2803.1	48141.0	48127.5	33695.3	33695.3	214.7	214.7
	7508.2	2000.0	18733.0	18733.0	16711.0	16711.0	9.0	9.0
10032.3	443780.3	274058.5	417919.7	408588.8	319693.4	315183.8	5261.7	5102.1
175.5	27100.9	8710.8	31203.9	31203.9	21633.9	21633.9	351.1	
1000.0	3341.3	600.0	3275.9	3053.8	1908.3	1840.8	32.8	32.8
2262.8	33179.5	15220.0	36489.2	36340.5	22109.0	22109.0	291.2	291.2
84574.1	389603.3	136095.0	531785.5	526054.2	441445.9	437837.5	1045.1	57.1
10.0	26143.7	4582.8	44534.3	44377.7	36028.7	35910.2	268.0	267.9
65480.7	**347957.2**	**222080.5**	**450638.6**	**447616.0**	**384480.1**	**382462.9**	**742.9**	**742.9**
65480.7	347957.2	222080.5	450638.6	447616.0	384480.1	382462.9	742.9	742.9

12-13 续表6

单位：万元

行 业	Sector	销售费用 Expenses for Sales	管理费用 Expenses for Management
四、计算机及办公设备制造业	**Computer and office equipment manufacturing**	**299.7**	**1840.7**
（一）计算机整机制造	Computer machine manufacturing		
（二）计算机零部件制造	Computer parts manufacturing		
（三）计算机外围设备制造	Computer peripheral equipment manufacturing	299.7	1840.7
（四）其他计算机制造	Other computer manufacturing		
（五）办公设备制造	Office Equipment manufacturing		
复印和胶印设备制造	Photocopying and offset printing equipment manufacturing		
计算器及货币专用设备制造	Calculator and money and special equipment manufacturing		
五、医疗设备及仪器仪表制造业	**Medical equipment and instrumentation manufacturing**	**35369.1**	**142157.1**
（一）医疗仪器设备及器械制造	Medical equipment and device manufacturing	3429.5	4733.8
医疗诊断、监护及治疗设备制造	Medical diagnosis, monitoring and treatment equipment manufacturing	1310.4	1907.1
口腔科用设备及器具制造	Stomatology manufacture equipment and appliances		
医疗实验室及医用消毒设备和器具制造	Medical laboratory and medical sterilization equipment and equipment manufacturing		
医疗、外科及兽医用器械制造	Medical, surgical and veterinary instruments manufacturing		
机械治疗及病房护理设备制造	Mechanical treatment and ward care equipment manufacturing	770.0	673.5
假肢、人工器官及植（介）入器械制造	Prostheses, artificial organs and implantable(interventional) device manufacturing	313.5	604.6
其他治疗设备及器械制造	Other treatment equipment and equipment manufacturing	1035.6	1548.6
（二）仪器仪表制造	Instruments manufacturing	31939.6	137423.3
工业自动控制系统装置制造	Manufacture of industrial automation control system devices manufacturing	5599.1	9814.4
电工仪器仪表制造	Electrical Instruments manufacturing	800.4	2058.5
绘图、计算及测量仪器制造	Drawings, calculation and measurement equipment manufacturing	1693.8	1132.4
实验分析仪器制造	Experimental analysis equipment manufacturing	1096.8	1514.1
试验机制造	Testing Machine Manufacturing		
供应用仪表及其他通用仪器制造	Supply of manufacturing devices and other general instrument Manufacturing	2940.5	3704.2
环境检测专用仪器仪表制造	Environmental testing special Instruments Manufacturing	5158.1	5547.7
运输设备及生产用计数仪表制造	Transport equipment and manufacturing with the counting instrument manufacturing		
导航、气象及海洋专用仪器制造	Navigation, meteorological and oceanographic special equipment manufacturing	88.3	6750.5
农林牧渔专用仪器仪表制造	Agriculture, forestry, animal husbandry and fishery special Instruments manufacturing	333.1	581.7
地质勘探和地震专用仪器制造	Geological exploration and seismic special equipment manufacturing	6347.0	31728.4
教学专用仪器制造	Teaching special equipment manufacturing		
核子及核辐射测量仪器制造	Nucleon and nuclear radiation measuring instruments manufacturing	1504.3	4047.5
电子测量仪器制造	Electronic Measuring Instruments Manufacturing	258.1	707.6
其他专用仪器制造	Other special equipment manufacturing	1395.8	3445.1
光学仪器制造	Optical Instruments Manufacturing	2387.3	63459.0
其他仪器仪表制造业	Other instrumentation manufacturing	2337.0	2932.2
六、信息化学品制造业	**Information chemicals manufacturing**	**4381.2**	**19647.8**
（一）信息化学品制造	Information Chemical Manufacturing	4381.2	19647.8

continued 6

(10 000 yuan)

财务费用 Financial cost	营业利润 Operating Profit	利润总额 Total Profits	亏损企业亏损额 Total Loss of Deficit Enterprises	利税总额 Total Pre-tax Profits	应付职工薪酬 Salary Payable	本年应交增值税 Value Added Tax Payable
136.3	**486.4**	**696.5**		**1120.1**	**1626.3**	**378.1**
136.3	486.4	696.5		1120.1	1626.3	378.1
11284.7	**125203.9**	**147930.6**	**4947.1**	**208943.4**	**244058.7**	**51122.2**
496.3	5798.9	5809.4	451.3	7610.7	2816.9	1568.4
394.5	-442.7	-449.5	451.3	-334.9	370.4	89.8
75.1	157.4	164.0		521.6	713.1	319.3
-1.0	1532.0	1531.8		2250.6	217.9	682.0
27.7	4552.2	4563.1		5173.4	1515.5	477.3
10788.4	119405.0	142121.2	4495.8	201332.7	241241.8	49553.8
571.3	18299.8	19433.5	2494.9	26225.4	13294.3	6002.2
112.1	953.5	1068.1	789.7	1449.0	2204.9	146.5
-106.3	136.5	329.0		751.6	1172.5	342.4
35.3	-1020.1	-611.8	798.6	-452.2	1632.7	128.0
78.6	2518.3	2892.5		4984.8	3378.3	1860.0
-952.7	14170.2	14706.2		18595.1	8512.4	3073.0
19.4	7324.5	7398.3		8821.2	9744.7	1208.2
101.8	996.4	1069.4		1103.7	415.4	25.3
2731.3	46178.5	49105.7	339.9	82726.7	101943.4	28359.3
361.0	7554.4	7539.1		9241.9	4236.1	1351.7
105.0	264.1	293.6		599.9	544.0	273.5
1070.5	8186.8	8726.6		9732.7	4060.7	714.9
6332.5	11315.7	27395.1		33153.3	87595.3	4713.1
328.6	2526.4	2775.9	72.7	4399.6	2507.1	1355.7
8043.6	**29676.5**	**32511.1**		**38070.5**	**36000.5**	**4816.5**
8043.6	29676.5	32511.1		38070.5	36000.5	4816.5

12-14 规模以上工业企业主要经济效益指标（2014年）

行　业	Sector	总资产贡献率（%） Ratio of Total Assets to Industrial Output Value (%)	资产负债率%） Assets-Liability Ratio (%)
总计	**Total**	**7.4**	**59.7**
按工业行业大类分	**Grouped by Sector**		
煤炭开采和洗选业	Mining and Washing of Coal		
石油和天然气开采业	Extraction of Petroleum and Natural Gas		
黑色金属矿采选业	Mining and Processing of Ferrous Metal Ores	16.2	184.3
有色金属矿采选业	Mining and Processing of Non-ferrous Metal Ores		
非金属矿采选业	Mining and Processing of Nonmetal Ores		
开采辅助活动	Mining Auxiliary Activities	5.8	69.6
其他采矿业	Mining of other Ores		
农副食品加工业	Processing of Food from Agricultural Porducts	9.2	75.5
食品制造业	Manufacture of Foods	16.3	41.2
酒、饮料和精制茶制造业	Manufacture of Alcohol,Beverages and Tea	12.5	59.4
烟草制品业	Manufacture of Tobacco	21.1	63.5
纺织业	Manufacture of Textile	10.5	59.9
纺织服装、服饰业	Textile, apparel industry	16.6	66.1
皮革、毛皮、羽毛及其制品和制鞋业	Leather fur feathers and its products and footwear	6.8	42.9
木材加工和木、竹、藤、棕、草制品业	Processing of Timber,Manufacture of Wood,Plam and Straw Products	6.9	59.8
家具制造业	Manufacture of Furniture	8.3	52.6
造纸及纸制品业	Manufacture of Paper and Paper Products	12.7	59
印刷和记录媒介复制业	Printing,Reproduction of Recording Media	16.6	37.2
文教、工美、体育和娱乐用品制造业	Manufacture of Articles For Cultural,Educational and Sports Activities	14.7	93.7

Main Indicators of Economic Benefit of Industrial Enterprises above Designated Size (2014)

流动资产周转率（次） Rate of Annual Turnover Working Capitals (times)	成本费用利润率（%） Ratio of Profits to Cost (%)	工业产品销售率（%） Proportion of Industrial Products Sold (%)	产值利税率（%） Ratio of Output Value to Profits and Tax (%)	每百元固定资产实现利税（元） Profit and Tax per 100 yuan of Fixed Assets (yuan)	每百元销售收入实现利税（元） Profit and Tax per 100 yuan of Sales Revenue (yuan)
1.4	**5.2**	**94.9**	**8.1**	**20.3**	**8.9**
1.8	1.4	100	5.6	63.4	7
2.6	3.6	100.8	8.2	12.5	4.3
3.9	1.7	99	3	32.4	3.4
4.3	5.6	94.2	6.9	49.7	8.1
1.6	7.9	110.6	14.6	35.1	15
1.2	48.9	104.3	47.7	125	42.8
1.2	9.1	82.7	11.6	51.6	12.8
1.3	10.3	84	12.7	115.3	14
1.3	6.7	100.9	8.1	109.2	8.1
1.7	3.2	88.1	6.4	18.4	8.4
1.8	4.7	90	6.4	31.8	7
2.5	7.7	98.6	8.3	60.2	10.2
1.8	13.8	96.1	16.9	41.1	19
2.6	0.7	99.9	5.3	298.2	5.9

12-14 续表1

行　业	Sector	总资产贡献率（%） Ratio of Total Assets to Industrial Output Value (%)	资产负债率%） Assets-Liability Ratio (%)
石油加工、炼焦和核燃料加工业	Processing of Petroleum, Cokeing,Processing of Nuclear and Nuclear Fuel	23.8	74
化学原料和化学制品制造业	Manufacture of Raw Chemical Materials and Chemical Products	5.7	57.6
医药制造业	Manufacture of Medicines	19	50.2
化学纤维制造业	Manufacture of Chemical Fibers	25.2	18.2
橡胶和塑料制品业	Manufacture of Rubber and Plastics	9	75.3
非金属矿物制品业	Manufacture of Non-metallic Mineral Products	15.9	59.9
黑色金属冶炼和压延加工业	Smelting and Pressing of Ferrous Metals	12	69.8
有色金属冶炼和压延加工业	Smelting and Pressing of Non-ferrous Metals	9	52.4
金属制品业	Manufacture of Metal Products	5.9	59.8
通用设备制造业	Manufacture of General Purpose Machinery	4.7	54.1
专用设备制造业	Manufacture of Special Equipment	6.4	45.3
汽车制造业	Manufacture of Motor Vehicle	8.6	65.6
铁路、船舶、航空航天和其他运输设备制造业	Railways,Shipbuilding,Aerospace and Other Transportation Equipment Manufacturing Industry	4	57
电气机械和器材制造业	Manufacture of Electric Equipment and Machinery	7.6	48.5
计算机、通信和其他电子设备制造业	Manufacture of Communication Equipment, Computers and other Electronic Equipment	3.3	61
仪器仪表制造业	Manufacture of Measuring Instruments and Machinery	9.2	50.7
其他制造业	Manufacture of Other Manufacturing	6	60.5
废弃资源综合利用	Recycling and Disposal of Waste		
金属制品、机械和设备修理业	Metal Products,Machinery and Equipment Repair Industry	10.8	61.6
电力、热力生产和供应业	Production and Supply of Electric Power and Heat Power	7.3	84.9
燃气生产和供应业	Gas Mining and Supplying Industry	7.7	61.6
水的生产和供应业	Production and Supply of Water	4.2	55.2

continued 1

流动资产周转率（次）Rate of Annual Turnover Working Capitals (times)	成本费用利润率（%）Ratio of Profits to Cost (%)	工业产品销售率（%）Proportion of Industrial Products Sold (%)	产值利税率（%）Ratio of Output Value to Profits and Tax (%)	每百元固定资产实现利税（元）Profit and Tax per 100 yuan of Fixed Assets (yuan)	每百元销售收入实现利税（元）Profit and Tax per 100 yuan of Sales Revenue (yuan)
6.3	-2.2	99.3	5.3	43.6	7.4
1.3	4.7	95.8	6.2	15.7	6.7
1.6	9.3	91	15.7	96.3	17.9
2.5	16.6	99.5	19.8	78.5	20
1.1	8.5	88.2	10.6	36.3	12.1
2.5	7.1	81.7	8.3	45.9	10.6
3	3.3	69.9	5.4	31.3	6.9
1.7	6.1	89	7	32.7	8.9
1.2	5.7	97.8	7.3	15.4	7.8
0.6	7.2	97.3	9.2	39.3	10.3
0.9	7.6	89.1	9.2	33.4	11.1
2	4.5	95.2	6	34	7.7
1	4.1	96.1	7.1	15.5	6.2
1.1	5.3	97.3	8.8	38.5	10
1.2	6.3	96.7	7.4	5	7.4
1	10.9	93.3	12.2	36.1	14.1
0.9	2.5	97.9	6.1	21.7	6.3
1.1	5.9	98.2	16.4	113.1	11.3
3.6	2.6	99.7	11.6	6	8.4
1.3	11.1	99.9	13.7	23.7	15.1
1.1	2.8	100	8.9	7.8	9

主要统计指标解释

工业 指从事自然资源的开采，对采掘品和农产品进行加工和再加工的物质生产部门。具体包括：（1）对自然资源的开采，如采矿、晒盐等（但不包括禽兽捕猎和水产捕捞）；（2）对农副产品的加工、再加工，如粮油加工、食品加工、缫丝、纺织、制革等；（3）对采掘品的加工、再加工，如炼铁、炼钢、化工生产、石油加工、机器制造、木材加工等，以及电力、自来水、煤气的生产和供应等；（4）对工业品的修理、翻新，如机器设备的修理、交通运输工具（如汽车）的修理等。

工业统计调查单位为独立核算法人工业企业。

独立核算法人工业企业指从事工业生产经营活动的单位。独立核算法人工业企业应同时具备以下条件：①依法成立，有自己的名称、组织机构和场所，能够承担民事责任；②独立拥有和使用资产，承担负债，有权与其他单位签订合同；③独立核算盈亏，并能够编制资产负债表。

国有及国有控股企业 指国有企业加上国有控股企业。国有企业（即原全民所有制工业或国营工业）指企业全部资产归国家所有，并按《中华人民共和国企业法人登记管理条例》规定登记注册的非公司制的经济组织。包括国有企业、国有独资公司和国有联营企业。1957年以前的公私合营和私营工业，后均改造为国营工业，1992年改为国有工业，这部分工业的资料不单独分列时，均包括在国有企业内。国有控股企业是对混合所有制经济的企业进行的"国有控股"分类。它是指这些企业的全部资产中国有资产（股份）相对其他所有者中的任何一个所有者占资（股）最多的企业。该分组反映了国有经济控股情况。

本篇涉及的其他企业登记注册类型的解释详见综合篇。

轻工业 指主要提供生活消费品和制作手工工具的工业。按其所使用的原料不同，可分为两大类：（1）以农产品为原料的轻工业，是指直接或间接以农产品为基本原料的轻工业。主要包括食品制造、饮料制造、烟草加工、纺织、缝纫、皮革和毛皮制作、造纸以及印刷等工业；（2）以非农产品为原料的轻工业，是指以工业品为原料的轻工业。主要包括文教体育用品、化学药品制造、合成纤维制造、日用化学制品、 日用玻璃制品、日用金属制品、手工工具制造、医疗器械制造、文化和办公用机械制造等工业。

重工业 指为国民经济各部门提供物质技术基础的主要生产资料的工业。按其生产性质和产品用途，可以分为下列三类：（1）采掘（伐）工业，是指对自然资源的开采，包括石油开采、煤炭开采、金属矿开采、非金属矿开采等工业；（2）原材料工业，指向国民经济各部门提供基本材料、动力和燃料的工业。包括金属冶炼及加工、炼焦及焦炭、化学、化工：原料、水泥、人造板以及电力、石油和煤炭加工等工业；（3）加工工业，是指对工业原材料进行再加工制造的工业。包括装备国民经济各部门的机械设备制造工业、金属结构、水泥制品等工业，以及为农业提供的生产资料如化肥、农药等工业。

根据上述划分原则，修理业中以重工业产品为修理作业对象的划为重工业，反之划为轻工业。

工业总产值

（1）定义：

工业总产值是工业企业在一定时期内生产的以货币形式表现的工业最终产品和提供工业性劳务活动的总价值量。它反映一定时间内工业生产的总规模和总水平。

（2）计算原则：

工业生产的原则，即凡是企业在报告期生产的经检验合格的产品，不管是否在报告期销售，均包括在内。

最终产品的原则，即凡是计入工业总产值的产品，必须是本企业生产的经检验合格的，不需要再进行任何加工的最终产品。如果企业有中间产品（半成品）对外销售，则对外销售的中间产品应视为企业的最终产品。

工厂法原则，即工业总产值是以下业企业作为基本计算（核算）单位，即按企业的最终产品计算工业总产值。按这种方法计算的工业总产值，不允许同一产品价值在企业内部重复计算，不能把企业内部各个车间（分厂）生产的成果相加，但允许企业间的重复计算。

（3）内容及计算方法：

1995年全国工业普查对工业总产值（原规定）的内容及计算原则和方法做了某些修订，修订后的工业总产值（新规定）包括三项内容：即本期生产成品价值、对外加工费收入、在制品半成品期末期初差额价值三部分。

本期生产成品价值指企业本期生产，并在报告期内不再进行加工，经检验、包装入库的全部工业成品（半成品）价值合计，包括企业生产的自制设备及提供给本企业在建工程、其他非工业部门和福利部门等单位使用的成品价值。本期生产成品价值为按自备原材料生产的产品的数量乘以本期不含增值税（销项税额）的产品实际销售平均单价计算；会计核算中按成本价格转帐的自制设备和自产自用的成品，按成本价格计算生产成品价值。生产成品价值中不包括用定货者来料加工的成品（半成品）价值。

对外加工费收入指企业在报告期内完成的对外承接的工业品加工（包括用定货者来料加工产品）的加工费收入和对外工业修理作业所取得的加工费收入。对外加工费收入按不含增值税（销项税额）的价格计算，可根据会计“产品销售收入”科目的有关资料取得。

对于本企业对内非工业部门提供的加工修理、设备安装的劳务收入，如果企业会计核算基础较好，能取得这部分资料，而且这部分价值所占比重较大，应包括在对外加工费收入中。

自制半成品在制品期末期初差额价值指企业报告期在制品期末减期初的差额价值，本指标一般可以从会计核算资料中取得。如果会计产品成本核算中不计算半成品、在制品的成本，则总产值中也不包括这部分价值，反之则包括。

（4）工业总产值统计范围变化和计算方法修订情况：

1984年以前工业总产值不包括村办工业，村办工业总产值划归农业。1984年以后工业总产值包括村办正业。

1995年工业普查对工业总产值计算方法做了修订，即从1995年始按新修订（新规定）方法计算工业总产值。新规定与原规定的区别如下：

全价与加工费的计算原则不同：新规定为凡自备原材料，不论其生产繁简程度如何，一律按全价计算工业总产值；凡来料加工，允许按加工费计算工业总产值。原规定则视生产加工的繁简程度不同，规定哪些行业按全价，哪些行业按加工费计算工业总产值。

自制半成品、在产品期末期初差额价值的计算原则不同：新规定要求，凡会计产品成本核算时计算了成本的差额价值，总产值中就应包括，否则可不包括；原规定则按生产周期六个月的界限区分，凡生产周期六个月以上的企业，总产值计算中应包括这部分差额价值，否则可不包括。

计算价格不同：新规定按不含增值税（销项税额）的价格计算；原规定则按含增值税（销项税额）的价格计算。

工业增加值 指工业企业在报告期内以货币表现的工业生产活动的最终成果。

工业增加值有两种计算方法：一是生产法，即工业总产出减去工业中间投入加上应交增值税；二是收入法，即从收入的角度出发，根据生产要素在生产过程中应得到的收入份额计算，具体构成项目有固定资产折旧、劳动者报酬、生产税净额、营业盈余，这种方法也称要素分配法。本年鉴中的工业增加值是以收入法计算的。

生产法工业增加值的计算方法为：

工业增加值＝工业总产出-工业中间投入+应交增值税

（1）工业总产出：指工业企业在一定时期内工业生产活动的总成果。工业总产出包括：成品生产价值，对外加工费收入，自制半成品、在产品期末期初差额价值。1995年后用新规定计算的工业总产值代替。

（2）工业中间投入：指工业企业在工业生产活动中消耗的外购物质产品和对外支付的服务费用。服务费用包括支付给物质生产部门（工业、农业、批发零售贸易业、建筑业、运输邮电业）的服务费用和支付给非物质生产部门（如保险、金融、文化教育、科学研究、医疗卫生、行政管理等）的服务费用。工业中间投入的确定须遵循以下原则：必须从外部购入的，并已计入工业总产出的产品和服务价值；必须是本期投入生产，并一次性消耗掉（包括本期摊销的低值易耗品等）的产品和服务价值。

工业中间投入包括直接材料费用、制造费用中的工业中间投入、管理费用中的工业中间投入、销售费用中的工业中间投入和利息支出五部分。

资产总计 指企业拥有或控制的能以货币计量的经济资源，包括各种财产、债权和其他权利。资产按流动性分为流动资产、长期投资、固定资产、无形资产、递延资产和其他资产。该指标根据企业会计“资产负债表”中“资产总计”项目的期末数增列。

流动资产 指企业可以在一年内或者超过一年的一个生产周期内变现或者耗用的资产，包括现金及各种存款、短期投资，应收及预付款项、存货等。

固定资产原价 指企业在建造、购置、安装、改建、扩建、技术改造某项固定资产时所支出的全部货币总额。它一般包括买价、包装费、运杂费和安装费等。

固定资产净值 指固定资产原价减去历年已提折旧额后的净额。计算公式为：

固定资产净值=固定资产原价-累计折旧

负债合计 指企业所承担的能以货币计量，将以资产或劳务偿付的债务，偿还形式包括货币、资产或提供劳务。负债一般按偿还期长短分为流动负债和长期负债。根据会计“资产负债表”中“负债合计”的年末数填列。

所有者权益合计 指企业投资人对企业净资产的所有权。企业净资产为企业全部资产与企业全部负债的差额，包括实收资本、资本公积、盈余公积、未分配利润等。根据会计“资产负债表”中“所有者权益”项的期末数填列。

主营业务收入 指会计“利润表”中对应指标的本年累计数。未执行2001年《企业会计制度》的企业，用“产品销售收入”的本期累计数代替。

主营业务成本 指会计“利润表”中对应指标的本年累计数。未执行2001年《企业会计制度》的企业，用“产品销售成本”的本期累计数代替。

主营业务税金及附加 指会计“利润表”中对应指标的本年累计数。未执行2001年《企业会计制度》的企业，用“产品销售税金及附加”的本期累计数代替。

利润总额 指企业在生产经营过程中各种收入扣除各种耗费后的盈余，反映企业在报告期内实现的盈亏总额，包括营业利润、补贴收入、投资净收益和营业外收支净额。根据会计“利润表”中的对应指标的本期累计数填列。

本年应交增值税 指企业按税法规定，从事货物销售或提供加工、修理修配劳务等增加货物价值的活动本期应交纳的税金。指企业在报告期应交增值税额。计算公式为：

本年应交增值税=销项税额–（进项税额–进项税额转出）–出口抵减内销产品应纳税额–减免税款+出口退税

本年进项税额 指工业企业在报告期内购入货物或接受应税劳务而支付的、准予从销项税额中抵扣的增值税额。

本年销项税额 指工业企业在报告期内销售货物或提供应税劳务应收取的增值税额。

从业人员平均人数 是指报告期内每天拥有的从业人员人数。其计算公式为：

月平均人数=报告月内每天实有人数之和／报告月日历日数

季平均人数=季内各月平均人数之和／3

年平均人数=年内各月平均人数之和／12

总资产贡献率 反映企业全部资产的获利能力，是企业经营业绩和管理水平的集中体现，是评价和考核企业盈利能力的核心指标。计算公式为：

总资产贡献率（%）=（利润总额+税金总额+利息支出）／平均资产总额×100%

公式中：税金总额为产品销售税金及附加与应交增值税之和；平均资产总额为期初期末资产之和的算术平均值。

资产负债率 该指标既反映企业经营风险的大小，也反映企业利用债权人提供的资金从事经营活动的能力。计算公式为：

资产负债率（%）=负债总额／资产总额×100%

资产与负债均为报告期期末数。

流动资产周转次数 指一定时期内流动资产完成的周转次数，反映投入工业企业流动资金的周转速度。计算公式为：

流动资产周转次数：产品销售收入／全部流动资产平均余额

公式中：全部流动资产平均余额为期初和期末的流动资产之和的算术平均值。

成本费用利润率 反映企业投入的生产成本及费用的经济效益，同时也反映企业降低成本所取得的经济效益。计算公式为：

成本费用利润率（%）=利润总额／成本费用总额×100%

公式中：成本费用总额为产品销售成本、销售费用、管理费用、财务费用之和。

产品销售率 该指标反映工业产品已实现销售的程度，是分析工业产销衔接情况，研究工业产品满足社会需求的指标。计算公式为：

产品销售率（%）=工业销售产值／工业总产值（现价）×100%

Explanatory Notes on Main Statistical Indicators

Industry refers to the material production sector which is engaged in the extraction of natural resources and processing and reprocessing of minerals and agricultural products, including (1) extraction of natural resources, such as mining, salt production (but not including hunting and fishing); (2) processing and reprocessing of farm and sideline produces, such as rice husking, flour milling, wine making, oil pressing, silk reeling, spinning and weaving, and leather making; (3) manufacture of industrial products, such as steel making, iron smelting, chemicals manufacturing, petroleum processing, machine building, timber processing; water and gas production and electricity generation and supply; (4)repairing of industrial products such as the repairing of machinery and means of transport (including cars).

In industrial statistics surveys, the units of enquiry are corporate industrial enterprises with independent accounting systems.

Corporate industrial enterprises with independent accounting systems refer to enterprises engaging in industrial production activities, which meet the following requirements: (1) They are established legally, having their own names, organizations, location and able to take civil liability; (2) They possess and use their assets independently, assume liabilities and are entitled to sign contracts with other units; (3) They are financially independent and compile their own balance sheets.

State-owned and State-holding Enterprises refer to state-owned enterprises plus State-holding enterprises. State-owned enterprises (originally known as State-run enterprises with ownership by the whole society) are non-corporate economic entities registered in accordance with the Regulation of the People's Republic of China on the Management of Registration of Legal Enterprises, where all assets are owned by the State. Included in this category are State-owned enterprises, State-funded corporations and State-owned joint-operation enterprises. Joint State- private industries and private industries, which existed before 1957, were transformed into state-run industries since 1957, and into State-owned industries after 1992. Statistics on those enterprises are included in the State- owned industries instead of being grouped them separately. State-holding enterprises are a sub- classification of enterprises with mixed ownership, referring to enterprises where the percentage of State assets (or shares by the State) is larger than any other single share holder of the same enterprise. This sub- classification illustrates the control of the State over a particular industry.

For explanation of enterprises of other types of registration covered in this chapter, please refer to General Survey.

Light Industry refers to the industry that produces consumer goods and hand tools. It consists of two categories, depending on the materials used:

(1) Industries using farm products as raw materials. These are the branches of light industry which directly or indirectly use farm products as basic raw materials, including the manufacture of food and beverages, tobacco processing, textile, clothing, fur and leather manufacturing, paper making, printing, etc.

(2) Industries using non-farm products as raw materials. These are the branches of light industry which use manufactured goods as raw materials, including the manufacture of cultural, educational articles and sports goods, chemicals, synthetic fibre, chemical products for daily use, glass products for daily use, metal products for daily use, hand tools, medical apparatus and instruments, and the manufacture of cultural and office machinery.

Heavy Industry refers to the industry which produces capital goods, and provides various sectors of the national economy with necessary material and technical basis for production. It consists of the following three branches according to the purpose of production or the use of products:

(1) Mining, quarrying and logging industry, which refers to the industry that extracts natural resources, including extraction of petroleum, coal, metal and non-metal ores.

(2) Raw materials industry refers to the industry that provides various sectors of the national economy with raw materials, fuels and power. It includes smelting and processing of metals, coking and coke chemistry, chemical materials and building materials such as cement, plywood, and power, petroleum refining and coal dressing

(3) Manufacturing industry which refers to the industry that processes raw materials. It includes machine-building industries which equip sectors of the national economy; industries producing metal structure and cement products; and industries producing means of agricultural production, such as chemical fertilizers and pesticides.

In accordance with the above principles of classification, the repairing trades, which are engaged primarily in repairing products of heavy industry, are classified as heavy industry while those which are engaged in repairing products of light industry are classified as light industry.

Gross Industrial Output Value

(1) Definition: Gross industrial output value is the total volume of final industrial products produced and industrial services provided during a given period in monetary terms. It reflects the total achievements and overall scale of industrial production during a given period.

(2) Principles for calculation:

Statistics on industrial production follow the principle that all products produced by the enterprises and accepted through quality check during the reference period are to be included no matter whether they are sold or not during the reference period.

Determination of final products follows the principle that all products that are included in the calculation of gross industrial output value are the final products of the enterprise which have been accepted through quality check and require no further processing. If an enterprise has intermediate (semi-finished) products to sell, these intermediate products are considered as the final products of the enterprise.

Gross industrial output value is calculated following the principle of factory approach, i.e. industrial enterprise is used as the basic accounting unit in calculating the gross industrial output value. By this approach, value of the same product is not to be double-counted, and the output value of different workshops (branch factories) within the enterprise should not be added. However, this approach allows the possibility of double counting between enterprises.

(3) Content and method of calculation: The old definition of gross industrial output value was modified during the 1995 National Industrial Census. The revised (new) definition of gross industrial output value consists of 3 components: value of the finished products during the reference period, income from processing for external parties, and value of change in semi-finished products between the end and the beginning of the reference period.

Value of finished products during the reference period: refers to the value of all finished (semi-finished) industrial products that are produced during the reference period without the need for further processing, checked for acceptance, packed and put into the warehouse of the enterprise, including the value of own-produced equipment and the value of products provided to the projects under construction of the enterprise, and to other non-industrial or welfare units. Value of finished products during the reference period is calculated by the quantity of products produced using own materials multiplied by the average unit prices at which products are sold (excluding value-added tax). Own-produced equipment and products produced for own use are valued at cost prices as in the case of enterprise accounting. Value of finished products does not include the value of finished products (semi-finished products) that are produced using the materials from the clients who place the orders.

Income from external processing: refers to income from contracted external processing of industrial products (including processing of industrial products using materials from the clients), and the income from industrial repairing work provided to other parties. Income from external processing is calculated using information from the item "products sales income" in the enterprise accounting at the prices with value-added tax excluded.

For income from services such as processing, repairing and installation of equipment provided to non- industrial units within the enterprise, if the accounting work of the enterprise is good enough to separate it from other records, and the share of such services is significant, it should also be included in the income from external processing.

Value of change in semi-finished products between the end and the beginning of the reference period: refers to the value of change in semi-finished products between the end and the beginning of the reference period, which generally can be obtained from accounting records of enterprises. If the enterprise accounting excludes the cost of semi-finished products, then it should not be included in the gross industrial output value, and the reverse if otherwise.

(4) Changes in the scope and method of calculation of the gross industrial output value

Prior to 1984, the value of rural industry run by villages was classified into agriculture instead of industry Since 1984, it has been included in the gross industrial output value. Method of calculation for the gross industrial output value was modified in the industriaLcensus in 1995. The difference in the new method as compared with the old one is outlined below:

Principle in using full value vs. processing fee: The new method stipulates that all products produced using own materials are to be calculated with full value in reporting the gross industrial output value irrespective of the complexity of production, and for external processing, it allows calculation using processing fee. In the old method, however, the use of full value or processing fee was determined by the degree of complexity of production in different branches of industries.

Principle in determining the value of change in semi-finished products: The new method requires that value of change in semi-finished products should be included in the gross industrial output value if it is included in the accounting record of the enterprise, otherwise it should not be included. In the old method, it is determined by the type of enterprises in terms of production cycle. If the production cycle is over 6 months, the value of change in semi-finished products is included in the gross industrial output value, otherwise it is not.

Difference in prices: The new method uses prices excluding value-added tax in the calculation of gross industrial output value, while the old method used prices including value-added tax.

Value–added of Industry refers to the final results of industrial production of industrial enterprises in money terms during the reference period.

Industrial value-added can be calculated by two approaches: the production approach, i.e. gross industrial output value minus intermediate input plus value-added tax, and the income approach, i.e. income for various factors used in the course of production, including depreciation of fixed assets, remuneration of labourers, net of production tax, and operating surplus. Value-added of industry in the Yearbook is calculated by the income approach as follows:

Value-added of industry = gross industrial output - industrial intermediate input + value-added tax

(1) Gross industrial output: refers to the total achievements of industrial production activities during a given period. Gross industrial output includes value of finished products, income from external processing, and value of change in semi-finished products between the end and the beginning of the reference period. Since 1995, the gross industrial output value obtained by the new method is used in the calculation.

(2) Industrial intermediate input: refers to purchased goods and paid services consumed during the industrial production of enterprises. Fees paid for services include fees paid for the services provided by material production sectors (industry, agriculture, wholesale and retail trade, construction, transport, post and telecommunications) and by non-material production sectors (insurance, banking, culture, education, scientific research, health and medical care, public administration, etc.). The determination of industrial intermediate input follows the principle that the goods and services must be purchased from outside and included in the gross industrial output, and that the goods and services are inputted into production and consumed (include low-value consumables) during the reference period.

Industrial intermediate input includes 5 components, namely direct consumption of materials, industrial intermediate input in manufacturing cost, industrial intermediate input in management cost, industrial intermediate input in marketing cost and expenditure on interest.

Total Assets refer to all economic resources, in monetary term, these are owned or controlled by enterprises, including properties, creditor's equity and other economic rights of all forms. Classified by the degree of liquidity, total assets include working capitals, long-term investment, fixed assets, intangible assets, deferred assets and other assets. Data on this indicator can be obtained by the year-end figures of total assets in the Assets and Liability Table of accounting records of enterprises.

Working Capital refers to capital that an enterprise can cash or use during one year or one production cycle that may exceed one year, including cash and savings deposits of various forms, short-term investment, money receivable and prepaid money, inventories, etc.

Original Value of Fixed Assets refers to the total value, in monetary terms, that an enterprise spent on fixed assets, through construction, purchase, installation, transformation, expansion or technical upgrading. Generally, it covers cost of purchase, packing, transportation and installation, etc.

Net Value of Fixed Assets refers to the original value of fixed assets minus depreciation over the years, i.e.:

Net value of fixed assets = original value of fixed assets - cumulative depreciation

Total Liabilities refer to payable liabilities of enterprises that have to be repaid in terms of money, assets or labour services. In terms of payment, it can be divided into liquid liabilities and long-term liabilities. Data on this item is obtained from the ending figures on total liabilities from the Assets and Liability Table from the enterprises.

Total Equity refers to the ownership of net assets of enterprise by its investors. Net assets equal total assets minus total liabilities of the enterprise, including the paid-in capital, accumulation of capital and operating surplus and non-distributed profits. Data are obtained from the ending figures on "total equity" from the "balance sheets" .

Revenue from Principal Business refers to the annual accumulation of the corresponding item in the "profit table" of the accountant. For enterprises that do not follow the 2001 Enterprise Accounting Standards, the year-end accumulation of revenue from the sales of products is used as a substitute.

Cost of Principal Business refers to the annual accumulation of the corresponding item in the "profit table" of the accountant. For enterprises that do not follow the 2001 Enterprise Accounting Standards, theyear-end accumulation of cost for the sales of products is used as a substitute.

Tax and Extra Charges from Principal Bosiness refer to the annual accumulation of the corresponding item in the "profit table" of the accountant. For enterprises that do not follow the 2001 Enterprise Accounting Standards, the year-end accumulation of tax and extra charges from the sales of products is used as a substitute.

Total Profits refers to the balance of various incomes minus various spendings in the course of operation, reflecting the total profits and losses of enterprises in reporting period. It includes: operating profits, income from subsidies, net investment income and net income from activities other than operation. Data are obtained from the annual accumulation of the corresponding item in the "profit table" of the accountant.

Value-added Tax Payable in the Current Year refers to the payable tax of enterprises which engaged in selling of goods or providing services that bring added value to the goods, such as processing, repairing, fitting and other activities should be paid according to Tax Law. It refers to the amount of the value-added tax which should be paid by the enterprises during the reference period. The formula is as tollows:

Value-added Tax Payable in the Current Year = tax on sales-(tax on purchase-transferred tax on purchase)- exports deduct tax payable on domestic sales-tax relief+the export tax rebate.

Tax on Purchase in Current Year refers to goods purchased by industrial enterprises or value added tax that should be paid but being granted the right to deduct from the tax on sales.

Tax on Sales in Current Year refers to value added tax on industrial enterprises from sales of goods or taxable services that should be charged value added tax.

Average number of employed persons refers to the number of employee everyday during the reference period, calculated with the following formula:

$$\text{Monthly average Number} = \frac{\text{sum of actual employees everyday in reference month}}{\text{number of calendar dates in reference month}}$$

$$\text{Quarterly average number} = \frac{\text{sum of monthly average number in reference quarter}}{3}$$

$$\text{Annual average number} = \frac{\text{sum of monthly average number in reference year}}{12}$$

Ratio of Profits, Taxes and Interests to Average Assets reflects the profit-making capability of all assets of the enterprise and is a key indicator manifesting the performance and management and evaluating the profit-making potential of the enterprise. It is calculated as

$$\text{Ratio of Profits, Taxes and Interests toAverageAssets(\%)} = \frac{\text{otal profits+ total taxes+ interest payment}}{\text{average assets}} \times 100\%$$

In the above formula, total taxes is the sum of tax and extra charges on the sales of products and value-added tax payable; and average assets is the arithmetic mean of the sum of beginning assets and ending assets.

Ratio of Debts to Assets reflects both the operation risk and the capability of the enterprise in making use of the capital from the creditors. It is calculated as follows:

$$\text{Ratio of Debts toAssets(\%)} = \frac{\text{total debts}}{\text{total assets}} \times 100\%$$

Both assets and debts are figures at the end of the reference period.

Turnover of Working Capital refers to the number of times of turnover of working capital in a given period of time, which reflects the speed of the turnover of working capital of industrial enterprises, and is calculated as follows:

$$\text{Turnover of Working Capital} = \frac{\text{sales revenue of products}}{\text{average balance of total working capital}}$$

In the above formula, average balance of total working capital refers to the arithmetic mean of the sum of working capital at the beginning and at the end of the reference period.

Ratio of Profits to Total Industrial Costs refers to the ratio of profits realized in a given period to the total costs in the same period, which reflects the economic efficiency of input cost and is calculated as follows:

$$\text{Ratio of Profits to Total Industrial Cost (\%)} = \frac{\text{total profits}}{\text{total costs}} \times 100\%$$

Total costs in the above formula are the sum of cost of products sold, marketing cost, management cost and financial cost.

Sales Ratio of Products is an indicator reflecting the actual sale of industrial products, analyzing the production-selling and supply-demand relations. It is calculated as:

$$\text{Sales Ratio of Products (\%)} = \frac{\text{value of industrial sales}}{\text{gross industrial output value (current prices)}} \times 100\%$$

13 能　源

ENERGY

资料整理：张　育　于元英　雷稳强
Data management：Zhang Yu　Yu Yuanying　Lei Wenqiang
数据审核：丁抗玲
Data audit：Ding Kangling

第十三部分　能源

一、简要说明

本章资料包括规模以上工业能源购销存情况、全市单位GDP能耗、规模以上工业单位增加值能耗、规模以上工业企业用水情况等，由西安市统计局能源处提供。

二、主要指标

规模以上工业综合能源消费量（万吨标准煤）	557.05	比上年下降	5.8%
单位GDP能耗（吨标准煤/万元）	0.486	比上年下降	5.89%
规模以上工业单位增加值能耗（吨标准煤/万元）	0.388	比上年下降	15.21%

13　ENERGY

Ⅰ.Brief Introduction

Data in this chapter reflects energy purchases consumption and inventory of industrial enterprises above designated size,energy consumption per unit of GDP in whole city,energy consumption per unit of industrial value-added above designated size and statistics on water use of industrial enterprises above designated size. data in this chapter are provided and compiled by Energy Division ransportation Division of the Xi'an Bureau of Statistics.

Ⅱ.Major Indicators

		Increase over Preceding Year
Comprehensive Energy Consumption Above Designated Size(10 000 Tons of Standard Coal)	557.05	-5.8%
Energy Consumption of GDP per Unit (Tons of Standard Coal /10 000 yuan)	0.486	-5.89%
Energy Consumption of value added per Unit of Industrial Enterprises Above Designated Size (Tons of Standard Coal/10 000 yuan)	0.388	-15.21%

13-1 全市及各区县单位GDP能耗（2014年）

Energy Consumption per Unit of GDP by City and District（2014）

单位：吨标准煤 / 万元 (ton of SCE/10 000 yuan)

地 区	Region	单位GDP能耗 Energy Consumption per unit of GDP	比上年增长（%） Growth Rate over the preceding Year
西安市	**Xi'an**	**0.486**	**-5.89**
新城区	Xincheng	0.479	-5.39
碑林区	Beilin	0.368	-6.06
莲湖区	Lianhu	0.430	-7.76
灞桥区	Baqiao	0.562	-5.20
未央区	Weiyang	0.563	-7.60
雁塔区	Yanta	0.441	-3.89
阎良区	Yanliang	0.444	-7.59
临潼区	Lintong	0.558	-8.07
长安区	Chang'an	0.555	-3.40
蓝田县	Lantian	0.924	-5.48
周至县	Zhouzhi	0.801	-7.63
户 县	Huxian	0.844	-3.40
高陵县	Gaoling	0.403	-7.32

注：GDP按2010年价格。

13-2 全市及各区县规模以上工业企业单位工业增加值能耗(2014年)

Energy Consumption per Unit of Industrial Value added above desiganated Size by City and District（2014）

单位：吨标准煤 / 万元 (ton of SCE/10 000 yuan)

地 区	Region	单位工业增加值能耗 Energy Consumption of value added per unit of Industrial Enterprises Above Designated Size	比上年增长（%） Growth Rate over the preceding Year
西安市	**Xi'an**	**0.388**	**-15.21**
新城区	Xincheng	0.318	-2.44
碑林区	Beilin	0.050	-16.18
莲湖区	Lianhu	0.114	-27.16
灞桥区	Baqiao	0.821	-11.29
未央区	Weiyang	0.396	-30.83
雁塔区	Yanta	0.159	-16.24
阎良区	Yanliang	0.113	-36.89
临潼区	Lintong	0.081	-35.39
长安区	Chang'an	0.169	28.64
蓝田县	Lantian	1.037	-25.90
周至县	Zhouzhi	0.152	-13.61
户 县	Huxian	2.353	-5.64
高陵县	Gaoling	0.115	-16.45

注：工业增加值按2010年价格计算，统计范围为主营业务收入2000万元及以上的法人工业企业。
能源消耗按当量值计算。

13-3 主要年份全社会用电量

单位：万千瓦时

行 业	Sector	2000	2007
总 计	**Total**	**732373**	**1482896**
#行业用电量合计	Total of Industry of Electricity	599855	1215799
1. 第一产业	Primary Industry	77579	120134
2. 第二产业	Secondary Industry	354245	700026
3. 第三产业	Tertiary Industry	168031	395639
一、农、林、牧、渔、水利业	Agriculture ,Forestry,Animal Husbandry and Fishery	77579	120134
二、工业	Industry	345175	674990
1. 轻工业	Light Industry	152125	187323
2. 重工业	Heavy Industry	193050	487667
三、信息传输、计算机服务和软件业	Information Transmission,Computer Service and Software		21938
四、建筑业	Construction	9070	25036
五、交通运输、仓储及邮政业	Traffic,Transport, Storage and Post	22904	53825
六、公共事业及管理组织	Public Utilities and Management Organization		144859
七、商业、住宿和餐饮业	Commercial,Hotels and Catering Services		107343
八、金融、房地产、商务及居民服务业	Finance,Real Estate,Business Affairs and Households Services		67674
九、城乡居民生活用电	Electricity Consumption of Urban and Rural Residents	132518	267097
1. 乡村	Rural	31281	38395
2. 城市	City	101237	228702

注：本表数据来源西安市供电局。

Electricity Consumption of the Whole Society in Representative Years

(10 000 kw. h)

2008	2009	2010	2011	2012	2013	2014
1605089	**1724067**	**1993751**	**2167453**	**2352571**	**2554679**	**2753213**
1293574	1358483	1499903	1590486	1706859	1854696	2002503
127054	99083	108720	117984	109086	110405	95997
724852	766029	883259	910360	932622	991202	1086105
441668	493371	507924	562142	665151	753089	820401
127054	99083	108720	117984	109086	110405	95997
696291	724920	838317	859796	875018	920024	998132
182176	167144	177362	183766	175392	170246	165933
514115	557776	660955	676030	699626	749778	832199
26680	29328	30760	33191	37444	39551	42662
28561	41108	44942	50564	57605	71179	87973
56614	62031	58509	66684	69633	78722	88805
165024	177409	154074	164473	207271	240866	254911
111676	122203	148418	166558	199970	228117	253199
81674	102400	116163	131236	150832	165833	180824
311515	365585	493848	576966	645713	699982	750710
63072	99941	142059	169898	197937	216148	235938
248443	265644	351789	407068	447776	483834	514773

13-4 规模以上工业企业能源购进、消费及库存（2014年）

Energy Purchases Consumption and Inventory of Industrial Enterprises above Designated size（2014）

能源名称	Name	年初库存量 Stock (year-beginning)	购进量 实物量 Quantity	Purchases 金额(万元) Sum (10 000 yuan)
原煤(吨)	Raw Coal (ton)	645664	9892030	456372
洗精煤(吨)	Washed Coal(ton)		1032	64
其他洗煤(吨)	Other Washed Coals(ton)		100	12
煤制品（吨）	Briquettes(ton)	76	3181	231
焦炭(吨)	Coke(ton)	226	2705	388
其他焦化产品(吨)	Other Coking Products(ton)	115	2500	431
焦炉煤气（万立方米）	Other Gases(10 000cu.m)			
天然气（气态）（万立方米）	Natural Gas(10 000cu.m)	25	20262	42877
液化天然气（液态）（吨）	Liquefied Natural Gas (Liquid)(ton)	13	4	3
原油(吨)	Crude Oil(ton)	61216	1494024	866534
汽油(吨)	Gasoline(ton)	63	24753	20711
煤油(吨)	Kerosene(ton)	16	196	155
柴油(吨)	Diesel Oil(ton)	688	66336	50608
燃料油(吨)	Fuel Oil(ton)			
液化石油气(吨)	LPG(ton)		551	374
其它石油制品(吨)	Other Petroleum Products(ton)	33	2797	3276
热力(百万千焦)	Heat (1 million kilo-joule)		6259546	32425
电力(万千瓦时)	Electricity(10 000kwh)		643722	446962
其他燃料（吨标准煤）	Other Fuels(ton of SCE)	20	2272	859
能源合计(吨标准煤)	Total Energy(ton of SCE)			

13-4 续表 continued

能源名称	Name	消费量合计 Consumption Total	工业生产消费 Industrial Production Consume	用于原材料 as Raw Material	非工业生产消费 Non-industrial Production Consume	年末库存 Stock (year-end)
原煤(吨)	Raw Coal (ton)	9624127	9605839	5350	18288	902783
洗精煤(吨)	Washed Coal(ton)	1032	1032			
其他洗煤(吨)	Other Washed Coals(ton)	100	100			
煤制品（吨）	Briquettes(ton)	3119	2599		520	137
焦炭(吨)	Coke(ton)	2624	2624			306
其他焦化产品(吨)	Other Coking Products(ton)	2500	2500			115
焦炉煤气（万立方米）	Other Gases(10 000cu.m)					
天然气（气态）（万立方米）	Natural Gas(10 000cu.m)	20209	19751	267	458	86
液化天然气（液态）（吨）	Liquefied Natural Gas (Liquid)(ton)	4	3		1	
原油(吨)	Crude Oil(ton)	1480503	1480503			74737
汽油(吨)	Gasoline(ton)	25261	21620	105	3641	26
煤油(吨)	Kerosene(ton)	197	195		2	7
柴油(吨)	Diesel Oil(ton)	65946	64229	1326	1717	1006
燃料油(吨)	Fuel Oil(ton)					
液化石油气(吨)	LPG(ton)	551	551	3		
其它石油制品(吨)	Other Petroleum Products(ton)	2768	2768			62
热力(百万千焦)	Heat (1 million kilo-joule)	7514531	7342059		172472	
电力(万千瓦时)	Electricity(10 000kwh)	719667	701276		18391	
其他燃料（吨标准煤）	Other Fuels(ton of SCE)	2272	2272			
能源合计(吨标准煤)	Total Energy(ton of SCE)	10326747	10270922		55825	

13-5 规模以上工业企业分行业主要能源品种消费量（2014年）

Major Energy Consumption above Designated Size by Sector (2014)

行 业	Sector	原煤 (吨) Raw Coal (ton)	天然气 (万立方米) Natural Gas(10 000 cu.m)	原油 (吨) Crude Oil (ton)
总 计	**Total**	**9624127**	**20209**	**1480503**
煤炭开采和洗选业	Coal Mining and Dressing			
石油和天然气开采业	Petroleum and Natural Gas Extraction			
黑色金属矿采选业	Ferrous Metals Mining and Dressing			
有色金属矿采选业	Nonferrous Metals Mining and Dressing			
非金属矿采选业	Nonmetal Minerals Mining and Dressing			
开采辅助活动	Ancillary activities for mining	390	114	
其他采矿业	Other Mining Industry			
农副食品加工业	Agricultural Products and Non-stable Food Processing Industry	169321	183	
食品制造业	Food Production	52763	2164	
酒、饮料和精制茶制造业	Wine, soft drinks and refined tea industry	115085	851	
烟草制品业	Tobacco Processing	16		
纺织业	Textile Industry	1529		
纺织服装、服饰业	Textile, apparel industry	260	2	
皮革、毛皮、羽毛及其制品和制鞋业	Leather, Fur, Feather (eiderdown) and Their Products Industry			
木材加工和木、竹、藤、棕、草制品业	Timber Processing,Bamboo,Cane,Palm Fiber and Straw Products	6128		
家具制造业	Furniture Manufacturing	103		
造纸及纸制品业	Papermaking and Paper products	11141		
印刷和记录媒介复制业	Printing,Record Medium Reproduction	371	514	
文教、工美、体育和娱乐用品制造业	Culture, education, Craft art, sports and entertainment goods manufacturing industry	129		
石油加工、炼焦和核燃料加工业	Petroleum Refining, Ccoke Making and Nuclear Fuel Processing Industry	25297	279	1480503
化学原料和化学制品制造业	Raw Chemical Materials and Chemical Products	26545	1715	
医药制造业	Medical and Pharmaceutical Products	19353	901	
化学纤维制造业	Chemical Fiber	1124	13	
橡胶和塑料制品业	Rubber and plastic products industry	128380	147	
非金属矿物制品业	Nonmetal Mineral Products	250548	548	
黑色金属冶炼和压延加工业	Smelting and Pressing of Ferrous Metals	7481	1218	
有色金属冶炼和压延加工业	Smelting and Pressing of Nonferrou Metals	2148	480	
金属制品业	Metal Products	20644	367	
通用设备制造业	General Equipment Manufacturing Industry	4415	238	
专用设备制造业	Special Purpose Equipment	6441	477	
汽车制造业	Automotive Manufacturing	43042	4950	
铁路、船舶、航空航天和其他运输设备制造业	Railroad, marine, aerospace and other transportation equipment manufacturing	22603	128	
电气机械和器材制造业	Electric Equipment and Machinery	3194	2252	
计算机、通信和其他电子设备制造业	Communication Equipment, Computer and Other Electronic Equipment Manufacturing Industry		1932	
仪器仪表制造业	Instrument manufacturing industry	640	241	
其他制造业	Other manufacturing	189		
废弃资源综合利用	Comprehensive utilization of waste resources			
金属制品、机械和设备修理业	Metal products, machinery and equipment repair industry			
电力、热力生产和供应业	Electric Power, Heating Power Generating and Supplying Industry	8704845	1	
燃气生产和供应业	Gas Mining and Supplying Industry		222	
水的生产和供应业	Water Processing and Supplying Industry		270	

13-5 续表 continued

行 业	Sector	汽油(吨) Gasoline (ton)	柴油(吨) Diesel Oil (ton)	热能(百万千焦) Heat (million kilo joule)	电力(万千瓦时) Electricity (10 000 kwh)
总 计	**Total**	**25261**	**65946**	**7514531**	**719667**
煤炭开采和洗选业	Coal Mining and Dressing				
石油和天然气开采业	Petroleum and Natural Gas Extraction				
黑色金属矿采选业	Ferrous Metals Mining and Dressing				93
有色金属矿采选业	Nonferrous Metals Mining and Dressing				
非金属矿采选业	Nonmetal Minerals Mining and Dressing				
开采辅助活动	Ancillary activities for mining	191	4886		415
其他采矿业	Other Mining Industry				
农副食品加工业	Agricultural Products and Non-stable Food Processing Industry	1245	1156	1190985	20353
食品制造业	Food Production	753	770	393048	17229
酒、饮料和精制茶制造业	Wine, soft drinks and refined tea industry	299	725	240392	20888
烟草制品业	Tobacco Processing	24		7239	225
纺织业	Textile Industry	81	19	295780	18931
纺织服装、服饰业	Textile, apparel industry	54	1		573
皮革、毛皮、羽毛及其制品和制鞋业	Leather, Fur, Feather (eiderdown) and Their Products Industry	37		12584	203
木材加工和木、竹、藤、棕、草制品业	Timber Processing,Bamboo,Cane,Palm Fiber and Straw Products	112			6653
家具制造业	Furniture Manufacturing	146	131		954
造纸及纸制品业	Papermaking and Paper products	139	263	29379	3649
印刷和记录媒介复制业	Printing,Record Medium Reproduction	496	258	81400	8794
文教、工美、体育和娱乐用品制造业	Culture, education, Craft art, sports and entertainment goods manufacturing industry	41	6		461
石油加工、炼焦和核燃料加工业	Petroleum Refining, Ccoke Making and Nuclear Fuel Processing Industry	3196	140		15642
化学原料和化学制品制造业	Raw Chemical Materials and Chemical Products	395	465	47523	33213
医药制造业	Medical and Pharmaceutical Products	649	56	176063	10617
化学纤维制造业	Chemical Fiber	21	9	771371	3402
橡胶和塑料制品业	Rubber and plastic products industry	339	3722	2205	19712
非金属矿物制品业	Nonmetal Mineral Products	2786	31986	33073	56542
黑色金属冶炼和压延加工业	Smelting and Pressing of Ferrous Metals	110	84		11846
有色金属冶炼和压延加工业	Smelting and Pressing of Nonferrou Metals	427	76	616095	40628
金属制品业	Metal Products	450	284	7293	10327
通用设备制造业	General Equipment Manufacturing Industry	1113	233	11350	9418
专用设备制造业	Special Purpose Equipment	2893	1137	81980	24890
汽车制造业	Automotive Manufacturing	3305	10162	588990	97905
铁路、船舶、航空航天和其他运输设备制造业	Railroad, marine, aerospace and other transportation equipment manufacturing	845	1074	107571	14049
电气机械和器材制造业	Electric Equipment and Machinery	2112	811	1027677	43404
计算机、通信和其他电子设备制造业	Communication Equipment, Computer and Other Electronic Equipment Manufacturing Industry	538	78	215541	90383
仪器仪表制造业	Instrument manufacturing industry	1320	5474	6750	3368
其他制造业	Other manufacturing	110	162		519
废弃资源综合利用	Comprehensive utilization of waste resources				
金属制品、机械和设备修理业	Metal products, machinery and equipment repair industry	92	47		70
电力、热力生产和供应业	Electric Power, Heating Power Generating and Supplying Industry	217	1637	1570243	118787
燃气生产和供应业	Gas Mining and Supplying Industry	438	79		6044
水的生产和供应业	Water Processing and Supplying Industry	285	14		9480

13-6 规模以上工业企业分行业综合能源消费量（2014年）

Comprehensive Energy Consumption by Sector above Designated Size （2014）

单位：吨标准煤 (ton of SCE)

行 业	Scetor	2014	比上年增长(%) Increase over Preceding Year (%)
总 计	**Total**	**5570466**	**-5.8**
煤炭开采和洗选业	Coal Mining and Dressing		
石油和天然气开采业	Petroleum and Natural Gas Extraction		
黑色金属矿采选业	Ferrous Metals Mining and Dressing	114	1.8
有色金属矿采选业	Nonferrous Metals Mining and Dressing		
非金属矿采选业	Nonmetal Minerals Mining and Dressing		
开采辅助活动	Ancillary activities for mining	9823	-16.6
其他采矿业	Other Mining Industry		
农副食品加工业	Agricultural Products and Non-stable Food Processing Industry	148067	-9.7
食品制造业	Food Production	102911	0.6
酒、饮料和精制茶制造业	Wine, soft drinks and refined tea industry	128223	-7.4
烟草制品业	Tobacco Processing	403	-24.5
纺织业	Textile Industry	30505	-19.9
纺织服装、服饰业	Textile, apparel industry	990	-26.0
皮革、毛皮、羽毛及其制品和制鞋业	Leather, Fur, Feather (eiderdown) and Their Products Industry	729	15.0
木材加工和木、竹、藤、棕、草制品业	Timber Processing,Bamboo,Cane,Palm Fiber and Straw Products	12720	5.1
家具制造业	Furniture Manufacturing	1652	5.2
造纸及纸制品业	Papermaking and Paper products	15402	-71.6
印刷和记录媒介复制业	Printing,Record Medium Reproduction	21027	22.3
文教、工美、体育和娱乐用品制造业	Culture, education, Craft art, sports and entertainment goods manufacturing industry	743	-37.1
石油加工、炼焦和核燃料加工业	Petroleum Refining, Ccoke Making and Nuclear Fuel Processing Industry	233720	-41.7
化学原料和化学制品制造业	Raw Chemical Materials and Chemical Products	84297	33.6
医药制造业	Medical and Pharmaceutical Products	45483	-18.2
化学纤维制造业	Chemical Fiber	31746	12.7
橡胶和塑料制品业	Rubber and plastic products industry	48201	-20.7
非金属矿物制品业	Nonmetal Mineral Products	304399	-3.4
黑色金属冶炼和压延加工业	Smelting and Pressing of Ferrous Metals	39303	-54.0
有色金属冶炼和压延加工业	Smelting and Pressing of Nonferrou Metals	81822	19.0
金属制品业	Metal Products	34212	-8.7
通用设备制造业	General Equipment Manufacturing Industry	17238	-8.4
专用设备制造业	Special Purpose Equipment	47524	-12.4
汽车制造业	Automotive Manufacturing	211352	4.7
铁路、船舶、航空航天和其他运输设备制造业	Railroad, marine, aerospace and other transportation equipment manufacturing	34419	9.2
电气机械和器材制造业	Electric Equipment and Machinery	124216	-7.7
计算机、通信和其他电子设备制造业	Communication Equipment, Computer and Other Electronic Equipment Manufacturing Industry	135072	179.4
仪器仪表制造业	Instrument manufacturing industry	17745	-15.2
其他制造业	Other manufacturing	1172	-11.3
废弃资源综合利用	Comprehensive utilization of waste resources		
金属制品、机械和设备修理业	Metal products, machinery and equipment repair industry	258	-1.0
电力、热力生产和供应业	Electric Power, Heating Power Generating and Supplying Industry	3581045	-3.8
燃气生产和供应业	Gas Mining and Supplying Industry	11081	13.7
水的生产和供应业	Water Processing and Supplying Industry	12852	7.6

13-7 规模以上工业企业用水情况（2014年）

Statistics on Water Use of Industrial Enterprises above Designated Size（2014）

指　标	Item	取水量（万立方米）Water Use (10 000 cu.m)	支付费用的取水量（万立方米）Paid WaterUse (10 000 cu.m)	取水支付金额（万元）Money Paid for Water Use (10 000 yuan)	外供水量（万立方米）Outward Water Supply (10 000 cu.m)
合　计	**Total**	**57946**			**48552**
地表淡水	Surface fresh water	37792			625
地下淡水	Underground fresh water	10247			
自来水	Tap Water	8790			47927
陆地苦咸水	Land lake Salt water	7			
矿井水	Mine Water	2			
雨水	Rain Water				
再生水	Reclaimed Water	1106			
其他水	Other Water	2			
外排水量	Efflux capacity	3978			
重复用水量	Repeated water consumption	9741			

13-8 规模以上工业企业分行业用水情况（2014年）

Volume of Water Use of Industrial Enterprises above Designated Size by Sector（2014）

行 业	Sector	取水量（万立方米）Water Use (10 000 cu.m)	外供水量（万立方米）Outward Water Supply (10 000 cu.m)
总 计	**Total**	**57946**	**48552**
煤炭开采和洗选业	Coal Mining and Dressing		
石油和天然气开采业	Petroleum and Natural Gas Extraction		
黑色金属矿采选业	Ferrous Metals Mining and Dressing	14	
有色金属矿采选业	Nonferrous Metals Mining and Dressing		
非金属矿采选业	Nonmetal Minerals Mining and Dressing		
开采辅助活动	Ancillary activities for mining	8	
其他采矿业	Other Mining Industry		
农副食品加工业	Agricultural Products and Non-stable Food Processing Industry	206	
食品制造业	Food Production	377	
酒、饮料和精制茶制造业	Wine, soft drinks and refined tea industry	848	
烟草制品业	Tobacco Processing	1	
纺织业	Textile Industry	99	5
纺织服装、服饰业	Textile, apparel industry	7	
皮革、毛皮、羽毛及其制品和制鞋业	Leather, Fur, Feather (eiderdown) and Their Products Industry	1	
木材加工和木、竹、藤、棕、草制品业	Timber Processing,Bamboo,Cane,Palm Fiber and Straw Products	2	
家具制造业	Furniture Manufacturing	2	
造纸及纸制品业	Papermaking and Paper products	14	
印刷和记录媒介复制业	Printing,Record Medium Reproduction	55	
文教、工美、体育和娱乐用品制造业	Culture, education, Craft art, sports and entertainment goods manufacturing industry	4	
石油加工、炼焦和核燃料加工业	Petroleum Refining, Ccoke Making and Nuclear Fuel Processing Industry	169	
化学原料和化学制品制造业	Raw Chemical Materials and Chemical Products	400	
医药制造业	Medical and Pharmaceutical Products	310	
化学纤维制造业	Chemical Fiber	23	
橡胶和塑料制品业	Rubber and plastic products industry	282	
非金属矿物制品业	Nonmetal Mineral Products	267	
黑色金属冶炼和压延加工业	Smelting and Pressing of Ferrous Metals	19	
有色金属冶炼和压延加工业	Smelting and Pressing of Nonferrou Metals	168	
金属制品业	Metal Products	50	
通用设备制造业	General Equipment Manufacturing Industry	70	
专用设备制造业	Special Purpose Equipment	219	4
汽车制造业	Automotive Manufacturing	759	
铁路、船舶、航空航天和其他运输设备制造业	Railroad, marine, aerospace and other transportation equipment manufacturing	118	
电气机械和器材制造业	Electric Equipment and Machinery	541	
计算机、通信和其他电子设备制造业	Communication Equipment, Computer and Other Electronic Equipment Manufacturing Industry	740	
仪器仪表制造业	Instrument manufacturing industry	126	
其他制造业	Other manufacturing	8	
废弃资源综合利用	Comprehensive utilization of waste resources		
金属制品、机械和设备修理业	Metal products, machinery and equipment repair industry	2	
电力、热力生产和供应业	Electric Power, Heating Power Generating and Supplying Industry	3067	
燃气生产和供应业	Gas Mining and Supplying Industry	17	
水的生产和供应业	Water Processing and Supplying Industry	48957	48543

主要统计指标解释

能源消费总量 指一定时期内，地区各行业和居民生活消费的各种能源的总和。该指标是观察能源消费水平、构成和增长速度的总量指标。能源消费总量包括原煤和原油及其制品、天然气、电力等，不包括低热值燃料、生物质能和太阳能等的利用。能源消费总量分为终端能源消费量、能源加工转换损失量和能源损失量三部分。

（1）终端能源消费量：指一定时期内，全国生产和生活消费的各种能源在扣除了用于加工转换二次能源消费量和损失量以后的数量。

（2）能源加工转换损失量：指一定时期内，全国投入加工转换的各种能源数量之和与产出各种能源产品之和的差额。该指标是观察能源在加工转换过程中损失量变化的指标。

（3）能源损失量：指一定时期内，能源在输送、分配、储存过程中发生的损失和由客观原因造成的各种损失量，不包括各种气体能源放空、放散量。

工业生产能源消费 指工业企业为进行工业生产活动所消费的能源。

非工业生产能源消费 指在工业企业能源消费中，除“工业生产能源消费”以外的能源消费，即非工业生产用能和工业企业附属的不从事工业生产活动的非独立核算单位用能。

运输工具消费 指在厂区内、外进行交通运输活动的交通运输工具所消费的能源。

能源加工转换投入 能源的加工转换是指为了特定的用途，将一种能源（一般为一次能源），经过一定的工艺，加工或转换成另外一种能源（一般为二次能源）。能源加工转换的投入即能源加工、转换消费。

一次能源 是指自然界中以现成形式存在，不经任何改变或转换的天然能源资源，即从自然界直接取得并不改变其形态和品位的能源。如原煤、原油、天然气、核燃料、植物燃料、风能、水能、太阳能、地热能、海洋能、潮汐能等。

二次能源 是指为了满足生产工艺和生活的特定需要以合理利用能源，将一次能源直接或间接加工转换产生的其它种类和形式的人工能源。如原煤加工产出的洗煤；由煤炭加工转换产出的焦炭，煤气；由原油加工产出的汽油、煤油、柴油、燃料油、液化石油气、炼厂干气等；由煤炭、石油、天然气转换产出的电力。

综合能源消费量 报告期内工业企业在工业生产活动中实际消费的各种能源的总和净值。计算综合能源消费量时，需要先将使用的各种能源折算成标准燃料后再进行计算。

单位生产总值能耗 指一定时期内，一个国家或地区每生产一个单位的生产总值所消耗的能源。计算公式为：

单位生产总值能耗=能源消费总量／生产总值

单位工业增加值能耗 指一定时期内，一个国家或地区每生产一个单位的工业增加值所消耗的能源。计算公式为：

单位工业增加值能耗=工业能源消费量／工业增加值

Explanatory Notes on Main Statistical Indicators

Total Energy Consumption refers to the total consumption of energy of various kinds by the production sectors and the households in the country in a given period of time. It is a comprehensive indicator to show the scale,composition and pace of increase of energy consumption. Total energy consumption includes that of coal,crude oil and their products,natural gas and electricity. However,it does not include the consumption of fuel of low calorific value, bio-energy and solar energy. Total energy consumption can be divided into three parts: end-use energy consumption; loss during the process of energy conversion; and energy loss.

（1）End-use Energy Consumption: It refers to the total energy consumption by the production sectors and the households in the country（region） in a given period of time. It does not include the consumption during the conversion of primary energy into secondary energy and the loss in the process of energy conversion.

（2）Loss During the Process of Energy Conversion: It refers to the total input of various kinds of energy for conversion, minus the total output of various kinds of energy in the country in a given period of time. It is an indicator to show the loss that occurs during the process of energy conversion.

（3）Energy Loss: It refers to the total of the loss of energy during the course of energy transport, distribution and storage and the loss caused by any objective reason in a given period of time. The loss of various kinds of gas due to gas discharges and stocktaking is not included.

Industry Consumption Energy refers to the volume of energy consumed by Industrial enterprises for industrial production activities.

Non–industry Consumption Energy refers to the energy consumed by industrial enterprises except for industrial production activities,means that energy consumed by non-industry production and not independent accounting units which was not engaged in industrial production activities affiliated to industrial enterprises.

Vehicle Energy refers to the energy consumed by vehicles which carried out transport activities in and out of factories.

Energy Processing Conversion Devoted energy processing conversion refers to for specialized application, a source of energy （normally primary energy）, after a certain technology , processed or converted to another kind of energy （normally secondary energy）. The input of energy conversion processing that is energy processing, and conversion consumption.

Primary Energy Source refers to natural energy resources as found naturally in the form of ready-made,without any change or conversion,as energy obtaineddirectly from natural and not change its shape and grade,such as raw coal, crude oil, natural gas, nuclear fuel, plantfuel, wind energy, water energy, solar energy,geothermalenergy, oceanic energy, tidal energy and so on.

Secondary Energy refers to other types and formsof artificial energy which was processed and conversed from primary energy sources directly or indirectly , in order to meet the specific needs in production process and life to use energy more effectively. Such as washing coalprocessed from raw coal; coke and coal gas processed andtransformed from raw coal; gasoline, kerosene, diesel oil, fuel oil, liquefied petroleum gas, dry gas refinery processed from crude oil; electric power conversed from coal, oil and natural gas.

Comprehensive energy consumption refers to the total and net energy actually consumed in industrial production activities by industrial enterprises in the reference period. When calculated the volume of consumption of comprehensive energy, should converted sorts of energy which was used into standards fuel firstly.

Energy Consumption per Unit of GDP refers to the energy consumption per unit of Gross Domestic Product in a country or the Gross Regional Product in a region in the same reference period. The formula is:

$$\text{Energy Consumption per Unit of GDP} = \frac{\text{Total Energy Consumption}}{\text{Gross Domestic Product}}$$

Energy Consumption per Unit of Industrial Value–added refers to the energy consumption per unit of industrial value-added in a country or region in the same reference period. The formula is:

$$\text{Energy Consumption per Unit of Industrial Value-added} = \frac{\text{Total Energy Consumption}}{\text{Industrial Value-added}}$$

14 建筑业

CONSTRUCTION

资料整理：陈海生
Data management：Chen Haisheng
数据审核：黄小丹
Data audit：Huang Xiaodan

第十四部分　建筑业

一、简要说明

本章资料主要包括建筑业基本情况、建筑业施工企业生产情况和财务状况，由西安市统计局固定资产投资处提供。

二、主要指标

企业个数（个）	539	比上年增长	28.3%
建筑业总产值（亿元）	2586.33	比上年增长	16.1%
#国有及国有控股企业	1981.24	比上年增长	16.4%
房屋建筑竣工面积（万平方米）	2536.71	比上年增长	13.8%
房屋建筑面积竣工率(%)	22.7	比上年下降	0.2个百分点

14 CONSTRUCTION

Ⅰ.Brief Introduction

This chapter consists of primarily the data basic situation of the construction industry, production situation and financial situation of the construction enterprises, provided by Fixed Asset Investment Division of the Xi'an Bureau of Statistics.

Ⅱ.Major Indicators

		Increase over Preceding Year
Number of Enterprises(item)	539	28.3%
Total Output Value of Construction(100 mil. yuan)	2586.33	16.1%
State-owned Or State Holding Majority Shares	1981.24	16.4%
Floor Space of Buildings Completed(10 000 sq.m)	2536.71	13.8%
Rate of Floor Space of Buildings Completed(%)	22.7	-0.2 percentage points

14-1 主要年份建筑业总产值

Total Output Value of Construction in Representative Year

单位：万元 (10 000 yuan)

年份 Year	单位数（个） Name of Enterprises (unit)	建筑业总产值 Total Output Value of Construction	国有及国有控股 State-owned Or State Holding Majority Shares	集体企业 Collective-owned Enterprises
2000	184	1059250	788704	148709
2001	205	1148091	918169	154749
2002	223	1334713	850278	153482
2003	204	1771126	1199911	134010
2004	244	2444242	2016792	165922
2005	235	3266535	2766785	196111
2006	217	4164782	3482016	236493
2007	279	6047524	4326279	326658
2008	328	9151199	6761190	4601423
2009	326	10745488	8751879	471533
2010	324	13339955	10340379	583928
2011	336	16190888	12783270	794189
2012	396	18742273	13647046	968291
2013	420	22284063	17020790	1548721
2014	539	25863267	19812354	950198

注：1、1996年以后建筑业年报统计范围由往年的县及县以上（含县级建制镇）各种经济类型的建筑企业，改为具有建筑业资质等级三级及三级以上的各种经济类型的建筑施工企业；2002年改为具有建筑业资质等级的各种经济类型的建筑施工企业。

2、本表资料含劳务分包企业。

3、由于统计口径变化，对部分年份建筑业总产值相关数据进行了修订。

14-2 全市建筑施工总承包企业基本情况（2014年）

Basic situation of construction general contracting business in whole city (2014)

指　　标	Item	合计 Total	国有及国有控股 State-owned Or State Holding Majority Shares
企业单位数（个）（施工总承包）	Number of Enterprises (unit) (Overall Contractor For Construction)	334	87
#二级以上企业（施工总承包）	First and Second Class Enterprise	276	76
计算劳动生产率的平均人数（人）（施工总承包）	Average Number of Employed Persons in Calculation of Labor Productivity (person) (Overall Contractor For Construction)	690584	504925
#二级以上企业（施工总承包）	First and Second Class Enterprise	675523	499129
建筑业总产值（亿元）（施工总承包）	Total Output Value of Construction(100 million yuan) (Overall Contractor For Construction)	2333.85	1799.1
#二级以上企业（施工总承包）	First and Second Class Enterprise	2283.56	1971.42
全员劳动生产率 按总产值计算(元/人)	Overall Labor Productivity Calculated by Total Output Value(yuan/person)	337953	356310

14-3 施工总承包和专业承包建筑企业生产情况（2014年）

分 组	Classify	签订的合同额（万元）Contract Value (10 000 yuan)
总计	**Total**	**57532699**
#国有及国有控股	State-Owned and State Holding Majority Shares	47830818
一、按登记注册类型分	**Grouped by Registion Status**	
内资	Domestic Investment Enterprises	56131367
国有企业	State-owned Enterprises	6025146
集体企业	Collective-owned Enterprises	1188449
股份合作企业	Share-holding Corperative Enterprises	9350
联营企业	Joint Ownership Enterprises	66455
有限责任公司	Limited Liability Corporations	41504822
股份有限公司	Share-holding Corperation Ltd.	1115782
私营企业	Private Enterprises	6221364
其他企业	Others	
港澳台商投资企业	Enterprises with Funds from Hong Kong,Macao and Taiwan	524
外商投资企业	Enterprises with Foreign Investment	1400808
二、按国民经济行业分	**Grouped by Sector**	
房屋建筑业	Building Engineering Construction	22595547
土木工程建筑业	Civil Engineering Construction	31664550
建筑安装业	Installation of Construction	1998981
建筑装饰和其他建筑业	Architectural decoration and other Construction	1273621
三、按隶属关系分	**Grouped by Administrative Relationship**	
中央	Central	30255037
地方	Region	27277662
四、按企业资质等级分	**Grouped by Class of Enterprises**	
1. 施工总承包	Overall Contractor for Construction	54262173
#特级	Special Class	11460492
一级	First Class	38279817
二级	Second Class	3690301
2. 专业承包	Special Contractor	3270527
#一级以上	First Class	2412906

Main Indicators on Overall Constructing Contractors and Professional Contractors by Registration Status（2014）

建筑业总产值（万元）Total Output Value of Constrution (10 000 yuan)	建筑工程产值 Output Value of Constrution	安装工程产值 Output Value of Installation	其他产值 Others	计算劳动生产率的平均人数（人）Average Number of Employed Persons in Calculation of Labour Productivity(person)
25863267	**22569034**	**2415317**	**878916**	**744893**
19812354	17981079	1307993	523282	526578
25407176	22114976	2413284	878916	734547
3281036	2634350	287215	359471	144027
950198	713257	205059	31882	52552
8100	8100			278
15636	10622		5014	669
16662765	15031223	1243980	387563	415571
585230	541613	37684	5933	15966
3904210	3175810	639346	89054	105484
510	510			14
455581	453549	2032		10332
10754026	9599957	904167	249902	333232
12785459	11738630	765367	281462	362219
1375442	748137	594909	32396	29236
948341	482310	150873	315157	20206
11251431	10535320	653462	62649	343506
14611836	12033714	1761854	816267	401387
23462837	21125335	1797252	540250	690330
2629240	2373253	222008	33980	25616
17708277	16102704	1157309	448263	558275
2623078	2238683	346795	37601	91415
2400430	1443699	618064	338666	15024
1762754	1192117	240629	330008	54563

14-3 续表

分 组	Classify	期末从业人员数（人） Number of Employment at Year-end (person)	工程技术人员 Technical Personnel
总计	**Total**	**394070**	**7015**
#国有及国有控股	State-Owned and State Holding Majority Shares	233624	4133
一、按登记注册类型分	**Grouped by Registion Status**		
内资	Domestic Investment Enterprises	384116	6959
国有企业	State-owned Enterprises	37270	886
集体企业	Collective-owned Enterprises	39552	190
股份合作企业	Share-holding Corperative Enterprises	33	
联营企业	Joint Ownership Enterprises	673	20
有限责任公司	Limited Liability Corporations	200362	3882
股份有限公司	Share-holding Corperation Ltd.	5919	171
私营企业	Private Enterprises	100307	1810
其他企业	Others		
港澳台商投资企业	Enterprises with Funds from Hong Kong,Macao and Taiwan	15	
外商投资企业	Enterprises with Foreign Investment	9939	56
二、按国民经济行业分	**Grouped by Sector**		
房屋建筑业	Building Engineering Construction	202107	3111
土木工程建筑业	Civil Engineering Construction	160268	2702
建筑安装业	Installation of Construction	21454	676
建筑装饰和其他建筑业	Architectural decoration and other Construction	10241	526
三、按隶属关系分	**Grouped by Administrative Relationship**		
中央	Central	119835	2462
地方	Region	274235	4553
四、按企业资质等级分	**Grouped by Class of Enterprises**		
1. 施工总承包	Overall Contractor for Construction	361659	5889
#特级	Special Class	16678	989
一级	First Class	264248	3918
二级	Second Class	71550	876
2. 专业承包	Special Contractor	32411	106
#一级以上	First Class	21073	1126

continued

房屋建筑 施工面积 （平方米） Number of Projects under Constrution (sq.m)	本年新开工 Beginning Projects in this year	房屋建筑 竣工面积 （平方米） Floor Space of Buildings Completed (sq.m)
111821838	**38159339**	**25367143**
85249003	25867957	17149330
111821838	38159339	25367143
15684504	4019074	2413901
4628340	2860343	2267401
74712	36571	14784
69297163	22127810	15005218
2036636	522457	225548
20100483	8593084	5440291
102294282	35131640	23224035
8368962	2546721	1696211
1126554	459088	435897
32040	21890	11000
27485974	8250005	3326924
84335864	29909334	22040219
111055592	37571949	25150487
9534626	2708515	1960434
90198887	29591772	19299201
10092762	4867602	3483636
766246	587390	216656
185000	91890	10200

14-4 施工总承包和专业承包建筑业企业财务状况（2014年）

单位：万元

指 标	Item	总 计 Total
一. 年初存货	**Stocks at the beginning of year**	**3986679**
二. 期末资产负债	**Total Assets and Liabilities of the final**	
流动资产合计	Total Circulating Funds	22600158
#应收工程款	Receivable Project Money	6789450
#存货	Stock	4094904
固定资产合计	Fixed Assets	1612105
固定资产原价	Original Value of Fixed Assets	2725867
累计折旧	Accumulative Total Depreciation	1402375
#本年折旧	Depreciation Within the Year	316374
在建工程	Projects Under Construction	157563
资产总计	Total Assets	27262571
流动负债合计	Total Liquid Liabilities	19777239
#应付帐款	Accounts Payable	8356357
非流动负债合计	Total Non-Liquid Liabilities	1205046
负债合计	Total Liabilities	21241384
所有者权益合计	Owner Rights and Interests	6021187
#实收资本	Actual Capital Hold	4582374
三. 损益及分配	**Profit or Loss and the Distribution**	
营业收入	Total Revenue	29497203
#主营业务收入	Revenue from Principal Business	29351276
营业成本	Total Cost	27079380
#主营业务成本	Cost of Principal Business	26837305
营业税金及附加	Taxs and Other Changes	906230
#主营业务税金及附加	Taxs and Other Changes on Principal Business	901199
其他业务利润	Profits from Other Operation	13654
销售费用	Sale Expenses	62167
管理费用	Managenment Expenses	809458
财务费用	Financial Expenses	136111
营业利润	Business Profits	576154
利润总额	Total Profits	587357
四. 人工成本	**Cost of Labor**	
应付职工薪酬	Salary Payable	3420201

Financial Status of Overall Constructing Contractors and Professional Contractors（2014）

(10 000 yuan)

国有及国有控股 State-Owned and State Holding Majority Shares Enterprises	中央企业 Enterprises Central	省属企业 Province Enterprises	市属企业 Municipal Enterprises
2923493	**2157326**	**635202**	**1194151**
17934937	12358812	4078337	6163010
5694988	3433010	1800797	1555643
3125385	2344931	518098	1231876
1067435	790939	198945	622221
2085967	1598706	351030	776132
1153964	894152	184971	323252
278087	222244	47386	46744
97453	61742	25985	69837
21431358	15052834	4737417	7472320
16819602	12060730	3657873	4058636
7545540	5390395	1612736	1353226
1058545	762712	146187	296147
17878191	12823443	3804105	4613836
3553168	2229391	933311	2858484
2573588	1539471	767647	2275256
23895140	15814714	6404687	7277802
23818792	15772418	6385259	7193600
22144200	14643302	5971554	6464525
22082340	14607333	5960100	6269872
724809	470264	201275	234691
722796	469189	200740	231270
9592	5943	5485	2226
20128	10887	3294	47986
607645	420853	144211	244393
98598	63496	20973	51642
372759	272537	67924	235693
385467	285533	67832	233992
2712175	1637633	852941	929627

14-5 劳务分包建筑业企业基本情况（2014年）

Basic Statistic on Enterprises of Work Subcontractors（2014）

单位：万元 (10 000 yuan)

指　标	Item	2014
一、期末资产负债	**Total Assets and Liabilities of the final**	
固定资产原价	Value of Fixed Assets	235
本年折旧	Depreciation In The Year	45
资产总计	Total Assets	20831
负债合计	Total Liabilities	17492
实收资本	Paid in Capital	1887
二、损益及分配	**Profit or Loss and the Distribution**	
营业收入	Total Revenue	39897
#主营业务收入	Revenue from Principal Business	39896
营业成本	Total Cost	37457
#主营业务成本	Cost of Principal Business	37053
营业税金及附加	Taxs and Other Changes	1313
#主营业务税金及附加	Taxs and Other Changes on Principal Business	1313
其他业务利润	Profits from Other Operation	
销售费用	Sale Expenses	19
管理费用	Managenment Expenses	1115
财务费用	Financial Expenses	72
营业利润	Business Profits	336
利润总额	Total Profits	324

14-6 各区县建筑业主要经济指标（2014年）

Main Indicators of Construction Enterprises by Region（2014）

区 县	Region	企业个数(个) Number of Enterprises (unit)	总产值(万元) Total Output Value (10 000 yuan)	计算劳动生产率的平均人数(人) Average Number of Employed Persons in Calculation of Labor Productivity(person)	全员劳动生产率(万元/人) Overall Labor Productivity (10 000 yuan/person)	利税总额(万元) Total Pre-tax Profits (10 000 yuan)
新城区	Xincheng	33	2822305	62005	46	120387
碑林区	Beilin	62	5836760	104269	56	345172
莲湖区	Lianhu	47	1798067	52141	35	94200
灞桥区	Baqiao	34	1076704	37778	29	74395
未央区	Weiyang	69	5389357	230212	23	315439
雁塔区	Yanta	183	6789521	162511	42	392813
阎良区	Yanliang	18	229185	10717	21	12032
临潼区	Lintong	22	115939	6612	18	5892
长安区	Chang'an	31	607583	23682	26	31267
蓝田县	Lantian	9	96552	3443	28	11213
周至县	Zhouzhi	11	88351	4480	20	5873
户 县	Huxian	5	164727	8411	20	6582
高陵县	Gaoling	7	848216	38891	22	78323

14-7 各区县建筑业房屋施工及竣工面积（2014年）

Floor Space of Buildings under Construction & Completed by Region（2014）

区 县	Region	房屋建筑施工面积（万平方米）Floor Space under Construction (10 000sq.m)	本年新开工面积 Newly Started This Year	房屋建筑竣工面积（万平方米）Floor Space of Buildings Completed (10 000sq.m)	竣工房屋价值（亿元）Value of Buildings Completed (100 million yuan)
新城区	Xincheng	1080.63	333.72	242.68	46.65
碑林区	Beilin	3363.75	1209.98	862.56	170
莲湖区	Lianhu	1608.47	360.99	275.57	52.42
灞桥区	Baqiao	119.03	49.48	18.82	3
未央区	Weiyang	1858.88	733.38	269.05	48.48
雁塔区	Yanta	2320.61	574.89	482.82	67.98
阎良区	Yanliang	84.06	40.56	19.39	2.63
临潼区	Lintong	47.85	17.15	21.07	3.18
长安区	Chang'an	182.06	121.93	56.57	9.33
蓝田县	Lantian	55.09	24.2	20.48	2.56
周至县	Zhouzhi	63.04	26.54	37.97	6.21
户 县	Huxian	145.37	78.83	58.49	10.5
高陵县	Gaoling	253.35	244.28	171.25	26.92

14-8 各区县建筑业企业主要经济效益指标（2014年）

Main Economic Benefit Indicators on Construction Enterprises by Region（2014）

区 县	Region	人均利润总额（元/人）Per Profit (yuan/person)	人均利税（元/人）Per Pre-tax Profits (yuan/person)	人均竣工产值（元/人）Per Output Value of Buildings Completed (yuan/person)	人均施工面积（平方米/人）Per Floor Space of Buildings Under Construcyion (sq.m/person)	人均竣工面积（平方米/人）Per Floor Space of Buildings Completed (sq.m/person)
新城区	Xincheng	5744	19416	263555	174	39
碑林区	Beilin	10306	33104	225941	323	83
莲湖区	Lianhu	7252	18066	171103	308	53
灞桥区	Baqiao	7159	19693	364869	32	5
未央区	Weiyang	5322	13702	49927	81	12
雁塔区	Yanta	10502	24171	187375	143	30
阎良区	Yanliang	5141	11227	91779	78	18
临潼区	Lintong	4235	8911	72344	72	32
长安区	Chang'an	5678	13203	50018	77	24
蓝田县	Lantian	25649	32567	105198	160	59
周至县	Zhouzhi	6869	13109	141092	141	85
户 县	Huxian	1641	7825	136274	173	70
高陵县	Gaoling	13163	20139	69223	65	44

14-8 续表 continued

区 县	Region	产值利润率（%）Ratio of Profits to Output Value (%)	产值利税率（%）Ratio of Pre-tax Profits to Output Value (%)	资产利润率（%）Ratio of Profits to Assets (%)	资产利税率（%）Ratio of Pre-tax Profits to Assets (%)	资产负债率（%）Ratio of Debts to Assets (%)
新城区	Xincheng	1.3	3.0	1.5	3.6	82.9
碑林区	Beilin	1.8	4.1	1.7	3.9	81.3
莲湖区	Lianhu	2.1	3.1	1.9	2.8	77.7
灞桥区	Baqiao	2.5	4.4	2.3	4.1	85.0
未央区	Weiyang	2.2	3.6	1.8	2.9	83.6
雁塔区	Yanta	2.4	3.3	2.3	3.1	76.2
阎良区	Yanliang	2.4	2.8	2.5	2.9	66.6
临潼区	Lintong	2.4	2.7	3.6	4.0	41.6
长安区	Chang'an	2.3	2.9	2.5	3.2	72.8
蓝田县	Lantian	9.1	2.5	28.9	7.8	59.4
周至县	Zhouzhi	3.8	3.2	5.8	4.8	53.3
户 县	Huxian	0.8	3.2	2.1	8.2	57.8
高陵县	Gaoling	6.0	3.2	7.0	3.7	3.8

主要统计指标解释

建筑业统计单位 指从事房屋、构筑物建造和设备安装活动的法人企业。建筑业法人企业应具有建筑业资质并能够独立核算，同时其应具备以下条件：①依法成立，有自己的名称、组织机构和场所，能够承担民事责任；②独立拥有和使用资产，承担负债，有权与其他单位签订合同；③独立核算盈亏，能够编制资产负债表。

建筑业总产值 是以货币形式表现的建筑业企业在一定时期内生产的建筑业产品和提供的服务的总和。建筑业总产值包括：

（1）建筑工程产值：指列入建筑工程预算内的各种工程价值。

（2）安装工程产值：指设备安装工程价值，不包括被安装设备本身的价值。

（3）其他产值：建筑业总产值中除建筑工程、安装丁程以外的产值。包括房屋构筑物修理产值、非标准设备制造产值、总包企业向分包企业收取的管理费以及不能明确划分的施工活动所完成的产值。

a. 房屋构筑物修理产值：指房屋和构筑物修理所完成的产值，但不包括被修理房屋、构筑物本身价值和生产设备的修理价值。

b. 非标准设备制造产值：指加工制造没有定型的非标准生产设备的加了费和原材料价值（如化工厂、炼油厂用的各种罐、槽，矿井生产统一使用的各种漏斗、三角槽、阀门等）以及附属加工厂为本企业承建工程制作的非标准设备的价值。

建筑业增加值 指建筑业企业在报告期内以货币形式表现的建筑业生产经营活动的最终成果。

从2004年第一次全国经济普查开始，建筑业现价增加值按生产法和分配法（收入法）两种方法计算，以收入法的计算结果为准，即从收入的角度出发，根据生产要素在生产过程中应得的收入份额计算。具体计算方法：经济普查年度建筑业增加值按照《经济普查年度GDP核算方案》计算，非经济普查年度建筑业增加值按照们≥经济普查年度GDP核算方案》计算。

房屋建筑施工面积 指在报告期内施过工的全部房屋建筑面积，包括本期新开工的房屋面积、上期施工跨入本期继续施工的房屋面积、上期停缓建在本期恢复施工的房屋面积、本期竣工的房屋面积及本期施丁后又停缓建的房屋面积。

房屋建筑竣工面积 指在报告期内房屋建筑按照设计要求全部完工，达到了使用条件，经验收鉴定合格，正式移交使用单位的房屋建筑面积。

Explanatory Notes on Main Statistical Indicators

Statistical Unit in the Construction Industry refers to a corporate enterprise engaged in the construction of buildings and structures and in the installation of equipment. A corporate construction enterprise should have qualification certificates with independent accounting system, and should meet the following 3 requirements: a) being set up in line with relevant legal basis, having its full name, organization and location, and capable of taking civil liabilities; b) independently possessing and using its assets and assuming its liabilities, and entitled to sign contracts with other institutions; and c) making independent accounts of its profits and losses, and capable of compiling its own balance sheet.

Gross Output Value of Construction refers to total of construction products and services, expressed in money terms, produced or rendered by construction and installation enterprises during a given period of time. It includes:

(1)Output value of construction projects: the value of projects covered by the project budgets;

(2) Output value of installation projects: the value of the installation of equipment, (excluding the value of the equipment to be installed);

(3)Other output values: the output value of construction industry apart from that of construction projects and installation projects. It includes: output value of repair of buildings and structures; output value of non-standard equipment manufacturing; overhead expenses received by contracted enterprises from the sub-contracted enterprises and the completed output value of construction activities for which there is no clear definition.

a. Output value of repair of buildings and structures: the value created through the repairs of buildings or structures. It does not include the value of buildings or structures being repaired and the value of the repair of production equipment;

b. Output value of manufactured non-standard equipment: the value of non-standard production equipment, including raw materials and manufacturing cost, made for the construction project (i.e., chemical plant; kettles or tanks used by refineries; various fillers, triangle tanks, valves used by mines). It also includes the output value of equipment manufactured by subsidiary workshops.

Value-added of Construction refers to the final result of the activities of production and operation of enterprises of the construction industry in monetary terms during the reference period.

Starting from the 2004 economic census, value-added of construction is calculated by both production approach and income approach, with the figures from the income approach as the final figures. Under the income approach, calculation starts from the perspective of income and is based on the share of income derived from the production process by the relevant factors of production. Specifically, value-added of construction for the Census years is calculated in accordance with the Programme of Compilation of GDP and National Accounts for the Year of Economic Census, and value-added of construction for other years is calculated in accordance with the Programme of Compilation of GDP and National Accounts for the Non Economic Census Years.

Floor Space of Buildings Under Construction refers to floor space of buildings under construction during the reference period, including the floor space of buildings for which construction has newly started; buildings for which construction has started earlier and is continuing during the reference period; and buildings for which construction has been suspended earlier but has restarted during the reference period; buildings completed during the reference period; and buildings under construction but construction has subsequently been during the reference period.

Floor Space of Buildings Completed refers to the floor space of buildings that are completed in the reference period in accordance with the requirements of the design, up to the standard for being put into use, and having been checked and accepted by departments concerned as qualified ones.

15 运输和邮电

TRANSPORT,POSTAL AND TELECOMMUNICATION SERVICE

资料整理：齐昆峰
Data management：Qi Kunfeng
数据审核：王金桂
Data audit：Wang Jingui

第十五部分　运输和邮电

一、简要说明

本章资料包括交通运输业和邮电通信业的基本情况，主要是交通运输工具、货物和旅客运输量、邮电业务、邮政局所及服务点等基本情况。资料由西安市统计局社会科技处根据有关部门提供资料整理。

二、主要指标

旅客周转量（亿人公里）	309.11	比上年增长	8.1%
货物周转量（亿吨公里）	623.41	比上年增长	9.4%
邮电业务总量（亿元）	292.20	比上年增长	17.9%
全社会车辆数（万辆）	213.90	比上年增长	14.9%
#民用小轿车	111.08	比上年增长	20.8%

15 TRANSPORT,POSTAL AND TELECOMMUNICATION SERVICES

Ⅰ.Brief Introduction

Data in this chapter consists of primarily basic data of communication, transportation and postal service industry, transportation facility, amount of goods and passenger transportation, basic data of postal service, post offices and service establishments of Xi'an City. Data in this chapter is compiled by Social & Science and Technology Division of the Xi'an Bureau of Statistics according to the data provided by department concerned of the municipal government.

Ⅱ.Major Indicators

		Increase over Preceding Year
Passenger-Km (100 mil. Person-km)	309.11	8.1%
Freight Ton-Km (100 mil. Ton-km)	623.41	9.4%
Amount of Postal and Telecommunication Service(100 mil. Yuan)	292.20	17.9%
Number of Vehides in the whole Sciety(10 000 unit)	213.90	14.9%
Civil Car	111.08	20.8%

15-1 主要年份各种交通线路和桥梁

Transportation Routes and Number of Bridges in Representative Years

年 份 Year	铁路营业 里程（公里） Length of Railways in Operation (km)	公路里程 （公里） Length of Highways (km)	桥 梁 （座） Bridges (seat)	桥梁长度 （公里） length of Bridge (km)
1978	555			
1979	555			
1980	555			
1981	569			
1982	569			
1983	569			
1984	569			
1985	697			
1986	697			
1987	1333			
1988	1339			
1989	1339	2563		
1990	1339	2586		
1991	1357	2785		
1992	1357	2786		
1993	1356	2801		
1994	1357	2830		
1995	1357	2852		
1996	1358	2877		
1997	1489	3026		
1998	1492	3047		
1999	1478	2789		
2000	1540	3010		
2001	1536	3298		
2002	1543	7862	629	29799
2003	1522	8360	629	29799
2004	1608	8360	629	29799
2005	202	8500	634	46973
2006	269	9530	634	46973
2007	269	9672	1319	91412
2008	269	11895	1710	151996
2009	269	12378	1856	154866
2010	269	12378	1856	154866
2011	269	12599	1863	149743
2012	269	13127	2190	214978
2013	269	13135	2213	224962
2014	269	13251	2213	224949

注：本表数据来自市交通局、西安铁路局，民航通航里程2013年统计口径发生较大变化。

15-1 续表 continued

年 份 Year	永久式桥梁 （座） Permanent Bridges (seat)	永久式桥梁 （公里） Length of Permanent Bridges (km)	民航通航里程 （重复航线）（公里） Length of Total Civil Aviation Routes(km)
1978			
1979			
1980			
1981			
1982			
1983			
1984			
1985			
1986			
1987			
1988			
1989			
1990			
1991			
1992			65007
1993			83215
1994			100800
1995			119753
1996			126433
1997			173010
1998			180000
1999			141284
2000			139764
2001			154614
2002	629	29799	211000
2003	629	29799	381800
2004	629	29799	386953
2005	632	46915	485749
2006	632	46915	418852
2007	1275	90716	553355
2008	1657	150980	515524
2009	1803	153850	587904
2010	1803	153850	742375
2011	1811	148810	898628
2012	2138	213985	981450
2013	2161	223970	70643568
2014	2171	224165	78626210

15-2 各种交通线路里程和桥梁数（2014年）

Length of Transportation Routes and Number of Bridges（2014）

指　　标	Item	2014
铁路营业里程（公里）	**Length of Railways in Operation (km)**	**269**
电气化营业里程	Length of Electrified Railways in Operation	
复线里程	Double-Tracking Length	
公路里程（公里）	**Length of Highways (km)**	**13251**
等级公路	Expressways and Class I to IV Highways	12733
高速	Expressway	471
一级	First Class	325
二级	Second Class	1471
三级	Third Class	1211
四级	Forth Class	9255
等外公路	Highways below Class IV	518
桥梁	Bridges	
永久式桥梁	Permanent	
座（座）	Seat (seat)	2213
长度（公里）	Length (km)	224949
民航通航里程(公里)(重复航线)	**Length of Total Civil Aviation Routes(km)**	**78626210**
国际航线（公里）	International routes	
民航航线条数（条）	**Length of Civil Aviation routes(Article)**	**269**
国际航线（条）	International routes	27

注：本表数据来自市交通局、西安铁路局。

15-3 主要年份全社会车辆数

Possession of Civil Vehicles in Representative Years

单位：辆、台 (unit)

年 份 Year	合计 Total	汽车 Motor	载客汽车 Passenget Vehicles	载货汽车 Ordinary Trucks	摩托车 Motorcycles	拖拉机 Tractors
1999	**279335**	133192	63772	44348		38023
2000	**310252**	138318	89783	44974		37177
2001	**369988**	172436	110744	55453		31355
2002	**454998**	206653	134527	64623	176960	36083
2003	**516719**	242599	163872	70781	191834	34733
2004	**512802**	276012	195524	74557	156709	34755
2005	**544586**	377628	240923	82463	131440	34741
2006	**608155**	393778	296078	89772	131449	33236
2007	**840376**	522616	360081	97614	284594	32028
2008	**875005**	595735	430472	89093	247079	30176
2009	**1012937**	754803	567326	113430	224121	31347
2010	**1253461**	961283	739038	145740	259239	29151
2011	**1445811**	1174874	928669	171649	241132	25600
2012	**1633257**	1380125	1123105	186412	224279	24458
2013	**1862063**	1634885	1372371	207058	200419	21898
2014	**2139024**	1926012	1658714	224409	190625	17484

注：本表数据来自市车管所。

15-4 全社会车辆数（2014年）

Possession of Civil Vehicles（2014）

指 标	Item	2014
合计（辆）	**Total (unit)**	**2139024**
民用汽车（辆）	Motor(unit)	1926012
#私人汽车拥有量	Possession of Private Vehicles	1705242
载客汽车	Passenget Vehicles	1658714
#大 型	Large	15004
轿 车	Car	1110760
普通载货汽车	Ordinary Trucks	224409
#重、中型	Heavy and Medium	58800
其他汽车	Others	42889
#三 轮	Three Wheelers	19375
拖拉机（台）	Tractors(unit)	17484
# 大中型	Large and Medium	
小 型	Small-sized	
摩托车（辆）	Motorcycle (unit)	190625
普通摩托车	Bicycle Motor	183994
挂车（辆）	Articulated Trailers (unit)	4832
其他类型车（辆）	Others (unit)	71

注：本表数据来自市车管所。

15-5 主要年份交通运输量及周转量

Passenger Traffic and Kilometers and Freight Traffic and Ton-kilometers in Representative Years

年份 Year	客运量（万人次） Passenger Traffic (10 000 person-times)	旅客周转量（万人公里） Passenger-Km (10 000 person-Km)	货运量（万吨） Freight Traffic (10 000 tons)	货物周转量（万吨公里） Freight Ton-Km (10 000 ton-Km)
1978	1334		3723	
1979	1420		3919	
1980	1508		3655	
1981	1839		3379	
1982	2340		4067	
1983	3054		4225	
1984	2899		4966	
1985	2404		5681	
1986	2186		5409	
1987	3781		6294	
1988	5721		6968	
1989	6092		8742	
1990	5748		6980	
1991	4193		3389	
1992	4368		8233	
1993	8036		8406	
1994	8321		8754	
1995	9069		9590	
1996	9854		10577	
1997	8922		9358	
1998	9223		9429	
1999	10311	2130383	9766	3452383
2000	10756	2507896	10191	3691963
2001	9078	2658037	7728	4229430
2002	12527	2524444	9484	4544040
2003	11413	2596402	9392	5037684
2004	10832	3112374	14845	5850029
2005	10479	1607568	12051	1249525
2006	11245	1721217	11832	1354318
2007	12466	1753464	15124	1473182
2008	26501	2529007	27560	3490707
2009	28693	2582025	30606	3766806
2010	30294	2942957	34323	4301680
2011	33375	3223544	39239	5212010
2012	36154	3387448	44924	5958742
2013	38289	3634915	50119	6471497
2014	25719	3091147	42039	6234128

注：本表数据由市交通局、西安铁路局、咸阳机场、长安航空公司、东方航空公司西北分公司提供。
2014年陕西省公路运输统计方法制度改变，因此与往年数据不可比。

15-6 交通运输量及运输周转量（2014年）

Passenger Traffic and Kilometers and Freight Traffic and Ton-kilometers（2014）

指　标	Item	2014年	2014比上年增长（%）Increase over Preceding Year（%）
一、客运量合计（万人次）	**Passenger Traffic(10 000 person-times)**	**25719**	**6.8**
铁路	Railway	3511	13.1
公路	Highway	19282	4.9
民航	Civil Aviation	2926	12.3
二、旅客周转量合计（万人公里）	**Passenger-Km (10 000 person-Km)**	**3091147**	**8.1**
铁路	Railway	659315	4.4
公路	Highway	1067456	5.0
民航	Civil Aviation	1364376	12.7
三、货运量合计（万吨）	**Freight Traffic(l0 000 tons)**	**42039**	**12.9**
铁路	Railway	900	4.9
公路	Highway	41120	13.1
民航	Civil Aviation	19	4.2
四、货物周转量（万吨公里）	**Freight Ton-Kin (10 000 ton-Km)**	**6234128**	**9.4**
铁路	Railway	2359484	2.9
公路	Highway	3863964	13.8
民航	Civil Aviation	10680	3.6

注：本表数据由市交通局、西安铁路局、咸阳机场、长安航空公司、东方航空公司西北分公司提供。

15-7 主要年份邮政电信情况

年份 Year	邮电业务总量（万元） Business Volume of Postal and Telecommunication Services(10 000 yuan)	电信业务总量 Business Volume of Telecommunication Services	#邮政业务总量 Business Volume of Postal Services
1978	1420		
1979	1616		
1980	1640		
1981	1713		
1982	2154		
1983	2250		
1984	2484		
1985	2972		
1986	3244		
1987	3911		
1988	5327		
1989	5973		
1990	7843		
1991	5700		
1992	6610		
1993	36581		
1994	54034		
1995	76450		
1996	104566		
1997	124601		
1998	204927		
1999	306457		
2000	461628		
2001	367620		
2002	515259	470492	44767
2003	820943	770673	50270
2004	1027415	975045	52370
2005	1320447	1261033	59414
2006	1867560	1796533	71027
2007	2267633	2191250	76383
2008	2646662	2564524	82138
2009	2989246	2900836	88410
2010	3231059	3167750	63309
2011	2005025	1944329	60696
2012	2162065	2098273	63762
2013	2479430	2313630	165800
2014	2922011	2695332	226679

注：2002年及以后，邮政电信机构分离；2001—2010年邮电业务总量按2000年不变价格计算；2011年邮电业务总量按2010年不变价格计算，故与以往年份不可比。

Basic Statistic on Postal and Telecommunication Service in Representative Years

固定电话年末用户数（户） Number of Immobile Telephone at Year-end (subscriber)	农村电话用户数 Number of Telephone in Rural Areas at Year-end	移动电话用户年末数（户） Number of Mobile Phone at Year-end (subscriber)	互联网年末宽带用户数（户） Number of Broad Band Net User (subscriber)
12828	1062		
13487	1052		
14024	1086		
14497	1125		
15357	1129		
16922	1156		
18611	1203		
21624	1239		
26373	1235		
30200	1290		
34265	1357		
39506	1498		
45267	1668		
49516	2479		
60727	2613		
101327	2671		
197398	5067		
299485	8386		
430270	13654		
573244	21202		
736998	37863		
874586	74761		
1242637	170199		
1711500	259374	1277400	17183
2095230	358803	1964200	35230
2538393	415593	2412392	160900
2934424	480276	3500900	243448
3214806	500847	4199570	339280
3159639	467526	5510720	508775
3145819	419446	6645863	586213
3068807	383869	7377575	813987
2891009	358238	11200566	1167916
2617691	335048	14230800	1461804
2703640	320189	16141463	1841027
3110176	335864	18035397	2023059
3191112	330602	21606662	2670473
3066575	372823	20253157	2779458

注：本表数据由市邮政管理局、市邮政局，中国联通、中国电信、中国移动和中国铁通等西安分公司提供。

15-8 邮政业务及服务网点

Postal Service and Branch Post Office

指　标	Item	2011	2012	2013	2014
一、邮政业务总量（万元）	**Business Volume of Postal Services(10 000 yuan)**	**60696**	**63077**	**165800**	**226679**
二、邮政业务收入（万元）	**Gross Income of Post Services (10 000 yuan)**	**65174**	**71778**	**177100**	**213893**
其中：快递业务收入（万元）	Express delivery business income (10 000 yuan)			97100	134306
三、函件（万件）	**Number of Letters (10 000 pcs)**	**3061**	**2769**	**2856**	**2112**
四、包件（万件）	**Parcels (10 000 pcs)**	**91**	**50**	**89**	**71**
五、汇票（万张）	**Money Order (10 000 pcs)**	**112**	**90**	**148**	**81**
六、报纸订销累计份数（万份）	**Accumulated Newspaper Prescribing and** Sales Volume (10 000 pcs)	**12603**	**13052**	**14495**	**14338**
七、杂志订销累计份数（万份）	**Accumulated Magazine Prescribing and** Sales Volume (10 000 pcs)	**564**	**613**	**1628**	**1572**
八、特快专递类业务（万件）	**Express Mail Service Volume (10 000 pcs)**	**1901**	**129**	**138**	**107**
九、集邮业务量（万枚）	**Stamps For Collection (10 000 pcs)**	**1060**	**2312**	**1431**	**1477**
十、邮政营销网点（处）	**Number of Post Office Branch Establishments (unit)**	**277**	**279**	**269**	**280**
#设在农村的局所	In it: number of post offices in rural area	50	115	110	123
十一、邮政信筒信箱（个）	**Number of Mailboxes(unit)**	**1108**	**1108**	**1108**	**1170**

注：本表数据来自市邮政管理局和邮政局，2013年邮政数据统计口径变化。

15-9 电信业务情况

Telecommunication Service

指　标	Item	2011	2012	2013	2014
一、电信业务总量（万元）	**Business Volume of Telecommunication Services (10 000 yuan)**	**1944329**	**2098274**	**2313630**	**2695332**
二、电信业务总收入（万元）	**Gross Income of Telecommunication Services (10 000 yuan)**	**1029629**	**1162257**	**1316435**	**1356705**
三、固定电话年末用户数（万户）	**Number of Immobile Telephone at Year-end (10 000 subscribers)**	**270.36**	**311.02**	**319.11**	**306.66**
#农村电话年末户数	Number of Telephone in Rural Areas at Year-end	**32.02**	**33.59**	**33.06**	**37.28**
四、电话交换机总容量（万门）	**Capacity (number) of Telephone Switchboard (10 000 lines)**	**441.49**	**420.38**	**378.02**	**230.01**
五、移动电话用户年末数（万户）	**Number of Mobile Phone at Year-end(10 000 subscribers)**	**1614.15**	**1803.54**	**2160.67**	**2025.32**
#3G电话用户数	3G Mobile Phone Subscribers	177.37	394.97	666.36	638.96
六、互联网年末用户数（万户）	**Number of Broad Band Net User (10 000 subscribers)**	**184.10**	**202.31**	**267.05**	**277.95**

注：本表数据由中国联通、中国电信、中国移动和中国铁通等西安分公司提供。

主要统计指标解释

铁路营业里程 又称营业长度（包括正式营业和临时营业里程），指办理客货运输业务的铁路正线总长度。凡是全线或部分建成双线及以上的线路，以第一线的实际长度计算；复线、站线、段管线、岔线和特殊用途线以及不计算运费的联络线都不计算营业里程。铁路营业里程是反映铁路运输业基础设施发展水平的重要指标，也是计算客货周转量、运输密度和机车车辆运用效率等指标的基础资料。

公路里程 指在一定时期内实际达到《公路工程技术标准JTJ01-88》规定的等级公路，并经公路主管部门正式验收交付使用的公路里程数。包括大中城市的郊区公路以及通过小城镇街道部分的公路里程和桥梁、隧道渡口的长度，不包括大中城市的街道、厂矿、林区生产用道和农业生产用道的里程。两条或多条公路共同经由同一路段，只计算一次，不得重复计算里程长度。它是反映公路建设发展规模的重要指标，也是计算运输网密度等指标的基础资料。

民用航空航线里程 指民航运输定期班机飞行的航线长度的总和。航线长度按机场之间的距离计算，通常有两种计算方法：一是将每条航线长度相加称为重复计算航线里程；一是将两线或两条以上航线经过同一区段里程，只计算一次航线长度称为不重复计算航线里程。一般常用的是后者，它能确切反映民航运输网的规模，是表明民航事业为国民经济服务和方便人民生活程度的主要指标。

货（客）运量 指在一定时期内，各种运输工具实际运送的货物（旅客）数量。它是反映运输业为国民经济和人民生活服务的数量指标，也是制定和检查运输生产计划、研究运输发展规模和速度的重要指标。货运按吨计算，客运按人计算。货物不论运输距离长短、货物类别，均按实际重量统计。旅客不论行程远近或票价多少，均按一人一次客运量统计；半价票、小孩票也按一人统计。

货物（旅客）周转量 指在一定时期内，由各种运输工具运送的货物（旅客）数量与其相应运输距离的乘积之总和。它是反映运输业生产总成果的重要指标，也是编制和检查运输生产计划，计算运输效率、劳动生产率以及核算运输单位成本的主要基础资料。计算货物周转量通常按发出站与到达站之间的最短距离，也就是计费距离计算。计算公式为：

货物（旅客）周转量=Σ货物（旅客）运输量×运输距离

民用汽车拥有量 指报告期末，在公安交通管理部门按照《机动车注册登记工作规范》，已注册登记领有民用车辆牌照的全部汽车数量。汽车拥有量统计的主要分类：根据汽车结构分为载客汽车、载货汽车及其他汽车；根据汽车所有者不同分为个人（私人）汽车、单位汽车；根据汽车的使用性质分为营运汽车、非营运汽车；根据汽车大小规格不同载客汽车分为大型、中型、小型和微型，载货汽车分为重型、中型、轻型和微型。

邮电业务总量 指以价值量形式表现的邮电通信企业为社会提供各类邮电通信服务的总数量。邮电业务量按专业分类包括函件、包件、汇票、报刊发行、邮政快件、特快专递、邮政储蓄、集邮、公众电报、用户电报、传真、长途电话、出租电路、无线寻呼、移动电话、分组交换数据通信、出租代维等。计算方法为各类产品乘以相应的平均单价（不变价）之和，再加上出租电路和设备、代用户维护电话交换机和线路等的服务收入。它综合反映了一定时期邮电业务发展的总成果，是研究邮电业务量构成和发展趋势的重要指标。计算公式为：

邮电业务总量=Σ（各类邮电业务量×不变单价）+出租代维及其他业务收入

移动电话用户 是指通过移动电话交换机进入移动电话网、占用移动电话号码的电话用户。用户数量以报告期末在移动电话营业部门实际办理登记手续进入移动电话网的户数进行计算，一部移动电话统计为一户。

电话用户 指接入国家公众固定电话网，并按固定电话业务进行经营管理的电话用户。1997年以前，电话用户分为市内电话用户和农村电话用户。“市内电话用户”是指接入县城及县以上城市的电话网上的电话用户；“农村电话用户”是指接入县邮电局农话台及县以下农村电话交换点，以县城为中心（除市话用户外）联通县、乡（镇）、行政村、村民小组的用户。从1997年起，电话用户数分组调整为以用户所在区域划分为“城市电话用户”和“乡村电话用户”，与过去的按市内电话和农村电话划分方法不同。而电话用户总数、电话机总部数统计范围不变。

农村电话用户 指县城关区以下的集镇和农村接入局用交换机的电话用户数。

局用交换机容量 是指安装在本地电信运营商内用于接续本地固定电话的电话交换机容量，有倍增设备按倍增后的数量计数。包括现用和备用的人工或自动交换机的全部容量。

互联网宽带接入端口 指用于接入互联网用户的各类实际安装运行的接入端口的数量，包括xDSL用户接入端口、LAN接入端口以及其他类型接入端口等，不包括窄带拨号接入端口。

Explanatory Notes on Main Statistical Indicators

Length of Railways in Operation refers to the total length of the trunk line under passenger and freight transportation(including both full operation and temporary operation). The calculation is based on the actual length of the first line even if this line has a full or partial double track or more tracks, excluding double tracks, station sidings, tracks under the charge of stations, branch lines, special-purpose lines and the non-payable connecting lines. The length of railways in operation is an important indicator to show the development of the infrastructure for the railway transport, and also the essential data to calculate volume of passenger freight transport,traffic density and utilization efficiency of the locomotives and carriages.

Length of Highways refers to the length of highways which are built in conformity with the grades specified by the highway engineering standard formulated by the Ministry of Communications, and have been formally checked and accepted by the departments of highways and put into use. The length of highways includes that of the suburb highways at large and medium- sized cities,highways passing through streets at small cities and towns,and also the length of bridges, tunnel and ferries. It does not include the length of streets in big and medium-sized cities and highways built for the production purpose at factories, mines, forest areas and agricultural areas. If two or more highways go the same section of the way, the length of the section is only calculated for once and no duplication is allowed. The length of highways is an important indicator to show the development of the highway construction and to provide essential information to calculate the transport network density.

Length of Civil Aviation Routes refers to the length of all routes for regular civil aviation flights. There are usually two ways to calculate the distance between airports connected by the route length: one is to put the length of all air routes together, called duplicated calculation of the length of the routes; the other is not to allow the duplication in calculation when two or more routes passing the same section of aviation routes. The latter is usually used, as it can precisely show the size of the civil aviation network and indicate the extent of civil aviation serving the national economy and the people.

Freight (Passenger) Traffic refers to the volume of freight (passenger) transported with various means. Freight transport is calculated in tons and passenger traffic is calculated in the number of persons. Despite the type of freight and travelling distance, the freight transport is calculated in the actual weight of the goods: and despite the travelling distance and ticket price, the passenger traffic is calculated by the principle that one person can be counted only once in one travel. The passenger who travel with a half price ticket or a child ticket is also calculated as one person. The freight (passenger) traffic provides a quantitative measure to show how the transport industry serves the national economy and people, and is also an important indicator for planning the transport industry and for studying the development scale and speed of the transport industry.

Freight Ton–kilometers(Passenger–kilometers) refer to the sum of the products of the volume of transported cargo (passengers) multiplying by the transport distance, usually using ton-kilometer and passenger-kilometer as units for measurement. Normally, the shortest distance between the departure station and the destination station (i.e., the payable distance) is the basis to calculate the freight ton-kilometers. This is an important indicator to show the total results of the transport industry, to prepare and examine the transport plan and to measure the efficiency, the labour productivity and the unit cost of transport.

The formula is as follows:

Freight Ton-kilometers(Passenger-kilometers)=Σ {Freight (Passenger) Traffic × Distance of Transportation}

Measuring unit: ton-kilometer (person-kilometer)

Possession of Civil Motor Vehicles refer to the total numbers of vehicles that are registered and received vehicles license tags according to the Work Standard for Motor Vehicles Registration formulated by the Transport Management Office under the department of public security at the end of the reference period. They are divided into categories. According to the structure of motor vehicles, they are divided into passenger vehicles, trucks and others; according to ownership into private vehicles and vehicles for the unit' s use; according to kind of usage into working vehicles and non-working vehicles; and according to size of vehicles into large passenger vehicles, medium-sized passenger vehicles, small passenger vehicles and mini passenger vehicles,heavytrucks, light-heavy trucks, light trucks and mini-trucks.

Business Volume of Post and Telecommunications refers to the total amount of post and telecommunications services, expressed in value terms, provided by the post and telecommunications departments for the society. Post and telecommunication services can be classified asletters, parcels, remittance, issue of newspapers and magazines, fast mail service, express mail service, savings deposits, stamps for collection, public and individual telegraph service, facsimiles, long-distance telephone service,leasing of telephone lines, urban paging service, mobile telephone service, data transfer and transmission, etc. The accounting approach is to multiply the service products of all types with their average unit price (constant price) to get sum of business value, plus income from other services such as leasing of telephone lines and equipment, maintenance of telephone switchboards and lines on behalf of customers. This indicator reflects the overall results of post and telecommunications service during a given period, and is important to study the composition of business service and the development of post and telecommunications service.

The formula is as follows:

Business Volume of Post and Telecommunications= Σ (Transaction of Post and Telecommunication Service x Constant Price) + Income from Leasing, Maintenance and other Services

Mobile Telephone Subscribers refer to the persons who own mobile telephone numbers and are connected with the mobile telephone communication network through the mobile telephone switchboards. The number of subscribers is calculated by the subscribers who have completed registration at mobile communication business centers and entered into the mobile telephone network. One mobile telephone is taken as a subscriber.

Telephone Subscribers refer to subscribers that are connected to the public line telephone network provided with telephone services. Before 1997, telephone subscribers were classified as city subscribers and village subscribers. City subscribers referred to those connected to city telephone networks in county towns and cities, while village subscribers referred to those connected to village telephone stations at and below counties. Since 1997, the classification of telephone subscribers was modified on the basis of physical location of the subscribers as Urban telephone subscribers and rural telephone subscribers , which is different from the previous classification of categorizing local telephones and rural telephones , while the definition of total subscribers and total number of telephones remain unchanged.

Rural Telephone Subscribers refer to telephone subscribers, located at towns under county town and country, that are connected to the public line telephone network.

Capacity of Office Telephone Exchanges refers to the capacity (measured in gate) of telephone exchanges installed in the offices of local telecommunication service providers for communication between fixed telephones. It includes the capacity of both manual and automatic exchanges in use and for stand-by purpose. Equipment with expansion function is to be counted by the expanded capacity.

Broadband Connection Terminals refer to the connection terminals to internet users actually installed and put into operation, including connection terminals for xDSL, connection terminals for LAN, and other connection terminals for xDSL. N-ISDN connection terminals are not included.

16 国内贸易

DOMESTIC TRADE

资料整理：马晓庆　杨　骏　左　宇　赵琳瑛　胡树建
Data management：Ma Xiaoqing　Yang Jun　Zuo Yu　Zhao Linying　Hu Shujian
数据审核：栾立森
Data audit：Luan Lisen

第十六部分　国内贸易

一、简要说明

本章资料主要包括社会消费品零售总额，批发零售贸易业商品购、销等情况，限额以上批发零售贸易业主要商品销售情况，限额以上批发零售贸易和住宿餐饮企业财务状况、经济效益，以及交易市场情况，由西安市统计局贸易外经处提供。

二、主要指标

社会消费品零售总额（亿元）	3093.89	比上年增长	12.8%
#批发零售贸易业零售额	2830.90	比上年增长	13.5%

16 DOMESTIC TRADE

Ⅰ.Brief Introduction

Content of this chapter consists of total retail sales of consumer goods, sails data on commodity purchasing and sails of wholesale and retail trade, sales data on primary goods exceeds quotation, financial, economic performance and market data on wholesale and retail trade and food services industry exceeds quotation. Data in this chapter is compiled and provided by Trade and Foreign Economy Division of the Xi'an Bureau of Statistics.

Ⅱ.Maior Indicators

		Increase over Preceding Year
Total Retail Sales of Consumer Goods (100 mil. yuan)	3093.89	12.8%
Retail Sales of Wholesale and Retail Enterprises	2830.90	13.5%

16-1 主要年份社会消费品零售额

Total Retail Sales of Consumer Goods in Representative Years

单位：亿元 (100 million yuan)

年 份 Year	社会消费品零售总额 Total Retail Sales of Consumer Goods	城镇 Urban	乡村 Village	批发和零售业 Wholesale Trades and Retail Trades	住宿和餐饮业 Accommodation and Catering Trade	其他行业 Others
1978	12.70	8.82	3.88	11.01	0.53	0.21
1979	13.94	9.88	4.06	11.88	0.60	0.21
1980	15.88	11.53	4.35	13.05	0.80	0.20
1981	17.41	12.85	4.56	14.31	0.80	0.19
1982	18.54	13.79	4.75	15.25	0.88	0.27
1983	20.82	15.14	5.68	16.95	1.03	0.32
1984	24.87	19.13	5.74	19.47	1.29	0.46
1985	32.92	26.09	6.83	25.04	1.69	0.48
1986	37.50	29.25	8.25	28.88	1.97	0.64
1987	43.86	34.62	9.24	33.32	2.50	0.49
1988	59.65	47.74	11.91	44.84	2.97	0.78
1989	68.05	54.60	13.45	54.41	2.98	0.76
1990	72.77	59.42	13.35	57.46	3.79	0.90
1991	81.04	66.93	14.11	60.35	4.43	1.26
1992	100.84	89.17	11.67	71.86	6.13	2.30
1993	115.38	104.41	10.97	75.99	7.49	2.71
1994	144.64	131.56	13.08	89.79	9.12	3.43
1995	186.60	165.98	20.62	115.46	11.97	3.73
1996	222.94	198.19	24.75	145.05	15.83	4.02
1997	264.47	238.17	26.30	169.08	22.12	4.17
1998	291.45	257.39	34.06	183.43	30.97	4.27
1999	323.37	283.32	40.05	207.96	34.78	4.85
2000	360.42	317.12	43.30	232.89	41.42	5.43
2001	406.21	358.97	47.24	265.25	48.87	5.86
2002	459.76	409.86	49.90	309.36	51.42	6.45
2003	502.65	449.62	53.03	440.28	53.30	9.07
2004	578.60	520.94	57.66	509.60	56.87	12.13
2005	670.56	604.63	65.93	592.77	63.59	14.20
2006	784.95	708.31	76.64	694.03	74.77	16.15
2007	936.21	845.59	90.62	828.63	89.32	18.26
2008	1176.58	1063.93	112.65	1033.00	122.90	20.68
2009	1398.37	1336.41	61.96	1250.41	147.96	
2010	1678.01	1610.88	67.13	1497.71	180.30	
2011	2039.24	1968.41	70.83	1825.79	213.45	
2012	2400.67	2326.84	73.83	2156.49	244.18	
2013	2742.89	2657.49	85.40	2494.74	248.15	
2014	3093.89	2996.43	97.46	2830.90	262.99	

注：依据2008年第二次经济普查数据，对2005-2007年数据进行调整。
依据2013年第三次经济普查数据，对2009年—2013年数据进行调整。
2009年以前按经营单位所在地分为市和县及县以下。
2002年以前按行业分组中不包括制造业零售额和农业对非农业居民零售额。

16-2 社会消费品零售总额

Total Retail Sales of Consumer Goods

单位：亿元　　　　(100 million yuan)

分 类	Classify	金额（2013年） Sum	金额（2014年） Sum
社会消费品零售总额	**Total Retail Sales of Consumer Goods**	**2742.89**	**3093.89**
（一）按销售单位所在地分	Grouped by Region		
（1）城镇	Urban	2657.49	2996.43
#城区	District	2251.84	2596.00
（2）乡村	Village	85.40	97.46
（二）按行业分	Grouped by Sector		
（1）批发业	Wholesale Enterprises	422.14	479.55
限额以上单位	Enterprises Above Designated Size	366.91	421.18
限额以下单位	Enterprises Below Designated Size and Self-employed Laborers	55.23	58.37
（2）零售业	Retail Enterprises	2072.60	2351.35
限额以上单位	Enterprises Above Designated Size	1513.83	1761.41
限额以下单位	Enterprises Below Designated Size and Self-employed Laborers	558.77	589.94
（3）住宿和餐饮业	Accommodation and Catering Trade	248.15	262.99
限额以下单位	Enterprises Above Designated Size	104.85	99.94
限额以上单位	Enterprises Below Designated Size and Self-employed Laborers	143.30	163.05
（4）其他行业	Others		

注：2013年为第三次经济普查数据。

16-3 各区县社会消费品零售总额

Total Retail Sales of Consumer Goods by Region

单位：亿元 (100 million yuan)

区 县	Region	社会消费品零售总额（2013年）Total Retail Sales of Consumer Goods（2013）	批发零售贸易业零售额 Wholesale and Retail Trade of Retail Sales	住宿餐饮业零售额 Accommodation and Catering Trade of Retail Sales	社会消费品零售总额（2014年）Total Retail Sales of Consumer Goods（2014）	批发零售贸易业零售额 Wholesale and Retail Trade of Retail Sales	住宿餐饮业零售额 Accommodation and Catering Trade of Retail Sales
新城区	Xincheng	446.06	423.22	22.84	499.78	475.72	24.06
碑林区	Beilin	445.11	396.53	48.58	505.87	453.88	51.99
莲湖区	Lianhu	368.62	334.63	33.99	413.00	377.21	35.79
灞桥区	Baqiao	132.26	124.31	7.95	154.28	145.90	8.38
未央区	Weiyang	423.72	403.48	20.24	480.79	459.33	21.46
雁塔区	Yanta	534.30	480.35	53.95	596.50	539.03	57.47
阎良区	Yanliang	31.37	26.42	4.95	34.93	29.68	5.25
临潼区	Lintong	64.08	57.17	6.91	72.63	65.36	7.27
长安区	Chang'an	144.94	114.52	30.42	164.00	131.96	32.04
蓝田县	Lantian	45.74	40.19	5.55	51.57	45.73	5.84
周至县	Zhouzhi	30.71	27.99	2.72	34.63	31.76	2.87
户 县	Huxian	50.97	44.13	6.84	57.52	50.32	7.20
高陵县	Gaoling	25.01	21.81	3.20	28.40	25.02	3.38

注：2013年为第三次经济普查数据。

16-4 限额以上批发零售贸易企业财务状况（2014年）

单位：万元

分类	Classify	单位数（个）Number (unit)	资产总计 Total Assets	流动资产合计 Circulating Funds	固定资产合计 Total Fixed Assets
总计	**Totai**	**803**	**17960643.9**	**13095063.4**	**1544862.6**
一、批发企业	**Wholesale Enterprises**	**342**	**9401683.8**	**7566349.5**	**481385.3**
1. 按登记注册类型分组	Grouped by Category of Commodities				
内资企业	Domestic Funded Enterprises	331	7864906.1	6361021	468727.3
国有	State-owned Enterprises	22	1245748.9	1052844.1	98199.3
集体	Collective-owned Enterprises	4	69569.6	34064.3	5379.3
股份合作	Corperative Enterprises				
联营	Joint Ownership Enterprises				
国有联营	State Joint Ownership Enterprises				
集体联营	Collective Joint Ownership Enterprises				
国有与集体联营	Joint State-collective Enterprises				
其他联营	Others Joint Ownership Enterprises				
有限责任公司	Limited Liability Corporrations	192	4104026.0	3567766.5	132758.5
国有独资公司	State Funded Corporations	8	1036579.1	854957	38927.3
其他有限责任公司	Other Limited Liability Corporrations	184	3067446.9	2712809.5	93831.2
股份有限公司	Other Limited Liability Corporrations	5	1058455.5	494716.8	156660.7
私营	Other Limited Liability Corporrations	106	1386281.1	1211426.3	75107.5
私营独资	Private-funded Enterprises	1	1419.3	1383.1	36.2
私营合伙	Private Partnership Enterprises				
私营有限责任公司	Private Limited Liability Corporations	102	1301332.4	1143375.1	73677.8
私营股份有限公司	Private Share-holding Corporations Ltd.	3	83529.4	66668.1	1393.5
其他	Other Enterprises	2	825.0	203.0	622.0
港澳台商投资	Enterprises with Funds from Hong Kong, Macao &Taiwan	4	140401.1	132536.3	6917.7
外商投资	Foreign Funded Enterprises	7	1396376.6	1072792.2	5740.3
2. 按国民经济行业分组	Grouped by Sector				

Financial Stares of Enterprises above Designated Size

in Wholesale and Retail（2014）

(10 000 yuan)

固定资产原价 Original Value of Fixed Assets	累计折旧 Accumulated Depreciation	负债合计 Total Liabilities	流动负债合计 Circulating Liabilities	非流动负债 Non-Circulating Liabilities	所有者权益合计 Total Owners' Equities	实收资本 Paid in Capital	营业收入 Total Revenue	主营业务收入 Revenue from Principal Business
2248552.5	**708293.5**	**13915709.2**	**13293326.7**	**619382.4**	**4044934.7**	**2347881.5**	**39599655.0**	**39287541.2**
721375.8	**240299.1**	**7638509.6**	**7496992.6**	**141516.9**	**1763174.2**	**1177153.3**	**24004290.4**	**23922291.1**
703236.5	234817.8	6317640.9	6176480.4	141160.4	1547265.2	1020181.8	20466105.6	20393595.2
155595.9	57717.7	810794.1	805458.2	5335.9	434954.8	63802.8	3392641.1	3369901.1
8710.4	3342.9	72539.1	44212.1	28327.0	-2969.5	4768.8	12414.1	12414.1
215675.8	82969.4	3471890.8	3411421.2	60469.5	632135.2	432843.7	11351179.9	11338269.5
54033.9	15106.6	843081.8	835385	7696.8	193497.3	51921.3	2584789.8	2583154.6
161641.9	67862.8	2628809.0	2576036.2	52772.7	438637.9	380922.4	8766390.1	8755114.9
207526.3	50747.5	782953	776037.2	6915.8	275502.5	278029.1	3233799.2	3207246.5
115044.1	39978.3	1179293.5	1139181.3	40112.2	206987.6	240082.8	2461308.3	2451001.0
125.5	89.3	1353.8	1353.8		65.5	50	4336.3	4336.3
112067	38430.9	1126686.3	1098000	28686.3	174646.1	220415	2293102.9	2282795.6
2851.6	1458.1	51253.4	39827.5	11425.9	32276	19617.8	163869.1	163869.1
684.0	62.0	170.4	170.4		654.6	654.6	14763.0	14763.0
9042.7	2125	120527.4	120527.4		19873.7	4073.6	357864.5	357385
9096.6	3356.3	1200341.3	1199984.8	356.5	196035.3	152897.9	3180320.3	3171310.9

16-4 续表1

单位：万元

分 类	Classify	营业成本 Total Cost	主营业务成本 Cost of Principal Business	营业税金及附加 Taxs and Other Changes	主营业务税金及附加 Taxs and Other Changes on Principal Business
总计	**Totai**	**36212534.9**	**36065497.0**	**206716.4**	**201731.5**
一、批发企业	**Wholesale Enterprises**	**22733888.7**	**22655548.0**	**89291.6**	**88548.6**
1. 按登记注册类型分组	Grouped by Category of Commodities				
内资企业	Domestic Funded Enterprises	19271612.6	19198028.0	88386.2	87643.2
国有	State-owned Enterprises	3050696.8	3024670.8	65842.5	65647.6
集体	Collective-owned Enterprises	9865.0	9865.0	548.9	548.9
股份合作	Corperative Enterprises				
联营	Joint Ownership Enterprises				
国有联营	State Joint Ownership Enterprises				
集体联营	Collective Joint Ownership Enterprises				
国有与集体联营	Joint State-collective Enterprises				
其他联营	Others Joint Ownership Enterprises				
有限责任公司	Limited Liability Corporations	10780741.8	10774099.0	11387.7	11271.5
国有独资公司	State Funded Corporations	2494961.2	2494915.1	1157.9	1139.0
其他有限责任公司	Other Limited Liability Corporations	8285780.6	8279183.5	10229.8	10132.5
股份有限公司	Other Limited Liability Corporations	3056459.7	3021460.8	4893.1	4659.7
私营	Other Limited Liability Corporations	2360249.3	2354332.8	5714.0	5515.5
私营独资	Private-funded Enterprises	4101.8	4101.8	1.3	1.3
私营合伙	Private Partnership Enterprises				
私营有限责任公司	Private Limited Liability Corporations	2208704.2	2202787.7	4837.8	4639.3
私营股份有限公司	Private Share-holding Corporations Ltd.	147443.3	147443.3	874.9	874.9
其他	Other Enterprises	13600.0	13600.0		
港澳台商投资	Enterprises with Funds from Hong Kong, Macao &Taiwan	308287.7	308283.5	565.0	565.0
外商投资	Foreign Funded Enterprises	3153988.4	3149236.9	340.4	340.4
2. 按国民经济行业分组	Grouped by Sector				

continued 1

(10 000 yuan)

销售费用 Sale Expenses	管理费用 Managenment Expenses	财务费用 Financial Expenses	营业利润 Business Profits	利润总额 Total Profits	应付职工薪酬 Salary Payable	本年应交增值税 Value Added Tax Payable
1374384.5	**656300.2**	**213728.8**	**956548.8**	**883976.3**	**672478**	**460727**
551234.7	**265393.8**	**93256.2**	**278665.7**	**242954.8**	**275637**	**150694**
513512.1	250511.5	81462.5	268012.5	231644.1	252992	139289
59005.0	54662.9	11193.7	151383.0	160663.0	73964	66921
641.2	1258.2	339.7	153.1	404.7	516	16
303930.1	140425.9	34162.7	86543.4	70218.3	103782	47065
46005.6	29943.4	1204.3	12654.8	8488.4	15693	15026
257924.5	110482.5	32958.4	73888.6	61729.9	88089	32039
107908.5	21859.4	9862.6	32356.2	7217.8	46896	15443
41872.4	32209.5	25804	-3235.9	-7340.3	27263	9844
159.2	20.2	48.8	5.0	5.0	48	13
37927.9	30367.9	24005.4	-11598.1	-11349.2	18583	9335
3785.3	1821.4	1749.8	8357.2	4003.9	8632	496
154.9	95.6	99.8	812.7	480.6	571	
29202.3	9561.9	5.1	10242.5	10257.4	17766	5236
8520.3	5320.4	11788.6	410.7	1053.3	4879	6169

16-4 续表2

单位：万元

分类	Classify	单位数（个）Number (unit)	资产总计 Total Assets	流动资产合计 Circulating Funds	固定资产合计 Total Fixed Assets
农、林、牧产品批发	Wholesale of Agricultural,Forestry and Animal Husbandry Products	3	76124.8	38879.9	8056.6
食品、饮料及烟草制品批发	Wholesale of food Beverages and Tobaccos	28	586223.1	455759.7	79177.0
纺织、服装及家庭服务器批发	Wholesale of Textiles, Garments and Daily Articles	26	590026	547065.1	30368.3
文化、体育用品及器材批发	Wholesale of Culture, Sports Applionces and Equipments	17	221388.8	138121.3	21266.0
医药及医疗器材批发	Wholesale of Medicines and Medical Appliances	57	971109.9	912489.9	11664.5
矿产品、建材及化工产品批发	Wholesale of Mineral Products, Building Materials and Chemical Products	135	5619110.9	4271811.5	251515.1
机械设备、五金产品及电子产品批发	Wholesale of Machinery, Hardware, and Electronic Equipment	70	1318857.3	1186201.6	76944.3
贸易经纪与代理	Trade Borker and Agency	2	10009.5	9657.9	351.6
其他批发	Other wholesale not Classified Elsewhere	4	8833.5	6362.6	2041.9
二、零售企业	**Retail Trade**	**461**	**8558960.1**	**5528713.9**	**1063477.3**
1. 按登记注册类型分组	Grouped by Category of Commodities				
内资	Domestic Funded Enterprises	419	6179168.6	4330397.2	860726.6
国有	State-owned Enterprises	10	172888.4	137533.4	34283.3
集体	Collective-owned Enterprises	21	10857.1	3973.0	5105.4
股份合作	Share-holding Cooperative Enterprises				
联营	Joint Ownership Enterprises				
国有联营	State Joint Ownership Enterprises				
集体联营	Collective Joint Ownership Enterprises				
国有与集体联营	Joint State-collective Enterprises				
其他联营	Others Joint Ownership Enterprises				
有限责任公司	Limited Liability Corporations	252	3539992.1	2483821.3	481433.2
国有独资	State Funded Corporations	4	93569.6	66017.0	20343.6

continued 2

(10 000 yuan)

固定资产原价 Original Value of Fixed Assets	累计折旧 Accumulated Depreciation	负债合计 Total Liabilities	流动负债合计 Circulating Liabilities	非流动负债 Non-Circulating Liabilities	所有者权益合计 Total Owners' Equities	实收资本 Paid in Capital	营业收入 Total Revenue	主营业务收入 Revenue from Principal Business
11555.0	3819.5	75314.5	47580.4	27734.1	810.3	9098.0	12663.6	12663.6
123476.3	44341.0	150360.9	133115.0	17245.9	435862.2	52654.7	1828650.2	1827250.5
61327.3	30959.0	515602.7	510629.8	4972.9	74423.3	48013.3	2545000.0	2540807.7
28855.7	7618.5	135815.9	127912.4	7903.5	85572.9	50161.0	337880.1	337243.1
21981.7	10340.5	876427.5	855417.2	21010.3	94682.4	79082.7	2109970.0	2105607.6
368879.9	117258.5	4673248.0	4625430.5	47817.4	945862.9	854772.0	14957596.5	14910670.7
101971.5	25027.2	1199212.3	1185899.8	13312.5	119645.0	77820.5	2155416.2	2131028.4
426.2	74.6	8810.2	8489.9	320.3	1199.3	1251.1	31939.6	31845.3
2902.2	860.3	3717.6	2517.6	1200.0	5115.9	4300.0	25174.2	25174.2
1527176.7	**467994.4**	**6277199.6**	**5796334.1**	**477865.5**	**2281760.5**	**1170728.2**	**15595364.6**	**15365250.1**
1239914.3	382602.1	4667298.5	4281495.1	385803.4	1511870.1	759843.3	11425392	11257226.5
40819.9	6536.6	135178.3	85638.7	49539.6	37710.1	3921.0	261813.3	255386.5
6057.5	997.7	8948.0	8280.6	667.4	1909.1	1874.6	49225.6	49225.6
663811.6	185747.3	2534783.5	2373534.5	161249.0	1005208.6	533173.6	7546920.9	7417356.2
28780.4	8436.8	76754.8	67373.8	9381.0	16814.8	4941.9	101300.3	98713.1

16-4 续表3

单位：万元

分 类	Classify	营业成本 Total Cost	主营业务成本 Cost of Principal Business	营业税金及附加 Taxes and Other Changes	主营业务税金及附加 Taxes and Other Changes on Principal Business
农、林、牧产品批发	Wholesale of Agricultural,Forestry and Animal Husbandry Products	10138.0	10138.0	859.3	859.3
食品、饮料及烟草制品批发	Wholesale of food Beverages and Tobaccos	1391524.1	1391508.2	66268.8	66268.3
纺织、服装及家庭服务器批发	Wholesale of Textiles, Garments and Daily Articles	2405759.4	2403340.4	4255.9	4248.2
文化、体育用品及器材批发	Wholesale of Culture, Sports Applionces and Equipments	301709.8	301625.9	1826.4	1807.5
医药及医疗器材批发	Wholesale of Medicines and Medical Appliances	2011555.3	2011485.2	1915.5	1823.9
矿产品、建材及化工产品批发	Wholesale of Mineral Products, Building Materials and Chemical Products	14554220.0	14492169.0	9677.7	9452.6
机械设备、五金产品及电子产品批发	Wholesale of Machinery, Hardware, and Electronic Equipment	2009281.7	1995581	4414.9	4015.7
贸易经纪与代理	Trade Borker and Agency	28632.3	28632.3	1.5	1.5
其他批发	Other wholesale not Classified Elsewhere	21068.6	21068.6	71.6	71.6
二、零售企业	**Retail Trade**	**13478646.2**	**13409948.5**	**117424.8**	**113182.9**
1. 按登记注册类型分组	Grouped by Category of Commodities				
内资	Domestic Funded Enterprises	9902413.0	9839220.1	102035.4	99909.7
国有	State-owned Enterprises	226687.9	226069.2	1488.3	1474.7
集体	Collective-owned Enterprises	44366.7	44366.7	866.8	866.8
股份合作	Share-holding Cooperative Enterprises				
联营	Joint Ownership Enterprises				
国有联营	State Joint Ownership Enterprises				
集体联营	Collective Joint Ownership Enterprises				
国有与集体联营	Joint State-collective Enterprises				
其他联营	Others Joint Ownership Enterprises				
有限责任公司	Limited Liability Corporations	6559692.2	6529367.1	61485.7	59542.8
国有独资	State Funded Corporations	82511.1	82413.2	201.0	85.0

continued 3

(10 000 yuan)

销售费用 Sale Expenses	管理费用 Managenment Expenses	财务费用 Financial Expenses	营业利润 Business Profits	利润总额 Total Profits	应付职工薪酬 Salary Payable	本年应交增值税 Value Added Tax Payable
835.7	1248.6	651.1	-677.1	1057.9	618	899
124591.5	74244.2	6441.8	167079.4	171026.7	82899	48297
54384.3	23797.2	350.8	56793.4	41337.0	40419	9111
9725.3	10489.8	-16.2	14214.5	14339.0	6802	858
41366.6	27565.8	15187.9	11884.6	11881.9	24895	12026
258285.4	88015.5	66369.8	-13613.6	-15563.9	85197	51941
57505.8	38309.9	4429.6	41724.3	18057.5	33583	27171
2229.1	456.2	-152.6	773.1	441.0	535	184
2311.0	1266.6	-6.0	487.1	377.7	689	207
823149.8	**390906.4**	**120472.6**	**677883.1**	**641021.5**	**396841**	**310033**
541640.5	307380.3	98427.5	487127.6	446069.6	295855	243250
13614.8	14731.2	155.6	4931.1	4888.6	14910	6352
1317.0	2001.2	53.9	618.0	633.8	1961	303
362698.4	189174.1	45384.0	324557.2	317530.9	192408	142039
11259.8	5373.1	-292.0	2244.7	3149.8	10974	12127

16-4 续表4

单位：万元

分类	Classify	单位数（个）Number (unit)	资产总计 Total Assets	流动资产合计 Circulating Funds	固定资产合计 Total Fixed Assets
其他有限责任公司	Other Limited Liability Corporations	248	3446422.5	2417804.3	461089.6
股份有限公司	Share-holding Corporations Ltd.	7	1454213.8	916163.9	254573.3
私营	Private Enterprises	126	999828.4	788258.8	84918.8
私营独资	Private-funded Enterprises	1	1511.6	613.7	110.2
私营合伙	Private Partnership Enterprises	2	1018.3	742.6	195.5
私营有限责任公司	Private Limited Liability Corporations	115	949796.1	759545.1	74818.0
私营股份有限公司	Private Share-holding Corporations Ltd.	8	47502.4	27357.4	9795.1
其他	Other	3	1388.8	646.8	412.6
港澳台商投资	Enterprises with Funds from Hong Kong, Macao &Taiwan	22	1786043.5	922782.1	113586.7
外商投资	Foreign Funded Enterprises	20	593748.0	275534.6	89164
2. 按国民经济行业分组	Grouped by Sector				
综合零售	Integrated Retail	101	2846751.9	1769516.9	422451.4
食品、饮料及烟草制品专门零售	Food, Beverages and Tobaccos Special Retail Trade	26	642836.2	409460.1	146873.6
纺织、服装及日用品专门零售	Special Retail of Textiles,Garments and Daily Consumer Articles	26	348063.8	116886.7	76291.7
文化、体育用品及器材专门零售	Retail of Culture,Sports Appliances and Equipments	21	285163.4	244418.5	32083.3
医药及医疗器材专门零售	Retail of Medicines and Medical Appliances	22	218340.3	199766.7	9231.1
汽车、摩托车、燃料及零配件专门零售	Retail of Motor Vehicles,Motorcycles, Fuel and Parts	190	3215125.7	2032763.2	225843.5
家用电器及电子产品专门零售	Special Retail of Household Electric Appliances and Electronic Products	39	621999.7	546360.9	51134.8
五金、家具及室内装饰材料专门零售	Special Retail of Hardware,Furniture and Decoration Materials	28	342327.0	187274.6	86938.4
货摊、无店铺及其他零售业	Non-shop and Other Retail	8	38352.1	22266.3	12629.5

continued 4

(10 000 yuan)

固定资产原价 Original Value of Fixed Assets	累计折旧 Accumulated Depreciation	负债合计 Total Liabilities	流动负债合计 Circulating Liabilities	非流动负债 Non-Circulating Liabilities	所有者权益合计 Total Owners' Equities	实收资本 Paid in Capital	营业收入 Total Revenue	主营业务收入 Revenue from Principal Business
635031.2	177310.5	2458028.7	2306160.7	151868.0	988393.8	528231.7	7445620.6	7318643.1
375641.4	121068.1	1218820.0	1081176.4	137643.6	235393.8	80531.8	1039993.7	1017723.7
153021.0	68102.1	768926.5	732455.7	36470.8	230901.9	139617.3	2520477.6	2510573.6
160.6	50.3	29.3	29.3		1482.3	78.7	5637.0	5637.0
249.9	54.4	1108.2	1058.2	50.0	-89.9	130.0	6387.5	6387.5
123849.7	49031.7	723898.9	687742.3	36156.6	225897.2	135798.6	2316119.6	2306323.3
28760.8	18965.7	43890.1	43625.9	264.2	3612.3	3610.0	192333.5	192225.8
562.9	150.3	642.2	409.2	233.0	746.6	725.0	6960.9	6960.9
157639.9	44053.2	1304195.9	1247823.6	56372.3	481847.6	151860.7	1996787.0	1950650.2
129622.5	41339.1	305705.2	267015.4	35689.8	288042.8	259024.2	2173185.6	2157373.4
605297.7	183133.2	2024384.4	1824919.4	199465.0	822367.5	361894.6	3199535.6	3020560.2
219060.4	72186.8	586261.3	512126.2	74135.1	56574.9	35352.3	193324.5	191381.2
92752.6	16506.5	136016.1	100027.0	35989.1	212047.7	97650.3	1347523.3	1344838.0
39746.2	10662.9	170767.6	150785.2	16982.4	114395.8	47924.8	269174.5	266231.1
14635.2	5404.1	207821.7	204625.1	3196.6	10518.6	20255.3	257346.4	255231.9
322287.9	97247.8	2603980.9	2489317.7	114663.2	611144.8	473801.3	6829560.6	6808282.0
72860.2	21725.4	283808.7	282553.5	1255.2	338191	57282.3	1686591.4	1670206.7
129317.1	42537.8	247108.2	215008.5	32099.7	95218.8	53264.9	1463312.4	1460066.7
31219.4	18589.9	17050.7	16971.5	79.2	21301.4	23302.4	348995.9	348452.3

16-4 续表5

单位：万元

分类	Classify	营业成本 Total Cost	主营业务成本 Cost of Principal Business	营业税金及附加 Taxs and Other Changes	主营业务税金及附加 Taxs and Other Changes on Principal Business
其他有限责任公司	Other Limited Liability Corporations	6477181.1	6446953.9	61284.7	59457.8
股份有限公司	Share-holding Corporations Ltd.	867243.9	866264.5	14304.8	14304.8
私营	Private Enterprises	2197845.7	2166576	23883.7	23714.5
私营独资	Private-funded Enterprises	4632.0	4632.0	81.5	81.5
私营合伙	Private Partnership Enterprises	5600.1	5600.1	42.1	42.1
私营有限责任公司	Private Limited Liability Corporations	2046360.9	2015091.3	23054.8	22965.7
私营股份有限公司	Private Share-holding Corporations Ltd.	141252.7	141252.6	705.3	625.2
其他	Other	6576.6	6576.6	6.1	6.1
港澳台商投资	Enterprises with Funds from Hong Kong, Macao &Taiwan	1643077.9	1638375.8	8134.1	7746.9
外商投资	Foreign Funded Enterprises	1933155.3	1932352.6	7255.3	5526.3
2. 按国民经济行业分组	Grouped by Sector				
综合零售	Integrated Retail	2547829.3	2528204.4	29500.3	26804.9
食品、饮料及烟草制品专门零售	Food, Beverages and Tobaccos Special Retail Trade	166207.5	163398.2	1155.8	1155.8
纺织、服装及日用品专门零售	Special Retail of Textiles,Garments and Daily Consumer Articles	1118010.2	1090499.7	17144.6	16551.5
文化、体育用品及器材专门零售	Retail of Culture,Sports Appliances and Equipments	211220.1	211012.3	4018.7	3899.9
医药及医疗器材专门零售	Retail of Medicines and Medical Appliances	220654.8	220490.0	670.0	670.0
汽车、摩托车、燃料及零配件专门零售	Retail of Motor Vehicles,Motorcycles, Fuel and Parts	6267986.3	6253680.7	9586.0	9499.3
家用电器及电子产品专门零售	Special Retail of Household Electric Appliances and Electronic Products	1422851.8	1422141.8	23975.6	23420.5
五金、家具及室内装饰材料专门零售	Special Retail of Hardware,Furniture and Decoration Materials	1236575.7	1233555.7	30577.1	30464.3
货摊、无店铺及其他零售业	Non-shop and Other Retail	287310.5	286965.7	796.7	716.7

continued 5

(10 000 yuan)

销售费用 Sale Expenses	管理费用 Managenment Expenses	财务费用 Financial Expenses	营业利润 Business Profits	利润总额 Total Profits	应付职工薪酬 Salary Payable	本年应交增值税 Value Added Tax Payable
351438.6	183801.0	45676.0	322312.5	314381.1	181434	129912
48406.4	44975.4	33761.6	47818.4	12130.5	22530	5619
115307.9	56458.6	19062.3	109170.6	110853.5	63834	88937
217.0	316.0	4.3	386.2	386.2	194	51
456.1	129.9		159.3	246.9	435	92
109445.6	52330.0	18112.2	68080.5	70248.9	59739	87102
5189.2	3682.7	945.8	40544.6	39971.5	3466	1691
296.0	39.8	10.1	32.3	32.3	212	
126612.1	49681.1	14148.0	156809.0	161895.8	53115	47406
154897.2	33845.0	7897.1	33946.5	33056.1	47871	19377
338604.7	151897	25467.7	104769.1	109855.6	161266	60117
17020.7	10924.2	16690.2	-2890.1	1492.5	8450	385
75478.6	27991.0	4851.8	104878.5	67091.9	20210	16218
22662.5	13172.3	805.8	16642.5	3728.1	17140	2357
22698.6	8814.2	1580.4	2922.7	3182.1	22092	3593
210357	114613.6	58342.9	166089.2	168063.0	122556	148697
93637.2	35029.2	2008.5	109995.6	120536.7	28584	38398
22456.1	24734.4	10290.4	138986.7	129908.5	11117	36844
20234.4	3730.5	434.9	36488.9	37163.1	5426	3424

16-5 限额以上住宿和餐饮企业财务状况（2014年）

单位：万元

分 类	Classify	单位数（个） Number (unit)	资产总计 Total Assets	流动资产合计 Circulating Funds	固定资产合计 Total Fixed Assets
总计	**Total**	**538**	**2746934.7**	**977478.4**	**1206238.1**
一、住宿业	**Hotel Services**	**223**	**1929339.9**	**583731.7**	**1022977.5**
1.按登记注册类型分组	Grouped by Type of Registration				
内资	Domestic Funded Enterprises	207	1559790.0	439866.1	828783.6
国有	State-owned Enterprises	26	171432.7	24140.5	105872.0
集体	Collective-owned Enterprises	2	2951.8	285.0	1446.9
股份合作	Cooperative Enterprises				
联营	Joint Ownership Enterprises				
国有联营	State Joint Ownership Enterprises				
集体联营	Collective Joint Ownership Enterprises				
国有与集体联营	Joint State-collective Enterprises				
其他联营	Others Joint Ownership Enterprises				
有限责任公司	Limited Liability Corporations	115	1099392.6	253552.3	640224.5
国有独资公司	State Sole Funded Corporations	4	88340.2	4226.8	42488.6
其他有限责任公司	Other Limited Liability Corporations	111	1011052.4	249325.5	597735.9
股份有限公司	Share-holding Corporations Ltd.	2	8791.3	1550.0	7113.3
私营	Private Enterprises	62	277221.6	160338.3	74126.9
私营独资	Private-funded Enterprises	3	1500.9	592.1	879.6
私营合伙	Private Partnership Enterprises	1	242.0	78.2	85.2
私营有限责任公司	Private Limited Liability Corporations	56	272147.6	159085.2	71362.7
私营股份有限公司	Private Share-holding Corporations Ltd.	2	3331.1	582.8	1799.4
其他	Other Enterprises				
港澳台商投资	Enterprises with Funds from Hong Kong, Macao &Taiwan	6	151024.4	34607.3	95758.7
外商投资	Foreign Funded Enterprises	10	218525.5	109258.3	98435.2
2.按国民经济行业分组	Grouped by Sector				
旅游饭店	Tourist Hotel	169	1811971.8	533232.2	980113.7
一般旅馆	Normal Hotel	49	83256	35717.1	34566.8
其他住宿业	Others	5	34112.1	14782.4	8297.0

Finacial Status of Catering Eenterprises Above Designated Size（2014）

(10 000 yuan)

固定资产原价 Original Value of Fixed Assets	累计折旧 Accumulated Depreciation	负债合计 Total Liabilities	流动负债合计 Circulating Liabilities	非流动负债 Non-Circulating Liabilities	所有者权益合计 Total Owners' Equities	实收资本 Paid in Capital	营业收入 Total Revenue	主营业务收入 Revenue from Principal Business
1858715.0	**653440.5**	**2146284.8**	**1655376.4**	**490908.4**	**600649.9**	**880636.0**	**1228877.5**	**1208660.4**
1553320.4	**530342.9**	**1537883.7**	**1099879.9**	**438003.8**	**391456.2**	**627342.6**	**545939.0**	**536373.8**
1184018.7	355235.1	1178096.0	909600.4	268495.6	381694.0	490788.5	444069.3	436744.7
168739.0	62867.0	110580.2	57780.3	52799.9	60852.5	40271.4	56999.4	56211.8
3037.6	1590.7	710.8	68.3	642.5	2241.0	2241.0	2392.8	2392.8
876516.8	236292.3	827335.2	703878.5	123456.7	272057.4	348145.8	276404.0	272495.4
82357.4	39868.8	75291.5	59492.5	15799.0	13048.7	29693.3	15689.5	14950.8
794159.4	196423.5	752043.7	644386.0	107657.7	259008.7	318452.5	260714.5	257544.6
10836.2	3722.9	7177.8	7177.8		1613.5	2185.5	4412.8	4412.8
124889.1	50762.2	232292.0	140695.5	91596.5	44929.6	97944.8	103860.3	101231.9
1090.0	210.4	1203.1	1203.1		297.8	930.0	1424.7	1424.7
110.5	25.3	27.0	27.0		215.0	200.0	324.1	324.1
121434.7	50072.0	228854.1	137267.6	91586.5	43293.5	93774.5	101015.1	98386.7
2253.9	454.5	2207.8	2197.8	10.0	1123.3	3040.3	1096.4	1096.4
166544.0	70785.3	96310.8	59051.4	37259.4	54713.6	69427.2	38944.6	38529.0
202757.7	104322.5	263476.9	131228.1	132248.8	-44951.4	67126.9	62925.1	61100.1
1488348.9	508235.2	1446045.5	1022119.8	423925.7	365926.3	581303.2	479619.8	471499.3
54380.8	19814.0	58802.2	45534.1	13268.1	24453.8	43859.4	53895.9	52451.2
10590.7	2293.7	33036.0	32226.0	810.0	1076.1	2180.0	12423.3	12423.3

16-5 续表1

单位：万元

分类	Classify	营业成本 Total Cost	主营业务成本 Cost of Principal Business
总计	**Total**	**524520.5**	**517471.7**
一、住宿业	**Hotel Services**	**181238.5**	**177719.2**
1.按登记注册类型分组	Grouped by Type of Registration		
内资	Domestic Funded Enterprises	150479.7	147583.0
国有	State-owned Enterprises	22915.9	22803.8
集体	Collective-owned Enterprises	1638.1	1638.1
股份合作	Cooperative Enterprises		
联营	Joint Ownership Enterprises		
国有联营	State Joint Ownership Enterprises		
集体联营	Collective Joint Ownership Enterprises		
国有与集体联营	Joint State-collective Enterprises		
其他联营	Others Joint Ownership Enterprises		
有限责任公司	Limited Liability Corporations	89158.9	88005.7
国有独资公司	State Sole Funded Corporations	4912.8	4912.8
其他有限责任公司	Other Limited Liability Corporations	84246.1	83092.9
股份有限公司	Share-holding Corporations Ltd.	848.2	848.2
私营	Private Enterprises	35918.6	34287.2
私营独资	Private-funded Enterprises	745.7	745.7
私营合伙	Private Partnership Enterprises	267.8	267.8
私营有限责任公司	Private Limited Liability Corporations	34347.5	32716.1
私营股份有限公司	Private Share-holding Corporations Ltd.	557.6	557.6
其他	Other Enterprises		
港澳台商投资	Enterprises with Funds from Hong Kong, Macao &Taiwan	12885.7	12723.3
外商投资	Foreign Funded Enterprises	17873.1	17412.9
2.按国民经济行业分组	Grouped by Sector		
旅游饭店	Tourist Hotel	160396.0	157380.8
一般旅馆	Normal Hotel	18813.2	18508.7
其他住宿业	Others	2029.3	1829.7

continued 1

(10 000 yuan)

营业税金及附加 Taxs and Other Changes		销售费用 Sale Expenses	管理费用 Managenment Expenses	财务费用 Financial Expenses	营业利润 Business Profits	利润总额 Total Profits	应付职工薪酬 Salary Payable	本年应交所得税 Value Added Tax Payable
	主营业务税金及附加 Taxs and Other Changes on Principal Business							
66521.9	**65927.4**	**427234.9**	**240148.8**	**32872.0**	**-61759.0**	**-56596.6**	**280461.4**	**6097.9**
30197.0	**29647.1**	**185720.6**	**163428.9**	**20732.8**	**-35651.9**	**-35021.2**	**138739.4**	**2711.0**
24672.6	24178.7	156272.6	133492.8	16432.0	-37567.6	-37220.8	116582.2	435.0
2982.8	2908.5	16910.0	16264.0	3027.8	-5112.2	-4064.7	14276.8	37.2
142.7	142.7	233.6	436.5	2.8	-60.9	-60.5	296.6	
15463.3	15109.1	99408.5	84826.6	8995.1	-21768.3	-21552.4	78236.2	268.1
759.4	759.4	5608.4	5092.8	304.4	-982.9	-1663.4	4631.3	
14703.9	14349.7	93800.1	79733.8	8690.7	-20785.4	-19889.0	73604.9	268.1
247.8	236.8	2209.0	513.4	2.3	591.0	595.8	956.8	
5836.0	5781.6	37511.5	31452.3	4404.0	-11217.2	-12139.0	22815.8	129.7
61.9	61.9	470.9	180.6	18.4	-52.8	-166.6	455.0	
16.2	16.2	65.0	20.0	9.0	-53.9	-53.9	66.0	
5712.7	5658.3	36322.4	30592.3	4340.1	-10255.0	-11063.0	21884.1	127.8
45.2	45.2	653.2	659.4	36.5	-855.5	-855.5	410.7	1.9
2051.1	2051.1	11991.5	11146.0	2588.5	-1706.3	-1378.9	8339.4	87.7
3473.3	3417.3	17456.5	18790.1	1712.3	3622.0	3578.5	13817.8	2188.3
26638.7	26274.0	163144.9	144535.7	18667.2	-34041.7	-33559.2	121772.0	2644.4
2856.4	2810.5	17363.1	13397.0	1627.5	-155.4	-66.4	12728.8	66.6
701.9	562.6	5212.6	5496.2	438.1	-1454.8	-1395.6	4238.6	

16-5 续表2

单位：万元

分 类	Classify	单位数（个） Number (unit)	资产总计 Total Assets	流动资产合 计 Circulating Funds	固定资产合 计 Total Fixed Assets
二、餐饮业	**Catering Trade**	**315**	**817594.8**	**393746.7**	**183260.6**
1.按登记注册类型分组	Grouped by Type of Registration				
内资	Domestic Funded Enterprises	301	652361.3	336071.5	134586.8
国有	State-owned Enterprises	3	5571.1	1535.5	3935.6
集体	Collective-owned Enterprises				
股份合作	Cooperative Enterprises				
联营	Joint Ownership Enterprises				
国有联营	State Joint Ownership Enterprises				
集体联营	Collective Joint Ownership Enterprises				
国有与集体联营	Joint State-collective Enterprises				
其他联营	Others Joint Ownership Enterprises				
有限责任公司	Limited Liability Corporations	172	404350.1	221662.6	101695.9
国有独资公司	State Sole Funded Corporations	2	3605.5	1301.7	2285.9
其他有限责任公司	Other Limited Liability Corporations	170	400744.6	220360.9	99410. 0
股份有限公司	Share-holding Corporations Ltd.	3	110257.3	43132.2	6404.9
私营	Private Enterprises	120	131501.4	69560.5	22423.8
私营独资	Private-funded Enterprises	12	3873.6	1095.9	796.6
私营合伙	Private Partnership Enterprises				
私营有限责任公司	Private Limited Liability Corporations	105	126830.7	67699	21595.8
私营股份有限公司	Private Share-holding Corporations Ltd.	3	797.1	765.6	31.4
其他	Other Enterprises	3	681.4	180.7	126.6
港澳台商投资	Enterprises with Funds from Hong Kong, Macao &Taiwan	7	105253.5	43194	30853.7
外商投资	Foreign Funded Enterprises	7	59980.0	14481.2	17820.1
2.按国民经济行业分	Grouped by Sdctor				
正餐服务	Dinner	306	656638.7	330674.5	118502.9
快餐服务	Fast Food	7	107743.8	43408.5	32471.9
饮料及冷饮服务	Beverages and Cold Drinks				
其他餐饮业	Other Catering Services	2	53212.3	19663.7	32285.8

continued 2

(10 000 yuan)

固定资产原价 Original Value of Fixed Assets	累计折旧 Accumulated Depreciation	负债合计 Total Liabilities	流动负债合计 Circulating Liabilities	非流动负债 Non-Circulating Liabilities	所有者权益合计 Total Owners' Equities	实收资本 Paid in Capital	营业收入 Total Revenue	主营业务收入 Revenue from Principal Business
305394.6	**123097.6**	**608401.1**	**555496.5**	**52904.6**	**209193.7**	**253293.4**	**682938.5**	**672286.6**
218936.8	85313.6	485067.6	438426.3	46641.3	167293.7	211298.5	514096.6	512061.8
4798.3	862.7	3448.7	824.4	2624.3	2122.4	2067.0	6546.3	6546.3
155050.3	54144.0	319855.1	289228.1	30627.0	84495.0	119813.1	316029.6	314160.8
3717.4	1431.5	4411.6	4411.6		-806.1	100.0	3784.3	3783.6
151332.9	52712.5	315443.5	284816.5	30627.0	85301.1	119713.1	312245.3	310377.2
15980.9	9591.0	35913.6	34669.0	1244.6	74343.7	50455.6	42816.5	42816.5
42449.6	20184.8	124575.1	112429.7	12145.4	6926.3	38799.8	142205.8	142039.8
1673.7	877.1	3655.5	3655.0	0.5	218.1	1914.9	6208.9	6197.6
40699.7	19262.9	120406.4	108261.5	12144.9	6424.3	36384.9	133662.0	133552.7
76.2	44.8	513.2	513.2		283.9	500.0	2334.9	2289.5
657.7	531.1	1275.1	1275.1		-593.7	163.0	6498.4	6498.4
57586.7	26733.0	80575.6	80114.8	460.8	24677.9	33447.3	68430.0	68318.2
28871.1	11051.0	42757.9	36955.4	5802.5	17222.1	8547.6	100411.9	91906.6
216785.2	99245.9	491069.3	441824.7	49244.6	165569.4	213471.8	599042.1	597142.0
54563.2	22091.3	74371.4	68668.5	5702.9	33372.4	28821.6	76295.4	67790.1
34046.2	1760.4	42960.4	45003.3	-2042.9	10251.9	11000.0	7601.0	7354.5

16-5 续表3

单位：万元

分类	Classify	营业成本 Total Cost	主营业务成本 Cost of Principal Business
二、餐饮业	**Catering Trade**	**343282.0**	**339752.5**
1.按登记注册类型分组	Grouped by Type of Registration		
内资	Domestic Funded Enterprises	271113.2	270030.9
国有	State-owned Enterprises	4935.0	4935.0
集体	Collective-owned Enterprises		
股份合作	Cooperative Enterprises		
联营	Joint Ownership Enterprises		
国有联营	State Joint Ownership Enterprises		
集体联营	Collective Joint Ownership Enterprises		
国有与集体联营	Joint State-collective Enterprises		
其他联营	Others Joint Ownership Enterprises		
有限责任公司	Limited Liability Corporations	170674.0	170300.3
国有独资公司	State Sole Funded Corporations	2771.5	2771.5
其他有限责任公司	Other Limited Liability Corporations	167902.5	167528.8
股份有限公司	Share-holding Corporations Ltd.	16281.6	16281.6
私营	Private Enterprises	73630.3	73477.0
私营独资	Private-funded Enterprises	3024.8	3024.8
私营合伙	Private Partnership Enterprises		
私营有限责任公司	Private Limited Liability Corporations	69564.5	69411.2
私营股份有限公司	Private Share-holding Corporations Ltd.	1041.0	1041.0
其他	Other Enterprises	5592.3	5037.0
港澳台商投资	Enterprises with Funds from Hong Kong, Macao &Taiwan	27699.2	27587.5
外商投资	Foreign Funded Enterprises	44469.6	42134.1
2.按国民经济行业分	Grouped by Sdctor		
正餐服务	Dinner	309349.5	308158.7
快餐服务	Fast Food	32293.3	29957.8
饮料及冷饮服务	Beverages and Cold Drinks		
其他餐饮业	Other Catering Services	1639.2	1636.0

continued 3

(10 000 yuan)

营业税金及附加 Taxs and Other Changes	主营业务税金及附加 Taxs and Other Changes on Principal Business	销售费用 Sale Expenses	管理费用 Managenment Expenses	财务费用 Financial Expenses	营业利润 Business Profits	利润总额 Total Profits	应付职工薪酬 Salary Payable	本年应交所得税 Value Added Tax Payable
36324.9	**36280.3**	**241514.3**	**76719.9**	**12139.2**	**-26107.1**	**-21575.4**	**141722.0**	**3386.9**
27715.8	27677.6	172629.7	57338.5	9870.5	-23291.4	-18561.8	112514.6	1797.7
323.2	323.2	660.6	385.2	-0.1	242.4	242.3	646.5	73.4
16031.4	15999.4	101179.3	36355.0	7762.2	-16273.2	-14801.3	65294.8	359.7
213.7	213.7	21.4	859.1	-8.5	-75.9	-73.2	1305.1	
15817.7	15785.7	101157.9	35495.9	7770.7	-16197.3	-14728.1	63989.7	359.7
2355.9	2355.9	21209.8	2783.1	677.9	302.3	4538.7	13739.9	1241.8
8738.3	8732.1	48744.1	17403.6	1379.8	-7243.8	-8222.4	32158.9	122.2
358.7	358.7	2635.2	529.3	10.6	-349.7	-358.7	1509.3	5.3
7925.3	7919.1	45109.7	16654.0	1361.9	-6847.7	-7822.0	30013.2	112.6
454.3	454.3	999.2	220.3	7.3	-46.4	-41.7	636.4	4.3
267.0	267.0	835.9	411.6	50.7	-319.1	-319.1	674.5	0.6
3619.2	3612.8	36714.3	6882.5	2209.7	-8842.1	-8776.1	11361.9	118.0
4989.9	4989.9	32170.3	12498.9	59.0	6026.4	5762.5	17845.5	1471.2
32239.9	32195.3	204555.0	65245.4	10658.3	-22148	-18006.7	127366.8	2350.6
3655.5	3655.5	34869.0	7548.6	1407.9	-3395.1	-3002.9	12917.8	1036.3
429.5	429.5	2090.3	3925.9	73.0	-564.0	-565.8	1437.4	

16-6 限额以上批发零售贸易业商品购进、销售、库存总额（2014年）

单位：个、万元

分 类	Classify	单位数 Number of Enterprises	商品购进额 Total Purchases	进口 Exports
总计	**Total**	**834**	**42138822.8**	**4093133.5**
一、批发企业	**Wholesale Enterprises**	**345**	**25888881.5**	**3222915.9**
1.按登记注册类型分组	Grouped by Type of Registration			
内资企业	Domestic Funded Enterprises	334	22157335.9	559609.6
国有	State-owned Enterprises	22	3325087.4	240220.0
集体	Collective-owned Enterprises	4	12198.7	
股份合作	Cooperative Enterprises			
联营	Joint Ownership Enterprises			
国有联营	State Joint Ownership Enterprises			
集体联营	Collective Joint Ownership Enterprises			
国有与集体联营	Joint State-collective Enterprises			
其他联营	Others Joint Ownership Enterprises			
有限责任公司	Limited Liability Corporations	193	12856146.9	260953.3
国有独资公司	State Sole Funded Corporations	8	3038119.4	35415.9
其他有限责任公司	Other Limited Liability Corporations	185	9818027.5	225537.4
股份有限公司	Share-holding Corporations Ltd.	7	3485199.6	
私营	Private Enterprises	106	2465273.3	58436.3
私营独资	Private-funded Enterprises	1	4232.6	
私营合伙	Private Partnership Enterprises			
私营有限责任公司	Private Limited Liability Corporations	102	2304020.5	48653.9
私营股份有限公司	Private Share-holding Corporations Ltd.	3	157020.2	9782.4
其他	Other Enterprises	2	13430.0	
港澳台商投资	Enterprises with Funds from Hong Kong, Macao &Taiwan	4	362247.5	216096.5
外商投资	Foreign Funded Enterprises	7	3369298.1	2447209.8
2.按国民经济行业分组	Grouped by Economic Sector			
农、林、牧产品批发	Wholesale of Agricultural,Forestry and Animal Husbandry Products	3	10231.3	

Total Sales of Enterprises above Designated Size in Wholesale and Retail Trades Grouped by Category of Commodities（2014）

(unit，10 000 yuan)

商品销售额 Sales Value	批发额 Wholesale Trade	出口 Exports	零售额 Retail Trade	期末商品库存额 Value of Stock at Final goods
45857866.9	**23876170.2**	**765444.9**	**21981696.7**	**2305762.7**
27428326.2	**23465761.7**	**764967.9**	**3962564.5**	**1072175.6**
23546173.6	19747010.7	764967.9	3799162.9	923549.8
3752816.2	3403728.2	23343.1	349088.0	153325.2
12333.1	11311.6		1021.5	1318.6
13264268.6	11113537.6	252331.5	2150731	551676.1
3052728.5	2193275.6	45269.1	859452.9	30963.1
10211540.1	8920262.0	207062.4	1291278.1	520713.0
3783397.7	2611527.7	419076.4	1171870.0	29752.1
2718595.0	2592142.6	70216.9	126452.4	187467.8
4336.3	4336.3			351.2
2549730.4	2455563.6	70216.9	94166.8	181227.4
164528.3	132242.7		32285.6	5889.2
14763.0	14763.0			10.0
410750.1	284419		126331.1	44808.1
3471402.5	3434332.0		37070.5	103817.7
12663.6	12663.6			2532.4

16-6 续表1

单位：个、万元

分类	Classify	单位数 Number of Enterprises	商品购进额 Total Purchases	进口 Exports
食品、饮料及烟草制品批发	Wholesale of Food, Beverages and Tobacco Products	28	1701413.9	
纺织、服装及家庭服务器批发	Wholesale of Textiles, Garments and Daily Articles	27	2944104.0	
文化、体育用品及器材批发	Wholesale of Culture, Sports Articles and Equipments	17	351474.5	
医药及医疗器材批发	Wholesale of Medicines and Medical Appliances	57	2159675.7	126645.8
矿产品、建材及化工产品批发	Wholesale of Mineral Products, Building Materials and Chemical Products	135	16422599.1	2792969.0
机械设备、五金产品及电子产品批发	Wholesale of Machinery, Hardwares, Transport Means and Electronic Products	72	2247907.7	302298.6
贸易经纪与代理	Trade Manage and Agent	2	27461.2	1002.5
其他批发	Other Wholesales	4	24014.1	
3.按经营形式分组	Grouped by Means of Operation			
独立门店	Independent Shop	255	19925398.8	2849385.7
连锁总店	Headquarter of Chain Store	3	924691.3	
连锁门店	Chain Store	2	633786.6	
其他	Other	85	4405004.8	373530.2
二、零售企业	**Retail Trade**	**489**	**16249941.3**	**870217.6**
1.按登记注册类型分组	Grouped by Registration Status			
内资	Domestic Funded Enterprises	420	11784131.9	434344.3
国有	State-owned Enterprises	11	286390.7	
集体	Collective-owned Enterprises	21	47802.6	
股份合作	Cooperative Enterprises			
联营	Joint Ownership Enterprises			
国有联营	State Joint Ownership Enterprises			
集体联营	Collective Joint Ownership Enterprises			
国有与集体联营	Joint State-collective Enterprises			

continued 1

(unit, 10 000 yuan)

商品销售额 Sales Value	批发额 Wholesale Trade	出口 Exports	零售额 Retail Trade	期末商品库存额 Value of Stock at Final goods
2030604.6	1803816.3	154.0	226788.3	89034.4
3014946.7	2036945.2	49553.9	978001.5	218726.0
379515.5	373882.5	7100.0	5633.0	27130.7
2323272.3	2147247.2		176025.1	170305.2
17019978.3	14868999.4	35599.3	2150978.9	379397.2
2588215.1	2163077.4	651821.5	425137.7	181625.6
30630.2	30630.2	20739.2		2296.9
28499.9	28499.9			1127.2
20624962	17208733.3	312741.7	3416228.7	643494.3
1227909.5	1227909.5			41243.2
679760.5	413543.2		266217.3	37526
4895694.2	4615575.7	452226.2	280118.5	349912.1
18429540.7	**410408.5**	**477.0**	**18019132.2**	**1233587.1**
13267906.2	324168.8	477.0	12943737.4	993848.8
293620.7	17130.9		276489.8	45955.5
50116.3	1587.4		48528.9	2126.0

16-6 续表2

单位：个、万元

分　类	Classify	单位数 Number of Enterprises	商品购进额 Total Purchases	进口 Exports
其他联营	Others Joint Ownership Enterprises			
有限责任公司	Limited Liability Corporations	252	7852655.4	335576.3
国有独资公司	State Sole Funded Corporations	4	116931.0	
其他有限责任公司	Other Limited Liability Corporations	248	7735724.4	335576.3
股份有限公司	Share-holding Corporations Ltd.	7	997547.0	37859.7
私营	Private Enterprises	126	2592162.2	60908.3
私营独资	Private-funded Enterprises	1	6940.2	
私营合伙	Private Partnership Enterprises	2	7523.8	
私营有限责任公司	Private Limited Liability Corporations	115	2380532.6	35947.8
私营股份有限公司	Private Share-holding Corporations Ltd.	8	197165.6	24960.5
其他	Other Enterprises	3	7574.0	
港澳台商投资	Enterprises with Funds from Hong Kong, Macao &Taiwan	22	1664429.6	381858.3
外商投资	Foreign Funded Enterprises	21	2336900.8	54015.0
2.按国民经济行业分组	Grouped by Registered Kind			
综合零售	General Retail Sales Trade	106	2620028.1	
食品、饮料及烟草制品专门零售	Retail of Food, Beverage and Tobaccos	30	226319.9	80.4
纺织、服装及日用品专门零售	Retail of Textiles, Garments and Daily Articles	31	1556657.4	
文化、体育用品及器材专门零售	Retail of Culture, Sports Articles and Equipments	23	263731.9	1584.4
医药及医疗器材专门零售	Retail of Medicines and Medical Appliances	22	291676.5	72.9
汽车、摩托车、燃料及零配件专门零售	Retail of Motor Vehicles, Motorcycles, Feuls and Parts	196	7411662.2	868479.9
家用电器及电子产品专门零售	Retail of Household Electronic Equipments and Products	42	1876657.6	

continued 2

(unit，10 000 yuan)

商品销售额 Sales Value	批发额 Wholesale Trade	出口 Exports	零售额 Retail Trade	期末商品库存额 Value of Stock at Final goods
8789874.8	216327.8		8573547	656160.8
113115.5			113115.5	32161.0
8676759.3	216327.8		8460431.5	623999.8
1161253	58414.1		1102838.9	103431.7
2965093.9	30708.6	477.0	2934385.3	185784.8
6960.1			6960.1	89.0
7588.5			7588.5	588.5
2752992.9	29760.8	477.0	2723232.1	172218.6
197552.4	947.8		196604.6	12888.7
7947.5			7947.5	390.0
2098881.5	20331.6		2078549.9	160857.0
2562628.4	52380.7		2510247.7	65720.8
3586359.7	2706.7		3583653.0	181291.3
335378	16129.2	477.0	319248.8	76198.1
1662074.3	71267.1		1590807.2	66205.5
295672.3	38732.4		256939.9	84314.5
306856.9	38243.0		268613.9	45359.0
7944435.8	33158.7		7911277.1	672026.3
2123624.0	192394.4		1931229.6	80253.5

16-6 续表3

单位：个、万元

分 类	Classify	单位数 Number of Enterprises	商品购进额 Total Purchases	进口 Exports
五金、家具及室内装饰材料专门零售	etail of Hardwares, Furniture and Room Decorative Building	31	1631567.6	
货摊、无店铺及其他零售业	No Fixed Stores and Other Retails	8	371640.1	
3.按经营形式分组	Grouped by Means of Operation			
独立门店	Independent Shop	413	12809941.1	726655.6
连锁总店	Headquarter of Chain Store	28	824114.5	
连锁门店	Chain Store	8	756981.2	
其他	Other	40	1858904.5	143562.0
4.按零售业态分组	Grouped by Retail Size			
有店铺	Retail of Shop	484	15891571.9	870217.6
食杂店	Grocery Store			
便利店	Convenience Store	8	31310.8	
折扣店	Dime Store			
超市	Supermarket	40	171008.4	
大型超市	Larget Supermarket	18	1209405.5	
仓储会员店	Warehouse Club	2	6804.0	
百货店	Department Store	56	1354946.6	
专业店	Special Store	169	5266358.3	336237.8
专卖店	Monopoly Store	145	4242207.9	533979.8
家居建材商店	Home-building Material Store	17	1245903.1	
购物中心	Shopping Center	12	1916309.3	
厂家直销中心	Factory Outlet Center	17	447318.0	
无店铺零售	Retail of No-shop	5	358369.4	
电视购物	TV Shopping	2	117535.9	
邮购	Mail Order			
网上商店	Online Stores	1	238322.8	
自动售货亭	Vending Machine			
电话购物	Tele Shopping			

continued 3

(unit，10 000 yuan)

商品销售额 Sales Value	批发额 Wholesale Trade	出口 Exports	零售额 Retail Trade	期末商品库存额 Value of Stock at Final goods
1789654.7	7861.9		1781792.8	24850.3
385485.0	9915.1		375569.9	3088.6
14320133.8	177110.7	477.0	14143023.1	880697.4
994224.4	22784.6		971439.8	69526.2
938693.3	55389.4		883303.9	87978.2
2176489.2	155123.8		2021365.4	195385.3
18059156.2	409780.5	477.0	17649375.7	1230682.9
38820.8			38820.8	4038.6
193621.9	11670.5		181951.4	20764.5
1395611.4			1395611.4	114603.3
7685.8			7685.8	877.7
2110140.7	1674.1		2108466.6	53795.6
5866597.4	139247.8	477.0	5727349.6	480128.6
4660693.2	93987.7		4566705.5	457954.3
1347195.9	7695.1		1339500.8	13500.7
1982312.5	144948.7		1837363.8	37185.3
456476.6	10556.6		445920.0	47834.3
370384.5	628.0		369756.5	2904.2
117686.8	628.0		117058.8	1355.5
250215.2			250215.2	1514.9

16-7 限额以上住宿和餐饮业经营情况（2014年）

Statistic on Hotel Services and Catering Services above Designed Size（2014）

单位：个、万元 (unit,10 000 yuan)

分 类	Classify	单位数 Number of Enterprises	营业额 Business Revenue	客房收入 From Hotel Room	餐费收入 From Meals	商品销售收入 From Commodities
总计	**Total**	**602**	**1416543.0**	**364337.4**	**914704.1**	**67707.0**
一、住宿业	**Lodging Services**	**237**	**630503.4**	**332360.7**	**238859.3**	**14845.3**
1. 按登记注册类型分组	Grouped by Registration Status					
内资企业	Domestic Funded Enterprises	220	515100.6	270880.1	199792.5	10946.8
国有	State-owned Enterprises	32	73763.1	32458.2	30130.9	4061.1
集体	Collective-owned Enterprises	2	2392.8	1531.5	154.6	192.9
股份合作	Cooperative Enterprises					
联营	Joint Ownership Enterprises					
国有联营	State Joint Ownership Enterprises					
集体联营	Collective Joint Ownership Enterprises					
国有与集体联营	Joint State-collective Ownership Enterprises					
其他联营	Other Joint Ownership Enterprises					
有限责任公司	Limited Liability Corporations	119	317944.1	169545.1	124468.8	3902.5
国有独资公司	State-funded Corporations	4	16170.9	6898.3	6916.5	238.3
其他有限责任公司	Other Limited Liability Corporations	115	301773.2	162646.8	117552.3	3664.2
股份有限公司	Stock Limited Corporation	4	14861.6	6534.5	6488	154.6
私营	Private Enterprises	63	106139	60810.8	38550.2	2635.7
私营独资	Private-funded Enterprises	3	1436.7	937	477.2	22.5
私营合伙	Private Partnership Enterprises	1	594.9	492.1	102.8	
私营有限责任公司	Private Limited Liability Corporations	57	103049.5	58795.4	37528.2	2583.6
私营股份有限公司	Private Share Holding Corporations	2	1057.9	586.3	442.0	29.6
其他	Others					
港澳台商投资	Enterprises Funded by Hong Kong, Macao and Taiwan	7	52498.3	26353.6	16080.4	2353
外商投资	Foreign Funded Enterprises	10	62904.5	35127.0	22986.4	1545.5
2. 按国民经济行业分组						
旅游饭店	Tour Restaurant	181	559276.3	290400.7	213776.5	13726.7
一般旅馆	Common Hotel	51	59335.9	35721.9	20572.1	1081.3
其他住宿业	Others	5	11891.2	6238.1	4510.7	37.3

16-7 续表1 continued 1

单位：个、万元 (unit, 10 000 yuan)

分类	Classify	单位数 Number of Enterprises	营业额 Business Revenue	客房收入 From Hotel Room	餐费收入 From Meals	商品销售收入 From Commodities
二、餐饮业	**Catering Trade**	**365**	**786039.6**	**31976.7**	**675844.8**	**52861.7**
1. 按登记注册类型分	Grouped by Registration Status					
内资	Domestic Funded Enterprises	310	534017.4	29738.7	441809.0	47602.9
国有	State-owned Enterprises	5	11420.3	960.2	7418.4	2413.8
集体	Collective-owned Enterprises					
股份合作	Cooperative Enterprises					
联营	Joint Ownership Enterprises					
国有联营	State Joint Ownership Enterprises					
集体联营	Collective Joint Ownership Enterprises					
国有与集体联营	Joint State-collective Ownership Enterprises					
其他联营	Other Joint Ownership Enterprises					
有限责任公司	Limited Liability Corporations	177	331187.7	25230.5	259985.1	36303
国有独资公司	State-funded Corporations	2	3783.6	1278.3	1500.3	109.6
其他有限责任公司	Other Limited Liability Corporations	175	327404.1	23952.2	258484.8	36193.4
股份有限公司	Stock Limited Corporation	3	42816.4	305.1	34740.8	3768.5
私营	Private Enterprises	121	141783.3	3138.2	133979	4098.3
私营独资	Private-funded Enterprises	12	6270.6		6026.6	189.9
私营合伙	Private Partnership Enterprises					
私营有限责任公司	Private Limited Liability Corporations	106	133177.8	3005.0	125842.3	3816.8
私营股份有限公司	Private Share Holding Corporations	3	2334.9	133.2	2110.1	91.6
其他	Others	4	6809.7	104.7	5685.7	1019.3
港澳台商投资	Enterprises Funded by Hong Kong, Macao and Taiwan	7	68845.1	1031.4	66024.5	1172.6
外商投资	Foreign Funded Enterprises	7	100411.9		91712.6	121.6
2. 按国民经济行业分						
正餐服务	Dinner Services	351	694904.3	28434.5	596781.3	52842.0
快餐服务	Fast Food Services	7	77353.0	615.4	68232.3	
饮料及冷饮服务	Beverage and Cold Beverage Services					
其他餐饮业	Other Catering Services	7	13782.3	2926.8	10831.2	19.7

16-8 限额以上批发和零售贸易业主要商品分类销售额（2014年）

Sale Values of Enterprises above Designated Size of Wholesale and Retail Trades by Category of Main Commodities（2014）

单位：万元 (10 000 yuan)

分类	Classify	销售合计 Total Sales Value	批发 Wholesale Value	零售 Retail Value
总计	**Total**	**47762144.2**	**25936274.6**	**21825869.6**
粮油、食品饮料、烟酒类	Grain and Oil, Food and Beverages,Alcoholic Drinks and Tobacco	3453568.1	1830760.8	1622807.3
#粮油、食品类	Cereals, Oils and Foodstuffs	1191894.4	226066.1	965828.3
#粮油类	Grain and Oil	494520	54543.8	439976.2
肉禽蛋类	Meat, Poultry and Eggs	112447.4	24745.1	87702.3
水产品类	Aquatic Products	159022.8	3879.0	155143.8
蔬菜类	Vegetables	121115.3	56884.8	64230.5
干鲜瓜果类	Fresh and Dried Fruit Category	89511.3	19619.5	69891.8
饮料类	Beverages	781023.1	353937.3	427085.8
烟酒类	Tobacco and Liquor	1480650.6	1250757.4	229893.2
服装、鞋帽、针、纺织品类	Clothing, Shoes, Hats and Textiles	5196229.0	1352713.3	3843515.7
#服装类	Clothing	4473858.3	1246564.5	3227293.8
鞋帽类	Shoes and Hats	457146.6	60172.2	396974.4
针、纺织品类	Knitwear and Textiles	265224.1	45976.6	219247.5
化妆品类	Cosmetics	374059.4	44169.6	329889.8
金银珠宝类	Gold,Silver and Jewelry	590959.2	101873.7	489085.5
日用品类	Articles for Daily Use	700750.1	126103.0	574647.1
#洗涤用品类	Bathing and Washing	195613.2	89702.1	105911.1
儿童玩具类	Children's Toys	71475.9	5963.4	65512.5
五金、电料类	Hardwear and Electrical Materials	251110.0	90832.1	160277.9
体育、娱乐用品类	Sports and Recreation Articles	266902.2	64819.3	202082.9
书报杂志类	Newspapers and Magazines	207283.4	117426.9	89856.5
电子出版物及音像制品类	E-journal and Video Products	41466.3	3692.9	37773.4
家用电器和音像器材类	Household Appliances and Video Products	1619593.1	691482.8	928110.3
中西药品类	Traditional Chinese and Western Medicine	2231461.5	1806570.4	424891.1
#西药	Western Medicine	1723968.6	1389678.4	334290.2
中草药及中成药	Chinese Herbal Medicine and Traditional Chinese Medicine	145123.9	117508.5	27615.4
文化办公用品类	Cultural and Official Goods	801131.8	349673.6	451458.2
家具类	Furniture	973936.3		973936.3
通讯器材类	Communication Appliances	612812.0	105792.1	507019.9
煤炭及制品类	Coal and Related Products	3606053.8	2747235.8	858818.0
木材及制品类	Wood and Wooden Products			
石油及制品类	Petroleum and Related Products	10601305.3	7816539.3	2784766.0
化工材料及制品类	Raw Chemical Materials	129981.1	129981.1	
#化肥类	Chemical Fertilizers	52298.9	52298.9	
金属材料类	Metal Materials	6460185.3	6460185.3	
建筑及装潢材料类	Buildings and Decoration Materials	1738245.3	484336.3	1253909.0
机电产品及设备类	Mechanical and Electrical Products	642730.1	622634.3	20095.8
#农机类	Agricultural Machinery	9268.9	9268.9	
汽车类	Automobile	6821410.4	918235.6	5903174.8
种子饲料类	Seeds and Feedstuff	2347.8	2347.8	
棉麻类	Cotton,Hemp	3053.6	3053.6	
其他类	Others	435578.2	65824.1	369754.1

16-9 亿元以上商品交易市场成交情况(2014年)

Basic Statistics on Commodity Exchange Markets of Transaction Value over 100 Million Yuan（2014）

分 类	Classify	年末出租摊位数（个）Number of Rental Booths at Year-end (unit)	成交额（万元）Turnover (10 000 yuan)
粮油、食品饮料、烟酒类	Grain and Oil, Food and Beverages,Alcoholic Drinks and Tobacco	5229	718159
#粮油、食品类	Cereals, Oils and Foodstuffs	3218	636646
#粮油类	Grain and Oil	404	287235
肉禽蛋类	Meat, Poultry and Eggs	969	69888
水产品类	Aquatic Products	606	19018
蔬菜类	Vegetables	849	206269
干鲜瓜果类	Fresh and Dried Fruit Category	344	53516
饮料类	Beverages	1918	79384
烟酒类	Tobacco and Liquor	93	2129
服装、鞋帽、针、纺织品类	Clothing, Shoes, Hats and Textiles	8471	664331
#服装类	Clothing	5952	418198
鞋帽类	Shoes and Hats	1311	169567
针、纺织品类	Knitwear and Textiles	1208	76566
化妆品类	Cosmetics	96	2483
金银珠宝类	Gold,Silver and Jewelry	50	1100
日用品类	Articles for Daily Use	963	36053
#洗涤用品类	Bathing and Washing		
儿童玩具类	Children's Toys	92	1565
五金、电料类	Hardwear and Electrical Materials	901	26548
体育、娱乐用品类	Sports and Recreation Articles	80	1750
书报杂志类	Newspapers and Magazines	3	40
电子出版物及音像制品类	E-journal and Video Products	103	9440
家用电器和音像器材类	Household Appliances and Video Products	182	14346
中西药品类	Traditional Chinese and Western Medicine	450	64312
#西药	Western Medicine		
中草药及中成药	Chinese Herbal Medicine and Traditional Chinese Medicine	450	64312
文化办公用品类	Cultural and Official Goods	1070	161661
家具类	Furniture	345	9230
通讯器材类	Communication Appliances	1157	62605
煤炭及制品类	Coal and Related Products		
木材及制品类	Wood and Wooden Products		
石油及制品类	Petroleum and Related Products		
化工材料及制品类	Raw Chemical Materials	24	170000
#化肥类	Chemical Fertilizers		
金属材料类	Metal Materials	55	280000
建筑及装潢材料类	Buildings and Decoration Materials	1591	78584
机电产品及设备类	Mechanical and Electrical Products	790	161000
#农机类	Agricultural Machinery		
汽车类	Automobile	1864	718900
种子饲料类	Seeds and Feedstuff		
棉麻类	Cotton,Hemp		
其他类	Others	222	37278

注：全市有亿元以上商品交易市场35个。

16-10 批发和零售业连锁经营情况(2014年)

Basic Statistics on Chain Business of Wholesale and Retail Trades（2014）

指　标	Item	本年合计 Total	上年合计 Total Last Year	本年直营店 Regular Chain
一、门店总数（个）	**Number of Stores(unit)**	**981**	**845**	**816**
二、年末从业人员数（人）	**Employees at Year-end(person)**	**20503**	**20962**	**18445**
三、年末零售营业面积（平方米）	**Operating Area of Retail at Year-end(sq.m)**	**886118**	**898349**	**718144**
四、连锁门店商品购进额（万元）	**Purchases Value of Chain Stores(10 000 yuan)**	**3436950**	**3583263**	**3297989**
其中：统一配送商品购进额	Centralized Purchases and Delivery	2789929	2913976	2772361
其中：自有配送中心配送商品购进额	Self Centralized Purchases and Delivery	2688357	2802840	2670789
非自有配送中心配送商品购进额	Non-self Centralized Purchases and Delivery	99709	93621	99709
五、连锁门店商品销售额（万元）	**Sales Value of Chain Store(10 000 yuan)**	**4053489**	**4164173**	**3847926**
其中：零售额	Retail Value	1845332	1931926	1639769

16-10 续表 continued

指　标	Item	上年直营店 Regular Chain Last Year	本年加盟店 Franchise	上年加盟店 Franchise Last Year
一、门店总数（个）	**Number of Stores(unit)**	**712**	**165**	**133**
二、年末从业人员数（人）	**Employees at Year-end(person)**	**18964**	**2058**	**1998**
三、年末零售营业面积（平方米）	**Operating Area of Retail at Year-end(sq.m)**	**730819**	**167974**	**167530**
四、连锁门店商品购进额（万元）	**Purchases Value of Chain Stores(10 000 yuan)**	**3440139**	**138961**	**143124**
其中：统一配送商品购进额	Centralized Purchases and Delivery	2891997	17568	21979
其中：自有配送中心配送商品购进额	Self Centralized Purchases and Delivery	2783346	17568	19494
非自有配送中心配送商品购进额	Non-self Centralized Purchases and Delivery	93621		
五、连锁门店商品销售额（万元）	**Sales Value of Chain Store(10 000 yuan)**	**3965402**	**205563**	**198771**
其中：零售额	Retail Value	1733155	205563	198771

16-11 住宿和餐饮业连锁经营情况(2014年)

Basic Statistics on Chain Business of Hotels and Catering Services（2014）

指 标	Item	本年合计 Total	上年合计 Total Last Year
一、门店总数（个）	**Number of Stores(unit)**	**181**	**174**
二、年末从业人员数（人）	**Employees at Year-end(person)**	**11049**	**11111**
三、年末餐饮营业面积（平方米）	**Operating Area of Retail at Year-end(sq.m)**	**77203**	**69084**
四、客房总数（间）	**Guest Rooms(room)**		
五、床位数（张）	**Guest Beds(bed)**		
六、餐位数（位）	**Dining Seats(set)**	**23110**	**22604**
七、连锁门店商品购进额（万元）	**Operating Area of Catering Services at Year end(room)(10 000yuan)**	**69358**	**64142**
其中：统一配送商品购进额	Centralized Purchases and Delivery	62848	61738
其中：自有配送中心配送商品购进额	Self Centralized Purchases and Delivery	59842	59554
非自有配送中心配送商品购进额	Non-self Centralized Purchases and Delivery		
八、连锁门店商品营业额（万元）	**Sales Value of Chain Store(10 000 yuan)**	**132962**	**127188**
其中：餐费收入	Catering Revenues	132108	126386
商品销售额	Sales Value	854	802

16-11 续表 continued

指 标	Item	本年直营店 Regular Chain	上年直营店 Regular Chain Last Year
一、门店总数（个）	**Number of Stores(unit)**	**181**	**174**
二、年末从业人员数（人）	**Employees at Year-end(person)**	**11049**	**11111**
三、年末餐饮营业面积（平方米）	**Operating Area of Retail at Year-end(sq.m)**	**77203**	**69084**
四、客房总数（间）	**Guest Rooms(room)**		
五、床位数（张）	**Guest Beds(bed)**		
六、餐位数（位）	**Dining Seats(set)**	**23110**	**22604**
七、连锁门店商品购进额（万元）	**Operating Area of Catering Services at Year end(room)(10 000yuan)**	**69358**	**64142**
其中：统一配送商品购进额	Centralized Purchases and Delivery	62848	61738
其中：自有配送中心配送商品购进额	Self Centralized Purchases and Delivery	59842	59554
非自有配送中心配送商品购进额	Non-self Centralized Purchases and Delivery		
八、连锁门店商品营业额（万元）	**Sales Value of Chain Store(10 000 yuan)**	**132962**	**127188**
其中：餐费收入	Catering Revenues	132108	126386
商品销售额	Sales Value	854	802

16-12 成品油批发企业（单位）能源购进、销售与库存(2014年)

Purchases,Sales and Stock of Refined Oil Wholesale Enterprises（2014）

单位：吨 (ton)

指 标	Item	年初库存量 Stock at Beginning of the Year	本年购进量 Purchases This Year	其中：购自省(区、市)外 From Other Provinces (Regions,Cities)	本年销售量 Sales This Year	其中：销往省(区、市)外 For Other Provinces (Regions,Cities)	售予省内批发和零售企业 For Wholesale and Retail Trades	年末库存量 Stock at End of the Year
汽油	Gasoline	46084	7841672	472861	5304243	1115050	3708819	134700
#93″	#93″	29442	4396277	369552	4430771	1072914	3115030	22242
柴油	Diesel Oil	210134	7967553	1874160	7909902	1408583	4971654	184697
#0″	#0″	204910	6641037	848722	6590401	406253	4689140	180109
煤油	Kerosene	23739	1020388	415476	1040852	419535	110	15732
燃料油	Fuel Oil		10383	1021	10383	9718	665	
润滑油	Lube	474	713		687		611	281

主要统计指标解释

批发业 指批发商向批发、零售单位及其他企事业、机关单位批量销售生活用品和生产资料的活动，以及从事进出口贸易和贸易经纪与代理的活动。批发商可以对所批发的货物拥有所有权，并以本单位、公司的名义进行交易活动；也可以不拥有货物的所有权，而以中介身份做代理销售商。还包括各类商品批发市场中固定摊位的批发活动。

零售业 指百货商店、超级市场、专门零售商店、品牌专卖店、售货摊等主要面向最终消费者（如居民等）的销售活动。包括以互联网、邮政、电话、售货机等方式的销售活动，还包括在同地点，后面加工生产，前面销售的店铺（如前店后厂的面包房）。不包括：谷物、种子、饲料、牲畜、矿产品、生产用原料、化工原料、农用化工产品、机械设备（用车、计算机及通信设备等除外）等生产资料的销售（批发业）；非零售单位附带的零售活动（如汽车修理单位销售汽车零件）；商业零售单位所在商厦的物业管理（物业管理）；商业零售单位所在的商品市场、商业大厦的市场管理活动（市场管理）。

住宿业 指有偿为顾客提供临时住宿的服务活动，不包括提供长期住宿场所的活动（如出租房屋、公寓等）。

餐饮业 指在一定场所，对食物进行现场烹饪、调制，并出售给顾客主要供现场消费的服务活动。

社会消费品零售总额 指批发和零售业、餐饮业、新闻出版业、邮政业和其他服务业等，售予城乡居民用于生活消费的商品和社会集团用于公共消费的商品之总量。社会消费品零售总额包括：

一、批发和零售业企业（单位）售予城乡居民用于生活消费和社会集团用于公共消费的商品。包括：

1. 售予城乡居民的各种生活消费品；

2. 售予入境旅游的外国人、华侨、港澳台同胞的各类商品；

3. 售予行政事业单位、社会团体、军队和武警等机构的商品，以及以零售方式售予各类企业的商品。具体包括：用于非生产和社会交往的办公用品，如通讯设备、计算器具和设备、电讯网络设备、文印设备、音像视听器材和设备、纸张、本册、文具及装订文印材料、家具、日用电器、针纺织品、清洁卫生用品、文体用品、奖品、纪念品、礼品等；供内部人员乘坐的交通工具和燃料；用于办公设施修缮的各类配件、材料、工具等；用于取暖和防暑降温的设备、燃料、材料及食品等；专用于教学的用品和设备；非营利医疗机构的中、西药品、中药材和医疗设备器材；非专用的劳动保护用品；不对外营业的内部食堂用的餐具、炊具、设备、清洁卫生工具和食品、燃料等；军队、武警用于其人员生活的衣着品和个人用品；其他各类非生产性设备和用品。

二、餐饮业出售的主食、菜肴、烟酒饮料和其他商品。

三、新闻出版业、邮政业售予城乡居民、企事业单位、军队和武警等机构的书报杂志、音像制品、邮品等。

四、其他服务业出售的食品、烟酒饮料、服装鞋帽、日常生活用品、医药保健用品、艺术品、工艺美术品、玩具、殡葬用品以及其他消费品。

批发和零售业商品购进、销售、库存总额 指各种登记注册类型的批发和零售业企业（单位）以本企业（单位）为总体的，从国内、国外市场购进的商品总量，销售和出口的商品总量、库存的商品总量等情况。该指标可以反映商品流转过程中商品的购进、销售、库存之间的比例关系和存在的问题。

购进总额 指从本企业（单位）以外的单位和个人购进（包括从境外直接进口）作为转卖或加工后转卖的商品总额。它反映批发和零售业从国内、国外市场上购进商品的总量。商品购进包括：（1）从工农业生产者购进的商品；（2）从出版社、报社的出版发行部门购进的图书、杂志和报纸；（3）从各种登记注册类型的批发和零售业企业（单位）购进的商品；（4）从其他单位购进的商品，如从机关、团体、企业等单位购进的剩余物资，从住宿和餐饮业、其他服务业购进的商品，从海关、市场管理部门购进的缉私和没收的商品，从居民手中收购的废旧商品等；（5）从国（境）外直接进口的商品。不包括企业（单位）为自身经营用和未通过买卖行为而收入的商品以及销售退回、商品升溢等。

销售总额 指对本企业（单位）以外的单位和个人出售（包括对境外直接出口）的商品总额。它反映批发和零售业在国内市场上销售商品以及出口商品的总量。商品销售包括：（1）售给城乡居民和社会集团消费用的商品；（2）售给工业、农业、建筑业、运输邮电业、批发和零售业、住宿和餐饮业、其他服务业等作为生产、经营使用的商品；（3）售给批发和零售业作为转卖或加工后转卖的商品；（4）对国（境）外直接出口的商品。不包括出售本企业（单位）自用的废旧包装用品，未通过买卖行为付出的商品，经本单位介绍、由买卖双方直接结算、本单位只收取手续费的业务，购货退出的商品以及商品损耗和损失等。

库存总额 指报告期末各种登记注册类型的批发和零售业企业（单位）已取得所有权的商品。它反映批发和零售业企业（单位）的商品库存情况和对市场商品供应的保证程度。商品库存包括：（1）存放在批发和零售业经营单位（如门市部、批发站、经营处）仓库、货场、货柜和货架中的商品；（2）挑选、整理、包装中的商品；（3）已记入购进而尚未运到本单位的商品，即发货单或银行承兑凭证已到而货未到的商品；（4）寄放他处的商品，如因购货方拒绝承付而暂时存放在购货方的商品和已办完加工成品收回手续而未提回的商品；（5）委托其他单位代销（未作销售或调出）尚未售出的商品；（6）代其他单位购进尚未交付的商品。不包括所有权不属于本单位的商品、委托外单位加工生产尚未收回成品的商品、外贸企业代理其他单位从国外进口尚未付给订货单位的商品、代国家物资储备部门保管的商品等。

住宿和餐饮业营业额 指住宿和餐饮业法人企业（单位）在经营活动中因提供服务或销售商品等取得的收入。包括：客房收入、餐费收入、商品销售额和其他收入。客房收入指住宿和餐饮业法人企业（单位）在经营活动中因提供住宿服务取得的收入。餐费收入指住宿和餐饮业法人企业、（单位）因为顾客提供就餐服务取得的收入，包括经烹饪、调制加工后出售的各种食品，如主食、炒菜、凉拌菜等的收入。商品销售额指住宿和餐饮业法人企业（单位）伴随服务而出售商品所取得的收入（含增值税）。其他收入指营业收入中除客房收入、餐费收入、商品销售额以外的其他收入，包括娱乐、健身和商务服务等。

连锁企业（或称连锁店、连锁公司） 指在核心企业或总店的领导下，由分散的、经营同类商品或服务的企业或活动单位，采取共同方针，实行集中采购和分散销售的有机结合，通过规范化经营，实现规模效益的经济联合组织形式。一般连锁店应由若干个分店组成。其经营特征：（1）经营同类商品；（2）使用统一商号；（3）统一采购配送，采购与销售相分离（部分商品可根据物流合理和保质保鲜原则，由供应商直接送货到门店，其余均由总部统一配送）。

连锁门店的形式分为直营连锁和加盟连锁。

直营连锁也叫正规连锁。指连锁门店均由总部独资或控股开设，在总部的直接领导下统一经营。总部采取纵深似的管理方式，直接下令掌管所有的零售门店，零售门店也必须完全接受总部指挥。这是大型垄断商业资本通过吞并、兼并或独资、控股等途径，发展壮大自身实力和规模的一种形式。

加盟连锁包括特许连锁和自由连锁两种形式。

特许连锁指各连锁门店（被特许人）通过合同形式，取得使用总部（特许人）商标、商号、经营技术和销售总部开发的商品的特许权，各加盟连锁门店为独立法人，在总部指导下统一经营。

自由连锁也称自愿连锁。指连锁公司的门店均为独立法人，各自的资产所有权关系不变，在公司总部的指导下共同经营。各成员店使用共同的店名，与总部订阅有关购、销、宣传等方面的合同，并按合同开展经营活动。在合同规定的范围之外，各成员店可以自由活动。根据自愿原则，各成员店可自由加入连锁体系，也可自由退出。

Explanatory Notes on Main Statistical Indicators

Wholesale Trade refers to the activities of wholesaler selling at wholesale commodities for daily use and capital goods to enterprises of wholesale and retail trades and other enterprises, institutions and government offices, including the activities of wholesaler engaged in import and export and acting as a trade agent. The wholesaler may have the right of ownership over the commodities of wholesale and trade in the name of its own or a company, the wholesaler may not have the right of ownership, only acts an agent. The wholesale trade also include the activities of wholesaler at the fixed stalls of the wholesale market of different commodities.

Retail Trade refers to the activities of department store,supermarket, franchised store, brand store, retail stall and on-the-spot-making-selling store selling commodities to the final consumers (citizens) by any means including internet, post, telephone, sales machine. Retail trade excludes the activities of sales of capital goods such a grain, seed, feed, livestock, mineral products, raw material for production, industrial chemicals, chemical products for farm, machine and equipment (vehicle, computer and communication equipment), and the activities of supplementary sales of non-retailer such as the sales of spare parts of car repair business

Hotel Services refer to the activities of enterprises providing paid services of lodging to the customer, excluding the activities of providing long period of services of lodging (such as leased house and apartments).

Catering Services refer to the activities of enterprises providing on-the-spot services of selling food cooked and prepared to the customer in certain sites

Total Retail Sales of Consumer Goods refer to the sum of retail sales of commodities sold by wholesale and retail trades, catering services, publishing, post and telecommunications and other service industries to urban and rural households for household consumption and to social institutions for public consumption. Retail sales of consumer goods include:

1) Sales sold by wholesale and retail trades to urban~thA and rural households for household consumption and to social institutions for public consumption.

a) of commodities to urban and rural households;

b) of commodities to foreigners, overseas Chinese and Chinese compatriots from Hong Kong, Macao and Taiwan visiting China;

c) of commodities to government agencies, institutions, social organizations, military and armed police units, and commodities to enterprises in the form of retail sales. More specifically, they include: office facilities and articles for non-production purposes such as communications equipment, computing equipment and instruments, TV and network equipment, printing and copying equipment, audio-visual equipment and instruments, paper, notebooks, stationeries, furniture, electric appliances, knitwear, sanitation and cleaning articles, cultural and sport articles, articles for prizes, souvenirs, etc.; transport vehicles and fuels for employees; materials, spare parts and tools for the maintenance of office facilities; equipment, fuels, materials and food for winter heating or summer cooling purposes; articles and equipment for teaching purpose; Chinese and western medicines and medical equipment and facilities purchased by non profit-making medical institutes; non- specialized work safety articles; cooking utensils, tableware, equipment, cleaning articles, food and fuels purchased by in-house cafeterias; clothes and personal articles purchased by military or armed police units for their officials and soldiers; and other equipment and articles for non-production purposes.

2) Sales of stable food, cooked dishes, beverages, tobaccos and other articles by catering units.

3) Sales of books, newspapers, magazines, audio-visual products and post products by publishing, post and telecommunications departments to urban and rural households and to enterprises, institutions, military and armed police units.

4) Sales of food, beverages, tobaccos, clothing, hats, footwear, articles for daily use, medicines, medical and health articles, work of art, handicrafts, toys, funeral articles and other articles by other service industries.

Purchase, Sales and Stock of Commodities by Wholesale and Retail Trades refer to the total volume of commodities purchased, total volume of sales and exports, and the stock of commodities by wholesale and retail enterprises (establishments) of different status of registration from domestic and overseas markets. This indicator reflects the relationship among purchase, sales and stock of commodities in the circulation of goods and reveals the existing problems.

Total Purchases of Commodities refer to the total value of purchases of commodities by enterprises (establishments)from other establishments or individuals (including direct import from abroad) for the purpose of re-selling, either with or without further processing of the commodities purchased. The commodities include: (1) commodities purchased from agricultural and industrial producer, wholesaler, retailer, publishing house and other service business; (2) commodities purchased from institutions and government departments; (3) confiscated goods purchased from the customs authorities or market management agencies; (4) second-hand goods and wastes purchased from residents; The commodities exclude 1 commodities purchased by enterprises (establishments) for use in their own business operation, commodities obtained without buying or selling procedures such as materials, consumable goods of low value, office appliances, etc. 2 received goods without trading, such as goods handed over from others, borrowed goods, preserved goods for others, donated goods from others, processed and retrieved goods, etc. 3. goods of direct settlement between buyer and seller with handling fees introduced by others, 4. goods returned or refused to pay by the buyer, 5. excessive goods.

Total Sales of Commodities refer to value of commodities sold by the establishments to other establishments and individuals (including goods sold for self consumption, including the value-added tax). The commodities include: (1) commodities sold to urban and rural residents and social groups for their consumption; (2) commodities sold to establishments in all industries for their production and operation, including agriculture, industry, construction, transportation, post and telecommunications, catering services, and public utility including commodities sold to wholesale and retail establishments for re-selling, with or without further processing; and (3) commodities for direct export to abroad.Excluded are (1) extended commodities without trading, such as goods handed over to other enterprises and institutions because of the change of organizations, lent goods, returned goods preserved for others, extended processing materials and samples donated to others, (2) goods of direct settlement between buyer and seller with handling fees introduced by others, (3)goods returned after purchase, (4) damaged and spoiled goods, (5) waste and used goods of selfuse,

Total Stock of Commodities refers to total commodities possessed by wholesaler and retailer of various types of registration status at the end of the reference period, reflecting the commodity stock level of various wholesaler and retailer and the potential for market supply. It includes: (1) commodities located in storage, garages, counters, and shelves of operating places (such as sale stores, wholesale centres, and operating offices) ; (2) commodities in the process of being selected, sorted, and packed; (3) commodities not arrived but recorded as purchase in the account, i.e. commodities not arrived but payment receipts for the commodities from the sellers or the banks arrived; (4) commodities deposited in other places rather than places mentioned above, for instance: commodities in the hold of purchasers temporarily due to the refusal of payment and commodities not taken back after going through the formalities; (5) commodities entrusted to other units to sell but not sold yet; (6) commodities purchased for other units but not delivered yet. Commodities not included as stock are those not owned by the enterprises (units), commodities on commission for processing but not yet delivered, imported commodities of agency of foreign trade enterprise but not yet delivered to ordering units and finally those put in stock on behalf of the state material reserves units.

Business Revenue of Hotels and Catering Services refers to revenue received from providing services or selling commodities by corporate enterprises and establishments engaged in hotels and catering services, including income from hotels, from catering services, from selling of commodities and from other services. Income from hotels refers to income of corporate enterprises and establishments engaged in hotels and catering services by providing lodging services. Income from catering services refers to income of corporate enterprises and establishments engaged in hotels and catering services by providing catering services, including selling of cooked or prepared foods such as staple food, cooked dishes or cold dishes. Income from selling of commodities refers to income of corporate enterprises and establishments engaged in hotels and catering services by selling commodities (including value-added tax) that accompany the services they provide. Income from other activities refers to income received other than income from hotels, catering services or selling of commodities, such as income from providing recreation, fitness or business services.

Chain Head Stores （headquarter） refer to the core leading stores responsible for development, allocation, administration and utilization of resources (name of stores, brand of stores, operation model, service standard, management way, ect.) of chain stores. Chain stores refers to the stores engaged in providing homogeneous commodities or services, with the central leadership of head store and guided by common policies, conduct centralized purchase and distributed selling of commodities, in order to gain better efficiency through standardized operation. The chain stores include regular chain stores, franchise chain stores and voluntary chain stores.

Regular Chain store refers to chain stores that are invested or controlled by the headquarters. They operate under direct and unified management from the headquarters.

Franchise chain store refers to the chain stores (franchisees) which are franchised with operation resources such as trade marks, names, patent and operation know-how by the franchisors in form of contract and pay the operation fees to the franchisors.

Voluntary chain store refers the stores operate jointly on the voluntary bases while maintaining their status of independent legal entities with full ownership of their assets. They sell goods of same brand from same channel of resource to the consumers.

17 对外经济贸易和旅游

FOREIGN TRADE AND ECONOMIC COOPERATION TOURISM

资料整理：马晓庆　赵琳瑛
Data management：Ma Xiaoqing Zhao Linying
数据审核：栾立森
Data audit：Luan Lisen

第十七部分　对外经济贸易和旅游

一、简要说明

本章资料包括对外经济贸易、利用外资和旅游等方面资料，由西安市统计局贸易外经处根据西安市商务局、海关和旅游局提供资料整理。

二、主要指标

进出口总额（亿元）	1532.15	比上年增长	38.9%
#出　口	734.68	比上年增长	41.1%
实际利用外商直接投资额（亿美元）	37.03	比上年增长	18.3%

17 FOREIGN TRADE AND ECONOMIC COOPERATION,TOURISM

Ⅰ.Brief Introduction

Data in this chapter consists of data on foreign trade, using of foreign capital and fund and tourism. Data on foreign economy and trade and tourism are compiled and provided by Foreign Economy Division of the Xi'an Bureau of Statistics according to the data from Xi'an Bureau of Commerce, Xi'an Custom Office and Xi'an Bureau of Tourism.

Ⅱ.Major Indicators

		Increase over Preceding Year
Total Imports and Exports (100 mil.yuan)	1532.15	38.9%
#Exports	734.68	41.1%
Total Amount of Foreign Direst zwestment (USD 100 mil.)	37.03	18.3%

17-1 主要年份外资、外贸和国际旅游基本情况

Main Indicators on Foreign Investments,International Trading and International Tourism In Representative Years

指　标	Item	1990	1995	2000	2005	2008
一、利用外资签定协议项目(个)	**Number of Projects of Foreign Capital Used through the Signed Agreements and Contracts (unit)**	**11**	**184**	**135**	**157**	**100**
利用外资签定协议金额 （万美元）	Value of Foreign Capital Used through the Signed Agreements and Contracts(USD 10 000)	415	28956	54123	121499	118230
外商实际直接投资额 （万美元）	Value of Foreign Direct Investment (USD 10 000)	1154	18653	15633	57113	114738
二、进出口总额（万美元）	**Total Imports and Exports (USD 10 000)**	**38229**	**137510**	**173696**	**390146**	**704029**
#进口总额	Total Imports	9939	27347	67634	126705	256916
出口总额	Total Exports	28290	110163	106062	263441	447113
进出口差额(出口-进口)	Balance of Imports and Exports	18351	82816	38428	136736	190197
三、国际旅游者人数总计（万人次）	**Total Number of International Tourists (10 000 person-times)**	**25.88**	**41.35**	**65.03**	**77.56**	**63.20**
#外国人	Foreigners	15.40	37.11	54.65	65.86	53.58
港、澳、台同胞	Chinese Compatriot From Hong Kong, Macao and Taiwan	10.07	4.16	10.38	11.70	9.62
四、国际旅游者人天数总计（万人天）	**Total Number of Days of International Tourists (10 000 person/day)**	**55.03**	**84.44**	**162.69**	**224.93**	**162.93**
#外国人	Foreigners	33.48	75.71	131.44	190.99	138.72
港、澳、台同胞	Chinese Compatriot From Hong Kong, Macao and Taiwan	21.55	8.56	31.15	33.94	24.21
五、国际旅游收入（亿元）	**Earning of International Tourism (100 millon yuan)**	**1.96**	**10.38**	**22.41**	**33.54**	**28.72**
#商品收入	Income from Mercantile	0.44	2.57	7.71	11.25	9.74
劳务收入	Income from Labour Service	1.52	7.81	14.70	22.29	18.98
六、国际旅游者在西安人均停留天数（天）	**Number of Days of Average Tourists Staying in Xi'an (day)**	**2.1**	**2.0**	**2.5**	**2.9**	**2.6**

注：1990年和1995年国际旅游者中含华侨。市旅游局未发布2014年国际旅游统计数据。
本表数据来源于市商务局、西安海关、市旅游局。

17-1 续表 continued

指　标	Item	2009	2010	2011	2012	2013	2014*
一、利用外资签定协议项目(个)	**Number of Projects of Foreign Capital Used through the Signed Agreements and Contracts (unit)**	**65**	**82**	**99**	**87**	**152**	**103**
利用外资签定协议金额 （万美元）	Value of Foreign Capital Used through the Signed Agreements and Contracts(USD 10 000)	60027	119689	120083	360264	251874	255321
外商实际直接投资额 （万美元）	Value of Foreign Direct Investment (USD 10 000)	121872	156653	200522	247800	312994	370310
二、进出口总额（万美元）	**Total Imports and Exports (USD 10 000)**	**724618**	**1039273**	**1260179**	**1301446**	**1798534**	**15321514**
#进口总额	Total Imports	391504	507544	677517	571568	950715	7974693
出口总额	Total Exports	333114	531729	582662	729878	847819	7346822
进出口差额(出口-进口)	Balance of Imports and Exports	-58390	24185	-94855	158310	-102896	-627871
三、国际旅游者人数总计（万人次）	**Total Number of International Tourists (10 000 person-times)**	**67.29**	**84.18**	**100.23**	**115.34**	**121.11**	
#外国人	Foreigners	59.09	73.21	88.63	101.40	106.89	
港、澳、台同胞	Chinese Compatriot From Hong Kong, Macao and Taiwan	8.20	10.97	11.60	13.94	14.22	
四、国际旅游者人天数总计（万人天）	**Total Number of Days of International Tourists (10 000 person/day)**	**195.14**	**241.67**	**287.09**	**334.44**	**351.11**	
#外国人	Foreigners	171.36	211.48	254.78	294.90	310.26	
港、澳、台同胞	Chinese Compatriot From Hong Kong, Macao and Taiwan	23.78	30.19	32.31	39.54	40.85	
五、国际旅游收入（亿元）	**Earning of International Tourism (100 millonyuan)**	**31.05**	**42.40**	**51.28**	**59.89**	**64.16**	
#商品收入	Income from Mercantile	8.94	11.87	11.38	14.19	14.69	
劳务收入	Income from Labour Service	22.11	30.53	39.90	45.70	49.47	
六、国际旅游者在西安人均停留天数(天)	**Number of Days of Average Tourists Staying in Xi'an (day)**	**2.9**	**2.9**	**2.9**	**2.9**	**2.9**	

注：2014年进出口数据计量单位为万元。

17-2 主要年份利用外资情况

Utilization of Foreign Capital In Representative Years

单位：万美元 (USD 10 000)

年份 Year	利用外资签订协议金额 Value of Foreign Capital Used through the Signed Agreements and Contracts	外商实际直接投资额 Direct Foreign Investment
1983	3500	800
1984	8	
1985	8361	1106
1986	19919	4010
1987	3218	5552
1988	2423	6758
1989	1645	11632
1990	415	1154
1991	591	1094
1992	24165	5200
1993	57289	8996
1994	20321	15240
1995	28956	18653
1996	35978	20510
1997	27214	22057
1998	40034	22286
1999	40390	13801
2000	54123	15633
2001	60736	17687
2002	70692	20281
2003	96380	25557
2004	78312	27595
2005	121499	57113
2006	182525	82463
2007	143978	111567
2008	118230	114738
2009	60027	121872
2010	119689	156653
2011	120083	200522
2012	360264	247800
2013	251874	312994
2014	255321	370310

注：本表数据来源于市商务局。

17-3 外国和港澳台地区在西安直接投资（2014年）

Direct Investments from Foreign Countries and Hong Kong, Macao and Taiwan in Xi'an（2014）

分类	Classity	新签协议情况 New-signed Agreement Circumstances		外商实际直接投资额（万美元） Value of Foreign Direct Investment (USD 10 000)
		合同数（个） Number of Constracts (unit)	利用外资签定协议金额（万美元） Value of Foreign Captial Used through the Signed (USD10 000)	
合　计	**Total**	**103**	**255321**	**370310**
一、按投资方式分	**Grouped by Investment Mode**			
1.中外合资经营企业	Joint-venture Enterprises	24	107704	95142
2.中外合作经营企业	Cooperation Enterprises		-860	10010
3.外资企业	Wholly Foreign-owned Enterprises	79	148477	255250
4.外资企业再投资	Re-investment from Foreign-funded Enterprises			
二、按国民经济行业分组	**Grouped by Sector**			
1.农、林、牧、渔业	Agriculture, Forestry, Animal Husbandry and Fishery		1250	1148
2.采矿业	Mining			
3.制造业	Manufacturing	27	109458	224487
4.电力、燃气及水的生产供应业	Production and Distribution of Electricity,Gas and Water			610
5.建筑业	Construction	5	1924	5
6.批发和零售业	Wholesale and Retail Trades	22	2392	21413
7.交通运输、仓储和邮政业	Traffic, Transport, Storage and Post		2674	3036
8.住宿和餐饮业	Hotels and Catering Services	7	502	2149
9.信息传输、软件和信息技术服务业	Information Transmission,Software and Information Technology Services	9	6030	9065
10.金融业	Financial Intermediation		1241	16152
11.房地产	Real Estate	8	97217	64631
12.租赁和商务服务业	Leasing and Business Services	19	9388	19362
13.科学研究和技术服务业	Scientific Research and Technical Service	1	7912	8167
14.水利、环境和公共设施管理业	Management of Water Conservancy,Environment and Public Facilities		1002	
15.居民服务、修理和其他服务业	Services to Households,Repairs and Other Services		169	11
16.教育	Education	2	12751	0
17.卫生和社会工作	Health and Social Work		1071	72
18.文化、体育和娱乐业	Culture, Sports and Entertainment	3	340	1
19.公共管理社会保障和社会组织	Public Management ,Social Security and Social Drganizations			
20.国际组织	International Organizations			
三、按投资国别、地区分组	**Grouped by Different Countries and Regions**			
香港	Hong Kong	47	193596	207112
澳门	Macao	1	4251	
台湾省	Taiwan	3	30	27
日本	Japan		111	2083
泰国	Thailand			
马来西亚	Malaysia	1	16	8
新加坡	Singapore	5	16185	10289
韩国	Korea	29	22207	126846
德意志联邦国	Germany	2	890	53
意大利	Italy	1	5	
法国	France	1	41	383
英国	United Kingdom	1	12	102
捷克共和国	Czechoslovakia			
加拿大	Canada			36
美国	America	4	682	8977
澳大利亚	Australia			307
维尔京群岛	Virgian Islands		969	1502
其它	Other	8	16327	12587

注：本表数据来源于市商务局。

17-4 各区县、开发区外商实际直接投资

Direct Investment by Foreign Entrepreneurs by Region and Development Zone

单位：万美元 (USD 10 000)

区县及开发区	Region and Economic Zone	2009	2010	2011	2012	2013	2014
区、县合计	**Sum of Region**	**29766**	**38855**	**49726**	**58119**	**45164**	**51423**
新城区	Xincheng	3740	4900	6765	7800	5012	6500
碑林区	Beilin	4780	5150	6273	7800	5103	5871
莲湖区	Lianhu	3953	5471	7405	7800	5100	5843
灞桥区	Baqiao	4300	5215	6001	7397	6124	6933
未央区	Weiyang	3902	5023	6202	7800	6000	6834
雁塔区	Yanta	4087	5488	6912	8190	6179	6847
阎良区	Yanliang	675	1208	2070	2200	2200	2346
临潼区	Lintong	970	1200	2000	2400	2400	2504
长安区	Chang'an	1219	1680	2300	2768	3003	3360
蓝田县	Lantian	605	950	1089	1100	1100	1182
周至县	Zhouzhi	315	550	600	650	660	707
户县	Huxian	560	970	1050	1100	1110	1210
高陵县	Gaoling	660	1050	1060	1115	1173	1288
开发区合计	**Sum of Development Zones**	**92107**	**117798**	**150797**	**189681**	**267830**	**318887**
高新区	GaoXin	40613	51130	64935	81776	132632	149387
经开区	JingKai	33661	42608	54201	68202	81423	103009
曲江新区	Qujiang	12589	17187	21002	26433	33870	41436
浐灞生态区	Chanba Eco-District	2400	3070	3856	4837	7266	8453
航空基地	Aviation Industry Base	1016	1239	1701	2072	2640	3082
航天基地	Aerospace Base	1208	1554	2030	2403	3000	3501
国际港务区	International Trade&Logistic Park	620	1010	1571	2082	3469	5050
沣东新城	FengDongXinCheng			1500	1876	3530	4970

注：本表数据来源于市商务局。

17-5 主要年份进出口总额

Total Imports and Exports In Representative Years

单位：万美元 (USD 10 000)

年 份 Year	进出口总额 Total Imports and Exports	出口总额 Total Exports	进口总额 Total Imports
1987	13596	7540	6056
1988	36750	24632	12118
1989	32715	21564	11151
1990	38229	28290	9939
1991	55356	41511	13845
1992	70467	53060	17407
1993	93330	62393	30937
1994	104752	76897	27855
1995	137510	110163	27347
1996	143187	91745	51442
1997	150668	107753	42915
1998	180589	100492	80097
1999	172919	94495	78424
2000	173696	106062	67634
2001	169914	87948	81966
2002	186966	112479	74487
2003	230932	140327	90605
2004	309295	203539	105756
2005	390146	263441	126705
2006	415403	272862	142541
2007	536162	347133	189029
2008	704029	447113	256916
2009	724618	333114	391504
2010	1039273	531729	507544
2011	1260179	582662	677517
2012	1301446	729878	571568
2013	1798534	847819	950715
2014*	15321514	7346822	7974693

注：本表数据来源于西安海关。*按照统计制度规定，2014年统计数据计量单位为人民币万元。

17-6 外贸商品进出口总额分国别和地区（2014年）

Total Value of Imports and Exports by Country and Region（2014）

单位：万元　　(10 000 yuan)

国别和地区	Country and Region	进出口总额 Total Imports and Exports	出口 Exports
亚洲	**Asia**	**8594363**	**4300280**
#香港	Hong kong	1642208	1620826
台湾省	Taiwan	2597378	487567
日本	Japan	833619	234355
菲律宾	Phiilippines	64906	34522
马来西亚	Malaysia	241928	116618
韩国	Korea	1689763	775067
非洲	**Africa**	**682768**	**350470**
#埃及	Egypt	36429	36348
突尼斯	Tunisia	1988	1830
埃塞俄比亚	Ethiopia	24211	24211
博茨瓦纳	Botswana	225	225
南非	South Africa	306849	36113
欧洲	**Europe**	**1909682**	**915789**
#德意志联邦国	Germany	362422	98421
法国	France	271591	207527
意大利	Italy	111230	44609
荷兰	Netherland	285650	63548
英国	England	331240	283239
瑞士	Switzerland	48686	3237
西班牙	Spain	21886	16045
俄罗斯联邦	Russia	74864	64698
拉丁美洲	**Latin America**	**525345**	**420722**
#哥伦比亚	Colombia	7226	7216
巴西	Brazil	51303	23312
阿根廷	Argentina	8101	6929
北美洲	**North America**	**3380565**	**1319005**
加拿大	Canada	97162	43732
美国	America	3283402	1275272
大洋洲及太平洋岛屿	**Oceanic and Pacific Islands**	**228678**	**40556**
#澳大利亚	Australia	219294	33284
新西兰	New Zealand	4987	2876

注：本表数据来源于西安海关。

17-7 主要商品分大类出口金额

单位：万美元

商品分类	HS Section and Division	2000	2004
食用蔬菜、根及块茎	Edible Vegetables, Certain,Roots amd Tubers	1095	1386
蔬菜、水果、坚果或植物其他部分的制品	Vegetables, Fruits, Nuts, or Products Made of Other Parts of Plants	2076	7786
矿砂、矿渣及矿灰	Ores,Slags and Ash	4083	30590
无机化学品；贵金属、稀土金属、放射性元素及其同位素的有机及无机化合物	Inorganic Chemicals,Organic or Inorganic Compounds of Precious Metals,of Rare Earth Metals,of Radioactive Elements or of Isotopes	3714	5806
有机化学品	Organic Chemicals	2367	4837
羊毛、动物细毛或粗毛、马毛纱线及其机织物	Wool ,Fine or Coarse Animal Hair; Horsehair Yarn and Woven Fabric	810	1640
棉花	Cotton	3197	3133
化学纤维短纤	Short Staple Chemical' Fibers	5061	1987
针织或钩编的服装及衣着附件	Articles of Apparel and Clothing Accessories, Knitted or Crocheted	6753	7465
非针织或非钩编的服装及衣着附件	Articles of Apparel and Clothing Accessories, not Knitted or Crocheted	7269	5543
其它纺织制成品；成套物品；旧衣着及旧纺织品	Other Made Up Textile Articles;Sets;Worn Clothing and Worn Textile Articles;Rags Articles	1649	2667
鞋靴、护膝和类似品及其零件	Footwear,Gaiters and The Like;Parts of Such Articles Headgear and Parts Thereof	1347	2687
玻璃及其制品	Glass and Glassware	3376	8083
钢铁	Iron and Steel	3534	5244
钢铁制品	Articles of Iron or Steel	5535	10398
铅及制品	Lead Areticles Thereof	1371	43
锌及制品	Zinc Areticles Thereof	4031	522
其他贱金属、金属陶瓷及其制品	Other Base Metals,Germets;Areticles Thereof	1066	6419
贱金属工具、器具、利口器、餐匙、餐叉及其零件	Tools,Implements,Cutlery,Spons and Forks, of Base Metal;Parts Thereof of Base Metal	2933	3406
核反应堆、锅炉、机器、机械器具及其零件	Nuclear Reactors ,Boilers, Machinery and Mechanical Appliances; and Parts Thereof	10915	24696
电机、电气设备及其零件；录音机及放声机、电视图象、声音的录制和重放设备及其零件、附件	Electrical Machinery and Equipment and Parts Thereof;Sound Recorders and Repreducers, Television Image and Sound Recordes and Repreducers, and Parts and Accessories of Such Articles	8339	19812
光学、照相、电影、计量、检验、医疗或外科仪器及设备、精密仪器及设备；上述物品的零配件、附件	Optical,Photographic,Cinematographic,Measuring, Checking,Precision Medical or Surgical Instruments and Apparatus;Parts and Accessories Thereof	2020	1847
家具、寝具、褥垫、弹簧床垫、软床垫及类似的填充制品；未列名灯具及照明装置；发光标志、发光名牌及类似品；活动房屋	Mattresses,Mattress Supports,Cushions and Similar Stuffed Furnishings;Lamps and Lighting Fittings, not Elsewhere Spcified or Included;Illumihated Signs,Illuminated	2587	4955

注：本表数据来源于西安海关。*2014年数据计量单位为人民币万元。

Export Value of Major Merchandise by Type

(USD 10 000)

2005	2006	2007	2008	2009	2010	2011	2012	2013	2014*
1190	1136	1232	1374	803	4740	2016	1961	2699	2686
10531	15374	37426	29270	21920	41289	36763	2576	49361	132663
63247	52046	47378	40502	6141	325	4709	1679	1686	14977
10997	10916	16508	15882	9774	24875	11735	8911	12588	67764
8569	11923	11182	13954	16294	982	20067	17890	28694	109986
903	1400	1065	720	460	10133	796	562	2433	15782
3240	3808	3255	3213	2346	98	2628	2185	5827	9252
1471	1556	1767	1181	2217	479	2586	2375	8245	13685
5736	5332	5345	4371	3617	3209	3366	12316	6491	29551
5068	4078	3875	3623	2919	3394	3262	7050	4861	33872
3000	3342	3090	3187	2813	544	2838	4412	4471	18906
1368	216	348	380	367	150	1003	5252	6293	20186
8576	8272	6246	6538	5574	928	8073	10995	13856	54453
5314	4900	11366	11966	4254	18549	16681	8407	6730	31854
13959	16903	17329	26568	11943	5998	25319	24259	33546	102720
12	158	1650	2	1	10	2	4913	16	3
135	4119	2470	46	78	28545	10	11	59	109
11233	17695	23414	27576	11276	3556	28092	21397	24030	106691
3052	3607	3917	4083	2777	2893	3641	5176	5992	30653
30832	36174	47381	75911	52372	130296	99631	127795	211009	1929864
23605	22801	33393	56758	53355	136	137105	183536	327931	3113155
2341	3521	4230	6348	5255	196	11066	14908	17879	112646
4773	5086	8301	8296	4769	5328	3860	25644	23595	52352

17-8 主要商品分大类进口金额

Import Value of Major Merchandise by Type

单位：万美元 (USD 10 000)

商品分类	HS Section and Division	2000	2005	2007	2008	2009
无机化学品；贵金属、稀土金属、放射性元素及其同位素的有机及无机化合物	Inorganic Chemicals,Organic or Inorganic Compounds of Precious Metals,of Rare Earth Metals,of Radioactive Elements or of Isotopes	1467	317	1039	6001	5040
有机化学品	Organic Chemicals	7257	15237	14536	15692	14186
塑料及其制品	Plastic and Articles Thereof	2559	4317	5149	2553	3134
钢铁	Iron and Steel	2467	752	1270	3888	2537
铜及制品	Copper and Articles Thereof	2367	689	22683	11097	41195
铝及制品	Aluminium and Articles Thereof	2652	3627	3223	4767	6505
核反应堆、锅炉、机器、机械器具及其零件	Nuclear Reactors ,Boilers, Machinery and Mechanical Appliances; and Parts Thereof	12990	38050	55243	68504	87493
电机、电气设备及其零件；录音机及放声机、电视图象、声音的录制和重放设备及其零件、附件	Electrical Machinery and Equipment and Parts Thereof;Sound Recorders and Repreducers, Television Image and Sound Recordes and Repreducers,and Parts and Accessories of Such Articles	5911	23337	25164	48008	113034
车辆及其零件、附件、铁道及电车道车辆除外	Vehicles Other Than Railway or Tramway Rolling-Stock, and Rarts and Accessories Thereof	1530	1387	1529	3789	1798
航空器、航天器及其零配件	Aircraft, Spacecraft and Parts Thereof	10443	8800	2463	26148	13057
光学、照相、电影、计量、检验、医疗或外科仪器及设备、精密仪器及设备；上述物品的零配件、附件	Optical,Photographic,Cinematographic,Measuring, Checking,Precision Medical or Surgical	3673	10424	17026	17737	24210

17-8 续表 continued

单位：万美元 (USD 10 000)

商品分类	HS Section and Division	2010	2011	2012	2013	2014*
无机化学品；贵金属、稀土金属、放射性元素及其同位素的有机及无机化合物	Inorganic Chemicals,Organic or Inorganic Compounds of Precious Metals,of Rare Earth Metals,of Radioactive Elements or of Isotopes	7513	19766	13329	11869	166549
有机化学品	Organic Chemicals	13949	18100	12331	12504	98293
塑料及其制品	Plastic and Articles Thereof	4091	3250	3107	8014	37082
钢铁	Iron and Steel	10949	10643	5928	1802	11893
铜及制品	Copper and Articles Thereof	43343	78482	11857	65170	169061
铝及制品	Aluminium and Articles Thereof	3116	5913	8649	11758	45295
核反应堆、锅炉、机器、机械器具及其零件	Nuclear Reactors ,Boilers, Machinery and Mechanical Appliances; and Parts Thereof	134753	135240	98802	186974	2017587
电机、电气设备及其零件；录音机及放声机、电视图象、声音的录制和重放设备及其零件、附件	Electrical Machinery and Equipment and Parts Thereof;Sound Recorders and Repreducers, Television Image and Sound Recordes and Repreducers,and Parts and Accessories of Such Articles	207937	230957	257444	444407	3919650
车辆及其零件、附件、铁道及电车道车辆除外	Vehicles Other Than Railway or Tramway Rolling-Stock, and Rarts and Accessories Thereof	3109	1527	2222	2966	17521
航空器、航天器及其零配件	Aircraft, Spacecraft and Parts Thereof	3620	4654	8516	9179	43191
光学、照相、电影、计量、检验、医疗或外科仪器及设备、精密仪器及设备；上述物品的零配件、附件	Optical,Photographic,Cinematographic,Measuring, Checking,Precision Medical or Surgical	37414	39317	48206	61727	452559

注：本表数据来源于西安海关。*2014年数据计量单位为人民币万元。

17-9 主要年份旅游人数及收入

Number of Tourists and Tourism Earnings In Representative Years

年 份 Year	接待旅游者人数（万人次） Number of Tourists (10 000 person-times)	国际旅游人数 Number of International Tourists	旅游总收入（万元） Total Tourism Earnings (10 000 yuan)	国际旅游收入 Earning of International Tourists	国际旅游者在西安人均停留天数（天） Number of Days of Average International Tourists Staying in Xi'an(day)
1980	4.00	4.00	1757	1757	3.8
1981	6.71	6.71	2314	2314	3.4
1985	21.15	21.15	7029	7029	2.2
1986	25.78	25.78	10886	10886	2.2
1987	30.15	30.15	16588	16588	2.1
1988	36.58	36.58	21152	21152	2.0
1989	21.20	21.20	14125	14125	1.9
1990	25.88	25.88	19628	19628	2.1
1991	31.00	31.00	29051	29051	2.3
1992	40.16	40.16	40966	40966	2.2
1993	43.50	43.50	48951	48951	1.9
1994	41.49	41.49	82000	82000	2.2
1995	791.35	41.35	440000	103818	2.0
1996	925.39	45.39	470000	149400	2.6
1997	1010.53	48.53	510000	166359	2.6
1998	1105.80	47.98	560000	160244	2.6
1999	1260.40	55.41	830000	186282	2.5
2000	1567.00	65.03	1050000	224100	2.5
2001	1752.20	67.20	1130000	240700	2.4
2002	1984.13	74.13	1310000	260000	2.2
2003	1647.67	33.66	1064200	121200	2.5
2004	2149.03	65.03	1544000	273900	2.9
2005	2423.60	77.56	1785000	335380	2.9
2006	2738.70	86.73	2043000	378270	2.9
2007	3118.01	100.01	2372000	424263	2.9
2008	3232.20	63.20	2435200	287200	2.6
2009	3929.29	67.29	2974000	310500	2.9
2010	5285.18	84.18	4051800	424000	2.9
2011	6653.23	100.23	5301500	512800	2.9
2012	7978.35	115.35	6543900	598900	2.9
2013	10130.00	121.11	8114400	641600	2.9
2014	12000.00		9500000		

注：本表数据来源于市旅游局。市旅游局未发布2014年国际旅游统计数据。

17-10 主要年份旅行社及A级景点

Statistics of Travel Agencies and Level-A Scenic Spots in Representative Years

项 目	Item	2007	2008	2009	2010	2011	2012	2013	2014
旅行社数（个）	Number of Travel Agencies (unit)	262	271	303	334	365	344	360	385
旅行社营业收入（亿元）	Revenue of Travel Agencies (100 million yuan)	26.48	17.85	21.34	31.22	44.31	49.49	57.93	45.70
旅游A级景点数（个）	Number of Level-A Scenic Spots(unit)	23	23	24	34	43	55	61	67
旅游A级景点年接待游客人次（万人次）	Number of Tourists Received at Level-A Scenic Spots (10 000 person times)	1410	1420	1504	2726	4295	5306	7163	7462

注：本表数据来源于市旅游局。

主要统计指标解释

进出口总额 指实际进出我国国境的货物总金额。包括对外贸易实际进出口货物，来料加工装配进出口货物，国家间、联合国及国际组织无偿援助物资和赠送品，华侨、港澳台同胞和外籍华人捐赠品，租赁期满归承租人所有的租赁货物，进料加工进出口货物，边境地方贸易及边境地区小额贸易进出口货物（边民互市贸易除外），中外合资企业、中外合作经营企业、外商独资经营企业进出口货物和公用物品，到、离岸价格在规定限额以上的进出口货样和广告品（无商业价值、无使用价值和免费提供出口的除外），从保税仓库提取在中国境内销售的进口货物，以及其他进出口货物。该指标可以观察一个国家在对外贸易方面的总规模。我国规定出口货物按离岸价格统计，进口货物按到岸价格统计。

商品经营单位所在地进、出口额 指在所在地海关注册登记的有进出口经营权的企业实际进、出口额。

商品目的地进口额和商品货源地出口额 目的地进口额指进口货物的消费、使用或最终抵运地的实际进口额；货源地出口额指出口货物的产地或原始发货地的实际出口额。

利用外资 指我国各级政府、部门、企业和其他经济组织通过对外借款、吸收外商直接投资以及用其他方式筹措的境外现汇、设备、技术等。

外商直接投资 指外国企业和经济组织或个人（包括华侨、港澳台胞以及我国在境外注册的企业）按我国有关政策、法规，用现汇、实物、技术等在我国境内开办外商独资企业、与我国境内的企业或经济组织共同举办中外合资经营企业、合作经营企业或合作开发资源的投资（包括外商投资收益的再投资），以及经政府有关部门批准的项目投资总额内企业从境外借入的资金。

旅游人数：

（1）入境旅游人数：指报告期内来我国观光、度假、探亲访友、就医疗养、购物、参加会议或从事经济、文化、体育、宗教活动的外国人、港澳台同胞等入境游客。统计时，外国人、港澳台同胞每入境一次统计1人次。

（2）出境人数：指中国（大陆）居民因公或因私出境前往其他国家、中国香港特别行政区、澳门特别行政区和台湾省观光、度假、探亲访友、就医疗养、购物、参加会议或从事经济、文化、体育、宗教活动的人数，即出境游客。统计时，按每出境一次统计1人次。

（3）国内旅游人数：指在报告期内在中国（大陆）观光游览、度假、探亲访友、就医疗养、购物、参加会议或从事经济、文化、体育、宗教活动的中国（大陆）居民人数，其出游的目的不是通过所从事的活动谋取报酬。统计时，国内游客按每出游一次统计1人次。

国际旅游（外汇）收入 指入境游客在中国（大陆）境内旅行、游览过程中用于交通、参观游览、住宿、餐饮、购物、娱乐等全部花费。

国内旅游收入 又称旅游总花费指国内游客在国内旅行、游览过程中用于交通、参观游览、住宿、餐饮、购物、娱乐等全部花费。

国际旅行社 指经营业务范围包括入境旅游业务、出境旅游业务和国内旅游业务的旅行社。

国内旅行社 指经营范围仅限于国内旅游业务的旅行社。

星级饭店 指设备、设施、服务符合《旅游饭店星级的划分与评定》（CB／T14308—2003），通过相关旅游管理部门评定，并取得星级饭店称号的饭店（含预备星级饭店）。

Explanatory Notes on Main Statistical Indicators

Total Imports and Exports at Customs refer to the real value of commodities imported and exported across the border of China. They include the actual imports and exports through foreign trade, imported and exported goods under the processing and assembling trades and materials, supplies and gifts as aid given gratis between governments and by the United Nations and other international organizations, and contributions donated by overseas Chinese, compatriots in Hong Kong and Macao and Chinese with foreign citizenship, leasing commodities owned by tenant at the expiration of leasing period, the imported and exported commodities processed with imported materials, commodities trading in border areas (excluding mutual exchange goods), the imported and exported commodities and articles for public use of the Sino-foreign joint ventures, cooperative enterprises and ventures with sole foreign investment. Also included is import or export of samples and advertising goods for which CIF or FOB value are beyond the permitted ceiling (excluding goods of no trading or use value and free commodities for export), imported goods sold in China from bonded warehouses and other imported or exported goods. The indicator of the total imports and exports at customs can be used to observe the total size of external trade in a country. In accordance with the stipulation of the Chinese government, imports are calculated at CIF, while exports are calculated at FOB.

Import Export Value by Location of China's Foreign Trade Managing Units refers to actual value of imports and exports carried out by corporations which have been registered by the local Customs house and are vested with right to run import export business.

Import Value of Commodities by Place of Destination and Export Value of Commodities by Place of Origin in China The former indicator refers to the value of import commodities of the places of their consumption, utilization or the places of their final destination. The latter indicator refers to the value of export commodities of the places of their origin or the places of the commodities dispatched.

Utilization of Foreign Capitals refers to remittance, equipment and technology financed from abroad, by loans, foreign direct investment and other forms undertaken by the Chinese governments at all levels, by various departments, enterprises and other economic units.

Foreign Borrowings refer to funds borrowed from abroad through formal signing of borrowing agreements with foreign institutions, including loans of foreign governments, loans of international financial institutions, commercial loans of foreign banks, export credit, and funds raised by Chinese bonds (and shares before 1996) issued abroad. It is an important part of China's utilization of foreign capitals.

Foreign Direct Investment refers to the investments inside China by foreign enterprises and economic organizations or individuals (including overseas Chinese, compatriots from Hong Kong, Macao and Taiwan, and Chinese enterprises registered abroad), following the relevant policies and laws of China, for the establishment of ventures exclusively with foreign own investment, Sino-foreign joint ventures and cooperative enterprises or for co-operative exploration of resources with enterprises or economic organizations in China.

Number of Tourists

(1) Visitor arrivals refer to the number of foreigners,Chinese compatriots from Hong Kong, Macao and Taiwan Chinese (mainland) who come to China (mainland) for sight-seeing,vacation,visiting relatives, medical treatment, shopping, attending conference, or to engage in economic, cultural, sports and religious activities. In compiling statistics, each time of entering China is counted as one person-time.

(2) Number of Chinese residents going abroad refer to the number of Chinese (mainland) residents going to other countries, Hong Kong Special Administrative region, Macao Special Administrative region and Taiwan for on official or private purposes, for sight-seeing, vacation, visiting relatives, medical treatment, shopping, attending conference, or to engage in economic, cultural, sports and religious

activities. In compiling statistics, each time of leaving is counted as one person-time.

(3) Number of domestic tourists refers to the number of Chinese (mainland) residents who travel within China (mainland) for sight-seeing, vacation, visiting relatives, medical treatment, shopping, attending conference, or to engage in economic, cultural, sports and religious activities. In compiling statistics, each time of travelling is counted as one person-time.

Foreign Exchange Earnings from International Tourism refer to the total expenditure of foreigners, overseas Chinese,Chinese compatriots from Hong Kong,Macao and Taiwan during their stay in the mainland of China on transportation,sighting,accommodation, food,shopping and entertainment.

Income from Domestic Tourism refer to expenditure of domestic tourists on transportation,sighting, accommodation, food, shopping and entertainment while they travel.

International Travel Agencies refer to travel agencies engaged in tourism entering China, Chinese residents going abroad and domestic tourism.

Domestic Travel Agencies refer to travel agencies only engaged in domestic tourism.

Star-rated Hotels refer to hotels rated with stars as assessed by the relevant tourism authorities according to GB/T14308-2003 standard with reference to their infrastructure, facilities and service levels.

18 规模以上服务业

SERVICE ENTERPRISES ABOVE DESIGNATED SIZE

资料整理：王家峰
Data management：Wang Jiafeng
数据审核：王金桂
Data audit：Wang Jingui

第十八部分　规模以上服务业

一、简要说明

本资料主要包括规模以上服务业（九个门类、两个中类）单位个数及主要经济指标，由西安市统计局社科处提供。

二、主要指标

单位数（个）	964		
资产总计（亿元）	5719.10	比上年增长	7.9%
营业收入（亿元）	1558.30	比上年增长	7.5%
利润总额（亿元）	128.83	比上年下降	8.5%

18　SERVICE ENTERPRISES ABOVE DESIGNATED SIZE

Ⅰ.Brief Introduction

The data in this chapter consists of The number of service units and main economic indicators of Service enterprises above designated size(Including nine categories, two in Class),data in this chapter is provided by Social Science&Technology Division of Xi'an Bureau of Statistics.

Ⅱ.Major Indicators

		Increase over Preceding Year
Number of units(units)	964	
Total assets (100 mil. yuan)	5719.10	7.9%
Operating income(100 mil. yuan)	1558.30	7.5%
The total profit (100 mil. yuan)	128.83	-8.5%

18-1 规模以上服务业按登记注册类型分主要经济指标

Main Economic Indicators for Services above the Designated Size grouped by Registration Type

单位：万元 (10 000 yuan)

指　标	Item	单位数（个）Number of Enterprises (unit)	资产总计 Total Assets	固定资产原价 Original Value of Fixed Assets
总计	**Totai**	**964**	**57191024.8**	**32084508.8**
按登记注册类型分组	**Grouped by Registration Type**			
内资企业	Domestic Funded Enterprises	917	56612502.4	31908194.9
国有	State-owned Enterprises	105	2898448	1168739.8
集体	Collective-owned Enterprises	18	64732.5	18823.5
股份合作	Corperative Enterprises	5	14524.1	4577.1
联营	Joint Ownership Enterprises			
国有联营	State Joint Ownership Enterprises			
集体联营	Collective Joint Ownership Enterprises			
国有与集体联营	Joint State-collective Enterprises			
其他联营	Others Joint Ownership Enterprises			
有限限责任公司	Limited Liability Corporrations	490	47355580.8	26842833.8
国有独资公司	State Funded Corporations	52	24144947.2	10434946.7
其他有限责任公司	Other Limited Liability Corporrations	438	23210633.6	16407887.1
股份有限公司	Other Limited Liability Corporrations	45	4614833.2	3634757.5
私营	Other Limited Liability Corporrations	241	1593328.9	219288.2
私营独资	Private-funded Enterprises	11	12534.8	6716.6
私营合伙	Private Partnership Enterprises	6	48025.6	13681.2
私营有限责任公司	Private Limited Liability Corporations	212	1434898.8	193469.4
私营股份有限公司	Private Share-holding Corporations Ltd.	12	97869.7	5421
其他	Other Enterprises	13	71054.9	19175
港澳台商投资	Enterprises with Funds from Hong Kong, Macao &Taiwan	14	360482.3	93289.3
合资经营	Joint Ventures	7	232339.2	81865.1
合作经营	Cooperation Enterprises	2	85686.5	5592.6
港澳台商独资经营	Enterprises with Sole Investment from Hong Kong Macau and Taiwan	5	42456.6	5831.6
港澳台商投资股份有限公司	Share-holding Corporations Ltd. with funds from Hong Kong, Macao & Taiwan			
外商投资	Foreign Funded Enterprises	33	218040.1	83024.6
中外合资经营企业	Sino-foreign Joint Ventures Enterprises	9	59344.9	19306.6
中外合作经营企业	Sino-Foreign Cooperation Enterprises	2	5016.5	3528.2
外资企业	Foreign Owned Enterprises	19	147169.9	58417.5
外商投资股份有限公司	Limited Company Funded by Foreign Investment	1	538	205.5
其他外商投资	Other Foreign Funded Enterprises	2	5970.8	1566.8

18-1 续表1

单位：万元

指 标	Item	负债合计 Total Liabilities	所有者权益合计 Total Owners' Equities	营业收入 Paid in Capital
总计	**Totai**	**35360374.1**	**21830650.7**	**15582963.5**
按登记注册类型分组	**Grouped by Category of Commodities**			
内资企业	Domestic Funded Enterprises	35136740.1	21475762.3	15236581.6
国有	State-owned Enterprises	1786506.3	1111941.7	1975607.1
集体	Collective-owned Enterprises	39446.1	25286.4	56590.6
股份合作	Corperative Enterprises	9031.4	5492.7	4544.7
联营	Joint Ownership Enterprises			
国有联营	State Joint Ownership Enterprises			
集体联营	Collective Joint Ownership Enterprises			
国有与集体联营	Joint State-collective Enterprises			
其他联营	Others Joint Ownership Enterprises			
有限限责任公司	Limited Liability Corporrations	30145121.2	17210459.6	10718703.3
国有独资公司	State Funded Corporations	16339020.7	7805926.5	1579539.7
其他有限责任公司	Other Limited Liability Corporrations	13806100.5	9404533.1	9139163.6
股份有限公司	Other Limited Liability Corporrations	2086544.2	2528289	1737998.5
私营	Other Limited Liability Corporrations	1022908	570420.9	670174.9
私营独资	Private-funded Enterprises	8694.4	3840.4	13075.5
私营合伙	Private Partnership Enterprises	33135.9	14889.7	38055.1
私营有限责任公司	Private Limited Liability Corporations	949953.7	484945.1	577045.3
私营股份有限公司	Private Share-holding Corporations Ltd.	31124	66745.7	41999
其他	Other Enterprises	47182.9	23872	72962.5
港澳台商投资	Enterprises with Funds from Hong Kong, Macao &Taiwan	132727.7	227754.6	175485.1
合资经营	Joint Ventures	96723.5	135615.7	106854.1
合作经营	Cooperation Enterprises	25245	60441.5	31725
港澳台商独资经营	Enterprises with Sole Investment from Hong Kong Macau and Taiwan	10759.2	31697.4	36906
港澳台商投资股份有限公司	Share-holding Corporations Ltd. with funds from Hong Kong, Macao & Taiwan			
外商投资	Foreign Funded Enterprises	90906.3	127133.8	170896.8
中外合资经营企业	Sino-foreign Joint Ventures Enterprises	32940.9	26404	31274.9
中外合作经营企业	Sino-Foreign Cooperation Enterprises	1437.9	3578.6	4208.4
外资企业	Foreign Owned Enterprises	54715.2	92454.7	121983.5
外商投资股份有限公司	Limited Company Funded by Foreign Investment	603	-65	6765.4
其他外商投资	Other Foreign Funded Enterprises	1209.3	4761.5	6664.6

continued1

(10 000 yuan)

主营业务收入 Revenue from Principal Business	营业成本 Total Cost	主营业务成本 Cost of Principal Business	销售费用 Sale Expenses
15269323.8	**10974917.9**	**10663582**	**1290467.9**
14925755.1	10790590.1	10482069.4	1271896.8
1942149.4	1830323.3	1753868.2	39841.6
56512.2	32182.5	29997	6144.1
4256.3	1696	1631	384.8
10476244.5	7256662.4	7046971.6	1036680
1558915.6	977887.4	961889.1	55151.6
8917328.9	6278775	6085082.5	981528.4
1712560.3	1166321	1154745.3	144436
664093.5	456715.7	448178.2	37900.5
13074	8819.4	8421.3	1120.5
38055.1	25306.5	25306.5	914.3
570965.4	393310.5	386633.3	35194.3
41999	29279.3	27817.1	671.4
69938.9	46689.2	46678.1	6509.8
173203.4	79816.7	79005.5	10080.1
105646	54470	53684.7	9279
30733	8246	8244	
36824.4	17100.7	17076.8	801.1
170365.3	104511.1	102507.1	8491
30887.9	19238.4	18821.7	1209.3
4208.4	1936.6	1936.6	216.4
121896.9	70812.1	69224.8	7061.6
6707.5	6568.1	6568.1	
6664.6	5955.9	5955.9	3.7

18-1 续表2

单位：万元

指 标	Item	管理费用 Management Expenses	财务费用 Financial Expenses	投资收益 investment income
总计	**Totai**	**1437213.6**	**721276.1**	**217220.1**
按登记注册类型分组	**Grouped by Category of Commodities**			
内资企业	Domestic Funded Enterprises	1356547.6	717688	216386.2
国有	State-owned Enterprises	234800.5	16280.9	11000.9
集体	Collective-owned Enterprises	14734.2	-0.5	383.8
股份合作	Corperative Enterprises	2420.7	0.7	-733.9
联营	Joint Ownership Enterprises			
国有联营	State Joint Ownership Enterprises			
集体联营	Collective Joint Ownership Enterprises			
国有与集体联营	Joint State-collective Enterprises			
其他联营	Others Joint Ownership Enterprises			
有限限责任公司	Limited Liability Corporrations	860581.1	644410.9	195128
国有独资公司	State Funded Corporations	114055.9	390157.1	113149.5
其他有限责任公司	Other Limited Liability Corporrations	746525.2	254253.8	81978.5
股份有限公司	Other Limited Liability Corporrations	114615.4	49377	7844.3
私营	Other Limited Liability Corporrations	119797.4	7319.9	2729.3
私营独资	Private-funded Enterprises	2889.2	94.7	
私营合伙	Private Partnership Enterprises	9551.9	240.6	139
私营有限责任公司	Private Limited Liability Corporations	100399.5	6749.8	2547.2
私营股份有限公司	Private Share-holding Corporations Ltd.	6956.8	234.8	43.1
其他	Other Enterprises	9598.3	299.1	33.8
港澳台商投资	Enterprises with Funds from Hong Kong, Macao &Taiwan	38357.9	2636.4	671.1
合资经营	Joint Ventures	22611.5	607.7	17.4
合作经营	Cooperation Enterprises	4692.6	1122.7	
港澳台商独资经营	Enterprises with Sole Investment from Hong Kong Macau and Taiwan	11053.8	906	653.7
港澳台商投资股份有限公司	Share-holding Corporations Ltd. with funds from Hong Kong, Macao & Taiwan			
外商投资	Foreign Funded Enterprises	42308.1	951.7	162.8
中外合资经营企业	Sino-foreign Joint Ventures Enterprises	6391.9	123.7	29.8
中外合作经营企业	Sino-Foreign Cooperation Enterprises	952.8	-29.7	
外资企业	Foreign Owned Enterprises	32977.6	835.7	133
外商投资股份有限公司	Limited Company Funded by Foreign Investment	753.3	5.1	
其他外商投资	Other Foreign Funded Enterprises	1232.5	16.9	

continued2

(10 000 yuan)

营业利润 Business Profits	利润总额 Total Profits	应付职工薪酬 Salary Payable	从业人员平均人数（人） Annual Average Employed Persons (person)
1115835.6	**1288292.6**	**2688897.9**	**307594**
1058689.2	1224236.9	2599296.9	298230
-73790.9	18847.6	549977.2	55528
2513.9	2604.5	27804.9	8710
-794.8	-644.1	1932.5	390
846235.5	897149.8	1599063.2	173031
18830.5	-1643	247428.1	31984
827405	898792.8	1351635.1	141047
240253	256562.3	262614.9	24387
38265.1	43949.8	143651.9	32692
98.1	140.3	2573.2	734
1881.3	2026.4	12191.3	1770
31461.5	36769.1	123014.5	28914
4824.2	5014	5872.9	1274
6007.4	5767	14252.3	3492
43975.4	47559.3	32713.7	3741
20115.7	23391.8	20483.1	2755
16471	16477.1	2606.9	296
7388.7	7690.4	9623.7	690
13171	16496.4	56887.3	5623
3934.1	4515.1	8370.5	834
932.1	930.9	838.3	185
9407.5	11487.8	41264	3840
-556.3	-242	2368.8	298
-546.4	-195.4	4045.7	466

18-2 规模以上服务业按规模分主要经济指标

单位：万元

指 标	Item	单位数（个）Number of Enterprises (unit)	资产总计 Total Assets	固定资产原价 Original Value of Fixed Assets
总计	**Total**	**964**	**57191024.8**	**32084508.8**
按规模分组	**Grouped by Size of Enterprises**			
大型企业	Large-size	106	37638379.1	25408278.2
中型企业	Medium-size	229	16012832	5992158.4
小型企业	Small-size	557	3409956.5	674339.3
微型企业	Microenterprise	72	129857.2	9732.9

18-2 续表1

单位：万元

指 标	Item	销售费用 Sale Expenses	管理费用 Managenment Expenses	财务费用 Financial Expenses
总计	**Total**	**1290467.9**	**1437213.6**	**721276.1**
按规模分组	**Grouped by Size of Enterprises**			
大型企业	Large-size	1077636	864126.8	432292.3
中型企业	Medium-size	111054	318080.9	247745.6
小型企业	Small-size	98505	245409.6	41159.7
微型企业	Microenterprise	3272.9	9596.3	78.5

Main Economic Indicators for Services above the Designated Size grouped by Size of Enterprises

(10 000 yuan)

负债合计 Total Liabilities	所有者权益合计 Total Owners' Equities	营业收入 Paid in Capital	主营业务收入 Revenue from Principal Business	营业成本 Total Cost	主营业务成本 Cost of Principal Business
35360374.1	**21830650.7**	**15582963.5**	**15269323.8**	**10974917.9**	**10663582**
22753032.7	14885346.4	10694616.9	10463364.9	7391951.2	7146238
10434542.7	5578289.3	3072847	3022065.5	2271117.9	2237257
2098568.9	1311387.6	1731674.7	1702255.7	1242436.9	1212339.9
74229.8	55627.4	83824.9	81637.7	69411.9	67747.1

continued 1

(10 000 yuan)

投资收益 investment income	营业利润 Business Profits	利润总额 Total Profits	应付职工薪酬 Salary Payable	从业人员平均人数（人） Annual Average Employed Persons (person)
217220.1	**1115835.6**	**1288292.6**	**2688897.9**	**307594**
92966.6	877685.2	1005476	1992071.6	186755
103900	116891.5	177655.1	438361.3	64479
20138.3	120689.4	103615.8	247780	52795
215.2	569.5	1545.7	10685	3565

18-3 规模以上服务业按行业分主要经济指标

单位：万元

指标	Item	单位数（个）Number of Enterprises (unit)	资产总计 Total Assets	固定资产原价 Original Value of Fixed Assets
总计	**Totai**	**964**	**57191024.8**	**32084508.8**
按国民经济行业大类分组	**Grouped by sector categories**			
铁路运输业	Railway transport industry	25	653446.3	116415.4
道路运输业	The road transport industry	77	18733220.8	10513078.7
水上运输业	Water transportation			
航空运输业	The air transport industry	13	7166496.4	10307504.2
管道运输业	Pipeline transportation	3	1064.3	193
装卸搬运和运输代理业	Handling and transport industry	27	914724.2	263077.5
仓储业	Warehousing industry	2	1015425.3	928213.3
邮政业	The postal service	29	416561.2	50894.9
电信、广播电视和卫星传输服务业	Telecommunication, broadcasting and satellite transmission services	5	4054965.9	2894367.2
互联网和相关服务	The Internet and related services	5	25465.1	7425.3
软件和信息技术服务业	Software and information technology services	18	60106.7	13157.7
物业管理	Property management	12	35081.1	9147.9
房地产中介服务	Real estate intermediary service	17	131393.7	60208
租赁业	Leasing industry	11	689439.4	103915.1
商务服务业	Business services	8	9669.5	1992
研究和试验发展	Research and development	129	1454310.4	336632
专业技术服务业	Professional and technical services	164	10001930.1	468659.5
科技推广和应用服务业	Promotion and application of science and technology services	4	131608.8	57722.9
水利管理业	Water resources management industry	2	1532.6	976.1
生态保护和环境治理业	Ecological protection and environmental control industries	7	32520.9	18266
公共设施管理业	Public facilities management industry	3	4237832.1	4277266.9
居民服务业	Resident services	37	213810.4	146721
机动车、电子产品和日用产品修理业	Motor vehicles, electronics and household goods-repairing	27	1308179.5	80636
其他服务业	Other service industries	117	722534.9	181317.6
教育	Education	23	327559.3	68481
卫生	Health	20	724415.8	221668.2
社会工作	Social work			
新闻出版业	Press and publishing industry	7	514248	423925
广播、电视、电影和影视录音制作业	Radio, television, film and video recordings	12	37723	10771.8
文化艺术业	Culture and arts	140	3484862.4	473211.6
体育	Physical education	16	41414.7	12580.5
娱乐业	The entertainment industry	4	49482	36082.5

Main Economic Indicators for Services above the Designated Size grouped by Sector Categories

(10 000 yuan)

负债合计 Total Liabilities	所有者权益合计 Total Owners' Equities	营业收入 Paid in Capital	主营业务收入 Revenue from Principal Business	营业成本 Total Cost	主营业务成本 Cost of Principal Business
35360374.1	**21830650.7**	**15582963.5**	**15269323.8**	**10974917.9**	**10663582**
577684.4	75761.9	640613.9	634546.5	631141.1	629182.8
12985423.5	5747797.3	1290592.5	1277199.2	917507.6	913085.2
3325786.7	3840709.7	3971753.4	3848822.8	2116102.8	1981658.5
1062.3	2	2503.2	2400.2	589.1	589.1
617203.9	297520.3	235790.7	235400.3	173572.3	172954.5
532010.5	483414.8	563495.6	559719.5	464665.7	463138.6
273434.6	143126.6	239471.3	235714.9	177112.2	175969.2
1650358.7	2404607.2	761434.2	710981.2	630557	607309.8
12754.6	12710.5	40561.3	40561.3	27519.3	27501.4
29904	30202.7	52198.9	51973.4	38987.9	37697.7
25249.7	9831.4	57363	54358.5	37300	36901.9
109244	22149.7	54585.6	54326.2	40238.5	37667.2
450818.7	238620.7	672950	672185.2	618368.9	618197.9
5205.7	4463.8	14447.1	14447.1	10564.8	9821.4
761242.7	693067.7	1236850	1220563.9	763070	750652.4
6489688.2	3512241.9	1148247.8	1110365	827090.4	817713.1
88655	42953.8	28986.5	28405.5	16113.1	15889.7
1513.1	19.5	2798.1	2681.4	2403.7	2313.4
29802.7	2718.2	14395.1	14395.1	2928.2	2928.2
2791069.5	1446762.6	547560	547107.3	359464.8	359076.3
127824.5	85985.9	187155	186600.8	131134.9	126099.4
621978.6	686200.9	77135.2	72249.4	34700.1	34147.1
616955	105579.9	378922.8	367912	302695.8	291579.9
186789.8	140769.5	195281.3	192481.3	155529.1	143793.6
273344.1	451071.7	381117.2	375910.2	264905.4	254044.6
355357.4	158890.6	397381.6	392468.3	429688.6	371732.2
25465.9	12257.1	11131.9	10031.8	5384.1	4919.5
2336794.5	1148067.9	2328857	2306553.6	1754828.3	1737939.9
22787.4	18627.3	43365	43148.5	34783.4	33170
34964.4	14517.6	6018.3	5813.4	5970.8	5907.5

18-3 续表1

单位：万元

指　标	Item	销售费用 Sale Expenses	管理费用 Management Expenses	财务费用 Financial Expenses
总计	**Totai**	**1290467.9**	**1437213.6**	**721276.1**
按国民经济行业大类分组	**Grouped by sector categories**			
铁路运输业	Railway transport industry	7388.5	15638.3	10799.3
道路运输业	The road transport industry	2344.1	90308.4	386717.8
水上运输业	Water transportation			
航空运输业	The air transport industry	918709.2	196579.5	10844.8
管道运输业	Pipeline transportation	1125.8	955.4	0.3
装卸搬运和运输代理业	Handling and transport industry	14406.1	33854	4140.7
仓储业	Warehousing industry	2387.8	14213.7	21671.2
邮政业	The postal service	21391.9	20093	5347.9
电信、广播电视和卫星传输服务业	Telecommunication, broadcasting and satellite transmission services	17105.1	69538.8	37683.7
互联网和相关服务	The Internet and related services	576.1	8732.8	-63.9
软件和信息技术服务业	Software and information technology services	2401	4952.9	403.4
物业管理	Property management	4669.7	7304.3	387.9
房地产中介服务	Real estate intermediary service	3731.1	6924.9	1471.5
租赁业	Leasing industry	4391	17204.6	-1283.3
商务服务业	Business services	948.1	1852.8	-39.5
研究和试验发展	Research and development	47851.2	306612	9910.3
专业技术服务业	Professional and technical services	66779	159869.9	68807.6
科技推广和应用服务业	Promotion and application of science and technology services	6722	2176.5	2086.1
水利管理业	Water resources management industry	70.1	275.9	7.1
生态保护和环境治理业	Ecological protection and environmental control industries	4830.3	3136.5	105.6
公共设施管理业	Public facilities management industry	1449.8	12401.3	141673
居民服务业	Resident services	9415.3	26939.1	1666.5
机动车、电子产品和日用产品修理业	Motor vehicles, electronics and household goods-repairing	24233.7	16845.4	12804.8
其他服务业	Other service industries	11434.7	42567	9879.6
教育	Education	25645.9	25152.3	237
卫生	Health	4151.2	49908.7	665.7
社会工作	Social work			
新闻出版业	Press and publishing industry	640.5	65594.3	1511.2
广播、电视、电影和影视录音制作业	Radio, television, film and video recordings	4194.3	2022.1	633.3
文化艺术业	Culture and arts	77459.5	229241.8	-8787.3
体育	Physical education	2702.8	4263.2	390.6
娱乐业	The entertainment industry	1312.1	2054.2	1603.2

continued 1

(10 000 yuan)

投资收益 investment income	营业利润 Business Profits	利润总额 Total Profits	应付职工薪酬 Salary Payable	从业人员平均人数（人） Annual Average Employed Persons (person)
217220.1	**1115835.6**	**1288292.6**	**2688897.9**	**307594**
2512.6	-11831.9	2253	15549.2	3201
7632.6	-102046	2228.5	295464.6	46471
1128.7	626645.6	622161.3	407277.6	39565
	-304.2	-305.5	1029.2	210
165.4	9236.6	10315.5	44171.6	9764
2334.9	58705.7	59001.2	28886.2	1841
605.1	9747.3	-23138.4	14191.4	1952
11807.6	7192.7	13951.8	147395.6	18249
0.3	4535	4569.6	14885.6	1858
	5205.9	5229	4322.4	965
26.1	3406.3	3456.5	10206.3	2579
62.2	1097.6	1540	19461.1	5754
2902	33437.2	34028.4	53969	2447
	1205.3	1182.8	4289.9	1265
1246.3	103657	142767	527532.9	26975
147502.4	123788.2	144648.8	141400.6	29866
-109.3	1355.9	1559.4	6545.7	855
3	-41.4	-35.5	485.7	98
	2758.3	2448.9	3401.8	841
	32228.7	30450.9	18767.8	3901
-981	17161.4	16721	44586.8	7702
25999.3	5865	15270.1	26732	4212
-465	3033.2	2833.9	114944.3	32670
402.2	4095.2	9050.5	31368.8	3481
4534.4	64637.9	70914.2	78478.1	5899
282.1	-46004.7	-46092.6	194798.2	15795
30.4	-1864.7	-1879.9	3205.5	1023
9597.8	163128.3	165267.9	428968.4	36683
	899.3	1745.8	4035.5	998
	-5095.1	-3851.5	2546.1	474

18-4 规模以上服务业按隶属关系分主要经济指标

单位：万元

指标	Item	单位数（个）Number of Enterprises (unit)	资产总计 Total Assets	固定资产原价 Original Value of Fixed Assets
总计	**Totai**	**964**	**57191024.8**	**32084508.8**
按隶属关系分	**Grouped by affiliation**			
中央	Central	61	15056081.9	15028426.9
省（自治州、直辖市）	Province (autonomous prefectures, municipalities)	138	24146682.3	14705040
地（区、市、州、盟）	Land (District, municipal, State, Union)	136	10116648.2	1117985.5
县（区、市、旗）	Counties (districts, cities, flags)	70	1103959.3	238188.1
街道	Street	2	23405.7	16941.7
镇	Town	1	170.9	16.3
乡	Township			
（社区）居委会	(Community) neighborhood	1	743	32.4
村委会	Village	4	27655.6	6181.8
其他	Others	551	6715677.9	971696.1

18-4 续表1

单位：万元

指标	Item	销售费用 Sale Expenses	管理费用 Managenment Expenses	财务费用 Financial Expenses
总计	**Totai**	**1290467.9**	**1437213.6**	**721276.1**
按隶属关系分	**Grouped by affiliation**			
中央	Central	972971.9	420543.1	133998.7
省（自治州、直辖市）	Province (autonomous prefectures, municipalities)	96445.4	251027.4	432001.7
地（区、市、州、盟）	Land (District, municipal, State, Union)	77621.4	294032.6	77649.9
县（区、市、旗）	Counties (districts, cities, flags)	14662.8	36930.5	12792.7
街道	Street	368.3	687.2	-0.7
镇	Town		80	
乡	Township			
（社区）居委会	(Community) neighborhood	92.9	78	-0.8
村委会	Village	1383.5	3164.5	-92.4
其他	Others	126921.7	430670.3	64927

Main Economic Indicators for Services above the Designated Size grouped by Affiliation

(10 000 yuan)

负债合计 Total Liabilities	所有者权益合计 Total Owners' Equities	营业收入 Paid in Capital	主营业务收入 Revenue from Principal Business	营业成本 Total Cost	主营业务成本 Cost of Principal Business
35360374.1	**21830650.7**	**15582963.5**	**15269323.8**	**10974917.9**	**10663582**
8577557.6	6478524.3	7340595.9	7196225.1	4857058.2	4649290.7
14631426.7	9515255.6	3744187.5	3665331.5	2908575.8	2864275
7129483	2987165.2	1444079.7	1411460.9	1130516.2	1111638.3
620791.1	483168.2	244655.8	236080.9	195982.5	195545.2
20523.6	2882.1	2514.6	2514.6	1436.5	1436.5
579.7	-408.8	333.4	333.4	318.6	318.6
534.9	208.1	473.9	473.9	262.4	262.4
24702.1	2953.5	11208.1	11148.7	6299.6	6299.6
4354775.4	2360902.5	2794914.6	2745754.8	1874468.1	1834515.7

continued 1

(10 000 yuan)

投资收益 investment income	营业利润 Business Profits	利润总额 Total Profits	应付职工薪酬 Salary Payable	从业人员平均人数（人） Annual Average Employed Persons (person)
217220.1	**1115835.6**	**1288292.6**	**2688897.9**	**307594**
5137.8	792229.1	808889.7	931171.4	73067
154941.1	161165.4	174696.5	483270.6	62331
23859.6	-123144.6	-38474.9	461009.7	66724
1932.2	-10799.7	16555.7	51919	14343
	-2.2	71.3	355.3	286
	-87.4	-87.4	170.3	58
	14.9	13.7	314	110
45.8	539.8	551.7	1497.1	346
31303.6	295920.3	326076.3	759190.5	90329

主要统计指标解释

国家统计局规模以上服务业单位统计标准：辖区内年营业收入1000万元及以上，或年末从业人员50人及以上服务业法人单位。包括：交通运输、仓储和邮政业，信息传输、软件和信息技术服务业，租赁和商务服务业，科学研究和技术服务业，水利、环境和公共设施管理业，教育，卫生和社会工作；以及物业管理、房地产中介服务等行业。辖区内年营业收入500万元及以上，或年末从业人员50人及以上服务业法人单位。包括：居民服务、修理和其他服务业，文化、体育和娱乐业。

固定资产原价 指固定资产的成本，包括企业在购置、自行建造、安装、改建、扩建、技术改造某项固定资产时所发生的全部支出总额。根据会计“固定资产”科目的期末借方余额填报。

资产总计 指企业过去的交易或者事项形成的、由企业拥有或者控制的、预期会给企业带来经济利益的资源。资产一般按流动性（资产的变现或耗用时间长短）分为流动资产和非流动资产。其中流动资产可分为货币资金、交易性金融资产、应收票据、应收账款、预付款项、其他应收款、存货等；非流动资产可分为长期股权投资、固定资产、无形资产及其他非流动资产等。根据会计“资产负债表”中“资产总计”项目的期末余额数填报。

执行2006年《企业会计准则》的企业：资产总计=流动资产合计+非流动资产合计；未执行2006年《企业会计准则》企业的资产包括流动资产、长期投资、固定资产、无形资产和其他资产等。

负债合计 指企业过去的交易或者事项形成的，预期会导致经济利益流出企业的现时义务。负债一般按偿还期长短分为流动负债和非流动负债。根据会计“资产负债表”中“负债合计”项目的期末余额数填报。

执行2006年《企业会计准则》的企业：负债合计=流动负债合计+非流动负债合计；未执行2006年《企业会计准则》企业的负债包括流动负债和长期负债。

所有者权益合计 指企业资产扣除负债后由所有者享有的剩余权益。公司的所有者权益又称股东权益。包括实收资本、资本公积、盈余公积、未分配利润等。根据会计“资产负债表”中“所有者权益合计”项目的期末余额数填报。

营业收入 指企业经营主要业务和其他业务所确认的收入总额。营业收入合计包括“主营业务收入”和“其他业务收入”。根据会计“利润表”中“营业收入”项目的本期金额数填报。

主营业务收入 指企业确认的销售商品、提供劳务等主营业务的收入。根据会计“主营业务收入”科目的期末贷方余额（结转前）填报。执行2006年《企业会计准则》的企业，如未设置该科目，以“营业收入”代替填报。

营业成本 指企业经营主要业务和其他业务所发生的成本总额。包括企业（单位）在报告期内从事销售商品、提供劳务等日常活动发生的各种耗费。包括“主营业务成本”和“其他业务成本”。根据会计“利润表”中“营业成本”项目的本期金额数填报。

主营业务成本 指企业经营主要业务所发生的成本总额。根据会计“主营业务成本”科目的期末借方余额（结转前）填报。执行2006年《企业会计准则》的企业，如未设置该科目，以“营业成本”代替填报。

销售费用 指企业在销售商品和材料、提供劳务的过程中发生的各种费用，包括保险费、包装费、展览费和广告费、商品维修费、预计产品质量保证损失、运输费、装卸费等以及为销售本企业商品而专设的销售机构（含销售网点、售后服务网点等）的职工薪酬、业务费、折旧费等经营费用。根据会计“利润表”中“销售费用”项目的本期金额数填报。未执行2006年《企业会计准则》的企业，根据会计“利润表”中“营业费用(或经营费用)”项目的本期金额数填报。

管理费用 指企业为组织和管理企业生产经营所发生的费用，包括企业在筹建期间内发生的开办费、董事会和行政管理部门在企业经营管理中发生的，或者应当由企业统一负担的公司经费等。根据会计“利润表”中“管理费用”项目的本期金额数填报。

财务费用 指企业为筹集生产经营所需资金等而发生的筹资费用，包括企业生产经营期间发生的利息支出（减利息收入）、汇兑损失（减汇兑收益）以及相关的手续费等。根据会计“利润表”中“财务费用”项目的本期金额数填报。

投资收益 指企业确认的投资收益或投资损失，反映企业以各种方式对外投资所取得的收益。根据会计“利润表”中“投资收益”项目的本期金额数填报。如为投资损失以“–”号记。

营业利润 指企业从事生产经营活动所取得的利润。执行2006年《企业会计准则》的企业，营业利润为营业收入减去营业成本、营业税金及附加、销售费用、管理费用、财务费用、资产减值损失，再加上公允价值变动收益和投资收益。未执行2006年《企业会计准则》的企业，营业利润为主营业务收入减去主营业务成本、主营业务税金及附加，加上其他业务利润后，再减去销售费用、管理费用、财务费用后的金额。根据会计“利润表”中“营业利润”项目的本期金额数填报。

利润总额 指企业在一定会计期间的经营成果，是生产经营过程中各种收入扣除各种耗费后的盈余，反映企业在报告期内实现的盈亏总额。根据会计“利润表”中“利润总额”项目的本期金额数填报。执行2006年《企业会计准则》的企业，利润总额为营业利润加上营业外收入，减去营业外支出后的金额；未执行2006年《企业会计准则》的企业，利润总额为营业利润加上投资收益、补贴收入、营业外收入，再减去营业外支出后的金额。

应付职工薪酬 指企业为获得职工提供的服务而给予各种形式的报酬以及其他相关支出。包括职工工资、奖金、津贴和补贴，职工福利费，医疗保险费、养老保险费、失业保险费、工伤保险费和生育保险费等社会保险费，住房公积金，工会经费和职工教育经费，非货币性福利，因解除与职工的劳动关系给予的补偿，其他与获得职工提供的服务相关的支出。执行2006年《企业会计准则》的企业，根据会计科目“应付职工薪酬”的本年贷方累计发生额填报；未执行2006年《企业会计准则》的企业，应将本年上述职工薪酬包含的科目归并填报。

从事服务业活动从业人员平均人数 指报告期内(年度、月度)平均拥有的从事服务业活动的人员数。按“谁用工，谁统计”的原则实施统计，包括参加企业服务业活动的正式人员，劳务派遣人员和临时聘用人员。不包括在本企业领取工资、股息、红利未参加服务业活动的人员。

Explanatory Notes on Main Statistical Indicators

Statistical standard of the services unit above the designated size of the National Bureau of Statistics: The legal entities of the area whose annual revenues are 10 million yuan and above, or at the end of the service sector whose employees are more than 50 people.Including: transportation, storage and postal services, information transmission, software and information technology services, leasing and business services, scientific research and technological services, water conservancy, environment and public facilities management industry, education, health and social work as well as property management and real estate services industries. The legal entities of the area whose annual revenues are 5 million yuan and above, or at the end of the service sector whose employees are more than 50 people.Including: service, repair and other services, cultural, sports and entertainment.

Original value of fixed assets: It refers to the cost of fixed assets, including the enterprise itself costs on the acquisition, construction, installation, alteration, expansion, technological innovation of an asset for all expenditure. Depending on the "fixed assets" account debit balance at the end of filling.

Total assets: It refers to the resourcesformed by past transactions or events, that the enterprise owns or controls, is expected to bring economic benefits to the enterprise. Asset is classified into current assets and non-current assets by its liquidity (realization of assets or spent time). Current assets can be divided into currency, tradable financial assets, notes receivable, accounts receivable, prepayments, other receivables and inventory; and non-current assets can be classified as equity investments, fixed assets, intangible assets and other non-current assets. It depends on the "balance sheet" of "total assets" closing balance number of items.

For business enterprises that implemented the 2006 accounting standard: total assets= total current assets +total non-current assets; for those who didn't implement the 2006 accounting standards, assets for business enterprises include current assets, long-term investments, fixed assets, intangible assets and other assets.

Total liabilities: It refers to the present obligations of the enterprise that formed by past transactions or events and are expected to lead to an outflow of economic benefits. Liability is divided into current and non-current liabilities according to the length of the repayment period. It depends on the "balance sheets" in the "total" closing balance number of items.

For business enterprises that implemented the 2006 accounting standard: total liabilities = total current liabilities+ total non-current liabilities; for those who didn't implement the 2006 accounting standards, liabilities include current liabilities and long-term liabilities.

Total owners ' equity: It refers to the residual rights and interests enjoyed by the owner after deducting the liabilities of an enterprise. The owner of the company is also called the shareholder's right. It includes the paid in capital, capital reserves, surplus reserves, undistributed profit and so on. According to the accounting "balance sheet", "the owner's equity total", the final balance of the project is reported.

Operating income: It refers to the total revenue recognized by the business and other business operations of the enterprise. Total operating income includes "main business income" and "other business income". It's reported according to the "business income" project of the "business income" in the accounting "profit statement".

The main business income: It refers to the income of the business of the main business, such as the sale of goods, services, etc.It's reported in accordance with the final credit balance of the accounts of the subject's "main business income" (before the transfer). For business enterprises that didn't implement the 2006 accounting standard, if not set up the subject, should fill the forms instead of the "operating income".

Operating cost: It refers to the total cost incurred by the business and other business of the enterprise. It includes a variety of costs of enterprises (units) in the reporting period to engage in sales of goods, services and other daily activities provided. It includes"the main business costs" and "other business costs". According to the "operating cost" of the "business cost" of the project in accordance with the accounting statement.

The main business cost: It refers to the total cost of the main business. It's reported in accordance with the final debit balance of the subject of accounting "main business cost". For business enterprises that didn't implement the 2006 accounting standard, if not set up the subject, should fill the forms instead of the "operating costs".

Selling expenses: It refers to the expenses of the enterprise in sales of goods and materials and providing services, including insurance, packing, exhibition fees and advertising fees, maintenance of commodity, expected to ensure product quality loss, transportation, loading and unloading charges and sales of the enterprise products and dedicated sales organizations (including sales network and after-sales service network) employee compensation, business expenses, depreciation charges and operating expenses. According to the "sales expense" in accounting "profit statement", the amount of the item in this period of the project is reported. For business enterprises that didn't implement the 2006 accounting standard, according to the number of "operating expenses (or operating expenses)" of the project in accordance with the "profit statement".

Management expenses: It refers to the expenses for the organization and management of enterprise production and management of the enterprises, including costs in construction occurred during the start-up costs, the board of directors and administrative departments in enterprise management, or shall be made by the enterprise unified burden of company funds. According to the "management fee" in the accounting "profit table", the amount of this period of the project is reported.

Financial expenses: It refers to the costs of the enterprise to raise the production and business operation required capital and funding, including occurred during the production and operation of enterprises interest payments (a reduction in interest income), exchange loss (less exchange gains) and related fees. It is reported according to the amount of the "financial expense" in the project of "financial expense" in the accounting "profit statement".

Investment income: It refers to the enterprise confirming the investment income or investment losses, reflecting the foreign investment income of the enterprise in various ways. According to the "investment income" in the accounting "profit statement", the amount of this period of the project is reported. Such as investment losses to "-".

Operating profit: It refers to the profits made by the enterprises in the production and operation activities. For business enterprises that implemented the 2006 accounting standard, operating profit is revenues minus operating costs, business taxes and surcharges, sales, management costs, financial costs, asset impairment loss and plus fair value changes in income and investment income. Without executing the 2006 "accounting standards for business enterprises" enterprises, operating profit equals the main business income minus the cost of major business, main business tax and surcharges, and plus profit from other operations, then minus the cost of sales and management costs, financial costs. It is reported according to the number of "operating profit" items in the accounting "profit table".

Total profit: It refers to the business results of the enterprise in a certain accounting period, and it is the production and operation of various kinds of income after deducting the cost of earnings, reflecting the enterprise in the reporting period to achieve total profit and loss. According to the amount of the total amount of the total profit of the project in accordance with the accounting profit table. For business enterprises that implemented the 2006 accounting standard, the total profit is operating profit plus operating income, and minus operating expenses; while who didn't execute the 2006 "accounting standards for business enterprises", a total profit is operating profit plus return on investment, income subsidies, camp outside the industry income, and minus operating expenses.

Employee compensation: It refers to various forms of remuneration and other related expenses paid by the company for the services provided by the staff and workers. It includes wages, bonuses, allowances and subsidies, employee welfare benefit expenses, medical insurance, endowment insurance, unemployment insurance, work-related injury insurance premiums and maternity insurance fees social insurance, housing provident fund, the trade union funds and employee education funds, non-monetary benefits, for the solution in addition to give labor relations and workers compensation, and obtain a worker to provide other services related expenditure. For business enterprises that implemented the 2006 accounting standard, according to accounting subjects "to deal with workers' compensation" this year, the accumulated credits is filled; those who didn't execute the 2006 "accounting standards for business enterprises", it should be the employee compensation including the amalgamative course reporting this year.

Average number of persons engaged in service activities: It refers to the number of persons engaged in the service industry in the reporting period (annual, monthly). The principles of statistics is implemented according to the principle that "who labor, who statistics," including the official personnel, labor sent contingent personnel and temporary employees who take part in the enterprise service activities. And it don't include employees who receive wages, dividends, bonus as well as not participate in the service activities of the enterprise.

19 金融业

FINANCIAL INTERMEDIATION

资料整理：刘　婷
Data management：Liu Ting
数据审核：陈　英
Data audit：Chen Ying

第十九部分　金融业

一、简要说明

本章资料包括金融、证券和保险业情况，由西安市统计局综合处根据人民银行西安分行营业管理部和市金融办提供资料整理。

二、主要指标

金融机构人民币（含外资）存款余额（亿元）	15166.78	比上年增长	10.2%
金融机构人民币（含外资）贷款余额（亿元）	11668.14	比上年增长	16.4%
保费收入（亿元）	219.49	比上年增长	8.4%

19 FINANCIAL INTERMEDIATION

Ⅰ.Brief Introduction

This chapter includes information of the financial, securities and insurance, compiled by Integration Division of the Xi'an Bureau of Statistics, according to data from Xi'an Branch Management Department of the People's Bank of China, Provincial Banking Bureau and Xi'an Financial Office.

Ⅱ.Major Indicators

		Increase over Preceding Year
Deposit in Financial Institution(100 mil. Yuan)	15166.78	10.2%
Loans in Financial Institutions(100 mil. Yuan)	11668.14	16.4%
Premiums(100 mil. Yuan)	219.49	8.4%

19-1 西安银行系统机构、人员数

Number of Institution and Employed Person in Finance System in Xi'an

机构名称	Name of Institution	2013		2014	
		机构数（个）Number of Institution (unit)	年末人数（人）Number of Staff and Workers (person)	机构数（个）Number of Institution (unit)	年末人数（人）Number of Staff and Workers (person)
合　计	**Total**	**1849**	**35577**	**1901**	**37311**
1. 人民银行西安分行营业管理部	Management Department of the People's Bank of China Xi'an Branch	1	389	1	386
2. 中国工商银行西安分行	Industrial and Commercial Bank of China Shaanxi Branch	193	4937	193	4976
3. 中国农业银行西安分行	Agricultural Bank of China Shaanxi Branch	169	3200	173	3249
4. 中国银行西安分行	Bank of China Xi'an Branch	124	3382	126	3384
5. 中国建设银行西安分行	Construction Bank of China Shaanxi Branch	189	4132	195	4255
6. 国家开发银行西安分行	National Development Bank Xi'an Branch	1	183	1	184
7. 中国农业发展银行西安分行	Agricultural Development Bank of China Xi'an Branch	10	263	10	258
8. 中国进出口银行	Export Import Bank of Xi'an Branch	1	74	1	64
9. 交通银行西安分行	Bank of Communication Xi'an Branch	49	1204	49	1169
10. 中信实业银行西安分行	CITIC Industrial Bank Xi'an Branch	22	855	26	869
11. 中国光大银行西安分行	China Everbright Bank Xi'an Branch	21	773	22	832
12. 华夏银行西安分行	China Huaxia Bank Xi'an Branch	13	393	14	467
13. 招商银行西安分行	China Merchants Bank Xi'an Branch	26	1161	42	1340
14. 上海浦东发展银行西安分行	Pufa Bank Xi'an Branch	15	623	19	656
15. 兴业银行西安分行	Fujian Industrial Bank Xi'an Branch	16	870	21	897
16. 民生银行西安分行	China Minsheng Banking Corp., Ltd Xi'an Branch	18	1044	20	1136
17. 浙商银行西安分行	China Zheshang Bank Xi'an Branch	5	255	5	290
18. 恒丰银行西安分行	Evergrowing Bank Xi'an Branch	4	126	6	276
19. 中国邮政储蓄银行西安分行	The postal savings bank branch in Xi'an	281	848	281	834
20. 西安银行	Bank of Xi'an	115	2545	114	2595
21. 重庆银行西安分行	Bank of Chongqing, Xi'an Branch	4	150	4	166
22. 北京银行西安分行	Bank of Beijing,Xi'an Branch	10	455	15	507
23. 长安银行	Bank of Changan	8	298	13	693
24. 昆仑银行西安分行	Kunlun Xi'an Branch Bank	5	317	7	390
25. 齐商银行西安分行	Qi Commercial Bank Xi'an Branch	5	168	7	219
26. 成都银行西安分行	Bank of Chengdu, Xi'an Branch	4	143	4	165
27. 宁夏银行西安分行	Bank of Ningxia Xi'an Branch	4	184	5	201
28. 农村信用社联合社	Rural Credit Cooperatives Association	523	5869	510	6080
29. 东亚银行西安分行	Dongya Bank Xi'an Branch	7	334	7	293
30. 汇丰银行西安分行	Huifeng Bank Xi'an Branch	3	60	3	50
31. 渣打银行西安分行	British Standard Chartered bank Xi'an Branch	1	41	1	46
32. 韩亚银行西安分行	Hanya Bank Xi'an Branch			1	32
33. 西安高陵阳光村镇银行	Xi'an Gaoling sunshine village bank	1	25	1	21
34. 平安银行西安分行	Pingan Bank Xi'an Branch	1	276	4	331

注：本表数据来源于人民银行西安营管部。

19-2 金融机构（含外资）本外币存贷款年末余额（2014年）

Financial institution Including Foreign-funded Balance of Bisic Currency and Foreign Currency at Year-end（2014）

单位：万元 (10 000 yuan)

指 标	Item	2014	比年初增加额 Increase or decrease compared with the beginning of the Year
存款余额合计（年均汇率：6.1428）	**Total Deposit (Exchange Rate: 6.1428)**	**153153889**	**14212813**
一、单位存款	**Company Deposit**	**86968927**	**8447704**
#活期存款	Demand Deposits	38426393	1217375
定期存款	Time Deposits	24841484	3497721
二、个人存款	**Personal Deposits**	**61812459**	**4748715**
#储蓄存款	Savings Deposits	57437557	3448744
三、财政性存款	**Fiscal Deposits**	**588674**	**24284**
四、临时性存款	**Temporary Deposit**	**164573**	**-4381**
五. 委托存款	**Consignment Deposits**	**956334**	**88893**
六. 其他存款	**Other Deposits**	**2662922**	**907598**
贷款余额合计（年均汇率：6.1428）	**Total Loans (Exchange Rate: 6.1428)**	**118788855**	**16259579**
一、境内贷款	**Domestic Loans**	**118622405**	**16254206**
短期贷款	Short-term Loans	26060775	1603720
中长期贷款	Medium-term and Long-term loans	87867093	13116207
融资租赁	Financial Leasing	30952	28188
票据融资	Bill Financing	4579328	1472858
各项垫款	Various Advance Funds	84258	33233
二、境外贷款	**Foreign Loans**	**166449**	**5373**

注：本表数据来源于人民银行西安营管部。

19-3 金融机构（不含外资）本外币存贷款年末余额（2014年）

Domestic Funded Financial institution balance of Bisic Currency and Foreign Currency at Year-end (2014)

单位：万元 (10 000 yuan)

指　标	Item	2014	比年初增加额 Increase or decrease compared with the beginning of the Year
存款余额合计	**Total Deposit**	**152014679**	**14119499**
一、单位存款	**Company Deposit**	**86098538**	**8309510**
#活期存款	Demand Deposits	38250594	1231144
定期存款	Time Deposits	24731463	3481994
二、个人存款	**Personal Deposits**	**61625187**	**4792370**
#储蓄存款	Savings Deposits	57312457	3482373
三、财政性存款	**Fiscal Deposits**	**588674**	**24284**
四、临时性存款	**Temporary Deposit**	**163050**	**-3137**
五、委托存款	**Trusted Deposits**	**956334**	**88893**
六、其他存款	**Other Deposits**	**2582896**	**907580**
贷款余额合计	**Total Loans**	**117848342**	**16282339**
一、境内贷款	**Domestic Loans**	**117685560**	**16280081**
短期贷款	Short-term Loans	25828789	1664593
中长期贷款	Medium-term&Long-term Loans	87193590	13101382
融资租赁	Financial Leasing	30952	28188
票据融资	Bill Financing	4549243	1452974
各项垫款	Various Advance Funds	82986	32944
二、境外贷款	**Foreign Loans**	**162782**	**2259**

注：本表数据来源于人民银行西安营管部。

19-4 主要年份金融机构（含外资）人民币存款年末余额

Year-end Balance of Deposit in Financial Institutions Including Foreign-funded in Representative Years

单位：亿元　　　　(100million yuan)

年 份 Year	合计 Total	其 中：Among 单位存款 Company Deposit	储蓄存款 Savings Deposits
1978	12.82		3.72
1980	20.99		5.48
1985	40.68		16.70
1990	112.37	31.10	62.23
1995	359.51	114.54	230.63
1996	619.98	199.85	394.02
1997	602.50	227.61	358.78
1998	799.54	245.44	499.68
1999	1014.27	347.49	586.40
2000	1335.63	540.19	675.83
2001	1629.72	674.49	800.86
2002	2191.47	884.69	988.04
2003	2665.87	1041.43	1210.56
2004	3061.66	1159.98	1432.86
2005	3599.70	1237.37	1716.76
2006	4066.16	1374.91	1950.53
2007	4582.71	1702.12	2002.38
2008	5749.35	2213.67	2513.70
2009	7522.08	3077.99	3084.20
2010	8933.23	3556.78	3641.09
2011	10430.27	5997.60	4155.65
2012	12125.53	6927.84	4787.03
2013	13763.19	7759.61	5357.05
2014	15166.78	8604.03	5698.15

注：本表数据来源于人民银行西安营管部。

19-5 主要年份金融机构（含外资）人民币贷款年末余额

Year-end Balance of Loans in Financial Institutions Including Foreign-funded in Representative Years

单位：亿元　　　　　　　　　　　　　　　　　　　　　　　　　　　(100 million yuan)

年　份 Year	合计 Total	其　中：Among 短期贷款 Short-term Loans	中长期贷款 Medium-term&Long-term Loans
1978	23.56		
1980	26.40		
1985	48.60		
1990	131.67	101.13	23.78
1995	334.50	252.30	73.32
1996	477.97	333.88	90.12
1997	443.76	342.79	87.27
1998	597.34	448.74	118.42
1999	786.20	589.52	150.64
2000	972.51	652.00	241.27
2001	1185.97	666.41	387.82
2002	1598.42	780.69	502.03
2003	1954.18	946.64	743.72
2004	2052.33	950.50	850.01
2005	2158.10	830.68	1013.32
2006	2344.77	812.33	1310.57
2007	2683.77	883.32	1593.37
2008	3275.12	1031.62	1905.08
2009	4482.63	1155.83	2908.75
2010	6482.28	1097.60	5075.98
2011	7564.93	1431.29	5776.48
2012	8635.22	1917.51	6378.88
2013	10023.63	2326.63	7385.37
2014	11668.14	2516.78	8685.74

注：本表数据来源于人民银行西安营管部。

19-6 金融机构（含外资）人民币存贷款年末余额（2014年）

Year-end Balance of Deposit and Loans in Financial Institutionst Including Foreign-funded（2014）

单位：万元 (10 000 yuan)

指　标	Item	2014	比年初增加额 Increase or decrease compared with the beginning of the Year
存款余额合计	**Total Deposit**	**151667815**	**14022593**
一、单位存款	**Company Deposit**	**86040266**	**8315904**
#活期存款	Demand Deposits	37964645	1297086
定期存款	Time Deposits	24602946	3345001
二、个人存款	**Personal Deposits**	**61333219**	**4702035**
#储蓄存款	Savings Deposits	56981480	3411021
三、财政性存款	**Fiscal Deposits**	**588674**	**24284**
四、临时性存款	**Temporary Deposit**	**127644**	**24411**
五、委托存款	**Trusted Deposits**	**955374**	**88182**
六、其他存款	**Other Deposits**	**2622639**	**867778**
贷款余额合计	**Total Loans**	**116681446**	**16064737**
一、境内贷款	**Domestic Loans**	**116674250**	**16062546**
（一）短期贷款	Short-term Loans	25167774	1516928
1. 个人贷款及透支	Individual Loans and Overdrafts	4021260	478195
2. 单位普通贷款及透支	Unit Loans and Overdrafts	19437806	907774
3. 普通并购贷款	Ordinary Merging Loans		
4. 银团贷款	Syndicated Loans	53412	-72018
5. 贸易融资	Trade Finance	1655296	202977
（二）中长期贷款	Medium-term&Long-term Loans	86857399	13007814
1. 个人贷款	Individual Loans and Overdrafts	21385756	2660176
2. 单位普通贷款	Unit Loans and Overdrafts	54566423	9051753
3. 普通并购贷款	Ordinary Merging Loans	429880	110750
4. 贸易融资	Syndicated Loans	8364	-14369
5. 银团贷款	Trade Finance	10466976	1199503
（三）融资租赁	Financial Leasing	30952	28188
（四）票据融资	Bill Financing	4579328	1472865
（五）各项垫款	Various Advance Funds	38798	36751
二、境外贷款	**Foreign Loans**	**7196**	**2190**

注：本表数据来源于人民银行西安营管部。

19-7 金融机构（不含外资）人民币存贷款年末余额（2014年）

Year-end Balance of Deposit and Loans in Financial Institutions Not Including Foreign-funded（2014）

单位：万元 (10 000yuan)

指　标	Item	2014	比年初增加额 Increase or decrease compared with the beginning of the Year
存款余额合计	**Total Deposit**	**150640969**	**13968743**
一、单位存款	**Company Deposit**	**85263575**	**8214225**
#活期存款	Demand Deposits	37825555	1320132
定期存款	Time Deposits	24548535	3356798
二、个人存款	**Personal Deposits**	**61164432**	**4748458**
#储蓄存款	Savings Deposits	56874866	3447419
三、财政性存款	**Fiscal Deposits**	**588674**	**24284**
四、临时性存款	**Temporary Deposit**	**126301**	**25834**
五、委托存款	**Trusted Deposits**	**955374**	**88182**
六、其他存款	**Other Deposits**	**2542613**	**867760**
贷款余额合计	**Total Loans**	**115762960**	**16082144**
一、境内贷款	**Domestic Loans**	**115756599**	**16080450**
（一）短期贷款	Short-term Loans	24939094	1576581
1. 个人贷款及透支	Individual Loans and Overdrafts	4002500	482003
2. 单位普通贷款及透支	Unit Loans and Overdrafts	19245999	970487
3. 普通并购贷款	Ordinary Merging Loans		
4. 银团贷款	Syndicated Loans	53412	-72018
5. 贸易融资	Trade Finance	1637183	196109
（二）中长期贷款	Medium-term&Long-term Loans	86199784	12986239
1. 个人贷款	Individual Loans and Overdrafts	21251075	2675838
2. 单位普通贷款	Unit Loans and Overdrafts	54043489	9014517
3. 普通并购贷款	Ordinary Merging Loans	429880	110750
4. 贸易融资	Trade Finance	8364	-14369
5. 银团贷款	Syndicated Loans	10466976	1199503
（三）融资租赁	Financial Leasing	30952	28188
（四）票据融资	Bill Financing	4549243	1452981
（五）各项垫款	Various Advance Funds	37526	36462
二、境外贷款	**Foreign Loans**	**6362**	**1694**

注：本表数据来源于人民银行西安营管部。

19-8 保险业务情况

Indicators of Insurance Business

指　标	Item	2013	2014
保险金额（亿元）	**Amount Insured(100 million yuan)**	**42596**	**51454**
保费收入（万元）	**Premiums(10 000 yuan)**	**2024067**	**2194924**
一、财产险	**Property Insurance**	**629947**	**741762**
（一）财产保险	Property Insurance	576666	668574
1. 机动车辆及第三者责任	Motor Vehicle and Outside Person Liability	513634	602905
2. 企业财产险	Enterprise Property Insurance	41140	41996
3. 货物运输险	Freight Transport Insurance	3944	4427
4. 家庭财产险	Family Property Insurance	296	584
5. 建工及安工保险及其责任险	Construction and Installation Projects Insurance and Related Libility Insurance	16133	16893
6. 其他	Others	1519	1770
（二）责任保险	Liability Insurance	13393	16328
（三）信用保险	Export Credit Insurance	8648	8401
（四）保证保险	Guarantee Insurance	21588	36868
（五）农业保险	Agriculture Insurance	9653	11590
二、人身险	**Personnel Insurance**	**1394120**	**1453162**
（一）人寿保险	Life Insurance	1221975	1238142
1. 非分红保险	Non Dividend Insurance	109810	444520
2. 分红保险	Dividend Insurance	1099986	780653
3. 投资连接保险	Insurance Connection Insurance	330	316
4. 万能保险	Universal Insurance	11849	12654
（二）意外伤害险	Unforeseen Injury Insurance	49541	52963
（三）健康保险	Health Insurance	122604	162057
赔款支出和各项给付（万元）	**Indemnity and Other Expenditure(10 000 yuan)**	**664905**	**807652**
一、财产险	**Property Insurance**	**339004**	**372906**
（一）财产保险	Property Insurance	325128	360384
1. 机动车辆及第三者责任	Motor Vehicle and Outside Person Liability	291390	327319
2. 企业财产险	Enterprise Property Insurance	24870	22257
3. 家庭财产保险	Freight Transport Insurance	93	107
4. 货物运输保险	Family Property Insurance	1224	2429
5. 建工及安工保险及其责任险	Construction and Installation Projects Insurance and Related Libility Insurance	6480	6719
6. 其他	Others	1070	1551
（二）责任保险	Liability Insurance	5192	5695
（三）信用保险	Export Credit Insurance	5414	1668
（四）保证保险	Guarantee Insurance	1450	2752
（五）农业保险	Agriculture Insurance	1820	2406
二、人身险	**Personnel Insurance**	**325900**	**434746**
（一）人寿保险	Life Insurance	268455	360895
1. 非分红保险	Non Dividend Insurance	48680	44359
2. 分红保险	Dividend Insurance	216911	313706
3. 投资连接保险	Insurance Connection Insurance	32	33
4. 万能保险	Universal Insurance	2832	2797
（二）意外伤害险	Unforeseen Injury Insurance Health Insurance	10685	11438
（三）健康保险	Health Insurance	46760	62414
退保金（万元）	**Withdrawal(10 000 yuan)**	**167446**	**405676**
#人寿保险	Life Insurance	165303	403099
1. 非分红保险	Ordinary Life Insurance	6192	20818
2. 分红保险	Dividend Insurance	159077	382274
3. 投资连接保险	Insurance Connection Insurance	9	
4. 万能保险	Universal Insurance	24	7

注：本表数据来源于市金融办。

19-9 西安地区证券期货系统机构、人员数

Number of Institution and Employed Person in Securities and Futures System in Xi'an

机构名称	Name of Institution	2013 机构数（个）Number of Institution (unit)	2013 年末人数（人）Number of Staff and Workers (person)	2014 机构数（个）Number of Institution (unit)	2014 年末人数（人）Number of Staff and Workers (person)
证券经营机构	**Securities Company and the Sales Department**				
一、证券公司	**Securities Company**				
西部证券股份有限公司	Western Securities Company Ltd.	71	2026	72	1995
陕西开源证券经纪有限责任公司	KaiYuan Securities Company Ltd.	22	463	22	472
西安华弘证券经纪有限责任公司	Xi'an Huahong Securities Brokerage Co., Ltd.	8	293	2	293
二、证券营业部（含外地公司在西安营业部）	**Sales Department (include Xi'an) departments of nonlocal companies.)**	**73**	**2533**	**92**	**2652**
期货经纪公司	**Futures Company**	**3**	**402**	**3**	**212**
迈科期货经纪有限公司	Maike Futures Company Ltd.	1	194	1	83
陕西长安期货经纪有限公司	Shanxi ChangAn Futures Company Ltd.	1	92	1	62
西部期货经纪有限公司	Western Futures Brokerage Co., Ltd.	1	116	1	67

注：证券公司包括三家公司及其在西安和外地的营业部。
本表数据来源于市金融办。

19–10 证券期货市场基本情况（2014年）

Basic Facts on Securities and Futures Markets（2014）

指　标	Item	2014
一、上市证券公司情况	**Listed Securities Companies**	
拥有上市股份公司（个）	Number of Listed Share-holding Companies(unit)	31
上市股份公司总股本（亿股）	Total Capital of Listed Share-holding Companies (100 millon shares)	356
#流通股(亿股)	Negotiable Shares(100 million shares)	219
总市值（亿元）	Total Market Capitalization(100 million yuan)	4229
累计证券市场筹措资金（亿元）	Accumulated Capital Raised by Securities Markets(100 millon yuan)	714
二、证券经营机构情况	**Securities Trading Organizations**	
拥有证券公司（个）	Number of Securities Companies(unit)	3
证券营业部（个）（含外地公司在西安营业部）	Number of Securities Business Departments(unit)	92
投资者开户数（万户）	Number of Investors Who have Opened an Account(10 000 accounts)	185
证券交易总额（亿元）	Total Turnover(100 million yuan)	18913
三、期货市场情况	**Futures Market**	
拥有期货经纪公司（个）	Number of Futures Business Management Companies(unit)	3
期货营业部（个）	Number of Futures Business,Departments(unit)	24
期货代理交易额（亿元）	Total Transaction Value in Futures Commissioning (100 million yuan)	25170
每个经纪公司平均拥有注册资金（万元）	Average Registered Capital of Each Business Management Company(10 000 yuan)	16511

注：本表数据来源于市金融办。

主要统计指标解释

信贷资金 指金融机构以信用方式积聚和分配的货币资金。金融机构信贷资金的来源有各项存款、金融债券、对国际金融机构负债、流通中现金、其他项目等；信贷资金的运用有各项贷款、有价证券及投资、金银占款、外汇占款、财政借款及在国际金融机构中的资产等。

存款 指企业、机关、团体或居民根据资金必须收回的原则，把货币资金存入银行或其他信贷机构保管并取得一定利息的一种信用活动形式。根据存款对象或性质的不同可划分为企业存款、财政存款、机关团体存款、城乡储蓄存款、农业存款、信托及委托类存款、其他存款等科目。它是银行信贷资金的主要来源。

贷款 指银行或其他信贷机构根据资金必须归还的原则，按一定利率，为企业、个人等提供资金的一种信用活动形式。我国银行贷款分为短期贷款、委托及信托类贷款、其他类贷款等。

保险公司 在中国境内的、经过保险监督管理部门批准设立，并依法登记注册的各类商业保险公司。

保险金额 指保险人承担赔偿或者给付保险金责任的最高限额。

保费 指投保人为取得保险人在约定范围内所承担赔偿责任而支付给保险人的费用。

赔款 指保险人根据保险合同的规定，向被保险人支付的赔偿保险责任损失的金额。

给付 包括死伤医疗给付和满期给付。死伤医疗给付是指保险人根据人寿保险及长期健康保险合同的规定，因被保险人在保险期内发生保险责任范围内的保险事故支付给被保险人（或受益人）的金额。满期给付是指被保险人生存期满，保险人按人寿保险合同规定支付给被保险人的满期保险金额。

Explanatory Notes on Main Statistical Indicators

Credit Funds refer to the monetary funds accumulated and distributed in the means of credit by the financial institutions. The sources of credit funds include various deposits, financial bonds, liabilities to international financial institutions, currency in circulation, other items. The uses of credit funds include loans, securities and investment, position for bullion and silver purchase, position for foreign exchange purchase, advances to treasury, and assets with international financial institutions..

Deposit is a form of credit by which enterprises, institutions, organizations or households can put money into banks and other credit institutions for safekeeping and interest earning under the principle of free withdrawal. According to different depositors, deposits are divided into enterprise deposits, fiscal deposits, deposits of government agencies and organizations, savings deposits of rural and urban households, agricultural savings deposits, entrusted deposits and other deposits. Deposits are major sources of the credit funds of banks.

Loan is a form of credit by which banks and other credit institutions provide funds at certain interest rate to enterprises and individuals in the light of the principle of unconditional repayment. Loans from Chinese banks include short-term loan, medium- term and long-term loans, entrusted loans, and other loans.

Insurance Companies refer to commercial insurance companies of various forms registered by law and established in China with the approval of insurance regulatory agencies.

Amount Insured refers to the maximum that the insurant will get for the claim of the case insured.

Premium is the fee paid by the insurant to the insurer to obtain the obligation of compensation from the insurance within the agreed terms.

Settled Claim is the compensation paid by the insurer to the insurant in accordance with the insurance contract.

Payment includes payment for death, injury or medical treatment and payment at maturity. Payment for death, injury or medical treatment refers to the money paid to the insurant (or the beneficiary) in accordance with the life or health insurance contract when the insurant encounters accidents within the insured period covered in the contract. Payment at maturity refers to the payment to the insurant in accordance with the life insurance contract at the end of the insured period.

20 教育和科技

EDUCATION,SCIENCE AND TECHNOLOGY

资料整理：郝　静　陈春光
Data management：Hao Jing Chen Chunguang
数据审核：王金桂
Data audit：Wang Jingui

第二十部分　教育和科技

一、简要说明

本章资料包括教育事业、科技事业基本情况，由西安市统计局社会科技处根据西安市教育局等有关部门提供资料整理。

二、主要指标

普通高等学校数（所）	63	比上年增加	持平
普通高等学校（本专科）在校学生（万人）	76.64	比上年增加	1.37万人
高等学校研究生在校人数（万人）	8.78	比上年增加	0.23万人

20　EDUCATION,SCIENCE AND TECHNOLOGY

Ⅰ.Brief Introduction

Data in this chapter consists of primarily data of educational undertakings, science and technology Activities of Xi'an city, compiled by Social & Science and Technology Division of the Xi'an Bureau of Statistics according to data from Xi'an Bureau of Education concerned.

Ⅱ Major Indicators

		Increase over Preceding Year
Number of Schools Regular Institutions of Higher Education(unit)	63	essentially on a par with last year's
Student Enrollment of Regular Institutions of Higher Education(10 000 persons)	76.64	1.37
Postgraduates(10 000 persons)	8.78	0.23

20-1 主要年份各类普通教育基本情况

Basic Statistics on Regular Eduction in Representative Years

指　标	Item	2006	2007	2008	2009	2010	2011	2012	2013	2014
学校数（所）	**Number of Schools (units)**									
普通高等学校	Regular Institutions of Higher Educatior	47	48	48	49	50	61	62	63	63
普通中等专业学校	Regular Specialized Secondary Schools	31	30	29	28	28	24	24	22	22
普通中学	Regular Secondary School	457	453	442	439	436	423	419	418	421
小学	Primary Schools	1929	1872	1781	1666	1531	1424	1322	1291	1257
幼儿园	Kindergarten	863	830	905	896	1004	1122	1239	1295	1343
毕业生人数（万人）	**Graduates (10 000 persons)**									
普通高等学校	Regular Institutions of Higher Educatior	13.0	15.8	17.6	16.9	18.3	19.7	20.9	20.2	21.3
普通中等专业学校	Regular Specialized Secondary Schools	1.8	2.0	2.6	2.7	2.5	2.3	2.1	1.9	1.8
普通中学	Regular Secondary School	18.0	18.4	18.0	17.8	17.0	16.4	15.6	15.2	14.5
小学	Primary Schools	11.5	11.4	10.6	10.0	9.6	8.9	8.9	8.5	8.3
幼儿园	Kindergarten						6.4	7.6	8.4	8.9
招生数（万人）	**New Enrollment (10 000 persons)**									
普通高等学校	Regular Institutions of Higher Educatior	17.1	19.0	21.5	21.3	21.7	23.1	25.2	23.9	23.6
普通中等专业学校	Regular Specialized Secondary Schools	2.6	2.9	2.6	2.2	2.1	2.0	1.7	1.4	1.3
普通中学	Regular Secondary School	18.6	18.0	17.2	16.6	16.2	15.4	15.0	14.5	14.0
小学	Primary Schools	9.2	8.7	8.3	7.8	8.6	8.8	8.9	9.6	10.1
幼儿园	Kindergarten	6.9	6.7	7.7	7.2	8.4	10.0	11.6	11.0	9.6
在校学生数（万人）	**Total Enrollment (10 000 persons)**									
普通高等学校	Regular Institutions of Higher Educatior	57.1	62.3	66.7	70.3	73.3	76.6	80.7	83.8	85.4
普通中等专业学校	Regular Specialized Secondary Schools	7.3	8.0	8.1	7.4	6.8	6.1	5.4	4.7	4.1
普通中学	Regular Secondary School	56.1	54.7	52.8	50.6	48.9	47.2	45.3	43.7	42.6
小学	Primary Schools	59.3	56.8	54.7	52.5	51.6	51.4	50.9	52.0	53.8
幼儿园	Kindergarten	13.4	14.1	15.5	16.3	18.4	24.0	27.1	28.6	29.0
教职工数（人）	**Staff and Teachers (persons)**									
普通高等学校	Regular Institutions of Higher Educatior	61414	65624	69048	70818	72247	72739	74041	74993	74954
普通中等专业学校	Regular Specialized Secondary Schools	3621	3548	3417	2965	3249	2868	2733	2599	2315
普通中学	Regular Secondary School	39341	39171	39088	39002	39207	41135	41197	41003	40576
小学	Primary Schools	34460	34901	34653	34389	34118	32457	32208	31863	32162
幼儿园	Kindergarten	12335	13468	14932	15928	18710	23680	27735	31989	33062
专任教师（人）	**Number of Full-time Teachers (persons)**									
普通高等学校	Regular Institutions of Higher Educatior	32891	36717	38926	40605	42098	42734	44487	46436	46766
普通中等专业学校	Regular Specialized Secondary Schools	2014	2011	1904	1720	1845	1723	1595	1474	1346
普通中学	Regular Secondary School	31203	31373	31425	31415	31506	33122	31526	31419	32615
小学	Primary Schools	30018	30533	30382	30334	29944	28453	29651	29421	28395
幼儿园	Kindergarten	7106	7951	8704	9240	10638	12577	14293	16238	17337

注：本表数据来源于市教育局。

本表中普通高等学校毕业生、招生、在校生数含研究生及普通高等学校中普通本、专科学生数。

本表中小学的学校数是指独立小学个数，其在校生、教职工等指标均为普通初等教育；幼儿园的校数是指独立的幼儿园个数，其在校生、教职工等指标均为学前教育。（下表同）

20-2 各级各类学校校数、教职工、专任教师数（2014年）

Basic Facts on Regular Education Teacher by School Type（2014）

指标	Item	学校数（所）Number of Schools (units)	教职工数（人）Number of Staff and Teachers (persons)	专任教师数（人）Full-time Teachers (persons)
一、高等教育	**Higher education**	**76**	**77495**	**48273**
（一）研究生培养机构	Postgraduate training institutions	(43)		
1、高等学校	Institutions of Higher Schools	(22)		
2、科研机构	Scientific Research Institution	(21)		
(二)普通高等学校	Regular Institutions of Higher Schools	63	74954	46766
1、 本科院校	Universities and Colleges of Undergraduate Course	42	64178	40074
其中：独立学院	Non-university Tertiary	11	7028	4530
2、专科院校	Higher Vocational Colleges	21	10776	6692
其中：高等职业学校	Higher Vocational College	19	9022	5853
(三)成人高等学校	Adult Higher Schools	13	2541	1507
二、中等职业教育	**Secondary Occupation Education**	**199**	**15731**	**11191**
1、普通中等专业学校	Regular Specialized Secondary Schools	22	2315	1346
2、成人中等专业学校	Adult Secondary Specialized Schools	7	1538	955
3、职业高中学校	Vocational Hight Schools	81	4860	3186
其中：市属	Municipal schools	80	4619	3085
4、技工学校	Technical Schools	89	7018	5704
其中：市属	Municipal schools	33	1410	1034
三、基础教育	**Elementary Education**	**3030**	**106185**	**78605**
（一）普通中等教育	Regular Institutions Education	421	40576	32615
1、高中	Senior High Schools	167		18184
完全中学	Complete Secondary Schools	100	12739	10266
高级中学	Senior Secondary Schools	52	7706	6247
十二年一贯制学校	Twelve-year Consistency Schools	15	2309	1671
2、初中	Junior Middle Schools	254		14431
初级中学	Junior Middle Schools	224	15589	12618
九年一贯制学校	Nine-year Consistency Schools	30	2233	1813
完全中学	Complete Secondary school	(100)		
十二年一贯制学校	Twelve-year Consistency schools	(15)		
附设普通初中班的学校	Senior Secondary Schools with Regular Junior Secondary Classes	(2)		(31)
（二）普通初等教育	Regular Primary Education		32162	28395
独立小学	Independent Primary Schools	1257		28058
教学点	Teaching Points	(107)		337
九年一贯制学校	Nine-year Consistency schools	(30)		
十二年一贯制学校	Twelve -year Consistency schools	(15)		
附设小学班的学校	Schools with Primary Classes	(4)		(74)
（三）特殊教育	Special Education Schools		345	238
特殊教育学校	Special Education Schools	8	345	238
附设特教班的学校	Schools with Special Edution Classes	(1)		(1)
（四）工读学校	Reformatory Schools	1	40	20
（五）学前教育	Preschool Education		33062	17337
幼儿园	Kindergarten	1343	33062	17337
附设幼儿班的学校	Schools with Nursery Classes	(262)		(172)
另有：技术培训机构	Technique Training Institution	2071	16056	9618

注：本表数据来源于市教育局。
本表为西安市行政区划内各级各类学校全口径数据（不含军事院校、党校）。
技工学校数据由西安市人力资源和社会保障局提供。
按照事业统计主体校原则，完全中学、十二年一贯制学校的学校数计入普通高中，九年一贯制学校的校数计入普通初中。
教职工数按照办学类型划分，为使用方便，专任教师同时按照办学层次列出。
( ) 内数据不计入总计。(下表同)

20-3 各级各类教育学生情况（2014年）

Basic Facts on Education Student by School Type（2014）

单位：人 (persons)

指　标	Item	毕业生数 Number of Graduates	招生数 New Enrollment	在校学生数 Total Enrollment	女生 Female Students
一、高等教育	**Higher education**	**310453**	**355767**	**1133436**	**549103**
(一)研究生	Postgraduates	24092	28636	88518	39490
1、高等学校	Institutions of Higher Schools	23881	28436	87826	39339
2、科研机构	Scientific Research Institution	211	200	692	151
（二）普通高等教育	Regular Institutions of Higher Schools	188801	207410	766373	383782
1、本科	Universities Course Schools	113634	128332	530606	266224
2、专科	Junior Colleges	75167	79078	235767	117558
（三）成人高等教育	Higher Vocational Colleges	50656	48204	138928	61781
其中：成人高等学校	Contains:Adult Higher Education	6043	5483	17092	9065
（四）网络本专科生	Network Undergraduate and clooege students	46904	71517	139617	64050
1、本科	Universities Course Schools	20431	30078	60159	29087
2、专科	Junior Colleges	26473	41439	79458	34963
二、中等职业教育	**Secondary Occupation Education**	**76940**	**60012**	**188306**	**52847**
1、普通中等专业学校	Regular Specialized Secondary Schools	17629	12451	40746	21172
2、成人中等专业学校	Adult Secondary Specialized Schools	3586	1108	4711	1163
3、职业高中学校	Vocational high Schools	19156	19508	60024	30512
其中：市属	Municipal schools	19156	19391	59413	30405
4、技工学校	Technical Schools	36569	26945	82825	
其中：市属	Municipal schools	10122	7914	21751	
三、基础教育	**Elementary Education**	**317484**	**336774**	**1254299**	**585628**
(一)普通中等教育	Regular Institutions Education	145398	139694	425651	199059
1、高中	Senior High Schools	58223	55516	167381	82245
完全中学	Complete Secondary Schools	24506	24221	72144	36433
高级中学	Senior Secondary Schools	32096	29589	90183	43431
十二年一贯制学校	Twelve-year Consistency schools	1621	1706	5054	2381
2、初中	Junior Middle Schools	87175	84178	258270	116814
初级中学	Junior Middle Schools	50508	44561	139755	62806
九年一贯制学校	Nine-year Consistency Schools	3773	4314	12897	5914
十二年一贯制学校	Twelve-year Consistency Schools	3080	4075	11392	5121
完全中学	Complete Secondary school	29814	31228	94226	42973
(二)普通初等教育	Regular Primary Education	82893	101348	537905	248334
小学	Pricmary Schools	77549	94107	501090	231290
九年一贯制学校	Nine-year Consistency schools	3411	4830	23699	11008
十二年一贯制学校	Twelve-year Consistency Schools	1933	2411	13116	6036
（三）特殊教育	Special Education Schools	172	222	1225	485
1、特殊教育学校	Special Education Schools	103	158	807	312
2、小学附设特教班	Primary Schools with Special Education Classes			5	1
3、小学随班就读	Elementary Inclusive	58	34	341	138
4、初中随班就读就读	Junior Mainstreaming	11	30	72	34
（四）工读学校	Reformatory Schools	12	15	31	11
（五）学前教育	Preschool Education	89009	95495	289487	137739
1、独立幼儿园	Independent Kindergartens	83232	89350	281191	133761
2、附设幼儿园	Attached Kindergartens	5777	6145	8296	3978
另有：职业技术培训机构	Vocational and Technical Institutions	410395		474608	252242

注：本表数据来源于市教育局。

20-4 主要年份普通高等学校和科研机构研究生情况

Basic Statistics on Regular Institutions Schools and Post-graduates of Scientific Research Institution in Representative Years

单位：人 (person)

年 份 Year	毕业生数 Number of Graduates	高等学校 Higher Schools	招生数 New Enrollment	高等学校 Higher Schools	在校学生数 Total Enrollment	高等学校 Higher Schools
1978					232	232
1980					651	651
1985					4799	4799
1990	2051	2051	1662	1662	5275	5275
1995	1769	1769	2712	2712	7974	7974
1998	2316	2316	3888	3888	10833	10833
1999	2903	2903	5020	5020	12986	12986
2000	3236	3236	6924	6924	16620	16620
2001	3881	3770	9274	8966	22564	21855
2002	4103	3952	11282	10882	28446	27471
2003	5971	5765	14322	13882	36936	35790
2004	8384	8127	17310	16871	45402	44169
2005	10416	10127	18583	18106	52699	51310
2006	12914	12552	19581	19105	58433	56951
2007	15506	15124	20570	20167	64137	62801
2008	17234	16788	21892	21443	67296	65834
2009	19025	18574	24879	24400	72366	70908
2010	19526	19129	25971	25477	76993	75483
2011	20965	20605	26686	26256	81696	80332
2012	22963	22578	28065	27618	84712	83306
2013	24778	24385	28786	28333	87002	85570
2014	24092	23881	28636	28436	88518	87826

注：本表数据来源于市教育局。

20-5 主要年份普通高等学校基本情况

Baisc Statistics on Regular Higher Education in Representative Years

单位：所、万人　　　　(units,10 000 persons)

年份 Year	学校数 Number of Schools	毕业生数 Number of Graduates	招生数 New Enrollment	在校学生数 Total Enrollment	教职工数 Number of Staff and Teachers	专任教师数 Full-time Teachers
1978	21	0.60	1.31	2.88	2.24	0.87
1980	24	0.21	1.08	4.17	2.55	0.97
1985	28	1.17	2.28	6.49	3.40	1.28
1990	31	2.11	2.00	7.50	4.15	1.56
1995	32	2.87	3.13	10.07	4.21	1.59
1998	29	2.61	3.30	11.58	3.91	1.50
1999	29	2.84	5.12	13.79	3.95	1.52
2000	25	2.71	6.79	17.75	3.81	1.57
2001	32	3.31	8.31	23.24	4.30	1.75
2002	35	3.82	10.75	30.15	4.67	2.06
2003	37	5.89	12.21	36.42	4.92	2.21
2004	41	7.66	13.17	40.29	5.45	2.69
2005	44	10.08	14.68	47.79	5.73	2.95
2006	47	11.75	15.15	51.40	6.14	3.29
2007	48	14.33	16.96	56.03	6.56	3.67
2008	48	15.82	19.31	60.10	6.90	3.89
2009	49	15.04	18.84	63.22	7.08	4.06
2010	50	16.33	19.16	65.74	7.22	4.21
2011	61	17.68	20.52	68.52	7.27	4.27
2012	62	18.64	22.46	72.40	7.40	4.45
2013	63	17.73	21.05	75.27	7.50	4.64
2014	63	18.88	20.74	76.64	7.50	4.68

注：本表数据来源于市教育局。
本表仅包括本、专科。
历史年份个别数据有调整，以此表数据为准。

20-6 主要年份普通中等专业学校基本情况

Baisc Statistics on Regular Specialized Secondary Schools in Representative Years

年 份 Year	学校数（所） Number of Schools (units)	毕业生数（万人） Number of Graduates (10 000 persons)	招生数（万人） New Enrollment (10 000 persons)	在校学生数（万人） Total Enrollment (10 000 persons)	教职工数（人） Number of Staff and Teachers(person)	专任教师数（人） Full-time Teachers(person)
1978	19	0.19	0.45	0.82	3937	1110
1980	31	0.18	0.42	1.50	3895	1474
1985	37	0.43	0.76	1.70	6071	2363
1990	44	0.56	0.68	2.09	7136	2891
1995	46	0.97	1.37	3.74	5903	2533
1996	47	1.15	1.61	4.18	5940	2573
1997	47	1.20	1.65	4.63	6124	2731
1998	47	1.26	1.62	5.08	6181	2840
1999	46	1.42	2.11	5.75	6385	2865
2000	47	1.63	1.90	6.02	6964	3172
2001	47	1.70	1.58	5.63	5252	2467
2002	46	1.60	1.69	5.57	5170	2508
2003	34	1.62	1.80	5.28	4562	2302
2004	35	1.40	2.09	5.71	4676	2388
2005	32	1.44	2.26	6.16	3924	2130
2006	31	1.84	2.61	7.30	3621	2014
2007	30	2.03	2.91	7.97	3548	2011
2008	29	2.58	2.55	8.06	3278	1814
2009	28	2.70	2.15	7.44	2965	1720
2010	28	2.45	2.08	6.75	3249	1845
2011	24	2.34	1.96	6.11	2868	1723
2012	24	2.15	1.67	5.43	2733	1595
2013	22	1.93	1.35	4.66	2599	1474
2014	22	1.76	1.25	4.07	2315	1346

注：本表数据来源于市教育局。
历史年份个别数据有调整，以此表数据为准。

20－7 主要年份普通中学基本情况

Baisc Statistics on Regular Secondary Schools in Representative Years

年 份 Year	学校数（所） Number of Schools (units)	毕业生数（万人） Number of Graduates (10 000 persons)	招生数（万人） New Enrollment (10 000 persons)	在校学生数（万人） Total Enrollment (10 000 persons)	教职工数（人） Number of Staff and Teachers(person)	专任教师数（人） Full-time Teachers(person)
1978	962			44.16	27380	20660
1980	1002	12.33	14.03	44.08	29867	22530
1985	563	10.72	13.05	38.24	30063	22050
1990	518	9.11	10.49	30.03	30739	22386
1995	485	8.13	12.40	32.32	30423	21984
1996	462	8.67	13.03	35.25	30902	22478
1997	466	9.96	13.83	37.16	31682	23129
1998	467	10.64	15.00	39.79	32371	23884
1999	469	11.21	16.58	43.49	33387	25114
2000	466	12.01	17.88	48.31	34385	26230
2001	470	13.85	18.98	52.50	35442	27190
2002	467	15.76	19.68	55.36	36706	28335
2003	467	16.76	18.78	56.44	38252	29887
2004	461	18.01	18.85	56.54	39121	30600
2005	460	18.82	18.83	55.74	39456	31094
2006	457	18.04	18.61	56.11	39341	31203
2007	453	18.37	17.96	54.68	39171	31373
2008	442	17.99	17.16	52.83	39088	31425
2009	439	17.80	16.57	50.63	39002	31415
2010	436	17.01	16.15	48.89	39207	31506
2011	423	16.44	15.42	47.20	41135	31675
2012	419	15.64	14.98	45.33	41197	31526
2013	418	15.24	14.47	43.73	41003	31419
2014	421	14.54	13.97	42.57	40576	32615

注：本表数据来源于市教育局。

20-8　各区县普通中学基本情况（2014年）

Baisc Statistics on Regular Secondary Schools by Region（2014）

单位：所、人　　(unit, person)

区　县	Region	学校数 Number of Schools	毕业生数 Number of Graduates	高中 Senior	招生数 New Enrollment	高中 Senior	在　校 学生数 Total Enrollment	女生 Female Students	高中 Senior	教职工数 Number of Staff and Teachers	专任教师数 Full-time Teachers
合　计	**Total**	**421**	**145398**	**58223**	**139694**	**55516**	**425651**	**199059**	**167381**	**40576**	**32615**
新城区	Xincheng	25	11710	4024	11989	3999	35501	16890	11473	2524	2051
碑林区	Beilin	35	15473	6268	16261	6662	48308	22680	19399	3827	2908
莲湖区	Lianhu	20	11061	3878	10990	3640	34260	16483	11284	2842	2205
灞桥区	Baqiao	28	6942	2498	8021	2380	23571	11351	7287	2315	1803
未央区	Weiyang	30	10532	4915	10221	4060	30727	15179	12887	3267	2575
雁塔区	Yanta	44	15596	5277	16127	5521	48056	22842	16124	4850	3954
阎良区	Yanliang	12	4270	1735	3624	1545	11507	5719	4738	1160	974
临潼区	Lintong	32	12257	4861	10214	4483	33021	16346	13982	3398	2830
长安区	Chang'an	49	14608	6559	13480	5913	41733	19419	18665	4116	3478
蓝田县	Lantian	45	11476	4647	10549	4780	32195	15402	13695	3378	2612
周至县	Zhouzhi	35	12900	5747	11162	5376	34076	13534	15682	3481	2658
户　县	Huxian	39	11444	5168	9965	4706	31532	13262	14639	3143	2724
高陵县	Gaoling	15	4056	1792	3428	1269	10890	5303	4408	1178	982
沣东新城	Fengdongxincheng	12	3073	854	3663	1182	10274	4649	3118	1097	861

注：本表数据来源于市教育局。
　　本表中教职工数按照办学类型划分，专任教师数按照办学层次划分。

20-9 主要年份职业高中基本情况

Baisc Statistics on Vocational Secondary Schools in Representatove Years

单位：所、人 (unit, person)

年 份 Year	学校数 Number of Schools	毕业生数 Number of Graduates	招生数 New Enrollment	在校学生数 Total Enrollment	教职工数 Number of Staff and Teachers	专任教师数 Full-time Teachers
1985	40	1661	8346	17621	1375	868
1990	58	5936	8095	20151	2674	1574
1995	71	8976	12490	32673	2394	1877
1996	67	9235	10563	25955	3098	1735
1997	73	8756	13390	29068	2993	1709
1998	89	7753	13949	31264	3152	1823
1999	91	8480	13062	31973	3217	1908
2000	95	9949	13903	32188	3311	1997
2001	85	10300	15591	34336	3517	2113
2002	78	8659	17231	39428	3461	2192
2003	87	10755	17310	44033	4036	2458
2004	83	12177	17865	46358	4101	2515
2005	91	15092	20603	51766	4750	2892
2006	96	14887	21158	53828	5193	3126
2007	86	14881	24434	56012	4899	3064
2008	84	15813	30201	62963	4878	3008
2009	84	14691	31042	72388	5129	3179
2010	84	18100	30042	78244	5222	3178
2011	78	22493	27641	75108	4849	3173
2012	77	24048	24995	67969	4775	3148
2013	74	21243	23043	61968	4699	3085
2014	81	19156	19508	60024	4860	3186

注：本表数据来源于市教育局。
本表仅包括市属部分。

20-10 各区县职业高中基本情况（2014年）

Basic Statistics on Vocational Secondary Schools by Region (2014)

单位：所、人 (unit, person)

区 县	Region	学校数 Number of Schools	毕业生数 Number of Graduates	招生数 New Enrollment	在校学生数 Total Enrollment	女生 Female Students	教职工数 Number of Staff and Teachers	专任教师 Full-time Teachers
合 计	**Total**	**80**	**19156**	**19391**	**59413**	**30405**	**4619**	**3085**
新城区	Xincheng	10	3072	3984	12324	7059	713	460
碑林区	Beilin	7	1122	1876	6483	2561	549	332
莲湖区	Lianhu	6	2145	2256	7558	4147	540	306
灞桥区	Baqiao	11	1138	1040	3713	2207	388	225
未央区	Weiyang	6	984	651	2233	1376	151	88
雁塔区	Yanta	13	2165	2111	6563	2690	603	361
阎良区	Yanliang	2	1063	1035	2702	1549	221	176
临潼区	Lintong	5	1960	1961	3240	1589	284	208
长安区	Chang'an	7	1799	1780	5436	2769	507	363
蓝田县	Lantian	2	475	337	1000	493	36	21
周至县	Zhouzhi	5	1782	775	3725	1944	300	254
户 县	Huxian	5	728	1087	2503	1099	259	229
高陵县	Gaoling	1	723	498	1933	922	68	62
沣东新城	Fengdongxincheng							

注：本表数据来源于市教育局。
　　本表仅包括市属部分。

20-11 主要年份小学基本情况

Basic Statistics on Primary Schools in Representative Years

年 份 Year	学校数（所） Number of Schools (units)	毕业生数（万人） Number of Graduates (10 000 persons)	招生数（万人） New Enrollment (10 000 persons)	在校学生数（万人） Total Enrollment (10 000 persons)	教职工数（人） Number of Staff and Teachers(person)	专任教师（人） Full-time Teachers(person)
1978	2667	13.07	14.10	74.03	29744	26428
1980	2337	11.91	12.57	73.36	31770	28360
1985	2337	11.21	9.57	62.16	31075	26430
1990	2343	8.67	10.85	61.87	37788	29090
1995	2360	9.93	14.09	79.36	35568	30270
1996	2362	10.48	13.63	81.81	35821	30267
1997	2368	10.98	12.48	82.67	35767	30117
1998	2361	12.18	11.88	82.03	35576	30089
1999	2354	13.65	11.61	79.81	35639	30196
2000	2323	13.83	11.51	77.81	35336	30215
2001	2277	14.20	11.07	74.51	34257	29281
2002	2137	13.89	10.13	70.78	34143	29428
2003	2084	12.97	9.28	66.78	34080	29531
2004	2016	12.37	9.12	63.75	33794	29367
2005	1980	11.92	8.47	60.47	33907	29674
2006	1929	11.53	9.16	59.33	34460	30018
2007	1872	11.38	8.67	56.83	34901	30533
2008	1781	10.58	8.33	54.66	34653	30382
2009	1666	9.96	7.84	52.52	34389	30334
2010	1531	9.61	8.64	51.56	34118	29944
2011	1424	8.92	8.77	51.39	32457	29900
2012	1322	8.88	8.88	50.85	32208	29651
2013	1291	8.51	9.56	51.95	31863	29421
2014	1257	8.29	10.13	53.79	32162	28395

注：本表数据来源于市教育局。

20-12 各区县小学基本情况（2014年）

Basic Statistics on Primary Schools by Region (2014)

单位：所、人 (unit, person)

区 县	Region	学校数 Number of Schools	毕业生数 Number of Graduates	招生数 New Enrollment	在校学生数 Total Enrollment	女生 Female Students	教职工数 Number of Staff and Teachers	专任教师 Full-time Teachers
合 计	**Total**	**1257**	**82893**	**101348**	**537905**	**248334**	**32162**	**28395**
新城区	Xincheng	34	6607	6283	36804	17083	1758	1522
碑林区	Beilin	42	6497	7446	41443	19263	2347	1938
莲湖区	Lianhu	47	7436	9375	49313	23083	2506	2196
灞桥区	Baqiao	73	5441	8000	39474	18272	1974	1604
未央区	Weiyang	57	7120	12350	58329	26731	1996	1714
雁塔区	Yanta	70	11149	15981	78732	36373	3767	3408
阎良区	Yanliang	22	2161	2480	13780	6679	1011	916
临潼区	Lintong	151	6388	6512	36776	17120	3128	2773
长安区	Chang'an	153	7521	10515	52230	24294	3602	3072
蓝田县	Lantian	218	5878	5059	30842	14418	2813	2594
周至县	Zhouzhi	146	6071	4784	32235	13953	2508	2305
户 县	Huxian	127	5369	5038	29944	13430	2109	2010
高陵县	Gaoling	70	2240	3344	15992	7631	1456	1308
沣东新城	Fengdongxincheng	47	3015	4181	22011	10004	1187	1035

注：本表数据来源于市教育局。
本表中教职工数按照办学类型划分，专任教师数按办学层次划分。

20-13 主要年份幼儿园基本情况

Basic Statistics on Kindergartens in Representative Years

年 份 Year	幼儿园（所） Number of Kindergartens (units)	班数（个） Number of Class (unit)	在园幼儿人数（万人） Student Enrollment (10000 persons)	教职工数（人） Number of Staff and Teachers(person)	专任教师数（人） Full-time Teachers(person)
1978	363		4	3568	1315
1980	186		10	5525	2657
1985	310	3135	10	6887	2770
1990	256	3816	14	6123	2058
1995	257	4464	16	6173	2659
1996	244	4313	15	5918	2661
1997	228	4243	15	6065	2748
1998	235	4195	13	6272	2910
1999	234	4222	13	6329	2982
2000	367	4142	13	6346	2995
2001	366	4306	12	6224	3069
2002	378	4186	12	6541	3397
2003	610	4470	12	8959	4853
2004	660	4507	12	9870	5577
2005	737	4712	13	10528	5959
2006	863	5037	13	12335	7106
2007	830	5081	14	13468	7951
2008	905	5506	15	14932	8704
2009	896	5710	16	15928	9240
2010	1004	6420	18	18710	10638
2011	1122	8010	24	23680	12577
2012	1239	8729	27.1	27735	14293
2013	1295	9408	28.56	31989	16238
2014	1343	9782	28.95	33062	17337

注：本表数据来源于市教育局。
幼儿园在园人数中包括学前班。

20-14 主要年份特殊教育基本情况

Basic Statistics on Special Education in Representative Years

单位：所、人 (unit, person)

年 份 Year	学校数 Number of Schools	毕业生数 Number of Graduates	招生数 New Enrollment	在校学生数 Total Enrollment	教职工数 Number of Staff and Teachers	专任教师数 Full-time Teachers
1978						
1980	1	48	64	315	66	43
1985	2	14	36	318	94	59
1990	5	35	111	451	142	96
1995	5	27	147	1363	204	141
1996	5	60	164	1520	210	150
1997	5	153	164	1655	210	148
1998	5	266	140	2145	232	157
1999	5	349	115	1912	235	160
2000	5	269	145	1880	230	156
2001	5	237	209	1915	238	162
2002	5	216	148	1661	232	157
2003	5	156	161	1380	237	166
2004	5	137	142	1290	236	167
2005	5	184	182	1445	240	169
2006	6	171	143	1425	254	178
2007	6	169	114	1342	259	190
2008	6	83	96	1286	259	190
2009	7	311	202	1523	335	234
2010	8	214	402	1529	340	235
2011	8	280	222	1393	343	231
2012	8	197	220	1392	352	248
2013	8	194	212	1174	338	243
2014	8	172	222	1225	345	238

注：本表数据来源于市教育局。

包括盲、聋、哑、弱智儿童教育在内。

20-15 基础教育监测评价情况（2014年）

Monitoring and Evaluation of Basic Education(2014)

指 标	Item	2014
入学率(%)	Enrollment Rate(%)	
小学	Primary Schools	99.98
初中	Junior Middle Schools	99.80
重读率(%)	Restduy-Rate(%)	
小学	Primary schools	0.04
初中	Junior Middle Schools	0.03
巩固率(%)	The Consolidation Rate (%)	
小学（六年）	Primary Schools (six years)	99.52
初中（三年）	Junior Middle Schools (three years)	95.29
毕业率(%)	The Graduate Rate(%)	
小学	Primary school	99.59
初中	Junior middle school	99.93
专任教师学历合格率(%)	Qualified Rate Of Full-time Teacher Education (%)	
小学	Primary Schools	99.64
初中	Junior Middle Schools	99.61
高中	Senior Middle Schools	97.79
幼儿园	Kindergartens	96.53
小学教师专科以上学历达到率(%)	Rate of Primary School Teachers with College degree or Above (%)	93.96
初中教师本科以上学历达到率(%)	Rate of Junior Middle SchoolTeachers with Bachelor degree or Above (%)	87.63
高中教师研究生以上学历达到率(%)	Rate of Senior Middle School Teachers with Postgraduate degree or Above (%)	11.92

注：本表数据来源于市教育局。

20-16 主要年份平均每万人口在校学生数及构成

单位：人、%

年 份 Year	平均每万人 高等学校在校学生 Per 10000 people on average Hight Education Students in the school	平均每万人 高中阶段在校学生 Per 10000 people on average Number of Senior high School Students in the school	平均每万人 初中在校学生 Per 10000 people on average Number of Junior Secondary School Students in the school
1978	58		
1980	84		
1985	117		
1990	123		
1995	168		
1996	177		
1997	180		
1998	189		
1999	224		
2000	282		
2001	366		
2002	470		
2003	560		
2004	618	463	517
2005	715	492	489
2006	760	534	484
2007	817	543	466
2008	863	571	444
2009	901	619	413
2010	939	635	361
2011	1090	576	337
2012	1132	541	319
2013	1146	448	307
2014	1157	414	301

注：本表数据来源于市教育局。

The Number of Students in the School in Major Years Per 10000 Pepole on Average

(persons,%)

平均每万人 小学在校学生 Per 10000 people on average Number of Primary School Students in the school	普通高等学校在校学生 占学生总数比重 Senior high School Students in the school in accounting for the proportion of the total number of students	中等学校在校学生 占学生总数比重 Junior Secondary School students in the school in accounting for the proportion of the total number of students	小学在校学生 占学生总数比重 Primary School students in the school in accounting for the proportion of the total number of students
1486	2.3	34.9	58.6
1434	3.1	33.2	55.3
1124	5.3	31.3	50.9
1016	6.7	25.1	51.7
1224	7.3	28.0	53.6
1249	7.6	28.8	53.5
1249	7.6	29.8	53.1
1228	8.0	31.3	52.0
1183	9.3	33.2	49.2
1131	11.5	34.8	46.0
1072	14.6	35.9	42.6
1007	18.2	36.4	39.0
932	20.1	33.8	33.5
879	22.2	35.2	31.6
815	26.4	36.2	30.1
788	27.7	37.1	28.7
744	29.3	36.3	26.7
708	30.8	36.1	25.2
672	31.8	36.5	23.7
660	33.0	35.0	23.2
604	29.8	30.1	19.9
595	31.0	28.2	19.5
605	32.6	25.3	20.2
626	33.2	23.8	20.9

20-17 民办教育情况(2014年)

Private Education Situation (2014)

单位：所、人 (unit, person)

指 标	Item	学校数 Number of Schools	毕业生数 Number of Graduates	招生数 New Enrollment
一、民办高等教育(民办高校)	**Private higher Education (Institutions)**	**16**	**67436**	**76656**
二、民办中等教育	**Private Secondary Education**	99	37688	42440
民办普通高中	Ordinary High School	31	5799	6348
民办中等专业学校	Specialized Secondary School	1	1971	617
民办职业高中	Vocational hight school	48	8345	10661
民办普通初中	Ordinary Junior middle school	19	18479	21128
民办的附设中职班	Private primary school class	(9)	3094	3686
三、民办普通小学	**Private Primary School**	**49**	**8133**	**12308**
四、民办幼儿园	**Private kindergarten**	**1064**	**60489**	**63239**
另有：民办培训机构（不计校数）	Private Training Institutions (Not included in the totals number of schools)	546	211456	

20-17 续表 continued

单位：所、人 (unit, person)

指 标	Item	在校学生数 Total Enrollment	教职工数 Number of Teachers and Staff	专任教师 Full-time Teachers	聘请外校教师 Teachers hired from Outside Schools
一、民办高等教育(民办高校)	**Private higher Education (Institutions)**	**283839**	**21035**	**13121**	
二、民办中等教育	**Private Secondary Education**	121817	8699	6259	694
民办普通高中	Ordinary High School	18707			
民办中等专业学校	Specialized Secondary School	2551	273	168	
民办职业高中	Vocational hight school	29391	2226	1313	552
民办普通初中	Ordinary Junior middle school	61390			
民办的附设中职班	Private primary school class	9778			
三、民办普通小学	**Private Primary School**	**58713**	**2716**	**2304**	**1**
四、民办幼儿园	**Private kindergarten**	**205444**	**24608**	**12538**	**36**
另有：民办培训机构（不计校数）	Private Training Institutions (Not included in the totals number of schools)	269053	8283	4190	5639

注：本表数据来源于市教育局。
毕业生数中幼儿园为离园人数。
民办高等教育在校生为民办高校普通、成人本专科学生数。
聘请校外教师中，小学、中学、幼儿园为代课教师和兼任教师之和。
民办普通高中含完全中学18所、高级中学5所、12年一贯制8所；民办普通初中含初级中学11所,9年一贯制8所。
民办中等教育教职工、专任教师、聘请校外教师合计中含民办普通中学教职工6200人，专任教师4778人，聘请校外教师142人，因此分项不等于合计。

20–18 研究与试验发展（R&D）情况

Research and Experiment Development Facts

指 标	Item	2013	2014
一、单位数（个）	**Number of Units(unit)**	**1684**	**1777**
#科研单位	Units of Scientific Research	80	63
高等院校	Institutions of Higher Education	46	47
规模以上工业企业	Industrial Enterprises above Designated Size	1061	1151
#有R&D活动单位数	Number of Units with R&D Activities	403	472
科研单位	Units of Scientific Research	48	44
高等院校	Institutions of Higher Education	46	46
规模以上工业企业	Industrial Enterprises above Designated Size	244	312
二、科技活动人员（人）	**Personnel Eagaged in Scientific and Technical Activities (person)**	**161004**	**173320**
科研单位	Units of Scientific Research	38423	39223
高等院校	Institutions of Higher Education	40454	43973
规模以上工业企业	Industrial Enterprises above Designated Size	65132	73783
三、R&D经费内部支出（万元）	**Interier Expenditures for R&D(10 000 yuan)**	**2567704**	**2871157**
科研单位	Units of Scientific Research	1350092	1529373
高等院校	Institutions of Higher Education	304608	334944
规模以上工业企业	Industrial Enterprises above Designated Size	800038	884957
四、R&D项目（课题）（个）	**Number of Projects of R&D(item)**	**30627**	**34898**
科研单位	Units of Scientific Research	2016	2095
高等院校	Institutions of Higher Education	24576	28392
规模以上工业企业	Industrial Enterprises above Designated Size	3629	3968

注：本表数据来源于省教育厅、省统计局、市科技局。本表单位数含规模以上工业企业、非工业企业和事业单位。

20-19 科研院所研究与试验发展（R&D）情况

Research and Experiment Development Facts in Scientific Research Institutions

指　标	Item	2013	2014
一、基本情况	**Basic Facts**		
单位数（个）	Number of Unit(unit)	80	63
#有R&D活动的单位数	Number of Units with Scientific and Technical Activities	48	44
科技活动人员（人）	Number of Personnel Engaged in Scientific Research (person)	38423	29223
# R&D人员	R&D Personnel	28004	28588
其中：女性	Female	8663	9117
其中：博士毕业	Doctor	1151	1439
硕士毕业	Master	8055	9440
本科毕业	Undergraduate	11198	11084
二、R&D人员折合全时当量（人/年）	**Full Time Equivalent of R&D Personnel (person/year)**	**25902**	**28036**
其中：研究人员	Personnel Engaged in Research	17978	18704
其中：基础研究	Basic Research	2077	1606
应用研究	Applied Research	7972	9549
试验发展	Experiment Development	15853	16881
三、R&D经费内部支出（万元）	**Raising and Use of Funds for Scientific and(10 000 yuan) Technical Activities**	**1350092**	**1529373**
在支出中：1、基础研究	Expenditure on: Basic Research	52265	63719
2、应用研究	Applied Research	310187	412146
3、试验发展	Experiment Development	987640	1053508
在支出中：1、日常支出	Expenditure on: Daily Expenditure	1045884	1179855
#人员劳务费	Service Fees of Personnel	214742	217267
2、资产性支出	Assets Expenditure	304208	350061
#仪器和设备	Instruments and Equipment	138702	174302
在支出中：1、政府资金	Expenditure on: Government Funds	1203551	1454904
2、企业资金	Enterpreises Funds	13085	31289
3、境外资金	Overseas Funds		2.9
4、其他资金	Others	133456	83180
四、R&D产出	**Achievements of R&D**		
专利申请数（个）	Number of Patent Applications (item)	2205	2726
#发明专利	Number of Invention Patents	1626	2201
专利授权数（个）	Number of Patents Awarded (item)	1138	15409
#发明专利	Number of Invention Patents	599	1067
有效发明专利数（件）	Number of Effective Invention Patents(item)	2135	3586
发表科技论文（篇）	Scientific and Technical Thesis (piece)	5663	5340
出版科技著作（种）	Scientific and Technical Works Published (book)	87	81

注：本表数据来源于市科技局。

20-20 大专院校研究与试验发展（R&D）情况

Research and Experiment Development Facts in Universities

指　标	Item	2013	2014
一、基本情况	**Basic Facts**		
单位数（个）	Number of Unit(unit)	46	47
#有R&D活动的单位数	Number of Units with Scientific and Technical Activities	46	46
科技活动人员（人）	Number of Personnel Engaged in Scientific Research (person)	40454	43973
# R&D人员	R&D Personnel	17395	17636
其中：女性	Female	5806	5875
其中：博士毕业	Doctor	5689	5901
硕士毕业	Master	5931	5965
本科毕业	Undergraduate	4717	4816
二、R&D人员折合全时当量（人/年）	**Full Time Equivalent of R&D Personnel (person/year)**	**8497**	8154
其中：研究人员	Personnel Engaged in Research	7462	7171
其中：基础研究	Basic Research	3837	3981
应用研究	Applied Research	3694	3168
试验发展	Experiment Development	966	1005
三、R&D经费内部支出（万元）	**Raising and Use of Funds for Scientific and(10 000 yuan) Technical Activities**	**304608**	334944
在支出中：1、基础研究	Expenditure on: Basic Research	93418	100094
2、应用研究	Applied Research	132607	178941
3、试验发展	Experiment Development	78584	55909
在支出中：1、日常支出	Expenditure on: Daily Expenditure	256710	288466
#人员劳务费	Service Fees of Personnel	31197	35745
2、资产性支出	Assets Expenditure	47889	46478
#仪器和设备	Instruments and Equipment	29578	33471
在支出中：1、政府资金	Expenditure on: Government Funds	186527	178990
2、企业资金	Enterpreises Funds	109480	147686
3、境外资金	Overseas Funds	1226	903
4、其他资金	Others	7375	7365
四、R&D产出	**Achievements of R&D**		
专利申请数（个）	Number of Patent Applications (item)	6153	6517
#发明专利	Number of Invention Patents	4180	4703
专利授权数（个）	Number of Patents Awarded (item)	4301	4668
#发明专利	Number of Invention Patents	2111	2588
有效发明专利数（件）	Number of Effective Invention Patents(item)	7283	8602
发表科技论文（篇）	Scientific and Technical Thesis (piece)	37542	37836
出版科技著作（种）	Scientific and Technical Works Published (book)	891	912

注：本表数据来源于省教育厅。

20–21 规模以上工业企业研究与试验发展（R&D）情况

Research and Experiment Development Facts in Large-size and Medium-size Industrial Enterprises

指　标	Item	2013	2014
一、基本情况	**Basic Facts**		
单位数（个）	Number of Unit(unit)	1061	1151
有（R&D）活动的单位数	Number of Units with Scientific and Technical Activities	244	312
从事科技活动人员（人）	Number of Personnel Engaged in Scientific Research (person)	65132	73783
#（R&D）人员	R&D Personnel	42229	45808
其中：女性	Female	11432	12811
二、R&D人员折合全时当量（人/年）	**Full Time Equivalent of R&D Personnel (person/year)**	**28715**	**31282**
其中：研究人员	Personnel Engaged in Research	13418	14261
其中：基础研究	Basic Research	26	61
应用研究生	Applied Research	895	1105
试验发展	Experiment Development	27794	30115
三、R&D经费内部支出（万元）	**Raising and Use of Funds for Scientific and Technical Activities(10 000 yuan)**	**800038**	**884957**
在支出中：1、基础研究	Expenditure on: Basic Research	501	773
2、应用研究	Applied Research	50533	31356
3、试验发展	Experiment Development	749004	852828
在支出中：1、日常支出	Expenditure on: Daily Expenditure	703539	801040
#人员劳务费	Service Fees of Personnel	153624	175172
2、资产性支出	Assets Expenditure	96498	83917
#仪器和设备	Instruments and Equipment	90290	80863
在支出中：1、政府资金	Expenditure on: Government Funds	188566	229893
2、企业资金	Enterpreises Funds	602911	646791
3、境外资金	Overseas Funds	62	175
4、其他资金	Others	8500	8098
四、R&D产出	**Achievements of R&D**		
专利申请数（个）	Number of Patent Applications (item)	4836	4714
#发明专利	Number of Invention Patents	2149	2030
有效发明专利数（件）	Number of Effective Invention Patents(item)	4017	4803
发表科技论文（篇）	Scientific and Technical Thesis (piece)	2821	3257

注：2014年规模以上工业企业科技年报为省统计局反馈数据。

20–22　主要年份企事业单位知识产权情况

Intellectual Property Right of Enterprises and Institutions in Representative Years

指　标	Item	2008	2009	2010	2011	2012	2013	2014
一、科技活动情况	**Science and technology activities**							
科技活动人员（人）	People involved into activities(person)	91994	137934	128559	147814	162232	161004	173320
科技活动机构数（个）	units involved into activities(unit)	411	569	490	625	616	634	656
二、知识产权拥有量情况	**Number of IPR**							
1. 专利情况（件）	Patents(item)							
（1）累计申请专利	Accumulated patent applications	42436	55208	74694	102411	139290	186401	233435
当年申请专利	Patent applictions in this year	9584	12772	19486	27717	36983	47111	47034
#发明专利	Invention patents	3049	5014	7176	11689	15029	23534	21189
（2）累计授权专利	Accumulated patents awarded	19256	23962	31999	41273	53118	69368	86639
当年授权专利	Patents awarded in this year	3285	4706	8037	9274	11862	16250	17271
#发明专利	Invention patents	749	1121	1651	2738	3475	3708	4272
2. 商标情况（件）	Trade marks(item)							
（1）当年注册商标申请	Trade mark registration claimed in this year	7613	8972	21562	15620	18230	12372	10023
（2）累计注册商标	Accumulated trade mark registrations	26386	23078	52387	39381	65733	69915	75515
#当年注册商标	Trade mark registrations in this year	3526	5278	18107	12278	12120	8850	8875
三、民事知识产权维权情况（件）	**IPR controversy(item)**	**212**	**427**	**241**	**512**	**631**	**476**	**385**
1. 专利纠纷	Patent controversies	47	37	69	104	107	77	48
2. 商标纠纷	Trade mark controversies	51	42	29	49	107	209	173
3. 著作权纠纷	Copyright controversies	91	319	110	315	365	141	126
4. 技术合同纠纷	Technological contract controversies	3	9	6	15	9	16	7
5. 其他知识产权纠纷	Others IPR controvers	20	20	27	29	43	33	31

注：本表数据由市科技局、陕西省工商局、陕西省新闻出版局、西安市中级人民法院等提供。

20-23 主要年份高新技术产业开发区情况

Basic Statistics of Hi-Tech Development Zone in Representative Years

指 标	Item	2008	2009	2010	2011	2012	2013	2014
1. 高新技术企业数（个）	Number of High-tech Enterprises(unit)	1324	592	672	774	690	802	827
2. 年末从业人员（人）	Number of Persons Employed at year-end (person)	388644	275141	287140	296723	320259	328707	346679
从事技术开发人数（人）	Number of Persons Engaged in Technology Development	48355	64212	67708	78636	81787	88179	101937
3. 技术开发经费支出总额（万元）	Expenditures on Technology Development(10 000 yuan)	777516	756767	1031223	1322923	1768282	1926100	3125766
研究与发展支出	Expenditures on Research and Development	581716	585449	669083	831822	1273311	1666389	2534456
4. 利润总额（万元）	Total Profits (10 000 yuan)	1231146	1308432	1707925	2224850	2905877	3539526	3896038
5. 上缴税费总额（万元）	Sum of tax (10 000 yuan)	1576472	1486556	1964820	2586712	3383678	4465587	4640297
6. 出口创汇总额（千美元）	Foreign Exchange Earnings of Exports(USD 1 000)	2188721	1177000	4951265	6447050	6591977	7880206	9488010

20-24 高新技术产业开发区发展规模（2014年）

Development Status of Hi-Tech Development Zone (2014)

指 标	Item	合计 Total	新建区 Newly constructed Zone
累计已开发面积（平方公里）	Accumulated Areas Developed (sq.km)	50	50
高新区工商注册（个）	Registered Enterprises in Hi-tech Zones (unit)	26452	26452
#工业型技术开发技术服务型企业数	Number of industrial technology developing enterprises	11117	11117
#三资企业数	Enterprises of Joiut Venture,Cooperation and Foreign-funded	1120	1120
已认定的高新技术企业数（个）	Hi-tech Enterprises Designated	827	827

注：本表数据来源于西安市高新技术开发区。

20-25 主要年份高新技术产业开发区建设与集资情况

Capital Construction and Funds-Raising of Hi-Tech Development Zone in Representative Years

指　标	Item	2008	2009	2010	2011	2012	2013	2014
一、基建投资（亿元）	**Investment on Capital Construction (100 million yuan)**							
本年基建投资	Investment on Capital Construction of this year	159.78	196.9	255.57	266.51	350.88	432.38	601.01
二、开发面积	**Area Developed**							
新建区累计开发土地面积（平方公里）	Accumulated Area Developed in Newly Constructed Zone (sq.km)	35	35	35	35	40	50	55
#当年新开发土地面积	Area Developed in this year					5	10	5
累计竣工建筑面积（万平方米）	Accumulated Floor Space Completed (10 000 sq.m)	1782.4	2085.7	2419.9	2748.1	3095.1	3433.9	3773.9
#当年竣工建筑面积	Floor Space Completed in this year	223.76	303.23	334.2	328.22	347	338.8	340
三、吸引外资（亿美元）	**Foreign Investment(100million USB)**							
年末累计境外客商协议投资额	Contracted Foreign Investment Accumulated at Year-end	36.26	43.76	52.76	56.71	74.11	150.61	170.61
年末累计境外客商实际投资额	Actual Foreign Investment	20.29	24.63	29.75	36.24	45.02	58.28	72.78
#当年实际投资额	Actual Investmen in this year	4.21	4.34	5.11	6.49	8.18	13.26	14.5

注：本表数据来源于西安市高新技术开发区。

主要统计指标解释

普通高等学校 指按国家规定的设置标准和审批程序批准举办的，通过全国普通高等学校统一招生考试，招收高中毕业生为主要培养对象，实施高等学历教育的全日制大学、独立设置的学院和高等专科学校、高等职业学校及其他机构（独立学院和分校、大专班）。

大学、独立设置的学院主要实施本科层次以上教育。高等专科学校、高等职业学校实施专科层次教育。其他机构是承担国家普通招生计划任务不计校数的机构，包括独立学院、普通高等学校分校、大专班和批准筹建的普通高等学校等。独立学院指由普通本科高校按新机制、新模式举办的本科层次的二级学院，一些普通本科高校按公办机制和模式建立的二级学院，“分校”或其他类似的二级办学机构不属此范畴。

成人高等学校 指按照国家规定的设置标准和审批程序批准举办的，通过全国成人高等教育统一招生考试，招收具有高中毕业或同等学历的人员为主要培养对象，利用函授、业余、脱产等多种形式对其实施高等学历教育的学校。包括职工高等学校、农民高等学校、管理干部学院、教育学院、独立函授学院、广播电视大学、其他机构等。其他机构是承担国家成人招生计划任务不计校数的机构。

小学学龄儿童净入学率 指调查范围内已入小学学习的学龄儿童占校内外学龄儿童总数（包括弱智儿童，不包括盲聋哑儿童）的比重。计算公式为：

小学学龄儿童净入学率（%）=已入学的小学学龄儿童数／校内外小学学龄儿童总数×100%

研究与试验发展（R&D） 指在科学技术领域，为增加知识总量，以及运用这些知识去创造新的应用进行的系统的创造性的活动，包括基础研究、应用研究、试验发展三类活动。国际上通常采用R&D活动的规模和强度指标反映一国的科技实力和核心竞争力。

基础研究 指为了获得关于现象和可观察事实的基本原理的新知识（揭示客观事物的本质、运动规律，获得新发现、新学说）而进行的实验性或理论性研究，它不以任何专门或特定的应用或使用为目的。其成果以科学论文和科学著作为主要形式。用来反映知识的原始创新能力。

应用研究 指为获得新知识而进行的创造性研究，主要针对某一特定的目的或目标。应用研究是为了确定基础研究成果可能的用途，或是为达到预定的目标探索应采取的新方法（原理性）或新途径。其成果形式以科学论文、专著、原理性模型或发明专利为主。用来反映对基础研究成果应用途径的探索。

试验发展 指利用从基础研究、应用研究和实际经验所获得的现有知识，为产生新的产品、材料和装置，建立新的工艺、系统和服务，以及对已产生和建立的上述各项作实质性的改进而进行的系统性丁作。其成果形式主要是专利、专有技术、具有新产品基本特征的产品原型或具有新装置基本特征的原始样机等。在社会科学领域，试验发展是指把通过基础研究、应用研究获得的知识转变成可以实施的计划（包括为进行检验和评估实施示范项目）的过程。人文科学领域没有对应的试验发展活动。主要反映将科研成果转化为技术和产品的能力，是科技推动经济社会发展的物化成果。

R&D人员 指参与研究与试验发展项目研究、管理和辅助工作的人员，包括项目（课题）组人员，企业科技行政管理人员和直接为项目（课题）活动提供服务的辅助人员。反映投入从事拥有自主知识产权的研究开发活动的人力规模。

R&D人员全时当量 指全时人员数加非全时人员按工作量折算为全时人员数的总和。例如：有两个全时人员和三个非全时人员（工作时间分别为20%、30%和70%），则全时当量为2+0.2+0.3+0.7=3.2人年。为国际上比较科技人力投入而制定的可比指标。

R&D经费内部支出 合计指调查单位用于内部开展R&D活动（基础研究、应用研究和试验发展）的实际支出。包括用于R&D项目（课题）活动的直接支出，以及间接用TR&D活动的管理费、服务费、与R&D有关的基本建设支出以及外协加工费等。不包括生产性活动支出、归还贷款支出以及与外单位合作或委托外单位进行R&D活动而转拨给对方的经费支出。

R&D经费内部支出中政府资金 指R&D经费内部支出中来自各级政府部门的各类资金，包括财政科学技术拨款、科学基金、教育等部门事业费以及政府部门预算外资金的实际支出。

R&D经费内部支出中企业资金 指R&D经费内部支出中来自本企业的自有资金和接受其他企业委托而获得的经费，以及科研院所、高校等事业单位从企业获得的资金的实际支出。

R&D项目（课题）数 指在当年立项并开展研究工作、以前年份立项仍继续进行研究的研发项目（课题）数，包括当年完成和年内研究：工作已告失败的研发项目（课题），但不包括委托外单位进行的研发项目（课题）数。

R&D项目（课题）人员全时当量 指实际参加研发项目（课题）活动人员折合的全时当量。

R&D项目（课题）经费内部支出 指调查单位内部在报告年度进行研发项目（课题）研究和试制等的实际支出。包括劳务费、其他日常支出、固定资产购建费、外协加工费等，不包括委托或与外单位合作进行项目（课题）研究而拨付给对方使用的经费。

新产品产值 指报告期企业生产的新产品的产值。新产品是指采用新技术原理、新设计构思研制、生产的全新产品，或在结构、材质、工艺等某一方面比原有产品有明显改进，从而显著提高了产品性能或扩大了使用功能的产品。新产品产值、新产品销售收入既包括经政府有关部门认定并在有效期内的新产品，也包括企业自行研制开发，未经政府有关部门认定，从投产之日起一年之内的新产品。

新产品销售收入 指报告期企业销售新产品实现的销售收入。

专利 是专利权的简称，是对发明人的发明创造经审查合格后，由专利局依据专利法授予发明人和设计人对该项发明创造享有的专有权。包括发明、实用新型和外观设计。反映拥有自主知识产权的科技和设计成果情况。

发明（专利） 指对产品、方法或者其改进所提出的新的技术方案。是国际通行的反映拥有自主知识产权技术的核心指标。

实用新型（专利） 指对产品的形状、构造或者其结合所提出的适于实用的新的技术方案。反映具有一定技术含量的技术成果情况。

外观设计（专利） 指对产品的形状、图案、色彩或者其结合所作出的富有美感并适于工业上应用的新设计。反映拥有自主知识产权的外观设计成果情况。

工业企业R&D投入强度 指研究与试验发展经费内部支出与主营业务收入的比值。

Explanatory Notes on Main Statistical Indicators

Regular Institutions of Higher Education refer to educational establishments set up according to the government evaluation and approval procedures, recruiting graduates from senior secondary schools as the main target by National Matriculation TEST. They include full-time universities, colleges, institutions of higher professional education, institutions of higher vocational education, institutions of higher vocational education and others (non-university tertiary, branch schools and undergraduate classes) .

Universities and colleges primarily provide undergraduate courses; institutions of higher professional education and institutions of higher vocational education primarily provide professional trainings; and others refer to educational establishments, which are responsible for enrolling higher education students under the State Plan but not enumerated in the total number of schools, including: branch schools of universities and colleges, and universities and colleges that have been approved and under plan for construction. Non-university tertiary refers to the regular undergraduate branch college which is running in new mechanism and mode, excluding the branch schools and other similar branches of educational institutions.

Institutions of Higher Education for Adults refer to educational establishments, set up in line with relevant rules approved by the government, enrolling staff and workers with senior secondary school or equivalent education, and providing higher education courses in many forms of correspondence, spare time, or full time for adults. Professionals thus trained receive a qualification equivalent to graduates studying regular courses at regular universities, colleges and professional colleges. Institutions of higher learning for adults include schools of higher education for staff and workers, schools of higher education for peasants, colleges for management cadres, pedagogical colleges, independent correspondence colleges, Radio and TV universities and other educational establishments. Other educational establishments have undertakings to enrol adult students but not enumerated in the schools under the State Plan.

Net Enrolment Ratio of Primary Schools refers to the proportion of school age children enrolled at schools to the total number of school age children both in and outside schools (including retarded children, but excluding blind, deaf and mute children) . The formula is:

$$\text{Net Enrolment Ratio Of Primary Schools} = \frac{\text{Total Primary School-age Children at Schools}}{\text{Total Primary School-age WnerdlihChether or Not Attending School}} \times 100\%$$

Research and Development (R&D) refers to systematic and creative activities in the field of science and technology aiming at increasing the knowledge and using the knowledge for new application. R&D includes 3 categories of activities: basic research, applied research and experimentation for development. The scale and intensity of R&D are widely used internationally to reflect the strength of S&T and the core competitiveness of a country in the world.

Basic Research refers to empirical or theoretical research aiming at obtaining new knowledge on the fundamental principles regarding phenomena or observable facts to reveal the intrinsic nature and underlying laws and to acquire new discoveries or new theories. Basic research takes no specific or designated application as the aim of the research. Results of basic research are mainly released or disseminated in the form of scientific papers or monographs. This indicator reflects the innovation capacity for original knowledge.

Applied Research refers to creative research aiming at obtaining new knowledge on a specific objective or target. Purpose of the applied research is to identify the possible uses of results from basic research, or to explore new (fundamental) methods or new approaches. Results of applied research are expressed in the form of scientific papers, monographs, fundamental models or invention patents. This indicator reflects the exploration of ways to apply the results of basic research.

Experiments and Development refer to systematic activities aiming at using the knowledge from basic and applied researches or from practical experience to develop new products, materials and equipment, to establish new production process, systems and services, or to make substantial improvement on the existing products, process or services. Results of experiment and development activities are embodied in patents, exclusive technology, and monotype of new products or equipment. In social sciences, experiment and development activities refer to the process of converting the knowledge from basic or applied researches into feasible programmes (including conduct of demonstration projects for assessment and evaluation) . There are no experiment and development activities in the science of humanities. This indicator reflects the capability of transferring the results of S&T into technique and products, and measures the realization of S&T in spearheading the economic and social development.

R&D Personnel refer to persons engaged in research, management and supporting activities ofR & D, including persons in the project teams, persons engaged in the management of S&T activities of enterprises and supporting staff providing direct service to the research projects. This indicator reflects the size of personnel engaged in R&D activities with independent intellectual property.

Full-time Equivalent of R&D Personnel refers to the sum of the full-time persons and the full-time equivalent of part-time persons converted by workload. For instance, if there are 2 full-time persons and 3 part-time workers (20%, 30% and 70% of working hours respectively on R&D activities) , the full-time equivalent are 2+0.2+0.3+0.7=3.2 person-years. This is an internationally comparable indicator of S&T manpower input.

Total Internal Expenditure of Funds on R&D refers to the real expenditure of surveyed units on their own R&D activities (basic research, application study, test and development) including direct expenditure on R&D activities, indirect expenditure of management and services on R&D activities, expenditure on capital construction and material processing by others. Excluding the expenditure on production activities, return of loan, and fees transferred to cooperated and entrusted agencies on R&D activities.

Internal Expenditure of Government Funds refersto the expenditure of funds on R&D activities from government agencies at different levels, including appropriate funds on science and technology from financial departments, scientific funds, operating expenses from education departments and the real expenditure of extra budgetary funds from government agencies.

Internal Expenditure of Funds of Enterprises refers to the expenditure of funds on R&D activities from self-raised funds of enterprises and funds from other enterprises through entrustment, and the expenditure of funds of institutions, such as institution of scientific research and universities, from enterprises.

Number of R&D Projects (subjects) refers to the number of R&D projects (subjects) set up and implemented at the reference year, and the number of R&D projects (subjects) set up in former years and under implementation, including the projects (subjects) finished and failed at the reference year, excluding the projects (subjects) implemented by others through entrustment.

Full-time Equivalent of R&D Personnel refers to the full-time equivalent of persons actually engaged in R&D projects. (subjects)

Internal Expenditure of Funds on R&D Projects (subjects) refers to the real expenditure of internal funds of the surveyed units on research and test of R&D projects (subjects) at the reference year, including service fee, other daily expenditure, cost for capital goods, cost of external process; excluding expenditure of funds transferred to other cooperated and entrusted units of the projects.

Output Value of New Products refers to the output value of new products during the reporting period. The new products refer to brand new products produced with new technology and new design, or product that represent noticeable improvement in terms of structure, material, or production process for improving significantly the character of function of the older versions. The output value and sales income of the new products include those of new products certified by relevant government agencies within the period of certification, as well as new products designed and produced by enterprises within a year without certification by government agencies.

Sales Income of New Products refers to the real sales income of new products of the enterprises at the reporting period.

Patent is an abbreviation for the patent right and refers to the exclusive right of ownership by the inventors or designers for the creation or inventions, given from the patent offices after due process of assessment and approval in accordance with the Patent Law. Patents are granted for inventions, utility models and designs. This indicator reflects the achievements of S&T and design with independent intellectual property.

Patented Inventions refer to new technical proposals to the products or methods or their modifications. This is universal core indicator reflecting the technologies with independent intellectual property.

Patented Utility Models refer to the practical and new technical proposals on the shape and structure of the product or the combination of both. This indicator reflects the condition of technological results with certain technical content.

Designs refer to the aesthetics and industrially applicable new designs for the shape, pattern and colour of the product, or their combinations. This indicator reflects the appearance design achievements with independent intellectual property.

Intensity of Input into R&D of Industrial Enterprises refers to the percentage of main operation income spent on R&D activities by industrial enterprises.

21 文化、体育、卫生、社会福利和其他

CULTURE,SPORTS,PUBLIC HEALTH,SOCIAL WELFARE INSTITUTIONS AND OTHER SOCIAL ACTIVITIES

资料整理：郝　静
Data management：Hao Jing
数据审核：王金桂
Data audit：Wang Jingui

第二十一部分　文化、体育、卫生、社会福利和其他

一、简要说明

本章资料主要包括文化、卫生、民政、体育、计划生育、共青团、妇联以及公检法等方面的内容，由西安市统计局社会科技处根据西安市文广新局、卫生局、民政局、体育局、妇联、共青团市委、计划生育委员会以及公安局、检察院、法院等部门提供资料整理。

二、主要指标

图书馆总藏量（千册件）	7585	比上年增加	938.4千册件
医院数（个）	281	比上年增加	持平
医院床位数（万张）	4.56	比上年增加	2808张

21　CULTURE,SPORTS,SANITATION,SOCIAL WELFARE INSTITUTIONS AND OTHER SOCIAL ACTIVITIES

Ⅰ.Brief Introduction

Data in this chapter primarily consists of data of culture, sanitation, civil administration, physical education, family planning, Communist Youth League, the Women's Federation, public security organs, procuratorial organs and people's court, compiled by Social Science & Technology Division of Xi'an Bureau of Statistics according to data from Xi'an Bureau of Cuture, Bureau of Sanitation, Bureau of Civial Adnimistration, Bureau of PE, the Women's Federation, Municipal Committee of Communist Youth League, Committee of Family Planning, Bureau of Public Security, Procuratorate, People's Court and other department concerned.

Ⅱ.Major Indicators

		Increase over Preceding Year
Number of Collections in Libraries(1 000 vol.)	7585	938.4
Number of Hospitals(unit)	281	essentially on a par with last year's
Number of Beds(10 000 units)	4.56	2808 units

21-1 文化事业机构和人数（2014年）

Number of Institutions and Personnel in Culture and Art（2014）

项　　目	Item	机构数（个）Number of Institutions (unit)	人员数（人）Number of Personnel (person)
一、电影事业	**Career of Film**		
制片厂	Studio	1	
发行放映管理机构	Number of Film Projection and Publication Administrating Institutions	2	8
电影放映单位	Unit of Film shows	171	1706
#电影院	Cinema	40	1494
影剧院	Theaters	5	65
放映队	Film Projection Team	126	147
二、艺术事业	**Art**		
艺术表演团体	Art Performance Troupes	18	2331
艺术表演场所	Art Centers	17	363
三、艺术科研机构	**Art Scientific Research Institution**	**2**	**61**
四、图书馆事业	**Libraries**	**15**	**552**
五、群众文化事业	**Mass Culture**		
群众艺术馆	Activities of Mass Art Centres	2	130
文化馆	Cultural Centers	14	238
文化站	Culture Stations	183	728
农村文化室	Rural Cultural Center	2515	
六、文化部门教育机构	**Educations Institution of Culture Department**	**2**	**117**

注：本表数据来源于市文广新局。

21-2 文化事业发展情况（2014年）

Basic Statistics on Culture Development（2014）

指　标	Item	2014
电影放映场数（千场）	Number of Film Shows (1 000 shows)	487.1
电影观众人数（千人次）	Number of Spectators (1 000 person-times)	16620
电影票房收入（万元）	Box-office Receipts(10 000 yuan)	56599
艺术表演团体演出场次（场）	Number of Art Performance Troupes Performers (shows)	5451
#国内演出场次	Number of domestic Performance	5190
艺术表演观众人次（千人次）	Number of Spectators(1 000 person-times)	5978
图书馆总藏量（千册件）	Number of Collections in Libraries (1 000 volumes)	7585
#电子图书（千册）	E-books (1 000 volumes)	1300
书刊文献外借人次（千人次）	Books, Journals and Documents Borrowing (1 000 person-times)	1020
书刊文献外借册次（千册次）	Books, Journals and Documents Borrowing (1 000 Volume-time)	2617
县以上公共图书馆购书经费（万元）	Book-purchase Fund of Public Library above the County Level(1 000yuan）	1596

注：本表数据来源于市文广新局。

21-3 主要年份群众艺术馆、文化馆（站）活动情况

Basic Statistics on Activities of Mass Art Centers and Cultural Centers in Representative Years

指　标	Item	2009	2010	2011	2012	2013	2014
机构数（个）	Number of Insititutions (units)	197	197	196	197	198	199
举办展览个数（个）	Number of Exhibitions (units)	716	705	592	652	658	627
举办展览参观人次（千人次）	Number of Exhibition Visitors(1 000 person-times)			375	416	301	326
组织文艺活动次数 （次）	Art Performances and Story-telling Sessions (times)	3158	3729	4544	3273	4114	3617
组织文艺活动参加人次（千人次）	Number of Culture Activities attendees (1 000 person-times)			1778	1377	1633	1576
举办训练班班次（个）	Number of Training Courses (units)	1467	3018	2224	1798	1616	1872
举办训练班结业人次（千人次）	Number of Certificate Trained Persons (1 000 person-times)	96	133	115	143	155	156
组织各类理论研讨和讲座次数（次）	Number of Theoretical Discussion and Seminars(1 000 person-times)			106	78	122	254
组织各类理论研讨和讲座参加人次（千人次）	Number of Persons in Theoretical Discussion and Seminars(1 000 person-times)			15	14	19	28
本年收入（千元）	Income of this year (1 000 yuan)	40891	42937	55367	88475	101365	89520
本年支出（千元）	Expenditure of this year (1 000 yuan)	42826	45160	62368	84522	93485	84827

注：本表数据来源于市文广新局。

21-4　文物保护业基本情况（2014年）

Basic Statistics on Cultural Relics Protection（2014）

指　标	Item	机　构（个）Insititution (unit)	人　员（人）Personnel (person)	文物藏品实际数量（件）Factual Number of Collections (piece)	一级品 Grade One	举办陈列展览次数(次) Times of exhibition (times)	参观人员（千人次）Number of Visitors (1000 person-times)
总　计	**Total**	**156**	**4530**	**1181978**	**5499**	**332**	**23816**
文物行政管理机关	Protection and Management Agencies	16	257				
文物保护管理机构	Cultural Relics administrative Departments	29	541	37150	32	22	2557
其他文物机构	Other Agencies	8	185	40321			
博物馆	Museums	100	3308	1071400	5281	310	21259
#免费开放馆		76	1902	883077	3098	218	12649
文物商店	Cultural Relics Agencies						
文物科研机构	Scientific Research of Historical Relics Preservation	3	239	33107	186		

注：本表数据来源于市文物局。

2010年前为省市直属文物单位数据，2011年及以后为全口径数据(含民营、院校等)。

21-5　主要年份广播电台及节目制作情况

Basic Statistics of Broadcasting Stations and Program Production in Representative Years

指　标	Item	2009	2010	2011	2012	2013	2014
省、地广播电台（座）	Broadcasting Stations at the Province and District Level(set)	2	2	1	1		
省、地广播电视台（座）	Broadcasting Station at Province and District Level(set)			1	1	2	2
县级广播电视台（座）	Number of Wire Broadcasting Stations and TV Relaying Stations(set)	6	6	6	6	6	6
中短波、调频发射台及转播台（座）	Medium/Short Ware and FM Broadcast Transmission Stations and Relaying Stations(set)	51	55	54	59	57	57
节目套数（套）	Number of Programs(set)	18	18	19	20	20	20
全年播出时间(时：分)	Broadcasting Hours annually(hour)	123005	124100	121723	129856	138278	143873
广播节目综合人口覆盖率 (%)	Broadcasts comprehensive population coverage(%)	99.37	99.4	99.42	99.45	99.47	99.49
制作广播节目(时：分)	Productions of Broadcasting(hour)	110455	110639	83368	104300	106554	104459
#新闻资讯类	News Programs		13786	13821	14025	14355	13208
专题服务类	Special Subject Programs		24451	16318	21891	30181	26884
综艺类	Variety Programs		37720	28679	28096	24516	27148
广播剧类	Literature Programs		2406	2014	1720	3083	3712
广告类	Advertisements		28339	14202	19547	20552	18465
其他类	Service Programs		3937	8334	19021	13867	15042

注：本表数据来源于市文广新局。

2010年制作广播节目时间分类发生变化，故2009年及以前无数据。

21-6 主要年份电视台及节目制作情况

Basic Statistics of TV Stations and Production of TV Program in Representative Years

指　标	Item	2009	2010	2011	2012	2013	2014
电视台（座）	Number of Television Stations (set)	2	2	1	1		
发射台及转播台（座）	Number of Television Transmission Stations and Relaying Stations (set)	10	10	10	11	11	11
无线电视节目（套）	Program Productions of Non-cable television Stations (set)	7	6	6	6	6	6
有线电视节目（套）	Program Productions of cable television Stations (set)	15	16	16	16	16	16
全年播出时间（时：分）	Broadcasting Hours annually(hour)	138372	141856	147003	137936	140927	143000
电视节目综合人口覆盖率(%)	TV shows comprehensive population coverage (%)	98.41	98.57	98.60	98.83	98.84	98.96
制作电视节目（时：分）	Earth Stations of Satellite TV (set)	27131	29626	43925	30091	46614	35182
#新闻资讯类	News and Information Programs		8930	10656	11169	13360	11797
专题服务类	Special Subject Programs		7762	19191	7689	7751	8289
综艺类	Variety Programs		3942	5202	5458	6508	5014
广播剧类	Literature Programs		1729	3781	113	1820	110
广告类	Advertisement		3313	3200	3663	8066	3491
其他类	Service Programs		3950	1894	1997	9109	6479
有线电视用户（万户）	Users of Cable television Stations (10 000 households)	146.84	164.64	179.29	188.71	207.48	216.55
有线广播电视干线网总长度(公里)	The total length of cable broadcasting and television arteries of communication(km)			62494	62494	37126	37551
有线电视入户率(%)	The Rate of Cable Television(%)			79.08	80.53	86.62	88.20

注：本表数据来源于市文广新局。

2010年制作电视节目时间分类发生变化，故2009年及以前无数据。

21-7 体育事业基本情况(2014年)

The Basic Situations of Sport（2014）

单位：人、枚　　(person, unit)

指　标	Item	2014
一、体育部门职工人数	**Number of Staffs and Workers in Physical Education System**	**419**
#运动员	Athletes	28
教练员	Coaches	85
二、等级裁判员发展人数	**Number of the Development of Grade Referees**	**961**
三、等级运动员发展人数	**Number of the Development of Grade Athletes**	**157**
四、全年获得奖牌数	**Number of Full-year Medals**	**420**
#国家级金牌	National Gold	14
国家级银牌	National Silver	11
省级金牌	Provincial Gold	230.5
省级银牌	Provincial Silver	148

注：本表数据来源于市体育局。

体育部门职工人数仅包含市本级人数。

21-8 少年儿童分项业余体校情况（2014年）

Basic Statistics of Youth Part-time Physical Training School（2014）

单位：人　(person)

指标	Items	2014
一、在读学生数	**Total Enrollment**	**7790**
田径	Track and Field	2000
游泳	Swimming	1200
体操	Gymnastics	100
举重	Weightlifting	70
国际式摔跤	Wrestling	80
柔道	Judo	60
射击	Shooting	280
射箭	Archery	190
足球	Football	500
篮球	Basketball	1700
排球	Volleyball	200
乒乓球	Table Tennis	700
拳击	Boxing	30
武术	Wu Shu	400
跆拳道	Kickboxing	120
跳水	Diving	80
棒球	Baseball	80
二、职工数	**Number of Staff and Workers**	**1260**

注：本表数据来源于市体育局。

21-9 群众体育事业（2014年）

Mass Sports（2014）

指标	Items	2013	2014
社会体育指导员（人）	Social Sports Instructor(persons)	9689	16609
晨晚健身站点（个）	Morning and Evening Fitness sites(units)	1600	1600
社区建有体育组织比重(%)	The community has a sports organization proportion (%)	90	97.6
全国、全省体育先进社区（个）	National, provincial advanced sports community (units)	25	25
体育人口(万人)	Sports population(10 000 persons)	420	420

注：本表数据来源于市体育局。
体育人口及晨晚站点2013年数据以此表为准。

21-10 主要年份卫生机构、床位、人员情况

Number of Health Care Institutions, Beds and Employed Persons in Health Care Institutions in Representative Years

年份 Year	卫生机构数（个） Number of Health Care Institutions (unit)	医院数（个） Number of Health Care Hospital (unit)	卫生机构床位数（张） Number of Health Care Bed (unit)	医院床位数（张） Number of Hospital Bed (unit)	卫生技术人员数（人） Number of Medical Technical Personnel (person)
2008	2239	276	34618	30582	47433
2009	2162	261	36849	32371	51641
2010	2385	258	39407	34274	56579
2011	5554	268	41010	35976	61281
2012	5576	276	44239	39213	66899
2013	5503	281	47867	42753	71134
2014	5554	281	51065	45561	76005

注：本表数据来源于市卫生局。
2008年及以后为新的统计口径、分类。

21-11 卫生机构、床位及人员情况(2014年)

卫生机构	Health Care Institutions	机构数（个）Number of Institutions (unit)	床位数（张）Number of Beds (unit)
总计	**Total**	**5554**	**51065**
一、医院	**Hospitals**	**281**	**45561**
综合医院	General Hospitals	209	35059
中医医院	Hospitals Specialized in Traditional Chinese Medicine	35	4649
中西医结合医院	Hospitals Integrating Traditional Chinese Medicine with Western Therapeutics in Practice	3	480
民族医院	Nationalities Hospitals		
专科医院	Specialized Hospitals	34	5373
护理院	Nursing Centets		
二、基层医疗卫生机构	**Commuting health care service centre**	**5198**	**3367**
社区卫生服务中心(站)	Community Health Care Center(Station)	202	1798
社区卫生服务中心	Community Health Care Center	123	1792
社区卫生服务站	Community Health Care Station	79	6
卫生院	Health Center	100	1514
街道卫生院	Urban Health-center	5	53
乡镇卫生院	Rural Health-center	95	1461
村卫生室	Village clinics	2944	
门诊部	Outpatient department	195	55
诊所、卫生所、医务室	Clinic, health center, Infirmary	1757	
三、专科公共卫生机构	**College of public health institutions**	**51**	**2015**
疾病预防控制中心	Center for Disease Control and Prevention	16	
专科疾病防治院（所、站）	Specialized disease prevention and cure center (place, station)	1	800
健康教育所（站、中心）	Health Education Institute (station, center)	2	
妇幼保健院（所、站）	Maternal and Child Health Hospital (Station)	15	1215
急救中心（站）	Emergency Center (Station)	1	
采供血机构	Blood Collection Agencies	1	
卫生监督所（中心）	Health Supervision Agencies (Center)	15	
四、其他卫生机构	**Other Health Institution**	**24**	**122**
疗养院	Nursing Centres	1	122
卫生监督检验(监测、检测)所(站)	Health Supervision and inspection Agencies (Station)		
医学科学研究机构	Medical scientific research institutions	3	
医学在职培训机构	Medical training institutions	5	
临床检验中心（所、站）	Clinical testing center (place, station)		
统计信息中心	Statistical information center	1	
其他	other	14	

注：本表数据来源于市卫生局。

本表人员合计中包括乡村医生3327人和卫生员381人。

Number of Health Care Institutions, Beds and Employed Persons in Health Care Institutions（2014）

人员合计（人） Total Number of Employed Persons (person)	卫生技术人员 Medical Technical Personnel	卫生技术人员中执业(助理)医师数 Licensed (Assistant) Doctors	#执业医师 Chartered Doctors
95633	**76005**	**24820**	**22145**
67376	**54884**	**16267**	**15411**
53884	44338	13186	12549
6012	4893	1486	1358
222	196	65	57
7258	5457	1530	1447
22500	**16896**	**7468**	**5754**
5706	4689	1560	1174
5101	4163	1358	1003
605	526	202	171
2833	2353	592	374
104	91	20	14
2729	2262	572	360
4592	884	738	260
2833	2572	1160	997
6536	6398	3418	2949
5074	**3853**	**954**	**858**
1069	781	295	268
481	373	81	78
67	28	5	5
2634	2083	529	467
119	50	28	26
149	96	16	14
555	442		
683	**372**	**131**	**122**
77	42	14	14
150	85	48	47
192	75	7	7
6			
258	170	62	54

21-11 续表1

卫生机构	Health Care Institutions	人员合计（人）	
		卫生技术人员中	
		注册护士 Registered Nurses	药师（士） Junior Paramedics
总计	**Total**	**32136**	**3709**
一、医院	**Hospitals**	**25441**	**2609**
综合医院	General Hospitals	20469	1985
中医医院	Hospitals Specialized in Traditional Chinese Medicine	2046	374
中西医结合医院	Hospitals Integrating Traditional Chinese Medicine with Western Therapeutics in Practice	103	12
民族医院	Nationalities Hospitals		
专科医院	Specialized Hospitals	2823	238
护理院	Nursing Centets		
二、基层医疗卫生机构	**Commuting health care service centre**	**5431**	**985**
社区卫生服务中心(站)	Community Health Care Center(Station)	1523	345
社区卫生服务中心	Community Health Care Center	1296	310
社区卫生服务站	Community Health Care Station	227	35
卫生院	Health Center	554	155
街道卫生院	Urban Health-center	20	7
乡镇卫生院	Rural Health-center	534	148
村卫生室	Village clinics	146	
门诊部	Outpatient department	891	185
诊所、卫生所、医务室	Clinic, health center, Infirmary	2317	300
三、专科公共卫生机构	**College of public health institutions**	**1176**	**105**
疾病预防控制中心	Center for Disease Control and Prevention	57	10
专科疾病防治院（所、站）	Specialized disease prevention and cure center (place, station)	190	18
健康教育所（站、中心）	Health Education Institute (station, center)	1	
妇幼保健院（所、站）	Maternal and Child Health Hospital (Station)	890	69
急救中心（站）	Emergency Center (Station)	10	2
采供血机构	Blood Collection Agencies	28	6
卫生监督所（中心）	Health Supervision Agencies (Center)		
四、其他卫生机构	**Other Health Institution**	**88**	**10**
疗养院	Nursing Centres	19	3
卫生监督检验(监测、检测)所(站)	Health Supervision and inspection Agencies (Station)		
医学科学研究机构	Medical scientific research institutions	13	4
医学在职培训机构	Medical training institutions		
临床检验中心（所、站）	Clinical testing center (place, station)		
统计信息中心	Statistical information center		
其他	other	56	3

continued 1

Total Number of Employed Persons (person)					
Among:Medical Technical Personnel			其他技术人员	管理人员	工勤技能人员
技师（士） Technicians	#检验师 Laboratory Technicians	其他 Other	Other Technical Personnel	Administrative Personnel	Logistics Technical Workers
4276	**3108**	**11064**	**621**	**7355**	**7944**
3066	**2180**	**7501**	**448**	**5856**	**6188**
2434	1775	6264	355	4461	4730
306	178	681	69	514	536
14	11	2		16	10
312	216	554	24	865	912
740	**502**	**2272**	**22**	**707**	**1167**
320	221	941	16	461	540
292	197	907	16	411	511
28	24	34		50	29
194	117	858	6	246	228
10	5	34		6	7
184	112	824	6	240	221
173	123	163			261
53	41	310			138
426	**390**	**1192**	**83**	**625**	**513**
222	214	197	18	142	128
30	22	54		59	49
		22	22	16	1
141	121	454	37	270	244
		10		39	30
33	33	13	4	40	9
		442	2	59	52
44	**36**	**99**	**68**	**167**	**76**
2	2	4		16	19
18	14	2	13	33	19
2	2	66	45	51	21
				6	
22	18	27	10	61	17

21-12 各区县卫生机构、床位及人员情况（2014年）

Number of Health Care Institutions, Beds and Employed Persons in Health Care Institutions By Region（2014）

区 县	Region	机构（个）Number of Health Care Institutions (unit)	床位（张）Number of Beds (unit)	人员合计（人）Total Number of Employed Persons (person)	#卫生技术人员 Total Number of Medical Technical Personnel
合 计	**Total**	**5554**	**51065**	**95633**	**76005**
新城区	Xincheng	281	7424	14772	11774
碑林区	Beilin	371	7495	14480	12011
莲湖区	Lianhu	339	6326	11916	9810
灞桥区	Baqiao	478	2944	5039	4130
未央区	Weiyang	310	3573	6873	5701
雁塔区	Yanta	508	9245	16615	13560
阎良区	Yanliang	159	1418	2500	1931
临潼区	Lintong	488	2309	3709	2578
长安区	Chang'an	770	3575	6384	4775
蓝田县	Lantian	594	1142	2275	1550
周至县	Zhouzhi	451	1398	3759	2617
户 县	Huxian	592	2780	4619	3454
高陵县	Gaoling	213	1436	2692	2114

注：本表数据来源于市卫生局。

21-13 主要年份卫生机构各类人员情况

Number of Employed Persons in Health Care Institutions in Representative Years

单位：人 (person)

指 标	Item	2009	2010	2011	2012	2013	2014
人员合计	**Total**	**65003**	**71230**	**79999**	**86096**	**90129**	**95633**
卫生技术人员	Medical Technical Personnel	51641	56579	61281	66899	71134	76005
执业（助理）医师	Licensed (Assistant) Doctors	19284	18763	21551	23051	23885	24820
#执业医师	Chartered Doctors	17286	16613	18904	20414	21205	22145
注册护士	Registered Nurses	20167	22640	25043	27837	29967	32136
药师(士)	Junior Paramedics	2814	3030	3127	3380	3551	3709
技师（士）	Technicians	3350	4589	3622	3953	4089	4276
#检验师	Laboratory Technicians	2290	2439	2622	2830	2974	3108
其他	Other	6026	7557	7938	8678	9642	11064
其他技术人员	Other Technical Personnel	1325	1156	895	633	590	621
管理人员	Administrative Personnel	6067	6416	6769	6939	7160	7355
工勤技能人员	Logistics Technical Workers	5970	7079	6789	7555	7437	7944

注：本表数据来源于市卫生局。
本表2011年人员合计中包括乡村医生3856人和卫生员409人；2012年人员合计中包括乡村医生3611人和卫生员459人。
2013年人员合计中包括乡村医生3477人和卫生员331人；2014年人员合计中包括乡村医生3327人和卫生员381人。

21-14　医疗卫生机构门诊、住院及病床使用情况（2014年）

指　标	Item	总诊疗人次数 总计 Total
总计	**Total**	**53281849**
一、医院	**Hospitals**	**27774500**
综合医院	General Hospitals	22459193
中医医院	Hospitals Specialized in Traditional Chinese Medicine	2242474
中西医结合医院	Hospitals Integrating Traditional Chinese Medicine with Western Therapeutics in Practice	86373
民族医院	Nationalities Hospitals	
专科医院	Specialized Hospitals	2986460
护理院	Nursing Centets	
二、基层医疗卫生机构	**Commuting health care service centre**	**23766432**
社区卫生服务中心（站）	Community Health Care Center(Station)	4231242
社区卫生服务中心	Community Health Care Center	3455775
社区卫生服务站	Community Health Care Station	775467
卫生院	Health Center	1279531
街道卫生院	Urban Health-center	40960
乡镇卫生院	Rural Health-center	1238571
村卫生室	Village clinics	10904869
门诊部	Outpatient department	1779092
诊所、卫生所、医务室	Clinic, health center, Infirmary	5571698
三、专业公共卫生机构	**College of public health institutions**	**1740613**
专科疾病防治院（所、站）	Specialized disease prevention and cure center (place, station)	31317
妇幼保健院（所、站）	Maternal and Child Health Hospital (Station)	1578964
急救中心（站）	Emergency Center	130332
四、其他卫生机构	**Other Health Institution**	**304**
疗养院	Sanatorium	304

注：本表数据来源于市卫生局。

Medical and Health Institutions Outpatient, Inpatient and Utilization of Beds(2014)

Total Number of Clinics (person time)				观察室 Observation Room	
门.急诊人次数 Number of Outpatient and Emergency	门诊人次数 Number of Outpatients	急诊人次数 Number of Emergency	死亡人数（人） Number of Deaths	留观病例数（人次） Number of Patients Receiving (person time)	死亡人数（人） Number of Deaths (persons)
52172883	**49341447**	**2831436**	**2811**	**26313**	**71**
27610105	**25117422**	**2492683**	**2806**	**26248**	**71**
22317932	20242428	2075504	2742	25932	69
2228543	2156689	71854	23	18	
85881	85083	798			
2977749	2633222	344527	41	298	2
22821861	**22691625**	**130236**	**5**		
4079767	3980181	99586	3		
3324770	3242167	82603	2		
754997	738014	16983	1		
1278542	1247892	30650	2		
40341	39783	558			
1238201	1208109	30092	2		
10226975	10226975				
1733582	1733582				
5502995	5502995				
1740613	**1532096**	**208517**		**65**	
31317	31306	11			
1578964	1500790	78174		65	
130332		130332			
304	**304**				
304	304				

21-14 续表1

指 标	Item	急诊死亡率（%） Emergency Mortality (%)	入院人数合计（人） Total Number of Admission Patients (person)
总计	**Total**	**0.10**	**1596884**
一、医院	**Hospitals**	**0.11**	**1480831**
综合医院	General Hospitals	0.13	1221876
中医医院	Hospitals Specialized in Traditional Chinese Medicine	0.03	113429
中西医结合医院	Hospitals Integrating Traditional Chinese Medicine with Western Therapeutics in Practice		6178
民族医院	Nationalities Hospitals		
专科医院	Specialized Hospitals	0.01	139348
护理院	Nursing Centets		
二、基层医疗卫生机构	**Commuting health care service centre**		**57064**
社区卫生服务中心（站）	Community Health Care Center(Station)		31372
社区卫生服务中心	Community Health Care Center		31372
社区卫生服务站	Community Health Care Station	0.01	
卫生院	Health Center	0.01	24795
街道卫生院	Urban Health-center		202
乡镇卫生院	Rural Health-center	0.01	24593
村卫生室	Village clinics		
门诊部	Outpatient department		897
诊所、卫生所、医务室	Clinic, health center, Infirmary		
三、专业公共卫生机构	**College of public health institutions**		**58755**
专科疾病防治院（所、站）	Specialized disease prevention and cure center (place, station)		5446
妇幼保健院（所、站）	Maternal and Child Health Hospital (Station)		53309
急救中心（站）	Emergency Center		
四、其他卫生机构	**Other Health Institution**		**234**
疗养院	Sanatorium		234

continued 1

出院人数合计 （人） Total Number of Discharge Patients (person)	死亡人数 （人） Number of Hospital Csualty (person)	病床周转次数 （次） Nnumber of Bed Rumover (time)	病床使用率 （%） Bed occupancy rate (%)	出院者平均住院日 （天） Average Stay Days in Hospital (day)
1594422	**8714**	**32.4**	**85.16**	**9.5**
1479408	**8663**	**33.6**	**88.67**	**9.5**
1222370	8000	35.9	89.12	9.0
112538	261	24.8	84.21	12.2
6245		25.2	66.94	9.2
138255	402	26.3	90.61	12.3
56513	**24**	**17.6**	**40.68**	**8.9**
31274	24	18.1	40.32	9.1
31274	24	18.2	40.46	9.1
24342		16.3	41.10	9.0
200		3.8	9.23	8.9
24142		16.8	42.28	9.0
897				
58277	**27**	**31.7**	**83.77**	**9.6**
5320	18	6.7	83.93	46.8
52957	9	50.9	83.65	5.9
224		**1.8**	**10.06**	**17.7**
224		1.8	10.06	17.7

21-15 社会福利事业单位基本情况（2014年）

Basic Statistics on Social Welfare Insititutions (2014)

指 标	Item	机构数（个）Number of Institutions	年末职工人数（人）Number of Staff at the Year End	床位数（张）Number of Beds	年末在院人数（人）Number of Persons Housed at the Year-end
社会福利院	Social Welfare Homes	3	71	1215	803
儿童福利院	Baby Welfare Homes	1	73	900	739
社会福利医院	Social Welfare Hospitals	1	138	500	448
收养性老年福利机构	Welfare units of adopting the elder	99	2103	16104	9372
城镇	Urban	70	1712	12666	7818
农村	Rural	29	391	3438	1554

注：本表数据来源于市民政局。

21-16 主要年份社会福利事业单位机构及人员情况

Number of Social Welfare Institutions and Employed Persons

单位：个、人 (unit, person)

指 标	Item	2009	2010	2011	2012	2013	2014
一、机构	**Insititutions**						
烈士纪念建筑物管理单位	Institutions Managing Memorial Buildings of Martyrs	2	2	2	2	2	2
救助类单位	Units Providing Assistance	8	8	8	8	8	9
殡仪服务单位	Funeral Service Units	20	22	21	22	25	26
殡仪馆	Funeral Homes	4	4	5	4	4	3
公墓	Cemeteries	12	14	12	12	15	16
殡葬管理单位	Funeral Management Units	4	4	4	6	6	7
二、人员	**Staff**						
烈士纪念建筑物管理单位	Institutions Managing Memorial Buildings of Martyrs	39	37	38	40	42	44
救助类单位	Units Providing Assistance	118	116	119	130	137	139
殡仪服务单位	Funeral Service Units	1046	1371	1313	1400	1430	1392
殡仪馆	Funeral Homes	218	375	408	442	491	470
公墓	Cemeteries	776	939	838	869	855	838
殡葬管理单位	Funeral Management Units	52	57	67	89	84	84

注：本表数据来源于市民政局。

21-17 全市及各区县福利企业单位基本情况（2014年）

Basic Statistics on Social Welfare Insititutions (2014)

单位：个、人 (unit, person)

区 县	Region	单位数 Number of Enterprise	年末职工人数 Number of Staff and Workers at the end of year	年末残疾职工人数 Number of Disabled Staff and Workers at the end of year	年末职工人数中女性 The number of female workers At the end of year
合 计	**Total**	**74**	**4334**	**1716**	**1555**
市本级	City Level	13	833	351	327
新城区	Xincheng	7	314	166	112
碑林区	Beilin				
莲湖区	Lianhu	13	968	405	418
灞桥区	Baqiao	3	101	37	38
未央区	Weiyang	7	348	128	66
雁塔区	Yanta	2	114	11	76
阎良区	Yanliang	3	141	68	37
临潼区	Lintong	1	90	23	32
长安区	Chang'an	10	551	219	171
蓝田县	Lantian	2	159	64	34
周至县	Zhouzhi	2	108	38	42
户 县	Huxian	11	607	206	202
高陵县	Gaoling				
沣东新城	Fengdongxincheng				

注：本表数据来源于市民政局。

21-18 社会保险基本情况

Basic Sitiation of Social Insurance

单位：万人 (10 000 persons)

指 标	Item	2014
基本养老保险参保人数	Number of Basic Old-age Insurance	563.88
1. 城镇企业职工养老保险参保人数	Number of Town Enterprise Worker Old-age Insurance	284.58
2. 机关事业单位养老保险参保人数	Number of Institution Old-age Insurance	28.33
3. 城乡居民养老保险参保人数	Number of Rural Residents Old-age Insurance	250.97
城镇基本医疗保险参保人数	Number of urban basic medical insurance	417.7
失业保险参保人数	Number of unemployed insurance	149.41
生育保险参保人数	Number of Maternity insurance	98.72
工伤保险参保人数	Number of industrial injury insurance	142.86

注：本表数据来源于市人社局。

21-19 全市及各区县新型农村合作医疗情况（2014年）

Situation of the New Rural Cooperative Medical Care of the Whole City and Area County（2014）

区 县	Region	参加新型农村合作医疗人数（万人）Participate in the new rural cooperative medical Population (10 000 persons)	新型农村合作医疗参合率(%) Participate in the new rural cooperative medical care ration (%)
合 计	**Total**	**407.18**	**99.21**
新城区	Xincheng		
碑林区	Beilin		
莲湖区	Lianhu		
灞桥区	Baqiao	29.65	100
未央区	Weiyang	12.81	100
雁塔区	Yanta	15.94	100
阎良区	Yanliang	16.81	99. 90
临潼区	Lintong	56.47	99.99
长安区	Chang'an	72.59	96.98
蓝田县	Lantian	56.53	99.35
周至县	Zhouzhi	57.92	99.44
户 县	Huxian	47.27	99.45
高陵县	Gaoling	23.06	100
沣东新城	Fengdongxincheng	18.13	100

注：本表数据来源于市卫生局。

21-20 全市及各区县优抚对象人员情况（2014年）

Statistics on Persons Enjoying Favoured Treatment by Region (2014)

单位：人 (person)

区 县	Region	革命伤残人员 Number of Disabled Veterans	烈军属人员 Number of Family Members of Martyrs and Soldiers	在乡复员军人 Demobilized Soldiers in Hometown	在乡退伍军人 Veterans in Hometown
全 市	**Total**	**4960**	**1015**	**4097**	**2064**
市本级	City Level	51			
新城区	Xincheng	633	32	9	
碑林区	Beilin	612	53	12	7
莲湖区	Lianhu	737	53	33	10
灞桥区	Baqiao	260	52	235	214
未央区	Weiyang	195	53	117	13
雁塔区	Yanta	699	64	82	225
阎良区	Yanliang	103	46	280	66
临潼区	Lintong	271	93	587	261
长安区	Chang'an	356	96	448	123
蓝田县	Lantian	212	79	404	184
周至县	Zhouzhi	337	241	901	212
户 县	Huxian	288	56	466	127
高陵县	Gaoling	137	64	319	172
沣东新城	Fengdongxincheng	69	33	204	450

注：本表数据来源于市民政局。

21-21 全市及各区县计划生育和婚姻登记情况（2014年）

Conditions of Birth Control and Marriage Registration by Region (2014)

区 县	Region	计划生育率（%）Family Planning Rate(%)	节育率（%）Birth control Rate(%)	独生子女领证率（%）Only-child Certificate Rate
合 计	**Total**	**94.2**	**90.7**	**46.2**
新城区	Xincheng	97.9	87.8	49.1
碑林区	Beilin	97.9	88.8	56.4
莲湖区	Lianhu	97.6	87	60.4
灞桥区	Baqiao	94.5	90.5	51.3
未央区	Weiyang	94.7	91.3	63.5
雁塔区	Yanta	94.7	89.9	61.9
阎良区	Yanliang	94.9	92.3	70.8
临潼区	Lintong	92.7	92.9	29.6
长安区	Chang'an	92.7	92.8	35.1
蓝田县	Lantian	92.6	91.1	23.9
周至县	Zhouzhi	92.4	92.6	13.5
户 县	Huxian	91.3	93.3	28.7
高陵县	Gaoling	94.4	90.7	38
沣东新城	Fengdongxincheng	93.7	93.4	52.6
高新区	GaoXin	97.9	75.4	54.5

注：本表数据来源于市计生委、市民政局、市法院。

21-21 续表1 continued 1

区 县	Region	结婚对数（对）Marriages (couple)	再婚人数（人）Remarriages (person)	离婚对数（对）Divorced Couple (couple)
合 计	**Total**	**91123**	**25775**	**21887**
新城区	Xincheng	5449	1948	1697
碑林区	Beilin	11063	2600	2245
莲湖区	Lianhu	7242	2827	2419
灞桥区	Baqiao	5502	1433	1409
未央区	Weiyang	5024	1658	1535
雁塔区	Yanta	9336	3009	2613
阎良区	Yanliang	3082	1248	970
临潼区	Lintong	7200	1928	1627
长安区	Chang'an	10993	3211	2504
蓝田县	Lantian	5847	1345	1108
周至县	Zhouzhi	7144	1393	946
户 县	Huxian	6537	1487	1132
高陵县	Gaoling	3557	1688	1011
沣东新城	Fengdongxincheng	3147		671
高新区	GaoXin			

21–22 全市及各区县妇幼卫生保健情况（2014年）

Care Health Conditions of Women and Child by Region(2014)

区 县	Region	5岁以下儿童死亡率（‰）Mortality rate of Children under 5-year-old（‰）	新生儿死亡率（‰）Infant Mortality Ratio in 2012（‰）	婴儿死亡率（‰）Neonatal Mortality Ratio（‰）
合　计	**Total**	**3.60**	**1.97**	**2.87**
新城区	Xincheng	0.44	0.44	0.44
碑林区	Beilin	3.02	1.13	3.02
莲湖区	Lianhu	3.13	1.74	2.43
灞桥区	Baqiao	2.57	1.28	1.80
未央区	Weiyang	2.00	1.43	2.00
雁塔区	Yanta	4.59	3.06	3.50
阎良区	Yanliang	7.31	5.00	6.54
临潼区	Lintong	1.33	0.83	1.00
长安区	Chang'an	5.42	2.62	4.30
蓝田县	Lantian	5.07	3.12	4.87
周至县	Zhouzhi	3.67	1.55	2.40
户　县	Huxian	2.60	1.67	2.04
高陵县	Gaoling	3.45	1.73	2.88

注：本表数据来源于市卫生局。

21–22 续表1 continued 1

区 县	Region	孕产妇死亡率（1/10万）Maternal Mortality Ratio (one in hundred thousandth)	产妇住院分娩比例（%）Proportion of maternal Hospital Births (%)
合　计	**Total**	**7.89**	**99.99**
新城区	Xincheng	87.76	100
碑林区	Beilin		100
莲湖区	Lianhu	34.78	100
灞桥区	Baqiao		100
未央区	Weiyang		100
雁塔区	Yanta		100
阎良区	Yanliang		100
临潼区	Lintong		100
长安区	Chang'an		100
蓝田县	Lantian		99.88
周至县	Zhouzhi	14.12	100
户　县	Huxian	18.58	100
高陵县	Gaoling		100

21–23 主要年份律师、公证及调解情况

Basic Statistics on Lawyer, Notaries and Mediation in Representative Years

指 标	Item	2009	2010	2011	2012	2013	2014
一、律师工作	**Lawyers**						
律师事务所（个）	Number of Law Offices (unit)	79	95	97	105	116	122
律师（人）	Lawyers(person)	1058	1202	1347	1522	1639	1846
专职	Full-time	1001	1139	1275	1439	1560	1738
兼职	Part-time	55	63	68	73	77	88
刑事诉讼辩护及代理（件）	The Criminal suit Defence andagents(suit)					3267	3118
民事诉讼代理（件）	Civil Litigation Agent(suit)					10754	9985
行政诉讼代理（件）	Administrative litigation(suit)					319	374
非诉讼法律事务（件）	Non-litigation legal affairs(suit)					2265	2352
二、公证工作	**Notarization**						
公证处（个）	Number of Notary Offices (unit)	14	14	14	14	14	14
公证人员（人）	Notarial Personnel (person)	194	202	233	235	222	298
#公证员	Notaries	102	112	118	116	115	118
办理公证件数（件）	Number of Notarized Documents Issued (case)	88637	106491	108120	119605	136471	135413
国内	Domestic	57190	72670	68239	79167	98572	90171
民事	Civil	22337	24813	24356	32442	32516	30121
经济	Economics	34853	47857	43883	46725	66056	60050
涉外	Foreign-related	31082	33410	39545	39888	37444	44773
港澳台	Hong Kong. Macao and Taiwan related	365	411	336	550	455	469
三、人民调解工作	**Number of People Mediations**						
已建调委会数（个）	Number of Mediation Committees (unit)	3961	3911	4031	4053	4040	4059
调解人员数（人）	Number of Mediators (person)	17198	15717	12848	15080	15240	15793
调解纠纷数（件）	Number of Civil Disputes Mediated (case)	23185	22247	33851	39230	33651	33641
#调解成功数	Number of Cases Successfully Mediated	21373	22164	32109	37510	32368	32537

注：本表数据来源于市司法局。

21-24 主要年份共青团组织情况

Basic Facts on Communist Youth League in Representative Years

单位：个、人 (unit,person)

指　标	Item	2008	2009	2010	2011	2012	2013	2014
一、基层团组织	**Grass-root Youth League Organisations**	**10985**	**9054**	**7006**	**11248**	**9097**	**10770**	**10152**
二、共青团员	**Youth League Members**	**348141**	**324785**	**308141**	**345682**	**336156**	**344096**	**343121**
#女团员	Female Youth League Members	145777	144027	142379	159725	157924	158287	153212
三、专职团干部	**Full-time Youth League Cadre**	**601**	**387**	**311**	**270**	**680**	**737**	**659**

注：本表数据来源于共青团西安市委员会。

21-25 妇联组织情况（2014年）

Women's Organizations Status (2014)

单位：个 (unit)

指　标	Item	2014
一、妇联组织	**Women's Organizations**	
市级妇联	Municipal Women's Federation	1
街道妇联	Street Women's Federation	123
社区妇联	Community Women's Federation	759
县（区）妇联	County (district) Women's Federation	13
乡（镇）妇联	Township (town) Women's Federation	92
村妇代会	Village Women's Representative Conference	2797
二、非公有制经济组织中妇女组织	**Women's Organizations in Non-public Economic Organizations**	
个体劳动者协会中的妇女组织	Women's Organizations in Association of Individual Workers	3
专业市场中的妇女组织	Women's Organizations in the Professional Market	5
私营企业中的妇女组织	Women's Organizations in the Private Sector	38
三资企业中的妇女组织	Foreign-funded Enterprises in the Women's Organizations	27
三、机关事业单位妇女组织	**Women's Organizations in Government Departments and Institutions**	
直属机关妇委会（妇工委）	Women's Committee of Direct-affiliated Departments	60
部门机关妇委会（妇工委）	Women's Committee of Affiliated Departments	279
事业单位妇委会（妇工委）	Women's Committee of Government Institutions	54
四、民主党派妇女组织	**Women's Organizations of Democratic Parties**	
民主党派妇委会	Women's Committee of Democratic Parties	7
五、团体会员	**Members of Organisation**	
工会女职工委员会	Women Staff Committee of Labor Unions	2970
民政部门登记注册的妇女社团	Women's Communities Registered at Civil Administration Departments	5

注：本表数据来源于市妇联。

21-26 妇联工作情况（2014年）

Basic Facts on Women's Federation (2014)

单位：个、人 (unit, person)

指　标	Item	2014
一、双学双比活动	**Double Learning and Double Competition Activities**	
（一）科技培训	Scientific and Technical Training	
接受技术培训人数	Number of People Receiving Technical Training	12365
获得绿色证书人数	Number of People Gaining Green Certificates	260
女农民技术员人数	The number of female farmer technician	165
妇代会主任中农民技术员数	Number of Farmer in Women's Head Technicians	134
（二）巾帼扶贫	Women Aid-the-poor Project	
脱贫户数	Households out of Poverty	375
扶贫项目数	Number of Poverty Alleviation Projects	7
二、巾帼建功活动	**Women Make Achievements**	
（一）巾帼建功	Women Make Achievements	
评选巾帼建功标兵数	Number of Pacemakes	205
巾帼建功先进工作者数	Number of Advanced Workers	51
巾帼建功先进协调单位数	Number of Advanced Supporting Units	56
巾帼文明示范岗数	Number of Model Workers	141
（二）下岗失业妇女再就业	Re-employment of Laid-off and Unemployed Women	
妇女就业服务机构数	Number of Institutions for Women's Employment Services	
妇联主办的劳务市场	Labor Markets Sponsored by Women's Federation	6
三、三八红旗手	**Models of Women**	**52**
四、三八红旗集体	**Models of Women Group**	**26**
五、实施春雷计划	**Carrying out of CHUNLEI Project**	
资助女童入学或返校数	Helping Women Children Enter School or Back School	67
社会捐资总额（万元）	Amount of Money That Social Attributes (10 000yuan)	24
六、来信来访情况	**Conditions of Letters and Visits(case)**	
女职工劳动保护信访案件(件)	Cases about Labor Protection of Employed Women through Letters and Visits	10
侵犯妇女财产权利信访案件(件)	Cases about Encroachment of Women's Property through Letters and Visits	146

注：本表数据来源于市妇联。

21-27 主要年份交通、火灾及安全生产情况

Transportation, Fire and Safety Production in Representative Years

指 标	Item	2008	2009	2010	2011	2012	2013	2014
全市合计	**Sum of Entire City**							
事故数(起)	Number of Cases (case)	4138	4225	4173	4199	5029	6329	5203
死亡人数（人）	Number of Deaths (person)	591	586	568	566	553	505	516
受伤人数（人）	Number of Injuries (person)	2472	2264	2529	2271	2492	2223	1840
损失（万元）	Economic Loss (10 000 yuan)	2802	3128.9	3666.8	2780.5	4524.8	4432.8	6122.6
道路交通事故	**Road Accidents**							
事故数(起)	Number of Traffic Accident (case)	2576	2702	2323	2264	2446	2252	1970
死亡人数（人）	Number of Deaths (person)	551	531	531	531	516	460	483
受伤人数（人）	Number of Injuries (person)	2464	2247	2520	2260	2486	2217	1832
损失（万元）	Economic Loss (10 000 yuan)	522.8	851.7	736.6	611.9	1011.1	1143.9	1264.0
火灾事故	**Fire Accidents**							
事故数(起)	Number of Cases (case)	1537	1485	1825	1920	2568	4062	3199
死亡人数（人）	Number of Deaths (person)	11	17	13	8	16	26	17
受伤人数（人）	Number of Injuries (person)	4	3	7	3	4	6	5
损失（万元）	Economic Loss (10 000 yuan)	1907.7	1850.6	2224.2	1587.2	2793.7	3011.9	4381.1
农机事故	**Farm Machinery Accidents**							
事故数(起)	Number of Cases (case)	2	11	5		2	1	24
死亡人数（人）	Number of Deaths (person)	1				2	1	1
受伤人数（人）	Number of Injuries (person)	1	2	2				3
损失（万元）	Economic Loss (10 000 yuan)		1.1	3.1		12.4	7.0	7.3
工矿商贸事故	**Accidents in Industry,Mine,Business and Trade**							
事故数(起)	Number of Cases (case)	22	27	20	15	13	14	10
死亡人数（人）	Number of Deaths (person)	27	38	24	27	19	18	15
受伤人数（人）	Number of Injuries (person)	3	12		8	2		
损失（万元）	Economic Loss (10 000 yuan)	366.5	425.5	703.0	581.5	707.7	270.0	470.2
特种设备	**Special Accidents**							
事故数(起)	Number of Cases (case)	1						
死亡人数	Number of Deaths (person)	1						
受伤人数	Number of Injuries (person)							
损失（万元）	Economic Loss (10 000 yuan)	5						

注：本表数据来源于市公安局及安监局。其中交通、火灾数据2011年及以前年份来自于市安监局，2012—2014年数据来自于市公安局。
2006年及以前道路交通数据不含高速公路数据。
2009年及以后工矿商贸事故数据含特种设备数据。
2014年农机及工矿商贸事故发生起数统计口径变化，数据与以前年份不可比。

21-28 主要年份刑事案件情况

Data on Criminal Cases in Representative Years

指 标	Item	2008	2009	2010	2011	2012	2013	2014
一、案件数情况	**Data on Number of Cases**							
立案数（起）	Number of Registered Cases(case)	41811	42321	48566	71499	61071	72611	77051
破案数（起）	Number of Cleared up Cases(case)	19284	21921	18906	17585	20788	26587	25830
破案率（%）	Percent of Cleared up Cases(%)	46.1	51.8	38.9	24.6	34.0	36.6	33.5
抓获作案成员(人)	Number of Criminals Caught(person)	12364	11870	13104	14672	16980	14255	14184
二、查获犯罪集团情况	**Data on Hunted down and Seized Criminal Gangs**							
查获犯罪集团个数（个）	Number of Hunted down and Seized Criminal Gangs (person)	211	154	186	209	853	695	359
查获犯罪集团人数（人）	Number of Members of Hunted down and Seized Criminal Gangs (person)	916	663	939	970	3332	2632	1508
涉及案件（起）	Number of Cases Involved(case)	1328	622	1172	485	2039	2439	1111
三、涉枪案件情况	**Data on Cases with Guns Involved**							
立案数（起）	Number of Registered Cases(case)	11	25	16	13	30	17	13
破案数（起）	Number of Cleared up Cases(case)	9	24	11	10	25	16	8
破案率（%）	Percent of Cleared up Cases(%)	81.8	96.0	68.8	76.9	83.3	94.1	61.5

注：本表数据来源于市公安局。

21-29 主要年份治安案件情况

Data on Public Order Cases in Representative Years

指 标	Item	2008	2009	2010	2011	2012	2013	2014
受理数（起）	Number of Accepted Cases(case)	45226	45925	58968	63289	60747	94853	108780
查处数（起）	Number of Investigated and Prosecuted Cases(case)	44202	45871	57151	62647	59949	93546	106811
查处率（%）	Percent of Investigated and Prosecuted Cases(%)	97.7	99.9	96.9	99.0	98.7	98.6	98.2
查处违法人数（人）	Number of Investigated and Prosecuted Law-breakers and Crime Committer(person)	38606	39214	45856	44199	34346	46253	52922

注：本表数据来源于市公安局。

21-30 各区县刑事、治安案件情况（2014年）

Data on Criminal Cases and Public Order Cases Grouped by Region (2014)

单位：起 (case)

区　县 Region	刑事案件 Criminal cases			治安案件 Public order cases		
	立案数 Number of Registered Cases	破案数 Number of Cleared up Cases	破案率（%） Percent of Ceared up Cases (%)	受理数 Number of Accepted Cases	查处数 Number of Investigated and Prosecuted Cases	查处率（%） Percent of Investigated and Prosecuted Cases(%)
新城区 Xincheng	7786	2273	29.2	8754	8754	100
碑林区 Beilin	7610	3558	46.8	11659	11659	100
莲湖区 Lianhu	9368	4631	49.4	10866	10079	92.8
灞桥区 Baqiao	4007	1406	35.1	5896	5888	99.9
未央区 Weiyang	6456	2259	35.0	11469	11208	97.7
雁塔区 Yanta	13447	2978	22.1	13167	13016	98.9
阎良区 Yanliang	1034	647	62.6	4038	3895	96.5
临潼区 Lintong	2148	1073	50.0	6912	6576	95.1
长安区 Chang'an	4400	903	20.5	12630	12630	100
蓝田县 Lantian	1148	428	37.3	1447	1395	96.4
周至县 Zhouzhi	1442	417	28.9	1992	1992	100
户　县 Huxian	1488	787	52.9	3740	3676	98.3
高陵县 Gaoling	1012	409	40.4	1384	1384	100

注：本表数据来源于市公安局。

21-31 主要年份西安市人民检察院案件办理情况

Data on Acceptance of Cases of Xi'an People's Procuratorate

指 标	Item	2008	2009	2010	2011	2012	2013	2014
一、贪污贿赂案件立案人数（人）	**Number of Persons Invovled in Case about Corporation and Bribery(person)**	**177**	**176**	**184**	**166**	**175**	**172**	**207**
二、渎职侵权案件立案人数（人）	**Number of Persons Invovled in Case about Misprison and Toetious(person)**	**40**	**32**	**40**	**33**	**38**	**42**	**56**
三、审查逮捕案件受理件数（件）	**Examination and Arresting(case)**	**3835**	**3656**	**4229**	**5741**	**5024**	**5748**	**6443**
四、逮捕各类案件人数（人）	**Arresting of Criminals of each kind(person)**	**5817**	**5429**	**6183**	**8787**	**7168**	**7177**	**7534**
决定逮捕贪污贿赂犯罪嫌疑人（人）	Suspects of Corporation and Bribery to be Arrested (person)	104	97	51	34	43	49	64
决定逮捕渎职、侵权犯罪嫌疑人（人）	Suspects of Misprision and Tortious to be Arrested (person)	11	11	2		6		18
批准逮捕刑事犯罪嫌疑人（人）	Suspects of Criminal to be Arrested (person)	5702	5321	6130	8753	7119	7128	7452
五、刑事立案监督、侦察活动监督（件）	**Supervision of Acceptance of Criminal Cases and Investigation (case)**	**222**	**173**	**623**	**89**	**263**	**368**	**284**
六、审查起诉案件受理件数（件）	**Examination and Prosecution (case)**	**4325**	**4242**	**4662**	**6298**	**6747**	**6371**	**7278**
七、起诉各类案件人数（人）	**Prosecution of Criminals of each kind(person)**	**5608**	**5614**	**5946**	**8276**	**7307**	**7615**	**8399**
起诉贪污贿赂犯罪被告人（人）	Prosecution of Criminals of Corruption and Bribery to be Defendants(person)	158	159	163	129	157	151	123
起诉渎职、侵权犯罪被告人（人）	Prosecution of Misprision and Tortious to be Defendants (person)	15	11	22	13	29	24	44
起诉刑事犯罪被告人（人）	Prosecution of Criminal to be Defendants (person)	5435	5444	5761	8134	7121	7440	8232

注：本表数据来源于市检察院。

21-32 西安市中级人民法院案件基本情况（2014年）

Xi'an Intermediate People's Court Basic Data of the Law Cases (2014)

单位：件、万元 (case,10 000 yuan)

指 标	Item	合 计 Total		中级人民法院theIntermediate People's Court	
		结案 Number of Case	诉讼标的总金额 Subject Matter of Litigation the Total Amount	结案 Number of Case	诉讼标的总金额 The Intermediate People's Court Litigation Total Amount
合 计	**Total**	**71715**	**1346418.75**	**8447**	**748859.4**
一、刑事	**Criminal**	**6414**	**9063.94**	**787**	**674.15**
二、民商事	**Civil and Commercial Matters**	**46684**	**701871.23**	**6099**	**367615.32**
三、行政	**Administration**	**1143**		**288**	
四、申诉、申请再审	**Appeals, Apply for Retrial**	**2041**		**388**	
五、司法赔偿	**Judicial Indemnification**	**4**	**666.26**	**4**	**666.26**
六、执行	**Execution**	**15429**	**634817.32**	**881**	**379903.67**

21-32 续表 continued

单位：件、万元 (case,10 000 yuan)

指 标	Item	基层人民法院 the Basic People's Court		人民法庭 People's Tribunal	
		结案 Number of Case	诉讼标的总金额 Litigation Total Amount	结 案 Number of Case	诉讼标的总金额 Total Number of Litigation
合 计	**Total**	**63268**	**597559.35**	**15483**	**80045.02**
一、刑事	**Criminal**	**5627**	**8389.79**		
二、民商事	**Civil and Commercial Matters**	**40585**	**334255.91**	**15483**	**80045.02**
三、行政	**Administration**	**855**			
四、申诉、申请再审	**Appeals, Apply for Retrial**	**1653**			
五、司法赔偿	**Judicial Indemnification**				
六、执行	**Execution**	**14548**	**254913.65**		

注：本表数据来源于市中级人民法院。

21–33 全市及分区县体育场地情况(2013年)

Sports venues in the city and district（2013）

区 县 Region		场地数量（个）Number of sites (unit)	场地面积（万平方米）Site area (10 000 sq.m)	建筑面积（万平方米）Built-up area (10 000 sq.m)	投资金额（万元）Investment amount (10 000 yuan)	场地从业人员（人）Site employees (person)
合 计	**Total**	**12185**	**1134.81**	**118.84**	**1682690**	**16297**
新城区	Xincheng	364	31.43	7.63	18889	738
碑林区	Beilin	575	72.37	28.98	68835	1222
莲湖区	Lianhu	388	25.43	5.08	15297	915
灞桥区	Baqiao	694	107.81	4.49	16473	1279
未央区	Weiyang	839	81.25	12.60	51996	1147
雁塔区	Yanta	724	102.64	21.16	386797	2151
阎良区	Yanliang	351	32.04	7.06	13447	403
临潼区	Lintong	919	65.07	6.68	14188	1151
长安区	Chang'an	2153	203.71	12.21	97491	2205
蓝田县	Lantian	1379	87.98	0.09	7860	1453
周至县	Zhouzhi	1191	78.71	6.26	8889	857
户 县	Huxian	2099	201.76	2.60	39751	2352
高陵县	Gaoling	509	44.61	4.00	942777	424

注：本表数据来源于陕西省第六次体育场地普查公报，为2013年数据。

主 要 统 计 指 标 解 释

艺术表演团体 指由文化部门主办或实行行业管理（经文化行政部门审批并领取营业性演出许可证），专门从事表演艺术等活动的各类专业艺术表演团体，含民间职业剧团。（不包括群众业余文艺表演团队）

艺术表演场馆 指由文化部门主办或实行行业管理（向文化行政部门备案或领取合资（合作）演出场所许可证），有观众席、舞台、灯光设备，公开售票、专供文艺团体演出的文化活动场所。附属于文化部门机构内非独立核算的剧场、排演场，公开营业的也应单独统计。

图书馆 指各类图书馆的管理与服务（对文献和信息的搜集、整理、存储、利用和管理，向社会公众开放并提供科学、文化等各种知识普及教育）。包括公共图书馆和各类机构内部举办的或单独举办的图书馆的管理与服务。不包括部队系统以及文化馆（文化中心、群众艺术馆）、文化站内设的图书室。

群众文化活动 指开展群众文化活动的场所的管理和组织活动。包括文化馆（含综合性文化中心、群众艺术馆）、文化站、文化宫、少年宫等群众文化活动。在本制度中，目前暂不统计文化部门以外的文化宫和少年宫。

文化馆 （含综合性文化中心、群众艺术馆）、文化站：指专门从事群众文化活动的群众文化场馆。不包括临时抽调人员组成、没有编制的农村和街道文化工作队、服务站等。

广播节目综合人口覆盖率 根据国家广电总局制定的《广播电视人口覆盖率统计技术标准和方法》进行统计调查的，分别反映中央、省级、地市级、县级广播节目在本行政区域的综合覆盖情况，反应以无线方式传输的广播节目综合覆盖情况，综合反映广播公共服务覆盖的规模、能力、水平。

电视节目综合人口覆盖率 根据国家广电总局制定的《广播电视人口覆盖率统计技术标准和方法》进行统计调查的，分别反映中央、省级、地市级、县级电视节目在本行政区域的综合覆盖情况，反应以无线方式传输的电视节目综合覆盖情况，综合反映广播公共服务覆盖的规模、能力、水平。

博物馆 指为了研究、教育、欣赏的目的，收藏、保护、展示人类活动和自然环境的见证物，向公众开放，非盈利性、永久性社会服务机构，包括以博物馆（院）、纪念馆（舍）科技馆、陈列馆等专有名称丌展活动的单位。

等级运动员人数 指经考核正式批准授予等级运动员称号的人数。运动员等级分为国际级运动健将、运动健将、一级运动员、二级运动员、三级运动员、少年级运动员。

等级裁判员人数 指经考核正式批准授予等级裁判员称号的人数。裁判员等级分为国际裁判、国家级裁判、一级裁判、二级裁判、三级裁判。

卫生机构 指从卫生行政部门取得《医疗机构执业许可证》，或从民政、工商行政、机构编制管理部门取得法人单位登记证书，为社会提供医疗保健、疾病控制、卫生监督服务或从事医学科研和教育等工作的单位。卫生机构包括医院、疗养院、社区卫生服务中心（站）、卫生院、门诊部、诊所（卫生所、医务室）、急救中心（站）、采供血机构、妇幼保健院（所、站）、专科疾病防治院（所、站）、疾病预防控制中心（防疫站）、卫生监督所、卫生监督监测机构、医学科研机构、医学在职培训机构、健康教育所（站）等其他卫生机构。

社区卫生服务中心（站） 指为本社区居民提供预防、医疗、保健、康复、健康教育、计划生育技术服务等的基层卫生机构。包括社区卫生服务中心和社区卫生服务站。

卫生人员 指在医疗、预防保健、医学科研和在职教育等卫生机构工作的职工，包括卫生技术人员、其他技术人员、管理人员和工勤人员。

卫生技术人员 包括执业（助理）医师、注册护士、药师（士）、检验和影像人员等卫生专业人员。不包括从事管理工作的卫生技术人员。

执业医师 指《医师执业证》"级别"为"执业医师"且实际从事医疗、预防保健工作的人员，不包括实际从事管理工作的执业医师。执业医师类别分为临床、中医、口腔和公共卫生四类。

执业助理医师 指《医师执业证》"级别"为"执业助理医师"且实际从事医疗、预防保健工作的人员，不包括实际从事管理工作的执业助理医师。执业助理医师类别同样分为临床、中医、口腔和公共卫生四类。

死亡率（疾病） 指在一定时期内，在一定人群中，死于某病的频率。

死亡率=某期间内（因某病）死亡总数／同期平均人口数×100%

社会福利企业 指以集中安置有一定劳动能力的残疾人员就业为目的（残疾职工占生产人员10%以上）、带有社会福利性质的企业总称。主要包括福利工厂、假肢厂和其他福利企业。

公证人员 指在国家公证机关依法办理公证事务的司法人员，包括公证员、助理公证员和在公证处工作的其他人员。

办理公证文书 指公证处在一定时期内办结的公证文书件数。公证文书按司法部规定或批准的格式制作，包括国内公证和涉外公证两部分。国内公证分为经济合同公证和民事法律关系公证两大类。

调解人员 指在人民调解委员会担负调解民间一般民事纠纷和轻微违法行为引起纠纷的工作人员，包括调解委员会的委员和调解小组的调解员。

立案 指检察机关对犯罪线索进行初步调查后，认为存在职务犯罪事实并需要追究刑事责任时，依法决定作为刑事案件进行侦查的诉讼活动，是追究犯罪的开始。

Explanatory Notes on Main Statistical Indicators

Arts Performance Troupes refer to the various professional performing arts groups, which sponsored by the cultural sectors or guided by the cultural society (Receive commercial performance license approved by the cultural administration authority),including non-governmental troupes. (The mass amateur arts performance troupes are not included.)

Arts Performance Places refer to the various sites for cultural activities, which sponsored by the cultural sectors or guided by the cultural society (approved by the cultural market administration, or receive joint/cooperative venues permit), with the facility of auditorium, stage and lighting, and selling tickets in public, including the opera halls and rehearse sites, etc. which are affiliated to the culture sectors without independent financial accounts and open to the public.

Library refers to all types of library management and services(collection, collation, storage, use and management of literature and information, open and provide scientific, cultural and other literacy education to the public). Including the management and services of public libraries and the libraries internally or separately organized by various sectors. Excluding the libraries in troops system and cultural palaces (cultural centers, mass art centers),cultural stations.

Mass Culture Center refers to the management and organization of the places where mass culture activities hold. Including cultural palace (cultural center ,mass art center), cultural stations, cultural palaces ,youth palaces and other mass cultural activities. In this system ,cultural palaces and youth palaces beyond cultural sectors are not counted at present.

Cultural Palaces (Cultural Centers, Mass Art Centers),Cultural Stations refers to the mass cultural venues specialized in mass cultural activities. Excluding rural and street cultural teams, service stations which made up by temporary without authorized strength.

Radio Coverage of Population refers to the comprehensive coverage which respectively reflected central ,province, city, prefecture and county radio programs by wireless in the administrative region, and comprehensively reflect the size, capacity, level of the public broadcasting services, according to Statistical Standard and Method on Television and Radio Coverage of Population established by the State Administration of Broadcasting ,Film and Television

Television Coverage of Population refers to the comprehensive coverage which respectively reflected central, province, city, prefecture and county television programs by wireless in the administrative region, and comprehensively reflect the size, capacity, level of the public broadcasting services, according to Statistical Standard and Method on Television and Radio Coverage of Population established by the State Administration of Broadcasting , Film and Television

Museum refers to the non-profit, permanent society service sectors which collect ,protect ,show human activities and the witnesses of natural environment, including the units that organize activities with the proper name such as museum, memorial hall , science and technology museum, exhibition hall, etc.

Number of Athletes in Grades refers to the number of athletes who have been given titles through examination. The titles of athletes include international masters of sports, masters of sports, first-grade, second-grade and third-grade sportsmen and young athletes.

Number of Referees in Grades refers to the number of referees who have been given titles after examination. They are classified as international referees, national referees and referees of the first, second and third grades.

Health Care Institutions refer to the units which have been qualified the Certification of Health Care Institution by the administration of public health, or qualified the Certification of Corporate Unit by the civil affairs, administration for industry and commerce, commission office for public sector reform, and engaging in medical care, disease prevention and control, health supervision and inspection, medicine research and health education, etc., including: hospitals, sanatoriums, community health service centers （stations）, health centers, clinics (health stations and infirmaries), first-aid centres (stations), blood gathering and supplying institutions, women and children care agencies (centres and stations), special disease prevention and curing agencies(centres and stations), disease prevention and control centres (epidemic prevention stations), health supervision and inspection agencies, sanitary inspection institutions, medicinal scientific research and on-job training institutions, health education centres and so on.

Community Health Service Centres (stations) refer to the primary units that provide the health care for community residents, such as disease prevention and control, medical treatment, health care, rehabilitation, health education, family planning technical services, including community health service centres and community health service stations.

Health Care Employee refer to all employee engaged in the health care institutions, such as medical organizations, disease prevention and control centres, health care agencies, medicinal scientific research and on-job training institutions, including medical technical personnel, other technical personnel, manager and labour.

Medical Technical Personnel refer to the professional staff engaged in health care, including licensed (assistant) doctors, registered nurse, pharmacists, laboratory technician, and imaging staff, excluding the medical technical personnel engaged in management job.

Licensed Doctors refer to the medical workers who have obtained the licenses of qualified doctors and are employed in medical treatment, disease prevention or healthcare institutions, excluding the licensed doctors engaged in management job. The licensed doctors are divided into 4 categories: clinician, Chinese medicine physicians, dentist and public health physicians.

Licensed Assistant Doctors refer to the medical workers who have obtained the licenses of qualified assistant doctors and are employed in medical treatment, disease prevention or healthcare institutions, excluding the licensed assistant doctors engaged in management job. The classification of licensed assistant doctors is cliniciam Chinese medicine, dentist and public health.

Mortality Rate refers to the ratio of deaths causedby diseases at reference period to the certain group of population.

Mortality Rate = total deaths (caused by diseases) at reference period/average population at same period x 100%.

Social Welfare Enterprises refers to those welfare-oriented enterprises employing a significant number of handicapped people with certain labour ability (handicapped employees shall exceed 10% of the production staff), including welfare factories, artificial limb plants as well as other welfare enterprises.

Notary Personnel refers to judicial workers of the state notary offices handling notarization work according to law. They include notaries, assistant notaries, and other people working for notary offices.

Notarized Documents refer to the documents settled by notary offices in a year. The notary documents are drawn up in accordance with the regulations of the Ministry of Justice, including domestic documents and foreign-related documents. Domestic documents are divided into two major categories, documents on economic contracts and documents on civil legal relations.

Mediators refer to workers on peoples mediation committees responsible for mediating in civil disputes and cases of slight infraction of the law. They include members of the mediation committees and mediators of mediation groups.

Acceptance of Case refers to the decision made by the procurators office to confirm the act of crime after initial investigation and to start legal proceedings of the case as criminal case.

22 企业调查

ENTERPRISES INVESTIGATION

资料整理：薛　燕
Data management：Xue Yan
数据审核：史安民
Data audit：Shi Anmin

第二十二部分　企业调查

一、简要说明

本章资料主要包括各行业企业景气调查指数和企业家信心指数等，由西安市统计局社会经济调查中心提供。

二、主要指标

企业景气指数（第四季度）	108.9
企业家信心指数（第四季度）	105.8

22 ENTERPRISES INVESTIGATION

Ⅰ.Brief Introduction

Data in this chapter consists prosperity survey indices of various industries and Entrepreneur Expectation Indicator, provided by Xi'an Municipal Bureau of Statics .

Ⅱ.Major Indicators

Business Climate Index（Fourth Quarter）	108.9
Entrepreneur Expectation Indicator（Fourth Quarter）	105.8

22-1 企业景气指数（2014年）

Business Climate Index（2014）

指　　标	Item	一季度 First Quarter	二季度 Second Quarter	三季度 Third Quarter	四季度 Fourth Quarter
企业景气指数	**Business Climate Index**	**126.6**	**117.3**	**115.3**	**108.9**
按行业门类分	**Grouped by Sector**				
工业	Industry	134.4	130.9	125.9	123.6
建筑业	Construction	142.1	128.7	114.4	112.3
交通运输、仓储及邮政业	Transport, Storage and Post	119.1	104.5	104.5	107.3
批发和零售业	Wholesale and Retail Sales	108.0	96.7	96.1	90.5
房地产业	Real Estate	127.0	100.0	100.9	78.3
社会服务业	Social Services	123.3	115.6	121.0	108.0
信息传输、计算机服务和软件业	Information Transmission, Computer Service and Safeware Service	146.0	120.0	122.0	116.0
住宿和餐饮业	Hotels and Catering Services	73.1	77.5	85.6	78.1
按企业(单位)登记注册类型分组	**Grouped by Registration**				
国有企业	State-owned Enterprises	119.0	112.6	112.9	110.9
集体企业	Collective-owned Enterprises	133.4	117.5	100.0	92.5
股份合作企业	Share-holding Cooperative Enterprises				100.0
联营企业	Joint Ownership Enterprises	100.0		100.0	100.0
有限责任公司	Limited Liability Corporations	121.4	101.0	97.0	86.3
股份有限公司	Share-holding Corporations Ltd.	113.6	110.8	110.0	106.7
私营企业	Privately Owned Enterprises	88.9	88.6	85.7	71.4
港澳台商投资企业	Enterprises Invested by Foreigners or Investors from Hongkong,Macro and Taiwan	102.9	114.3	105.7	91.4
外商投资企业	Foreign Funded Enterprises	130.0	160.0	110.0	130.0
按企业规模分	**Grouped by Size of Enterprises**				
大型企业	Large-size	136.2	123.1	128.9	122.8
中型企业	Medium-size	131.7	133.8	125.4	122.5
小型企业	Small-size	113.5	112.7	109.3	105.9

22-2 企业家信心指数（2014年）

Entrepreneur Expectation Indicator（2014）

指　标	Item	一季度 First Season	二季度 Second Season	三季度 Third Season	四季度 Fourth Season
企业家信心指数	**Entrepreneur Expectation Indicator**	**123.9**	**115.4**	**114.5**	**105.8**
按行业门类分	**Grouped by Sector**				
工业	Industry	129.0	125.1	118.2	118.7
建筑业	Construction	131.3	115.4	101.5	91.8
交通运输、仓储及邮政业	Transport, Storage and Post	122.7	100.9	111.8	100.0
批发和零售业	Wholesale and Retail Sales	106.3	98.4	101.3	97.4
房地产业	Real Estate	98.3	71.3	76.5	70.4
社会服务业	Social Services	130.0	122.6	132.6	111.7
信息传输、计算机服务和软件业	Information Transmission, Computer Service and Safeware Service	150.0	150.0	140.0	120.0
住宿和餐饮业	Hotels and Catering Services	84.4	87.5	91.3	85.0
按企业(单位)登记注册类型分组	**Grouped by Registration**				
国有企业	State-owned Enterprises	112.9	110.2	107.8	108.2
集体企业	Collective-owned Enterprises	146.7	97.5	67.5	82.5
股份合作企业	Share-holding Cooperative Enterprises			60.0	60.0
联营企业	Joint Ownership Enterprises	100.0	100.0	100.0	100.0
有限责任公司	Limited Liability Corporations	112.8	101.2	98.6	87.1
股份有限公司	Share-holding Corporations Ltd.	127.2	121.7	125.8	109.2
私营企业	Privately Owned Enterprises	84.5	85.7	91.4	62.8
港澳台商投资企业	Enterprises Invested by Foreigners or Investors from Hongkong,Macro and Taiwan	114.3	128.6	114.3	100.0
外商投资企业	Foreign Funded Enterprises	200.0	180.0	160.0	100.0
按企业规模分	**Grouped by Size of Enterprises**				
大型企业	Large-size	133.1	122.8	122.0	121.8
中型企业	Medium-size	130.4	133.5	127.2	125.5
小型企业	Small-size	112.9	113.0	112.3	103.7

主 要 统 计 指 标 解 释

企业景气指数：是根据企业家对本企业综合生产经营情况所作的判断与预期（通常是对“良好”、“一般”、“不佳”的选择）而编制的指数，用以综合反映企业的生产经营状况。企业景气指数也称“企业综合生产经营景气指数”。

企业家信心指数：是根据企业家对企业外部市场经济环境与宏观政策的认识、看法判断和预期（通常是对“乐观”、“一般”、“不乐观”的选择）而编制的指数，用以综合反映企业家对宏观经济环境的感受与信心。企业家信心指数也称“宏观经济景气指数”。

景气指数的表示方式：景气指数的表示范围在0~200之间，其含义：100为景气指数的临界值，表明景气状况变化不大；100~200为景气区间，表明景气状况趋于上升或改善，越接近于200，状况越景气；0~100为不景气区间，表明经济状况趋于下降或恶化，越接近于0，状况越不景气。

Explanatory Notes on Main Statistical Indicators

Business Climate Index it is an index worked out according to the judgment and anticipation (normally a choice from good, ordinary, not good) of entrepreneurs made based on synthetic productive and operational situation of the enterprise. It is used to reflect synthetically the productive and operational situation of the enterprise. It is also referred to as synthetic and productiveoperational prosperity index of enterprise.

Confidence index of entrepreneur it is an index worked out according to the judgment and anticipation (normally a choice from optimistic , ordinary , not optimistic) of entrepreneurs made based on their understandings and views of the market and economic environment outside the enterprise and the macro policies. It is used to reflect synthetically the confidence and feelings of the entrepreneurs to the macro economic environment. It is also referred to as macro-economy prosperity index.

The way to express prosperity index the range of prosperity index is from 0 to 200; 100 is the critical value, and means economic situation didn't change largely; from 100 to 200 is the interval of prosperity; and from 0 to 100 is the interval of not prosperity, meaning economic situation is going down or worse, the closer to 0, the worse the economic situation.

中国统计出版社最新图书简目

(仅供参考,以实际出版为准)

统计资料

中国统计年鉴 中国统计摘要 中国发展报告
中国经济普查年鉴2013 国际统计年鉴 金砖国家联合统计手册
中国-东盟国家统计手册 中国区域经济统计年鉴 中国县域统计年鉴
中国城市统计年鉴 中国农村统计年鉴 中国地区经济监测报告
中国贸易外经统计年鉴 中国对外直接投资统计公报 中国商品交易市场统计年鉴
大中型批发零售和住宿餐饮企业统计年鉴 中国零售和餐饮连锁企业统计年鉴 中国住户调查年鉴
中国价格统计年鉴 中国农产品价格调查年鉴 全国农产品成本收益资料汇编
中国环境统计年鉴 中国能源统计年鉴 国外资源、能源和环境统计资料汇编
中国工业统计年鉴 中国建筑业统计年鉴 中国房地产统计年鉴
中国城市建设统计年鉴 中国城乡建设统计年鉴 中国第三产业统计年鉴
中国证券期货统计年鉴 中国科技统计年鉴 中国高技术产业统计年鉴
工业企业科技活动资料 中国劳动统计年鉴 中国人口和就业统计年鉴
中国人才资源统计报告 中国社会统计年鉴 中国文化及相关产业统计年鉴
文化及相关产业统计概览 中国教育经费统计年鉴 中国民政统计年鉴
中国民族统计年鉴 中国工会统计年鉴 中国残疾人事业统计年鉴
中国妇女儿童状况统计资料（英） 中国乡镇街道行政区域简册

省级综合统计年鉴系列

北京 天津 河北 山西 内蒙古 辽宁 吉林 黑龙江 上海 江苏 浙江 安徽 福建 江西 山东 河南 湖北 湖南 广东 广西 海南 重庆 四川 贵州 云南 西藏 陕西 甘肃 青海 宁夏 新疆 新疆生产建设兵团

市(县)级综合统计年鉴系列

天津滨海新区 石家庄 唐山 邯郸 保定 沧州 邢台 廊坊 承德 衡水 秦皇岛 张家口 太原 大同 阳泉 长治 晋城 朔州 晋中 运城 忻州 临汾 呼和浩特 呼和浩特新城区 鄂尔多斯 包头 沈阳 大连 长春 四平 哈尔滨 齐齐哈尔 黑龙江垦区 上海浦东新区 南京 无锡 徐州 常州 苏州 南通 连云港 淮安 盐城 扬州 镇江 泰州 宿迁 江阴 丹阳 杭州 宁波 温州 嘉兴 绍兴 金华 衢州 舟山 台州 丽水 合肥 安庆 马鞍山 福州 厦门 宁德 南昌 九江 上饶 新余 抚州 济南 青岛 枣庄 滕州 郑州 洛阳 平顶山 三门峡 南阳 商丘 济源 武汉 十堰 荆州 宜昌 荆门 咸宁 长沙 广州 深圳 惠州 东莞 南宁 柳州 桂林 来宾 海口 三亚 成都 贵阳 昆明 西安 兰州 庆阳 银川 乌鲁木齐 兵团一师 兵团十师

调查年鉴系列

天津 山西 内蒙古 辽宁 吉林 上海 福建 河南 湖北 湖南 广西 重庆 四川 云南 甘肃 宁夏 新疆

“十二五”规划教材

统计学（经济管理类专业本科适用，单薇 等） 抽样调查理论与方法（冯士雍 等）
贝叶斯统计（茆诗松 等） 统计学（黄良文 等） 试验设计（茆诗松 等）
统计学：从数据到结论（吴喜之） 医学统计学（于浩） 统计学（经济、管理类专业基础教材，张小斐）
概率论与数理统计三十三讲（魏振军） 概率论与数理统计三十三：学习指导与习题解答（魏振军）
非参数统计（吴喜之 等） 统计学：经济与管理中的数据分析（李慧云 等）
卫生管理统计学（新编医学院校基础课教材，尚磊） 医院统计学（新编医学院校基础课教材，徐天和 等）
社会统计学（蒋萍 等） 现代金融投资统计分析（李腊生 等）
国民经济核算初级教程（经济类、统计类、管理类专业适用，蒋萍 等）

重点图书

图解中国经济2015 新编英汉汉英统计大词典 中华医学统计百科全书
挑大学选专业2016—考研择校指南 挑大学选专业2015—高考志愿填报指南